# WORLD ERAS

## VOLUME 7

### IMPERIAL CHINA
617 - 1644

# WORLD ERAS

## VOLUME 7

## IMPERIAL CHINA
### 617 - 1644

# GUANGQIU XU

## A MANLY, INC. BOOK

GALE®

**THOMSON**

★

™

**GALE**

Detroit • New York • San Diego • San Francisco • Cleveland • New Haven, Conn. • Waterville, Maine • London • Munich

**World Eras**
**Volume 7: Imperial China, 617–1644**
Guangqiu Xu

**Editorial Directors**
Matthew J. Bruccoli and Richard Layman

**Series Editor**
Anthony J. Scotti Jr.

**LIBRARY OF CONGRESS CATALOGING-IN-PUBLICATION DATA**

World Eras vol. 7: Imperial China, 617-1644 / edited by Guangqiu Xu.
      p.  cm.—(World eras; v.7)
"A Manly, Inc. book."
      Includes bibliographical references and indexes.
      ISBN 0-7876-1708-3 (alk. paper)
      1. China—Civilization—221 B.C.–960 A.D.
      2. China—Civilization—960–1644.
      I. Xu, Guangqiu, 1951–. II. Series.

DS749.3 .I46 2002
951'.02—dc21

2002007914

Printed in the United States of America
10 9 8 7 6 5 4 3 2 1

# ADVISORY BOARD

*For my father, Xu Quanqing,*
*and my mother, Liang Peiying*

# CONTENTS

**Significant People**

**Documentary Sources**

## CHAPTER 6: POLITICS, LAW, AND THE MILITARY

**Chronology**

**Overview**

**Topics in Politics, Law, and the Military**

**Significant People**

**Documentary Sources**

## CHAPTER 7: LEISURE, RECREATION, AND DAILY LIFE

**Chronology**

**Overview**

**Topics in Leisure, Recreation, and Daily Life**

# ABOUT THE SERIES

## PROJECT DESCRIPTION

Patterned after the well-received *American Decades* and *American Eras* series, *World Eras* is a cross-disciplinary reference series. It comprises volumes examining major civilizations that have flourished from antiquity to modern times, with a global perspective and a strong emphasis on daily life and social history. Each volume provides in-depth coverage of one era, focusing on a specific cultural group and its interaction with other peoples of the world. The *World Eras* series is geared toward the needs of high-school students studying subjects in the humanities. Its purpose is to provide students—and general reference users as well—a reliable, engaging reference resource that stimulates their interest, encourages research, and prompts comparison of the lives people led in different parts of the world, in different cultures, and at different times.

The goal of *World Eras* volumes is to enrich the traditional historical study of "kings and battles" with a resource that promotes understanding of daily life and the cultural institutions that affect people's beliefs and behavior.

What kind of work did people in a certain culture perform?

What did they eat?

How did they fight their battles?

What laws did they have and how did they punish criminals?

What were their religious practices?

What did they know of science and medicine?

What kind of art, music, and literature did they enjoy?

These are the types of questions *World Eras* volumes seek to answer.

## VOLUME DESIGN

*World Eras* is designed to facilitate comparative study. Thus volumes employ a consistent ten-chapter structure so that teachers and students can readily access standard topics in various volumes. The chapters in each *World Eras* volume are:

1. World Events
2. Geography

3. The Arts
4. Communication, Transportation, and Exploration
5. Social Class System and the Economy
6. Politics, Law, and the Military
7. Leisure, Recreation, and Daily Life
8. The Family and Social Trends
9. Religion and Philosophy
10. Science, Technology, and Health

*World Eras* volumes begin with two chapters designed to provide a broad view of the world against which a specific culture can be measured. Chapter 1 provides students today with a means to understand where a certain people stood within our concept of world history. Chapter 2 describes the world from the perspective of the people being studied—what did they know of geography and how did geography and climate affect their lives? The following eight chapters address major aspects of people's lives to provide a sense of what defined their culture. The ten chapters in *World Eras* will remain constant in each volume. Teachers and students seeking to compare religious beliefs in Roman and Greek cultures, for example, can easily locate the information they require by consulting chapter 9 in the appropriate volumes, tapping a rich source for class assignments and research topics. Volume-specific glossaries and a checklist of general references provide students assistance in studying unfamiliar cultures.

## CHAPTER CONTENTS

Each chapter in *World Eras* volumes also follows a uniform structure designed to provide users quick access to the information they need. Chapters are arranged into five types of material:

- **Chronology** provides an historical outline of significant events in the subject of the chapter in timeline form.

- **Overview** provides a narrative overview of the chapter topic during the period and discusses the material of the chapter in a global context.

- **Topical Entries** provide focused information in easy-to-read articles about people, places, events, institutions, and matters of general concern to the people of the time. A references rubric includes sources for further study.

- **Biographical Entries** profiles people of enduring significance regarding the subject of the chapter.
- **Documentary Sources** is an annotated checklist of documentary sources from the historical period that are the basis for the information presented in the chapter.

Chapters are supplemented throughout with primary-text sidebars that include interesting short documentary excerpts or anecdotes chosen to illuminate the subject of the chapter: recipes, letters, daily-life accounts, and excerpts from important documents. Each *World Eras* volume includes about 150 illustrations, maps, diagrams, and line drawings linked directly to material discussed in the text. Illustrations are chosen with particular emphasis on daily life.

## INDEXING

A general two-level subject index for each volume includes significant terms, subjects, theories, practices, people, organizations, publications, and so forth, mentioned in the text. Index citations with many page references are broken down by subtopic. Illustrations are indicated both in the general index, by use of italicized page numbers, and in a separate illustrations index, which provides a description of each item.

## EDITORS AND CONTRIBUTORS

An advisory board of history teachers and librarians has provided valuable advice about the rationale for this series. They have reviewed both series plans and individual volume plans. Each *World Eras* volume is edited by a distinguished specialist in the subject of his or her volume. The editor is responsible for enlisting other scholar-specialists to write each of the chapters in the volume and of assuring the quality of their work. The editorial staff at Manly, Inc., rigorously checks factual information, line edits the manuscript, works with the editor to select illustrations, and produces the books in the series, in cooperation with Gale Group editors.

The *World Eras* series is for students of all ages who seek to enrich their study of world history by examining the many aspects of people's lives in different places during different eras. This series continues Gale's tradition of publishing comprehensive, accurate, and stimulating historical reference works that promote the study of history and culture.

The following timeline, included in every volume of *World Eras,* is provided as a convenience to users seeking a ready chronological context.

# TIMELINE

This timeline, compiled by editors at Manly, Inc., is provided as a convenience for students seeking a broad global and historical context for the materials in this volume of World Eras. *It is not intended as a self-contained resource. Students who require a comprehensive chronology of world history should consult a source such as Peter N. Stearns, ed.,* The Encyclopedia of World History, *sixth revised edition (Boston & New York: Houghton Mifflin, 2001).*

## CIRCA 4 MILLION–1 MILLION B.C.E.
Era of *Australopithecus,* the first hominid

## CIRCA 1.5 MILLION–200,000 B.C.E.
Era of *Homo erectus,* "upright-walking human"

## CIRCA 1,000,000–10,000 B.C.E.
Paleothic Age: hunters and gatherers make use of stone tools in Eurasia

## CIRCA 250,000 B.C.E.
Early evolution of *Homo sapiens,* "consciously thinking humans"

## CIRCA 40,000 B.C.E.
Migrations from Siberia to Alaska lead to the first human inhabitation of North and South America

## CIRCA 8000 B.C.E.
Neolithic Age: settled agrarian culture begins to develop in Eurasia

## 5000 B.C.E.
The world population is between 5 million and 20 million

## CIRCA 4000–3500 B.C.E.
Earliest Sumerian cities: artificial irrigation leads to increased food supplies and populations in Mesopotamia

## CIRCA 3000 B.C.E.
Bronze Age begins in Mesopotamia and Egypt, where bronze is primarily used for making weapons; invention of writing

## CIRCA 2900–1150 B.C.E.
Minoan society on Crete: lavish palaces and commercial activity

## CIRCA 2700–2200 B.C.E.
Egypt: Old Kingdom and the building of the pyramids

## CIRCA 2080–1640 B.C.E.
Egypt: Middle Kingdom plagued by internal strife and invasion by the Hyksos

## CIRCA 2000–1200 B.C.E.
Hittites build a powerful empire based in Anatolia (present-day Turkey) by using horse-drawn war chariots

## CIRCA 1792–1760 B.C.E.
Old Babylonian Kingdom; one of the oldest extant legal codes is compiled

## CIRCA 1766–1122 B.C.E.
Shang Dynasty in China: military expansion, large cities, written language, and introduction of bronze metallurgy

## CIRCA 1570–1075 B.C.E.
Egypt: New Kingdom and territorial expansion into Palestine, Lebanon, and Syria

## CIRCA 1500 B.C.E.
The Aryans, an Indo-European people from the steppes of present-day Ukraine and southern Russia, expand into northern India

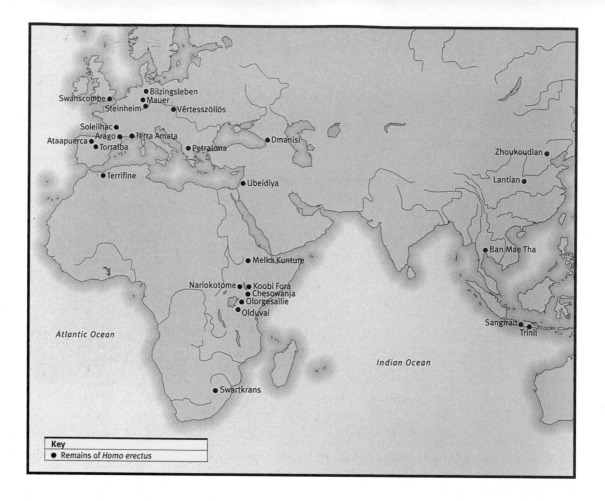

**Key**
● Remains of *Homo erectus*

**CIRCA 1500 B.C.E.**
Phoenicians create the first alphabet

**CIRCA 1400-1200 B.C.E.**
Hittites develop the technology of iron-smelting, improving weaponry and agricultural implements as well as stimulating trade

**CIRCA 1200-800 B.C.E.**
Phoenicians establish colonies throughout the Mediterranean

**CIRCA 1122-221 B.C.E.**
Zhou Dynasty in China: military conquests, nomadic invasions, and introduction of iron metallurgy

**CIRCA 1100-750 B.C.E.**
Greek Dark Ages: foreign invasions, civil disturbances, decrease in agricultural production, and population decline

**1020-587 B.C.E.**
Israelite monarchies consolidate their power in Palestine

**CIRCA 1000-612 B.C.E.**
Assyrians create an empire encompassing Mesopotamia, Syria, Palestine, and most of Anatolia and Egypt; they deport populations to various regions of the realm

**1000 B.C.E.**
The world population is approximately 50 million

**CIRCA 814-146 B.C.E.**
The city-state of Carthage is a powerful commercial and military power in the western Mediterranean

**753 B.C.E.**
Traditional date of the founding of Rome

**CIRCA 750-700 B.C.E.**
Rise of the polis, or city-state, in Greece

**558-330 B.C.E.**
Achaemenid Dynasty establishes the Persian Empire (present-day Iran, Turkey, Afghanistan, and Iraq); satraps rule the various provinces

**509 B.C.E.**
Roman Republic is established

**500 B.C.E.**
The world population is approximately 100 million

The ROMAN EMPIRE
before the Barbarian Invasions

**Circa 400 b.c.e.**
Spread of Buddhism in India

**338-323 b.c.e.**
Macedon, a kingdom in the central Balkan Peninsula, conquers the Persian Empire

**323-301 b.c.e.**
Ptolemaic Kingdom (Egypt), Seleucid Kingdom (Syria), and Antigonid Dynasty (Macedon) are founded

**247 b.c.e.-224 c.e.**
Parthian Empire (Parthia, Persia, and Babylonia): clan leaders build independent power bases in their satrapies, or provinces

**215-168 b.c.e.**
Rome establishes hegemony over the Hellenistic world

**206 b.c.e.-220 c.e.**
Han Dynasty in China: imperial expansion into central Asia, centralized government, economic prosperity, and population growth

**Circa 100 b.c.e.**
Tribesmen on the Asian steppes develop the stirrup, which eventually revolutionizes warfare

**1 c.e.**
The world population is approximately 200 million

**Circa 100 c.e.**
Invention of paper in China

**224-651 c.e.**
Sasanid Empire (Parthia, Persia, and Babylonia): improved government system, founding of new cities, increased trade, and the introduction of rice and cotton cultivation

**340 c.e.**
Constantinople becomes the capital of the Eastern Roman, or Byzantine, Empire

**Circa 320-550 c.e.**
Gupta dynasty in India: Golden Age of Hindu civilization marked by stability and prosperity throughout the subcontinent

**395 c.e.**
Christianity becomes the official religion of the Roman Empire

**Circa 400 c.e.**
The first unified Japanese state arises and is centered at Yamato on the island of Honshu; Buddhism arrives in Japan by way of Korea

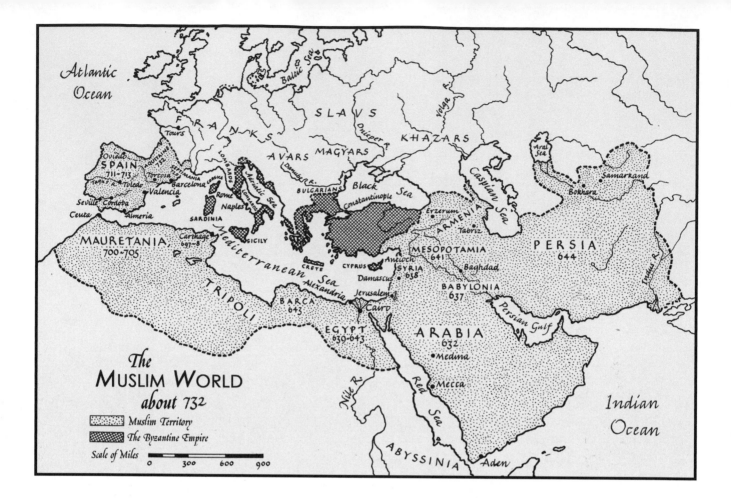

The
MUSLIM WORLD
about 732

- ⣿ Muslim Territory
- ▨ The Byzantine Empire

Scale of Miles
0    300    600    900

## CIRCA 400 C.E.
The nomadic Huns begin a westward migration from central Asia, causing disruption in the Roman Empire

## CIRCA 400 C.E.
The Mayan Empire in Mesoamerica evolves into city-states

## 476 C.E.
Rome falls to barbarian hordes, and the Western Roman Empire collapses

## CIRCA 500-1500 C.E.
Middle Ages, or medieval period, in Europe: gradual recovery from political disruption and increase in agricultural productivity and population

## 618-907 C.E.
Tang Dynasty in China: territorial expansion, government bureaucracy, agricultural improvements, and transportation and communication networks

## 632-733 C.E.
Muslim expansion and conquests in Arabia, Syria, Palestine, Mesopotamia, Egypt, North Africa, Persia, northwestern India, and Iberia

## CIRCA 700 C.E.
Origins of feudalism, a political and social organization that dominates Europe until the fifteenth century; based on the relationship between lords and vassals

## CIRCA 900 C.E.
Introduction of the horseshoe in Europe and gunpowder in China

## 960-1279 C.E.
Song Dynasty in China: civil administration, industry, education, and the arts

## 962-1806 C.E.
Holy Roman Empire of western and central Europe, created in an attempt to revive the old Roman Empire

## 1000 C.E.
The world population is approximately 300 million

## 1096-1291 C.E.
Western Christians undertake the Crusades, a series of religiously inspired military campaigns, to recapture the Holy Land from the Muslims

## 1200-1400 C.E.
The Mali empire in Africa dominates the trans-Saharan trade network of camel caravans

## 1220-1335 C.E.
The Mongols, nomadic horsemen from the high steppes of eastern central Asia, build an empire that includes China, Persia, and Russia

## CIRCA 1250 C.E.
Inca Empire develops in Peru: Civil administration, road networks, and sun worshiping

## 1299-1919 C.E.
Ottoman Empire, created by nomadic Turks and Christian converts to Islam, encompasses Asia Minor, the Balkans, Greece, Egypt, North Africa, and the Middle East

## 1300 C.E.
The world population is approximately 396 million

## 1337-1453 C.E.
Hundred Years' War, a series of intermittent military campaigns between England and France over control of continental lands claimed by both countries

## 1347-1350 C.E.
Black Death, or the bubonic plague, kills one-quarter of the European population

## 1368-1644 C.E.
Ming Dynasty in China: political, economic, and cultural revival; the Great Wall is built

## 1375-1527 C.E.
The Renaissance in Western Europe, a revival in the arts and learning

## 1428-1519 C.E.
The Aztecs expand in central Mexico, developing trade routes and a system of tribute payments

## 1450 C.E.
Invention of the printing press

## 1453 C.E.
Constantinople falls to the Ottoman Turks, ending the Byzantine Empire

## 1464-1591 C.E.
Songhay Empire in Africa: military expansion, prosperous cities, control of the trans-Saharan trade

## 1492 C.E.
Discovery of America; European exploration and colonization of the Western Hemisphere begins

LATIN
AMERICAN
STATES
*after the*
REVOLUTIONS

## CIRCA 1500-1867 C.E.
Transatlantic slave trade results in the forced migration of between 12 million and 16 million Africans to the Western Hemisphere

## 1500 C.E.
The world population is approximately 480 million

## 1517 C.E.
Beginning of the Protestant Reformation, a religious movement that ends the spiritual unity of western Christendom

## 1523-1763 C.E.
Mughal Empire in India: military conquests, productive agricultural economy, and population growth

## 1600-1867 C.E.
Tokugawa Shogunate in Japan: shoguns (military governors) turn Edo, or Tokyo, into the political, economic, and cultural center of the nation

## 1618-1648 C.E.
Thirty Years' War in Europe between Catholic and Protestant states

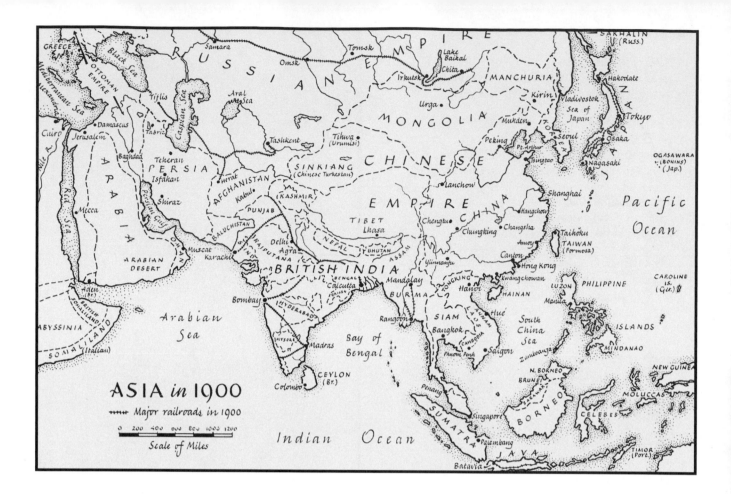

ASIA in 1900

⊪⊪⊪ Major railroads in 1900

Scale of Miles

**1644-1911 C.E.**
Qing Dynasty in China: military expansion and scholar-bureaucrats

**1700 C.E.**
The world population is approximately 640 million

**CIRCA 1750 C.E.**
Beginning of the Enlightenment, a philosophical movement marked by an emphasis on rationalism and scientific inquiry

**1756-1763 C.E.**
Seven Years' War: England and Prussia versus Austria, France, Russia, Saxony, Spain, and Sweden

**CIRCA 1760-1850 C.E.**
Industrial Revolution in Britain is marked by mass production through the division of labor, mechanization, a great increase in the supply of iron, and the use of the steam engine

**1775-1783 C.E.**
American War of Independence; the United States becomes an independent republic

**1789 C.E.**
French Revolution topples the monarchy and leads to a period of political unrest followed by a dictatorship

**1793-1815 C.E.**
Napoleonic Wars: Austria, England, Prussia, and Russia versus France and its satellite states

**1794-1824 C.E.**
Latin American states conduct wars of independence against Spain

**1900 C.E.**
The world population is approximately 1.65 billion

**1914-1918 C.E.**
World War I, or the Great War: the Allies (England, France, Russia, and the United States) versus the Central Powers (Austria-Hungary, Germany, and the Ottoman Empire)

**1917-1921 C.E.**
Russian Revolution: a group of Communists known as the Bolsheviks seize control of the country following a civil war

**1939-1945 C.E.**
World War II: the Allies (China, England, France, the Soviet Union, and the United States) versus the Axis (Germany, Italy, and Japan)

**1945 C.E.**
Successful test of the first atomic weapon; beginning of the Cold War, a period of rivalry, mistrust, and, occasionally, open hostility between the capitalist West and communist East

**1947-1975 C.E.**
Decolonization occurs in Africa and Asia as European powers relinquish control of colonies in those regions

**1948**
Israel becomes the first independent Jewish state in nearly two thousand years

**1949**
Communists seize control of China

**1950-1951**
Korean War: the United States attempts to stop Communist expansion in the Korean Peninsula

**1957 C.E.**
The Soviet Union launches *Sputnik* (fellow traveler of earth), the first man-made satellite; the Space Age begins

**1965-1973**
Vietnam War: the United States attempts to thwart the spread of Communism in Vietnam

**1989 C.E.**
East European Communist regimes begin to falter, and multiparty elections are held

**1991 C.E.**
Soviet Union is dissolved and replaced by the Commonwealth of Independent States

**2000 C.E.**
The world population is 6 billion

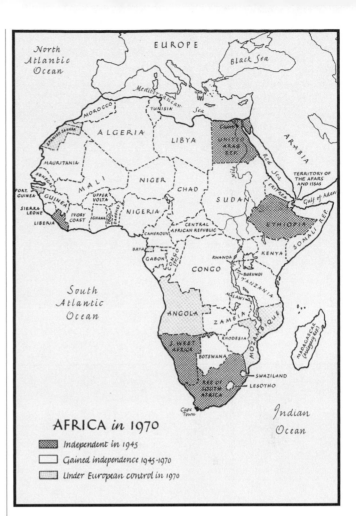

AFRICA in 1970

Independent in 1945

Gained independence 1945-1970

Under European control in 1970

# INTRODUCTION

**Objective.** This volume is meant to serve as an introduction to the history of imperial China and its four major dynasties following the decline of the Sui empire in 617: the Tang (618–907), Song (960–1279), Yuan or Mongol (1279–1368), and Ming (1368–1644). It has been prepared for general readers who have little knowledge of Chinese history from the seventh century to the seventeenth century and who may wish to compare and contrast the achievements of the Chinese during this time period with those of other civilizations. An understanding of the rich historical past of China is critical to an appreciation of present-day Chinese culture.

**The Land.** The land we know as China is an immense mountainous area bounded by the Pacific Ocean to the East and South, the massive Himalaya and Pamir mountain ranges to the West and Southwest, and the steppes to the North. Mountains, deserts, rivers and other topographical features have had a profound effect upon China Proper throughout its history. They frequently represented insurmountable barriers; the southern hills in particular were havens for various rebel groups during the period of 617–1644. However, four major dynasties managed to arise, achieve cultural and political unity, and maintain near economic self-sufficiency during this period. The Pacific Ocean is the source of the moisture-laden winds that provide China with rains, but it also effectively isolates China, more so than the great land masses to the North and West.

**Isolation.** Throughout the period under consideration, the Chinese did not look for territorial expansion until the seventeenth century, when many began to migrate to Taiwan and other places. Isolation also contributed to intense national pride in China. *Zhongguo,* the Chinese term for China, means "Middle Kingdom," reflecting the Chinese belief that their country was the center of the earth under heaven. To the Han Chinese, all other peoples—the non-Chinese—were barbarians, and their cultures were held in low regard. This outlook, however, did not prevent the Han Chinese from periodically borrowing ideas from these inferior groups. At the same time, these barbarians, such as Tibetans and Uighurs, influenced Chinese thinking. Indeed, the period from 617 to 1644 has been called a "transition to modern times," although some historians argue that modern Chinese history did not begin until the arrival of Westerners in the thirteenth century.

**Non-Chinese Elements.** A great external force for change came from the tribal people along China's northern and western borders. Beginning in the fourth century, the Chinese were unable to defend the empire against invasion, and raiders ravaged most of North China. In the following centuries the Chinese empire endeavored to survive and by 600 China was reunified, but it was a different China from the Han dynasty (206 B.C.E.–220 C.E.). Non-Chinese aristocrats in the new elites dominated the military and the administrations throughout the Tang dynasty. Indeed, these foreigners helped to create a worldview for the Chinese.

**Intellectual Development.** The imperial era was one of the richest and most complex with regard to intellectual development. It was marked by the expansion of neo-Confucianism, the growth of religious passion, and the confirmation of an artistic and literary dilettantism, a pursuit of aesthetic pleasure for its own sake that was in conflict with the classical tradition. Chinese civilization eventually radiated far beyond the boundaries of China Proper to central Asia and East Asia, where local groups inherited the moral, artistic, and intellectual traditions of China.

**The Arts.** The artworks of the Tang dynasty and Song dynasty were romantic, optimistic, and energetic. Under the Yuan court the arts flourished, and by the time of the Ming empire a distinct division had developed between northern and southern schools of artists. Song architectural structures were smaller than earlier edifices but more ornate, complicated, and integrated with their natural settings. Simplicity and grace characterized Ming residential architecture and furniture. Many great poets arose during the Tang dynasty, and Song and Yuan poets established an important tradition of vernacular poetry. The Ming dynasty represented the glory days of Chinese literature with significant novels and short stories that promoted orthodox forms concentrating on ideology rather than aesthetics. Music during the Tang period could generally be categorized as either folk or palace music, and by the Song dynasty public theater had appeared, indicating a rise in urban music. During the Yuan dynasty many new orchestral instruments and schools of musicians were created. Folk songs became popular among the literati during the Ming era.

**Society.** Imperial society was typified by isolated village communities, comprehensive public-works projects (especially in education and defense), the absence of private ownership of land, and a significant class struggle. Since the Chinese farm economy relied heavily on the control of water resources, the government had to be capable of assembling hundreds of thousands of people to administer irrigation and flood-control projects. These circumstances led to the rise of despotic administrations and the stagnation of commercial and industrial development. In Tang times Chinese society was stratified, but the Song transformed China from an extremely aristocratic nation into a nearly egalitarian society. The development of a commercial economy and civil service examinations in the Song times enlarged the size and prestige of the office-holding gentry class. (Civil service exams based on merit continued until the Qing [Manchu] dynasty of 1644–1911.) By the Ming era local landlords and government officials constituted the crucial governing structure of society.

**Economy.** From the fourth century onward, many Chinese migrated to the less populated South, and the old metropolitan regions of the Northwest began to lose their strategic significance. The Yangzi (Yangtze) River valley soon turned out to be the chief rice-producing area and the basis of the imperial administration. Large private manors appeared in the early Song dynasty, but there was no feudal system based along Western lines. Revolutions in agricultural techniques, transportation, and the money economy occurred between the tenth and thirteenth centuries. New types of rice grown in paddy fields contributed to the development and expansion of wet farming. The manor had the resources to coordinate the projects to build the requisite dams, sluices, and irrigation machinery. Multiple crop growing became practicable. In the early Ming era the Chinese economy continued to grow; serfdom declined gradually; and small market towns arose. From the fifteenth century onward, the economy faltered. The Ming court failed to improve its technology at a pace sufficient to counterbalance the improvements made by other peoples, especially Europeans.

**Dynastic Cycle.** Historians have traditionally divided Chinese history into dynastic stages. Although powerful monarchs established dynasties, their heirs many times did not uphold the principles that their forefathers had set. If successive monarchs did not respond to frequent signals, which took the form of portents, the mandate of Heaven was transmitted to the founder of a new dynasty. Some modern historians, while admitting that the personal character of its leaders had some influence on a dynasty's fate, argued that the dynastic cycle was fundamentally the result of economic and administrative factors. When a new dynasty was established the ruler removed his rivals, created an efficient government, collected taxes, and defended the frontiers. As successive rulers installed new administrations, however, the expenses of government rose; strong families avoided paying taxes; officials became more corrupt; public works were abandoned; and the frontiers became overextended. Given such conditions, the peasants frequently revolted. The core of the Tang armies consisted of aristocrats. Song military forces were weak, although the government adopted new technologies such as gunpowder. The Mongols had a superb army in terms of overall direction, organization, and prowess. The Ming regime restored the glories of Tang times by creating strong armies and strengthening the Great Wall.

**Family.** Gradual but momentous changes in family life occurred in the period 618–1644. Crucial changes led to the solid formation of what is now viewed as the core of Chinese familial institutions. The development of marriage in imperial China was closely tied to the development of familiar patrilineality, filial piety, and patriarchy. From the Tang dynasty onward, the main characteristics of marriage included exogamy and polygamy. While social customs varied from one area to another over several centuries, they adhered to the same cultural heritage and interactive patterns. Common home life usually involved ritual rites being performed for a variety of purposes, mainly in the forms of ancestral worshiping, child rearing, weddings, and funerals. The patterns of such home-life customs had become regularized without much significant alteration since the Song dynasty, and some of the traditions still prevail in present-day Chinese society.

**Religion and Philosophy.** In imperial China, several religions and philosophies played important roles in justifying political powers, establishing administrative authority, upholding peace and order, maintaining civil values, inspiring faith in the government, and raising public morale in times of crisis. Confucianism, Buddhism, and Daoism were the three major religions. Buddhism began to spread from India to China in the fourth century and gradually gained strength by the eighth century. It stimulated the institutionalization of local cults and practices, but it never appealed to the masses. Both Confucianism and Daoism were developed by the Chinese. Although Confucianism and Daoism had much in common, Confucianism stressed the patriarchal extended family and the performance of worshiping dead ancestors while Daoism stressed personal freedoms and harmony with nature. In the Song dynasty neo-Confucian philosophers returned the philosophy of Confucius to its leading place as the ideology of the imperial government and adopted both Buddhist and Daoist concepts. Neo-Confucianism became the major orthodoxy until late in the Ming period. The tendency to combine Confucianism, Buddhism, and Daoism attracted many intellectuals.

**Science and Technology.** Major advances in mathematics, engineering, shipbuilding, chemistry, and biology occurred in the Song era. The Mongols respected Chinese craftsmen and technicians and encouraged their work.

Woodblock printing, invented in the ninth century, led to the rapid spread of knowledge.

**Medicine and Health**. Chinese medicine from the seventh century to the seventeenth century strongly stressed public health measures, providing many diagnostic and prognostic options, therapeutic alternatives for most health problems, and a rational philosophical basis that could be applied to psychological illnesses. More important, centralization and bureaucratization resulted in open access to the medical system for both the rich and poor. The greatest weakness of Chinese medicine during this time was the limited improvement in surgical procedures.

**Significance**. According to the scholar F. W. Mote, the development of Chinese civilization over the millennium covered in this volume is the story of "the largest society in human history." The period 617–1644 was not characterized only by autocracy and elitism but also by sophisticated cultural and social achievements. Nevertheless, Chinese advancements during this time did not ensure the creation of a modern nation-state. Although the Manchus established a prosperous and powerful dynasty at the end of the imperial era, that empire became plagued by foreign manipulation and internal disorder by the nineteenth century.

**Spelling**. In this volume all Chinese personal names are given in the traditional order, with family name first, followed by the given name (for example, Zhu Yuanzhang), except for overseas Chinese, whose names are given in the Western manner. The romanization of Chinese words has generated many and often confusing variations in spelling. Two romanization systems are used to write Chinese names and terms: the Wade-Giles system and the pinyin system. The Wade-Giles system has been used for more than one hundred years and remains the major one used outside of mainland China, especially on Taiwan. The Chinese Communists who established the People's Republic of China in 1949 created the pinyin system. The choice of which system to be employed is becoming a political issue: whether to use the pinyin system of Communist China or the Wade-Giles system preferred by Nationalist Taiwan. This volume adopts the pinyin system because of its increasing use all over the world today. There are some exceptions here to the pinyin system, particularly the retention of some names, which have long been assimilated into the English language. Thus, Hong Kong, Macao, Tibet, and others have not been converted to pinyin. Wade-Giles equivalents are noted and cross-referenced. Also, in some cases, this volume occasionally uses the Wade-Giles version of a name or term because it is familiar that way to Western readers.

**Acknowledgments**. This volume has benefited from the hard work of many people. I wish to thank George Wei, Jieli Li, and Huping Ling for their professionalism, dedication, and willingness to work with a tight deadline. All of them received their education in China and the United States, and they are currently professors at major American universities. These contributors are distinguished experts in their respective fields, and their educational background and competence in Chinese history help to make this reference book valuable in terms of scholarship. I am also grateful to Anthony Scotti, who has worked hard to bring the manuscript into conformity with the series' requirements. I am deeply indebted to him for his kindness in reading, criticizing, and offering suggestions at various stages of the editing process.

Guangqiu Xu
Friends University
Wichita, Kansas

# ACKNOWLEDGMENTS

This book was produced by Manly, Inc. Karen L. Rood is the senior editor and Anthony J. Scotti Jr., series editor, was the in-house editor.

Production manager is Philip B. Dematteis.

Administrative support was provided by Ann M. Cheschi, Carol A. Cheschi, and Amber L. Coker.

Accountant is Ann-Marie Holland.

Copyediting supervisor is Sally R. Evans. The copyediting staff includes Phyllis A. Avant, Brenda Carol Blanton, Caryl Brown, Melissa D. Hinton, Philip I. Jones, Rebecca Mayo, Nancy E. Smith, and Elizabeth Jo Ann Sumner. Freelance copyeditor is Brenda Cabra.

Editorial associates are Michael S. Allen, Michael S. Martin, Catherine M. Polit, and James F. Tidd Jr.

Permissions editor is Amber L. Coker.

Database manager is Amber L. Coker.

Layout and graphics supervisor is Janet E. Hill. The graphics staff includes Zoe R. Cook and Sydney E. Hammock.

Office manager is Kathy Lawler Merlette.

Photography supervisor is Paul Talbot. Photography editor is Scott Nemzek.

Digital photographic copy work was performed by Joseph M. Bruccoli.

SGML work was done by Linda Dalton Mullinax.

Systems manager is Marie L. Parker.

Typesetting supervisor is Kathleen M. Flanagan. The typesetting staff includes Patricia Marie Flanagan, Mark J. McEwan, and Pamela D. Norton.

Walter W. Ross supervised library research. He was assisted by Jo Cottingham and the following librarians at the Thomas Cooper Library of the University of South Carolina: circulation department head Tucker Taylor; reference department head Virginia W. Weathers; reference department staff Brette Barron, Marilee Birchfield, Paul Cammarata, Gary Geer, Michael Macan, Tom Marcil, Rose Marshall, and Sharon Verba; interlibrary loan department head John Brunswick; and interlibrary loan staff Robert Arndt, Hayden Battle, Alex Byrne, Jo Cottingham, Bill Fetty, Marna Hostetler, and Nelson Rivera.

# WORLD ERAS

## VOLUME 7

### IMPERIAL CHINA
617 - 1644

# WORLD EVENTS:
## SELECTED OCCURRENCES OUTSIDE IMPERIAL CHINA

by GUANGQIU XU

| | |
|---|---|
| **617** | • Alexandria, Egypt, is captured by the Persians. |
| **619** | • Spanish prelate Isidore of Seville presides at the second Council of Seville in Spain. He promotes the protection of monasteries throughout Europe. |
| **620** | • Heraclius buys peace with the Avars, who thereafter, with the Byzantines, fight against the Persians. |
| **621** | • Japanese crown prince and regent Shotoku Taishi, who imported Chinese culture into Japan as well as compiled the first written history of his country, dies. |
| **622** | • The founder of Islam, Muhammad, who was forced to leave Mecca in 619, migrates to Yathrib (Medina) with his followers. His flight is known as the Hegira. This date is used as the traditional start of the Muslim calendar. |
| **625** | • Muhammad begins dictating his beliefs, which will be gathered into the Koran. |
| **627** | • Bishop Paulinus of Kent, an Anglo-Saxon kingdom of England, converts Edwin to Christianity. |
| **628** | • Muhammad and his followers, by the treaty of Hudaybiya, are granted permission to make a pilgrimage from Yathrib to Mecca. Later, the Meccans lift a siege of Yathrib. |

*DENOTES CIRCA DATE

**630\*** • Hindu king Narasimhavarman I Mahamalla, of the Pallava dynasty, begins his reign in southern India. He rules until 668.

**632** • Muhammad dies. His successor, Abū Bakr, puts down an anti-Islamic Arab revolt with the assistance of general Khālid ibn al-Walīd and begins military campaigns against Syria.

**637** • A small Arab army defeats a Persian force of fifty thousand men in a three-day battle at al-Qādisīyah (Kadisiya) in Persia (modern Iraq). The Arabs occupy the Persian capital at Ctesiphon three months later.

**638** • Muslim Arabs under 'Umar I capture Jerusalem.

**641** • Heraclius dies. After a period of internal struggle, Constans II Pogonatus emerges as the Byzantine emperor.
• Germanic Lombards capture the cities of Oderzo and Genoa in Italy.

**642** • Narasimhavarman attacks the Deccan ruler Pulakesin II and captures southern India.

**643** • Egypt is conquered by the Arabs.
• King Rothari of the Lombards issues a Germanic civil and criminal code.

**645** • A palace revolt in Japan leads to a more closely knit state; an authoritarian, monarchial government is established by the Taikwa reforms the following year.

**646** • Arab general 'Amr ibn al-'As defeats an uprising in Alexandria.

**647** • The Arabs invade the Byzantine province of Africa, kill the usurper Gregory, and put down an African rebellion.

**648** • Byzantine emperor Constans II Pogonatus declares that Christian teachings will be limited to those defined in the first five ecumenical councils.

**654** • The Mediterranean island Rhodes is attacked by Arabs. Surviving portions of the Colossus of Rhodes, which was destroyed in an earlier earthquake, are dismantled and sold for scrap by the Arabs.

\* DENOTES CIRCA DATE

**655**
- The Arabs take Kabul and Kandahār (in present-day Afghanistan).
- A Byzantine fleet is destroyed by an Arab fleet in the Battle of Attaleia (Battle of the Masts) off the coast of Asia Minor.

**657**
- Wulfhere becomes king of the Mercians in southern England; he helps spread Christianity on the island.

**661**
- The Khariji, a fanatical sect, breaks away from 'Alī and members of the group assassinate him. Mu'āwiyah becomes caliph and establishes the Umayyad dynasty, making Damascus his capital. The Muslim Shia sect is created.

**663**
- Japanese troops are withdrawn from Korea after being defeated by the Chinese.

**664**
- Catholics in England, from the rival Celtic and Roman traditions, meet at the monastery of St. Hilda for the Synod of Whitby to debate doctrinal differences, especially concerning the celebration of Easter. The dispute is settled in favor of the Roman tradition.

**666**
- The newly elected Bishop of Canterbury, the Saxon Wighard, travels to Rome and announces the conversion of all of England to Catholicism. He will, however, never become bishop, having been blocked from reentry into England by an outbreak of plague.

**668**
- Constans II is assassinated while he is in Sicily to protect Italy from Arab invasion and making plans to retake North Africa. His son, Constantine IV, becomes the Byzantine ruler.

**669**
- Muslims conquer Morocco. They also sack Syracuse on Sicily.

**671**
- English prelate Wilfrid, later bishop of York, who was instrumental in converting northern Englishmen to Roman Catholicism, is given a monastery at Ripon, where he builds a great abbey.
- The reign of Japanese emperor Tenchi (Nakano-Oe) ends, sparking a dynastic struggle between his eldest son and his eldest brother.

**676**
- A Catholic nunnery is established at Bath, England, which is an important health resort.

*DENOTES CIRCA DATE

**677**
- The siege of Constantinople is lifted after the Arab fleet is destroyed. This defeat leads to thirty years of peace between the Byzantine and Arab empires.

**678**
- Pope Donus, who served from 676, dies. During his short reign he brought the Archbishopric of Ravenna back into the Roman church.

**680**
- Mu'āwiyah dies and a war of succession occurs. Yazīd I seizes power and wipes out a small revolt led by Husayn ibn 'Ali, who is killed in the Battle of Karbala. The town becomes a holy site for the Shiite branch of the Muslim faith.

**681**
- Bulgarians and Byzantines, who have been at war since 679, forge a peace treaty that gives the latter the province of Moesia.

**682**
- The Thirteenth Council of Toledo issues many anti-Jewish restrictions.
- Ah Cacau takes the throne of the Mayan city of Tikal (in modern northern Guatemala) and begins building great temples.

**683**
- Yazīd I—who reformed the political and administrative functions of his empire—dies. Marwān I succeeds to the Baghdad throne.

**685**
- Constantine IV dies; the Byzantine throne is taken by his son, Justinian II.
- Marwān I dies; he is succeeded by his son, 'Abd al-Malik ibn Marwān, who continues efforts to expand the influence of the Umayyad empire against the Byzantines and the North Africans.

**686**
- Citizens of the Isle of Wight are converted to Christianity.

**687**
- Pépin II (the Younger) of Heristal bests a rival for mayorship of the palace, in which the power of the kingdom resides, defeats the Neustrian nobles at the Battle of Tertry, and unites the Frankish empire.

**688**
- King Cadwalla of Wessex, one of the last holdouts to Christianity in the British Isles, travels to Rome and is baptized by the Pope.

\*Denotes Circa Date

**690** • Benedict Biscop, responsible for spreading Benedictine monasticism in Britain and allegedly introducing glassmaking and stone-constructed churches to the island, dies.

**691** • The ornate Dome of the Rock in Jerusalem, built by 'Abd al-Malik ibn Marwān to protect the site where Muhammad allegedly ascended into heaven, is completed. Work on this Islamic structure, designed to compete with Christian and Jewish sacred buildings in the city, was begun in the late 680s.

**692** • An Episcopal meeting in Constantinople, the Council of Trullo (or Quinisext Ecumenical Council), confirms Eastern customs (such as the marriage of priests) against Western ways and declares that the patriarch of Constantinople is equal to the pope. Sergius I refuses to sign the decrees.

**694** • Marwān I appoints a governor in North Africa who continues Muslim attacks against the Berbers and Byzantines in the region.

**695** • An army officer, Leontius, stages a coup and deposes Emperor Justinian II, who is exiled to the Crimea. Leontius rules for only three years, being deposed by Tiberius III Apsimar in 698.

**698** • Arabs occupy Carthage and end Byzantine rule in North Africa.

**700\*** • The North American Indians begin to use bows and arrows in place of spears as the favorite weapons for hunting. Invention of the hoe improves the efficiency of agriculture.

• The Srivijayas, who originate in Sumatra, take control of maritime trade routes in Indonesia.

**701\*** • Anglo-Saxon scholar Aldhelm, later bishop of Sherborne, translates the Psalms from Latin into Old English.

**702** • The Bala Bhramma temple, principal site in the Hindu Nava Brahamma temple complex in southern India, is constructed.

**703** • Anglo-Saxon scholar and monk the Venerable Bede is ordained at Jarrow. He is the author of ecclesiastical histories—as well as works on grammar, physical science, and biblical commentary.

*Denotes Circa Date

**705**
- Justinian II returns to the Byzantine throne and captures Constantinople with a Bulgarian army. He beheads Tiberius III Apsimar and kills Leontius.

**708**
- Sisinnius is elected Pope, but he dies after serving for only twenty days. His place is taken by Constantine, who travels to Constantinople in 711 at the invitation of Justinian II to confer about the differences between the Eastern and Western rites.

**710**
- The Buddhist center of Nara is made the capital of Japan, an honor it holds until 784.
- Roderick becomes king of the Visigoths in Spain.

**711**
- Led by Mohammed ibn al-Kassim, the Arabs invade India.
- Mūsa ibn Nusayr sends general Tāriq ibn Ziyād to invade Iberia with a Berber army of seven thousand soldiers; Tāriq defeats the Visigoths under Roderick at the Battle of Río Barbate.
- Justinian II is captured by his rebellious general Philippicus (Philip Bardanes) and is put to death. Philippicus rules Constantinople for two years and then is defeated by an Arab army.

**712**
- Liutprand becomes king of the Lombards in Italy.
- O no Yasumaro compiles the *Kojiki* (Records of Ancient Matters), a collection of Japanese creation stories and legends sacred to the Shinto sect, and presents it to the Imperial Court. This work is considered the start of Japanese literature.

**713**
- A treaty between Muslim invaders and Visigoth defenders of Orihuela, Spain, is signed. Terms were favorable to the defeated citizenry, as Christians and Jews were permitted to keep their property, practice their religion, pay fairer taxes, and retain local leadership.

**714**
- Pépin II dies; by force of arms, his illegitimate son, Charles Martel, wins the Frankish throne.

**715**
- Byzantine government official Theodosius III becomes emperor after the fall of Anastasius II.
- Gregory II is elected Pope. He concentrates on converting Germanic tribes to Christianity.
- Shōmu becomes the forty-fifth emperor of Japan. He promotes Buddhism and temple construction.

*DENOTES CIRCA DATE

**716**
- Aethelbald becomes king of Mercia. He begins to make it the strongest of the Anglo-Saxon kingdoms.

- Muslims invade Portugal.

- The newly crowned king of the Neustrians, Chilperic II, is defeated by forces of Charles Martel at the Battle of Amblève. He is recalled from exile to retain the kingship of the Franks in 719.

**717**
- The Khamis Mosque, the oldest Islamic structure in Bahrain, is built.

**718**
- Because of Byzantine superiority at sea, Emperor Leo III (the Isaurian), who deposed Theodosius III in 717, successfully raises the Arab siege of Constantinople.

**719**
- English Benedictine missionary Boniface (Wynfrid) is sent by Pope Gregory II to work with the Germanic people. He organizes many churches and becomes archbishop. In 725 he chops down the Donar Oak, spiritual symbol of Germanic spirituality, in his attack on heathen belief in the region. He is killed by a mob in 754.

**720**
- The second oldest collection of Japanese myths is gathered in the *Nihon shoki* (Chronicles of Japan).

**724**
- Lalitaditya becomes ruler of Kashmir and begins to conquer portions of northern India. His kingdom will stretch from Tibet to Iran and from southern India to Central Asia.

**725**
- Following the Sycthian Christian monk Dionysius Exiguus in reckoning dates from the birth of Christ, the Venerable Bede publishes *De Temporum ratione* (On the Reckoning of Time); this system is rapidly accepted in Western Europe.

**726**
- Leo III condemns and bans the use of icons and begins destroying these religious works of art. He also revises the law code, known as the *Ecloga*, and devises new rules for the military and maritime trade.

**730**
- Pope Gregory II excommunicates Leo III.

- The Khazars, an Eastern European people with Turkish roots, defeat an Arab army at the three-day Battle of Ardabil and then conquer Azerbaijan, Armenia, and northern Iraq. Their military presence helps block the spread of Islam into the Caucasus Mountain region. Khazar rulers, and many of their people, convert to Judaism, possibly in an effort to avoid being subjugated or dominated by their Muslim and Christian neighbors.

*Denotes Circa Date

**731**
- Pope Gregory II dies. The Pope elected to replace him also adopts the name Gregory (III) and takes up the fight against Iconoclasm.

**732**
- An army led by Charles Martel defeats the Arabs at the Battle of Tours (Poitiers) in central Gaul, effectively blocking the expansion of Islam into southern Europe.

**734**
- The Hindu Siva temple complex Eklingji, located near Udaipur, India, is carved from sandstone and marble.

**736**
- The Mayan Temple of the Masks is constructed in Tikal (modern Guatemala).

**738**
- Mayan warriors from Quiriguá defeat the defenders of Copán, capture its ruler and behead him, gaining for the victors control of trade to the Caribbean.

**739**
- Charles Martel and Luitprand unite their forces and attack Rome.

**740**
- At the battle of Akroinon, Byzantine forces, with the help of the Khazars and the Georgians, defeat the Arabs, who had invaded Asia Minor.

**741**
- The Japanese government of Shōmu pronounces that Buddhist temples will be constructed throughout the nation.
- Charles Martel dies; his lands are divided between his sons Pepin III (the Short) and Carloman.
- Leo III dies and is replaced on the Byzantine throne by his son Constantine V, who has served as coruler since 720. Constantine defeats a challenge from his brother-in-law Artabasdus.

**743**
- Shōmu begins construction of the Tōdai Temple in Nara, which is completed in 752.

**744**
- Umayyad caliph al-Walid II, who cultivated the arts, dies. The Abbāsid movement emerges and contests the leadership of the Umayyads.

**745**
- Bubonic plague sweeps Constantinople and spreads to Europe.

**746**
- Daibutsu Hall, the largest wooden structure in the world, is built in the Tōdai Temple complex in Nara, Japan.

*DENOTES CIRCA DATE

**749**
- The reign of Shōmu comes to an end. Japanese society was dominated by a widespread imitation of Chinese culture during his administration. His daughter Kōken takes the throne.
- Indian monk Padmasambhava introduces Buddhism to Tibet and establishes a monastery.

**750**
- The Mayan city Teotihuacan in Mexico is destroyed and the seat of power shifts to southern Mexico.
- Marwān II, last of the Umayyad rulers, is defeated by the Abbāsids at the Battle of Great Zab. Abu al-'Abbās as-Saffāh becomes caliph (establishing the Abbāsid dynasty), murders Umayyad leaders, and moves the capital to Baghdad.

**751**
- Arabs defeat the Chinese on the Talas River after occupying Tashkent, Samarqand, and Bukhara; they begin to spread Islamic influence through central Asia.
- Pepin the Short deposes Childeric III and becomes king of the Franks, starting the Carolingian dynasty.

**753**
- Two Chinese prisoners disclose the technique of making paper to the Arabs, and thereafter the first paper mill in the Arab world is founded in Baghdad.

**754**
- Constantine V calls the Synod of Constantinople to sustain his fight against the use of icons.

**756**
- Pepin the Short defeats the Lombards; the Papal States are declared an independent territory under the authority of the Pope. Pepin the Short gives the Pope control of Ravenna.

**759**
- Pepin the Short drives Muslims out of southern France.
- Mountain tribes in Lebanon revolt against Abbāsid rule.
- A collection of more than 4,500 Japanese poems from the Nara period is compiled in the *Man'yoshu* (The Anthology of Ten Thousand Leaves).

**760**
- Construction begins on Borobudur, a great Buddhist temple fashioned from lava rock, on the island of Java in Indonesia. More than 1900 bas-reliefs and statues were featured in the complex.

**761**
- Abd ar Rahman ibn Rustum founds the Rustumid dynasty at Tahirt in Algeria.
- The Abbāsids in Mesopotamia adopt the Indian system of numerals.

*DENOTES CIRCA DATE

| | |
|---|---|
| **763** | • The Abbāsids improve irrigation, repair the Nahrwan canal on the Tigris River near Baghdad, and construct a dam. |
| **764** | • Japanese Buddhist priest Dōkyō instigates a coup against Emperor Junnin and installs Kōken as Empress Shōtoku. Dōkyō remains, however, the power behind the throne. |
| **766** | • The Mayan Temple of the Inscriptions is constructed in Tikal (modern Guatemala). |
| **768** | • Charlemagne, son of Pepin the Short, becomes king of the Neustrians upon the death of his father; he becomes king of all the Franks in 771 when his brother, Carloman, dies.<br>• The Celtic Church in Wales officially reunites with the Roman Church. |
| **770** | • Empress Shōtoku dies; she is replaced on the Japanese throne by Emperor Konin. Her death also marks the end of influence of the priest Dōkyō, who is banished from the royal city. |
| **771** | • Charlemagne makes Aachen (Aix-la-Chapelle), probably the town of his birth and where he has resided since 668, capital of his empire. By this date most of what will be modern France, Belgium, and Germany is controlled by the Franks. Charlemagne also marries Hildegarde, a fellow native of Aachen. |
| **774** | • After occupying the Lombard Kingdom, Charlemagne declares himself king. He also occupies much of Italy. The first Frankish king to visit Rome, he agrees to give Ravenna to the Pope, a donation originally made by Pepin the Short, his father and predecessor. |
| **775** | • On the death of Constantine V, his eldest son, Leo IV (the Khazar), succeeds as Byzantine emperor. Although also an iconoclast, he carries out a more appeasing religious policy. |
| **776\*** | • Arab alchemist Jābir ibn Hayyān, considered by some the father of chemistry, works in the city of Al-Kufa, south of Baghdad. |
| **778** | • The rear guard of Charlemagne's army is caught and massacred by Basques at the pass at Roncesvalles, Spain, in the Pyrenees Mountains. The Basques, fighting with lighter arms—and therefore more mobile than their opponents—probably sought to plunder the baggage train. The attack is memorialized as *La Chanson de Roland* (The Song of Roland, circa 1100s), in honor of one of the knights who died. |

\* DENOTES CIRCA DATE

**780**
- Alp Qutlug, *Kagan* (emperor) of the Uighurs in Central Asia, opens his empire to Sino-Persian influence by adopting Manichaeism as the state religion.

**781**
- Pépin, son of Charlemagne, becomes king of Italy, while his brother, Louis I (the Pious), is made king of Aquitaine. Charlemagne brings Alcuin, headmaster of the cathedral school in York, England, to Aachen, which sparks a revival of learning.

**782**
- Charlemagne, who is trying to establish the Christian Church in Saxony, massacres 4,500 Saxon hostages by beheading them, possibly in revenge for an earlier defeat suffered at their hands. He faces several insurrections, deports many Saxons, and fails to subdue the region until 804.

**784**
- Japanese emperor Kammu moves the capital from Nara to Nagaoka to lessen the influence of the Buddhist priests.

**786**
- Hārūn ar-Rashīd becomes fifth caliph of the Abbāsid dynasty after the short rule of his brother Musa al-Hādi (785–786). He extends the power of the Islamic caliphate from Asia to Africa, with Baghdad the centerpiece of Arabic culture.

**787**
- Pope Adrian I calls and presides over the Second Nicean Council, the seventh ecumenical council of the Catholic Church, which was initially planned to be held in Constantinople. Empress Irene, however, replaces rebellious officers, and the meeting is held in Nicea. Among the decisions made at the council is approval of the use of icons.

**788**
- Tassilo III is deposed by Charlemagne; Bavaria is added to the kingdom of the Franks.

**789**
- Münster, Germany, is founded.

**790***
- Jayavarman II returns from Javan exile to Cambodia, initially serving as a puppet ruler; he asserts independence (802), unites the people, establishes Hindu Brahminism as the state religion, and founds the Khmer Empire.

**792**
- Empress Irene is called back from a two-year retirement to become coruler with her son, Constantine VI.

**793**
- Viking invaders attack Lindisfarne (Holy Island), which is located off the coast of Northumberland, England. A monastery, founded there in 635, is destroyed and the monks are carried off.

*DENOTES CIRCA DATE

**794**
- The imperial court is moved to Kyoto, which is the traditional start of the Heian period of Japanese history.

**795**
- Charlemagne establishes a frontier province south of Pyrenees (Spain) between the Frankish and Arab empires.
- Viking raids, particularly aimed at monasteries, are carried out against Ireland and England.

**796**
- Charlemagne defeats the Avars after five years of conflict.

**799**
- Rijeka (Fiume), Croatia, is destroyed by Charlemagne's forces.
- A rebellion in Rome against Leo III is put down by Charlemagne.

**800\***
- Irish monks on the island of Iona copy and illuminate the Four Gospels in a manuscript known as the Book of Kells (or Book of Columba). It is a masterpiece of medieval Celtic art.

**800**
- Pope Leo III crowns Charlemagne the first Emperor in the West since the downfall of the Roman Empire in 476.
- Iceland and the Faeroe Islands are allegedly discovered by Irish monks.

**801**
- Charlemagne recaptures Barcelona from the Moors, who have held the city since 713.

**802**
- Jayavarman II establishes Angkor as his capital. The city features beautiful temples and palaces, as well as advanced irrigation.
- The khan and warrior Krum takes the Bulgar throne by defeating the Avars; he then wages war against the Byzantine Empire.

**804-806\***
- Japanese Buddhist monk Kūkai founds the Shingon sect.

**806**
- Ashot IV becomes the first king of the Bagratid dynasty of Armenia and remains in power until 826.
- Venetia and Dalmatia, two former Roman provinces, submit to the authority of Charlemagne.

\*Denotes Circa Date

**806**
(CONT'D)

- Hārūn ar-Rashīd renews Arab incursions into Byzantine territory and forces new terms of peace with the empire.

**807**

- Krum's Bulgar army advances on Constantinople.
- The Kiyomizu Temple is founded in Kyoto, Japan.

**808***

- Charlemagne founds a fortress on the Elbe River to serve against the Slavs; the citadel becomes the town of Hamburg.

**809**

- Emperor Saga takes the Japanese throne upon abdication of Heizei.

**810***

- The Temple of the Jaguar Priest is constructed by the Mayans in Tikal.
- King Harold I (Harald) begins his reign in Denmark.

**811**

- Nicephorus I dies in battle while attacking the capital of Bulgar leader Krum. Allegedly, the khan drinks from a cup fashioned from the slain emperor's skull. Nicephorus I's successor, Stauracius, is unable to serve because of a debilitating injury and is replaced on the throne by his son-in-law, Michael Rangabe, who becomes Michael I.

**812**

- Michael I sends an embassy to Charlemagne and formally recognizes him as emperor of the West. In return, Charlemagne concedes Venice and Dalmatia to the Byzantine Empire.

**813**

- Leo V (the Armenian), a Byzantine general, overthrows Michael I and takes the crown. He continues to fight against the Bulgars; Krum dies the following year; Leo leads the Byzantines until he is assassinated in 820.
- Al-Amīn is captured at Baghdad and killed by his rebellious brother al-Ma'mūm (Mamūm the Great), who rules as caliph until 833.

**814**

- Charlemagne dies; his son, Louis I (the Pious), becomes emperor of the West. Louis has served as coruler since 813.

**817**

- In accordance with Frankish custom, Louis I divides the kingdom among his three sons (Lothair I [Italy], Pepin I [Aquitaine and Burgundy], and Louis II the German [Bavaria]), and bitter rivalry and warfare break out among the brothers thereafter.
- Paschal I becomes Pope and secures control over the papal territories.

*DENOTES CIRCA DATE

**817**
**(CONT'D)**

- Leo V defeats the Bulgarians at Mesembria and concludes a peace that lasts for thirty years.
- Moorish ruler al-Hakam I defeats and expels rebels in Córdoba.

**819**

- Sāmān-khodā founds the Sāmānid dynasty in Persia. The Sámánids remain controlled, however, by the caliph in Baghdad.

**820\***

- Arab mathematician Muhammad ibn Musa al-Khwārizmī advances the concepts of algebra, algorithms, and decimal notation; he greatly influences scientific and mathematical knowledge in the Middle East and Europe.

**823**

- Japanese emperor Saga abdicates the throne to follow cultural pursuits and is replaced by Junna.
- Vikings plunder Bangor in Ulster in northern Ireland.
- Kanak Pal becomes the first ruler of the Himalayan state of Garhwal.

**824**

- Crete is invaded by Saracens and is used as a base for pirates. They found in 825 the city of Khandak (later Candia, and now Heraklion) on the northern coast. Conquest of the island is completed in 826.

**825**

- The dominance of the Mercians comes to an end after West Saxon (Wessex) king Egbert defeats the forces of Beornwulf at the Battle of Ellendune.

**826**

- Benedictine missionary Ansgar enters Denmark, Norway, and Sweden to evangelize for the Church. He is made archbishop for Scandinavian (as well as Slavic) missions and is later canonized for his efforts.

**827**

- Sicily is invaded by Arabs from North Africa, who are invited in by a local governor. The conquest is slow, as many strongholds do not fall until the turn of the century.

**829**

- Emperor Michael II dies; he is succeeded on the Byzantine throne by his son, Theophilus, who initiates a renaissance of learning and art.

**830**

- Louis I's three sons attempt to overthrow him as Holy Roman Emperor, but they fail. Another coup attempt in 833 also fails.
- Viking raiders sail up the Thames River in England.

*Denotes Circa Date

**831**
- French Benedictine theologian Paschasius Radbertus of the abbey at Corbie introduces the concept of transubstantiation in *De corpore et sanguine Christi*.
- Pannonia is conquered by the Bulgars.
- Omortag, leader of the Bulgarians, dies and is succeeded by his son, Malamir.

**832**
- Approximately one thousand Viking warriors raid deep into Ireland.

**834\***
- Kenneth I MacAlpin becomes king of Dalriada and begins a campaign to unite the Scots under one rule. He is traditionally credited with establishing the kingdom of Scotland.
- Al-Mu'tasim succeeds al-Ma'mūm as caliph, initiating the decline of the Abbāsid dynasty.

**837**
- The Muslim Empire ruled by al-Mu'tasim is invaded by Byzantine forces.
- A revolt by Christians in Spain is put down by the Moors.

**838**
- The Saxons, led by Egbert, defeat a combined Danish-Cornish army at the Battle of Hingston Down.

**840\***
- The Norsemen found Limerick and Dublin as trading bases on the Irish coast.

**840**
- Invaded by Kirghiz Turks coming from the west, the Central Asian empire of the Uighur Turks collapses.

**841**
- The armies of Louis the German and Charles the Bald defeat their brother Lothair I at the Battle of Fontenoy.
- Scandinavians settle in Normandy.

**842**
- Byzantine emperor Theophilus dies; his wife, Theodora, serves as regent for their son, Michael III. She is forced to retire in 858.

**843**
- Charles the Bald, Louis the German, and Lothair I meet and sign the Treaty of Verdun; they agree to divide Carolingian lands among themselves. Charles the Bald obtains the western part of the empire, Louis the German gains the eastern, and Lothair I, the oldest brother, retains the title of emperor and obtains the middle kingdom.

*Denotes Circa Date

**844**
- Pope Gregory IV dies. He tried, and failed, to mediate among warring Frankish rulers. A popular uprising tries to install John as the next Pope, but the nobility succeeds in electing Sergius II.

**845**
- Viking raiders sack Paris.

**846**
- Rome is attacked by the Saracens, who desecrate many holy Christian shrines, including the Basilica of St. Peter, from which they strip gold and silver.

**847**
- Pope Leo IV builds the Leonine Wall to protect the Vatican.

**849**
- Muslim raiders are defeated at the Battle of Ostia by a fleet and army from united Italian seaport cities led by the Duke of Naples.

**850**
- Irish-born theologian John Scotus Erigena writes *De divisione naturae*.
- Vijalaya founds the Cōla (Chola) dynasty of southern India.

**851**
- Danish sea forces are defeated by the Saxons off the coast of Kent; after sacking London, a Danish army is beaten by Aethelwulf at the Battle of Ockley.

**852**
- Construction, started in 842, is completed on the largest Muslim mosque in the world, the Great Mosque of Samarra in Iraq, which features a fifty-foot spiral tower.
- Boris I becomes ruler of Bulgaria and converts (in 865) to Orthodox Christianity. He makes his subjects adopt Christianity as well.

**855**
- Lothair I dies; his lands are divided among his three sons: Louis II obtains Italy, Charles gets Provence, and Lothair II gains Lotharingia. Louis II is crowned Holy Roman Emperor.

**856**
- Michael III serves as Byzantine emperor after ending the regency of his mother, who enters a convent. He is heavily influenced by Bardas, who raises eyebrows by living with the widow of his son.

**857**
- The patriarch of Constantinople, Ignatius, excommunicates Bardas for living in an allegedly incestuous arrangement.

*DENOTES CIRCA DATE

**858**
- Michael III removes Ignatius from the patriarchy and puts Photius in his place, a move opposed by Pope Nicholas I, who excommunicates Photius, sparking the Photian Schism.

**860**
- Rus Vikings, living in the Kiev region (modern Ukraine), travel down the Dnieper River into the Black Sea and attack Constantinople, but they fail to capture the city.

**862**
- Byzantine Orthodox missionaries Constantine (Cyril) and Methodius are sent by Michael III to convert the Slavs of Moravia and Bohemia. The former develops a written language, Cyrillic, adapted for the Slavs from Greek.
- Varangians, of Scandinavian origins and led by Rurik, arrive in Novgorod, an area dominated by the princes of Kiev.

**865***
- Persian physician Abū Bakr Muhammad ibn Zakarīyā ar-Rāzī (Rhazes) writes a treatise detailing the differences between smallpox and measles.

**865**
- Louis the German divides his kingdom: Carloman gets Bavaria and Carinthia; Charles III (the Fat) obtains Swabia; and Louis the Younger is given Franconia, Thuringia, and Saxony.

**866**
- Danish invaders capture Northumbria and begin building settlements.

**867**
- Basil I murders Michael and sits as emperor until 886. A strong leader who reforms the laws, finances, and military, Basil starts a dynasty that lasts until 1056. He also deposes Photius and restores Ignatius as patriarch of Constantinople.

**868**
- The first known book printed on paper, the Buddhist text *Diamond Sutra*, is produced in Japan.

**869**
- Lothair II dies and his lands are divided between his uncles Louis the German and Charles the Bald.

**869–870**
- The Fourth Council of Constantinople, called by Basil I and Byzantine patriarch Ignatius in hopes of mending fences among the contesting parties to the patriarchy, is held to determine the status of clerics assigned under Photius. Adrian II sends delegates; Photius is condemned; and Ignatius is confirmed.

*Denotes Circa Date

**871**
- The son of Aethelwulf and brother of the deceased King Aethelred, Alfred (the Great) becomes king of Wessex. Nine battles are fought this year between Saxons and Danes.

**872**
- King Harold I consolidates control of Norway, defeating his rivals at the Battle of Hafrsfjord.

**874**
- Viking legend claims that Ingolfur Arnarson sails to Iceland and founds a settlement that becomes Reykjavik.

**875**
- After the death of Holy Roman Emperor Louis II, Charles the Bald rushes to Italy and is crowned Emperor by Pope John VIII.

**876**
- Louis III (the Younger) defeats his uncle, Charles the Bald, who was trying to control territory held by Louis the German, at the Battle of Andernach.

**877**
- Charles the Bald dies. His son, Louis II (the Stammerer), becomes king of France but not Holy Roman Emperor.

**878**
- King Alfred defeats a Danish army commanded by Guthrum at Edington in Wiltshire and forces the Danes to accept the Peace of Wedmore. Guthrum is baptized and removes his settlements to East Anglia.

**879**
- The Khmers of Cambodia begin building temples at Angkor.
- Pope John VIII recognizes Photius as the patriarch of Constantinople.

**880**
- Louis the Stammerer dies; his sons, Carloman and Louis III, divide the kingdom of the West Franks.
- King Amoghavarsha of northern India, a patron of Jainism and regional literature, dies.

**881**
- Charles becomes the first eastern Frankish ruler to be crowned Holy Roman Emperor. His empire is divided into several small, entirely independent, kingdoms.

**882**
- Kiev is captured by Rus king Oleg, who succeeded Rurik; Oleg makes the town his capital.

*Denotes Circa Date

**883**
- The Zinj—East African slave laborers—who began a revolt near Basra, Iraq, in 869, are put down by al-Muwaffaq, regent for caliph al-Mu'tamid.

**885**
- Count Eudes defends Paris against a Norse siege; he defeats the invaders in 886, despite receiving no help from Charles the Fat.

**886**
- Alfred the Great captures London and rules England south of the Danish-controlled areas.
- Byzantine emperor Basil I dies and is succeeded by his son, Leo IV (the Wise), who has been co-emperor since 870.

**887**
- Charles the Fat is deposed and the Carolingian empire falls apart; Germany and France are founded; southern France, Burgundy, and Italy become competing kingdoms. Carloman's illegitimate son Arnulf becomes king of Germany.
- Uda Tennō, who is dominated by the civil dictator Fujiwara Mototsune, becomes emperor of Japan.

**888**
- Eudes, defender of Paris, becomes king of the west Franks, but he is opposed by Charles III (the Simple).

**889**
- The Magyars are pushed out of the Danube River region by invading Turkic peoples.
- Boris I abdicates the Bulgarian throne in favor of his son Vladimir, although Boris is forced to return in 893 to put his third son, Simeon (the Great), in power.
- King Anand Dev founds the Nepalese city of Bhadgaon (Bhaktapur, the "city of devotees") in the Himalayas.

**890\***
- Thyra, wife of Danish king Gorm the Old, has an immense rampart (Dannevirke) erected across the peninsula to protect the Danes against German attacks.

**891**
- German king Arnulf defeats the Vikings at the Battle of the Dyle (in modern Belgium). He also attacks the Moravians and invades Italy.
- Arnulf is unable to come to Rome to accept the coronation as Emperor of the Holy Roman Empire; Guy of Spoleto forces Pope Stephen V to crown him instead. Guy's young son, Lambert, becomes coruler in 892. Stephen dies and is replaced as Pope by the reluctant Formosus, who follows his predecessor's policies.

**894**
- Simeon (the Great) leads the Bulgarians against Constantinople, initiating a series of wars that last until 924, although he never captures the Byzantine capital.

\***Denotes Circa Date**

**896**

- Arnulf captures Rome, whereupon he becomes Holy Roman Emperor. Formosus, who crowns the conqueror, dies and is replaced by Boniface VI, who lives only fifteen days after becoming Pope and is possibly an assassination victim. Stephen VI then is elected Pope.

- Magyar chief Arpád leads his people out of the Black Sea region into Hungary and captures territory from local tribes.

**897**

- Pope Stephen VI, who may be deranged, exhumes Pope Formosus's corpse at the behest of Lambert (who regained the crown) and makes it undergo trial for capital crimes at the "Cadaver Synod." After Formosus is convicted, three fingers are severed and the body is tossed into the Tiber River; the cadaver is later buried. An uprising deposes Stephen, and he is strangled while imprisoned. Romanus is made Pope, but he is deposed after four months; his replacement, Theodore II, is also perhaps murdered, his reign lasting only about a month.

**899**

- Arnulf dies, after having suffered paralysis during the wars in Italy, and is succeeded on the German throne by his six-year-old son, Louis IV (the Child), with the archbishop of Mainz serving as regent.

- Japanese emperor Uda Tennō appoints scholar Sugawara Michizane as minister to counter the influence on the imperial house by the Fujiwaras.

**900\***

- Magyar raiders conduct incursions, which continue into the 950s, in central Europe.

- Bantu-speaking people establish city-states in eastern Africa.

- Mayan civilization is in disarray as the lowland cities of Central America are abandoned, while in the highlands the Mayans continue to flourish.

- Toltecs migrate into Mexico and drive remnants of native inhabitants from Teotihuacán.

**901**

- Muslim raiders capture the Balearic Islands in the western Mediterranean Sea, located off the coast of Spain.

**902**

- Muslim invaders complete their conquest of Sicily.

**903**

- The Saffārid dynasty in Iran ends and is replaced by the Sāmānids.

- Returned from exile for having supported Stephen VI, Sergius III orders the deaths of the antipope Christopher and Pope Leo V in 903, and takes the pontificate (904).

**904**

* Denotes Circa Date

- By treaty, the Byzantines acknowledge Bulgarian territorial acquisitions in northern Greece.

**905**
- The Muslim Tūlūnid dynasty of Egypt, founded in 868 by Ahmad ibn Tūlūn, is defeated by the armies of Caliph al-Maktafī.

**907**
- Kievan prince Oleg defeats Constantinople and obtains an indemnity; he follows up this victory by negotiating a trade agreement in 911.

**909**
- 'Ubayd Allāh founds the Muslim Fātimid dynasty of North Africa.

**910**
- The largest Benedictine abbey is founded at Cluny, France. The monastery starts a reform movement that will sweep Europe by establishing a sanctuary that promotes a prayerful Benedictine life.

**911**
- The final Eastern Carolingian king, Louis the Child, dies; Germany is divided into rival principalities. Conrad I is elected king but is forced to renounce the throne in 919.
- Charles the Simple gives Rollo, who converted to Christianity, land that becomes known as Normandy. Rollo is baptized Robert and becomes Charles's vassal.
- Edward the Elder takes London and Oxford after the death of Mercian king Aethelred II. Queen Aethelflaed continues as ruler in Wessex and fortifies Mercia against Viking attacks. She rules until her death in 918.

**913**
- The scholarly Constantine VII (Porphyrogenitus) becomes Byzantine emperor and reigns until 959.
- Umayyid emir 'Abd ar-Rahman III an-Nasir captures Seville and controls the Iberian Peninsula.

**915**
- A united Italian army, supported by a Greek navy and led by Pope John X, destroys a Saracen force encamped near the Gagliano River in southern Italy.

**919**
- Henry I (the Fowler) is elected King of Germany and forms an alliance with Charles the Simple.
- Southwest Anasazi Indians begin construction of Pueblo Bonito (in modern Chaco Canyon, New Mexico); the structure will eventually have 650 rooms and is not completed until 1085.

**920**
- Admiral of the fleets, Romanus I Lecapenus, becomes the power behind the Byzantine throne while serving as co-emperor with Constantine Porphyrogenitus.

*DENOTES CIRCA DATE

**923**
- Charles the Simple is defeated by Hebert, Count of Vermandois, and dies while in his custody.

**925**
- Bulgarian leader Simeon the Great becomes tsar of the Romans and Bulgarians.

**926**
- Aethelstan annexes Northumbria.
- Manchuria and northern Korea are annexed by the Mongol Khitan empire.

**927**
- The Heveller, a Slavic tribe living along the Havel River, are defeated by Henry the Fowler.

**928**
- Marozia (Little Mary), an influential Italian noblewoman, succeeds in having Pope John X imprisoned. He dies in prison.
- Vikings reputedly massacre one thousand Irish taking refuge in Dunmore Cave.

**929**
- Stephen VII becomes Pope and serves until his death in 931. He may have been the first Pope to be clean-shaven in office and to promote the practice in Italy.

**930**
- A constitutional law code and parliament, the Althing, are established in Iceland. Representatives meet in a natural amphitheater yearly to elect leaders and settle disputes.

**931**
- Marozia gets her son, possibly conceived from a union with Pope Sergius III, installed as Pope John XI; he wields little power, as he is dominated during his pontificate either by his mother or his brother, Alberic II, the ruler of Rome.

**933**
- The Second Kingdom of Burgundy (Kingdom of Arles) is formed by Rudolf II from the united provinces of Cisjurane and Transjurane Burgundy, which had been separated after the fall of the Carolingian empire.
- Henry the Fowler leads German forces, newly trained in mounted warfare, in defeating Magyar invaders at Riade.

**935**
- The Silla dynasty, which has ruled Korea since 618, comes to an end and is replaced by the Koryo dynasty, which rules until 1392.

*DENOTES CIRCA DATE

**936**
- Otto I (the Great) is placed on the German and Holy Roman thrones after the death of his father, Henry.
- Harold II (Bluetooth), son of Gorm the Old, becomes king of Denmark upon the death of his father.

**937**
- Aethelstan gains greater control of Anglo-Saxon England after defeating a combined Pict-Viking army at the Battle of Brunanburh in Scotland.

**938**
- Vietnamese leader Ngo Quyen defeats the Chinese at the Battle of Bach Dang River and proclaims an independent Vietnam.

**941**
- A Greek fleet defending Constantinople destroys an invading Russian force led by Igor, Duke of Kiev.

**942**
- After a peace was arranged between Hugh of Provence and the Vatican, Pope Stephen VIII dies and is followed in the patriarchy by Marinus II, who is dominated by Alberic II.

**944**
- Co-emperor Romanus I Lecapenus is deposed by his sons, but Constantine V remains in power; the fratricides are banished from the Byzantine Empire.
- Rebellious Slavs (Drevelans) capture and kill Prince Igor. His wife, Olga, serves as regent for their son and exacts revenge upon the murderers by killing their emissaries and burning their city.
- Edmund expels the Norsemen, led by Olaf Sihtricson, from Northumbria.

**945**
- The Būyids seize Baghdad and establish a Shiite state that rules central Iraq until 1055. Abbāsid caliphs remain as puppet rulers.

**946**
- Edmund is murdered while attending a banquet at Pucklechurch. His brother, Eadred, succeeds to the English crown.

**949**
- The Cōlas of southern India, ruled by Paranthaka I, are defeated by invading Rashtrakutas from the north at the battle of Takkolam, North Arcot, which slows the expansion of the Cōlas empire.

**950\***
- The Toltecs build a capital city, Tula, in Central America on a site near modern-day Mexico City.

\***DENOTES CIRCA DATE**

**950\***
**(CONT'D)**

- The central Indian kingdom of Chandela reaches new heights of influence and prosperity.

- Polynesians begin settling in New Zealand.

**953**

- Duke Liudof of Swabia leads a revolt against his father, Otto the Great; coconspirators Conrad the Red of Lotharingia and Archbishop Frederick of Mainz desert him in 955 and the revolt is ended.

**955**

- A Magyar army, raiding into Bavaria, is defeated by Otto the Great at the Battle of Lechfeld and pushed back into Hungary. Rather than ransoming captured Magyar leaders, Otto the Great has them killed; the Magyars stop raiding Germany and settle in Hungary.

**957**

- Arab historian and geographer al-Masūdī, who traveled as far south as Mozambique and wrote several important books, including *Akhbar āz-Zamān* (The History of Time), dies in Cairo.

**959**

- Constantine Porphyrogenitus, patron of art and literature, dies and is replaced on the Byzantine throne by his son, Romanus II.

**960**

- Romanus II names his young sons, Basil II (two) and Constantine VIII (one), co-emperors. Their guardians—their mother Theodora, Nicephoras II Phocas, and John I Tzimisces—actually run the empire until 976. Romanus II dies in 963.

**961**

- Nicephoras Phocas recaptures Crete, as well as much of Sicily, from Muslim occupiers. He challenges the young emperors, marries their mother, and effectively rules Byzantium until he is assassinated in 969 in a plot orchestrated by his wife and John I Tzimisces, who had been a trusted lieutenant.

**962**

- After an appeal by Pope John XII for aid, Otto the Great invades Italy again and is later crowned emperor in St. Peter's Basilica (Vatican).

- Svyatoslav I, the duke of Kiev, comes of age and takes control of his kingdom; he creates a strong kingdom in the Volga region by defeating the Khazars and spreads his influence into the Balkans.

**964**

- Pope John XII, who conspired against Otto the Great the previous year and was deposed by Leo VIII, regains his position but then dies. The newly elected Pope, Benedict V, is quickly overthrown in favor of Leo VIII, who serves for only one year.

\*DENOTES CIRCA DATE

**965**

- Nicephoras II Phocas recaptures Cyprus from the Muslims.

**966***

- The Fātimids gain control of Jerusalem.

**969**

- John I Tzimisces takes effective control of the Byzantine Empire as guardian of the minor emperors. The Byzantines end three hundred years of Arab rule in Antioch (Syria).
- Egypt is conquered by the Fātimids. They make their capital, Cairo, the center of Islamic culture.

**971**

- John I Tzimisces besieges Duke Svyatoslav I at Dristra and forces a peace treaty between the Byzantines and Kievans, which also forces the duke to give up territory in the Balkans. During his return trip to Kiev, Svyatoslav is killed by Pecheneg raiders.

**972**

- Construction of the Al-Azhar mosque and accompanying school for Shiites in Cairo (begun in 970) is completed; it will become the oldest university for religious and secular studies in the world.

**973**

- Otto the Great dies and his son, Otto II, becomes Holy Roman Emperor.

**974**

- While Otto II is busy dealing with a revolt in Bavaria, the short pontificate of Benedict VI ends with his death by strangulation, ordered by Boniface VII at the behest of rebellious factions in Rome. Boniface is quickly removed from power when Otto returns. The new Pope takes the name Benedict VII.

**975**

- Fātimid caliph al-Mu'izz, who captured Syria and Mesopotamia, dies. His son, al-Aziz, takes power and rules for fifteen years.
- English king Edgar dies. He had conquered Northumbria but allowed the Vikings local rule. His son, Edward (the Martyr), takes the throne.

**977**

- Sebüktigin founds the Ghaznavid dynasty. These Turkish rulers defeat the Sāmānids and control Afghanistan and northern India until 1186.

**979**

- Vietnamese emperor Dinh Bo Linh—who established a bureaucracy, set up judicial courts, organized an army, unified the people, and secured independence—dies.

*DENOTES CIRCA DATE

**980**

- Vladimir I, who was forced to flee in 972, returns and becomes Grand Prince of Kiev.

- Macedonian leader Samuel is crowned tsar of Bulgaria and engages in almost constant warfare with the Byzantine Empire.

- Le Dai Hahn becomes emperor of Vietnam; he extends the road network and deals with rebellious factions.

**981**

- Danish king Olaf Sihtricson of Dublin and Northumbria dies. His forces were defeated the previous year at Tara.

**982**

- Norwegian sailor Erik the Red, banished from Iceland after killing two men with which he was feuding, discovers Greenland and explores the coast. A colony is planted there in 986.

**983**

- Three-year-old Otto III becomes Holy Roman Emperor upon the death of his father, Otto II; Theophano serves as her son's regent. Pope Benedict VII dies and is replaced by John XIV, who was put forward by Otto II, but the new pontiff dies the following year.

- A fifty-seven-foot statue of Gomateswara, sacred saint of the Jains, is carved at Sravanabelgola, India.

**984**

- The exiled Boniface VII returns from Constantinople to Rome to claim the pontificate, only to be murdered and skinned by a mob the next year.

**985**

- Rājarajā I is made king of southern India. He extends his Cōla kingdom to include the Maldive Islands, Sri Lanka, and parts of the Malay Peninsula.

**986**

- The coast of Labrador, Newfoundland, is allegedly sighted by Viking sailors who have been driven off course.

**987**

- Louis V, the final king of the Western Carolingians, dies and is succeeded by Hugh Capet.

**988**

- Vladimir I converts to Christianity when he marries Anne, the sister of the Eastern emperor Basil II, thus opening Russia to Byzantine influence. Basil II establishes the Varangian Guard, a well-paid loyal private honor guard, from a contingent of six thousand soldiers detailed to his use by Vladimir.

*DENOTES CIRCA DATE

**989**
- The Council of Charroux, a synod sanctioned by Hugh Capet, issues the "Peace of God," a call for limiting warfare to certain times of the year; protecting churches, clergymen, and noncombatants; and ending robbery of the poor.

**990**
- Mande (Ghanian) warriors from West Africa defeat the Saharan Berbers. The Ghanians control trade across the Sahara to Muslim regions in North Africa.

**991**
- Anglo-Saxons are defeated by a Viking army at the Blackwater River in the Battle of Maldon (Northey Island). Aethelred the Unready is forced to pay tribute to the Danes.

**992**
- Boleslaw I (the Brave) succeeds his father Mieszko (founder of the Piast dynasty) as prince of Poland.

**994**
- Danish invaders led by Sweyn I Forkbeard enter England.

**996**
- Otto III crowns Boleslaw the Brave as king of Poland. Otto also names the first German Pope, Gregory V; although contested, he remains Pope until 999.

**997**
- Stephen I becomes king of Hungary, establishing the Arpád dynasty. He is credited with establishing the state of Hungary; he promotes evangelical efforts and suppresses paganism.

**1000\***
- Iroquois peoples in northeastern North America establish village communities and cultivate maize and beans. Navajo and Apache tribes migrate south into the Pueblo areas and compete for territory with the more-stable native communities.
- The Ghaznavids defeat the Sāmānids and control northern Iran. They make frequent military incursions into India as well.
- Norwegian explorer Leif Eriksson, the son of Erik the Red, allegedly sails west from Iceland and discovers Nova Scotia and Vinland.
- An advanced metalworking society, Benin, emerges in West Africa.
- Islamic scientist Ibn Sīnā (Avicenna) begins his travels through Persia, where he writes the important medical treatise *al-Qanum fi at-tibb* (The Canon of Medicine).

**1002**
- Danish raiding parties begin a twelve-year cycle of attacks on England in response to the massacres of Danish settlers on the island.

*Denotes Circa Date

**1003**

- Pope Sylvester II, who helped introduce Arabic science and mathematics to the West and served as tutor to Otto II, dies. He had been elected to the pontificate after the death of Gregory V in 999; the man chosen to replace him, John XVII, reigns for only six months. Crescentius II succeeds in placing John XVIII, who rules until his abdication in 1009.

- Norse settlements along the North American coast (Baffin Island and Labrador), established as early as 1000, are abandoned.

**1004**

- Construction begins on the Brihadeswara temple, built by the Cōlas, in Tamil Nadu in southern India. The structure is made of granite, including its eighty-ton cupola.

**1005**

- The Sāmānid empire crumbles under the combined assault of the Ghaznavids and Qara-khanids.

**1007**

- Javanese king Dharmavamsa, who has ruled since 991, dies. During his reign he codified a law code, translated the Bhagavat Gita into Javanese, and spread Hindu philosophy.

**1009**

- The Byzantine Church of the Holy Sepulchre in Jerusalem, built over the alleged site where Jesus was crucified, is destroyed by the Fātimids. News of the act galvanizes interest in the site in western Christendom.

**1010**

- Thang Long (Hanoi) becomes the capital city of Vietnam.

**1012**

- Sergius IV, best known for combating famine in Rome during his reign, dies. Benedict VIII ascends to the papal throne.

**1013**

- Aethelred the Unready flees from England to France to escape the campaigns of Danish king Sweyn I, who now controls the country.

- Hishām II, who had temporarily been removed as leader of Córdoba by Muhammad II, dies.

**1014**

- Rājarajā I dies and is replaced on the Cōla throne by his son, Rājendra, who continues his father's policy of expansion.

- Bulgarian tsar Samuel's forces are defeated by the Byzantines at the Battle of Belasica (Cleidon Pass) in southeast Macedonia. Thousands of defeated soldiers are blinded and sent to their king, who dies at Prilep soon after seeing the results of the battle.

- Irish king Brian Boru is killed fighting Viking rebels from Dublin and their Scandinavian allies at the Battle of Clontarf. Despite the loss of their leader, the Irish triumph.

**1016**
- The Dome of the Rock collapses in an earthquake. The structure is rebuilt in 1022.
- An army led by Edmund II Ironside is defeated at Assandun by Canute (the Great), who becomes king of England and Denmark and rules until 1035.

**1018**
- Lombard nobleman Melus, with the help of Norman mercenaries, invades Italy but is defeated by Byzantine forces (the Varangian Guard) at Cannae.

**1019**
- England and Scandinavia are unified under the rule of Canute the Great.
- Mahmūd establishes the great mosque at Ghazni, capital of a Muslim kingdom comprising the territory between the Tigris and Ganges. His armies now occupy most of northern India.
- Yaroslav (the Wise) becomes Grand Prince of Kiev. He undertakes building programs, promotes Christianity, codifies laws, and develops relations with Western Europe during his thirty-five year reign.

**1021**
- Fātimid caliph al-Hākim dies. The empire experiences decline under the rule of his replacement, al-Zāhir.

**1024**
- German king and Holy Roman Emperor Henry II dies; Conrad II takes the German throne but waits several years before he is crowned Emperor.

**1026**
- Danish king Canute the Great defeats an attempt by the Swedes and Norwegians to conquer his country.

**1027**
- Conrad II is crowned Holy Roman Emperor in the presence of Canute the Great and Rudolf III of Burgundy.

**1028**
- Japanese noble Fujiwara Michinaga dies. He had been the power behind the emperor.
- Romanus III Argyrus becomes emperor of the Byzantines and rules until 1034.
- Canute the Great names his son, Hardecanute, as king of Denmark.

**1030**
- Mahmūd dies; his son, Ma'sūd, blinds his brother, Mohammed, and takes the throne. His empire expands from Persia to the valley of the Ganges.
- Norwegian king Olaf II Haraldsson, who actively spread Christianity in his country, is killed while making an attempt to recapture Norway from Canute.

*DENOTES CIRCA DATE

**1031**
- The last Ummayid ruler of Córdoba, Hishām III, dies. A series of petty kings will rule Córdoba.

**1034**
- Romanus III Argyrus is murdered by his wife, Zoë, who conspired with her lover Michael V. They rule until a rebellion deposes Michael and places her as co-empress with her sister Theodora.
- Casimir I (the Restorer) becomes king of Poland. He is deposed three years later by Polish nobles but regains the crown in 1040 with the help of Conrad II and Henry III of Germany.

**1039**
- Henry III becomes king of Germany. He is crowned Holy Roman Emperor in 1046.
- Arab scientist, astronomer, and mathematician Abū 'Alī al-Hasan ibn al-Haytham (Alhazen), who specialized in optics, dies.

**1040**
- Hardecanute, who was blocked from taking the English throne by his half brother Harold I (Harefoot), arrives in England and forces the English to crown him.
- Macbeth seizes the Scottish kingdom by killing in battle his cousin Duncan I.
- Seljuk Turks defeat the Ghazanavids, led by Ma'sūd, at the Battle of Dandanqan.

**1042**
- Constantine IX, Zoë's third husband, joins the co-empresses as Byzantine rulers.
- Hardecanute dies and his brother, Edward (the Confessor), becomes the last Anglo-Saxon ruler of England.

**1043**
- The Rus raid Constantinople for the final time.
- Norwegian and Danish king Magnus I Olafsson (the Good) defeats a Wend army in the Battle of Lyrskog, killing more than fifteen thousand of the enemy and ending their raids into Denmark.

**1044**
- Anawrahta, ruler of Upper Burma, defeats the states of Lower Burma and becomes king of Burma, establishing his capital at Pagan on the Irrawaddy River. He establishes a strong military, fortifies towns, builds pagodas and dams, and rules until 1077.

**1046**
- Rival candidates for the papacy—Benedict IX, Sylvester III, and Gregory VI—struggle to gain primacy in Rome. A synod is called at Sutri to resolve the problem; the bishops depose all three candidates and elect Clement II.

*DENOTES CIRCA DATE

**1047**
- Pope Clement II convenes a synod in Rome that outlaws simony. He dies while on a return trip from Germany and the bishops elect Damasus II, but he reigns for just twenty-three days.

- Norman general Robert Guiscard invades Italy, conquering Apulia and Calabria. He fights against the Byzantines, driving them from Italy by 1071.

- Sweyn II becomes king of Denmark. After several years of conflict with Norway, a peace is established between the two countries.

**1048**
- Leo IX is elected Pope and undertakes to reform and revitalize the Church.

**1053**
- The Normans, who control most of southern Italy and raid against the Byzantines, raise the ire of Pope Leo IX, who gathers an Italian and Greek army against them. They, however, defeat the Italians and capture the Pope at the Battle of Civitella (Civitate).

**1054**
- Pope Leo IX excommunicates the Byzantine patriarch Michael I Cerularius, who has closed Latin churches and insisted that he is equal to the Roman patriarch, causing a schism between the two churches. Leo falls ill and is removed from Benevento, where he was being held by the Normans, to Rome, where he dies. A German rector is elected Pope as Victor II.

**1055**
- Seljuk Turks capture northern Syria, central Iraq, and Palestine.

**1056**
- Henry III dies; his six-year-old son, Henry IV, is made king of Germany, with his mother, Agnes, serving as regent. He takes sole rulership in 1066 but is not crowned Holy Roman Emperor until 1084.

**1057**
- Byzantine military leaders revolt against Michael VI Stratioticus and force him to abdicate in favor of Isaac I Comnenus, who rules until forced to retire because of illness in 1061.

**1058**
- Boleslaw II (the Bold) becomes king of Poland.

**1059**
- Isaac I Comnenus defeats a Pecheneg-Hungarian raid into Byzantine territory. He becomes ill, abdicates, and is replaced on the throne by a former imperial minister, Constantine X Ducas.

*DENOTES CIRCA DATE

**1060**

- Seljuk Turk leader Togril Beg captures Baghdad and controls the Abbāsid caliphate.

- Norman raiders, led by Roger I, begin attacks on Sicily; they capture Messina the following year.

**1062**

- The Moroccan city of Marrakech is founded by Yūsuf ibn Tāshfin, who became king of the Almoravids in 1061 and conquered Algeria.

**1065**

- Earl Tostig of Northumbria is exiled by Edward the Confessor, who dies the following year. Westminster Abbey, founded by Edward, is consecrated.

**1066**

- William of Normandy and an army of five thousand men cross the English Channel and defeat King Harold Godwinsson at Hastings. William I (the Conqueror) becomes king of England and thereafter introduces the Norman system of feudalism into England.

- The Normans attempt to capture Rome but are dissuaded by defensive tactics and payment of tribute.

**1069**

- Danish king Sweyn II sends troops to Northumbria to help Anglo-Saxon rebels against William the Conqueror.

**1070**

- The Second Earl of Pembroke, Richard Strongbow, takes a force to Ireland to aid his father-in-law, Dermot MacMurrough; he captures Dublin and opens the door to Norman conquest.

**1071**

- Turkish troops under Alp Arslan defeat Byzantine mercenary troops at the Battle of Manzikert (Malazgirt) and capture Emperor Romanus IV Diogenes, who dies shortly after being exiled. The combined effect of the Schism of 1054 and conquest by the Turks have reduced the power of the Byzantines and shifted Christian religious locus back to Rome.

**1072**

- Palermo falls to the Normans.

- In order to block any claim to the English throne, William the Conqueror marches a large army into Scotland and forces Malcolm III MacDuncan to renounce any such intentions.

**1073**

- The reformer Pope Alexander II, who battled against simony and for clerical celibacy, dies in Rome. The tough reformer Gregory VII is consecrated Pope.

*DENOTES CIRCA DATE

**1075**

- The Acoma (People of the White Rock) move to the top of a mesa in the Southwest (modern New Mexico) and establish the oldest continuously occupied settlement in what will become the United States.

**1076***

- Almoravids attack the African kingdom of Ghana, which experiences a decline in power.

**1077**

- Pope Gregory VII receives Henry IV of Germany in penance at Canossa and grants him absolution (Henry had been excommunicated the previous year for supporting lay investitures).

**1078**

- Byzantine emperor Michael VII Ducas, who became sole ruler in 1071, enters a monastery in the face of serious civil unrest. Anatolian general Nicephorus III Botaneiates takes control of the crown, but he faces continued rebellion and attacks from the Turks. He abdicates in 1081 and also becomes a monk.

**1079**

- Persian poet and scholar Omar Khayyám joins seven academics in reforming the Islamic calendar. Khayyám, who dies is 1131, is best known for his quatrains in the *Robā'īyāt*.

- On their third attempt, Norse (Viking) invaders capture the Isle of Man from Celtic defenders at the Battle of Sky Hill.

**1080**

- German king Henry IV defeats a rebellion led by Duke Rudolf of Swabia, who is killed. The victory opens the door for Henry to invade Italy and end his dispute with Pope Gregory VII over the lay investiture of bishops.

**1081**

- The able military leader Alexius I Comnenus takes the Byzantine throne and defends the empire from foreign invasions. He rules until his death in 1118.

**1082**

- To quell civil unrest caused by the teaching of Byzantine Neoplatonist philosopher John Italus, the scholar is condemned as a heretic and forced by Alexius I Comnenus to live in a monastery outside of Constantinople.

- Macedonia is captured from the Byzantines by the Norman prince of Antioch, Bohemond I, the son of Robert Guiscard.

**1084**

- Henry IV attacks Rome, deposes Pope Gregory VII, and puts Clement III on the papal throne. Clement reciprocates by crowning Henry the Holy Roman Emperor. Gregory returns with Norman allies but retreats after his supporters plunder the city.

*Denotes Circa Date

**1085\***
- Thule Eskimo culture spreads across the North American Arctic area as far as Greenland and Siberia. Thule Eskimos achieve supremacy by developing essential skills and technologies to a more complicated level than that attained by existing Arctic peoples. They use dog sleds to cross the continent and large canoes to hunt whales.

**1085**
- Alfonso VI (the Valiant) of León defeats the Muslims and occupies Toledo, the old capital of Visigothic Spain and the greatest city that the Christians have captured in the reoccupation. Alfonso takes the title Emperor of Toledo. Loss of the city is a disaster for the Muslims.

**1086**
- Alfonso VI is defeated by Yūsuf ibn Tāshfin of the Almoravids, a Berber dynasty that rules North Africa and much of Spain, with the help of the Arab princes of Spain. After the Battle of Sagrajas, carts loaded with Christian heads are sent to the major cities of Spain and North Africa to demonstrate that the enemy is suppressed.
- William the Conqueror orders a census of property in the shires of England, particularly to improve tax collection. Information gathered by his commissioners is collected in the Domesday Book.

**1087**
- Fatally injured when his horse stumbles during military action against the French, William the Conqueror dies. He is replaced on the English throne by his second surviving son, William Rufus, who becomes William II at his coronation at Westminster Abbey.
- The much-reluctant-to-serve and fragile Victor III is enthroned as Pope but soon dies.

**1091**
- Alexius I Comnenus pushes the Pechenegs northward out of Crimea and beyond the Danube River.
- The Normans complete their conquest of Sicily.

**1093**
- Malcolm III MacDuncan, his wife Margaret, and one of his sons are killed in an ambush while attacking Northumbria. His brother, Donaldbane, briefly reigns but is overthrown by Duncan II, who is in turn killed by forces loyal to Donaldbane.

**1095**
- Alexius I Comnenus writes a letter to Pope Urban II requesting assistance in his fight against Islamic invaders. Urban, at the Council of Clermont, responds by calling for a campaign to free the holy places from the control of Muslims and starts the First Crusade in November in France. Urban accuses the Muslims of committing unspeakable atrocities.

**1096**
- The first university in the West is founded at Salerno, a city and seaport of Italy.
- German Crusaders, preparing to join the trek to the Middle East, massacre Jews in Worms and other German cities.

**\* DENOTES CIRCA DATE**

**1098**
- French Benedictine abbot Robert of Molesmes founds Cîteaux Abbey, which will become the Cistercian Order; its members seek a stricter, more-austere observance of monastic orders.

**1099**
- Crusaders of the First Crusade capture Jerusalem and massacre the Muslims. A Muslim relief column traveling toward Jerusalem is destroyed by Crusaders at the Battle of Ascalon (Ashdod).
- Pope Urban II dies; Paschal II is elected Pope and continues his predecessor's calls for crusades against the Muslims.

**1100**
- An arrow fatally strikes William II in the eye while he is hunting. His brother, Henry I, takes the English throne.
- Bohemond I, a Crusader leader, is captured by the Muslims but is released three years later.
- Baldwin I of Boulogne is made king of Jerusalem; he captures Acre (1104).

**1102**
- Boleslaw III (the Wrymouth) becomes ruler of Poland.

**1104**
- The Christian state of Edessa (modern Urfa) in Turkey, established by the Crusaders in 1098, is attacked by Turks, who defeat a Christian army at Harran; the Turks are unable to capture Edessa.

**1106**
- Henry I defeats his sibling, the Duke of Normandy, Robert II (Courteheuse), at Tinchebrai and captures his kingdom. The younger brother imprisons his elder rival, who had tried to unseat him by invading England earlier, at Cardiff for twenty-eight years.

**1108**
- Philip I dies and his son, Louis VI (the Fat), becomes king of France.

**1109**
- Scholastic Benedictine monk and philosopher Anselm, archbishop of Canterbury and author of *Cur Deus Homo* (1063) on atonement, dies.

**1110***
- Chichimec Aztecs migrate southward, possibly in response to drought conditions, into Mexico.
- Seljuk Turks invade Anatolia.

**1111**
- Islamic Iraqi theologian, teacher, jurist, and mystic al-Ghazālī, who promoted Sūfism, dies.
- Henry V is crowned Holy Roman Emperor.

*Denotes Circa Date

**1112**
- The Order of the Hospital of St. John of Jerusalem (Knights of St. John, and commonly called the Knights Hospitalers) is formed in Jerusalem. Originally organized to provide medical care to pilgrims to the holy city, it is reconstituted as a military order (although hospital work continued). Retreating in the face of constant Muslim pressure, the order moves to several locations in the Mediterranean, settling in Malta in 1530.

**1113**
- Vladimir II (Monomakh), a scholar and warrior, becomes prince of Kiev. Theodosian Russian monk Nestor, who is credited (possibly with several monks) with writing the chronicle *Povesti vremennykh let,* dies.

**1115**
- Matilda, Countess of Tuscany, who has ruled her northern Italian kingdom for sixty-nine years, dies. She supported Pope Gregory VII during the Investiture Crisis and opposed Henry IV.

**1118**
- Pope Paschal II, a mild and weak patriarch who had been driven from Rome by rioting in 1116 but returned, dies. Elected to replace him is Gelasius II, who is driven by Henry V from Rome to Cluny, where he dies in 1119.
- Alfonso I captures the Moorish stronghold of Saragossa in northeast Spain and makes it the capital of Aragon.

**1119**
- Henry V installs the antipope Gregory VIII, but he is excommunicated by Calixtus II, who is elected by the cardinals to replace Gelasius.
- French king Louis VI is defeated at the Battle of Brémule by an English army under King Henry I, who is defending his newly won province of Normandy.
- Burgundian knight and crusader Hugues de Payens founds in Jerusalem the military order known as the Knights Templars, whose duty it is to protect religious travelers. The order becomes wealthy and powerful.

**1120**
- Henry I's only legitimate son, William, dies while crossing the English Channel on a return trip from warfare in France. Also lost in the wreck are many nobles and other family members.
- Norwegian king Sigurd I (Jerusalemfarer), the first Scandinavian king to participate in the Crusades (1107–1111), begins a crusade at home to eliminate pagan Viking religion.

**1122**
- Pope Calixtus II issues the Concordat of Worms, which states that the Holy Roman Emperor can invest bishops with secular, but not sacred, authority; Henry V accepts the decree.

**1123**
- Calixtus II calls the Lateran Council in Rome, attended by most bishops in the West. The Concordat of Worms is ratified; priests are forbidden to marry or keep concubines; and pilgrims to the Holy Land are given protection. The Orthodox Church rejects the provisions.

*DENOTES CIRCA DATE

**1124**
- The Cumans, a nomadic Turkish people from southern Russian lands, begin entering the Bulgarian region. They will clash with the Byzantines, Slavs, and later, the Mongols.

**1125**
- Henry V dies without an heir. The main candidates for successor are Frederick of Hohenstaufen, the duke of Swabia, and Lothar of Supplinburg, the duke of Saxony. Lothair is finally chosen (1133).

**1128**
- Construction on the Neminath temple, sacred to the Jain Hindus, is begun on Mt. Girnar in western India. The building is completed in 1159.

**1130**
- Pope Honorius II withdraws to a monastery and dies. Two challengers, Innocent II and Anacletus II, are elected by rival factions to replace Honorius. Both men serve periods in Rome until Anacletus dies in 1139 and Innocent takes the throne unchallenged.
- Roger II, who supports Anacletus in the papal contest, becomes the second Norman king of Sicily.

**1132**
- Baldwin I of Jerusalem builds a fortress at Kerak, in modern Jordan, to serve as capital of that province.

**1135**
- English king Henry I dies, and his nephew Stephen of Blois seizes the crown. Supporters of the chosen successor, Matilda, rebel, sparking a civil war that lasts until 1141.

**1137**
- French king Louis the Fat dies and is succeeded by his son, Louis VII (the Young), who is only about seventeen years old.
- Raymond of Antioch is defeated by Byzantine forces in Cilicia; Armenian resistance, however, continues against the Byzantines.

**1138**
- The Scots, led by King David I, are defeated by the Anglo-Normans of York at the Battle of the Standard.

**1139\***
- English bishop and chronicler Geoffrey of Monmouth completes *Historia regum Britanniae,* a work that introduces the Arthurian legend into English literature.
- Pope Innocent II convenes a Lateran Council in Rome to oust appointments made by Anacletus II and to excommunicate Roger II of Sicily for having supported him.

\*DENOTES CIRCA DATE

**1141**
- Forces loyal to Matilda capture Stephen at the Battle of Lincoln, but she does not gain the support of Londoners, and Stephen is released and made king.

**1142**
- French philosopher and abbot Peter Abelard, whose writings were condemned at the Council of Sens (1140), dies at Cluny monastery.

**1143**
- The independence of the Kingdom of Portugal is established with the Treaty of Zamora; Alfonso I is the first king.
- Pope Innocent II dies, and the Romans declare their independence from papal control. His replacements, Celestine II and Lucius II, each serve for less than a year, the latter being killed fighting against the Roman rebels.

**1144**
- On Christmas Eve, troops led by Seljuq leader Zangī break the walls protecting Edessa, kill thousands of inhabitants, especially soldiers from the West, and send thousands more into slavery. The French cleric Bernard of Clairvaux is inspired by the catastrophe to promote a new Crusade.

**1145**
- Eugenius III is elected Pope but is expelled from Rome. After helping to prepare plans for the Second Crusade, he returns to Rome in 1148.

**1146**
- Boleslaw IV (the Curly) becomes king of Poland.

**1147**
- Spanish king Louis VII and German king Conrad II initiate the Second Crusade, which turns into a disaster because of Turkish victories and the inability of the crusaders to capture Damascus.

**1150***
- Cotton looms begin to appear in West Africa, and windmills are constructed in Europe.

**1152**
- Before he dies, Conrad III designates Frederick III of Swabia as his successor to the German kingship. Frederick is crowned Holy Roman Emperor in 1155 as Frederick I (Barbarossa).

**1153**
- Eugenius III establishes the terms for Frederick I taking control of the Holy Roman Empire in the Treaty of Constance, largely trading support from the German king against internal and external threats for the crown. He then dies and is replaced on the papal throne by Englishman Adrian IV, who as Nicholas Breakspear had helped promote Christianity in Scandinavia.

*DENOTES CIRCA DATE

**1155**
- Frederick I captures the Roman rebel Arnold of Brescia and is rewarded by Pope Adrian IV (as had been promised by Eugenius III) with the Holy Roman crown.

**1156**
- Former Japanese emperor Sutoku attempts to unseat his brother Shirakawa II, sparking the Hōgen civil war. Sutoku loses and is exiled.

**1158**
- The Bohemian king Vladislav I, who aided Frederick I in Lombardy, establishes his capital in Prague. Frederick declares at the Diet of Roncaglia that he has authority over the communities of Lombardy.

**1159**
- Pope Adrian IV is driven from Rome by Frederick I. Alexander III is elected to replace him but is forced to step aside by the candidate of Frederick, Victor IV, who controls the papacy for five years.

**1160**
- King Erik IX Jedvardsson, who conquered the Finns and forced them to accept Christianity and who is considered the patron saint of Sweden, dies.
- Tiara Kiyomori wins control of Japan, ending the Fujiwara period.

**1162**
- Indian leaders Ghiyas-ud-Dīn and Mu'izz-ud-Dīn conquer Ghūr. From this base they command an empire that eventually includes Afghanistan, Turkmenistan, eastern Iran, and northern India.
- Adviser to Henry II and English cleric Thomas à Becket is made the archbishop of Canterbury. He protects the rights of the church, even opposing secular trials for clerics.
- Frederick I captures Milan.

**1163**
- The cornerstone for the Gothic cathedral of Notre Dame (Our Lady) is laid on an island in Paris. Construction on the structure will continue until around 1250.

**1165**
- Arab geographer al-Idrisi, who under the patronage of Roger II helped spread Muslim knowledge of the world into Europe, dies.

**1167**
- Cities in northern Italy found the Lombard League in opposition to Frederick I, after he occupies Rome and forces Pope Alexander III to leave the city.

**1168**
- After Henry II bans English students from attending the University of Paris, an institution is officially established at Oxford, where teaching had been undertaken as early as 1096.

*DENOTES CIRCA DATE

**1169**
- Danish king Valdemar I captures Rügen and ends the power of the Wends in his kingdom.

**1170***
- Toltec civilization in central Mexico, pressured by Chichimec invasions, crumbles and its citizens leave the great cities.

**1170**
- Thomas à Becket is murdered by defenders of Henry II in his fight against the power of the church. Only three years after his death, Becket is canonized a saint.

**1171**
- Saladin puts an end to the Fātimid caliphate in Cairo and reestablishes Sunnism, the great branch of Islam that follows orthodox tradition and accepts the first four caliphs as rightful successors of Mohammed. Saladin becomes the effective sovereign of Egypt and Syria, founding the Ayyūbid dynasty.

**1172**
- Saladin conquers Tripoli.

**1174**
- Scottish king William the Lion is captured at the Battle of Alnwick by English king Henry II but is released when he recognizes Henry's authority.

**1176**
- Troops from the Lombard League, in support of Pope Alexander III, defeat the forces of Frederick I at the Battle of Legnano.
- The first stone-made London Bridge is built across the Thames River.

**1177**
- Saladin attacks Jerusalem but is surprised and defeated by King Baldwin IV (the Leper King) at Montgisard. Two years later Saladin gains revenge by defeating the Christians at Marj Ayun (Valley of the Springs).
- The Chams, a Hindu-Muslim people of central Vietnam, attack and sack the Khmer capital of Ankgor, though their control of the Cambodian region is short. They control much of southern Vietnam until the 1400s.

**1178**
- Byzantine troops under Manuel I Comnenus are defeated by the Turks in Anatolia. The Byzantines are forced to concede Turkish dominion over Anatolia.

**1179**
- The Third Lateran Council, held in Rome, ends the papal schism, establishes the two-thirds vote of cardinals to elect a pope, and sets age limits for advancement.

*DENOTES CIRCA DATE

**1180**
- French king Louis the Young dies. His son, Philip II, succeeds him and begins a campaign to drive Jews out of France.
- An-Nāsir becomes caliph of Baghdad; he rules until 1225.

**1182**
- Canute VI becomes king of Denmark following the death of his father, Valdemar I; he rules for twenty years.

**1183**
- The Treaty of Constance ends the conflict between Emperor Frederick I and the Lombard League.

**1185**
- The child emperor of Japan, Antoku, who is but seven years old, is killed at the naval battle of Dannoura; Minamoto Yoritomo establishes a military government that dominates the imperial family in Japan.

**1186**
- Ivan Asen I revolts against Byzantine control and establishes the second Bulgarian empire.

**1187**
- Saladin defeats a Christian army in Palestine at the Battle of Hattin and captures the Latin kingdom of Jerusalem.
- Pope Urban III dies; his replacement, Gregory VIII, serves for only two months, although during that time he calls for a renewed crusade to the Holy Land.

**1188***
- A text on English common law is allegedly written by jurist and royal adviser Ranulf de Glanville.

**1189**
- Henry II's sons rebel against their father for the second time, but he dies before being able to face and defeat the upstarts. One son, Richard I (Lion-hearted), takes the throne. He unites his forces with crusaders from Germany, under Frederick I, and France, following Philip II, and initiates the Third Crusade.

**1190**
- Frederick I dies while leading crusaders across the Saleph River in Anatolia. His successor to the German throne is his son, Henry VI.
- A new crusader knight organization, the Teutonic Order, is founded during the siege of Acre (which falls in 1191) to aid sick Germans in the Holy Land.

**1191**
- Richard I captures Cyprus. Two orders of knights in succession control the island.

*DENOTES CIRCA DATE

**1192**
- Mu'izz-ud-Dīn defeats the Rajput kings and establishes Muslim control over most of northern India.

- Japanese emperor Shirakawa II dies, and Minamoto Yoritomo grabs the throne, establishing a shogunate.

- The Third Crusade ends with only minor victories for the crusaders. Saladin cedes a portion of the coastline and allows pilgrimages to the holy sites in Jerusalem. Richard I is captured by King Leopold V of Austria during his return trip from the Holy Land.

- Cypriots revolt against the Knights Templar, and the island comes under the dominion of the King of Jerusalem.

**1193**
- Saladin dies, leaving Egypt more prosperous and militarily strong; he also reformed education and government.

**1194**
- The English raise a large ransom to free Richard I from his captivity. He returns home, quells a rebellion led by his brother John, and then turns his attention to France.

**1195**
- Byzantine emperor Isaac II Angelus is deposed and blinded by his brother, Alexius III Angelus. Isaac regains the throne but is again deposed, in 1203, by Alexius V (Alexius Ducas Murtzuphus).

**1197**
- Holy Roman Emperor Henry VI dies, sparking a contest among rival nobles to gain the crown. His son, four-year-old Frederick, is made king of Sicily and is not crowned as Holy Roman Emperor until 1220.

**1199**
- Richard I is fatally wounded while campaigning in France. He dies from an infection of the arrow wound. His brother, John Lackland, takes the throne.

**1200***
- The Great Zimbabwe kingdom, made up of Bantu-speaking peoples, forms in southern Africa.

- Mandinka people begin developing the Muslim state of Mali, successor to Ghana.

**1201**
- Pope Innocent III recognizes Otto IV as Emperor and is crowned in 1208. Otto IV and Philip of Swabia go to war with each other over who is the true Emperor.

**1202**
- Italian mathematician Leonardo Fibonacci introduces the Arabic numeral system to Europe when he publishes *Liber abaci*.

*DENOTES CIRCA DATE

**1202**
(CONT'D)

- A fleet carrying soldiers for the Fourth Crusade leaves Venice; they capture Zara on the Dalmatian coast.

**1203***

- West African leader Sumanguru captures Ghana.

**1204**

- The Fourth Crusade ends with the capture and pillage of Constantinople by the Crusaders. Byzantine emperor Alexius Ducas Murtzuphus is killed by the invaders. The new emperor, Alexius I (Grand Comnenus), who founds the Trebizond dynasty, controls only the northern coast of Anatolia at this time.

- Theodore I Lascaris, a Byzantine general, forms an eastern empire based at Nicea.

- Philip II annexes formerly English-held French provinces, including Normandy.

**1205**

- Venetians capture Corfu, the Ionian Islands, and portions of Greece.

**1206**

- Temüjin is declared Genghis Khan (Universal Ruler) of the Mongols.

- Muslims capture the Indian province of Delhi. Mu'izz-ud-Dīn Muhammad is murdered and General Qutb-ud-Dīn Aybak, a former slave, becomes ruler.

**1208**

- After a papal legate is assassinated by the Albigenses of southern France, a group that espoused heretical views of Christianity, Pope Innocent declares a crusade against them.

**1209**

- Italian friar Francis of Assisi founds an organization of friars known as the Franciscans. A similar organization, the Clares, is established for women three years later.

**1210**

- Qutb-ud-Dīn Aybak dies and is replaced as ruler of the Slave Dynasty of India by Iltutmish, who captures additional Indian lands, including the Punjab, and puts his capital at Delhi.

**1212**

- Portuguese king Afonso II (the Fat), along with armies from several Christian Spanish kingdoms, such as Aragon (led by Peter II), defeats a Muslim army led by An-Nāsir at the Battle of Navas de Tolosa in southern Spain. This victory turns the tide against the Moors in Spain.

- An army of adolescents is raised in France and Germany to go on a crusade to the Holy Land. Known as the Children's Crusade, most of the youthful warriors are blocked from fighting the Muslims, though a handful arrive in England, where they are sold into slavery.

*DENOTES CIRCA DATE

**1213**
- French crusaders led by Simon de Montfort defeat a combined Aragonese and Albigensian army at the Battle of Muret. Peter II of Aragon is killed in action.

**1214**
- A French army headed by Philip II defeats a combined English and German army, led by King John and Otto IV respectively, at the Battle of Bouvines in Flanders.

**1215**
- King John is forced by English barons to sign the Magna Carta, which reforms the relationship between the Crown and the nobility, standardizes measures, limits the seizure of private property or persons, establishes the rule of consent for taxation, and requires a trial by one's peers.
- Pope Innocent III calls the Fourth Lateran Council in Rome, which ratifies a body of canon law and acknowledges territorial gains of Simon de Montfort in France. The Pope also calls for another Crusade to capture Jerusalem.

**1216**
- King John of England dies, and his nine-year-old son, Henry III, is made king, with William Marshal, Earl of Pembroke, serving as regent.
- The Dominican Order is founded.
- Scottish king Alexander II invades England.

**1217**
- French troops, who arrived in England in 1216 at the behest of dissatisfied English barons, are defeated at the Battle of Lincoln near London. The French are cut off from leaving the island when their fleet is defeated in a naval engagement known as the Battle of Sandwich; they sue for peace, giving up any claims on English territory.

**1218**
- The Fifth Crusade begins. French and German armies, along with Frisian sailors, travel to Acre and then on to Egypt. They capture the town of Damietta but are unable to hold their advantage and are forced to withdraw in 1221. During the Crusade, Al-Malik al-Kāmil becomes sultan of Egypt.
- Genghis Khan occupies Kashgar and the Tarim basin in Central Asia and makes Korea his vassal state.

**1220**
- Mongol invaders begin incursions into Eurasia and the Middle East.

**1223**
- The Pandyas regain control of their northern Indian kingdom.
- Mongol invaders crush a much larger force of Russian soldiers at the Battle of Kalka River, opening the way for further incursions into the region.

*DENOTES CIRCA DATE

**1224\*** • The Mayan city of Chichen Itza in the Yucatan is abandoned.

**1226** • French king Louis VIII finally gains submission from the Albigenses; he dies later in the year and is succeeded by his son, Louis IX.

**1227** • After his return from China, Japanese monk Dōgen establishes Zen Buddhism in Japan.

• Innocent III's nephew is elected Pope and takes the name Gregory IX.

• Genghis Kahn dies; his son Ögödei becomes khan.

**1228** • Holy Roman Emperor Frederick II, who claims the kingship of Jerusalem through his marriage, leads Crusaders to the Holy Land. Delayed by opposition from the Lombard League, he captures Jerusalem (1229) and establishes a peace treaty with the Egyptians but becomes ill and is forced to return home.

**1230** • The Mongols capture Central Asia and Iran.

**1231** • Frederick II establishes a law code (*Liber Augustalis*) for Sicily.

• The towering Muslim monument Qutb Mīnār is constructed by Iltutmish in his capital city, Delhi.

**1233\*** • Pope Gregory IX establishes the Inquisition, a tribunal in the Roman Catholic Church to suppress heresy.

**1235\*** • Frederick II establishes an imperial court to handle property cases in Germany, while he is at the Diet of Mainz.

• Mandingo warriors led by Sundiata defeat the Susu kingdom of Sumanguru at the Battle of Kirina, capture the old kingdom of Ghana, and expand the kingdom of Mali.

**1236** • Iltutmish, who spent the last years of his life fending off Mongol incursions into India, dies. He is succeeded by his daughter, Raziya, who reigns for three years until she is killed by Hindus.

**1238** • The Moors establish an independent kingdom of Granada in Spain.

\***Denotes Circa Date**

**1240**
- Mongol general Batu Khan, under the authority of Ögödei, sacks Kiev. His armies have conquered most of Russia, Hungary, and Poland, and threaten Western Europe.

**1241**
- Batu Khan leads troops in the defeat of Silesian duke Henry at Liegnitz. Ögödei, however, dies, and Batu is made supreme khan of the Western Kipchaks.

**1242**
- The Mongols withdraw from Hungary and return to the lower Volga.
- German Crusaders are defeated by a Russian army led by Alexander Nevsky at the Battle of Lake Peipus (Battle of the Ice) in Estonia.

**1243**
- Innocent IV is elected Pope but spends most of his papacy in Lyons.

**1244**
- Egyptian Ayyūbid ruler Sālih Ayyūb allies with the Khwārezmians and recaptures Jerusalem from the Crusaders.

**1245**
- At the First Council of Lyons, Innocent IV tries to have Frederick II deposed; the demand comes to nothing, but it renews conflict between the imperial house and the papacy.

**1248**
- French king Louis IX answers the call of Innocent IV for a Seventh Crusade. His troops arrive in Cyprus.

**1249**
- Sālih Ayyūb is killed while fighting the Crusader invasion against Jerusalem. The Crusaders, however, fail to retake the city and withdraw.

**1250**
- After the Crusaders are turned back from Cairo and removed from Damietta, Ayyūbid rule of Egypt is put to an end by the Mamlūks.
- Frederick II dies while on campaign in Italy; his son, Conrad IV, assumes the throne the following year.

**1253**
- Louis IX sends Franciscan Willem van Ruysbroeck to the Great Khan of Mongolia in an effort to establish an anti-Muslim alliance.
- English theologian, scholar, and bishop Robert Grosseteste, supporter of the Franciscans and advocate of the policy that the Church stay out of the political realm, dies.
- Mongol invaders hasten the downfall of the Khmer regime in Siam.

*DENOTES CIRCA DATE

**1254**
- Byzantine emperor John III Ducas dies, and his son, Theodore II Lascarius, takes the crown. Theodore successfully defeats Bulgarian incursions and maintains good relations with the Turks.

**1258**
- Led by Simon de Montfort, rebellious English nobles obtain various concessions known as the Provisions of Oxford from Henry III. It provides the establishment of a permanent council to advise the king and a parliament that meets three times a year.
- Mongols capture Baghdad and end Seljuk rule in Iraq.

**1259**
- After serving a short regency for John IV, Michael VIII Palaeologus becomes Byzantine co-emperor and attacks Latin control of Constantinople, forcing the Latins out in 1261.
- Mamlūks block and destroy a Mongol army invading Palestine at the Battle of Ain Jalut near Nazareth.

**1262**
- Norwegian king Haakon IV Haakonsson gathers Iceland and Greenland under his control. He dies the following year.

**1263**
- A civil conflict, known as the Second Baron's War, breaks out in England. Simon de Montfort again leads the opposition against Henry III, who failed to live up to previous bargains with the British nobles.

**1264**
- At the Battle of Lewes, Henry III and his son are captured by Simon de Montfort, who then forms the House of Commons.

**1266**
- After defeating his rival, Manfred, at the Battle of Benevento, Charles I (Charles of Anjou) is crowned king of Naples and Sicily by Pope Clement IV, who took the papal throne in 1265.
- Turkish general Balban becomes Sultan of Delhi. During his reign he must defend his empire against Mongol incursions and domestic rebellions.

**1268**
- The Duke of Swabia, Conradin, the last Hohenstaufen ruler, who had been given Sicily in 1258 by Manfred, returns to the island to attempt to retake it from Charles I, but he is captured at Tagliacozzo and executed.
- English scientist Roger Bacon, with patronage from the papacy, writes *Opus majus*, an encyclopedia on science, mathematics, and philosophy. He is also credited with producing lenses, the camera, and gunpowder.

*Denotes Circa Date

**1270**
- French king Louis IX dies of plague while on the Seventh Crusade, which is supported by Edward I, against Tunisia. Edward continues the Crusade and provides support to the defenders at Acre.

**1273**
- Rudolf I of Habsburg is elected (recognized by the Pope in 1274) as the Holy Roman Emperor, beginning the Habsburg dynasty.
- Persian Sūfī poet and mystic Jālal ad-Dīn ar-Rūmī, whose disciples become known as the Whirling Dervishes because their meditation is based on dance, dies.

**1274**
- Edward returns from Acre and takes the English throne.
- Pope Gregory X—who hopes to end the break with the Eastern Church, obtain peace in Italy, and continue the Crusades—assembles the Second Council of Lyons. A short-lived union is achieved, though no Crusade is undertaken.

**1280\***
- Anasazi Indians disappear from their cities.

**1282**
- Welsh prince Llywelyn ap Gruffudd and his brother David, who were subjugated by Edward I (1277), lead a rebellion against the English. Edward puts down the revolt and kills Llywelyn. David is executed a year later.

**1289**
- Tripoli falls to forces led by Mamlūk sultan Qalā'ūn of Egypt; he also has blocked further Mongol incursions into the Middle East.

**1290**
- Jalāl-ud-Dīn Fīrūz Khaljī becomes the sultan of Delhi after the end of the Slave Dynasty; he establishes the Khaljī dynasty and rules until his murder in 1296.

**1291**
- Acre, defended by the Knights Templar, falls to the Muslims.
- The Swiss Confederation is formed from three states: Uri, Schwyz and Unterwalden.

**1292**
- Despite claims to the Scottish throne by Robert Bruce and John Hastings, Edward I awards the crown to John de Baliol.

**1294**
- Boniface VIII becomes Pope; in 1296 he issues a bull declaring that priests will not pay taxes on church properties without his consent.

\*Denotes Circa Date

**1295**
- Mongol leader Mahmūd Ghāzān captures northern Iran and establishes himself as Il-khan. He makes Islam the dominant religion in Iran.

**1296**
- 'Ala-ud-Dīn, sultan of Delhi, extends his power over much of India.
- Edward I forces John de Baliol to relinquish the Scottish crown after defeating his forces at the Battle of Dunbar. Edward removes the "Stone of Destiny" from Scotland to Westminster Abbey.

**1297**
- Scottish noble William Wallace and his army defeat an English force at the Battle of Stirling Bridge.

**1298**
- The Scots are defeated by the English at the Battle of Falkirk.

**1299**
- Mahmūd Ghāzān invades Syria, although he abandons the area in 1303.

**1300**
- Osman I founds the Ottoman Empire and rules for approximately thirty-six years.

**1302**
- Flemish common soldiers defeat an army of French knights, sent by Philip the Fair to force Flemish towns to submit to his authority, at the Battle of Courtrai (Battle of the Golden Spurs).
- Philip the Fair calls representatives from the nobility, the towns, and the clergy in the first Estates General to gain support for his political struggle with the Pope.

**1303**
- William Wallace is captured and executed by the English.

**1304**
- Mahmūd Ghāzān dies; Mongol control of Persia soon crumbles because of internal strife among the ruling family.

**1305**
- Clement V, with support from Philip the Fair, is elected Pope.

**1306**
- Robert I (the Bruce) kills the nephew of John de Baliol and is crowned king of Scotland.

**1307**
- Edward I, after defeating Robert the Bruce at Loudon Hill, dies enroute to Scotland; his son, Edward II, takes the throne.

*Denotes Circa Date

**1307**
(CONT'D)

- Mansa Musa, a patron of the arts and Islam, becomes ruler of Mali.

**1308**

- The influential Franciscan theologian John Duns Scotus, who founded a scholastic system and who argued that faith was an act of will, dies.

**1309**

- Pope Clement V moves the papal residency to Avignon, where it will remain until 1377.

**1311**

- Pope Clement V, heavily influenced by Philip the Fair, calls the Council of Vienne to take up the issue of the Knights Templar.

**1312**

- The Knights Templar, who own considerable property in France and have been accused of heresy, are repressed by order of Pope Clement V, who dies in 1314.

**1314**

- Scottish independence is won at the Battle of Bannockburn; an army of Scots led by Robert the Bruce defeats the English forces led by Edward II.
- A widespread famine, which lasts three years, spreads through Europe.

**1315**

- An army led by Austrian king Leopold I is defeated by Swiss Confederation forces at the Battle of Morgarten.

**1316**

- John XXII becomes Pope and resides in Avignon.

**1320**

- Ghiyās-ud-Dīn Tughluq becomes the sultan of Delhi, founding the Tughluq dynasty.

**1321**

- Italian poet Dante Alighieri finishes *Commedia*, or *Divina commedia* (The Divine Comedy).

**1322**

- French king Philip V (the Tall), who persecuted Jews and attempted monetary and weight reforms, dies.

**1324**

- Mali leader Mansa Musa makes a grand pilgrimage to Mecca.
- Cannons are allegedly used in France. Firearms also appear among Muslim fighters in Spain.

*DENOTES CIRCA DATE

**1325\***
- The grand capital Tenochtitlán is constructed by the Mexica (Aztecs) in central Mexico (present-day Mexico City).

**1326**
- Orhan, the son of Osman I, founder of the Ottoman Empire, takes Bursa from the Byzantines and makes it his capital.
- Isabella, the wife of Edward II, returns to England with a French army led by Roger de Mortimer and defeats the English.

**1327**
- Edward II is captured and forced to relinquish the English crown to his son Edward III, with his mother Isabella serving as regent; Edward II is later murdered.

**1328**
- Edward III recognizes Scottish independence and the rights of the King of Scotland by signing the Treaty of Northampton.
- Ivan I (Moneybag) becomes Grand Prince of Moscow and begins expanding the power of the Muscovite kingdom.

**1330**
- Alfonso XI of Castile, who became king in 1312 as a one-year-old, forms the secular Order of the Band.

**1331**
- Stephen Urosh IV overthrows Urosh III and continues to maintain his father's control over Bulgaria. He later conquers Macedonia and Epirus. In 1346 he assumes the title "Emperor of the Serbs."

**1332**
- Lucerne joins the Swiss Confederation.

**1333**
- A Scottish army is cut down while attacking fortified English positions on Halidon Hill.
- Casimir III (the Great) becomes ruler of Poland.
- The Kamakura shogunate is overthrown by Emperor Go-Daigo, which sparks a civil war in Japan.

**1336**
- Emperor Go-Daigo moves his court to Yoshino, south of Kyoto, Japan, and then is driven from the throne by shogun Ashikaga Takauji, who puts Kogon in as emperor.

**1337**
- The Hundred Years' War begins as French king Philip VI and English king Edward III compete for control of Normandy.

\*DENOTES CIRCA DATE

**1339**
- Construction starts on a grand ducal palace, called the Kremlin, in Moscow.

**1340**
- Edward III claims the French throne.
- An English fleet destroys a rival French fleet and gains control of the English Channel at the Battle of Sluys.
- Alfonso XI of Castile and Alfonso IV of Portugal defeat the Moroccan Marinids at the Battle of Río Salado.

**1341**
- Byzantine emperor Andronicus III Palaeologus, who took the throne as co-emperor sixteen years earlier, dies. His son, John V Palaeologus, takes the crown and rules for fifty years, although ten years of his reign are dominated by other men.

**1342**
- Pope Benedict XII, who imposed stricter rules—including ending the wandering tradition—for religious orders, dies; elected to replace him is Clement VI.

**1346**
- The English under Edward III invade Normandy and destroy a French army, leaving more than 1,500 French knights dead, at the Battle of Crécy.
- Scottish king David II is captured by the English at Neville's Cross and imprisoned until 1357.

**1347**
- Bubonic plague (Black Death) spreads into Sicily and within a year reaches North Africa and mainland Europe. Between twenty million and thirty-five million people will perish in Europe.
- The fortified city of Calais in France is besieged for eleven months and the people inside starved by the English into submission.

**1350**
- Bubonic plague reaches the Scandinavian countries.
- Hayam Wuruk becomes king of Majapahit and extends Javan rule throughout Indonesia.
- Utong general Ramathibodi I becomes the Thai king and establishes his capital near Bangkok; he defeats the Cambodians, but Khmer culture spreads throughout the region.

**1351**
- Zurich joins the Swiss Confederation.

**1352**
- Pope Clement VI, a princely Pope who enjoyed entertainments but also is credited with protecting Jews who were accused of causing plague, dies; Innocent VI is elected to the throne.

*DENOTES CIRCA DATE

**1352**
(CONT'D)

• Zug and Glarus, along with Bern the following year, join the Swiss Confederation.

**1353**

• The Genoans triumph in a three-year naval war with Venice.

• Ivan II (the Red) becomes Grand Duke of Moscow.

• The Laotians are united under the leadership of Fa Ngum.

**1354**

• The Ottomans invade Thrace.

**1355**

• Stephen Urosh IV dies while marching to invade Constantinople. During his administration he established a powerful empire in Serbia.

• Venetian naval commander Marino Falier is executed for conspiracy a year after his forces are defeated by the Genoese.

• Charles IV is crowned the Holy Roman Emperor.

**1356**

• Edward, the Black Prince, captures French king John II at the Battle of Poitiers and imprisons him in England until 1360. After the French people fail to raise a required ransom, John is returned to England, where he dies in 1364.

**1358**

• Etienne Marcel leads an uprising in Paris, but he is assassinated. Another revolt, led by Guillame Cale in Compiègne, breaks out, and peasant soldiers march to aid Marcel, but the army is defeated at Clermont-en-Beauvais.

**1359**

• The Ottomans capture Angora (later known as Ankara).

**1360**

• Edward III attempts to capture the French crown but is forced to relinquish this demand in the Treaty of Calais, although Aquitaine is awarded to the English.

• Murad I becomes sultan of the Ottoman Turks, who capture Adrianople. He establishes an elite force of soldiers comprised of Christian youths and prisoners of war who are called the Janissaries.

• Mari Jata II becomes leader of Mali.

**1361**

• King Valdemar IV Atterdag of Denmark initiates a war against the Hanseatic League (Hansa) and defeats its fleet the following year.

*DENOTES CIRCA DATE

**1364**
- Polish king Casimir III founds the University of Cracow.

**1365**
- French mercenaries are sent by Charles V to aid Henry of Trastámara (later Henry II) in Spain.

**1366**
- The Statute of Kilkenny, forbidding intermarriage between English settlers and Irish inhabitants, is established in Ulster.

**1367**
- The Brahmans massacre approximately four hundred thousand Hindus after the Battle of Vijayanagar in India.

**1368**
- A coalition army of Hansa, Swedes, and Germans defeats the forces of Valdemar IV Atterdag of Denmark.
- The Arab author Ibn Battūttah, who traveled to areas from Africa to China, dies.
- Shogun Ashikaga Yoshimitsu takes power in Japan.

**1369**
- Henry of Trastámara captures and executes Peter the Cruel, king of León and Castile, and then invades Portugal.
- Thai king Ramathibodi I dies; his son, Prince Ramesuan, rules for one year and then abdicates in favor of Boromaraja.

**1370**
- The Hanseatic League is granted trade concessions in the Baltic by the Treaty of Straslund.
- Timur (Tamerlane) becomes king of Samarghand.

**1371**
- The Ottoman Turks under the leadership of Murad I defeat the Bulgarian forces, and most of Macedonia except Salonika falls to the hands of the Turks.

**1372**
- The French navy beats an English force at La Rochelle, regaining control of the English Channel.
- Henry of Trastámara captures Lisbon and forces King Ferdinand I to end his alliance with the English prince, John of Gaunt.

**1373**
- Laotian king Sam Sene Thai begins a forty-four-year reign.

*Denotes Circa Date

**1375\***

- English poet Geoffrey Chaucer begins writing *The Canterbury Tales.*

**1375**

- The Songhai, led by Suleiman-Mar, win independence from the Mali Kingdom.

**1376**

- John of Gaunt is impeached by the "Good" Parliament but regains power after the death of Edward III the following year.

**1377**

- Pope Gregory XI returns the papacy to Rome from Avignon.

**1378**

- Florence is wracked by civil war. Initially, a rebellion of lower-class citizens led by the Ciompi (wool carders) triumphs, placing Michele de Lando in power, but a counter-revolution by the major guilds defeats the upstarts.

**1380**

- Charles VI (the Well-Beloved) takes the French throne upon the death of his father, Charles V.
- A Russian army under Grand Duke Donskoy of Moscow defeats a Tartar army at the Battle of Kulikova.

**1381**

- A Genoese fleet is trapped at Chiogga by the Venetians and forced to accept the Peace of Turin, conceding trade concessions to the victors.
- An English peasant army, its members angry over serfdom and oppressive taxation, is defeated by Richard II; its leader, Wat Tyler, is executed. The uprising does force the government to abolish poll taxes.

**1385**

- John of Aviz becomes King John I of Portugal after defeating the forces of John I of Castile at Aljubarrota and establishes the independence of his kingdom.

**1386**

- Murad I occupies Salonika; the Byzantine Empire is now completely under the control of the Ottoman Empire, except for a small area around Constantinople. The Turks, however, are defeated by the Serbs, led by Lazar Hrebeljanović, at the Battle of Pločnik.
- Polish queen Jadwiga marries Lithuanian grand duke Jagiello and unites their kingdoms.
- Portugal and England form an official alliance with the Treaty of Windsor and the marriage of the daughter of John of Gaunt to John I.

**1387**

- Sigismund becomes king of Hungary and later rules over Rome, Bohemia, and Lombardy.

\*DENOTES CIRCA DATE

**1388**
- The Scots defeat an English army at the Battle of Otterburn in Northumbria.

**1389**
- Murad I leads his Turkish troops to victory over the Serbian forces of Prince Hrebeljanović at the Battle of Kosovo. Both leaders, however, are killed. Bayazid I becomes ruler of the Ottoman Empire.
- Albert of Mecklenburg is imprisoned after the defeat of his army by Danish and Swedish troops.

**1391**
- The archdeacon of Ecija, Ferrant Martinez, foments unrest against the Jewish population of Seville, and approximately four thousand Jews are massacred.

**1392**
- The Koryŏ dynasty is ended with Korean general Yi Sŏnggye taking the throne; he establishes his capital at Hanyang (Seoul).

**1393**
- Cambodia is captured by the Thais.

**1394**
- Richard II invades Ireland with an army of more than eight thousand men.
- Timur captures Baghdad and Mesopotamia.

**1396**
- A peace is established between England and France that lasts for twenty-eight years.
- Turkish sultan Bayezid I's army destroys a crusading European army led by John the Fearless near the Danube River at the Battle of Nicopolis.

**1397**
- Erik of Pomerania becomes the first Danish king of the Union of Kalamar, which unites the kingdoms of Sweden, Denmark, and Norway.
- The English Parliament is forced by Richard II to award him an annual stipend for life and to seat members favorable to his rule.

**1398**
- Turkish troops under Timur invade India, capturing Delhi and killing thousands of Hindus.

**1399**
- Richard II is deposed and imprisoned by Henry of Bolingbroke, Duke of Hereford, who is proclaimed king of England as Henry IV.
- Faraj becomes the ruler of Egypt, though he is later captured by Turkish invaders.

*DENOTES CIRCA DATE

**1400**
- Holy Roman Emperor Wencelas is deposed.
- Timur captures Damascus and Aleppo in Syria.

**1400***
- The Iroquois nations (Oneida, Mohawk, Cayuga, Seneca, and Onondaga) form in northeastern North America.

**1402**
- Archibald Douglas leads a Scottish invasion of England and sacks Durham; Henry Percy, utilizing effective English archers, catches the Scots off guard and defeats them at the Battle of Homildon Hill.
- Ethiopian ambassadors visit Europe.

**1403**
- A Scottish army is defeated by the English at the Battle of Shrewsbury.
- Malacca (Melaka), a major spice-growing region on the Malay Peninsula, is founded by Paramesvara.

**1404**
- Albert V takes the German throne upon the death of his father, Albert IV.

**1406**
- James I becomes king of Scotland but is captured by the English while in flight to France.
- A copy of Ptolemy's *Geography* is brought to Italy from Constantinople and translated into Latin by James Angelus. Its availability gives a significant boost to geographical knowledge in Europe.

**1407**
- A civil war breaks out in France between supporters of the Armagnacs and the Burgundians.

**1408**
- An army of Teutonic knights is defeated by a combined army of Polish, Tartar, Lithuanian, Russian, and Bohemian troops at the Battle of Tannenburg.

**1411**
- Aragon and Portugal reach a peace agreement after thirty years of fighting and truces. Peace at home allows John of Portugal to begin a policy of overseas expansion.
- The Polish king is unable to gain greater advantage in his war against the Teutonic knights and signs the Peace of Thorn.

**1412**
- Erik of Pomerania becomes king of Denmark upon the death of Margaret I.
- The Egyptians attempt to recapture Syria from the Turks, but their leader Faraj is killed.

*DENOTES CIRCA DATE

**1413**
- Henry IV dies and is succeeded on the English throne by his son, Henry V, who had proven himself by leading the war against the Welsh (1402–1408). He arrests Sir John Oldcastle for heresy and then puts down a rebellion against his rule.

- Another revolt breaks out in Paris, led by Simon Caboche, and the rebels win some concessions, although they are later defeated and the reforms withdrawn.

**1414**
- The Sayyid dynasty of Delhi is established with the start of Khizr Khan's reign.

**1415**
- English troops under Henry V invade and recapture Normandy by defeating the forces of Charles VI at the Battle of Agincourt.

- Czech leader Jan Hus, advocate of church reform and opponent of indulgences, is seized (possibly by Sigismund) while on alleged safe-conduct to the Council of Constance and burned at the stake for heresy.

- Prince Henry the Navigator becomes the governor of Ceuta in Morocco. He will become more famous as the sponsor of maritime voyages of exploration and for helping to improve navigaton and shipbuilding.

**1418**
- Vietnamese living along the Red River basin, led by Le Loi, begin a revolt against the Chinese.

**1419**
- The Hussites present King Sigismund with demands known as the Four Articles of Prague, which include provisions for freedom of religion and reduction of church finances; Sigismund attempts to put down the revolt and fails.

- Sejong becomes king of Korea.

**1420**
- The Treaty of Troyes recognizes English king Henry V as the heir to the French throne.

- Hussite military innovator and leader of the Taborites, Jan Zizka, who transformed the use of mobile artillery, defeats forces sent by Sigismund to quell his rebellion. He dies in 1424.

**1421**
- Henry V dies and his one-year-old son, Henry VI, takes the English throne, under the regency of the Duke of Gloucester.

- Gypsies arrive in the city of Bruges. Established in Eastern Europe by the end of the last century, they start to move westward.

**1422**
- Charles VI dies, and despite the Treaty of Troyes, his son Charles VII takes the French throne.

*Denotes Circa Date

**1424**
- James I is crowned in Scotland following his release by the English the previous year in recognition of his service to Henry V in the French campaigns.
- A civil war breaks out in Siam, each faction led by a son of the deceased ruler. Boromaraja II emerges as king.

**1427**
- Emperor Yeshaq of Ethiopia sends envoys to Aragon in Spain to establish an alliance against Islam.
- An income tax (*catàsto*) is instituted in Florence.

**1428**
- Itzcóatl begins his rule over the Aztecs of Central America.

**1429**
- The Order of the Golden Fleece, dedicated to the Virgin Mary and St. Andrew to defend Roman Catholicism and chivalry, is founded by Philip II (the Good), Duke of Burgundy.
- Charles VII is crowned king of France after defeating the English at Orléans and the Battle of Patay.

**1431**
- Joan of Arc, who helped raise the siege of Orléans but was captured and given to the English, is burned at the stake for allegedly having practiced witchcraft, after a trial by French clerics.

**1434**
- A Swedish revolt against the rule of Erik of Pomerania breaks out. It is led by Engelbrekt Engelbrektsson and the Council of Aristocrats.
- Florentine banker Cosimo de' Medici returns home from a temporary exile and begins to dominate politics and arts in Florence.
- Phnom Penh is established as the capital of Cambodia, because Angkor is vulnerable to attacks by the Thais.

**1435**
- The Treaty of Arras between Charles VII and Philip of Burgundy establishes Charles as supreme king of France.

**1436**
- The Portuguese, having sailed past the Sahara coast, begin to explore the Rio de Ouro (the Gold River) in West Africa.
- Swedish rebels capture Stockholm, but their leader Engelbrektsson dies.

**1437**
- Prince Henry the Navigator fails to capture Tangiers.

*DENOTES CIRCA DATE

**1438**
- In order to restrict papal rights in France, Charles VII issues the Pragmatic Sanction of Bourges.

**1439**
- Hungarian king Albert II, who gained the crown the previous year, is killed in battle against the Turks.
- The French develop a standing army by instituting such reforms as standard pay, discipline, and troop organization.

**1440**
- A conspiracy of French nobles attempts to overthrow the king, but they are defeated.
- Venetian and Florentine troops defeat the Milanese.
- Montezuma I becomes ruler of the Aztecs and begins conquering tribes outside the valley of Mexico. A triple alliance established in 1428 by Tenochtitlán, Texcoco, and Tlacopan contributes to the final defeat of Tepanec power.

**1441**
- Slaves and gold are directly imported from West Africa into Portugal.

**1442**
- A Hungarian army led by János Hunyadi defeats a Turkish army in Transylvania, breaking Ottoman control in the Balkans.
- North African Berbers are enslaved by the Portuguese.

**1444**
- The Ottomans defeat the Hungarians at Varna (Bulgaria) on the shores of the Black Sea, which opens their way to Constantinople. Mehmed II (the Conqueror) takes the crown from his father, although he is displaced two years later.
- Portuguese explorers arrive in Cape Verde.

**1446**
- Alfonso V issues a law code for Portugal, called the *Ordenaçoes Affonsinas*.
- Murad II returns from retirement to quell a revolt of the Janissaries.

**1447**
- The Ngamo people of the Daniski Hill are displaced by an influx of Bolewa people from the Lake Chad region.

**1448***
- Leaving Strasbourg, where he has lived for several years, Johannes Gutenberg, who has invented movable printing characters, goes back to his native town of Mainz.
- Hussite leader George of Podebrady captures Prague from the Habsburgs.

*Denotes Circa Date

**1449**
- A civil war breaks out in Portugal, the opposing sides seeking control of royal politics. An army led by Pedro, Duke of Coimbra, is defeated by the forces of the Duke of Bragança at the Battle of Alfarrobeira.
- The Timurid Empire of Central Asia begins to collapse after the death of Tartar leader Ulūgh Beg.

**1450***
- A smoothbore matchlock gun, the arquebus, is invented in Germany.

**1450**
- A rebel army of property owners in Kent, angry about high taxation and led by John Cade, defeats a royal army sent by Henry VI at the Battle of Sevenoaks. Cade is later captured and killed at London Bridge.
- An English army is defeated and approximately five thousand soldiers killed by the French at the Battle of Formigny, opening the way for the recovery of Normandy.

**1451**
- Mehmed II takes control of the Ottoman Empire upon the death of his father.
- The Lodī dynasty of Afghanistan is established with the start of the kingship of Bahlūl Lodī.

**1452**
- Frederick III is crowned Holy Roman Emperor.

**1453**
- France defeats England at the Battle of Castillon, ending the Hundred Years' War.
- Constantinople falls to Ottoman troops, led by Mehmed II, and the city is renamed Istanbul. He installs Islam as the official religion, although he shows toleration toward Jews and Orthodox Christians, and encourages European scholars to settle in the city.
- Uzun Hasan becomes ruler of the Turkmen Ak Koyunlu dynasty.

**1454**
- Prussians and Poles unite in opposition to the Teutonic Order.
- Venice and Milan forge the Peace of Lodi and establish a mutual defense in opposition to the Turks, who threaten established trade routes.

**1455**
- The English defeat in the Hundred Years' War raises discontent in England, helping lead to a civil war between two powerful factions—the houses of Lancaster and York—in what becomes known as the War of the Roses, so named because rival sides wore red or white roses to signify their allegiance. Richard, Duke of York, triumphs over opposing forces at St. Albans.

*Denotes Circa Date

**1460**
- Le Thanh Tong becomes ruler of Vietnam.

**1461**
- Charles VII dies and is succeeded on the French throne by his son, Louis XI. Influenced by Pietro Barbo, who will become Pope Paul II in three years, the new king abolishes the Pragmatic Sanction of Bourges.
- Henry VI is deposed from the English throne after a royal army is defeated by the Yorkists at the second Battle of St. Albans. Lancastrian troops are later routed at the Battle of Towton and the Duke of York is proclaimed king as Edward IV.
- Mehmed II occupies Trebizond, the last territory of the Byzantine Empire to be conquered by the Turks.

**1462**
- Vasily II dies and his son, Ivan III Vasilyevich (the Great), becomes Grand Prince of Moscow; Ivan rules until 1505.

**1464***
- Charles the Bold, Duke of Burgundy, who seeks independence of Burgundy, leads the League of Public Weal against Louis XI, defeating royal forces at the Battle of Montl'héry the following year.
- Sonni 'Alī (the Great) becomes ruler of the Songhai kingdom.

**1466**
- The Second Peace of Thorn between the Poles and Teutonic Order gives Poland a port on the Baltic Sea.

**1467**
- Japan is torn by the Ōnin War, lasting ten years, concerning who will replace Shogun Ashikaga Yoshimasa when he retires, which will not be until 1473.

**1468**
- Charles the Bold and Louis XI establish a truce.
- Sonni 'Alī conquers Timbuktu.

**1469**
- The brothers de' Medici, Lorenzo and Giuliano, establish their control over Florence.
- The kingdoms of Aragon and Castile are drawn together and eventually united by the marriage of Ferdinand II and Isabella I.

**1470**
- A Lancastrian revolt, led by the earl of Warwick and the duke of Clarence in support of Henry VI, is defeated by the forces of Edward IV at the Battle of Stamford.

*DENOTES CIRCA DATE

**1471**
- Mehmed II takes the last surviving Turkish emirate, Karamania. As a result, all territories from the Taurus Mountains to the Adriatic are now under Ottoman rule.
- Ulászló I, the son of Polish king Casimir IV, becomes king of Bohemia.
- Champa is captured by the Vietnamese, who will begin attacking the border areas of Cambodia.

**1474**
- Isabella I succeeds her father, John II, as queen of Castile.

**1475**
- Edward IV invades France but takes a subsidy offered by Louis XI, money that gives Edward greater financial latitude in his struggles with Parliament; the two kings sign the Treaty of Picquigny.

**1476**
- Charles the Bold's Burgundian troops are defeated and seriously reduced in number at the Battles of Grandson (2 March) and Morat (22 June).
- Portuguese troops sent to capture Castile are defeated by Spanish troops at the Battle of Toro. Alfonso V renounces any claims to Castile in the Treaty of Alcáçovas, signed three years later.

**1477**
- Swiss Confederation troops defeat the Burgundians near Nancy, France, and Charles the Bold is killed.

**1478**
- Hungarian king Matthias Corvinus wins Moravia, Silesia, and Lusatia through the Treaty of Olomouc, signed by the Bohemian king Ulászló I.
- Giuliano de' Medici is assassinated by conspirators inspired by the Pazzi family and Pope Sixtus IV. Lorenzo gathers support in Florence, kills many of the conspirators, and initiates a war with the Vatican.

**1480**
- The Ottomans capture and destroy the southern Italian town of Otranto.

**1481**
- The Diet of Stans strengthens the Swiss Confederation by bringing in the cantons of Solothurn and Fribourg.
- Bayezid II becomes the Ottoman ruler after the death of his father, Mehmed II. He defeats a challenge to his rule by his brother, Cem.

**1482**
- The Kongo people are discovered by Portuguese explorers; trade and Christian evangelization commence.

*DENOTES CIRCA DATE

**1483**
- Edward IV dies, and his brother, Richard, Duke of Gloucester, takes the throne after the illegitimate son of Edward is blocked from becoming king. Richard III eliminates other rivals to the throne and defeats a rebellion led by the Duke of Birmingham.

**1485**
- The Earl of Richmond defeats royal forces at the Battle of Bosworth Field and kills Richard III; the earl becomes king as Henry VII (Henry Tudor).
- Saluva Narasimha becomes ruler of India.

**1487**
- Henry VII establishes the Star Chamber, a secretive and oppressive court established to try English nobles. An army of a pretender to the throne, Lambert Simnel, is defeated at Stoke-on-Trent.

**1488**
- Portuguese explorer Bartolomeu Dias rounds the Cape of Good Hope, the southern tip of Africa.
- Anti-English Scots murder King James III and replace him with James IV.
- Boroomaraja III becomes ruler of the Thais.

**1491**
- Ottomans and Mamlūks reach a peace agreement after six years of fighting.
- Cilicia in Anatolia is now under Egyptian control.

**1492**
- Christopher Columbus arrives at San Salvador (in the Bahamas). He later lands on Cuba, believing that it is Japan.
- Granada, the last stronghold of the Muslims in Spain, falls to Castilian and Aragonese troops under Ferdinand and Isabella.
- Spanish Jews who refuse to be converted to Catholicism are forced into exile.

**1493**
- The Habsburg archduke Maximilian becomes Holy Roman Emperor as Maximilian I.
- Mohammed I Askia becomes ruler of the Songhai Empire after the defeat at the Battle of Anfao of the son of Sonni 'Alī, who had died the previous year.

**1494**
- English rule is firmly established in Ireland, weakening the power of the Irish Parliament, by Poyning's Law (Statute of Drogheda).
- Spain and Portugal sign the Treaty of Tordesillas, by which they agree not to encroach on territories controlled in the parts of the world demarcated by a line west of the Cape Verde Islands. Spain gets the west and Portugal the east; other European nations ignore the agreement.

*Denotes Circa Date

**1495**
- The Holy League—comprised of the Vatican, the Holy Roman Empire, Spain, Venice, and Milan—aligns against Charles VIII.
- James IV of Scotland supports Perkin Warbek, who claims to be the Duke of York, in an invasion of England. Warbek fails and is executed in 1499.
- Limited constitutional reforms, such as a supreme court and Roman law, are introduced to Germany through the Diet of Worms.
- Gonja, a new state on the Ghana-Ivory Coast, is ruled by Sumayla Ndewura Dyakpa.

**1497**
- Jews are expelled from Portugal.
- Leaders of a tax revolt in Cornwall, England, are defeated at the Battle of Blackheath; they are captured and executed.

**1498**
- Louis XII becomes king of France upon the death of Charles VIII.

**1499**
- French troops capture Milan. An attempt by Ludovico, who became Duke of Milan in 1481, to liberate the city the following year fails, and he is imprisoned by Louis XII. In 1508 he dies in France.
- A Venetian fleet is destroyed by the Ottomans at Sapienza after a renewal of warfare between the kingdoms.
- The Treaty of Basel establishes the independence of the Swiss Confederation after the Swiss defeat an army sent by Maximilian I at the Battle of Dornach.

**1500**
- The French and Spanish partition Naples, though France gains sole control the following year.

**1501**
- Basel joins the Swiss Confederation.
- Shah Esmāʿīl of Iran begins his reign and starts converting the Sunnis to the Shīʿah faith.

**1502**
- A peasant revolt occurs in Germany; seeking confiscation of church property and an end to the nobility, the rebels are betrayed and defeated.
- Montezuma II becomes leader of the Aztecs upon the death of his uncle, Ahuitzotl.

**1503**
- Lithuania and Russia establish peace; Russia gains territory along the Baltic Sea.
- Pope Alexander VI dies, and the nephew of Sixtus IV is elected as Julius II.

*DENOTES CIRCA DATE

**1504**

- English guilds and trade companies are placed under the supervision of the Crown.
- The Funj Sultanate is established in central Sudan by Amara Dunkas.

**1505**

- Ivan the Great dies, leaving his strengthened kingdom to his son, Vasily III.
- Benin king Ozolua, who established contacts with the Portuguese, dies.

**1506**

- The Habsburgs are established in Spain by the one-year reign of Philip I (the Handsome).
- Portuguese citizens massacre *conversos* (converted Jews) in Lisbon; survivors are allowed to emigrate.
- Kongo ruler Afonso I converts to Roman Catholicism.

**1508**

- The Pope grants the Spanish crown rights to establish and build churches, especially in the Americas.
- The Holy League of Cambrai—formed by Pope Julius II, Louis XII, Maximilian I, and Ferdinand II—send forces against Venice.
- Michelangelo begins painting his ceiling frescoes for the Sistine Chapel in Rome.

**1509**

- Henry VIII succeeds to the English throne upon the death of his father, Henry VII.
- A Portuguese fleet captained by Francisco de Almeida destroys an Arab fleet off the coast of Diu (India).

**1510**

- Pope Julius II leaves the Holy League of Cambrai and allies with Venice in an attempt to force the French out of Italy.

**1511**

- The first African slaves arrive in the New World after Nicolás de Ovando, the Spanish governor of Hispaniola, was authorized in 1503 to transport them to the island after enslavement of the natives proves troublesome.

**1512**

- Despite their victory over the Holy League at the Battle of Ravenna, French forces are forced out of Milan.
- Bayezid II abdicates the Ottoman throne to Selim I (the Grim).

**1513**

- The Holy League is disbanded after the defeat of French forces by a combined English-German army at the Battle of Spurs.

*DENOTES CIRCA DATE

**1513**
**(CONT'D)**

- Scottish king James IV is killed at the Battle of Flodden Field by the Earl of Surrey, whose troops are defending against a combined French-Scottish invasion of England.

- A French and Venetian army is destroyed by a Swiss army at the Battle of Novarra.

**1515**

- The Spanish found the city of Havana, though the site is changed in 1519 by Diego Velázquez.

- Swiss mercenary troops defending Milan are defeated by the French and Venetians; the Swiss establish peace with the French the following year with the Treaty of Fribourg.

**1516**

- Charles I becomes king of Spain after the death of his grandfather Ferdinand II.

- Frances I obtains the right to nominate church officials in France by the Concordat of Bologna, negotiated by Pope Leo X, who was elected in 1513.

- The Ottomans annex Syria.

- Ang Chan becomes king of Cambodia.

**1517**

- The Protestant Reformation begins when German monk Martin Luther publishes his Ninety-five Theses against the sale of indulgences granting the forgiveness of sins. He maintains that salvation comes by faith and not by works.

- Egypt falls to the Ottomans.

**1518**

- Italian diplomat Baldassare Castiglione writes *Il cortegiano* (The Courtier).

**1519**

- Charles of Spain is elected Holy Roman Emperor and takes the name Charles V, although both Francis of France and Henry VIII of England are candidates.

- Spanish conquistador Hernán Cortés enters Tenochtitlán.

- Italian artist, scientist, and architect Leonardo da Vinci dies. His works include *The Last Supper* (circa 1495) and *Mona Lisa* (circa 1502).

**1520**

- During a conference at the Field of Cloth of Gold, Francis I tries to get Henry VIII to support a French attempt to control the Holy Roman Empire.

- Spanish cities rebel against Charles V, but the uprising is put down.

- A rebellion against Christian II, Danish king of Scandinavia, leads to the Bloodbath of Stockholm, in which hundreds of nobles are murdered; Gustavus Vasa leads a Swedish invasion of Denmark.

- The last two emperors of the Aztecs, Montezuma II and Cuauhtémoc, are executed by Cortés.

*DENOTES CIRCA DATE

**1520**
**(CONT'D)**

- Süleyman I (the Magnificent) begins his rule in the Ottoman Empire.

**1521**

- The Spanish and English unite against France. Francis I declares war against the Holy Roman Empire.

- Portuguese explorer Fernão de Magalhães (Ferdinand Magellan) reaches the Polynesian Islands; he visits Guam and the Philippines, where he dies the following year.

**1522**

- The Knights Hospitalers are defeated by the Turks on Rhodes; some survivors escape and resettle in Malta.

- Spain recaptures Milan and expels the French.

- Juan de Elcano captains the last surviving ship from the Magellan expedition to its home port, completing the first circumnavigation of the earth.

**1523**

- Vasa topples King Christian II and takes the throne as Gustavus I.

- Charles V gains most of Lombardy after defeating the French at the Battle of La Bicocca.

**1525**

- Francis I is defeated and taken prisoner by Charles V at the Battle of Pavia. He is later forced to sign the Treaty of Madrid and cede his claim to Italy.

- Huáscar and Atahualpa become co-emperors of the Incan Empire.

**1526**

- England, Venice, France, Florence, and the Vatican form the League of Cognac to oppose Charles V.

- In response to the creation of the Catholic Dessau League, Philip, the landgrave of Hesse, and Johann of Saxony establish the League of Torgau. Most Protestant kingdoms of the German empire participate in it later.

- Turkish troops led by Süleyman I defeat the Hungarians at the Battle of Mohács and kill Louis II.

**1527**

- Pope Clement VII is taken prisoner by Charles V, whose troops sack Rome.

- A civil war breaks out in the Incan Empire; Atahualpa wins the conflict in 1530.

- Mac Dang Dung becomes ruler of Vietnam.

**1528**

- Genoese admiral Andrea Doria sets up an oligarchy in Genoa.

- A typhus epidemic thwarts French plans to capture Naples.

*DENOTES CIRCA DATE

**1528**
(CONT'D)

- Influential German painter and engraver Albrecht Dürer, famous for woodcuts and engravings of religious themes, dies.

**1529**

- Papal authority in England is renounced by Henry VIII and the "Reformation Parliament."
- The Viceroyalty of New Spain is established, with Mexico City (formerly Tenochtitlán) its capital city.

**1531**

- The Schmalkaldic League—a defensive alliance including Hesse, Saxony, Brunswick, Anhalt, Magdeburg, Strasbourg, Ulm, and Bremen—is formed to counter Charles V.
- Swiss Protestant reformer Ulrich Zwingli is killed defending Zurich from Catholic opponents.

**1532**

- Italian philosopher Niccolò Machiavelli's *Il principe* (The Prince) is published.

**1534**

- The Act of Supremacy, separating the English Church from papal control, is established.
- French explorer Jacques Cartier, who discovered the St. Lawrence River, claims the area that will become Canada for France.

**1535**

- Tunisian pirates are defeated by the forces of Charles V.
- Antonio de Mendoza, viceroy of New Spain, brings the first printing press to the Americas.

**1536**

- Turks raid the Italian coast. Turin falls to the French.
- Several rebellions in England are caused by the enclosure movement and heavy taxation begun by Henry VIII; they are put down.
- Dutch scholar Desiderius Erasmus, who helped promote learning in Europe, dies.
- French theologian John Calvin publishes *Christianae religionis Institutio* (Institutes of the Christian Religion).

**1540**

- Moghul emperor Humāyūn is forced to leave India by Afghans under the leadership of Shēr Shāh, who becomes emperor of Delhi.
- The Privy Council in England is established.

**1541**

- The Spanish begin to occupy Peru.
- The Somalis are forced out of Ethiopia by a Portuguese army.

*Denotes Circa Date

**1542**

- An English army defeats the Scots at the Battle of Solway Moss.

- Antonio da Mota is the first European to reach Japan. In 1543 Portuguese sailors arrive at the island of Tanegashima; their three matchlock guns are purchased by the Japanese, who have not seen firearms since the unsuccessful Mongol invasion of Japan in the thirteenth century.

- Portuguese explorer João Cabrilho, sailing for Spain, discovers California.

- Spanish colonists in the Americas protest the New Laws of the Indies, issued by Charles V. Among other reforms, the laws seek to control abuses of the native populations.

- The French establish a colony in New France (Canada).

**1543**

- Polish astronomer Mikolaj Kopernik (Nicolas Copernicus) publishes *De revolutionibus orbium coelestium* (On the Revolutions of the Celestial Orbs).

**1544**

- In order to restore Catholic unity in Europe, Francis I and Charles V sign the Treaty of Crépy. Francis assures his support to the Emperor against the Protestants if they refuse to recognize decisions of the forthcoming Council of Trent.

- The English invade Scotland.

**1545**

- Silver is discovered at Potosí, Bolivia; the Spanish begin using native laborers as miners.

**1546**

- Charles V declares war on the Schmalkaldic League.

- Spanish conquistadors suppress a Mayan uprising in Mexico.

- French printer Etienne Dolet, accused of producing the works of humanist reformers such as Erasmus, is hanged in Paris and burned at the stake for blasphemy, sedition, and heresy.

**1547**

- Ivan IV (the Terrible) is made the Grand Duke of Moscow.

- The Schmalkaldic League is defeated by Charles V at the Battle of Mühlberg.

**1548**

- Queen Tao Sri Sudachan takes the Thai throne after killing her husband the previous year; she and her lover are murdered by Khun Pirentoratep, who serves as regent for King Chakrapat. The Burmese invade Thailand.

**1549**

- Robert Kett leads a rebellion against the enclosure movement in England. After defeating an English army sent against them, the rebels are defeated and Kett is executed.

- Spanish Jesuit missionary Francis Xavier arrives in Japan to convert the locals. He works in Japan for two years, then returns to India, where he dies.

*DENOTES CIRCA DATE

**1550**
- Iceland prelate Jón Arason is beheaded for opposing the introduction of Lutheranism into his country.

**1551**
- Burmese ruler Tabinshweti is assassinated, and his brother-in-law, Bayinnaung, places himself on the throne.

**1552**
- Ivan the Terrible begins the occupation of Kazan and Astrakhan, which are held by the Tartars.

**1554**
- Edward VI dies and Mary Tudor takes the throne. The Parliament repeals all religious laws passed under Henry VIII and Edward VI; Roman Catholicism is reestablished in England and the power of the Pope is recognized.

**1555**
- An anti-Calvinist uprising in Geneva is cruelly suppressed.
- The Peace of Augsburg recognizes the practice of Lutheranism in the Holy Roman Empire.
- Tobacco is first shipped to Spain from the Americas.

**1556**
- Akbar, who has succeeded as Mughal emperor of India upon the death of Humāyūn, defeats the Afghans at Panipat.

**1557**
- Bukhara is captured by Shaybanid ruler 'Abd Allāh, who then attacks Persia.

**1558**
- Mary I dies and Elizabeth I, daughter of Henry VIII, takes the English throne.
- The Nguyen dynasty is established in southern Vietnam.

**1559**
- Henri II is mortally wounded in a tournament; he is replaced on the French throne by his son Francis II, who dies the following year, whereupon Charles IX succeeds, with Catherine de' Medici serving as regent.
- The French and Spanish end their contest for control of Italy; the Habsburgs control Italy for the next century and a half.

**1560**
- Akbar conquers the Rajput and Lower Bengal kingdoms in India.

*Denotes Circa Date

**1561***
- The Luba Empire is established in southern Zaire.

**1561**
- Madrid is made the capital of Spain.
- Mary, Queen of Scots, returns to Scotland.

**1562**
- French Huguenots (Protestants) are massacred at Vassy, sparking the Wars of Religion in France. A Huguenot army is defeated at the Battle of Dreux.
- John Hawkins begins the English slave trade across the Atlantic; he leaves Sierra Leone in West Africa with a shipment of three hundred slaves, sailing to Hispaniola (Santo Domingo) in the Caribbean.

**1563**
- Protestantism is strengthened in England with the extension by Parliament of the Act of Supremacy.
- The Peace of Amboise temporarily quells fighting in the French Religious Wars and allows Protestants to worship freely.
- Ivan IV occupies Polotsk in Eastern Livonia, taking it from Poland. A war between Russia and Poland erupts immediately and continues until 1582.
- Burma invades Siam.

**1564**
- An outbreak of plague in Europe spreads to England and kills more than twenty thousand inhabitants of London.
- Hawkins introduces the sweet potato from North America into Europe; the following year he returns to London from North America with a shipload of tobacco.
- Francesco de' Medici becomes the ruler of Florence.

**1565**
- Protestants are massacred in France following a meeting between the duke of Alba and Catherine de' Medici, wife of Charles IX.
- The Knights Hospitaler successfully defend Malta against a Muslim invasion.
- The Spanish found Saint Augustine in Florida.

**1566**
- Margaret of Parma, at the request of the "Beggars," relaxes religious restrictions on Protestants in the Netherlands.
- Selim II becomes sultan of the Ottoman Empire.

*DENOTES CIRCA DATE

**1567**
- Rebels in the Netherlands revolt against Spanish rule.
- Mary, Queen of Scots, abdicates; her thirteen-month-old son takes the Scottish crown as James VI.
- French settlers are expelled by the Portuguese from the Brazilian area that later becomes Rio de Janeiro.

**1568**
- Mary, Queen of Scots, is imprisoned after the English defeat the Scots at the Battle of Langside. Catholics are persecuted in England.
- Nobleman Omura Sumitada, baptized by the Jesuits in 1562, allows foreign traders to set up posts at a small fishing village called Fukue (near Nagasaki) in Japan.

**1569**
- The Earl of Sussex puts down a Catholic rebellion in Northumberland and Westmoreland, known as the Revolt of the Northern Earls.
- The Union of Lublin unites Poland and Lithuania.
- Cosimo de' Medici becomes the Grand Duke of Tuscany.

**1570***
- Chiefs Hiawatha and Dekanawidah help establish the Iroquois League.

**1570**
- Huguenots achieve freedom of worship in France after the Peace of St. Germain is signed.
- Converted Muslims (*moriscos*) in Spain revolt, are defeated, and are then expelled from Spain (1609).
- A conspiracy, known as the Ridolfi plot, calling for Spanish troops from the Netherlands to invade England, is uncovered.

**1571**
- Ottoman expansion into the eastern Mediterranean is blocked when their fleet is defeated by Venetian and Spanish ships at the Battle of Lepanto in the Gulf of Patras.

**1572**
- The Dutch War of Independence, sparked by William of Orange, begins. The Sea Beggars harass the Spanish and capture Brielle. William is forced to retreat to the northern provinces, where he continues to lead the resistance.
- The last of the Incan chiefs, Tupac Amarú, is executed by the Spanish.

**1573**
- The Ottomans capture Cyprus, forcing the Venetians to sign the Peace of Constantinople.

*DENOTES CIRCA DATE

**1574**

- Murad III becomes sultan of the Ottoman Empire.

- The Spanish lose control of Tunis to the Ottomans but gain a colony in Angola.

**1575**

- Plague breaks out in Sicily and spreads to Italy, killing many inhabitants in Milan and Florence.

- The first European imitation of Chinese porcelain is produced at Florence.

**1576**

- Spanish troops riot and kill about six thousand Antwerp citizens in a rampage known as the Spanish Fury.

- William of Orange is placed over the northern provinces after the Pacification of Ghent.

- Maximilian II dies; he is succeeded as Holy Roman Emperor by his brother, Rudolf II.

**1577**

- Huguenots in France rebel; peace and their freedom to worship is restored with the Peace of Bergerac.

- English admiral Sir Francis Drake begins a sea voyage that ends in the circumnavigation of the earth; the trip ends in 1580, making him the first Englishman to accomplish this feat.

**1578**

- A Portuguese army, led by Sebastian, invades North Africa and is defeated by the Moors at the Battle of the Three Kings. Sebastian is killed and is replaced on the Portuguese throne by his uncle, Henry I.

**1579**

- The Union of Utrecht is signed, establishing the Dutch Republic.

**1581**

- The Act of Abjuration against Philip II of Spain is passed by the Estates General of the Netherlands.

- Russians begin to conquer Siberia; they completely occupy it by 1598.

- Burmese king Bhueng Noreng dies; he is succeeded by his son, Nanda Bhueng.

**1582**

- After twenty-five years of warfare, Russia reaches peace with Poland and gives up its claims to the Baltic state of Livonia.

- Scottish king James VI is forced by William Ruthven, Earl of Gowrie, to denounce the Catholic Duke of Lennox.

- A commission formed by Pope Gregory XIII introduces the Gregorian calendar.

* DENOTES CIRCA DATE

**1583**
- Francis Throckmorton is captured and executed for his participation in a conspiracy to help France invade England and overthrow Queen Elizabeth I.

**1584**
- William of Orange is assassinated by Balthazar Gérard. Maurice succeeds as leader of the Union of Utrecht.

**1585**
- The English agree to aid the Dutch against Philip I in the Treaty of Nonsuch.
- The War of Three Henris begins in France in response to a rebellion of Protestants, who have been ordered to convert to Catholicism or be exiled.

**1586**
- Mary Stuart is tried for treason after the uncovering of a plot, allegedly led by Antony Babbington, to overthrow Elizabeth I. Mary is beheaded early the following year.
- Spanish painter El Greco (Doménikos Theotokópoulos), who produced many important pieces with religious themes, starts work on *Burial of the Conde de Orgaz*, which he finishes in 1588.

**1587**
- Protestant Henri of Navarre's troops defeat those of rival Catholic Henri III in France at the Battle of Coutras.
- The Burmese and Cambodians invade Siam.

**1588**
- Henri III escapes a rebellion known as the Day of the Barricades, in Paris.
- The Spanish Armada is destroyed, partly by bad weather and partly by an English fleet.

**1589**
- Henri III is assassinated, and Henri of Navarre takes the French throne as Henry IV, initiating the rule of the Bourbon dynasty. The Catholic League is defeated at the Battle of Arques and then again, in the following year, at the Battle of Ivry.

**1590**
- Toyotomi Hideyoshi unifies Japan under his rule. His powerful vassal Tokugawa Ieyasu transfers his administrative and military base to Edo (Tokyo), a strategic city for control of the great plain of eastern Japan.

**1591**
- The Songhai Empire collapses as Moroccan troops, most of whom are mercenaries, capture Gao and Timbuktu.

**1592**
- Japan invades Korea and captures the castle at Pusan after the Korean government refuses to accept Japanese trade terms.

*Denotes Circa Date

**1593**
- The Thais defeat the Burmese and attack Cambodia.

**1594**
- Irish soldiers defeat an English army at the Battle of the Ford of Biscuits near Enniskillen.

**1595**
- Spanish troops in France are defeated at the Battle of Fontaine-Française.
- Akbar's troops occupy Kandahār. All of India north of the Narmada River, as well as Kabul and Ghazni, is now under his control.
- Ottoman sultan Murad III dies; he is succeeded by Mehmed III.

**1596**
- The War of the Catholic League ends with the Articles of Folembray.

**1597**
- English playwright William Shakespeare writes *Henry VI*, an historical drama in three sections, each consisting of five acts.

**1598**
- Irish rebels, led by Hugh O'Neill, Earl of Tyrone, defeat a British army at Yellow Ford in Ulster.
- The Persians defeat the Uzbeks in a battle near Herāt.

**1599**
- The Swedes overthrow Polish king Sigismund III Vasa; Charles IX establishes Lutheranism as the state religion in Sweden.

**1600**
- Tokugawa Ieyasu defeats his rivals at the Battle of Sekigahara, becoming the most powerful warlord in Japan.
- The English East India Company is founded.
- Dutch stadtholder Maurice of Nassau leads an army in defeat of the Spanish at the Battle of Nieuport.

**1601**
- Irish and Spanish forces are defeated by the English at the Battle of Kinsale.
- Danish astronomer Tycho Brahe dies. His *Tabulae Rudolphinae* is completed by his assistant, German astronomer Johannes Kepler, and published in 1627.

**1602**
- Spanish traders arrive at Japan.
- The Dutch East India Company is founded.

*Denotes Circa Date

**1603**
- Scottish king James VI becomes king of England as King James I.
- French mathematician François Viète dies; he was the first person to use alphabetical symbols in algebra.
- The first beaver pelts arrive at the port of La Rochelle in France from Canada.

**1604**
- Protestants in Hungary, led by István Bocskay and aided by the Turks, revolt against the Habsburgs.
- Dmitri, an imposter posing as the son of Tsar Ivan IV, leads an army of Lithuanians and Poles into Russia.

**1605**
- The Dutch seize Ambon (Amboyna), Malaysia, from the Portuguese.
- European diseases are devastating the American Indian population. Smallpox, measles, dysentery, typhoid, and tuberculosis are transmitted by trade and warfare; alcohol is also becoming a disaster for Indian communities.
- English Catholic Guy Fawkes, along with fellow conspirators, attempts to blow up the House of Parliament. He is executed the following year.
- Spanish novelist Miguel de Cervantes completes the first part of *El ingenioso hidalgo Don Quijote de la Mancha;* the second portion will be completed by 1615.

**1606**
- The Dutch ship *Duyfken* lands at the Gulf of Carpentaria in Australia.

**1607***
- The Powhatan Indians form a confederacy of approximately thirty tribes in Virginia.

**1607**
- Under the leadership of Captain John Smith, Jamestown is founded in Virginia as an English colony in North America.

**1608**
- Samuel de Champlain founds Quebec.
- A defensive alliance of German Protestant cities, called the Evangelical League, is formed; a corresponding entity, the Catholic League, is formed the following year.

**1609**
- Kepler publishes his laws of planetary motion.
- The Dutch East India Company first transports tea from China to Europe.

*DENOTES CIRCA DATE

**1610**

- English navigator Henry Hudson, sailing aboard *Discovery*, reaches Hudson Bay.

**1611**

- Jesuits, authorized by Philip III of Spain to control the Indian missions, establish their first mission at San Ignacio Guazu in Paraguay.

- The first English settlers arrive at Masulipatam (Machilipatnam), Madras, on the east coast of India.

- Englishman Thomas Harriott, German Johannes Fabricius, German Jesuit Christoph Scheiner, and Italian Galileo Galilei all discover sunspots.

- Denmark declares war on Sweden; the Kalamar War ends in 1613 with the Peace of Knäred.

- The King James Version of the Bible is published.

**1612**

- Rudolf II dies; his brother, Matthias, who had taken the kingship of Hungary in 1608, becomes Holy Roman Emperor.

- The Dutch first use Manhattan Island as a center for the fur trade.

- Tobacco cultivation is introduced by John Rolfe into Virginia.

**1613**

- Michael Romanov becomes tsar of Russia.

**1614**

- Christians are ordered out of Japan.

- Scottish mathematician John Napier invents logarithms; he later works with the use of the decimal point and constructs an early calculating machine.

**1616**

- Tokugawa Ieyasu dies; his son, Tokugawa Hidetada, becomes shogun and continues his father's campaign against Christian influences in Japan, including ordering the executions of missionaries the following year.

- The western coast of Australia is explored by the Dutch.

**1618**

- An uprising in Prague sparks the Thirty Years' War, a series of conflicts fought primarily on German soil between Protestant and Catholic factions.

- A smallpox epidemic sweeps through New England and spreads down the coast as far as Virginia. Indian tribes are the hardest hit, losing up to 90 percent of their population.

- Explorer and adventurer Sir Walter Ralegh, who helped establish the English colony in Virginia, is executed on a charge of treason.

*DENOTES CIRCA DATE

**1619**
- A Dutch frigate arrives in Jamestown, leaving behind twenty Africans as indentured servants, one of the first cargoes of its kind to go to British North America.
- The House of Burgesses (parliament) meets for the first time in Virginia.

**1620**
- A Catholic army defeats a Bohemian (Protestant) army at the Battle of White Mountain.
- The *Mayflower*, carrying more than one hundred Protestant dissenters called the Pilgrims, leaves England and sails to Massachusetts.

**1621**
- Spanish king Philip III dies; his son, Philip IV, takes the throne.

**1623**
- Pope Gregory XV, who introduced secret voting for election, dies; Urban VIII is elected to replace him.

**1624**
- The first English settlers arrive in the West Indies after Sir Thomas Warner occupies the island of St. Christopher (St. Kitts).
- Dutch settlers arrive in New Amsterdam (later renamed New York by the British).

**1625**
- Virginia is made a royal colony; James I dies, and his brother, Charles I, becomes king of England.

**1626**
- Catholic forces in Germany defeat a Protestant army at the Battle of Dessau during the Thirty Years' War.

**1628**
- The English Parliament passes the Petition of Right, which restricts the right of the king to impose taxes, declare martial law, and imprison citizens.

**1631**
- Swedish king Gustav II Adolph leads his troops to victory over Flemish forces, led by Johann Tserclaes (Tilly), at the Battle of Breitenfeld; the Flemish also lose an engagement at the Lech River the following year.

**1632**
- Galileo publishes *Dialogo sopra i due massimi sistemi del mondo* (Dialogue of the Two Chief Systems of the World), although he was ordered by the Pope to denounce the Copernican system. He dies in 1642.
- Shāh Jahān begins construction, finished in 1649, of the Taj Majal.

*DENOTES CIRCA DATE

**1634**
- The first English settlers arrive in Maryland and establish their capital at St. Mary's, on property given to George Calvert in 1632.

**1635**
- Emperor Ferdinand II and Elector John George of Saxony sign the Peace of Prague, which is accepted by Brandenburg and most Lutheran states.

**1636**
- Dissident clergyman Roger Williams founds Providence (Rhode Island).

**1637**
- The foundation for modern philosophical inquiry is developed by French philosopher René Descartes in *Discours de la méthode* (Discourse on the Method).
- New England settlers attack neighboring Native Americans in a short conflict known as the Pequot War.

**1638**
- Christians are persecuted in Japan, which is closed to foreigners except the Dutch and Chinese, who are allowed only to maintain trading posts under guard in a walled compound on the island of Deshima.

**1640**
- Portugal regains its independence from Spain.

**1642**
- The English Civil War commences between the royalist forces of Charles I and the Roundheads, those who support Parliament.
- The Dutch obtain a monopoly of foreign trade in Japan on final exclusion of the Portuguese, but the Japanese government imposes severe limitations on their activities.
- Dutch captain Abel Tasman discovers New Zealand and Tasmania; the following year he finds the Fiji Islands.

**1643**
- Louis XIV (the Great, or Sun, King) becomes king of France.

**1644**
- Pope Urban VIII, who promoted Catholic missionary activities in Asia and Latin America, dies; Innocent X becomes the new Pope.

*Denotes Circa Date

CHAPTER TWO

# GEOGRAPHY

by GUANGQIU XU

## CONTENTS

*Sidebars and tables are listed in italics.*

**618**

- The Tang dynasty is founded and rules until 907. It encompasses what is known as "China Proper," the present-day People's Republic of China except for Manchuria and the island of Hainan. The Tang capital is Chang'an, located in east central China along the southern bank of the Wei River, approximately eighty miles above its juncture with the Huang, or Yellow, River.

**630***

- Tang armies advance northward and defeat the Tujue, a nomadic people who control an empire stretching from present-day Mongolia to the Black Sea. Because Tang forces expand beyond the original frontier they let the Great Wall, a series of fortifications first connected in the third century B.C.E., fall into disrepair.

**644**

- Tang armies advance into Korea, a peninsula on the east coast of Asia.

**661**

- The Tang empire annexes the valley of the Amu Dar'ya (Oxus) River, Kashmir, Bokhara, and the borderlands of present-day eastern Iran.

**821**

- Both the Tang and Tibetan governments reach a treaty at Chang'an, ratified at Lhasa the following year, which recognizes the independence of Tibet and the occupation of Gansu in northern China by the Tibetans.

**893**

- The Yellow River breaks its dikes and changes course.

**902**

- The Ten Kingdoms rule South China until 979; their capital cities include Guangling, Jinling, Xidu, Chengdu, Canton, Changsha, Xifu, Changle, Jiangling, and Taiyuan.

**907**

- The Five Dynasties rule North China until 960; one of their capitals is Luoyang in present-day Henan Province.

**936**

- The Later Jin dynasty, one of the Five Dynasties, arises and rules for ten years. The founding emperor relinquishes control of the Sixteen Prefectures (strategic border regions along the northern frontier) to the Khitans (Qidans). This event allows the Liao empire (916–1115) to have full access to North China.

**939**

- The present-day Southeast Asian country of Vietnam (called Annam by the imperial Chinese) wins its autonomy from China. It is later reconquered by Mongol and Ming armies.

* DENOTES CIRCA DATE

**960**
- The Song dynasty is established and rules until 1279. The Northern Song capital is at Kaifeng or Bian in east central China in the Yellow River Valley. One of the most historic cities in China, it is the site of early settlements and the junction point of important trading routes. The Southern Song capital is Hangzhou in eastern China at the mouth of the Fuchun River. The Venetian traveler Marco Polo visited this city in the thirteenth century when it was called "Kinsai."

**1056**
- The Khitans make limited repairs on the Great Wall in the area between the Yazuo and Hongtong Rivers.

**1077**
- The Yellow River shatters its dikes downstream from Kaifeng.

**1115**
- The Jurchens (Ruzhens) establish the Jin empire in Manchuria. They make improvements on the Great Wall at Mingchang.

**1148**
- The Yellow River alters its course again.

**1194**
- The mouth of the Yellow River changes from the north of the Shandong Peninsula to the south of it.

**1279**
- The Yuan, or Mongol, dynasty is founded and rules China Proper until 1368; its capital is Beijing, located on an extensive plain in northeastern China. A frontier town for many centuries, Beijing was called Chi or Yen by previous dynasties; Marco Polo identifies it as "Cambaluc."
- The Mongols garrison certain forts along the Great Wall in order to guard the Silk Road or Silk Route (an ancient trade route that linked China with the West) from brigands and to limit the threat of insurrection from their Han (Chinese) subjects.

**1289**
- Over the span of the next fifty years, the Yellow River shifts its course at least three times.

**1368**
- The Ming dynasty overthrows the Mongols and rules China Proper until 1644; Nanjing (located in eastern China along the southern bank of the Chang or Yangzi River) serves as the capital until 1403, when it is replaced by Beijing.

* DENOTES CIRCA DATE

**1487**
- The Ming government begins to connect more sections of the Great Wall in order to protect the entire northern frontier. The Great Wall as it stands today is the result of this building project.

**1549**
- The geographer Zheng Ruozeng completes *Yanhai Tuben*, an atlas of the Chinese coastline from the Liaodong Peninsula southward to Guangdong.

**1560**
- Zheng Ruozeng finishes *Chouhai Tubian*, a massive reference work dedicated to the study of the Chinese coastal provinces.

**1606**
- Cheng Dayue completes a catalogue of ink tablets called *Chengshi Moyuan*, which contains illustrations of mountains, rivers, and other geographic features.

\* DENOTES CIRCA DATE

Mountains near Linxia in western Gansu Province

# OVERVIEW

**Terrain.** China Proper is an immense mountainous area bounded by the Pacific Ocean to the east and south, the massive Himalaya and Pamir mountain ranges to the west and southwest, and the steppes to the north. Although the North China Plain is large, it is actually much smaller than the plain that extends across northern India, the North European Plain, or the American Middle West. The Qinling mountain range divides China into two drainage systems: the Yellow River in the North and the Yangzi (Yangtze) River in the South.

**Loess.** The winds blowing outward from the continent are cold and dry. These winds, producing vast dust storms, deposited in ancient times the fine loess soil that now covers about one hundred thousand square miles of northwestern China south of the Great Wall. The loess is from one hundred feet to three hundred feet thick. The Yellow River spread some of it over the North China Plain as alluvium. The loess region has never been forested except on mountains above the level of the loess itself. Although the Chinese made efforts during the imperial period (617–1644) to hold back the steady process of erosion by the Yellow River and its tributaries, they failed. Since the North has little rainfall, the loess does not have its minerals washed away, and it, therefore, makes a fertile soil.

**Climate.** Most of China has a temperate climate. Its location between the sea and the Asian landmass gives it more rainfall than most of western Eurasia and a much greater temperature range than the Mediterranean countries and western Europe. The seasonal monsoon winds of China are increased by cyclonic storms. An average of eight or nine typhoons originate in the region of the Philippines during the final part of each summer and blow into China with wind velocities up to 150 miles an hour.

**Agricultural Conditions.** South China has a perfect climate for agriculture, but its soils have been leached by heavy rainfall and exhausted by many centuries of intensive farming. South of the Yangzi River only 15 percent of the uplands are flat enough for farming. During the imperial era, most of the area produced two crops annually: winter wheat in the fall and rice in the summer. In the West River Delta in South China two rice crops could be grown annually. As a result, South China had a denser population than the North and higher standards of nutrition. North China, in spite of its fertile loess, balanced dangerously on the edge of famine. Even today the northern peasants face the continual threat of drought. The growing season is short and rainfall is light. It is not astonishing that in the last one thousand years more than eight hundred famines affecting one or more regions in China have been recorded. The North China Plain, the richest and most populous part of the region, faces the additional threat of floods by the Yellow River. As an alluvial plain it has a high water table, often not far below the surface. Soluble salts are carried onto the surface through capillary action and set down there when the water evaporates. Consequently, these salts cannot be washed away in the rainy season, rendering the land infertile.

**People.** The people of imperial China were divided into two major groups: the Han or Chinese and the non-Han minorities. The Han formed the vast majority of the population. Like the Europeans, the Han Chinese were the product of constant intermingling of ethnic groups caused by invasions, colonization, trade, migrations, and other contacts among neighbors. From 617 to 1644 non-Han minorities such as the Turks, Mongols, Tungus, Koreans, Tibetans, Burmese, Thais, Miaos, Yaos, Indians, and Persians appeared. Non-Han elements lived chiefly in Southwest China, where colonization went on for more than one thousand years.

# TOPICS IN GEOGRAPHY

## BORDER REGIONS

**Tibet.** Beyond China Proper are continental and insular border areas that had periodically been incorporated into Chinese empires from 617 to 1644. These areas include Tibet, Xinjiang, Mongolia, and Manchuria. Derived from a Mongolian term, the name *Tibet* was used in Europe by the thirteenth century. A mountainous area, Tibet covers about 500,000 square miles, half of which is more than 15,000 feet in altitude. The source of the principal Chinese and Asian rivers, Tibet had a population of about two million during the period under consideration. Agricultural and mineral resources were insignificant. Chinese interest in Tibet began in 650 when a military expedition occupied Lhasa, the capital. In the thirteenth century the Mongols incorporated Tibet into their empire, and Kublai Khan established a regime in Tibet under the control of priest-kings. After the Mongols, Ming rulers from time to time tried to reincorporate Tibet into their domains.

**Xinjiang.** Called Chinese or Eastern Turkestan, Xinjiang has an average elevation lower than Tibet's. The oasis Turfan is a little below sea level. With an area of 635,000 square miles

Xinjiang had a population of about 5 million by Ming times (1368–1644), the majority of whom were Turkish-speaking Islamic peoples, mainly Uighurs. (The Uighurs had relations with the tribes of central Asian Russia.) Xinjiang is separated into two sections by the Tian Shan range with the Dzungarian Plain to the north and the Tarim Basin to the south. The main areas of settlement are the oases along the northern and southern borders of the Tarim Basin. Across Xinjiang, overland trade routes existed from the seventh to seventeenth centuries. One main route followed the northern side of the Tarim Basin to such cities as Kashgar and Yarkand at the eastern foot of the Pamirs, which was the barrier between China and India and the trans-Caspian regions. Another route started from north of the Tian Shan to Kuldja near the head of the Ili River and then down the valley of the Ili to the grasslands east of the Aral Sea. The routes, known as the Silk Road, connected imperial China and the outside world in the West. These routes were used not only by the merchants and travelers but also by the Buddhist pilgrims during the time period.

**Mongolia.** The semiarid northern region of Mongolia, a plateau of 3,000–5,000 feet elevation, was an intermediary

Caves near the Turfan depression in eastern Xinjiang

Section of the Great Wall, initially built in the third century B.C.E. to thwart raids by northern tribes

between the Chinese and barbarian ways of life. The Gobi Desert and the adjacent Ordos are primarily rocky, gravelly, and sandy wastes crossed by low mountains and hills. The northern and western sections of Mongolia have adequate grazing lands, and some parts are well irrigated by rivers. The higher mountains in the northwest are forested. Because of their poor soil and limited resources, the Mongols had to expand their territories in order to gain more resources during the thirteenth century. Well-known conquerors, they created one of the largest empires in the history of the world. They dominated most of Eurasia, including Russia and Persia, and all of central Asia, China, and Korea. Mongol armies attacked as far as the Adriatic Sea in the West. In the East they sailed to attack Japan and Java. For a while communication between the East and the West was promoted by Mongolian domination and international trade. The territory, however, was too vast, and local cultures were too varied. The Mongol empire ultimately disintegrated at the end of the fourteenth century.

**Manchuria.** Located to the northeast of China, Manchuria is bordered by Mongolia to the west and by mountains and the Amur River to the north. On the east, mountains separate Manchuria from the valley of the Ussuri River and the Sea of Japan. To the south the Gulf of Zhili and the Yellow Sea provide access to the Pacific. The only easy land route into China Proper from Manchuria lies along the coast. Extensive plains, valleys, and low hills largely make up the central portion of Manchuria. The valleys and plains are rich and quite well irrigated. Forests cover many of the mountains, and mineral deposits include coal and some gold. Severe winters and hot summers make the climate one of extremes. During the imperial era the Jurchen tribes of Manchuria were not well developed culturally. The Ming government, facing dangers from the North, often kept peace and order in Manchuria by careful diplomacy. As long as the Ming empire was powerful and the local Jurchen tribes were weak, the frontier area was relatively peaceful. In the early seventeenth century the descendants of the Jurchens founded the Manchu state and continued to send tributes to Beijing. When strong enough, however, they began to defy the Ming empire and finally occupied the capital in 1644.

**Sources:**

Patricia B. Ebrey, ed., *Chinese Civilization and Society: A Sourcebook* (New York: Free Press, 1981).

John K. Fairbank and Merle Goldman, *China: A New History* (Cambridge, Mass. & London: Belknap Press of Harvard University Press, 1992).

Paul S. Ropp, ed., *Heritage of China: Contemporary Perspectives on Chinese Civilization* (Berkeley: University of California Press, 1990).

## CHINA PROPER

**Cultural World.** China's cultural world can be divided into three parts: China Proper, its border regions, and various remote areas. China Proper during the imperial era (617–1644) constituted only one-third of the total area of the Chinese world, but it embraced 95 percent of the population. In spite of the fact that China Proper possesses a variety of topographical features and a continental climate

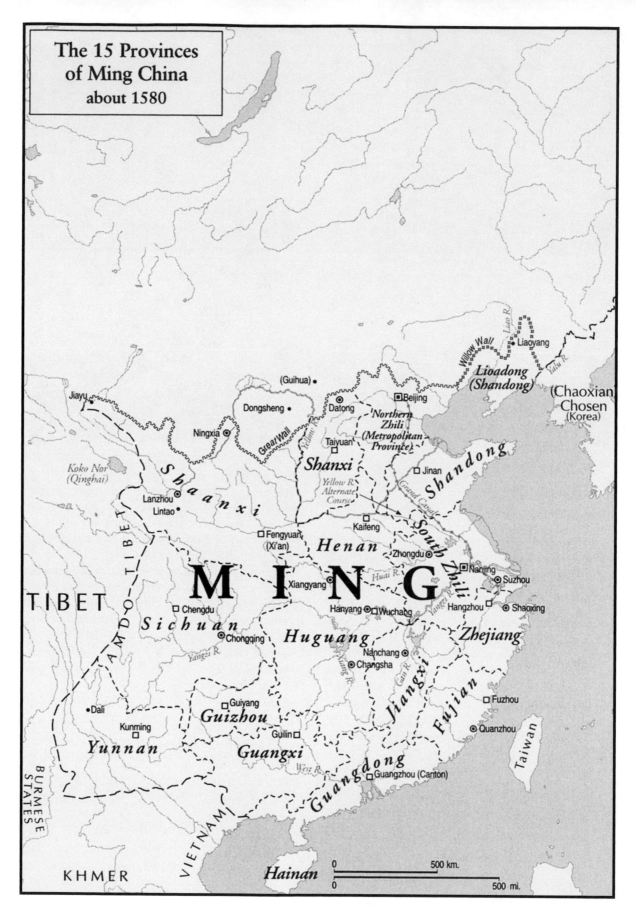

The 15 Provinces
of Ming China
about 1580

(Guihua)

Jiayu

Dongsheng

Ningxia

*Koko Nor
(Qinghai)*

Great Wall

Datong

*Northern
Zhili
(Metropolitan
Province)*

Beijing

Liaoyang

Willow Wall

*Lioadong
(Shandong)*

(Chaoxian
Chosen
(Korea)

Lanzhou

Lintao

*Shaanxi*

Taiyuan

*Shanxi*

*Yellow R.
Alternate
Course*

Jinan

*Shandong*

Grand Canal

Fengyuan
(Xi'an)

Kaifeng

*Henan*

Zhongdu

*South
Zhili*

Nanjing

Suzhou

**MING**

Xiangyang

*Huai R.*

Hangzhou

Shaoxing

*AMDO — TIBET*

Chengdu

Hanyang

Wuchang

*TIBET*

*Sichuan*

Chongqing

*Yangzi R.*

*Huguang*

Nanchang

*Zhejiang*

Changsha

*Gan R.*

*Yangzi R.*

*Jiangxi*

*Fujian*

Fuzhou

Dali

Guiyang

*Guizhou*

Kunming

Guilin

Guangzhou (Canton)

Quanzhou

*Yunnan*

*Guangxi*

*West R.*

*Guangdong*

Taiwan

BURMESE STATES

VIETNAM

KHMER

*Hainan*

0        500 km.

0        500 mi.

Map of China Proper as it was near the end of the imperial era (from F. W. Mote, *Imperial China*, 1999)

of extremes, the Chinese people succeeded in forming a unified empire thanks to a common written language and political philosophy. Naturally, regionalism exists in such a large country, but obstacles were never so great that they partitioned the Chinese culture to the same extent as the Europeans were divided.

**Internal Boundaries.** Physical features such as mountain ranges and large rivers help to define internal boundaries of China Proper, which is divided into three parts: North, Central, and South. North China is watered by the Huang or Yellow River, which travels approximately 2,903 miles from Tibet across the North China Plain to the Yellow Sea. (This river and the plain represent the source of livelihood for one-fourth of China's people today.) The imperial capitals were usually located in the region, and North China became an important political center of the medieval period. Central China has the Chang (Yangzi or Yangtze) River, which starts in the mountains of Tibet and descends into the vast central plain. It is an estimated 3,434 miles long. The region is a transitional zone in terms of geography, culture, and crops. The growing season is longer than in the North, and important crops are wheat, rice, and tea. The mountains contain some mineral deposits. South China, with its many mountain ranges, has many small valleys and short rivers, of which the most important is the Xi (West) River. Approximately 1,200 miles in length, it pours into the South China Sea close to Guangzhou. There are other rivers in the region that flow into the West River or directly into the ocean. The climate is wet, and typhoons hit with terrible force in the summer. Rice and tea are the chief crops of South China, and because the growing season is from six to twelve months, up to three rice crops a year are possible. There are some mineral deposits in this area, such as bauxite, antimony, mercury, and tungsten. South China was never important as a political center during the period from 617 to 1644 because it was far from the imperial capitals. Thereafter it became a base of peasant rebellions.

**Eurasian Continent.** The Chinese world maintained relations with peoples whose modes of life and culture were different from its own. The Chinese world was in contact with the western and southern parts of the Eurasian continent during the Middle Ages (814–1350). There were four kinds of contacts: military campaigns, official diplomacy, commercial trade, and religious pilgrimages. The oasis routes played a significant role in establishing relations between China and other civilizations by the ninth century. The steppe routes, further to the north, linked Mongolia and North China closely to Europe and the countries of the Middle East from the thirteenth to fourteenth centuries. Maritime traffic along the coast also played an important role.

**Interactions.** The commercial centers situated at the ends of the main routes across the Eurasian continent and on the borders of the Chinese world were visited by traders, embassies, and missionaries from Central Asia, India, and the Middle East. In the same way the harbors on the Chinese coast were the meeting sites of Korean, Japanese, Indian, Persian, Arab, and later, European sailors and merchants. The big Chinese cities, especially the capitals, had been cosmopolitan centers since the Tang dynasty (618–907), and in turn Chinese soldiers, ambassadors, pilgrims, merchants, and craftsmen went to almost every area of Asia.

Sources:
George B. Cressey, *Asia's Lands and People: A Geography of One-third of the Earth and Two-thirds of Its People* (New York: McGraw-Hill, 1963).

John K. Fairbank, *Chinese Thought and Institutions* (Chicago: University of Chicago Press, 1957).

Michael Loewe, *The Pride That Was China* (New York: St. Martin's Press, 1990).

## CLIMATE

**Rainfall.** China is impacted by cold, dry, continental air, but the warm, humid, oceanic air brings in most of its rainfall. During the summer this sea air reaches further into the continent, sometimes as far as Mongolia. Naturally, a great deal more rain falls on South China than on North China. To the south, near the sources of cloud-carrying winds, rainfall is heavy because the coast is backed by mountains and this situation gives rise to moisture as it comes in from the ocean. Rain in the South averages almost sixty inches a year, and some coastal mountains receive as much as a hundred inches. This rainfall, together with run-off from the central Asian massif, supplies South China with plenty of water, which is used not only for irrigating rice fields but also for transportation. The network of navigable streams and canals, which covers most of the central and lower Yangzi basin and the less mountainous regions south of it, has been a great economic resource. In Central China the rain averages about forty inches, and in the Yangzi delta forty-five. In both South and Central China the summer humidity is high and temperatures range from sixty to eighty degrees Fahrenheit. In the North, far from the sources of moisture, rainfall declines and averages usually between twenty inches and thirty inches on the coast, and much less inland. The Northwest receives less than the twenty inches of minimum rainfall necessary for cultivating unirrigated lands and has little or no water transportation.

**Boundary.** An equally significant climatic boundary is the one between the farming areas of China Proper and the steppes to the north, which (unless some parts of the steppes are farmed) too arid for crops. This region also marks the linguistic and cultural border between the agricultural Chinese and the pastoral, Altaic-speaking nomads. During the imperial era (617–1644) the Chinese continued to rebuild and extend the Great Wall in order to defend themselves from their northern neighbors and distinguish themselves from other peoples.

**Temperate Zone.** China Proper lies almost entirely in the temperate zone. Seasonal differences are marked. In the spring and summer, moisture-laden winds carrying rain sweep northward from the ocean; in the autumn and winter the process is reversed. The air over the great northern and western land barriers cools more rapidly than that over the

Rice paddies in Guizhou Province, southwestern China

tropical and subtropical seas to the south, and it moves southward, bringing cloudless skies and comfortable temperatures. Therefore, China Proper has most of its rain in the spring and summer.

**Crops.** Differences between the North and the South in rainfall and temperature help to distinguish North China from the Yangzi Valley and the south coast in terms of geographical appearance and crops. During the imperial era in the South the plains and hills were more green than they are today, the growing season was from six to nine months in length, two or three crops a year were produced, and the widespread grain was rice. In the North the hills and plains were brown and dust blown during the winter, the growing season was only about four to six months, only one crop a year was planted, and the most prevalent crops were wheat, *kaoliang* (Chinese sorghum), millet, and beans. In the North trees did not grow easily, and the characteristic forests were of broad-leaved, deciduous varieties. Because of the climate and the nature of the soil only parts of North China were heavily timbered. In contrast, the longer growing season and the heavier rains of the South were favorable to trees. Vegetation was more abundant, and forests grew much faster.

**Society.** In the North little rainfall meant many famines, and the bitter winters adversely affected people's health. The cold and the dust storms often kept people indoors in unhygienic conditions. Since fuel was expensive, houses remained badly heated. Heavy clothing was normal, and winter laundry and bathing were hard. Under such conditions disease thrived. Furthermore, the short growing season demanded intense activity for only several months in a year and enforced idleness during the rest of the year. Home industries occupied only part of the time during the slower seasons. In the Yangzi Valley

and the South, on the other hand, the winter temperatures were milder. Dust storms did not occur, outdoor life was frequent, and bathing was possible.

**Animals and Architecture.** The climate contributed in part to the small number of domestic animals in the South. The humid, damp summers produced coarse grasses that proved difficult for cows, sheep, and horses to eat and digest. The climate also had an impact on Chinese architecture to a certain extent. During the imperial era, heavy summer rains forced the Chinese to use sound, heavy, tiled or thatched roofs to protect their houses.

**Sources:**
Caroline Blunden and Mark Elvin, *Cultural Atlas of China* (New York: Facts on File, 1983).

Albert Hermann, *Historical and Commercial Atlas of China* (Chicago: Aldine, 1966).

Pierre Pfeffer, *Asia: A Natural History* (New York: Random House, 1968).

## CULTURAL GROUPS

**Sedentary People.** Imperial China had a population consisting of three cultural groups: sedentary people, nomadic people, and mountain people. The sedentary people engaged primarily in agriculture. As in other parts of the world, it was agriculture that contributed to population expansion and formation of organized states. Sedentary people spread over all the plains, valleys, and fertile high plateaus of China. They grew two different kinds of crops: "dry" and "wet." "Dry" crops included cereals, barley, wheat, and different types of millet. Irrigation was irregularly practiced in "dry" areas. Despite the prevalence of agriculture in these regions, the raising of livestock, such as cattle, sheep, and horses, was comparatively significant from the seventh century onward. The major "wet" crop was rice, and its mass production originated during the Tang dynasty (618–907). This agricultural product began

Farmland at Roungshui in southeastern China

in the lower basin of the Yangzi (Yangtze) River and proved successful, spreading to all the warm, damp areas where irrigation was possible. The development of rice growing from the seventh to tenth centuries onward signified a new stage in the history of the Chinese people, and it became the major food of the country.

**Nomadic People.** Nomadic cattle raisers lived in the grasslands and desert regions, extending from the Siberian taiga (subarctic forest) to the agricultural lands of North China. These people played a fundamental role in the history of the Chinese world and exerted a strong influence on its civilization. They had large herds of oxen, sheep, horses, camels, and yaks. Consummate horsemen, these nomads possessed a mobility that turned them into a formidable military power. From the seventh to seventeenth centuries their contacts and trade relations with sedentary peoples helped to strengthen the political organization of the steppe societies and to enrich them. Nevertheless, internal tensions and rifts developed, and eventually some of the nobles adopted the lifestyles of the sedentary people.

**Mountain People.** The mountain people of the Himalayas and adjoining areas practiced both livestock raising and agriculture. These mountaineers lived in an area approximately four million square kilometers in size. They grew poor but hardy cereals such as barley, millet, rye, buckwheat, and sometimes wheat in sheltered valleys. They also raised cows, yaks, horses, sheep, and goats. Cattle raising on a grand scale, like that of the nomadic people of the steppe areas, was conducted on the high plateau of Tibet and Qinghai, but mountain rearing, with the animals driven to stables in winter, prevailed in the more hilly areas. The aggressive mountain peoples of the Himalayan complex used to attack caravans and invade the domains of the sed-

entary people. From the Tang dynasty to the Ming dynasty (1368–1644) they moved eastward into Gansu, Sichuan, and Shanxi as well as northward into the farmlands.

Sources:
George B. Cressey, *Asia's Lands and People: A Geography of One-third of the Earth and Two-thirds of Its People* (New York: McGraw-Hill, 1963).

Milton W. Meyer, *China: An Introductory History* (Totowa, N.J.: Littlefield, Adams, 1978).

Thomas R. Tregear, *A Geography of China* (London: University of London Press, 1965).

David C. Wright, *The History of China* (Westport, Conn. & London: Greenwood Press, 2001).

## THE ENVIRONMENT AND CHINA

**Unity.** Mountains, deserts, rivers, and other topographical features have had a profound effect upon China throughout its history. They frequently represented insurmountable barriers; the southern hills in particular were havens for various rebel groups during the period 617–1644. However, four major dynasties (Tang, Song, Yuan or Mongol, and Ming) managed to arise and achieve cultural and political unity from the seventh to seventeenth centuries. Moreover, these empires achieved economic self-sufficiency.

**Isolation.** The Pacific Ocean is the source of moisture-laden winds that provide China with rain, but it is even more effective in isolating China than are the great land masses to the north and west. To the east the Koreans and Japanese were the only civilized people with whom trade was possible. Culturally, both of these groups borrowed more from than contributed to China Proper. The Pacific coast of North America was too far away for the Chinese to have any relations with the people living there. Southeastern Asia was considered to be civilized, but the nearest

## BARBARIANS

Wang Fuzhi was a famous philosopher of the seventeenth century. In the following excerpts from the opening portion of his *Yellow Book*, he makes observations on barbarian tribes:

The strength of the barbarians lies in the paucity of their laws and institutions. As long as their shelter, food, and clothing remain crude and barbaric, as long as they continue to foster a violent and savage temper in their people and do not alter their customs, they may enjoy great advantage. And at the same time, because of this China may escape harm. But if they once begin to change and to adopt Chinese ways, then the advantage of their situation will also change. They may there in time grow braver and mightier than the Chinese, which will be an advantage gained, but they will also open the way for eventual weakness. Therefore it is said that, as fish forget each other in the rivers and lakes, so men should forget each other and follow their own ways and principles. While the barbarians are content to roam about in pursuit of water and pasture, practicing archery and hunting, preserving no distinctions between ruler and subject, possessing only rudimentary marriage and governmental systems, ranging back and forth over their territory in accordance with seasonal demands, then China can never control or rule them. And as long as the barbarians do not realize that cities can be fortified and maintained, that markets bring profit, that fields can be cultivated and taxes exacted, as long as they do not know the glory of elaborate marriage and official systems, then they will continue to look upon China as a perilous and inhospitable bed of thorns. In like manner the Chinese who are seized and carried off to the lands of the barbarians will regard them with hatred and bitterness and refuse to serve them. The two lands will ignore each other to the advantage of both. It is in accordance with the ordinances of Heaven and the dictates of human feeling that each should thus find delight only in his own ways.

**Source:** William Theodore de Bary, ed., *Sources of Chinese Tradition* (New York: Columbia University, 1963), pp. 597–601.

lands represented the Middle Kingdom, and all other peoples were barbarians.

Sources:

John K. Fairbank and Edwin O. Reischauer, *East Asia: Tradition and Transformation* (Boston: Houghton Mifflin, 1989).

Charles O. Hucker, *China to 1850: A Short History* (Stanford, Cal.: Stanford University Press, 1978).

F. W. Mote, *Imperial China, 900–1800* (Cambridge, Mass. & London: Harvard University Press, 1999).

## MOUNTAINS AND RIVERS

**Mountains.** China is broken up into a sort of checkerboard by intersecting mountain chains. One major range is traced from southwestern China northeastward through Shansi and western Manchuria. A parallel range extends from Guangzhou northward along the coast to the lower reaches of the Yangzi (Yangtze) River and then reappears in the Shandong Peninsula and along the Korean and Manchurian borders. Intersecting these two southwest-to-northeast ranges, three parallel mountain chains are spaced at roughly equal intervals from west to east. Across the center of South China the southernmost chain creates the watershed dividing the West River system of the Guangzhou region from the Yangzi Valley. In the extreme North another east-west range divides North China from the Mongolian plateau. The eastward extension of the massive Kunlun Mountains of northern Tibet creates the dividing line between the Yangzi and the Yellow Rivers, marking the boundary of North China and South China. Overall, this crosshatching of mountain ranges produces

Mount Tian Zi, Hunan Province

kingdoms had little cultural impact upon China. India, the closest great cultural center noticeably different from China, was difficult to reach either by sea or land. Enjoying the natural protection of the ocean, the Chinese did not need to worry about any major invasions from the east and southwest, although Japanese pirates plagued the coast in Ming times. Throughout the imperial era the Chinese were extremely isolated, and they did not look outside for an outlet for their surplus population until the seventeenth century, when many began to migrate to Taiwan and other places.

**Superiority.** Isolation contributed to intense national pride in China. To the Chinese all other civilizations with which they had close contacts were actually derived from them and were considered to be inferior. Chinese

Yangzi River near the Yangzi Gorges in South China

several separate geographical regions, which contributed to the lack of economic and political unity during the imperial era (617–1644).

**Yellow River.** The Yellow River, approximately 2,700 miles in length and located in North China, is the fifth longest river in the world. It begins in Tibet at 14,000 feet, then drops precipitously to 5,800 feet within the first seven hundred miles and gradually descends in great bends through western and northern China. A wide but relatively shallow river, it is not navigable for deep-draft ships. After entering the North China Plain about five hundred miles from the sea, it crosses a wide floodplain. The riverbed slopes only about one foot per mile. Along the banks of the Yellow River there is a great problem with silt. In the summer flood season the waters from the great treeless mountain ranges to the west bring with them a heavy deposit of yellow silt, which gives the river its name. The river, continually building up its own bed, rose from ten to forty feet above the surrounding areas, and the imperial governments from the Tang dynasty (618–907) to the Ming dynasty (1368–1644) had to construct dikes to keep it within its channel.

**Insoluble Problem.** Because of its alternating droughts and floods the Yellow River represented death, as well as life, to the Chinese. Only one breach in the dikes could spread water over hundreds of square miles and cut millions of peasants off from their provisions. When the river bursts the dikes, its mouth changes too, emptying into the Yellow Sea at various points. The immensity of the Yellow River problem was graphically demonstrated by the historic shifts of its bed from the north to the south of the Shan-

dong promontory and back again. After 1191 water of the Yellow River primarily entered the Yellow Sea south of the peninsula. The Yellow River gave the Chinese an apparently insoluble problem, one that the Chinese emperors were never able to conquer.

**Yangzi River.** The Yangzi (Yangtze) River, the fourth longest river in the world, is 3,200 miles in length. With a catchment basin double the size of the Yellow River's, the Yangzi collects double the amount of rainfall. In its upper reaches the Yangzi is called the "Golden River," and it is navigable. In flood season the river dashes through the well-known Yangzi gorges above Hubei at fourteen knots. Joined by a great network of tributaries, the Yangzi itself takes an enormous volume of silt, approximately four hundred million tons a year, into the ocean. As a result, during the imperial era the Yangzi River extended the rich Shanghai delta region at the rate of about one mile in seventy years. The Dongting and Poyang Lakes serve as water catchment and storage basins for the lower Yangzi, but the rainy season can raise the water level in places as much as forty or fifty feet between the dikes. Disastrous floods, however, did not occur as much as they did with the Yellow River during the imperial era. The Yangzi River played an important role in the economic development of the Yangzi areas.

Sources:

George B. Cressey, *Asia's Lands and People: A Geography of One-third of the Earth and Two-thirds of Its People* (New York: McGraw-Hill, 1963).

Leo J. Moser, *The Chinese Mosaic: The Peoples and Provinces of China* (Boulder, Colo.: Westview Press, 1985).

Christopher J. Smith, *China: People and Places in the Land of One Billion* (Boulder, Colo.: Westview Press, 1991).

## NEIGHBORING COUNTRIES

**Korea.** Chinese cultural influences spread into outlying countries during the imperial period (617–1644). Korea, a mountainous peninsula situated among more powerful states, suffered politically from its position. In the seventh century, Buddhism spread to Korea from China, and Koreans in turn played an important role in exporting it to Japan. In the tenth century, when Chinese control declined, a rebel founded the Koryo dynasty, from which the name *Korea* is derived. The Koryo dynasty continued as a vassal of imperial China from the Yuan or Mongol dynasty (1279–1368) through the Ming dynasty (1368–1644).

**Japan.** As an insular country Japan came within the cultural, but not the territorial, sphere of Chinese interest. The Japanese, emerging from a relatively primitive society, began to adopt much of Chinese culture, including the written script, the Buddhist religion, and the concepts of centralized economic and political power. Tang dynasty (618–907) architecture, dances, and literary forms had a great impact on the Japanese. At the end of the ninth century, after attaining a degree of cultural complexity and with the decay of Tang political order at home, the Japanese began to lose their interest in Chinese society and lifestyles. Good relations between China and Japan were revived sporadically in the following centuries, but they suffered when Japanese pirates began to assault the eastern Chinese coastline at the beginning of the fifteenth century.

**Southeast Asia.** Another region that had been subjected to Chinese expansion was Southeast Asia. Chinese interest there was predominantly directed toward present-day Vietnam. A Chinese general established an independent southern kingdom with its capital at Guangzhou, which embraced Vietnam and some southern Chinese provinces. Despite native rebellions the incorporation of Vietnamese territory into the Chinese empire continued until 939. By this time the Chinese had designated the southern region as Annam, a term still used today. During the imperial era the Chinese had a great influence on the system of writing, law codes, administrative structures, and bureaucracy in Vietnam. The Chinese established merchant communes in other areas of Southeast Asia where native kingdoms were under Indian influences through Hinduism and Buddhism. In the thirteenth century Mongols dispatched armies into Burma and Vietnam and sent naval forces as far as Java. In

## RELATIONS WITH JAPAN

In 1266 the Yuan government appointed the vice president of the Ministry of War as envoy to Japan and granted him the Tiger Seal for his specific mission. The vice president of the Ministry of Rites was appointed as his deputy bearing the Golden Seal. They were to carry with them a letter from the Mongol emperor to the king of Japan. The message read as follows:

> I have heard that since ancient times even a small nation emphasizes the importance of mutual trust and reciprocal friendship in its relationship with neighboring states. How can we be any more different? Our ancestor received the mandate of Heaven to establish a great empire and brought a large number of peoples under their jurisdiction. Even peoples in the remotest areas feared our military might and longed for the benevolent influence we might be able to extend to them. I can assure you that their number was very large indeed.

> When I ascended the throne as the emperor, I immediately ordered the cessation of hostilities and the restoration of Korea the territories we had conquered, feeling compassionate for the innocent Korean people who had suffered so much during the previous war. Grateful for the favor we had shown to them, the Korean King and his ministers bore tribute to China, and the relationship between China and Korea, though legally a relationship between lord and vassal, has been as cordial as a relationship between a father and his son. Of this fact I am sure that you are fully aware.

Source: Dun J. Li, ed., *The Essence of Chinese Civilization* (Princeton: D. Van Nostrand, 1967), pp. 227–278.

the early fifteenth century Ming emperors periodically dispatched naval expeditions into waters as far west as the Persian Gulf. These expeditions, however, brought no significant results, and as the European powers began their expansion in Asia, Ming China stopped sending any overseas expeditions.

Sources:

Kang Chao, *Man and Land in Chinese History: An Economic Analysis* (Stanford, Cal.: Stanford University Press, 1986).

Mark Elvin, *The Pattern of the Chinese Past* (Stanford, Cal.: Stanford University Press, 1973).

Pierre Pfeffer, *Asia: A Natural History* (New York: Random House, 1968).

# SIGNIFICANT PEOPLE

## CHENG DAYUE

### 1541-1616
### INK TABLET DESIGNER

**Ink Tablets.** Cheng Dayue was the youngest of three sons of a prosperous merchant in a village south of Nanjing. In 1564 he attempted to enter the National University in Beijing, but he failed to pass the provincial examination. He soon became interested in nature and geography. He also engaged in the making of ink tablets and purchased a large collection of nature scenes, many of which had been made by master craftsmen of earlier times. In the meantime, Cheng Dayue also began an ink-manufacturing enterprise.

**Ink Sticks.** In 1592 he obtained a position as an usher in the Court of State Ceremonial. He left that petty official position the next year and returned home, where he was accused of murder and sent to prison. Appealing the conviction, Cheng Dayue was ultimately acquitted and released in 1600. He then became involved in producing ink sticks and ink cakes on which he imprinted elaborate artistic designs. Samples of his products circulated among the elite, including the emperor.

**Great Achievement.** After 1600 he invented a new formula to make ink (oil mixed with lacquer). His devotion to the art was inspired by the success of the illustrated catalogue of ink tablets of a former partner. In 1606 he produced his own catalogue of ink tablets, a book of designs and illustrations together with essays, poems, eulogies, and testimonials from grateful recipients. In releasing his album Cheng Dayue spared neither effort nor expense in engaging the best talents, persuading well-known artists to furnish the bulk of the illustrations and famous scholars and important officials to contribute literary pieces and calligraphy. He arranged the illustrations under such categories as natural and unusual phenomena, geography, famous personalities, animal kingdoms, and Confucian, Buddhism, and Daoist teachings.

**Later Life.** In his life Cheng Dayue made more than 130 revisions to his catalogue, complaining of a lack of cooperation on the part of certain scholars. He also became interested in Buddhism. Accused of murder a second time, he starved himself to death in prison.

**Sources:**
L. Carrington Goodrich and Chaoying Fang, eds., *Dictionary of Ming Biography* (New York: Columbia University Press, 1976).

F. W. Mote, *Imperial China, 900–1800* (Cambridge, Mass. & London: Harvard University Press, 1999).

## ZHENG RUOZENG

### 1505-1580
### GEOGRAPHER

**Early Life.** A native in the prefecture of Suzhou, Zheng Ruozeng was born into a literary family that spanned many generations. His father, however, was a businessman. In his teens Zheng Ruozeng studied at the National University in Beijing, but it took him several attempts to pass the examination. He then taught at home and became a pupil of an older scholar.

**Geographic Book.** In the mid sixteenth century the coastal provinces of China suffered from Japanese pirate attacks. Many cities from the Yangzi (Yangtze) River Valley to Guangdong were sacked and the civilian population killed. In the 1540s Zheng Ruozeng determined to improve the coastal defenses. Encouraged by his friends, he took several years to complete the *Yanhai Tuben,* a strategic atlas of the Chinese coastal region ranging from the Liaodong Peninsula to southern Guangdong, including the offshore islands. It had a total of twelve maps with brief descriptions.

**Serious Scholar.** After finishing *Yanhai Tuben,* he began to work on another book, *Chouhai Tubian.* He was such a serious scholar that when Japanese pirates besieged his home city in 1554 he went to that area, observing that only field investigations would provide him with better knowledge of the strategies of the interlopers and the weapons they utilized. As piratical raids on the coast of Zhejiang multiplied, Zheng Ruozeng was encouraged by the governor of Zhejiang to continue his research.

**Interviews.** To gain more dependable information, Zheng Ruozeng conducted interviews with captured Japanese pirates. He also obtained access to government documents and archives, including classified reports of officials who went to Japan to petition Japanese leaders to control the raiders. Therefore, he received firsthand material not generally available. During the interviews he learned that the Japanese had little geographic knowledge of the Chinese coast. Their incursions on China mostly relied upon native guides and river pilots. As a result Zheng Ruozeng recommended that the governor create conflicts between Japanese and Chinese collaborators so as to reduce their military power. Because of his dedication Zheng Ruozeng was granted a military rank in 1560, but he refused to accept it.

**Expanded Work.** By 1560 Zheng Ruozeng finished a draft of the *Chouhai Tubian*. The first edition was fairly small because Zheng attempted to compile only a handbook of pirate activities so as to help Chinese coastal officials. Later, the book was expanded into an encyclo-pedic reference book on coastal affairs. Divided into eight parts, the book had thirteen volumes and was called one of the most scholarly works in its field. From 1564 to the end of the Ming dynasty (1368–1644) the *Chouhai Tubian* was republished at least three times.

**Significance.** The *Chouhai Tubian* was significant because it was not only the first book of its kind but also marked a turning point in the Ming period. Before 1560 China's foremost threats came from the North, and geographers had thus far emphasized those frontier regions and paid relatively little attention to other sections of the empire. Only after the publication of the *Chouhai Tubian* did the government start to endorse other geographical studies. In addition to this book, Zheng Ruozeng later compiled ten other texts. In his sixties he enjoyed good health and was twice recommended in the late 1570s to serve as an official historian, but he rejected the posting.

Sources:

L. Carrington Goodrich and Chaoying Fang, eds., *Dictionary of Ming Biography* (New York: Columbia University Press, 1976).

F. W. Mote, *Imperial China, 900–1800* (Cambridge, Mass. & London: Harvard University Press, 1999).

# DOCUMENTARY SOURCES

Cheng Dayue, *Chengshi Moyuan* (1606)—Catalogue of ink tablets contained in twenty-three volumes. It includes essays, poems, eulogies, laudatory compositions, correspondence, articles, and stories relating to ink and ink making. There are also five hundred detailed illustrations pertaining to geographical as well as religious and biological subject matter.

Zheng Ruozeng, *Chouhai Tubian* (1560)—Encyclopedic reference book of thirteen volumes on the coastal affairs of China. Called one of the most scholarly works in its field, this book stimulated the study of shorelines, estuaries, marshlands, and so forth.

Zheng Ruozeng, *Yanhai Tuben* (1549)—Atlas with twelve maps on the coastal areas of China, ranging from the Liaodong Peninsula to southern Guangdong and including nearby islands.

# THE ARTS

by C. X. GEORGE WEI

## CONTENTS

*Sidebars and tables are listed in italics.*

**618-907**
- China is ruled by the Tang dynasty.

**629-645**
- Theologian Xuanzang travels in India and brings important Buddhist texts back to China.

**630**
- Orders are given to erect Confucian temples at schools all over China.

**633**
- Tang emperor Taizong invents the dance known as *pozhenyue* (breaking battle array).

**634**
- The Palace of Great Clarity, an imperial resort including residential and official buildings, is constructed northwest of Chang'an in Shanxi Province.

**636**
- The Zhaoling (Clarity Tomb) of Emperor Taizong is built in Liquan County, Shanxi Province. The tomb includes the well-known stone sculpture *Six Horses of the Clarity Tomb.*

**637-642**
- Tang-dynasty *duobuyue* (multinational music), also called "the ten melodies," incorporates many foreign melodies.

**641**
- Ouyang Xun, one of the four master calligraphers of the early Tang dynasty, dies.

**648-703**
- Sun Guoting writes *Shupu* (Guide to Calligraphy).

**649**
- Intercultural exchanges take place as China controls Kucha and Khotan of Central Asia, begins to conquer Korea (known as Great Silla), and establishes relations with Japan as well as Funan and Champa in Southeast Asia.

**651**
- After Muslim envoys visit the Tang court, Islamic religion and architecture spread to China. Construction begins on the Huaishengsi (Mosque in Memory of the Sage) in Guangzhou, Guangdong Province.

**651-718**
- Painters Li Sixun and his son Li Zhaodao create the School of Golden and Green Landscape Painting.

\* DENOTES CIRCA DATE

**669**
- The Xuanzhangta, the tomb-pagoda of the monk Xuanzhang, is built at Xingjiao Temple in Chang'an.

**673**
- Yan Liben, the most-celebrated court painter of the early Tang dynasty, dies. Known for his portraits of emperors and scholars, he and his brother Yan Lide brought about a renaissance in figure painting.

**675**
- The Fengxian (Ancestral Reverence) Temple is completed at the Longmen (Dragon Gate) Cave in Henan Province.

**680**
- Poet Lu Zhaolin dies. With Luo Binwang, Wang Bo, and Yang Jiong, he is considered one of the "Four Talents" of the early Tang period.

**683**
- Construction begins on Qianling Tomb (the mausoleum of Emperor Li Zhi) in Qianxian County, Shanxi Province.

**700**
- Poet Chen Ziang dies. With poems such as "Deng Youzhoutai ge" (Upon the Yuzhou Terrace) he initiated a new trend in Chinese literature.

**700\***
- Zhang Haiquan writes *Shuduan* (Analysis of Calligraphy), which describes the artistic features and evolution of ten calligraphic styles.
- The Great Wild Goose Pagoda is built at Cien Temple in Chang'an.

**700-750**
- Duan Shanben, master of the lute, is well known throughout China.

**708**
- Poet Du Shenyan dies. With Li Qiao, Su Weidao, and Cui Rong he was one of the palace literati of the early Tang dynasty known as the "Four Friends of Literary Works."

**712**
- The Japanese book *Kojiki* (Records of Ancient Matters) is written partly in Chinese script and partly in Chinese characters used phonetically to represent Japanese syllables.

**712-756**
- During his reign, Tang emperor Xuanzong, musician and patron of the arts, reorganizes multinational music and composes "Nishang Yuyi" (Rainbow and Feather Dress).

\* DENOTES CIRCA DATE

**717-734**
- Japanese monk Kibi-no-Mabi spends seventeen years at Chang'an, the capital of the Tang dynasty. He then takes back to Japan the Chinese art of embroidery, the *biwa* (four-stringed lute), and the game of *go* (Chinese chess). He invents *kana*, which employs simplified Chinese characters for phonetic purposes.

**720**
- *Nihongi* (Chronicles of Japan) is the first Japanese book written in pure Chinese characters.
- The Tianchang Daoist Temple is built in Youzhou (present-day Beijing). During the early Ming dynasty (1368–1644) it is renamed Baiyun Guan (Temple of White Clouds).

**740**
- Zhang Jiuling dies. A great politician of the early Tang dynasty and a successful prime minister, he was also an important poet.

**741***
- Painter Zhang Xuan dies. He was one of the artists known for their portraits of "Court Ladies on Silk."

**742**
- Poet Wang Zhihuan, known for his frontier poems, dies.

**751**
- *Kaifuso* (Fond Recollections of Poetry) collects 120 Japanese poems written in Chinese language and literary forms over the past seventy-five years.

**755**
- Yang Yuhuan, dancer and consort of Tang emperor Xuanzong, is killed during the An Lushan revolt.

**758**
- Wu Daozi, an influential court artist known as the "Saint Painter," dies. His hundreds of works contributed to the development of genre and landscape painting.

**759***
- The Golden Hall of the Toshodaiji in Japan is founded by the Chinese monk Ganjin (Jianzhen in Chinese).

**761**
- Poet and artist Wang Wei dies. He is known as the father of the Southern School and of monochrome landscape painting in ink.

**762**
- Li Bai, one of the greatest poets in Chinese history, dies.

*Denotes Circa Date*

**770**
- Du Fu, the "Sage of Poetry," dies.

**782**
- One of the two Tang temples still extant, Nanchan (Temple of the Southern Chan), is built on Wutaishan (Mountain of Five Terraces) in Shanxi Province.

**785**
- Monk and calligrapher Huai Su dies. He earned the nickname "Crazy Su" because of his "cursive script."
- Yan Zhenqing dies. One of the four Tang-dynasty masters of calligraphy, he invented the "Yan style" of calligraphy.

**804**
- Painter Zhou Fang, best known for his paintings of "Court Ladies on Silk," dies.

**805**
- Japanese monk Saicho returns to Nara, Japan, after studying in China.

**806**
- The monk Kukai leaves China, where he has been studying, to return to Nara, Japan.

**819**
- Essayist Liu Zongyuan dies. With Han Yu, he has been a leader of a prose movement exalting Confucianism.

**824**
- Poet and essayist Han Yu dies. He and Liu Zongyuan led the Confucian prose movement.

**835**
- Japanese official Tenyuan Zhenmin arrives in China, where he studies lute playing for several years.

**838-847**
- Ennin, a monk of Nara, visits China as a member of the last official Japanese embassy to the Tang dynasty.

**846**
- Poet Yuan Zhen, author of "The Story of Yingying (Little Oriole)," dies.
- Bai Juyi—government official, musician, music critic, and poet—dies. He created *Xinyuefu* (New Music Bureau Ballads), which became popular in Korea and Japan as well. Japanese emperor Saga has had Bai Juyi's works stored in the Imperial Secretariat.

\* **DENOTES CIRCA DATE**

**847**
- Zhang Yanyuan writes *Records of Famous Paintings of All the Dynasties,* the first comprehensive history of Chinese paintings.

**851**
- An Arabic work, *The Story of China and India,* informs the Muslim world about Chinese pottery.

**858**
- Japanese monk Enchin takes works of Chinese literature and art back to Nara, Japan.
- Li Shangyin, author of poems characterized by sensitivity and sorrow, dies.

**865**
- Liu Gongquan dies. One of the four Tang-dynasty masters of calligraphy, he invented the "Liu Style" of calligraphy.

**870**
- Poet Wen Tingyun dies. His lyrics, along with those of Wei Zhuang and Li Yu, mark the maturation of Chinese lyric poetry.

**877**
- The Minghui dashita (Pagoda of Master Minghui) is built at the Haihuiyuan (Academy of Ocean Meeting) in Pingshun County, Shanxi Province.

**902-979**
- Southern China is broken into the Ten Kingdoms: Wu (902–937), Southern Tang (937–975), Former Shu (907–925), Later Shu (935–965), Southern Han (917–971), Chu (927–951), Wu-Yue (907–978), Min (909–945), Nanping/Jingnan (924–963), and Northern Han (951–979).

**905**
- A Chinese scholar of Japan compiles the *Kokinshu* (Ancient and Modern Collection), an anthology of Japanese poems.

**907-960**
- Northern China is ruled by the Five Dynasties: Later Liang (907–923), Later Tang (923–936), Later Jin (936–946), Later Han (947–950), and Later Zhou (951–960).

**960-1125**
- The Song dynasty rules Northern China, with the Liao empire of the Khitans (Qidans) on its northern border.

**962**
- Painter Dong Yuan dies. With Jing Hao, Guan Tong, and Ju Ran, he is called one of the "Four Masters of Landscape Painting."

* DENOTES CIRCA DATE

**967**
- Li Cheng, an influential landscape painter, dies.

**971**
- The Foxiangge (Pavilion of Buddha Fragrance) is built at the Longxingshi (Temple of Prosperity) in Zhengding County, Hebei Province. It houses a twenty-four-meter-high bronze statue of Avalokitesvara, or Guanyin (Goddess of Mercy).

**978**
- Li Yu, the last emperor of the Southern Tang, dies. He was also a poet who wrote lyrics for such well-known tunes as "Yumeiren" (The Beautiful Lady Yu), "Pozhenzi" (Dance of the Cavalry), and "Langtaosha" (Ripples Sifting Sand).

**980**
- Painter Gu Hongzhong dies. He is best known for his painting *Night Feast,* which realistically depicts various palace figures.

**984**
- Guanyin Hall is built at the Duleshi (Temple of Lonely Happiness) in Jixian County, Hebei Province. The three-story hall features an open center to accommodate a tall Buddha.

**996**
- The Niujie libaisi (Mosque of Ox Street) is built in Beijing.

**1000\*-1090\***
- Guo Xi's *Linquan gaozhi* (A Father's Instructions), a classical book on landscape painting, is compiled and edited by his son Guo Si.

**1009**
- The Tiankuangdian (Hall of Godsend) is built at the Daimiao (Temple of Eastern Sacred Mountain) at the foot of Mount Tai in Shandong Province.
- The Ashab Mosque is constructed at Quanzhou in Fujian Province.

**1020**
- Izumi Shikibu, a female writer of Heian, Japan, dies. She is the author of *Honcho Monzui* (Chinese Prose Written by a Japanese).

**1023-1032**
- Shengmudian (Goddess Hall) is built at the Jinci (Jin Temple) in Taiyuan, Shanxi Province. The hall contains statues of forty-three female servants; the statues are considered the best works of Song-dynasty sculpture.

**1031**
- Fan Kuan, an influential landscape painter, dies.

\* DENOTES CIRCA DATE

**1048**
- Su Shunqin, an influential poet who created a new poetic style, dies. He and Mei Yaochen were called "Su-Mei" by contemporaries.

**1056**
- The Pagoda of Sakyamuni, the oldest extant wooden pagoda in China and one of the tallest wooden buildings in the world, is erected in the Fogongshi (Temple of the Buddhist Palace) in Ying County, Shanxi Province.

**1060**
- The innovative poet Mei Yaochen dies. He and poet Su Shunqin were called "Su-Mei" by contemporaries.

**1067**
- Cai Xiang, one of the "Four Master Calligraphers of the Song Dynasty," dies.

**1072**
- Poet, essayist, and literary reformer Ouyang Xiu dies.

**1075**
- Empress Yide dies. She wrote *Huixinyuan* (The Court for the Returning Heart), which contains some of the best-known Liao-dynasty poems.

**1079**
- Wen Tong dies. He belonged to the Song-dynasty School of Literati Painters.

**1086**
- Poet-politician Wang Anshi dies. He served the Song dynasty as a reformist prime minister.

**1089**
- Jueshanshi (Temple of Enlightenment Hill) is built in Lingqiuxian (Soul Hill County), Shanxi Province.

**1098**
- Musician Zhu Changwen dies. His *Qinshi* (The History of Zither), the earliest book on the subject, is later published by his grandnephew Zhu Zhengda.

**1099**
- A typical Song-dynasty landlord or merchant tomb is completed at Baisha (White Sand) in Yu County, Henan Province.

**1100**
- Chen Yang, a composer of palace-feast music, dies. He compiled the *Yueshu* (Music Dictionary), the first Chinese encyclopedia of music.

**1100***

- Guo Mian, a great composer of the Song dynasty, founds the School of Two Zhes.

- Zhang Zeduan paints *Qingming Festival on the River,* a major contribution to the development of genre painting.

- Li Di is the most important flower and bird painter of the Song dynasty.

- Han Tuozhou builds his private Southern Garden in Linan (present-day Hangzhou).

- Han Shizong builds his private garden on Plum Blossom Ridge in Linan.

**1101**

- Painter, poet, calligrapher, lyricist, essayist, and theorist Su Shi dies. His writings represent the greatest achievement of the neoclassical movement in Song-dynasty literature.

**1102**

- The Shengmudian (Goddess Hall) at the Jinci (Jin Temple) in Taiyuan, Shanxi Province, is restored.

**1105**

- Huang Tingjian dies. He was the founder of the Jiangxi School, and—along with Su Shi, Cai Xiang, and Mi Fei—he is known as one of the "Four Master Calligraphers of the Song Dynasty."

**1106**

- Artist Li Gonglin, developer of traditional Chinese line-drawing technique, dies.

**1107**

- Painter, calligrapher, and connoisseur Mi Fei, one of the "Four Master Calligraphers of the Song Dynasty," dies. His paintings and those of his son Mi Youren are known collectively as "The Landscapes of the Mi Family."

**1119-1125**

- *Xuanhe yinpu* (Xuanhe Guide to the Seal), the first systematic record of engraved seals in Chinese history, is published.

**1127-1279**

- The Southern Song dynasty rules southern China, with the Jin empire of the Jurchens (Ruzhens) in northern China.

**1135**

- Song emperor Huizong Zhao Ji, art collector and a notable painter of flowers and birds, dies.

* DENOTES CIRCA DATE

**1140\***

- The Huayanshi (Grand Hall of the Temple of Chinese Rigorousness), the largest building in the ancient style of single-eave architecture, is constructed in Datong, Shanxi Province.

**1150**

- Li Tang dies. With Ma Yuan, Liu Songnian, and Xia Gui, he is known as one of the "Four Master Painters" of the Southern Song Dynasty.

**1151\***

- Li Qingzhao, the great female lyricist of the Song dynasty, dies. She is considered the successor to Su Shi and the predecessor of Xin Qiji.

**1190–1208\***

- Playwright Dong Jieyuan writes *Xixiangji zhugongdiao* (The Western Chamber—Multiple Palace Tunes).

**1191**

- Eisai, a Heian monk, returns to Japan with tea from China.

**1193**

- Poet Fan Chengda dies. Along with Yang Wanli, Lu You, and You Mao, he is known as one of the "Four Masters of Restoration."

**1198**

- Musician Cai Yuanding dies. His works include *Lülü xinshu* (The New Classic Temperament) and *Yanyueshu* (Classic Palace Feast Music).

**1200\***

- Monk Fa Chang is the most important Song-dynasty painter of flowers and birds. The Japanese call him the "Great Benefactor of Painting."

**1206**

- Poet Yang Wanli, advocate of the style of Chengzhaiti (Honest Study) and one of the "Four Masters of Resurgence," dies.

**1207**

- Nationalist poet Xin Qiji dies.

**1210**

- Poet and patriotic writer Lu You, one of the "Four Masters of Resurgence," dies.

**1221**

*DENOTES CIRCA DATE

- Poet and musician Jiang Kui dies. Considered one of the greatest musicians in all Chinese history, he published the four-volume *Baishi daoren shiji* (Songs of the White Stone Daoist), a collection of ancient and Song-dynasty songs.

**1222**
- The Kamakura monk Dogen arrives in China and later takes works of Chinese art and literature back to Japan.

**1240**
- The Yonglegong (Palace of Perpetual Happiness), a Daoist temple, is built in memory of Lu Dongbin, one of the Eight Daoist Immortals, at Lu Dongbin's reputed birthplace, Yongle Town, in Yongji County, Shanxi Province.

**1244**
- Yelü Chucai, one of the best-known poets of the invading Mongol empire, dies.

**1250\*-1300\***
- The carved-lacquer technique is invented.

**1257**
- Poet and critic Yuan Haowen dies. He compiled *Zhongzhouji* (The Collection of the Central Plains), an anthology of works by 240 Jin-dynasty poets. Yuan's literary criticism and poems are considered the most important literary legacy of the Jin dynasty in northern China.

**1260\*-1263\***
- The pipe organ reaches China from the West via Central Asia.

**1264-1272**
- The Grand Capital of Dadu (present-day Beijing) is built. It is reconstructed and enlarged after 1403.

**1271**
- The Miaoyingshi (Temple of Wonderful Response), a lamasery, is erected in the Grand Capital of Dadu. It includes the White Pagoda, the most important example of Lamaist architecture of China and the earliest intact pagoda in China.

**1275**
- The Tomb of Puhading, constructed for a sixteenth-generation descendant of Mohammed, is built in Yangzhou, Jiangsu Province.
- The Xianhesi (Mosque of the White Crane) is erected in Yangzhou.

**1279-1368**
- The Mongol Yuan dynasty rules China.

**1282**
- Nationalist poet Wen Tianxiang, who was loyal to the Song dynasty and taken prisoner by the Yuan, dies.

\* DENOTES CIRCA DATE

**1297**
- The great playwright Guan Hanqing dies. With Wang Shifu, Ma Zhiyuan, and Ji Junxiang, he is considered one of the "Four Masters" of Variety Plays of the Yuan dynasty.

**1302**
- The Confucian Temple in Dadu (present-day Beijing) is built.

**1306**
- Poet Deng Mu dies. With Qiu Yuan, Dai Biaoyuan, and Zhao Mengfu, he is considered one of the "Four Masters" of Yuan-dynasty poets.

**1310**
- Gao Kegong, an influential religious painter of the Yuan dynasty, dies.

**1320**
- Artist Li Gan dies. Along with Zhao Mengfu, Ke Jiusi, and Wang Mian, he is called one of the "Four Gentlemen" painters of the Yuan dynasty.

**1320***
- Jingdezhen in Jiangxi Province is established as a major center for the production of high-quality ceramics.

**1322**
- Painter, calligrapher, and poet Zhao Mengfu dies. He is known as one of the "Four Gentlemen" painters and one of the "Four Masters" of poetry of the Yuan dynasty.

**1324**
- Shuishenmiao (Temple of the River God), an important example of Yuan religious architecture, is built in Hongdongxian, Shanxi Province.
- Musician Zhou Deqing publishes *Zhongyuan yinyun* (Musicology of the Central Plain).

**1325***
- Daoist murals are painted in the Yonglegong (Palace of Perpetual Happiness), Yongji County, Shanxi Province.

**1341-1368**
- Wu Qiuyan publishes the first scholarly work on the occult, *Learning from the Ancients*.

**1342**
- Tian Ru, a Buddhist abbot, builds the Shizilin (Garden of Lion Grove) in Suzhou, Jiangsu Province.

**1350*-1380***
*\* Denotes Circa Date*
- Shi Naian compiles *Water Margins,* one of the great novels of imperial China.

**1354**
- Artist Huang Gongwang dies. With Wang Meng, Ni Zan, and Wu Zhen, he is considered one of the "Four Masters" of Yuan-dynasty painting.

**1356**
- The Mosque of Dongsi is built in Beijing. It is renovated in 1447.

**1368-1644**
- The Ming dynasty rules China.

**1370**
- Playwright Gao Zecheng (Gao Ming) dies. He wrote *Pipaji* (The Story of the Lute, or The Lute Song), which marked the maturity of southern drama.

**1373**
- Construction of the capital city of Nanjing, including the imperial palace, is completed.

**1381-1405**
- The Xiaoling (Mausoleum of Emperor Taizu) is constructed in Nanjing.

**1392**
- A mosque is built in the Huajuexiang (Lane of Conversion and Enlightenment) in Xian, Shanxi Province.

**1400\***
- Luo Guanzhong, author of *The Romance of the Three Kingdoms,* one of the great novels of imperial China, dies.

**1407-1420**
- The Gugong (Forbidden City), the residence of Ming emperors, is built in Beijing.

**1421**
- The Three Great Halls of the Gugong are destroyed by fire. They are rebuilt in 1615.

**1424**
- The largest Ming imperial tomb, the Changling (Long Tomb) of Emperor Chengzu, is built in Beijing.

**1425**
- Prince Zhu Quan, a musician, selects zither compositions for and sponsors the publication of *Shenqi mipu* (Secret Scores of Mystery and Wonder).

**1462**
- Dai Jin dies. He and Wu Wei were important artists in the Zhi School of painting.

\* DENOES CIRCA DATE

**1473**
- The Vajrasana (Diamond Throne) Pagodas, a cluster of five pagodas, and the Da zheng-jueshi (Temple of True Awakening) are built in Beijing.

**1500\***
- The long stories *Fengshen yanyi* (The History of Granting God Titles) and *Xingshi yinyuanzhuan* (Shocking Love Legends) are written.

**1500\*-1570\***
- A literary revival is launched by the "Former Seven Youths," including Li Mengyang and He Jingming (1483–1521), and the "Four Geniuses of the Middle Wu," including Tang Yan and Zhu Yunming. These groups are challenged by the orthodox "Tang-Song School," including Gui Youguang, which is countered by the "Latter Seven Youths," including Li Panlong and Wang Shizhen.

**1509**
- Wang Xianchen, a censor at the imperial court, is dismissed from office and returns to his hometown, Suzhou, where he builds a garden that he calls the *Zhuozhengyuan* (Humble Administrator's Garden).
- Painter and calligrapher Shen Zhou dies. He and Wen Zhengming, Tang Yin, and Lan Ying are known as the "Wu School" of Ming-dynasty painters.

**1515-1527**
- The Feihongta (Pagoda of the Flying Rainbow) is built at the Guangsheng Shangshi (Upper Temple of Wide Victory) in Hongdong County, Shanxi Province.

**1519**
- Having been destroyed by fire in 1514, the Palace of Heavenly Purity and the Palace of Earthly Tranquility are rebuilt in the Forbidden City of Beijing.

**1522-1566**
- The Liuyuan (Lingering Garden) is built in Suzhou. It is later restored in the Qing dynasty.

**1526**
- Calligrapher and poet Zhu Yunming dies. Called one of the "Four Geniuses of the Middle Wu," he helped to launch a revival in poetry.

**1530**
- The Altar of the Earth, the Altar of the Sun, and the Altar of the Moon are constructed on the outskirts of Beijing. The Temple of Agriculture in the Forbidden City is rebuilt.

**1534**
- The Altar of Heaven and Earth in Beijing is turned into the Temple of Heaven, and its main hall is rebuilt and renamed the Hall of Prayer for Good Harvest.

* DENOTES CIRCA DATE

**1551**
- Calligrapher Wen Zhenming dies. He is the ancestor of several prominent Ming artists.

**1559**
- Pan Yunduan, a retired official, builds Yu Yuan, a private garden in Shanghai. Its rockery is created by Zhang Nanyang.

**1573**
- Wen Peng dies. He founded the "School of Wu," the first school of seal art.

**1582**
- Novelist Wu Chengen dies. He is the author of *The Journey to the West*, one of the great novels of imperial China.

**1583**
- Construction begins on the mausoleum of Emperor Wanli in Changping, Beijing.

**1594**
- An important contributor to the development of Kunshan tunes, or Kun melodies, the singer Liang Chenyu dies.

**1596–1617**
- The erotic *Gold Vase Plum*, one of the great novels of imperial China, is written by the pseudonymous "Scoffing Scholar of Lanling."

**1600\***
- Influenced by Western painting styles, Zeng Jing reforms traditional Chinese painting technique with his Pochenpai (School of Barbarian Officials).

**1602**
- The influential philosopher Li Zhi dies. In his *Fenshu* (Books to Be Burned) he was the first Chinese scholar to challenge traditional values, and he developed prose forms that began the transformation of conventional Chinese literature into modern writing.

**1605**
- Influential seal artist He Zheng dies.

**1610**
- Playwright Shen Jing dies. The leader of the School of Wujiang, he challenged the dramatic style of Tang Xianzu.
- Yuan Hongdao, essayist and founder of the "School of Gongan," dies.

\* DENOTES CIRCA DATE

**1616**

- Musicologist Zhu Zaiyu dies. He published *Yuelü quanshu* (The Complete Work on Temperament) and *Yayue wupu* (The Dance Scores of Palace Feast Music).

- The great Ming-dynasty playwright Tang Xianzu dies.

**1624**

- Essayist Zhong Xing dies.

**1625**

- *Da Qin Jingjiao liuxing Zhongguobei* (The Popular Chinese Melodies of Nestorianism of the Great Qin) are discovered near Xian.

- Musician Yan Cheng dies. Founder of the School of Yushan, he composed *Songxuan guanqinpu* (Scores of Pine String and Studying Zither).

**1634**

- Ji Cheng's *Yuanye* (Garden Enterprise) is published.

**1636**

- Painter and calligrapher Dong Qichang dies. He wrote the influential theoretical work *The Objective of Painting*.

**1644**

- Novelist Ling Mengchu dies.

**\* DENOTES CIRCA DATE**

Moni Hall at the Longxingshi (Temple of Prosperity), Zhengding County, Hebei Province, 1030

# OVERVIEW

**Art.** The artworks of the Tang dynasty (618–907) are romantic, optimistic, and energetic. Buddhist influences led to the development of vigorous and colorful figure painting, such as the religious works in the Mogao Caves of Dunhuang in Gansu Province. Artists also created animal, flower, and landscape paintings that derived many elements from Chinese brush calligraphy. New styles and theories of calligraphy developed, and the cutting of seals became an art. Impressive Tang-era sculpture groups and stone carvings have survived at several sites. Tang porcelain, silks, and metal arts were the most advanced in the world. By the Song dynasty (960–1125) the Buddhist influence had declined. The extraordinary Song-era Buddhist paintings and sculptures in Sichan and the Mogao Caves are more secular in appearance than earlier Buddhist works. Song landscape painting became abstract, symbolic, impressionistic, and playful, and painting styles diverged. Song porcelain was created in three colors: green, white, and black, and beautiful new embroidery techniques were invented. Under the Mongol Yuan dynasty (1279–1368) the arts flourished as many artists used painting and calligraphy as a means of escape. Multilayered painting and gold-outlining techniques were used in lacquerware. Calligraphy and seal art also flourished, and many scholarly works on painting and calligraphy were published. By the Ming dynasty (1368–1644) a distinct division had developed between the Northern and Southern Schools of artists. White and red porcelain, cloisonné, and folk-miniature sculptures were created. Textile production was significantly increased, and several production centers developed, with distinct regional styles.

**Architecture.** After the ambitious building projects of the Han dynasty (206 B.C.E. – 220 C.E.) a second tide of architectural advances occurred during the Tang era. Many great palaces, temples, pagodas, and imperial tombs were constructed in the grand capital of Chang'an and the eastern capital of Luoyang. Architectural technology developed significantly. Song structures were smaller in scale than earlier architecture but were more beautiful, more complex, and more integrated with their natural settings than previous buildings. The oldest surviving wooden pagoda dates from the Song dynasty, during which many multi-eaved pagodas were built of stone and brick. During the Yuan dynasty many religious buildings, including Lamaist temples and Islamic mosques, were constructed. Because many of these early structures were constructed with wood, they are no longer standing. The brick and stone buildings from the Ming and the Manchu or Qing (1644–1912) dynasties have fared better. During the Ming dynasty the Great Wall and the grand capital at Dadu (Beijing) were significantly reconstructed and expanded. Imperial and private gardens were built. Ming residential architecture and furniture were characterized by simplicity and grace.

**Literature.** Many great poets emerged during the Tang dynasty, including Li Bai (701–762) and Du Fu (712–770). Han Yu (768–824) and Liu Zongyuan (773–819) launched a prose movement. The *chuanqi* (marvel tales, or strange stories) of this period are considered the roots of the Chinese novel. *Ci* (lyrical poetry) reached its high point during the Song dynasty. Song poets formed different schools. Many wrote in the styles of great Tang poets. Su Shi (1037–1101) and Ouyang Xiu (1007–1072) led a neoclassical movement in Song literature. By the middle of the Song era, itinerant poets of the lower classes had become a dominant force in Chinese poetry. During the Song and Yuan dynasties vernacular novels focused on the lives of ordinary people, and classic novels depicted the upper class. Poetry of the Yuan dynasty departed from the Song tradition and became diverse in style. Two important long novels, *The Romance of the Three Kingdoms* and *Water Margins,* were written during the late Yuan and early Ming dynasties. Early Ming despotism led to the emergence of orthodox court poetry and prose in the "Style of Stage and Pavilion," which emphasized "the harmony of the writing and the way" and placed ideology over aesthetics. By the middle Ming period, relaxation of political control led some writers to launch a revival movement to liberate poetry from ideological and political control. They were opposed by the orthodox Tang-Song school, which was in turn countered by a second revival movement. The Ming dynasty was the heyday of Chinese drama, and many great novels and short stories were written as well. Folk songs attracted the attention of the literati.

**Music.** By the Tang dynasty several kinds of Chinese music had developed. In general they fell into two major categories: palace feast music and folk music. About three hundred different musical instruments and many great musicians emerged during this period. During the Song dynasty public theater developed, marking the rise of urban music. Great musicians used several forms of musical notation and published the first scholarly works on vocal theory. Musicians of the Liao (916–1115) and Jin (1115–1234) dynasties in the North added diversity to Chinese music. During the Yuan dynasty many new orchestral instruments and schools of musicians appeared. Folk songs became popular among the literati during the Ming dynasty, and important musicians, especially players of ancient stringed instruments, emerged.

**Theater Arts.** By the Tang dynasty the earliest types of the Chinese genre show—which included various kinds of vocal and instrumental music, storytelling, and skits—had established their basic forms. Dance had evolved into two types: the graceful, expressive, and relatively slow *ranwu* (soft dance) and the powerful, explosive, and rhythmically complicated *jianwu* (vigorous dance). There were also many acrobatic programs. By the Song dynasty, after many years of evolution, the *zaju* (variety play) had developed into northern and southern regional forms, which led to the cohesively plotted dramas of the Yuan era. New forms of genre shows appeared, and large dance troupes emerged. Military men—as well as actors and actresses from the new urban amusement areas called "spontaneous markets"—performed acrobatics. Recitations of *san qu*, a folk version of lyrical poetry, enjoyed popularity during the Yuan dynasty, as did a southern dramatic form that developed from traditional folk song and dance and absorbed the elements of Song music and lyrical poetry. As theatrical performances gained in popularity during the Yuan dynasty, dance and acrobatics declined. By the Ming dynasty, palace dance performances were chiefly limited to ceremonial occasions, but many folk dances and minority dances were popular and were introduced at the court. The genre show had become more diverse, but the overall quality of Ming drama was inferior to that of Yuan plays.

**International Cultural Exchange.** By the seventh century, Chinese music had absorbed elements from many regions outside its borders. The main Tang-dynasty musical instruments of *duobuyue* (multinational music) were based on instruments from Persia, India, and Egypt, while the music itself was influenced by that of India, Central Asia, Korea, and the Uighurs. Burma sent a dance troupe to perform at the Tang court, and the Chinese lion dance was performed in Southwest China, Korea, and Japan. Many Chinese acrobatic troupes traveled to Central Asia, Korea, and Japan. The shapes and motifs of Tang ceramics reveal strong foreign influences, while fragments of Tang-era white ware have been found in Japan, Korea, Indonesia, Sri Lanka, India, Pakistan, Iran, Iraq, Syria, and Egypt. During the Yuan dynasty many instruments—such as the *huobusi* (three-stringed lute) and *xinlongsheng* (pipe)—were introduced into China from Central Asia. Musical exchanges among China, Japan, Korea, India, and Thailand were frequent. Nestorian Christian hymns introduced into China by missionaries in the seventh century are the earliest instance of Sino-Western musical exchange, and they influenced Daoist music. Later, Western missionaries brought the piano, as well as the Western stave and scale, to China.

**Japan and Korea.** Except for certain periods when cultural exchange was slowed by domestic political concerns, China had been an enormous cultural influence on Japan and Korea since the Tang dynasty. In Japan the city of Nara and the temples of Horyuji, Toshodaiji, and Todaiji are not only built in the Chinese architectural style but also contain many Chinese paintings and art. Japanese monks studied in China and returned home with Chinese instruments and music. The popular Japanese "Ming and Qing Music" was derived from Chinese melodies. The Japanese monk Kibi-no-Mabi invented simplified Chinese characters for writing Japanese. The paintings of the Song-dynasty artist Fa Chang, whom the Japanese called the "Great Benefactor of Painting," were exhibited and much admired in Japan. Many Japanese books of history and poetry were written in Chinese or with Chinese style. The fame of Chinese poet Bai Juyi reached to Korea and Japan.

# TOPICS IN THE ARTS

## ARCHITECTURE

**Tang Architecture.** The architecture of the Tang dynasty (618–907) is magnificent, lofty, symmetrical, elegant, and not fragile. Architectural technology significantly developed during this era, and various materials were used—including earth, stone, brick, iron, wood, and bamboo. They were decorated with tiles, glaze, bronze, and various kinds of paint. Many Tang palaces and temples consisted of groups of buildings. Usually, two or more main buildings were constructed along an axis line with other smaller structures on either side of the line. This arrangement resulted in the formation of subordinate compounds. In front of the major building was a large central courtyard, and the entire square compound was surrounded by walls.

**Tang Capitals.** The Tang capital of Chang'an in Shanxi Province, originally constructed in 582, was one of the largest cities in the world during that era. Based on the principle of the square, the city was built on a symmetrical plan with the 108 square or rectangular blocks defined by streets and alleys running north-south and east-west, reflecting the ideal order and hierarchy to which the ruler aspired. Each block was enclosed by its own wall and had gates that were closed at nightfall. Shops were clustered in east and west markets, each occupying a single block. The palaces and the forbidden city were in the northern section of the city. The forbidden city, where the political and military offices and the imperial temples were located, was 2,820.3 meters long and 1,843.6 meters wide. It had three gates each on its north and south sides and two gates each on its east and west sides. A 220-meter path to the north linked the forbidden city to the city of palaces, which was the same length as the forbidden city and 1,492.1 meters in width. The Taijigong (Ultimate Palace), the office and residence of the emperor, was at the center of the city of palaces with other residential and official palaces on its east and west. The city palaces had five gates on its southern side, four each on its northern and western sides, and one on its eastern side. To the north of the city of palaces was the forbidden garden. The Tang had another capital at Luoyang, whose scale and layout were similar to those at Chang'an, but the plan of this eastern capital conformed more to the physical features of its location.

**Tang Palaces.** The Palace of Great Clarity was built in 634 on the plain of Dragon Head Hill in the northwest section of Chang'an, from which one could overlook the entire city. An imperial resort with residential and official structures, it was built with great attention to security. The city wall was 10.5 meters wide at the bottom. With double walls on three sides and triple gates on the northern wall, the palace complex included three great halls as well as several pavilions and small halls. North of the palace was the garden with a lake, a hill, halls, and pavilions. The Hanyuandian (Hall of Origin), the principal hall in the palace complex, was flanked by two pavilions to which it was linked by winding passageways. Designed and constructed in accordance with the natural shape of the Hill of Dragon Head, this magnificent palace represented the power of the Tang emperors, whose symbol was the dragon. Northwest of the Hall of Origin was the Lindedian (Hall of Unicorn Virtue), which was used for feasts, entertainment, Buddhist ceremonies, and meditation. It had pavilions at its back, center, and front. None of the Tang palaces have survived, and modern knowledge of them is based on archaeological discoveries.

**Tang Temples.** Most Tang-dynasty temples have also been destroyed. Only two have survived: the Nanchan (Temple of the Southern Chan), built in 782, and the Foguang Shizheng (Temple of Buddhist Light), built in 857—both located on the Wutaishan (Mountain of Five Terraces) in Shanxi Province. The Temple of Buddhist Light perfectly combines art and architecture. The roof beams and pillars of the temple were placed to create three independent arches beneath the roof, creating maximum space and a sense of symmetry. The temple looks dignified, stable, and beautiful.

**Tang Pagodas.** Among the existing Tang pagodas, the oldest and most important example is the Xuanzhangta, built in 669, the five-story tomb-pagoda of a monk named Xuanzhang. It has five stories and is known for its simplicity. The well-known Dayanta (Great Wild Goose Pagoda), built in the early eighth century at Cien Temple in Chang'an, has lost its original appearance through extensive reconstruction during the Ming dynasty. The Qianxunta (Thousand Xun Pagoda), built late in the Tang era at the Chongshenshi (Lofty and Saint Temple) of Dali in

Guanyin Hall at the Duleshi (Temple of Lonely Happiness), Jixian County, Hebei Province, 984

Yunnan Province, is an example of the multi-eaved pagoda, which typically has a high first story topped by many courses of eaves, which do not necessarily correspond with the number of stories in the pagoda. With sixteen sets of eaves the Thousand Xun Pagoda is one of the tallest surviving Tang pagodas. The Minghui dashita (Pagoda of Master Minghui), built in 877 at the Haihuiyuan (Academy of Ocean Meeting) in Pingshun County of Shanxi Province, is an exquisite one-story square stone pagoda with four layers of beautifully crafted sculptures of gods. During the second half of the seventh century, Sutra towers became a part of Buddhist architecture and were built in multistory shapes with beautiful carvings. Sutra towers were similar to pagodas, but they were used to hold sutra texts instead of for worshiping Buddha.

**Tang Gardens and Private Residences.** There are no remaining examples of Tang residential architecture. Knowledge of Tang building practices comes from paintings on the walls of the Mogao Caves of Dunhuang in Gansu Province, as well as other paintings and books of the period. A Tang house usually had a central axis with a symmetrical arrangement of rooms on each side, and they were grouped in a rect-angular compound (siheyuan). There were also simpler thatched cottages in a triangular compound (sanheyuan) enclosed by a wooden fence. Tang noble families followed the tradition of building a garden in the back of their residence or constructing a resort in a suburban area. Hills and ponds were the main features in Tang gardens, which also might have included bridges, small islands, pavilions, flowers, trees, and stones. Gardens were intended to convey "poetic feeling and pictorial ideas." For instance, at the home and garden of the well-known poet Bai Juyi (772–846) in Luoyang, housing occupied one-third of the 2.9 acres of land, with ponds on one-fifth, bamboo trees on one-ninth, and the rest given over to paths, trees, halls, platforms, and pavilions. Three small islands, each with a pavilion, were connected to each other by bridges. A path ran along the water. The focus was on bamboo trees and water. Rough and rare stones were piled up to make a hill—a feature that became a prevalent Tang garden feature.

**Song Architecture.** The architecture of the Song dynasties (960–1279) was smaller in scale but more beautiful and more splendid than that of the Tang era. By this time the use of brick for city walls, city roads, pagodas, and tombs had significantly increased. The heights of pillars and the degree of roof slope increased, while the size of the cantilever bracket supporting the roof was reduced, simplifying the architectural structure and increasing space within a house. Song architectural styles varied and included complexly designed pavilions and buildings with sophisticated decorations and paintings. Construction parts became standardized. In northern China, Liao (916–1115) architecture inherited the Tang style, while that of the Jin (1115–1234) followed the style of the Song dynasty. The use of wood imitating stone was widespread. Flat and coffered ceilings became more common, and painted decorations became more colorful.

**Song Cities.** By the Song era, commercial development had broken up the traditional block-style urban plan with concentrated and fixed marketplaces. The Song government destroyed the walls that enclosed blocks, but for its convenience still used the lanes to divide cities into administrative units. Many streets were developed along business and professional lines, and many restaurants, stores, and entertainment centers were also established. There were also many market fairs and Buddhist gardens. Kaifeng, the eastern capital of the Northern Song dynasty (960–1125), included three walled enclosures, each protected by a moat. The perimeter of the outer city was nineteen kilometers. There were three land gates and two water gates on the south border, four gates each on the north and the east borders, and five gates on the west border. At each gate a defense tower was built. The inner city—with a perimeter of nine kilometers and three gates on each of the four sides—was located in the center of the outer city. The palace city, with one gate each on four sides and a tower on each corner of its wall, was almost in the center of the inner city. Within the palace city were many halls and a large imperial garden. Pingjiang (Suzhou), a major city during the Tang and Song dynasties, had water and land transportation systems. Each residential and official building faced a street and had a river behind it.

**Song and Liao Temples.** The Shengmudian (Goddess Hall), built in 1023–1032, at the Jinci (Jin Temple) in Taiyuan, Shanxi Province, is an ancestral temple with a front hall and main hall as well as a garden. Flying beams designed in harmony with the terrain support a bridge across a square fishpond in front of the main hall and a platform within. The inside of the main hall looks spacious because extra-long beams bear the roof and the only pillars are in the corners. The external features of the hall are soft and feminine and quite different from the masculine style of Tang architecture. The Longxingshi (Temple of Prosperity) in Zhengding County, Hebei Province, is an important surviving example of Song Buddhist temples. The first rectangular courtyard has bell towers on the left and the right sides. The Hall of the Sixth Master, in its center, has been destroyed. To the north is another rectangular courtyard with the Moni Hall in the center and secondary halls on either side. The Moni Hall is built on a square base with a projecting portico on each of its four sides. It has thick

## THE GREAT WALL OF CHINA

The Great Wall of China, or the Chinese Wall, is one of the major architectural achievements of the premodern world. Around the seventh century B.C.E., the state of Chou in North China started to construct a permanent frontier-defense system, and by the third century B.C.E. various other northern kingdoms had followed suit. Although subsequent dynasties, such as the Han (206 B.C.E. –220 C.E.) and the Sui (589–618), improved various sections of wall, it was not until the Ming empire (1368–1644) that many fragments were connected into one continuous wall. The emperor Hongzhi (reigned 1487–1505) ordered most of the work on the existing Great Wall in order to repel another Mongolian invasion.

The Ming Great Wall is approximately 4,500 miles long, extending from the mountains of Korea to the Gobi Desert (the distance between Miami, Florida, and the North Pole). It follows the contours of the mountains, some of which are seven thousand feet above sea level and have ridges that climb at an angle of seventy degrees. The wall is made of beaten earth, bricks, and stones. It has thousands of towers and individual forts. During the Ming empire the fortifications were garrisoned by one million troops. At each strategic pass there is a fortified gate. The height of the wall varies from fifteen feet to thirty feet, and its width at the base measures anywhere from fifteen feet to twenty-five feet; the walkway on top of the wall is thirteen feet wide.

Sources: Jonathan Fryer, *The Great Wall of China* (London: New English Library, 1975).

William Lindesay, *The Great Wall* (Hong Kong: Odyssey, 1998).

Arthur Waldron, *The Great Wall of China: From History to Myth* (Cambridge: Cambridge University Press, 1990).

Luo Zewen and others, *The Great Wall* (New York: McGraw-Hill, 1981).

walls, and the only window is in its front door. Further north, beyond a second gate, is a grand temple complex, including towers, pavilions, and halls. This complex was constructed along a central axis extending northward, with interrelated courtyards and buildings of varying heights. The major buildings have two or three stories, illustrating the Song tendency to construct multistory structures, as well as tall buildings to accommodate large Buddhist sculptures. One example of such a building is the Guanyin Hall, built in 984 at the Duleshi (Temple of Lonely Happiness) in Jixian County, Hebei Province, when it was occupied by the Liao empire (916–1115). Combining the masculine style of the Tang and the feminine style of the Song, the hall seems from the outside to be a two-story building, but it has a "secret" story inside and an open center to accommodate its tall statue of the Buddha. The base of the build-

Pagoda of Sakyamuni at the Fogongshi (Temple of the Buddhist Palace), Ying County, Shanxi Province, 1056

ing is low, and its pillars lean inward. An external balcony circles the building under the upper eaves. Also dating from the Liao period, the Huayanshi (Grand Hall of the Temple of Chinese Rigorousness)—built about 1140 in Datong, Shanxi Province—is the largest surviving early single-eave wooden building. The two-story Hall of Sakya Sutra at the Huayanshi is also an important Liao building. The two sets of cabinets for sutra manuscripts in this library building are connected by a bridge on which a five-room pavilion is built.

**Song and Liao Pagodas.** The Pagoda of Sakyamuni, built in 1056 at the Fogongshi (Temple of the Buddhist Palace) in Ying County, Shanxi Province, is the oldest extant wooden pagoda in China and one of the tallest wooden buildings in the world. Octagonal in shape, it is 30.27 meters wide at its base and is 67.3 meters tall. It has only five stories but has six levels of eaves because the first floor has two sets of eaves. Inside, each of the four upper stories has a mezzanine level; thus, it may be said to have four "secret" stories for a total of nine. Although it is huge, this building does not have a heavy appearance because its sets of eaves form an elegant shape and give the observer a sense of upward motion. Among all Song sutra towers, the one in the Zhao County of Hebei Province is the most representative and the largest. Entirely made of stone and more than 15 meters tall, it has a beautiful shape and features vivid carvings of gods, noblewomen, and dancing girls. The stone pagoda reached the peak of its development during the Song dynasty.

**Song Houses and Gardens.** A rural house during the Song dynasty was typically a simple, one-story dwelling with either a thatched roof or a half-thatched, half-tiled roof. Several houses were usually grouped together. Under the eaves and near the ceiling were windows covered by bamboo material. There were also windows near the roof peak at the gable ends for cross ventilation. Urban mansions were usually constructed as compounds with tile roofs. The entry room was often built to allow a horse and wagon to be driven into the central courtyard. Galleries or halls began to connect the various buildings in a compound. Song private gardens developed differently in various regions. The gardens in Luoyang usually tended to be natural and were built on a large scale with only a few halls and pavilions. "Borrowing scenes," purposely constructing a high point or window from which to view a neighbor's scenery, was a significant characteristic of many Song gardens. The gardens of the South were subtle and complicated. Symmetry was emphasized, and gardens were organized into different "rooms" separated by gargles stones (or, gargled lake stones, which were of various shapes and could be found only in certain lakes; such as Panyang Lake in South China) paths, walls, and flower beds. Poetry, painting, calligraphy, and carving became integral parts of the garden. Appreciation of lake stones was widespread, and a water feature was always included. Flowers were arranged in patterns but not according to strict conformity. Several flowers had their symbolic implications. Chrysanthemums represented culture; water lilies stood for purity and peace; and the bamboo tree was a token of lasting friendship, loyalty, and flexibility. The salt merchants of Yangzhou built many gardens. Suzhou, home to many nobles and landlord families, is also renowned for its gardens, including the Canglangting (Garden of the Blue-Waves Pavilion), which was built during the Song dynasty, and the Shizilin (Garden of the Stone Forest), dating to the Yuan dynasty. The Xiyuan (Western Garden) in Beijing was initially built during the Liao dynasty and was later enlarged by the Jin and Yuan dynasties. Combining features of the natural landscape with manmade components, this garden has water as its main feature. At its center is the White Tower on Jade Island in a naturally existing lake. The long lakeshore is dotted by several exquisite pavilions.

**The Yuan Capital at Beijing.** In 1264 the Yuan dynasty (1279–1368) began to construct Dadu (Grand Capital) on the site of present-day Beijing. Completed eight years later, the Yuan capital is a well-designed, large-scale city (7,400 meters by 6,650 meters) with many grand palaces. The wall had two gates on the north side and three gates on each of the other three sides. The city was divided into sixty administrative sections, which were not walled. The city drainage system was well planned and built of brick. The grand canal was used as the water supply and for transportation. Yuan palaces were located in the Imperial City and the Palace City. The Imperial City had a pond, garden, and three groups of palaces. The Palace City wall had four gates in the front and back and a tower on each corner. The palaces were symmetrically arranged on each side of a central axis line. Yuan palaces were extravagant and built with many precious materials.

**Yuan Religious Architecture.** The Deningdian (Hall of Virtue and Peace) at the Beiyuemiao (Temple of North Mountain) in Quyang County, Hebei Province; the Yonglegong (Palace of Perpetual Happiness) in Yongji County, Shanxi Province; and the Shuishenmiao (Temple of the River God), built in 1324 near the future site of the Ming-era Guangshengshi (Temple of Wide Victory, built in 1515–1527) in Hongdong, Shanxi Province, are representatives of Yuan religious architecture. They are built in the styles of Song temples or those of the Jin empire in northern China but on a larger scale. During the Yuan dynasty the spread of Lamaism resulted in the construction of several Lamaist buildings, of which the pagoda of the Miaoyingshi (Temple of Wonderful Response), built in 1271 in the Grand Capital, is the most notable. This brick pagoda was 50.86 meters tall and painted with white lime. Although it is uncarved and quite plain, it looks magnificent and powerful. The guojieta (street pagoda) was a common form of Lamaist architecture, but no complete street pagoda has survived. The Temple of Shajia (mid thirteenth century) and the Temple of Xialu (mid fourteenth century) are typical Lamaist temples. Mosques built during the Yuan dynasty sometimes adopted Central Asian models, while others were based on traditional Chinese models.

Aerial view of the Tiantan or Temple of Heaven, Beijing, 1534

The Huajuexiang mosque in the Lane of Conversion and Enlightenment of Xian, Shanxi Province, was established in 1392.

**Ming Architecture.** By the Ming dynasty (1368–1644) many roof shapes had developed, and the use of brick had become common. The framework for the city gate became a brick arch instead of wood pillars and a cross beam. The production of glazed tiles to cover walls reached its height in terms of both quality and quantity. Ming official architecture, interior design, and construction practices became much standardized, which to a certain extent stifled creativity. In his *Book of Wood* carpenter Yu Hao recorded the accumulated knowledge of Chinese architects.

**Ming Beijing.** After the Ming dynasty decided to move its capital from Nanking to Beijing in 1403, Beijing was significantly reconstructed and enlarged according to the feudal hierarchical concept for convenience of political control. All the important buildings were built along a 7.5-kilometer axis with a central path running north from the Yongdingmen (Gate of Lasting Peace) at the south wall of the outer city through the Zhengyangmen (Meridian Gate) of the Gugong (Forbidden City) to the palace complex.

Ming imperial architecture followed exactly the feudal rules of "three halls" in the front for court gatherings, "three palaces" in the back for imperial residences, and "five gates." They also followed the ritual requirement that the temple for ancestor worship should be on the left (east) and the ceremonial altar for community ceremonies on the right (west). On either side of the central axis, near the Gate of Lasting Peace, were two large architectural complexes, the Tiantan (Temple of Heaven) and the Xiannongtai (Temple of Agriculture).

**The Temple of Heaven.** The Temple of Heaven is considered the best example of Ming ceremonial architecture. Built in 1534 on the site of the Altar of Heaven and Earth, it occupies 280 acres of land planted with many cypress trees and is surrounded by walls. The enclosed area is nearly square. The north corners of the wall are rounded, however, to symbolize the ancient belief in "round heaven and square earth." On the southern end of a 360-meter axis (representing the days in a Chinese year) is a large circular white-stone altar from which the emperor prayed to heaven. It has three levels and looks massive and solemn. At the north end of the axis is the Qiniandian (Hall of

Feihongta (Pagoda of the Flying Rainbow) in Hongdong County, Shanxi Province, 1515–1527

Prayer for Good Harvest). Built on a high base of white stone, it is a huge, round, wooden building with three tiers of eaves. The roof is covered with blue tiles representing heaven and curves gracefully upward to a golden point.

**The Forbidden City.** From 1407 to 1420 the Ming court employed 20,000–30,000 laborers to build the Forbidden City, which was divided into outer and inner courts. The outer court was used mainly for administrative and ceremonial activities. The inner court, with an imperial garden, was designed as living space for the emperor, his wives, and their servants and eunuchs. To avoid creating hiding places for assassins, no trees were planted in the outer court, and the ground was covered with fifteen large rock slabs to prevent enemies of the emperor from tunneling into the Forbidden City. The front gate—the Noon

Gate—was not only a gate but also a palace hall for announcing government proclamations and emperors' edicts. Within the Forbidden City the path continued northward from the Noon Gate to the Damingmen (Gate of Great Clarity), which opened onto a vast, paved courtyard bordered on the north by five stone bridges crossing the Inner Golden River to the stone lions and ornamental columns on the Tiananmen (Gate of Heavenly Peace). Inside this gate the Ming emperors built three halls for the administration of their imperial government: the Taihedian (Hall of Ultimate Peace), the Zhonghedian (Hall of Central Peace), and the Baohedian (Hall of Lasting Peace), as well as smaller government buildings in the same style. The similarity between the major and minor buildings reinforced the relationship among the buildings. The Hall of

Vajrasana or Diamond Throne Pagodas, Beijing, 1473

Ultimate Peace, which was the site of the most important ceremonies, was taller and more elaborate than the other buildings, with two sets of eaves supported by a large number of cantilevered brackets, and three tiers of white-stone steps.

**The Inner Court.** From the three halls the path then continues north to the Duanmen (Gate of Origin), which leads to the complex of royal palaces. The emperor's palace, the Qianqinggong (Palace of Heavenly Purity), has been destroyed by fire several times, and the present palace was rebuilt according to the original plans after a major fire in 1797. To the north of this palace is a square pavilion, which was used as the empress's throne room, and her palace, the Kunninggong (Palace of Earthly Tranquillity), with the Imperial Garden on its north. The inner court also includes smaller residences. Toward the northern end of the axis, in the Forbidden City, is the Jingshan (Prosperity Hill), which at fifty meters tall is the highest point of the city. The imperial path then continues north through the Dianmen (Gate of Earthly Peace) and ends at the Bell Tower and the Drum Tower.

**The Center of Government.** This plan met the needs of the ruling class by putting the government at the center of

the city, but it severely impeded city transportation. Throughout the Forbidden City the imperial colors, gold and red, were liberally employed, as were images of the dragon and the phoenix, symbols of the emperor and empress.

**Ming Temples.** The magnificent Tiantan (Temple of Heaven) in Beijing, constructed in 1534, is the best example of a Ming imperial ceremonial temple, demonstrating the ability of its architect to organize space. It consists of two groups of buildings connected by a broad path that is 360 meters long, representing the number of days in the Chinese year. In addition to the two main buildings, there are others for preparing sacrifices, ceremonial dancing, and fasting.

**Ming Pagodas.** The Feihongta (Pagoda of the Flying Rainbow)—built in 1515–1527 at the Guangsheng Shangshi (Upper Temple of Wide Victory) in Hongdong County, Shanxi Province—is a typical Ming pagoda. This octagonal, thirteen-story structure is 47.63 meters high. Its surface is decorated with terra-cotta gods and animal figures glazed in various colors. The diamond-shaped pagodas originated in India. They appeared in Tang-era paintings on the walls of the Mogao Caves of Dunhuang in Gansu

Province, but the earliest surviving example in China is the Vajrasana (Diamond Throne Pagodas), built in 1473 at the Da zhengjueshi (Temple of True Awakening) in Beijing. This five-pagoda cluster sits on a single, tall, diamond-shaped base on which gods, lions, peacocks, and the "eight treasures" of Lamaist Buddhism are carved. The five multi-eaved pagodas and the small hall that is also on the base have similar carvings. The Tai minority community built a distinctive style of pagoda complex during the Ming dynasty. Typically, a tall slim pagoda was surrounded by smaller pagodas and strange animal figures. The various shapes and elaborate carvings of these pagodas made them especially attractive.

**Uighur Mosques.** In the fifteenth century the Uighur people of Mongolia and eastern Turkestan converted to Islam, and the Uighur architectural style has influenced the construction of Chinese mosques ever since. Uighur Muslim structures—including mosques, religious schools, and tombs—are decorated with colorful tiles, carved plaster, paintings, and elaborate window lattices.

**Ming Houses and Gardens.** The Ming dynasty began many grand imperial gardens—such as the Yuanmingyuan (Garden of Perfect Clarity), the Yiheyuan (Summer Palace), and the Bishu shanzhuang (Summer Imperial Village), all in Beijing—that were not completed until the Qing dynasty. During the same period more much-admired gardens were built in the town of Suzhou: the Zhuozhengyuan (Humble Administrator's Garden), the Liuyuan (Lingering Garden), and the Wufengyuan (Garden of Five Mountains). Together with earlier Suzhou gardens, they formed a vast garden of forest and mountain. Ming gardening became a science with the publication in 1634 of Ji Cheng's *Yuanye* (Garden Enterprise). By the Ming period various styles of residential architecture had developed. In Beijing and elsewhere in the north, quadrangular compounds of buildings with thick roofs and walls became standard. Walled courtyards with thin roofs and walls prevailed in the South. Hakka people, northern Chinese people who migrated to Southern China during the last years of the Song dynasty, lived together as clans in large group residences. In western China, cave rooms were built on the sides of mountains, while in rainy tropical areas houses were raised to prevent water damage. Tibetan houses were made of stone, while Uighur people lived in beaten-earth houses with openings in the ceiling to release heat. The nomadic Mongolians lived in yurts, collapsible circular domed tents.

Sources:

Andrew Boyd, *Chinese Architecture and Town Planning, 1500 B.C.–A.D. 1911* (Chicago: University of Chicago Press, 1962).

Liang Ssu-ch'eng, *A Pictorial History of Chinese Architecture: A Study of the Development of Its Structural System and the Evolution of Its Types*, edited by Wilma Fairbank (Cambridge, Mass. & London: MIT Press, 1984).

Liu Dunzhen, *Zhongguo gudai jianzhushi* (Taipei, Taiwan: Enlightening Literature Press, 1994).

Liu and Liu Xujie, *Liu Dunzhen jianzhushi lunwen xuanji* (Beijing: Chinese Architectural Industry Press, 1997).

Michèle Pirazzoli-T'Serstevens, *Living Architecture: Chinese,* translated by Robert Allen (London: Macdonald, 1972).

Ru Jinghua and Peng Hualiang, *Palace Architecture: Ancient Chinese Architecture,* translated by Zang Erzhong and others (Vienna & New York: Springer, 1998).

Laurence Sickman and Alexander Soper, *The Art and Architecture of China* (New York: Penguin, 1984).

Michael Sullivan, *The Arts of China,* fourth edition, expanded and revised (Berkeley: University of California Press, 1999).

Wang Tianxing and Liang Faming, *Tiantan* (Beijing, China: China Esperanto Press, 1993).

Xiao Mo, *Zhongguo Jianzhu* (Beijing: Culture and Arts Press, 1999).

## CALLIGRAPHY AND SEAL MAKING

**Masters of Calligraphy.** The Tang dynasty (618–907) required that its officials practice the art of calligraphy, and the study of calligraphy was one of the six disciplines in higher education. Ever since that time calligraphy has been considered a cultural symbol of China and a sign of an individual's character and personality. Because Tang emperor Taizong (ruled 626–649) loved his adviser Wang Xizhi, the four best-known early Tang calligraphers—Yu Shinan (558–638), Ouyang Xun (557–641), Zhu Suiliang (596–659), and Xue Ji (649–713)—all followed Wang's style. Ouyang Xun and two other calligraphers who learned from Wang Xizhi—Yan Zhenqing (709–785) and Liu Gongquan (778–865)—established the three schools of Tang calligraphy. They developed the new style of *kaishu* (normal script). Ouyang's writing is stiff and vigorous, with open structure and strong strokes, showing the influence of the *lishu* (clerical script) style. Yan's calligraphy is dignified and full, with thin, straight, and firm horizontal strokes and curving, thick vertical and diagonal strokes. His writing, which was called "The Second Calligraphy of the World," is natural and unrestrained, with tight and majestic structure. In contrast, Liu absorbed the power of Yan's calligraphy but invented a writing style that is lean, stiff, and stern. Zhang Xu (who flourished in the seventh and eighth centuries) and Huai Su (725–785) earned the nicknames "Lunatic Zhang" and "Crazy Su" because their *caoshu* (cursive script, grass writing, or rough writing) has been compared to scudding clouds, running water, violent thunderstorms, or lively music and dancing. During the Song dynasty (960–1279) Emperor Taizong (ruled 976–997) purchased the best-known calligraphy of past dynasties and had it printed in ten volumes. Most of this calligraphy was written by the "Two Wangs"—Wang Xizhi (321–379) and his son Wang Xianzhi (344–386). They dominated calligraphy during the Song period, except for the "Four Master Calligraphers of the Song Dynasty": Cai Xiang (1012–1067), Su Shi (1037–1101), Huang Tingjian (1045–1105), and Mi Fei (1057–1107)–all of whom were unconventional. Cai's writing is natural, steady and smooth, round and vigorous, harmonious and balanced. Su was a great author and painter, and his writing is artistic and flowing. He could write in several styles. His "grass writing" is characterized by its changing strokes: long and thin or short and thick. Huang's calligraphy has been likened to the movement of an oar through waves: tight in the

Song seal (left) with its imprint, 1055 (Field Museum of Natural History, Chicago)

middle and radiating outward at the ends of strokes. Mi was excellent at using a brush, and his writing has been described as running like a horse, fast and calm, shifting and powerful, with strong rhythms and clear structural features. The calligraphers of the Yuan dynasty (1279–1368), including the great master Zhao Mengfu (1254–1322), all lacked creativity, trying to follow the style of Tang or Jin calligraphers rather than create new styles. Though he lacked originality, Zhao's calligraphic skill was renowned. He could write in any style and with amazing speed. His writing is adept, smooth, graceful, and powerful, with a harmonious and natural structure. The only creative Yuan-era calligrapher may have been Yang Weizhen (1296–1370), who was also a writer and known as the "Literary Ghost" for his fantastic fairy tales and stories of historical events. He was aloof from politics and material pursuits and loved nature. His writing is alternately tight and open, with varying thin and thick strokes, a modulating rhythm, and a surprising pattern. The calligraphy of the Ming dynasty (1368–1644) is also conservative, an attempt to copy the calligraphy of past dynasties. The only truly creative Ming calligraphers were Song Ke (1327–1387), Zhu Yunming (1460–1526), Wen Zhenming (1470–1539), Xu Wei (1521–1593), and Dong Qichang (1555–1636), with their cursive script, which became more popular than *zhuanshu* (seal script) and *lishu* (official script).

**Theories of Calligraphy.** The study of calligraphy during the Tang dynasty was widespread. Of the many calligraphy books published during the era, the best are *Shupu* (Guide to Calligraphy) by Sun Guoting (648–703) and *Shuduan* (Analysis of Calligraphy) by Zhang Haiquan (seventh and eighth centuries). Zhang's work introduced and analyzed the artistic features and historical evolution of ten calligraphic styles. Sun fully and profoundly expounded on the rules of calligraphy. During the Song dynasty Mi Fei,

Su Shi, and Huang Tingjian all wrote influential books on calligraphic theory. Mi's work was the most influential. For instance, he characterized the calligraphic styles of the "Four Masters" with four characters: *le, miao, hua, shua.* When they were writing, he believed, Cai was "carving"; Huang was "tracing"; Su was "painting"; and he was "brushing." The theory of Zhao Mengfu in the Yuan era was as influential and conservative as his calligraphy.

**Seal Cutting.** Seal cutting before the Tang era was more practical than artistic. Seal art was initiated by Emperor Taizong, who loved painting and calligraphy and ordered a craftsman to cut the characters *Zhenguan* (Emperor's View) into a seal that was to be stamped on the paintings and calligraphic works he owned and appreciated. Moreover, Prime Minister Li Mi engraved the name of his study room onto a seal, with thick and round lines appearing steady, ancient, and simple. As a result, the seal as a means of personal and official identification evolved into an artistic medium, as artists cut words into seals that had no practical use. Folk seal art developed in a natural and simple style characterized by "normal script" or "clerk script" characters, but the nine-line *jiudiezhuan* (multiple-line seal) of the upper classes revealed the negative impact of the disintegrating social and political system on art. The official seals of the Song dynasty still followed the multiple-line pattern, but the lines became thinner, softer, more numerous, and more complex. Meanwhile, the artistic development of the *xianzhang* (idle seal), which used the titles of studies, halls, buildings, or years, surpassed that of the official seal. The popularity of the idle seal has been partially attributed to the use of red seal ink. A red seal applied to a painting or calligraphic work enhanced its artistic effectiveness. The adaptation of tablet inscriptions (scripts carved into stone tablets) to seals challenged the style of the official nine-line seal. There also emerged a new seal called *huayayin* (sophisticated security seal), which turned a personal name into a mysterious symbol, or cipher, that was hard for others to recognize. The first systematic record of the seal in Chinese history, *Xuanhe yinpu* (Xuanhe Guide to the Seal), was published in 1119–1125 and greatly promoted the development of seal art. In 1341–1368 Wu Qiuyan published the first scholarly work on sigillography, *Learning from the Ancients,* which describes the evolution of calligraphic and seal arts and techniques and denounces the nine-line seal style. Meanwhile, instead of cutting seals into metal or ivory, cutters began engraving seals into softer and more colorful stones, ending the long-lasting division of labor between seal designer and seal cutter. Now an artist could design and cut a seal by himself. As a result, many literati were attracted to seal art, and seal cutting went from a craftsman's job to an artist's work. This change led to the further development of seal art. The *yuanzhuwen* (round and red seal script) invented by Zhao Mengfu during the Yuan dynasty was the first step in bringing calligraphic art to seal art. His *yuanzhuwen* had thin, vigorous, graceful, and flowing lines and varying compositions. By the Ming dynasty the rising "Seals of Flowering Schools" stood in sharp contrast to the "Ancient Seals" from before the Tang era. Wen Peng (1498–1573) created the School of Wu, the first school in seal art. His seal cutting shows the influence of an ancient style. It is steady, balanced, classic, and graceful. He Zheng (?–1605) absorbed various styles of ancient seal arts and tablet inscriptions and established the School of Wan (Anhui Province). He used several cutting methods to create seals that appear ancient, simple, and vigorous, with thick, heavy, and powerful lines, stiff turnings of characters, and a variety of structures. Wen and He were followed by a group of seal artists, including Su Xuan (1553– ?), Wang Guan (flourished 1600–1631), and Zhu Jian (circa 1570– ?). Zhu was not only a great seal artist but also an influential seal theorist. He spent fourteen years writing *Yinpin* (Seal Articles) and many other books on the subject.

**Sources:**

Craig Clunas, *Art in China* (Oxford & New York: Oxford University Press, 1997).

Laurence Sickman and Alexander Soper, *The Art and Architecture of China* (New York: Penguin, 1984).

Michael Sullivan, *The Arts of China,* fourth edition, expanded and revised (Berkeley: University of California Press, 1999).

Wang Qisen, *Zhongguo yishu tongshi* (Jiangsu, China: Jiangsu Arts Press, 1999).

## CRAFT WORK

**Metal Arts.** By the Tang dynasty (618–907), Chinese metal art—especially engraved gold or silver objects—had become elaborate and exquisite. Metal ornaments and utensils with elegant and colorful decoration were produced. Bronze mirrors became smooth and shiny, and their backs were decorated with gold and silver relief or inlay. Designs for these mirrors included clouds and dragons, flying horses, grapevines, hunting scenes, flowers, and polo players. The technology for making metal sculpture devel-

Covered jar decorated with parrots amid peonies, mid eighth century (from Michael Sullivan, *The Arts of China,* 1973)

oped during the Song dynasty (960–1279). The twenty-four-meter-tall Buddha in Guanyin Hall at the Duleshi (Temple of Lonely Happiness) in Jixian County, Hebei Province, is the largest bronze figure made in imperial China. Its body proportions are balanced, and the lines of its drapery are smooth. Cloisonné enamel was the greatest product of the Ming period (1368–1644). Thin brass wires were welded to bronze to form various designs, and the spaces were filled with colorful enamels and gilded with silver or gold. Cloisonné became prevalent during the reign of Ming emperor Jingtai (ruled 1449–1457), so it was called "Jingtailan" in Chinese. Jingtailan is sumptuous and beautiful and was admired by the court and the nobles. As a result, there emerged a series of Jingtailan products and designs, which the court and noble families collected. During the reign of Ming emperor Xuande (1425–1435), craftsmen made gracefully shaped and richly decorated bronze stoves, which became popular and were called Xuande stoves.

**Silk.** During the Tang dynasty the craftsmanship of silk textile workers developed rapidly all over China. Various regional silk products flourished, including *liangkeling* (double-nest silk) and *dukeling* (single-nest silk) in Dingzhou, *fanyangling* (fanyang silk) in Youzhou, *kepaojin*

Earthenware figure of a tomb guardian trampling a demon, Tang dynasty, 618–907 (Asian Art Museum, San Francisco)

names such as "Green Plants and Cloud Goose," "Green Grass and Cloud Crane," "Green Lion," and "True Red Blanket Path and Snow Flowers." *Ke si*, a form of tapestry woven from fine silks and gold thread, required excellent craftsmanship. *Ke si* designs could be woven in different colors and shading to copy paintings and calligraphic works, and thus design styles changed along with those of contemporary painting and calligraphy. The Mongolian rulers of the Yuan dynasty loved silk and promoted its production. The term *duan* (satin) was coined during this time. The scale of silk production was significantly enlarged during the Ming dynasty. Several new regional production centers were founded, including Jiaxing and Songjiang. All the various silk regions developed their own artistic styles. For instance, the high-quality "Song Brocade" of Suzhou imitated designs of the Song dynasty, and the sturdy "Cloud Brocade" of Nanjing was produced in strong colors. The new technique of embroidering the edges of silk pictures with gold thread was striking. The Ming technique of weaving *Ke si* could produce large silk pictures that observers mistook for paintings or calligraphy. The embroidery techniques of the Ming varied according to region. The Gu embroidery of Shanghai, Xiang embroidery of Hunan, Yue embroidery of Guangdong, Lu embroidery of Shandong, and Su embroidery of Suzhou each had its distinctive artistic features. Gu embroidery was especially popular and well known for its strict and balanced stitching, artistic designs, vivid colors, and refined workmanship.

**Lacquerware and Carving.** During the Tang dynasty craftsmen began to inlay gold or silver into lacquerware. By the Song and the Yuan dynasties lacquer craftsmanship had considerably advanced. Usually, ten layers of lacquer were painted on wood, and then the object was engraved with various pictures and designs—such as landscapes, flowers, plants, birds, animals, stones, and human figures—producing an object that looked three-dimensional. Sometimes, different colors were applied after the lacquerware was engraved, and gold outlining was introduced. During the Ming dynasty, lacquerware became still more advanced. Ming carved lacquerware (*tihong*) was made in graceful shapes with smooth carving and rich designs. Red lacquerware was made on gold, silver, or wood bases, often with a hundred layers of red lacquer, and it was then carved into various designs. If yellow lacquer was used, it was called *tihuang*. Black lacquerware was called *tihei*. Craftsmen also began to inlay lacquerware with mother-of-pearl. Jiaxing in Zhejiang Province and Yangzhou in Jiangsu Province were important centers for lacquerware production. The technique of carving jade, ivory, and bamboo reached a high level of sophistication during the Ming era. A Ming craftsman could carve a piece of bamboo into an imitation of an ancient bronze vessel. Zhu Min of Jiading in Jiangsu Province was famous for his bamboo carving. Carved jade, because of its precious raw material, was confined to the nobility. Ivory carvings were produced in many complex designs.

(guest-robe brocade) and *beijin* (quilted brocade) in Yangzhou, and *jiaoling* (mixed silk) and *shiyang hualing* (ten-flower silk) in Yuezhou. These bright, high-quality textiles were named after features of their colors, designs, or weaving techniques. Tang embroidery was greatly enhanced by the development of new techniques such as *wangxiu* (nest embroidery), *mandixiu* (all-over embroidery), *suosi* (blocked silk), *nasi* (sewed silk), *lusha* (united sand), and *panjin* (plate gold). Tang brocade was especially elegant because the jacquard-weaving technique used by its weavers could produce a variety of designs. New techniques of dyeing, printing, or color drawing on silk were introduced. Most Tang silk designs were made with line drawings in such designs as Buddhist images, flying horses, double phoenixes, peacocks, dragons, unicorns, flowers, grass, leaves, and stems. They are imaginative, harmonious, and colorful. During the Song and Yuan dynasties, silk production and markets increased, as did the quality of materials and designs. There emerged several production centers: Kaifeng, Luoyang, and Huzhou of the empire of the Northern Song, as well as Hangzhou, Suzhou, and Chengdu in that of the Southern Song. Song brocade is known for its riotous profusion of colors, and its jacquard weaving is well-done. Its many designs have imaginative

Sources:

Craig Clunas, *Art in China* (Oxford & New York: Oxford University Press, 1997).

Laurence Sickman and Alexander Soper, *The Art and Architecture of China* (New York: Penguin, 1984).

Michael Sullivan, *The Arts of China,* fourth edition, expanded and revised (Berkeley: University of California Press, 1999).

Wang Qisen, *Zhongguo yishu tongshi* (Jiangsu, China: Jiangsu Arts Press, 1999).

## LITERATURE

**Palace Literati and the Regulated Poem.** Tang emperor Taizong (ruled 626–649) had an excellent understanding of literature and was tolerant and supportive of the literati. Therefore, several groups of palace literati emerged, competing with each other to extol the great successes of the Tang dynasty (618–907). The result was the so-called palace style, which emphasized antithesis and rhetoric. Palace literati wrote in an ornate style and contributed a great deal to the poetic form known as *lüshi,* a "regulated," eight-line poem written in couplets. Each of its eight lines has five or seven characters. In a couplet each character in the odd-numbered line should be antithetical to the character in the same position in the even-numbered line, both in tone and meaning. The last characters in each couplet should rhyme in a soft tone, and there are also rules governing the rhyming of the other characters. Du Shenyan (circa 645 – 708), Song Zhiwen (circa 656 – circa 713), and Shen Quanqi (circa 656 – 673) are representative of the palace literati. Du's poems are well knit and vigorous. One of his regulated poems, "He jinling lucheng zaochun wangyou" (Sightseeing in Early Spring: Echoing Official Lu of Jinling), has been called the best regulated five-character poem of the time. Song Zhiwen and Shen Quanqi expressed their true feelings in their poetry, avoided the awkward expression of the regulated five-character poem, and perfected the regulated seven-character poem. Before Song and Shen, regulated poems were not accepted by the public.

**The "Four Talents" of the Early Tang.** Four young and handsome geniuses of the early Tang era became known as the "Four Talents": Lu Zhaolin (630–680), author of *Youyou ziji* (The Collection of Deep Sorrow); Luo Binwang (circa 640 – circa 684), author of *Luo Binwang wenji* (The Collection of Luo Binwang); Wang Bo (650–676), author of *Wang Zian wenji* (The Collection of Wang Zian); and Yang Jiong (650–693), author of *Yingchuanji* (The Collection of the Full River). Luo began writing poems at the age of seven. When he was only ten Yang passed the civil examination for teenagers, and the following year he entered the Hongwenguan (Grand Literary Academy). The "Four Talents" were confident, ambitious, and unrestrained by convention, but none was able to secure a high position in the government. These career failures affected their writing. They expressed the feelings of lower-class people who have been suppressed and anticipate changes. They explored broad social themes and wrote about their goals of contributing to society. They attacked court litera-

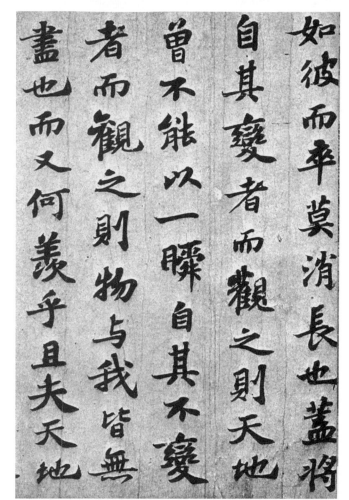

Section of the first Red Cliff Ode, copied by Su Shih, early twelfth century (National Palace Museum, Taipei, Taiwan)

ture for its devotion to rhetoric and decorative perfection, calling it lifeless, without passion and vitality. Two long poems, Lu's *Chang'an guyi* (The Ancient Implication of Chang'an) and Luo's *Jingdipian* (The Imperial Capital), deny the values of noble society. Luo and Yang, both of whom served in the army, wrote many poems depicting the western frontier and wilderness. They were the pioneers of Tang frontier poetry. Luo and Wang wrote many regulated five-character poems, fully demonstrating their individualism in works such as "Zaiyu yongchan" (On the Cicada: In Prison) by Luo and "Song Dushaofu zhiren Shuzhou" (See Junior Du to the Appointment at Shuzhou) by Wang. The "Four Talents" also absorbed the elements of ancient verse (*fu*) mixed with rhythmical prose (*pian*) to create a new form that allowed them to express their emotions and that was embraced by the later poets. They thus initiated poetic reform though they did not make any theoretical contribution to the movement.

**Chen Ziang.** Chen Ziang (659–700) truly initiated a new tide in Chinese literature. He criticized flowery poetic style and correctly pointed out that the problem of the current style resulted from its overemphasis on form. His rem-

## FIVE-CHARACTER QUATRAINS

The five-character quatrain has been popular since the early years of the Tang dynasty (618–907), and many well-known poems in this form have been memorized by generation after generation of Chinese people. Children are able to recite many ancient five-character quatrains, often without understanding them. The following poems are among the most popular:

**Wang Zhihuan (688–742), "Climbing the Stork Pavilion"**
The white sun leaning on the mountain disappears,
The Yellow River flows on into the sea;
To stretch your gaze a thousand leagues,
Climb up still another story.

**Meng Haoran (689–740), "Spring Dawn"**
Asleep in spring unaware of dawn,
And everywhere hear the birds in song.
At night the sound of wind and rain,
You'll know how much from the flowers gone.

**Li Bai (701–762), "Quiet Night Thought"**
Before my bed the moonlight glitters
Like frost upon the ground.
I look up to the mountain moon,
Look down and think of home.

**Li Shen (772–846), "Sympathy for the Peasants"**
When crops are worked at noon,
It is sweat that moistens the soil.
Who stops to think, before a bowl of food,
That every grain comes only through long toil?

Sources: Victor H. Mair, ed., *The Columbia Anthology of Traditional Chinese Literature* (New York: Columbia University Press, 1994).

Zhang Tingchen and Wei Bosi, trans., *100 Tang Poems* (Beijing: Chinese Translation Company / Hong Kong: Business Press, 1994).

---

edy was to revive the vigorous and heroic literary style of the Han (206 B.C.E.–220 C.E.) and Wei (386–535) dynasties. Chen's poems are notable for his pursuit of integrity and the romantic dream. The thirty-eight poems titled *Ganyu* (Empathetic Experiences) are his most widely acclaimed work. His "Deng Youzhoutai ge" (Upon the Yuzhou Terrace) is known by nearly all educated Chinese.

**Great Tang Poets.** The Tang era is known as the golden age of Chinese classical poetry. *The Complete Tang Poetry* in its present version includes almost fifty thousand poems written by more than 2,200 poets. In addition to the famous poets Li Bai (701–762) and Du Fu (712–770), the Tang period produced many other great poets, including Zhang Shui (667–731), Zhang Jiuling (678–740), Wang Zhihuan (688–742), Meng Haoran (689–740), Wang Changling (690?–756?), Li Jin (690–753?), Cui Hao (?–

754), Wang Wei (700?–761), Gao Shi (704–765), Cen Can (715–769), Yuan Jie (719–772), Liu Changqing (? – circa 790), Wei Yingwu (circa 737 – circa 791), Gu Kuang (?–806), Meng Jiao (751–814), Zhang Ji (circa 766 – circa 830), Han Yu (768–824), Wang Jian (768–833), Bai Juyi (772–846), Liu Yuxi (772–842), Liu Zhongyuan (773–819), Yao He (circa 775 – circa 846), Yuan Zhen (779–831), Jia Dao (779–843), Li He (790–816), Du Mu (803–853), Li Shangyin (813–858), Wei Zhuang (836–910), and Wen Tingyun (circa 813 – 870). They produced many poems that enjoyed great popularity and are still recited. Zhang Jiuling was a great prime minister during the early Tang era, as well as an important poet. He also patronized several great poets, including Wang Wei, Meng Haoran, and Du Fu. Zhang's poems, which express his feelings metaphorically by transplanting his emotions to objects and natural scenes, paved the way for the poetic styles of Wang and Meng. The reclusive Meng was the first Tang poet to write a great many landscape poems, developing Zhang Jiuling's style and melding his feelings with nature. His best-known verse is "Spring Dawn." Wang had many talents. He was an accomplished musician, an innovative painter, a great calligrapher, and a master of poetry in all its forms. Called the "Great Master of the Five-Character Quatrain," he wrote more poems in that form than any other Chinese poet. Wang's idylls were especially influential on later poets. One of his idylls, "Deer Enclosure," depicts a quiet, secluded, peaceful valley. Cui Hao was a friend of Wang Wei and is often ranked with him. His poems are also heroic and lofty. Li Bai admired Cui's "Yellow Crane Tower," which has been called the "best seven-character quatrain of the Tang." Wang Zhihuan and Wang Changling were well known for their frontier poems. Wang Zhihuan, who quit his official positions at the county level, left only six poems—all strikingly impressive regulated quatrains, of which the best known is "Climbing the Stork Pavilion." Wang Changling was regarded by his contemporaries as "the supreme poet of the empire" and was friends with almost all the well-known poets of his time. His poems address three themes: the frontier, parting, and unhappy palace women. One of his poems is "Reproach in the Women's Chamber." Du Mu liked to comment on history and wrote many oft-quoted lines in poems such as "Passing by the Huaqing Palace," "Red Cliff," "Anchor at Qinhuai," and "A Mountain Walk." The extremely sensitive Li Shangyin wrote deep, sad, lonely poems such as "Without Title."

**The New Music Bureau Ballads.** Around 755, when Mongol general An Lushan revolted against the Tang dynasty, Du Fu adopted the Music Bureau style, an old ballad tradition associated with social protest, to expose the problems of the day, in effect initiating what became known as the New Music Bureau movement. Later, the realistic poets Zhang Ji, Wang Jian, Yuan Zhen, and Bai Juyi, who were all government officials, explicitly raised the concept of New Music Bureau poetry and initiated a movement to promote it through theory as well as practice. Pur-

Two illuminations from *The Journey to the West,* mid sixteenth century (from Arnold Toynbee, *Half the World,* 1973)

posely using poetry as a tool to advocate their political ideas, they chose simple and plain words to describe serious social issues and made their poems natural, smooth, and readable. The four poets echoed each other's work. Their movement reached its peak around 809 when Bai Juyi created what he termed the *Xinyuefu* (New Music Bureau Ballads), narrative poems dramatizing what he saw and felt.

**The Prose Movement.** Toward the end of the Tang dynasty the master essayist Han Yu initiated a prose movement to exalt Confucianism over Daoism and Buddhism, which was totally accepted in the Song era (960–1279). Han believed that scholars should learn the way (*Dao*) and the writing style from ancient prose. He urged writers to replace clichés, dead words, and overworked metaphors with the purity and vividness exhibited in the classics of the Han dynasties and the period before the Qin dynasty (221–206 B.C.E.). Han, who paid great attention to sentence structure and organization, wrote many pieces of theoretical prose with strict structure and logic but no great literary value, including "On the Origin of the Way," "On the Origin of Destruction," and "A Talk on Instruction." Yet, his short critical essays are compelling and touching. Also a master essayist, Liu Zongyuan (773–819) did not belong to Han's circle and was much less influential than Han, but he made an important contribution to the prose movement. His prose theory was similar to Han's, but Liu accepted Buddhism. He stressed the need for depth of ideas and implicit, but subtle, expression and invented a kind of prose that is more literary and more lyrical. His nature essays,

such as "Eight Sketches of Yongzhou," are beautiful and broke with the tradition that the themes of essays should be limited to politics and philosophy. His best-known essays include "The Snake Catcher," "Song Qing," "Camel-Back Guo," "The Nurseryman," and "The Carpenter."

**The Rise of the Marvel and Colloquial Tales.** The term *chuanqi* (marvel tales) was coined by Yuan Zhen, whose "Story of Yingying [Little Oriole]" was originally titled "A Marvel Tale." Marvel tales evolved from *zhiguai* (mysterious records), accounts of unexplained, supernatural events, and were influenced by the writing style of history books, which often used fictional methods to attract readers. While mysterious records are religious and superstitious rather than literary, the marvel tale is a kind of short story with plot, character development, and psychological analysis. The appearance of marvel tales during the Tang dynasty marked the beginning of the Chinese novel. Many popular marvel tales— such as "The Ancient Mirror," "The Story of Li Yi," "The Story of a Pillow," "The Story of a Singsong Girl," "The Story of Liu Yi," and "The Story of Huo Xiaoyu"—emerged during this period and later became source materials for novelists and dramatists in the Yuan (1279–1368) and Ming dynasties (1368–1644).

**The Development of Lyrics.** *Ci* (lyrics) are a kind of folk song, or poetry in a broad sense. Ancient poems were closely associated with music, but with the decline of old music they gradually became known as a literary form. During the Tang dynasty the music imported from Central Asia, combined with that of ancient China, became known as *yanyue* (feast music). The words to these songs were written in lines of unequal length to fit the rhythms and structure of feast music. During the late Tang, Five Dynasties (907–960), and Ten Kingdoms (902–979) periods, these lyrics became an independent poetic form. The works of Wen Tingyun, Wei Zhuang, and Li Yu (937–978) marked the maturity of the lyric form. The first group of five lyrics set to "Pusaman" (Bodhisattva Barbarian) is Wen's best-known work, while Wei is known for a second group of five lyrics for the same tune. Li, the last ruler of the Southern Tang dynasty (937–975), wrote several well-known poems, including lyrics for the tunes "Yumeiren" (The Beautiful Lady Yu), "Pozhenzi" (Dance of the Cavalry), and "Langtaosha" (Ripples Sifting Sand).

**The Song Neoclassical Movement.** During the early years of the Song dynasty, most poets followed the styles of Tang poets Bai Juyi, Jia Dao, and Li Shangyin. Writers of lyrics followed the Tang style as well. Many progressive literati were not happy about this literary situation. Poetry-prose writers Ouyang Xiu (1007–1072) and Su Shi (1037–1101) started a neoclassical movement for literary reform that launched not only their careers but also those of important poets such as Mei Yaochen (1002–1060), Su Shunqin (1008–1048), and Wang Anshi (1021–1086). Ouyang had developed a great admiration for Tang essayist Han Yu, echoed Han's call for a return to the ancient style, and emphasized the importance of simplicity, vigor, rationality, and tolerance. Su Shi represented the greatest achievement of the neoclassical movement in Song literature.

**Lyrics of the Song Era.** During the Song dynasty there emerged many great lyric writers, including not only Ouyang Xiu and Su Shi but also Yan Shu (991–1055), Liu Yong (flourished 1034), Qin Guan (1049–1100), He Zhu (1052–1125), Zhou Bangyan (1056–1121), Li Qingzhao (1084 – circa 1151), Lu You (1125–1210), Xin Qiji (1140–1207), Chen Liang (1143–1194), Jiang Kui (1155–1221), and Wu Wenying (circa 1200 – circa 1260). Lyrics of the Song period may be divided into two groups, one characterized by its grace and tenderness and the other by its vigor. The first group includes lyrics by Liu Yong, Qin Guan, Zhou Bangyan, and Li Qingzhao. Their lyrics are mostly devoted to love and sorrow at parting; Li is the best poet of this school. The second group includes the works of the "Three Sus"—Su Xun (1009–1106) and his sons Su Shi and Su Che (1039–1112)—and nationalist poets Lu You and Xin Qiji. Lu was a prolific writer who destroyed virtually all the poems he wrote before his middle age. He excelled in several verse forms, and more than ten thousand poems are included in his eighty-five volumes of *Jiannan shigao* (Poetic Manuscripts of Jiannan) and fifty volumes of *Weinan wenji* (Collection from Weihan). The style of his poems was first influenced by the scholarly School of Jiangxi, then became expansive and vigorous, and eventually developed a tranquil tone. Patriotic sentiments permeated his lyrics. Some critics consider Lu's seven-character regulated poems as good as Du Fu's. Among Lu's best works are "For My Sons" and "Expressing Indignation." Xin's literary style and life experience were similar to Lu's. Xin was determined to recapture North China from the Jin dynasty (1115–1234), and his six hundred lyrics express his longing for national unity and his frustration at the Song dynasty's failure to achieve this goal. Xin also wrote fresh and romantic landscape lyrics, significantly contributing to the divorce of lyrics from their musical background. His best poem is probably "Written on a Wall En Route to Poshan." After the Southern Song dynasty fell to the Mongols in 1279, patriotic literati such as Wen Tianxiang, who remained loyal to the Song while a prisoner of the Mongol Yuan dynasty, used their poems to express their sadness and concern about their nation.

**The School of Jiangxi and Its Detractors.** The "Four Scholars of the Su School" followed in the style of Su Shi. One of them, Huang Tingjian (1045–1105), went on to develop his own poetic style and founded the Jiangxi School, which stressed the importance of book knowledge as the foundation of poetic writing. Attempting to develop a method of composition that would allow the creative transmutation of ancient literature into contemporary poetry, Huang advocated the techniques of "changing the bones" and "snatching the embryo"—that is, borrowing images and phrases from past writers but altering the meaning or expressing the ideas of other writers but changing their words. He also tried to avoid politics and social issues and believed in detaching emotion from the artistic process. The Jiangxi School prevailed until the new *Chengzhaiti* (Style of Honest Study) was developed by Yang Wanli (1127–1206). This style is characterized by natural and humorous language and a philosophical view of life and nature. Yang, Fan Chengda (1126–1193), Lu You (1125–1210), and You Mao (flourished 1170) were called the "Four Masters of Restoration." In his *Changlang Shihua* (Poetry Talks from Changlang) Yan Yu (flourished 1200) praised Tang poetry and criticized the Jiangxi School, calling on poets to reinstate the magic quality of spirituality in poetry. His work had profound influence on later poets. Reacting against the Jiangxi School, many lower-class literati—including Yan Yu and the other poets called the "Four Souls of Yongjia"—divorced themselves from politics and became itinerant poets sponsored by a rich merchant, Chen Qi. They became a dominant force in Chinese poetry.

**The Poetry of the Yuan Dynasty.** The few surviving poems from the Liao dynasty, which ruled an empire on the northern border of China in 916–1115, create a poetic transition from the rationality of the Song poets to the emotion that characterizes the poems written during the Yuan era. The best-known Liao poems are ten works in *Huixinyuan* (The Court for the Returning Heart), written by Empress Yide (1040–1075). The most important legacy of the Jin dynasty is the literary criticism and poetry of Yuan Haowen (1190–1257). He compiled *Zhongzhouji* (The Collection of the Central Plains), an anthology of works by 240 Jin poets. During the Yuan dynasty, poets of the North such as Yelü Chucai (1190–1244), Hao Jing

(1223–1275), and Liu Yin (1249–1293) followed in the Liao and Jin traditions, writing bold, unconstrained, and artistically rough works. Poets of the South included the "Four Masters of the Yuan": Deng Mu (1247–1306), Qiu Yuan (1247–1326), Dai Biaoyuan (1244–1310), and Zhao Mengfu (1254–1322). Among them, Zhao was the most influential. His poems were written in the styles of the Han, Wei (386–535), and Six Dynasties (220–589) periods and were as subtle and beautiful as his calligraphy.

**Song and Yuan Fiction.** The short and medium-length novels of the Song and the Yuan dynasties can be divided into two types: vernacular and classic. The vernacular novel is closely related to the folk art of storytelling and developed alongside the growth of cities. Such fiction portrayed the lives, taste, and ideas of the urban lower class and was more popular than the classic novel, which appealed mainly to the upper class. Only twenty to thirty storytellers' scripts of the Song and the Yuan periods have survived. Among the most popular of these vernacular stories are "The Jade Worker" and "Fifteen Strings of Cash." Such stories have complex plots and realistic narratives and employ popular language that is lively, simple, and witty. Unlike the "marvel tales" of the Tang dynasty, most Song classic novels, especially the early ones, were neither imaginative nor skillfully written. Influenced by neo-Confucianism, the authors of these works were more concerned with morality and justice than with character development and psychological analysis. Notable exceptions include Song classic novels such as *Jiaohongji* (The Story of Charming Red) by an unknown author and *Yijianzhi* (The Records of Eliminating the Toughest), a work of 420 volumes by Hong Mai (1123–1202).

**Literary Restoration.** The despotism and political-cultural suppression of the early Ming era resulted in the executions or suicides of well-known literati and led to a change in poetic style, as represented by the pessimistic poems of Gao Qi (1336–1374), who was executed by the Ming government. Song Lian (1310–1381) and other poets supported by the imperial court promoted orthodox literature that placed ideology over aesthetics. They were followed by the so-called Three Yangs, who developed the *Taigeti* (Style of Platform and Pavilion) in court poetry and prose, which voiced the official ideology of neo-Confucianism and focused on the lives and social activities of bureaucrats and the nobility. By the middle of the Ming era, economic development and a relative relaxation of political and cultural suppression provided the conditions for literary change. The "Former Seven Youths," including Li Mengyang (1473–1530) and He Jingming (1483–1521), and the "Four Geniuses of the Middle Wu," including Tang Yan (1470–1524) and Zhu Yunming (1460–1526), launched a revival in poetry. They criticized the "Style of Platform and Pavilion" and neo-Confucianism and tried to liberate literature from ideological and political control, advocating the role of literature in expressing individual feelings and desires. Their efforts were attacked by the orthodox Tang-Song School, including Gui Youguang (1507–1571),

Illumination from the Ming-era novel *Water Margins*. Wu Sung holds the head of his adulterous sister-in-law while her lover lies dead on the ground (from Arnold Toynbee, *Half the World*, 1973).

whose influence was soon challenged by the "Latter Seven Youths," including Li Panlong (1514–1570) and Wang Shizhen (1526–1590).

**Great Ming Novels.** Writers of the Ming era produced many important long novels. Typically episodic in nature, they relate the adventures of a large number of characters in a string of loosely connected events. The thematic range of Ming novels is broad, including historical romances, chivalric tales, ghost stories, social satires, and love stories. *The Romance of the Three Kingdoms*, originally attributed to Luo Guanzhong (circa 1330 – circa 1400) and extensively revised by later hands, chronicles in great detail the fall of the Han Empire and the rise and decline of the three competing kingdoms that followed it. Written in a combination of vernacular and classic language, the novel holds its characters to a clear-cut moral standard. *The Journey to the West*, attributed to Wu Chengen (circa 1506 – 1582), is a mythological, comic fantasy based on the seventeen-year-long journey of the Tang monk Xuanzang (596–664) to India to collect Buddhist scriptures. Four disciples with superhuman abilities accompany and protect the monk from all sorts of demons and monsters that threatened his life at various points of his pilgrimage. The true protagonist of the novel is the most capable, intelligent, and faithful disciple, the "Monkey King," who—assisted by other disciples and various deities—invariably rescues the monk. Among the various versions of the anonymous *Water Mar-*

gins, the best is the one made by Shi Naian during the late Yuan and early Ming periods. The novel tells the story of a band of 108 colorful, daredevil bandit-heroes—men and women—who have been forced by unjust officials to rebel against the government. Celebrating loyalty and the code of brotherhood, the novel is written in northern colloquial language—fresh, lively, and humorous. *Gold Vase Plum*, by the pseudonymous "Scoffing Scholar of Lanling," is considered the greatest pornographic novel of imperial China. (The Chinese title, *Jinpingmei*, is made up of the name of the three main female characters.) Through skillfully borrowed plots, materials, and several characters from *Water Margins*, *Gold Vase Plum* tells the story of a wealthy merchant and his sexual adventures and exploits. With brutal realism and satiric style, it also depicts the corrupt life and customs of Chinese society. *Sanyan* (Three Words), a collection of short novels compiled by Feng Menglong (1574–1646), comprises *Yushi mingyan* (Instructive Words to Enlighten the World), *Jingshi tongyan* (Popular Words to Admonish the World), and *Xingshi hengyan* (Lasting Words to Awaken the World). These works are derived from storytellers' scripts of the Song and the Yuan dynasties. Focusing on friendship, love, passion, fidelity, and corruption, the novels are fraught with moral lessons and admonitions. Ling Mengchu (1580–1644) followed the style of *Three Words* when he wrote books 1 and 2 of *Paian jingqi* (Striking the Table in Amazement at the Wonders)—known collectively as *Erpai* (Two Strikes). *Two Strikes* depicts more vividly than *Three Words* the urban social consciousness and resentment of tradition and corruption. Other notable fiction of the Ming era includes *Fengshen yanyi* (The History of Granting God Titles) and *Xingshi yinyuanzhuan* (Shocking Love Legends).

**Li Zhi and the Schools of Gongan and Jingling.** In his *Fenshu* (Books to Be Burned) Li Zhi (1527–1602) became the first Chinese scholar to criticize feudal and traditional values, challenging orthodox ideology and the authorities. His most influential literary theory is "the heart of a child," in which he argues that the best and most genuine essays come from an innate, original self. Anything that is not genuine should be avoided, and the genuine should not be corrupted by learning and society. Li Zhi was greatly admired by the three Yuan brothers of Gongan, most notably Yuan Hongdao (1568–1610), who developed the School of Gongan, which advocated the free expression of "natural spirit." The School of Jingling, which included Zhong Xing (1574–1624), continued to promote creativity and "exclusively express natural spirit." These two schools and Li Zhi developed the prose style that began to transform conventional Chinese writing into modern writing. The last great Ming essayist was Zhang Dai (1597–1679), whose many talents also included music and dance.

**Sources:**

Cyril Birch, ed., *Anthology of Chinese Literature: From Early Times to the Fourteenth Century* (New York: Grove, 1965).

Jonathan Chaves, ed. and trans., *The Columbia Book of Later Chinese Poetry: Yüan, Ming, and Ch'ing Dynasties (1279–1911)* (New York: Columbia University Press, 1986).

Wu-chi Liu and Irving Yucheng Lo, eds., *Sunflower Splendor: Three Thousand Years of Chinese Poetry* (Bloomington: Indiana University Press, 1975).

Victor H. Mair, ed., *The Columbia Anthology of Traditional Chinese Literature* (New York: Columbia University Press, 1994).

Mair, ed., *The Columbia History of Chinese Literature* (New York: Columbia University Press, 2001).

Stephen Owen, ed. and trans., *An Anthology of Chinese Literature, Beginning to 1911* (New York: Norton, 1996).

Burton Watson, ed. and trans., *The Columbia Book of Chinese Poetry: From Early Times to the Thirteenth Century* (New York: Columbia University Press, 1984).

Zhang Peiheng and Luo Yuming, eds., *Zhongguo wenxueshi* (Shanghai: Fudan University Press, 1996).

## MUSIC

**Tang Palace Music.** The Tang dynasty (618–907) established two music-management systems, one controlled by the court and the other by the government. The Taichangsi (Temple of Ultimate Normalcy) was the governmental institution in charge of ritual and music. The court had the *Jiaofang* (Training Center) for teaching court musicians and the *Liyuan* (Pear Garden) for palace musicians. Tang music falls into three basic genres: the *gequ* (song melody), the *wuqu* (dance melody), and the *jiequ* (instrumental melody). It is also grouped in four different styles: *yanyue* (palace-feast music), *duobuyue* (multinational music), *daqu* (grand melody), and *faqu* (Buddhist melody). Broadly speaking, Tang palace music included Chinese, foreign, and minority music of the Sui (589–618) and the Tang dynasties. Narrowly speaking, it included only the categories of music known as the "ten melodies." In fact, during the early Tang era there were only "nine melodies" inherited from the Sui dynasty. Between 637 and 642, however, one more "melody," multinational music, was added. Tang emperor Xuanzong (ruled 712–756) divided multinational music into two parts: sitting players (for the hall) and standing players (for the garden). The grand melody, also called the grand palace-feast melody, combined instrumental and vocal music with dance into a harmonious large-scale performance with changing rhythms, pace, and dynamics. Its structure included three parts: instrumental music, vocal music with instrumental accompaniment, and dance accompanied by vocal and instrumental music. Unfortunately, the scores for most Tang grand melodies have not survived. The Tang Buddhist melody included elements of traditional Chinese, Buddhist, Daoist, and foreign music and faded after the middle of the Tang alongside the decline of Buddhism.

**Later Palace Music.** Palace music became more luxurious during the Northern Song dynasty (960–1125). During this period there were 599 palace musicians who played 351 musical instruments of 25 different varieties. Palace music declined for a while early in the Southern Song dynasty (1127–1279) but revived again later. During the 1110s, 1,422 woodwind and percussion players were employed as palace musicians. Song-era musicians developed several kinds of orchestral music. The palace-feast music of the Northern Liao dynasty (916–1115) has been

Figurines of female musicians from Chinese Turkestan, seventh century
(from Bradley Smith & Wan-go Weng, *China: A History in Art*, 1973)

classified as national music, foreign music, the grand music of the Tang, and a category called *sanyue* (variety music), which included instrumental compositions as well as accompaniments for poetic drama, singing, and acrobatics. The palace-feast music of the northern Jin dynasty (1115–1234) included ancient music, variety music, wind-and-percussion music, ritual music, and national music. By the Ming dynasty (1368–1644) orchestral music was divided into string music and wind-and-percussion music. String music included Canton music, string-and-bamboo music of the South, poetic string music, and Han music. Wind-and-percussion music included music for the Xian drum and other drums and gongs.

**Tang Musicians and Composers.** A staunch supporter of all the arts, Tang emperor Xuanzong composed and conducted music and played several musical instruments, including the flute and drums. He was good at composing Buddhist melodies and at translating the titles of foreign melodies into meaningful Chinese. During the nearly three hundred years of the Tang dynasty there were more than 100,000 musicians. The Tang government followed the tradition of retaining foreign musicians from well-known families, including Cao Bao, Cao Shuxin, Cao Zhesu, Shan Cai, Kang Kulun, Kang Nai, An Chinu, An Wanshan, and An Peixin. Duan Shanben (flourished 700) enjoyed nationwide renown and trained dozens of lute players. Yongxin, Nian Nu, and He Manzi—all of whom flourished around 710—were excellent singers. The prominent poet Bai Juyi (772–846) was also a musician and music critic. He wrote more than one hundred poems describing and commenting on various musical instruments and songs. Nan Zhuo was a well-known drummer of the Tang era. His *Jiegulu* (Record of the Jie Drum) describes the evolution of the Jie drum, includes many stories about drummers, and records 128 names of Jie-drum compositions.

**Song Musicians and Composers.** Jiang Kui (circa 1155 – 1221) is considered the greatest musician of the Song dynasty and possibly of all Chinese history. A composer and player of the vertical bamboo flute and the zither, he was also a poet and calligrapher. His four-volume *Baishi daoren shiji* (Songs of the White Stone Daoist) is a collection of ancient and Song works and his own compositions. Two of his best-known compositions are *Yangzhouman* (Slow Yangzhou) and *Xinghua tianying* (Apricot Flowers Reflecting Heaven). Song string players were divided into several schools. The School of the Capital preserved many ancient palace scores, and its style was bold and vigorous. The School of Jiangxi liked music with rich and diverse sounds, and its performance style was delicate and beautiful. The style of the School of the "Two Zhes" was refined and civilized. The founder of the School of "Two Zhes" was Guo Mian (flourished 1110). His "Water and Cloud of Xiaoxiang," "Autumn Wind," "Walking Moon," and "Floating on Blue Waves" were famous string compositions, but their scores have been lost.

**Ming Musicians and Composers.** During the reign of Ming emperor Wanli (1573–1620) the so-called Eight Unsurpassed Musicians of the Capital in Beijing were considered the best players of the lute, strings, flute, and drum. The Song-era School of the Two Zhes evolved into two schools of zither playing during the Ming era: the School of Jiang and the School of Zhe, each of which carried on some features of the Two Zhes' style. The influential School of Yushan, founded by Yan Cheng (1547–1625), played in a subtle but profound style.

**Sui and Tang Music Historians and Theoreticians.** The 173-volume *Beitang shuchao* (Collected Writings of the North Hall), compiled by Yu Shinan during the Sui dynasty, preserved many historical materials on ancient music for later eras. *Yueshu yaolu* (The Brief Record of

Music Books), published in 700, is an important theoretical book, but only volumes five through seven are extant, having been preserved in Japan. *Jiaofangji* (Record of the Training Centers) written by Cui Lingqin (flourished 713–741), documents the Tang training centers, which were also the subject of Duan Anjie's *Yuefu zalu* (The Miscellaneous Records of Music Institutions), written late in the Tang period. During the Tang era there were two forms of music notation. The first, which used Chinese characters, was extremely complex until it was reformed and simplified by Cao You. His system could accurately record high pitches and changing timbre but not rhythm. The second, which used some characters and some signs, has yet to be deciphered by modern scholars.

**Music Historians and Theoreticians of the Song Dynasty.** During the Song dynasty at least four methods of musical notation were developed: *gongchepu* (traditional musical notation), *suzipu* (conventional character notation), *lülü zipu* (character notation based on twelve temperaments, or semitones), and *guqin jianzipu* (simplified character notation for the ancient zither). Song musician Cai Yuanding (1135–1198) invented notation based on "eighteen temperaments" and published *Lülü xinshu* (The New Classic of Temperament) and *Yanyueshu* (Classic Palace Feast Music). Chen Yang (1096–1100), a composer of palace-feast music, compiled a 200-volume *Yueshu* (Music Dictionary), the first Chinese encyclopedia of music. During the Southern Song dynasty, Wang Zhuo wrote *Biji manzhi* (The Informal Record of a Green Rooster), which traces the evolution of music from remote ages to the Tang dynasty, examining the origins of twenty-eight Tang melodies and their relationship to Song lyrics. During the same period Zhang Yan wrote *Ciyuan* (Lyrical Dictionary). Volume one covers musical and vocal temperaments, and volume two expounds on lyrical principles.

**Yuan Music Historians and Theoreticians.** Written during the Yuan era, *Changlun* (Vocal Theory), by Zhi An, is the first Chinese scholarly work on vocal music. It has thirty-one sections and wide-ranging subject matter, including the famous melodies of the Song, Jin, and Yuan dynasties. In 1324 Zhou Deqing published *Zhongyuan yinyun* (Musicology of the Central Plain). The first part covers the notation system of northern musicology, and the second part discusses phonology and "ten rules of lyrical work." *Shenqi mipu* (Secret Scores of Mystery and Wonder), published in 1425, is the earliest Chinese collection of zither compositions, comprising sixty-two works selected from thousands by Prince Zhu Quan.

**Ming Music Historians and Theoreticians.** The main text of the Ming-era School of Yushan is *Songxuan guanqinpu* (Scores of Pine String and Studying Zither). One member of this school, Xu Shangyin (died circa 1661), wrote *Xishan qinkuang* (Zither Conditions from Creek Hill), which includes important aesthetic views of music and was necessary reading for any zither player. Philosopher Wang Shouren (1472–1528) discussed music in his *Wang Wencheng Gong quanshu* (The Complete Collection of the Revered Wang Wencheng). Wang Fuzhi's (1619–1692) opinions about music were scattered throughout his voluminous writings. Zhu Zaiyu (1536–1616) separated the study of musicology from that of temperament, introduced the music pedagogy and quantitative notation, and invented the "twelve equal temperaments" of what became the standard division of a musical scale into equal semitones. He also published the forty-seven-volume *Yuelü quanshu* (The Complete Work on Temperament) and *Yayue wupu* (The Dance Scores of Palace Feast Music).

**Musical Instruments.** There were about three hundred kinds of musical instruments during the Tang dynasty, including eighteen kinds of wind instruments, fifteen kinds of string instruments, and twenty-one kinds of percussion instruments. The lute, reed pipe, bamboo flute, and Jie drum were the most important, and various kinds of bells were also used. Two new musical instruments appeared during the Tang period: the *yazheng*, a seven-string zither played with a piece of bamboo, and the *xiqin*, a form of violin that was the predecessor to the *huqin*. Musical instruments from the Tang and earlier dynasties still played an important role during the Song dynasty. Many new instruments, some of which are no longer extant, appeared, including the *maweihuqin*, which is related to the later two-string violin known as the erhu.

**Genre Music.** The folk and popular music of China is generally called genre music. Genre music of the Tang era included *quzi* (melody) or *xiaoqu* (mini melody), *shujiang* (storytelling) or *bianwen* (Buddhist scripts), *canjunxi* (adjutant play), and *sanyue* (variety music). The mini melody was a kind of folk music that originated during the Sui dynasty and developed during the Tang dynasty. Popular Tang mini melodies—such as "Eternal Longing," "Magpie on the Branch," "Memories of the South," "The Charm of My Wife," "Willow Branches," "Lingering at Dawn," "Twelve Hours," "Memories of Fish," "Worshiping the New Moon," and "Corn Poppy"—were sung with various lyrics or played for dancing and theatrical performances. The development of mini melodies reached its peak during the Song dynasty, when they were classified as ancient, foreign, folk, or "new." "Storytelling" music was derived from Buddhist preaching and texts. The "adjutant play" was a form of skit with vocal accompaniment that prevailed during the Tang and the Song periods and greatly influenced the development of Chinese drama. "Variety music" was played for large variety shows that included skits, wrestling, acrobatics, magic, dancing, and martial arts. These shows were still popular during the Song and Yuan dynasties. The rise of urban music during the Song and the Ming dynasties paralleled that of the urban *washe*, or *washi* (spontaneous market), an outdoor entertainment center, where several shows could take place at the same time. A spontaneous market usually had several dozen stages and entertainment tents, the largest of which could hold several thousand people. During the Song dynasty several forms of music developed for the genre show, a folk-art performance that included singing. One of these forms was *sanqu* (loose melody), whose rise occurred along with the decline of *zaju* (variety plays). Loose melody was much more sentimental than that of variety plays and revealed the personal feelings of playwrights such as Yuan-era dramatists Guan Hanqing (circa 1213 – circa 1297), Bai Pu (1226–1306), and Ma Zhiyuan (circa 1250 – 1324), whose scripts show little trace of earlier variety plays. Another popular form of the Song era was *guzici* (poetic drum) music, which evolved into the "drum melody," a short sung narrative, during the Ming dynasty and was popular in the North. A musician played a wooden drum and sang or chanted a rhyming verse to the accompaniment of stringed instruments. Eventually an instrumental introduction and interludes were added to create what became known as *dagu* (big drum) songs. During the Ming dynasty folk songs became popular among the literati, a development that ensured the preservation of this music. Feng Menglong (1574–1646) published two large collections of folk songs: *Guizhier* (Cassia Twigs), comprising 435 songs, and *Shange* (Mountain Songs), comprising 383. The *bangziqiang* (wooden clapper tune), or "Qin Qiang," originated in Shanxi Province during the Ming dynasty and spread east, evolving into various regional forms. It usually has one basic melody with changing rhythms and has strong expressive power. The earliest surviving script of *tanci* (musical storytelling), or *pingtan* (talking music), is by Yuan writer Yang Jizhen. Musical storytelling used Beijing or Wu dialects and was accompanied by strings and flute. *Yugu daoqing* (fish-drum singing) is one of the oldest forms of genre shows. The singer is accompanied only by a wooden clapper and a fish-shaped drum. The development of the northern folk form known as *Kunqu* (Kunshan tune, or Kun melody) was a major and influential achievement. Its creation has been attributed to Wei Liangfu, a blind doctor and famous singer, and his disciple, Liang Chenyu (circa 1521 – circa 1594). Wei transformed the Kun melody from plain, uncouth, countrified music into a new tune that retained the best features of the Kun tune and other northern melodies. The result was soft, clear, sweet, relaxing music often described as "water polished."

**Dance Music.** The "seeding" dance of rural folk during the Southern Song dynasty went through three stages of development. It began as a diversion during labor, then became an independent folk show, and finally became a short dramatic performance. It was accompanied by singing, percussion, and a woodwind instrument called the *suona*. The flower-drum dance also originated in the Southern Song era and was usually performed by a man and a woman who danced and sang. Many regions have their own versions of flower-drum dances, among which the flower-drum dance of Gengyang is especially notable. The classic Uighur *mukamu*—combining song, dance, and instrumental music—dates from the fifteenth century. There are three major types: *Keshe mukamu*, popular in Keshe and Yili; *Duolan mukamu*, a hunting dance popular around Yeerqiang River and the Talimu Valley; and *Hami mukamu*, popular in Hami and Yiwu. "Slender Music of White Sand" is the traditional dance music of the Naxi minority in Ilijiang County of Yunnan Province. A legacy of the Yuan, it combines instrumental and vocal music.

Sources:

Cai Yuanli and Wu Wenke, *Zhongguo Quyishi* (Beijing: Culture and Arts Press, 1998).

Ma Wenqi, Xie Yongjun, and Song Bo, *Zhongguo Xiqushi* (Beijing: Culture and Arts Press, 1998).

Zang Yibing, *Zhongguo yinyueshi* (Wehan, China: University Press of Survey Drawing and Science Technology, 1999).

## PAINTING AND PRINTMAKING

**Tang Painting.** The great international successes of the Tang empire (618–907) provided Chinese artists with an excellent working environment and exposure to other cultures, leading to a wide range of artistic innovations. The rich myth of a supernatural universe gave way to a rational view of a mundane world. Depicting a tangible reality, Tang painting is vigorous, colorful, and optimistic. Various styles, techniques, and theories of painting all thrived. Generally speaking, Chinese painting uses dark outlines, a limited color palette, flat images, and a blank background. It is also known for its shifting (but not foreshortened) perspective. That is, while the Western painter generally locates the viewer in one spot and paints everything in the picture as it would appear from that viewpoint, the traditional Chinese painter employs multiple points of view in a

Detail of the eighth-century painting *Ladies Preparing Newly Woven Silk* by Zhang Xuan; twelfth-century copy (Museum of Fine Arts, Boston)

Detail of the painting *Emperors of the Successive Dynasties,* by Yan Liben, circa 650 (Museum of Fine Arts, Boston)

single work. Figure painting reached a new height during the Tang era. The most celebrated painter of the early Tang period, Yan Liben (died 673), is known for his lucid and ponderous portraits of emperors and scholars. He and his brother Yan Lide (died 656) brought about a renaissance in figure painting. The extremely influential Wu Daozi (circa 688 – 758), called the "Saint Painter," was renowned for his realistic style, knowledge of anatomy, painting technique, vivid imagination, and enthusiasm. He painted hundreds of magnificent Buddhist murals and is well known for his habit of painting after bouts of heavy drinking. Court painters such as Zhang Xuan (flourished 713–741) and Zhou Fang (flourished 766–804) portrayed many beautiful palace ladies engaged in work or play. Known collectively as "Court Ladies on Silk," the works of Zhang and Zhou are usually voluptuous, opulent portraits with rounded motifs and draperies. Gu Hongzhong (circa 910 – 980) realistically depicted various palace figures in his well-known painting *Night Feast.* The famous figure painters Li Zhen (flourished late eighth and early ninth centuries) and Sun Wei (flourished late ninth century) influenced many later painters. The inventor of ink-wash painting, Wang Wei (701–761) is called the father of monochrome landscape painting in ink and of the Southern School of painter-poets. He was also a writer, a musician, and scholar of Chan (Zen Buddhism). His painting has been called a harmonious fusion of painting and poetry, and he became a model for landscape painters of later generations. Zhang Zhao (flourished late eighth century) employed a new technique of "splashing ink," which gave his pictures a sense of haziness and movement. Li Sixun (651–718) and his son Li Zhaodao (flourished 700), known as "Big Li" and "Little Li," liked to use blue and green and to outline objects in a shade of gold. They created the School of Golden and Green Landscape Painting. The rise of flower and bird painting is attributed to Xue Ji (649–713), Jiang Jiao (flourished 720), Bian Luan (flourished late eighth century), and Diao Guangyin (flourished late in the Tang era). During the early or mid eighth century Cao Ba, Han Gan, and Wei Yan were well known for their paintings of horses and human figures. Han Kuang (723–787) and Dai Song (flourished late eighth century) specialized in genre paintings depicting cows, pastoral scenes, and peasant life. The ten-volume *Lidai minghuaji* (Records of Famous Paintings of All the Dynasties) by Zhang Yanyuan (circa 815 – circa 875) is the first comprehensive history of Chinese painting.

**Five Dynasties Landscapes.** During the chaotic period of the Five Dynasties (907–960), many painters secluded themselves in the mountains and began to paint landscapes on large screens, employing a shifting focus that suggests unlimited space. In viewing a single work the spectator might imagine himself looking at the same scene from the middle distance and from a great elevation. The Chinese

*A Solitary Temple amid Clearing Peaks* by Li Cheng; hanging scroll, circa 960
(Nelson-Atkins Museum of Art, Kansas City, Missouri)

artist carefully selected the details he included in a painting, concentrating on what he felt was the true essence of his subject. A landscape represented nature as a whole; a spray of bamboo was a microcosm of the universe. Chinese classical artists painted the ideal they saw in the real, focusing on their interpretation of nature and humanity's relationship with it. Chinese landscape painters tried to connect to four principles: the divine, in which there appears no trace of human effort; the sublime, which flows spontaneously from the artist's brush as a result of his grasp of the universe and the nature and circumstances of all things; the marvelous, which possesses truth even though it may be contrary to reality; and skill, which allows the artist to piece together fragments of beauty into a masterpiece. The tenth-century artists known as the "Four Masters of Landscape Painting" included Jing Hao and his student Guan Tong, both of whom liked to depict the mountains and rivers of North China. Their paintings are bold and uninhibited, with vigorous strokes and grand vistas. The other two painters of this group were Dong Yuan and his student Ju Ran, who loved the topography of South China. Their paintings are charming and gentle, yet elegant and splendid.

**Song Landscapes.** Landscape painting reached the peak of its development during the Song dynasty (960–1279). Li Cheng (flourished tenth century) had a preference for wild fields, wintry scenes, broken bridges, stony crags, and gnarled trees with leafless branches. His personal feelings permeate his paintings. Fan Kuan (circa 950 – 1031) also liked to paint winter landscapes, as well as places popular with tourists. His paintings are magnificent, weighty, elegant, and misty with refined strokes and smooth rhythms. In the early eleventh century Guo Xi painted changing seasons and a variety of natural scenes. His painting theory is fully elaborated in his *Linquan gaozhi* (A Father's Instructions), compiled and edited by his son Guo Si. Another important book on painting theory is Guo Ruoxu's twelfth- or thirteenth-century *Tuhua jianwenzhi* (Record of Paintings). Wang Shen (1036–?) worked in the style of Li Cheng and Guo Xi, and liked to paint tiny horizontal scenes. Around the twelfth or thirteenth century, Ma Yuan preferred to depict "a corner of nature" and emphasize one part of a scene as a microcosmic representation of all nature. Ma Yuan was one of the "Four Master Painters" of the Southern Song dynasty, a group that also included Li Tang (circa 1066–1150), Liu Songnian, and Xia Gui. They changed the painting style of the Northern Song period (960–1125) by combining landscape painting and figure painting, using empty spaces to depict substance, and replacing complexity with simplicity. Mi Fei (1057–1107) and his son Mi Youren (1086–1165) brought the romantic, intimate style of the Literati Painters to landscape painting. Their paintings were known collectively as "The Landscapes of the Mi Family."

**Yuan Landscapes.** Landscape painting continued to flourish during the Yuan dynasty (1279–1368). Combining the painting styles of Dong and Ju, Gao Kegong (1248–1310) exercised great influence. Huang Gongwang (1269–1354), Wang Meng (1301–1385), Ni Zan (1301–1374), and Wu Zhen (1280–1354) were called the "Four Masters" of the Yuan dynasty. They were Daoists or Chan Buddhists who were

*Six Gentlemen* by Ni Zan; hanging scroll, 1345
(Shanghai Museum)

aloof from the world and immersed themselves in nature. Their paintings have religious implications of transcendence and enlightenment. Another group of landscape artists—including Tang Di (1296–1364), Zhu Derun (1294–1365), and Cao Zhibai (1272–1355)—painted in a style resembling that of Li Cheng and Guo Xi.

**The Painting Academy and the Literati Painters.** An Imperial Painting Academy existed in some form as early as the Five Dynasties period (907–960) but did not develop as a full-scale formal entity until it became an integral part of the civil-examination system during the Song dynasty. This development was encouraged by Emperor Huizong Zhao Ji (1082–1135), who was an incompetent ruler but an excellent painter of flowers and birds. Painting Academy artists became known as the Literati Painters. The Painting Academy tightly controlled subject matter and style, emphasizing intellectual agility, elitist elegance, exquisite precision, delicate taste, colorful expression, and faultless drawing. The result was often stiff composition. Painters from western China played an important role. The eleventh-century painter Cui Bai, who was already well known when the emperor ordered him to join the academy, brought a fresh style to the school. Su Shi (1037–1101), Wen Tong (1018–1079), and Mi Fei, were intuitive, playful, witty, and romantic, creating vivid works with simple compositions and shapes but rich implications. They were gentlemen first and painters second, playing with their paintings.

**Flower and Bird Painting.** The rise of the Literati Painters brought changes to flower and bird painting. Xu Xi (flourished tenth century) and Huang Quan (903–968) occupied a similar rank in the history of Chinese painting but employed different painting styles. Xu emphasized the application of ink, and Huang—who, as an imperial painter, painted in a style that reflected the taste of the emperor—is known for his use of color. By the Song dynasty, flower and bird painting had become realistic and popular. Distinctive regional painting styles and distinct schools of painters developed, and the Academic School of Huang enjoyed a dominant position in the genre. During the Southern Song dynasty the school shrank to a small group who emphasized detail and careful line drawing. The monk Fa Chang (flourished thirteenth century) and Li Di (flourished early twelfth century) were masters of flower and bird painting. Fa Chang invented an ink-splash style that revealed the aesthetic perception and emotional state of the painter, emphasizing simple composition and images. Li Di's poetic paintings had strict composition and were executed with steady, lively strokes. Yuan painters of flowers and birds continued to be influenced by Literati Painting and developed a solemn and simple style that combined heavy ink and light color. Among the best-known flower and bird painters of the period are Zhao Mengfu (1254–1322), Li Gan (1245–1320), Ke Jiusi (1290–1343), and Wang Mian (died 1359)—known as the "Four Gentlemen" painters of the Yuan dynasty. By the Ming dynasty many Literati painters had developed a casual and unconstrained attitude to life. The ink-splash style, which does not require meticulous detail and neat strokes, became the tool by which they could express their hopes in a playful way. Lin Liang (late fifteenth century), Chen Chun (1483–1544), and Xu Wei (1459–1508) were influential ink-splash flower and bird painters.

**Figure Painting.** During the Five Dynasties and the Ten Kingdoms periods, religious influences in painting began to decline, and the themes of figure painting became increasingly secular. Realism dominated figure painting. During the early part of the Song dynasty, Wu Zongyuan (died 1050) painted religious works in the style of Tang artist Wu Daozi, and Shi Ge (flourished tenth century) and Sun Zhiwei (976–1022) revealed Daoist mysteries in paintings known for their wild and unconventional style. Yet, most Song painters concentrated on secular themes. Among them, Mu Xi and Ruo Feng worked with brevity, clarity, and simplicity, painting at a pace identical to the rapidity of their thought. Liang Kai (circa twelfth or thirteenth centuries) was unconstrained both in his

*Old Trees by a Cold Waterfall* by Wen Zhengming; hanging scroll, 1549 (National Palace Museum, Taipei, Taiwan)

personality and his painting. His style is simple. His method of "reducing" brush strokes is in striking contrast to the style of Li Gonglin (1049–1106), who developed the traditional line-drawing technique and created a simple and clear method of delineation. Song-dynasty figure painting tended to be realistic, exquisite, and vivid, focusing on the personality of the subject. Song painters broadened their subject matter, painting portraits of working people such as peasants, fishermen, and woodcutters. As a result of Mongol suppression and conflicts between the majority and minorities during the Yuan dynasty and the despotism of the early Ming dynasty, painters lost interest in figure painting. Not until late in the Ming period, when the economy developed and the merchant class arose, did figure painting began to revive. Chen Hongshou (1598–1652), the best of the Ming figure painters, developed a style that tended to exaggerate forms and used rounded, vigorous strokes to emphasize the personalities of his subjects. Learning from Western art, Zeng Jing (1566–1650) reformed traditional Chinese painting technique and formed the *Pochenpai* (School of Barbarian Officials), which eventually dominated the field of figure painting.

**Genre Painting.** *Qingming Festival on the River,* painted during the twelfth century by Zhang Zeduan, is an historic painting, which—along with Wang Juzheng's *Weaving,* depicting rural women—contributed a great deal to the development of genre painting. Zhang's painting realistically depicts market life in Kaifeng, the capital of the Northern Song dynasty. The original work was painted on a scroll that was longer than the surviving seventeen feet, which shows in great detail a bustling main thoroughfare crowded with officials, noblewomen, peddlers, laborers, carpenters, and peasants at a festival along the banks of the Bian River. The composition is magnificent and multilayered, offering a grand view as well as subtle portraits. This painting is reminiscent of a mural painted at the Temple of Yanshang during the Jin dynasty (1115–1234). During the Yuan dynasty, figure painting declined among the literati but not folk painters, who depicted human figures on the walls of tombs or temples. The best collections of folk genre paintings are the murals in the Guangshengshi (Temple of Wide Victory) in Hongdong County and in the Yonglegong (Palace of Perpetual Happiness) in Yongji County, both in Shanxi Province.

**Writings about Painting.** During the Yuan dynasty scholarly works on painting theory—such as *Tuhui baojian* (Valuable Examination of Paintings) by Xia Wenyan (flourished thirteenth century) appeared along with scholarly works on painting technique—such as *Xie shanshui jue* (Key to Landscape Painting) by Huang Gongwang and *Huazhupu* (Guide to Bamboo Painting) by Li Gan. Various theories were also scattered in writings by the Yuan Literati, including Zhao Mengfu's claim that brush technique should be the same in painting and calligraphy. During the Ming dynasty, Dong Qichang (1555–1636) accounted for the divergence of the Northern and Southern Schools of painting in his *Huazhi* (The Objective of Painting).

**The Zhe School and the Wu School.** The Ming dynasty endeavored to restore the tradition of the Han emperors (206 B.C.E. – 220 C.E.) and the Song system, which included the restoration of the Painting Academy. Ming despots suppressed the creativity of painters until a group of painters in the Zhejiang area, including Dai Jin (1388–1462) and Wu Wei (1459–1508), developed a new painting style known as the "Zhe School" or the "Northern School." Influenced by the Song-era landscape paintings of Li Tang and Ma Yuan, the Zhe School paid great attention to technique but was not restrained by convention. By the middle of the Ming era the painters of the "Wu School" or "Southern School"—who lived in the area of Suzhou, which was then an economic and cultural center—gradually replaced the Zhe group as the leading school. The Wu School included the so-called Four Masters of Ming painting: Shen Zhou (1427–1509), Wen Zhengming (1470–1559), Tang Yin (1470–1523), and Qiu Yin (flourished sixteenth century). Tang Yin, who was also called Tang Bohu, was called "the first truly great man of the south," and some scholars classify Qiu Yin as a member of the Painting Academy School. The Wu School focused on tradition, technique, and use of brush and ink. Their paintings are poetic, elegant, cultured, and much looser in style than those of the Zhe School. The Zhe School enjoyed a kind of revival in the late Ming era because of the paintings of Lan Ying (1585–1664) and his Martial School (*wulin,* the ancient name of Hangzhou).

**Printmaking.** Printing pictures from carved wooden blocks originated as a tool for preaching during the Sui dynasty (589–618) and rapidly developed during the Song and Yuan dynasties with the rise of new technology and the printing business. Wood-block printing reached new heights in quality and quantity during the Ming dynasty. Realistic, detailed prints were used in all kinds of publications, including novels, plays, classics, history books, biographies, and scientific documents. They were also used to promote plays and novels. Wood-block prints made in Beijing and Jianan are plain and rough and usually placed on the upper half of a page with printed text beneath. Diverging from the "School of Jianan," the "Jinling School" of Nanjing enlarged its prints to a full page. Its style became quite detailed, with sharp and powerful lines, though its human figures were unsophisticated and naive. The best wood-block prints were made by the "School of Hui" in Xinan (Huizhou), Anhui Province. Hui prints include accurately depicted human figures and vivid images. The excellent carving skills of their creators are apparent in their fine lines.

**Sources:**

Cheng Chen-to, Xu Bangda, and Zhang Anzhi, *Qingming shanghe tu yanjiu yu xinshang* (Hong Kong: Scene Press, 1978).

Craig Clunas, *Art in China* (Oxford & New York: Oxford University Press, 1997).

He Yanzhe, *Zhongguo huihua shiyao* (Tianjin, China: People's Arts Press, 2000).

Laurence Sickman and Alexander Soper, *The Art and Architecture of China* (New York: Penguin, 1984).

Michael Sullivan, *The Arts of China,* fourth edition, expanded and revised (Berkeley: University of California Press, 1999).

Nicole Vandier-Nicolas, *Chinese Painting: An Expression of a Civilization,* translated by Janet Seligman (New York: Rizzoli, 1983).

Zhou Baozhu, *"Qingming shanghe tu" yu Qingming shanghe xue* (Kaifeng: Henan University Press, 1996).

*Whispering Pines on a Mountain Path* by Tang Yin; hanging scroll, Ming dynasty, 1368–1644
(National Palace Museum, Taipei, Taiwan)

# PORCELAIN

**Tang Pottery.** The strong economy and effective government of the Tang era (618–907), coupled with the Tang dynasty's openness to foreign influences, stimulated the development of porcelain as early as the seventh century or as late as the early ninth century. The kilns of the Yue region produced greenish-colored porcelain well known for its hardness and craftsmanship. Tang porcelain from the kilns of Xing is white and known for its strength and elegant shapes. The *Tang San Cai* (The Three Colors of Tang), well-known lead glazes developed in the Tang period, allowed the craftsman to decorate porcelain and other ceramics in yellows (ranging to amber and brown), green, and blue. Tang figurines decorated with Tang San Cai are colorful, and their shapes are rounded, natural, and dynamic.

**Song and Yuan Porcelain.** During the Song (960–1279) and Yuan (1279–1368) dynasties, economic growth and the flourishing of the arts established a solid foundation for the development of the porcelain industry. Official and unofficial management systems efficiently organized craftsmen through a highly developed division of labor, which allowed the quality and quantity of porcelain and other ceramics to reach new heights. Combining art, craftsmanship, and utility, many porcelain products appeared in various elegant shapes, bright new colors, and beautiful decorations. Song porcelain in green, white, and black came from many production centers. Ruyao (Ru Kiln), located in and around Linru County of Henan Province, is known for its green porcelain, and the translucent porcelain produced by the official kilns there is exquisite and elegant.

The "shrimp green" of Ruyao is among the best green porcelains. The Guanyao (Official Kiln) was established by the Song court in Kaifeng and moved to Hangzhou during the Southern Song dynasty (1127–1279). The porcelain produced by the Official Kiln has a fine, smooth, even glaze in shades of green and milk white. Its thickness creates a translucent quality. The craftsmen at the Longquanyao (Dragon Fountain Kiln) in Longquan County, Zhejiang Province, were masters of technique and produced porcelain carved in relief and glazed with beautiful colors, mostly shades of green. Craftsmen at another kiln in Longquan County, the Geyao (Brothers' Kiln), invented the popular crackle-glazed porcelain. Jianyao (Strong Kiln) of Chidun Village in Shuiji County, Fujian Province, was the center for black porcelain. The earth there contains a lot of iron, which turns porcelain made from it black during the process of firing and cooling. The black porcelain produced at this site—in patterns with names such as such as *Tuhao* (Rabbit Hair), *Zheguban* (Partridge Speckle), and *Yinxingban* (Silver Star Spots)—had thick, translucent glazes. In contrast, Dingyao (Ding Kiln) in Ding County, Hebei Province, was famous for its white porcelain, which is extremely refined and decorated with various designs and methods of carving.

**Jingdezhenyao from the Yuan to the Ming Eras.** Jingdezhenyao (Jingdezhen Kiln) at Jingdezhen in Jiangxi developed into a major porcelain center during the Yuan dynasty, and official and nonofficial (or folk) kilns sprang up all over the town. Jingdezhen porcelain is characterized by its elegant, exquisite shapes and beautiful glazes. By the Ming dynasty (1368–1644), Jingdezhen porcelain glazes

Green porcelain bottle; Yaozhou ware, circa 1100 (Museum of Oriental Ceramics, Osaka)

Lidded porcelain vase with dragons in blue glaze;
Jingdezhen ware, fourteenth century
(British Museum, London)

huang in Gansu Province, the Longmen (Dragon Gate) Cave in Henan Province, the Tianlongshan (Mountain of the Heavenly Dragon) in Shanxi Province, the cave temple of Binglin near Lanzhou in Gansu Province, and the Qianling tomb in Qianxian County of Shanxi Province. Unlike Buddhist stone sculptures of earlier eras, Tang Buddhist figures are secular, emotional, and possessed of humanized characteristics. For instance, the large Buddha in the Mogao Caves has a full, round face, smiling and wide-spaced eyes, thick lips, and a kindly and affable expression, while in earlier Buddhist sculptures his facial expression is majestic, solemn, and awe inspiring. In addition to the large Buddha, the Mogao caves are filled with many other graceful and touching Buddhist sculptures with clear body lines and expressive facial features. Many are actually portraits of male and female members of the Tang nobility. Among the more than ten caves at Longmen, the most notable sculpture is at the Fengxian (Ancestral Reverence) Temple, completed in 675. The colossal Buddha there is quite symmetrical, full-bodied, and solid. A few folds in his

came in some fifty-seven colors. Craftsmen there also perfected true-white porcelain and a red porcelain, breakthroughs in the history of Chinese ceramics. They also developed methods of underglaze and overglaze painting, which allowed craftsmen to add many more layers of color to porcelain.

**Sources:**
Craig Clunas, *Art in China* (Oxford & New York: Oxford University Press, 1997).

Lan Pu, *Jingdezhen taolu* (Daibei, China: Eastern Culture Press, 1984).

Rosemary E. Scott, ed., *The Porcelains of Jingdezhen* (London: Percival David Foundation of Chinese Art, 1993).

Laurence Sickman and Alexander Soper, *The Art and Architecture of China* (New York: Penguin, 1984).

Michael Sullivan, *The Arts of China,* fourth edition, expanded and revised (Berkeley: University of California Press, 1999).

Wang Qisen, *Zhongguo yishu tongshi* (Jiangsu: Jiangsu Arts Press, 1999).

## SCULPTURE

**Tang Stone Sculpture.** The great economic power and social stability of the Tang dynasty (618–907) provided the necessary environment, manpower, and financing for the creation of large-scale stone carvings and sculptures, including those at the Mogao (Highest) Caves of Dun-

Porcelain phoenix-head ewer; white ware with
green-tinged glaze, circa twelfth century
(British Museum, London)

Located at the midpoint of the Silk Road, the world-renowned Mogao Caves of Dunhuang in Gansu Province comprise 492 manmade caves decorated with many Buddhist paintings, carvings, and sculptures. The earliest caves were begun circa 366–439, and the latest date from the Yuan dynasty (1279–1368).

The golden age of activity at Mogao was during the Tang dynasty (618–907)—the period in which Buddhism was at its height of influence in China—when more than two hundred caves were completed. In general Mogao cave decorations may be described as depictions of four subjects: the Buddhist Paradise, Buddhist stories, Bodhisattvas (Buddhists who have achieved enlightenment), and Buddhist worshippers, including donors and patrons. In addition to revealing much about Buddhist religious beliefs, the cave decorations document information about the daily life, social mores, and aesthetic tastes of their creators. The drawing and composition of the Tang-era murals are refined and elegant. While their religious contents are spiritual and intangible, their forms and style are concrete and mundane. The Buddhist stories Tang artists chose to illustrate often had secular moral messages and appealed to rationality rather than mysticism. They were often entertaining as well and later provided source material for the popular form of folk entertainment known as the genre show. Paradise was the most popular theme, and was usually depicted with great imagination as magnificent, romantic, and harmonious. The plump, extravagantly dressed female figures in many Mogao paintings reveal a Tang aesthetic trend. Magao paintings of the Song era (960–1125) remain in the Tang style. Their scenes are magnificent and drawings are exquisite. One of the best-known paintings is the Guanyin Buddha with a thousand hands and a thousand eyes in cave 3. He has a gentle expression, and each of his thousand hands is in a different posture. Since the painter used the technique of painting before the plaster on the cave wall was dry, the colors are slightly blurred, giving the painting an impressionistic beauty.

Sources: Roderick Whitfield, Susan Whitfield, and Neville Agnew, *Cave Temples of Dunhuang: Art and History on the Silk Road* (London: British Library, 2000).

Peng Huashi, *Art Treasures of Dunhuang* (Beijing: Cultural Objects Press, 1981).

the human beauty of his body. The best-known sculptor of the Tang era is Yang Huizhi.

**Song and Yuan Sculpture.** By the Song (960–1279) and Yuan (1279–1368) dynasties the mysterious element of stone sculptures had faded further and was replaced with realism. Stone carvings became more exquisite, more rigorous, and simpler. The Song sculptures in the Magao Caves have relatively slim bodies and graceful body lines. The forty-three statues of female servants in the Shengmudian (Goddess Hall), built in 1023–1032 at the Jinci (Jin Temple) in Taiyuan, Shanxi Province, are great works of Song sculpture. Each of the bright and life-like painted sculptures has a different posture and expression. The portrayal is subtle, and the body proportions are accurate. The forty statues of arhats (Buddhists who have reached the stage of enlightenment) in the Linyanshi (Spirit Rock Temple) in Changqing, Shandong Province, depict male beauty. Each of the forty arhats is an independent sculpture as well as an integral part of the whole group, with each echoing the others. The statues of arhats in the Baoshengshi (Temple of the Protecting God) in Luzhi, Wu County, Jiangsu Province, are more relaxed and realistic. The sculptor of the great stone carvings of Baoding and Beishan in Sichuan applied techniques borrowed from painters in an exquisite display of carving skill. The secularity of these sculptures far exceeds their religious spirit. The sixteen-

Seated Buddha (with restored head) from T'ien-lung-shan, Shanxi Province, Tang dynasty, 618–907 (Shansi Fogg Art Museum, Cambridge, Massachusetts)

robe skillfully reveal the contours of his body, and his face is full and round. All the other figures at Fengxian also have varied facial expressions. Among them is the Lushena Buddha, a masterpiece of Chinese stone sculpture. His facial expression is vivid and emotional, dignified and kindly, sincere and wise. His right hand is raised to his chest, symbolizing power and stability. The large Buddha at Tianlongshan is magnificent. He looks calm and concerned, and the graceful folds of his clothing fully delineate

Vairocana Buddha flanked by Ananda, Kasyapa, and attendant bodhisattvas, from Feng-hsien-ssu, Lungmen, Honan Province, circa 672–675

meter-high Guanyin in the Duleshi (Temple of Lonely Happiness) in Jixian County, Hebei Province, is the largest existing Song statue.

**Ming Sculpture.** The carving technique of sculptors during the Ming dynasty (1368–1644) was more skillful than that of earlier artists. They used precious materials such as brass and gold and worked in new styles. The Guanyin Buddha with a thousand hands and a thousand eyes at the Chongshanshi (Temple of Holy Goodness) in Taiyuan, Shanxi Province, has a warm and pleasant expression; his hands and eyes are ingeniously made; and his clothing is flowing. The style of Ming arhats is freer than the carving of earlier figures, but, generally speaking, most Ming sculptures are mediocre and lack sophistication.

**Tang Imperial Tomb Sculpture.** Departing from the style of earlier imperial tombs, Tang imperial tombs made use of existing topography. Fifteen of the eighteen Tang imperial tombs were built into hills. Completed in 637, the Zhaoling (Clarity Tomb) of Tang emperor Taizong (ruled 626–649), was constructed in Liquan County, Shanxi Province. Situated between three hills, it was built under the supervision of Yan Lide, elder brother of the poet Yan Liben (died 673), who designed the fourteen stone carvings of foreign noblemen that line the path to the tomb. These figures appear to be doing homage to the emperor, indicating the superior position of the Tang dynasty in the world of that time. The tomb includes the well-known *Six Horses of the Clarity Tomb*, which portrays the emperor's favorite horses, which carried him through many victorious battles. Executed in high relief

and half-round carving, the horses are vivid, powerful, and realistically individualized. The stone sculptures at the Qianling Tomb of Tang emperor Li Zhi (ruled 649–683) and his wife, Empress Wu (ruled 660–704), in the Qian County, Shanxi Province, are grand and noble. In front of the tomb and on the two sides of the path approaching the tomb are sculpted pairs of ornamental columns, lions, flying horses, phoenixes, human figures, tablets, and sixty foreign kings. These sculptures are three-dimensional and convey a sense of motion, demonstrating the clarity of Tang artists' rationalistic concept of the universe.

**Song Tomb Sculpture.** The imperial tombs of the Northern Song dynasty (960–1125) were built in Gong County, Henan Province, at a site selected by geomancy, about 130 kilometers from the Song capital of Kaifeng. Their scale is smaller than that of Tang imperial tombs. Moreover, the scale of Tang tombs and the number and styles of Tang tomb sculptures varied, while those of the Song were quite consistent. Over time, carving of humans and animals at these tombs became increasingly refined, and the figures appear realistic rather than mythic. Expecting that their remains would later be moved back to central China and reburied with those of their ancestors, the emperors of the Southern Song dynasty (1279–1368) constructed temporary tombs without stone sculptures. While the tombs of Northern Song emperors and empresses are separated, those of Southern Song rulers and their wives are situated together on the same axis. The builders of Ming imperial tombs were influenced by this arrangement.

Buddhas in Guanyin Hall at the Duleshi (Temple of Lonely Happiness), Juxian County, Hebei Province, 984

arranged symmetrically on either side. These huge, simply carved statutes have great symbolic and political significance, but aesthetically they lack strength and vitality.

**Pottery and Miniature Sculpture.** The many pottery figurines made during the Tang dynasty are in the traditional style of earlier dynasties but tend to be more rounded and opulent. They are often humorous, and their colors are bright and beautiful. Most of them depict real life. Surviving Song pottery figures do not match those of the Tang in quality or quantity. They continued to be realistic, and—as folk arts began to influence their style—Song pottery figures became more exquisite and lively. Yuan pottery figures gradually lost realism and became more stereotypical. Miniature folk-art figurines of the Ming dynasty were carved from materials such as jade, ivory, wood, bamboo, tree roots, and cores of fruit. The Ming folk artist Xia Baiyan could carve sixteen playing children on a tiny olive pit, each vividly individualized. The "Three Pines"—Zhu Songlin, Zhu Xiaosong, and Zhu Sansong—of Jiading County, Jiangsu Province, were known for their bamboo figures.

**Sources:**

Craig Clunas, *Art in China* (Oxford & New York: Oxford University Press, 1997).

Li Xixing, Chen Zhiqian, Han Wei, and Zhang Chongzin, *Zhaoling wenwu jinghua* (Xian, China: Shanxi People's Arts Press, 1991).

Liu Dunzhen, *Zhongguo gudai jianzhushi* (Taipei, Taiwan: Enlightening Literature Press, 1994).

Ru Jinghua and Peng Hualiang, *Palace Architecture: Ancient Chinese Architecture,* translated by Zang Erzhong and others (Vienna & New York: Springer, 1998).

Shi Yongnan and Wang Tianxing, *Gugong: The Former Imperial Palace in Beijing* (Beijing: China Esperanto Press, 1995).

Laurence Sickman and Alexander Soper, *The Art and Architecture of China* (New York: Penguin, 1984).

Michael Sullivan, *The Arts of China,* fourth edition, expanded and revised (Berkeley: University of California Press, 1999).

Wang Qisen, *Zhongguo yishu tongshi* (Jiangsu, China: Jiangsu Arts Press, 1999).

A tomb completed in 1099 at Baisha (White Sand), in Yu County, Henan Province, is a typical landlord or merchant's tomb. It is built of brick and divided into two rooms. The front room, which was possibly a "living room," forms a "T" shape with the entry path, and the back room, which was perhaps a "bedroom," is hexagonal. The murals and carvings in the tomb depict the life of its resident.

**Ming Imperial Tomb Sculpture.** The scale of Ming imperial tombs approaches that of Tang tombs. Thirteen Ming emperors are buried in Beijing in thirteen tombs built between the early fifteenth century and the mid seventeenth century. This enormous construction project employed huge quantities of manpower and material and followed contemporary Ming architectural designs for palaces, temples, and government buildings. The largest of the Ming tombs in Beijing is the Changling (Long Tomb) of Emperor Chengzu (ruled 1402–1424), completed in 1424. Like the Xiaoling (Filial Piety Tomb) of Emperor Taizu (ruled 1368–1398) in Nanjing, the Changling is approached by a long path with groups of sculptures

## THEATER ARTS: ACROBATICS

**Styles.** During the prosperous Tang period (618–907) many styles of acrobatics appeared, including tightrope walking, pole climbing, horseback acrobatics, mock sword fighting, sword swallowing, fire breathing, and juggling pieces of jade. Some acrobats were also magicians or circus performers with trained monkeys, horses, rhinoceroses, and elephants. Tang acrobatic programs were often an integral part of dance and music shows. Members of ethnic minorities brought new skills to such shows. For example, a Tibetan was able to lie naked on the sharp points of two upright swords. During the Song dynasty (960–1125) military acrobatics were developed. Two of the ten Song armies, the "Left Army" and the "Right Army," were primarily acrobats who raised money and provisions through their public performances. To demonstrate their benevolence, Song emperors announced amnesties every year, and acrobatic shows were considered an essential part of such ceremonies. To the repertoire they inherited from earlier performers, Song-era acrobats added new elements such as the "mute variety play," which included acrobatics and vocal imitations of hundreds of birdcalls. Song-period acrobatics were mingled with dancing, music, and the folk performances known as genre shows. The newly invented gunpowder increased the effectiveness of magic shows. Song circuses included small trained animals such as fish, turtles, birds, bees, butterflies, crickets, and ants. During the Yuan dynasty (1279–1368) ordinary people were forbidden to carry any kind of weapon, though swords and knives were allowed as stage props. Because swords and other weapons were essential to several kinds of acrobatic acts, many acrobats became dramatic performers, and acrobatics began to be absorbed into drama.

**Sources:**

Cai Yuanli and Wu Wenke, *Zhongguo Quyishi* (Beijing: Culture and Arts Press, 1998).

Liu Junxiang, *Zhongguo Zajishi* (Beijing: Culture and Arts Press, 1998).

Wang Kefen, ed., *Zhongguo gudai wudao shihua* (Beijing: People's Music Press, 1998).

Wang Ningning, Jiang Dong, and Du Xiaoqing, *Zhongguo wudaoshi* (Beijing: Culture and Arts Press, 1998).

## THEATER ARTS: DANCE

**Tang Dance.** During the Tang dynasty (618–907) dances were usually performed by one or two people and were divided into two styles: *ranwu* (soft dance) and *jianwu* (vigorous dance). With names such as *lüyao* (green waist) and *chunyingzhuan* (twitter of spring oriole), soft dances were graceful and expressive with relaxed and relatively slow movements. Vigorous dances such as the *jianqi* (sword dance) were powerful and explosive with quick and complicated rhythms. Tang dance absorbed many elements from foreign dances, including the *huxuan* (barbarian spin) and *huteng* (barbarian jump) from western Asia. The barbarian spin was mostly performed by female dancers who could make quick and agile turns. The barbarian jump demonstrated the performer's ability to leap and quickly change steps. Tang actors and actresses also created new dances. *Zhezhiwu* (Cudrania twig), which included dance elements imported from Central Asia, was classed as both soft and vigorous because it is graceful and expressive as well as energetic and unrestrained. It could be performed by one or two dancers or by a group of dancers and required strict training. When a dancer performed it well, her body was so flexible that it seemed to have no bones at all. Three well-known early Tang dances were the *qidewu* (seven virtues dance), *jiugongwu* (nine achievements dance), and *shangyuanwu* (superior primary dance). Following the tradition of previous dynasties, Tang rulers kept at their court many foreign dancers of well-known families, including Mi Jiarong, He Liang, Mi Hejia, and Mi Wanchui.

**Tang Palace Dance.** Tang palace dancers inherited the palace-dance system of the Sui dynasty (589–618) and continued to perform to the accompaniment of music in the categories known as "the nine melodies." Between 637 and 642, a tenth melody, multinational music, was added. The Tang developed dance scores and established a dance school at the *Liyuan* (Pear Garden), where palace musicians were trained. Among the Tang dance programs, the best known was *pozhenyue* (breaking battle array), performed to music played by sitting players and standing players. Tang emperor Taizong (ruled 626–649), who was the Prince of Qin before he became emperor, sketched a *pozhenyue* performance in 633. "The Prince of Qin's Breaking Battle Array" has three sections, each with 120 dancers dressed and armed like warriors. They were accompanied by big drums and vigorous music. In "Longevity of the Majesty" about one hundred colorfully dressed dancers formed the shapes of sixteen Chinese characters extolling the emperor. The "Great Peace," or "Lion Dance of Five Dimensions," was a elaborate version of the folk performance known as the lion dance. The dancers wore fake lion skins and portrayed five lions facing in five directions. Two dancers teased each lion into moods of excitement, indifference, happiness, or anger—all to the accompaniment of instrumental music and 140 singers. The dance section of *nishang yuyi* (rainbow and feather dress), one of the well-known Tang musical entertainments known as grand melody, was performed by dancers dressed like goddesses and was vividly described by the poet Bai Juyi (772–846) in his "Song of Rainbow and Feather Dress." Yang Yuhuan was considered the best performer of this dance. After she became the favorite concubine of Emperor Xuanzong (ruled 712–756), performances of this dance became increasingly elaborate.

**Song Palace Dance.** By the Song dynasty (960–1279) many dances were no longer performed, and the remaining dance programs were reformed and developed. Classic dance programs were performed on a much larger and more elaborate scale and combined singing and speaking parts with dancing. A new dance program, *zhuanta* (stepping repeatedly), appeared. The Song court continued to stage annual *nuoli* (nuo ritual) performances. (Nuo are gods who are able to keep demons away.) Every year the dancers of the palace dance schools performed ritual dances wearing masks of various gods.

**Liao and Jin Dances.** Dancers for the northern Liao dynasty (916–1115) performed many traditional works, especially Tang palace-dance programs, as well as Liao national dances, especially the Liao shaman dance. Following Tang protocol, the Liao court honored foreign emissaries with toasting and entertainments during a feast. After the toasts, foreign emissaries were requested to show their dances. The northern Jin dynasty (1115–1234) absorbed Song dance culture to a great extent and invented a dance called "lyrics linking wing rooms," which separated the roles of dancer and singer.

**Yuan and Ming Dance.** Dance continued to decline during the Yuan dynasty (1279–1368), becoming increasingly absorbed into or replaced by dramatic performances. Large-scale dance performances were influenced by the Yuan mask dance, hunting dance, and Buddhist dance. The best-known Yuan palace dance is "Sixteen Female Demons in Heaven," which the government would not permit to be shown to common people. Another popular Yuan dance is

Pottery figures of a flutist and dancer, Yuan dynasty, 1279–1368 (from Colin Mackerras, *Chinese Theatre*, 1983)

*daola,* meaning "singing and dancing" in the Mongolian language. *Daola* dancers perform to graceful music, attempting to imitate wind and snow while holding bamboo in their mouths and lamps on their heads. Dramatic performances became the main entertainment during the Ming dynasty (1368–1644), and palace dance was largely reserved for ceremonial activities. Meanwhile, many folk dances and the dances of minority cultures were introduced at court.

**The Rise of Folk Dancing.** During the Song dynasty there emerged large folk-dance troupes that combined dance, music, martial arts, and acrobatics into shows they performed during holidays in the outdoor entertainment areas called spontaneous markets. Their dances included the *wuxuan* (spinning dance), based on the skill of spinning fibers into thread; a barbarian musical dance; *shuadatou* (tease the monk), a humorous dance inspired by a Ming marvel tale about a monk; and the *huagu* (flower-drum dance), one of the most popular dances. The dancers beat a drum while singing and dancing vigorous, unrestrained, and sophisticated steps. There were a total of twelve sets in the flower drum dance. The bold, powerful, and graceful *wujian* (sword dance) began evolving from martial arts in the Han dynasty (206 B.C.E. – 220 C.E.) and had become an exquisite dance by the Tang era. It has been said that many calligraphers absorbed the elements of the sword

dance into their writings. *Wupan* (dancing judge) was about an ugly god destined to eliminate demons, and in *puqizi* (play with flags) dancers with colorful army flags depicted battle scenes. Other folk dances included *chuntianle* (happy farmland and village), *hanlongzhou* (land-dragon boat), *zhumaer* (bamboo horse), *shizailang* (ten Zailang officials), *baolao* (old Bao), *baoluo* (hold gongs), *manpai* (barbarian tune), *tage* (go to songs), *shiziwu* (lion dance), *yaogu* (waist drum), *liangsanwu* (sunshade-umbrella dance), *huabanwu* (flower-plate dance), and *tengpaiwu* (cane shield dance). Folk-dance dramas of the Tang era, such as *tayaoniang* (stepping and singing woman), *botou* (move with head), and *damian* (big face) were the predecessors to later, full-fledged theater plays. Beautiful and talented female folk dancers were often called to palaces to perform. The Tai minority's dances included *chelile* (happiness in a wagon), *kongquewu* (peacock dance), and *mianyue* (Burmese music). The Zhuang minority performed the *dazhuangwu* (pile-driving dance). The Miao minority had the *lushengwu* (reed-pipe dance), *guwu* (drum dance), and *tiaoyue* (jumping on the moon). The Yi minority loved its traditional torch festival, during which people danced *Axi tiaoyue* (Axi jumping on moon), *sanyuesan* (third of March), and *tiaozuojiao* (jump with the left foot). The Yao and Tu minorities were fond of the *changguwu* (long-drum dance) and *baishouwu* (sway-hand dance). Mongol dances spread widely during the Yuan dynasty, including *daola*, a "mast dance," and a shaman dance known as *andaiwu* (peace-spokesman dance). The *taipinggu* (great-peace drum) dance and *mangshiwu* (rash dance) were legacies from the Manchu minority. The Tibetans often stood hand in hand in a circle and performed the *tiaoguozhuang* (dance around the hearth). They also liked the *xuanziwu* (string dance), *reba*, and *mianjuwu* (mask dance). Tibetan palace-feast dances included the *naoma* and an ardent *duixie* (tap dance).

**Sources:**

Liu Junxiang, *Zhongguo Zajishi* (Beijing: Culture and Arts Press, 1998).

Wang Kefen, *Zhongguo wudao fazhanshi* (Shanghai, China: Shanghai People's Press, 1989).

Wang, ed., *Zhongguo gudai wudao shihua* (Beijing: People's Music Press, 1998).

Wang Ningning, Jiang Dong, and Du Xiaoqing, *Zhongguo wudaoshi* (Beijing: Culture and Arts Press, 1998).

Zang Yibing, *Zhongguo yinyueshi* (Wehan, China: University Press of Survey Drawing and Science Technology, 1999).

## THEATER ARTS: DRAMA

**The Rise of Drama.** The beginning of Chinese drama may be located in the *zaju* (variety play) of the Song era (960–1279), which evolved over a long period from primitive songs and dances and many ancient palace and folk shows. Theater art of the Song period is generally categorized as Northern variety play or Southern drama.

**Origins of the Northern Variety Play.** The Northern variety play emphasized comedy and dialogue and inherited characteristics from court- and folk-dance dramas such as *tayaoniang* (stepping and singing woman), *botou* (move with head), and *damian* (big face), as well as the *canjunxi* (adjutant play), a sort of skit with musical accompaniment, which by the Song era already had many theatrical elements. By the Northern Song dynasty (960–1125) characters in an adjutant play were no longer limited to two, and instrumental and vocal music were incorporated into the plot. A genre known as "multiple palace tunes," invented by actor Kong Sanchuan during the middle of the Northern Song dynasty, reached its maturity with *Xixiangji zhugongdiao* (The Western Chamber—Multiple Palace Tunes) by Dong Jieyuan (flourished 1190–1208). Sometimes called the father of the Northern variety play, Dong arranged various palace tunes into several suites and interspersed them with spoken dialogue to tell a story. The play was structured on a large scale and developed characters in much detail. Meanwhile, the *washi* (spontaneous market), which also developed during the Song era, provided theater art with a stimulating milieu for its development. The spontaneous market was an outdoor entertainment center that usually had several dozen stages and entertainment tents, some large enough to hold several thousand people. By the Southern Song dynasty (1127–1368) the Northern variety play was strictly systematized. Usually the main play consisted of a single and complete story in four acts or song sequences. Only the protagonist, either male or female, sang the songs. This *zhengzaju* (core variety play) was preceded by a *yanduan* (colorful piece) that included dialogue, martial arts, dance, songs, and

various means to attract an audience. It was often, but not always, followed by *zaban* (variety acts) such as comic patter and dancing. The *zhengzaju* included music in the form of palace or Buddhist melodies, as well as humorous dialogue. There were usually five characters: the *moni* (male protagonist), the *yintou* (introducer, who also often played the female character), *fujing* (the object of teasing), the *fumo* (teaser), and the *zhuanggu* (official). Song variety plays were rich and colorful but were more loosely structured than variety plays of the Yuan dynasty (1279–1368), which were cohesively plotted dramas. The *yuanben*, a Jin dynasty (1115–1234) version of the variety play, was even more important than the *zaju* to the development of the Yuan variety play. Nearly seven hundred Jin variety plays were written, as opposed to fewer than three hundred Song variety plays. The Jin plays had more interesting stories than those of the Song, and many—such as *Zhuangzhoumeng* (The Dream of Zhuangzhou), *Chibi aobing* (The Fierce Battle at Red Cliff), *Du Fu youchun* (Du Fu's Spring Tour), and *Zhangsheng zhuhai* (Mr. Zhang Boils the Ocean)—were adapted for later variety plays.

**Yuan Variety Plays.** The variety play reached its full development in the Yuan era, during which some two hundred playwrights wrote about seven hundred to eight hundred plays, of which only 530 have survived intact. The subjects of these plays may be divided into several categories: crimes and lawsuits or corrupt versus honest officials; love and marriage; religion and the supernatural; family and ethics; and revenge and the bandit-hero.

**The Four Masters of the Yuan Variety Play.** Guan Hanqing (circa 1213 – circa 1297), Wang Shifu (flourished late thirteenth and early fourteenth centuries), Ma Zhiyuan (circa 1250 – 1324), Ji Junxiang (flourished late thirteenth century) were called the "Four Masters" of Yuan variety plays. The greatest of these playwrights is Guan Hanqing, who wrote about sixty-seven plays, including *Dou E yuan* (Snow in Midsummer), a classic Chinese tragedy. Eighteen of Guan's plays are extant. Wang Shifu wrote fourteen plays, of which only three have survived in complete form. One is his version of *Xixiangji* (The Western Chamber), based on a well-known marvel tale, "The Story of Yingying (Little Oriole)" by Yuan Zhen (779–831), which was earlier the basis for Dong Jieyuan's *The Western Chamber—Multiple Palace Tunes*. The best of the Yuan romantic dramas, Wang's play is the love story of a beautiful girl, Cui Yingying, and the talented young Zhang Junrui, who falls in love with her in defiance of feudal tradition and values. The play challenged and satirized conventional ethics, extolling the sacred nature of pure love and advocating freedom of choice in marriage. Wang was a master of dramatic language. He employed the vernacular with occasional and sometimes witty recourse to poetic and historical terms. Ma Zhiyuan wrote thirteen plays, of which seven are extant. His best work is *Hangongqiu* (Autumn in the Han Palace), the story of patriotic princess Wang Zhaojun, who is married to a foreign ruler to make peace with that country and ends up committing suicide after her mission. Ma used graceful, pure language and was a master of expressing feelings. Ji Junxiang wrote six plays, of which only *Zhaoshi*

Illumination of a scene from the play *Western Chamber,* Yuan dynasty, 1279–1368
(from Bradley Smith and Wan-go Weng, *China: A History in Art,* 1973)

*guer* (The Orphan of Zhao) has survived. The play is based on a classic story about people who sacrifice themselves and their child to rescue the orphan of the Zhao family. The play is a pioneering tragedy and was one of the first Chinese plays to be translated into a European language. Another well-known Yuan playwright was Bai Pu (1226–1306), who wrote sixteen plays, of which only two survive. His *Wutongyu* (Rain on the Plantain Tree) is a dramatic version of Tang poet Bai Juyi's "The Song of Everlasting Sorrow," about the fatal love between Tang emperor Xuanzong (ruled 712–756), also known as Minghuang, and his concubine Yang Yuhuan. Bai's *Qiangtou mashang* (Over the Wall and on Horseback) is a comedy about the elopement of a young couple who fell in love at first sight. Playwrights of the late Yuan era include Zhen Guangzu, Qin Jianfu, Qiao Jie, and Gong Tianxiang. Yuan playwrights produced many plays that employed stories from the novel *Water Margins,* of which more than thirty sur-

vive, including eight by Gao Wenxiu, who took Li Kui from *Water Margins* as his protagonist.

**The Rise of Southern Drama.** A famine in the North, the shift of the economic center from the North to the South, and the restoration of the civil-examination system that attracted literati away from dramatic activities—as well as an ossification of the Northern variety play—all contributed to its decline in the early fourteenth century, after it had prospered for a century. It was gradually replaced by Southern drama. Originally called "the variety play of Wenzhou" or "the variety play of Yongjia," the Southern drama or variety play developed from traditional folk song and folk dance and absorbed elements of Song music and lyrics. One of the few surviving early Southern Song dramas, the anonymous *Zhangxie Zhuangyuan* (Top Graduate Zhangxie), does not have separate sections like those of Song-era Northern variety plays. Rather, all parts of *Top Graduate Zhangxie* are smoothly interconnected with dances and songs. These Southern plays synthesize various performing arts and stage methods, and give all the characters, not just the protagonist, a chance to sing, solo, in duets, or in the chorus. The appearance of *Pipaji* (The Lute Song) by Gao Zecheng (circa 1301 – 1370, also known as Gao Ming) marked the maturity of the Southern drama. The play is about Cai Boxie, whose father forces him to leave his parents and wife to take the civil examination. After he gets the highest score, he is forced to take an official position and to marry the daughter of the prime minister. Eventually, the wrong is corrected by the prime minister after he witnesses the filial piety of Cai and his former wife toward his now-deceased parents. *The Lute Song* successfully unfolds two twisted and contrasting plotlines, exhibiting none of the disorder and monotony of previous Southern dramas. It also led to the reorganization of song sets. As a result of such reforms, Southern drama became characterized by intriguing plots, humorous and intelligent dialogue, resonant arias, penetrating music, appropriate and graceful dancing, colorful costumes, and exquisite stage design—offering its audiences an exciting experience. Yet, Southern drama received less attention than Northern drama and was even suppressed because it was folk drama and often exposed and criticized the injustice and corruption of the ruling class. The total number of Southern plays was perhaps 150, but most of them are lost.

**Four *Chuanqi* Masterpieces.** The term *chuanqi* originally referred to the marvel tales of Tang-era fiction, but it was later used in reference to a dramatic form that reached its peak during the Ming dynasty (1368–1644). Differing from Southern drama, the marvel-tale play was long, and had a complicated plot and a fixed structure. It followed stricter rules than the Southern drama and—unlike the Southern drama, which has no internal divisions—it was divided into scenes. Four anonymous plays are considered the greatest marvel tales. *Jingchai ji* (The Thorn Hairpin) and *Baiyue ting* (The Moon Prayer Pavilion) are about a man who has to leave behind his loyal wife, who suffers maltreatment rather than betray him during his absence. *Baitu ji* (The White Rabbit) portrays the unconditional and eternal love between mother and son. In *Shagou ji* (Killing a Dog) a wife kills a dog to persuade her husband to leave fox-like and dog-like "friends" and restore harmony with his brother. Unlike previous, tragic Southern dramas that portray the male protagonist as a greedy and ungrateful betrayer of his wife, all these plays have happy endings in which virtuous women are rewarded. These plays reflected the changing morality of the Ming era, which was influenced by neo-Confucianism and reinforced the dominant role of the man and the subordinate role of the woman in the family and society.

**The Height of Ming Drama.** After the middle of the Ming era, when drama critic Li Zhi (1527–1602) denounced neo-Confucianism and advocated human rights and individual freedom, Southern drama reached its high point. Meanwhile, the Northern variety play became more like the Southern play. More than five hundred plays by more than one hundred playwrights were written during the Ming dynasty. Of these, some 180 plays have survived. The overall quality of Ming plays is far below that of Yuan plays. Notable late-Ming plays included *Du Fu youchun* (Du Fu's Spring Tour) by Wang Jiusi (1468–1551), *Zhongshanlang* (The Wolf of Mount Zhong) by Kang Hai (1475–1540), the 4-play cycle *Sishengyuan* (Four Shrieks of a Monkey) by Xu Wei (1521–1593), *Baojianji* (The Story of a Sword) by Li Kaixian (1502–1568), *Huangshaji* (Washing Gauze) by Liang Chenyu (circa 1521 – circa 1594), *Yuzanjin* (The Story of a Jade Hairpin) by Gao Lian (late sixteenth century), *Yiwenqian* (One Penny) by Xu Fuzhuo (1560–?), *Yuyang sannong* (Three Plays of Yuyang) by Shen Zizhi (1591–1641), and the anonymous *Mingfengji* (The Story of a Singing Phoenix).

**Tang Xianzu and the "Linchuan School."** The greatest Ming playwright was Tang Xianzu (1550–1616) from Linchuan in Jiangxi Province, who was renowned for a group of plays known as "The Four Dreams of Linchuan." One of Tang's "Four Dreams," *Mudanting* (The Peony Pavilion), has fifty-five scenes and focuses on the love story of Liu Mengmei, a young scholar, and Du Liniang, the daughter of a high official. Du falls asleep in her family's garden and dreams that she has an affair with an ideal lover in the Peony Pavilion. After awakening, she becomes lovesick and dies from a broken heart. Before she dies she draws a self-portrait. Having discovered the self-portrait near Du's grave, Liu begins longing for Du, whose soul has been freed by the sympathetic judge of the underworld. After she appears in Liu's dream, Liu exhumes her body, brings her back to life, and marries her. Later Du sends Liu to find her parents, who were lost during the Tartar invasion. Du's father cannot believe that his daughter has been resurrected nor can he forgive her for marrying without his permission. Eventually, however, an imperial intervention brings reconciliation and reunion. Tang never established a dramatic school or movement, but his influence on his contemporaries was so profound that many playwrights from different regions claimed to belong to the "School of Linchuan."

**Shen Jing and the School of Wujiang.** Shen Jing (1553–1610) of Wujiang in Jiangsu Province challenged Tang's dramatic style, stimulating the development of theories on drama and marvel tales. Shen criticized Tang's stress on lyric sentiments and his characters' passions to the extent that he neglected rhyme and versification. A master of metrical rules, Shen angered Tang by revising his *Peony Pavilion*. Except for *Yixiaji* (The Righteous Chivalry), which was fairly popular, Shen's seventeen plays lack imagination and passion. He was most respected for his *Nanjiugong shisandiao qupu* (Thirteen Tables of Southern Prosody) and became the leader of the School of Wujiang. It included many well-known playwrights, including Feng Menglong (1574–1646), Ruan Dacheng (1587–1646), Wu Bing (died 1646), and Meng Chengshun (flourished 1600–1640).

Sources:

Cai Yuanli and Wu Wenke, *Zhongguo Quyishi* (Beijing: Culture and Arts Press, 1998).

Ma Wenqi, Xie Yongjun, and Song Bo, *Zhongguo Xiqushi* (Beijing: Culture and Arts Press, 1998).

Colin Mackerras, *Chinese Drama: A Historical Survey* (Beijing: New World Press, 1990).

Mackerras, ed., *Chinese Theater: From Its Origins to the Present Day* (Honolulu: University of Hawaii Press, 1983).

Victor H. Mair, ed., *The Columbia Anthology of Traditional Chinese Literature* (New York: Columbia University Press, 1994).

Meng Kui, *Xiqu wenxue: A Comprehensive Art Held by Language (Dramatic Literature: Yuyan tuoqi de zonghe yishu)* (Guilin, China: Guangxi Normal University Press, 2000).

Stephen Owen, ed. and trans., *An Anthology of Chinese Literature, Beginning to 1911* (New York: Norton, 1996).

Xu Muyun, *Zhongguo Xiqushi (The History of Chinese Drama)*, edited and translated by Duo Zai (Shanghai: Shanghai Ancient Books, 2001).

Zhang Peiheng and Luo Yuming, eds., *Zhongguo wenxueshi* (Shanghai: Fudan University Press, 1996).

## THEATER ARTS: THE GENRE SHOW

**The Tang and Song Genre Show.** The *quyi* (genre show) is a folk-art performance including elements such as ballad singing, storytelling, comic dialogues, and clapper talks. The genre show originated during the Tang dynasty (618–907) when Buddhists discovered that they were more successful with the masses when they sang Buddhist texts, using music to attract audiences. This earliest form of genre show is called *zhuanbian,* which means "singing Buddhist texts"; *bian* refers to the murals in Buddhist temples, and *bianwen* (Buddhist scripts) initially referred to the all-genre shows from Dunhuang literature in Gansu Province. A thorough study of Dunhuang literature, however, revealed that another form of folk drama, the *shuohua* (storytelling show), existed during the Tang era and was already quite advanced. It differed from the early *zhuanbian* mostly in having secular rather than religious content. In the early *zhuanbian* the singer used Buddhist paintings to illustrate his subject. Later, there emerged *subian* (secularized Buddhist texts)—mainly telling historical, folk, and contemporary tales—and improved acting skills made the use of Buddhist paintings unnecessary. *King Geshaer* is a Tibetan epic without written text that has been told and passed on by genre-show actors from generation to generation. It includes more than sixty stories and more than a million lines of song lyrics, which is the longest among the world's epics. All its song tunes are derived from one melody.

**Song Genre Shows.** During the Song dynasty (960–1279), genre shows gradually moved from the court to urban areas, following the development of the spontaneous market, an urban amusement area with stages and entertainment tents. The subjects of Song genre shows could be secular, military, religious, or historic. Several forms of genre-show performances developed during the Song era. *Guzici* (poetic drum) was singing with or without spoken

Detail of a handscroll depicting storytellers and puppeteers entertaining city dwellers, fourteenth century
(Art Institute of Chicago)

lines, accompanied by the drum and including only one kind of melody. Zhang Wuniu, an actor of the Southern Song era (1227–1279), developed the *changzhuan* (singing show) from the *guban* (wooden drums) performances of the Northern Song (960–1125). The singing show was accompanied by metal and wooden drums as well as flutes. It had two forms: *chanling* (winding lyrics), which had an introduction and a coda and could use several melodies, and *chanda* (winding expression), which had an introduction but no coda and used only two alternating melodies. The singing show required advanced performance skills because its music was complex and hard to play. Kong Sanchuan, an actor of the Northern Song era, invented the *zhugong-diao* (multiple palace tunes), a large-scale genre show that included some spoken lines with the singing. This style of genre show could tell a long story with a complicated plot and had a profound influence on the later development of Chinese drama. The *huolanger* (peddler) show was derived from the hawking of peddlers in the streets. It always began and ended with a tune called "peddler," with other tunes in between. Urbanites were fond of *yaci* (boundless lyrics), which were relatively graceful. *Taozhen* (real selection), whose form and content appealed to the common folk, was popular among peasants. *Sanqu* (loose melody) mostly depicted love affairs and sentiments such as disappointment, sorrow at parting, and world-weary pessimism. The loose melody usually had no plot. It could be long or short and was accompanied by string and wind instruments but no drums. It had three forms: a *xiaoling* (minor songs), or *yeer* (leaves), has a single, short, and vigorous melody; a *daiguoqu* (take along tune) has two or three melodies in sequence; and a *santao* (loose set) combines from three to thirty palace tunes and melodies into one set. *Rewafu kexiake* is a Uighur genre show that originated during the Song dynasty and is still popular in northwest China. One to three actors sing stories with short rhyming lyrics in the Uighur language to the accompaniment of a Uighur musical instrument called the *rewafu*.

**Jin and Yuan Genre Shows.** In the North during the Jin (1115–1234) and Yuan dynasties (1279–1368) genre-show forms became much more diverse, expanding to include various kinds of narrative storytelling. *Manasi*, one of three national epics performed as a genre show during the Jin and Yuan periods, depicted the life of the Aerkezi people, who lived in northwest China. How this drama was originally performed is undocumented, but it may have been similar in style to the *Manasi* that is still popular in the northwestern areas of Xinjiang Province.

**Ming Genre Shows.** By the Ming dynasty (1368–1644) many kinds of genre shows had developed into their final forms. In the northern *Gugu* (drum melody) show a single actor told a story while accompanying himself with drumbeats. The *paiziqu* (well-known melody) show combined various popular songs. The instruments used for the show also varied according to which songs were sung. The *qinshu* (string talking) show was performed with a *yangqin*, which is similar to a zither with several sets of strings that are struck rather than plucked. In the late Ming period there were two kinds of *cihua* (lyric storytelling). In the North, *mupi guci* (wood-and-skin-drum lyrics) shows were narrated by actors such as the popular Jia Fuxi (1590–1674), who told stories about Chinese history from prehistoric times to the days of the last Ming emperor. In the South, *tanci* (singing lyrics), which had evolved from the *taozhen* (real selection) of the Song era, was popular. It had various forms and was performed by blind singers accompanied by a small drum and string instruments. *Yugu daoqing* (fish-drum singing) evolved from Daoist songs sung a capella during the Tang and Song eras; by the Ming era they were accompanied by the rhythmic beating of a fish-shaped bamboo drum and a wooden clapper. *Shefuqian*, or *shibuqian* (busy show), quite popular in the South during the late Ming period, was performed by a single actor, who used his hands and one foot to play many gongs and drums while he sang. *Lianhuayue* (lotus music), or *lianhualuo* (lotus falling), was originally Buddhist "spreading flower" music, which was sung and widely disseminated by beggars. It was sung by one person—or occasionally two people—who accompanied himself with percussion instruments. The *taoli* (epic) and *haolaibao* (linked songs) were popular Mongolian genre shows. The *taoli* originated during the seventh century and reached its present form early in the thirteenth century. Still popular in Inner Mongolia, it is spoken or sung or a combination of both, and it is accompanied by string music. The epic is usually extremely long. In fact, each actor plays in only part of the epic and none can remember the entire epic from beginning to end. *Haolaibao* originated during the Yuan dynasty and became popular during the Ming period. It is performed by one person, or several people, who sit and sing to string accompaniment. Liu Jingting (circa 1587 – 1670), a student of the well-known genre-show master Mo Houhuang (flourished 1600), was the most popular late-Ming genre-show actor.

**Publications on the Genre Show.** Five documents that appeared during the Song era include important information relating to the genre show. Volumes two and five of *Dongjing menghualu* (The Record of the Splendid Dream in the East Capital), written in 1147 by Meng Yuanlao, recorded the locations of spontaneous markets and information about various performers and genre shows from 1102 to 1125. Parts 1, 7, and 8 of *Ducheng jisheng* (The Record of the Prosperity of the Capital City), written in 1235 by Nai Dewong, provided similar information. *Xihu Laoren fanshenglu* (The Record of an Old Man from the Western Lake), written between 1241 and 1252 by Xihu Laoren, covered much of the same ground but in more detail. Volumes nineteen and twenty of *Mengliangglu* (The Record of a Dream), written in 1274 by Wu Zimu, are about genre shows. Written early in the Yuan era, volumes three and six of *Wulin jiushi* (The Old Story of Martial Arts Masters), by Zhou Mi, includes much information about genre shows. During the Jin and Yuan dynasties there appeared many works of Song genre-show scripts—

including *Xinbian wudaish pinghua* (The New History of Storytelling) and *Xinkan da Song Xuanhe yishi* (The New Legacies of the Great Song)—as well as a collection of Yuan scripts, *Quanxiang pinghua wuzhong* (The Complete Five Storytelling Scripts). Theoretical works on the genre show were also written during the Yuan period. In his twenty-volume *Zuiwong tanlu* (The Conversation of a Drinker), Luo Ye discussed the genre show and the performing arts in general and established new training and technical standards for actors and actresses. Hu Zhijue listed nine standards for actresses in his *Zishan daquanji* (Complete Collection of Purple Hill).

**Sources:**

Cai Yuanli and Wu Wenke, *Zhongguo Quyishi* (Beijing: Culture and Arts Press, 1998).

Ma Wenqi, Xie Yongjun, and Song Bo, *Zhongguo Xiqushi* (Beijing: Culture and Arts Press, 1998).

Colin Mackerras, *Chinese Drama: A Historical Survey* (Beijing: New World Press, 1990).

Mackerras, ed., *Chinese Theater: From Its Origins to the Present Day* (Honolulu: University of Hawaii Press, 1983).

Xu Muyun, *Zhongguo Xiqushi (The History of Chinese Drama)*, edited and translated by Duo Zai (Shanghai: Shanghai Ancient Books, 2001).

Zang Yibing, *Zhongguo yinyueshi* (Wehan, China: University Press of Survey Drawing and Science Technology, 1999).

## WESTERN AND EASTERN CULTURAL EXCHANGE

**Background.** The prosperity of China during the Tang dynasty (618–907) may be partially attributed to the development of the Silk Road and other land and water routes to the West as early as the Han period (206 B.C.E. – 220 C.E.). By 649 China controlled Kucha and Khotan in Central Asia and was beginning to conquer Korea (then known as Great Silla). By that time the Chinese had also established relations with Japan, as well as Funan and Champa in Southeast Asia. Between 629 and 645 the great Chinese theologian Xuanzang traveled in India and then brought home the texts of Mahayana Buddhism as well as Buddhist culture. By the middle of the eighth century, Zoroastrianism, Manichaeanism, Nestorian Christianity, and Islam had all arrived in China from the Near East and were established in Chang'an, the capital of the Tang dynasty. Prince Shotoku of Nara, Japan, sent his first embassy, led by Ono-no-Imoko, to China in 607. The prince sent another the following year and a third in 614. Between 630 and 838, Japan sent thirteen missions to China, each with several hundred people—including monks, officials, painters, musicians, doctors, and students—thus establishing a cultural bridge between the two countries. Many Japanese visitors, including the Nara monks Saicho (767–822), Kukai (774–835), and Ennin (flourished 838–847), as well as Kamakura monk Dogen (1200–1253), visited China and took Chinese literature and artwork back to Japan. Eisai (1141–1215), a Heian monk, returned to Japan with tea in 1191. Among the most distinguished Japanese visitors to China was Kibi-no-Mabi, who went to China in 717 and spent seventeen years at Chang'an. He went back to Japan with the art of embroidery, the *biwa* (a four-stringed lute),

and the game of *go* (Chinese chess). After his return home, he invented *kana*, which employs simplified Chinese characters phonetically to represent sounds in Japanese that are similar to the Chinese words the characters signify.

**Music.** The main instruments used to play the *duobuyue* (multinational) music of the Tang period all developed from instruments that had been brought to China from Persia, India, and Egypt. Some parts of the music itself are Indian, Central Asian, Korean, and Uighur. *Da Qin Jingjiao liuxing Zhongguobei* (The Popular Chinese Melodies of Nestorianism of the Great Qin), discovered at an excavation near Xian in 1625, and other so-called Nestorian hymn scripts discovered at the Dunhuang Cave in 1900 were brought to China from Persia during the eighth century. The arrival in China of the Nestorian Christian hymn, which influenced Daoist music, is the first instance of Sino-Western musical exchange. During the Song (960–1279) and Yuan (1279–1368) dynasties a Chinese two-stringed lute evolved from a Muslim three-stringed instrument. Around 1260–1263 a pipe organ was imported from the West via Central Asia to be used only for palace feasts. Western missionaries introduced the piano and the Western stave and scale to China. Musical exchanges with Japan, Korea, India, and Thailand were common. "Nishang yuyi" (Rainbow and Feather Dress), composed by Tang emperor Xuanzong (ruled 712–756), is a version of an Indian Brahman melody. The music for the Tang-era dance *pozhenyue* (breaking battle array) was lost in China but preserved in Japan, where it was taken by Litian Zhenren. In 716 a twenty-two-year-old Japanese student named Jiebei Zhenbei took home to Nara a piece of music for a brass band, writings on how to compose band music, and ten volumes of *Yongle yaolu* (The Important Record of Yongle), a collection of important music from the Yongle reign. Japanese official Tenyuan Zhenmin, who was sent to Tang China in 835, spent several years taking lute lessons in Chang'an and Yangzhou. Upon his departure for Japan his teacher in Chang'an sent him two lutes and ten volumes of music, including *Piba zhudiaozi pin* (Various Types of Lute Melody). In the imperial warehouse at Nara many Chinese musical instruments that have disappeared in China were preserved. Volume 347 of *Da Ribenshi* (Great Japanese History) recorded information about various forms of Chinese music. Various kinds of music were imported by Japan, where the Japanese government encouraged musicians to study and play it. Japanese palace-feast music includes Chinese and Korean elements. Chinese music also greatly impacted medieval Japanese pastoral music. The popular Japanese "Ming and Qing Music" was based on Chinese melodies imported into Japan during those dynasties (1368–1644 and 1644–1912).

**Dance and Acrobatics.** Tang dances included many from the West. For example, *fulinwu* (stroking forest) was from the Byzantine Empire. Many Chinese acrobatic routines were introduced into Central Asia, Korea, and Japan. *Tangwuhui* (The Record of Tang Dance), a Japanese book that has been lost, is said to have recorded more than fifty dance, magic, and acrobatic routines. Nanzhao (Yunnan) and Burma sent dance teams to the Tang court to present their dances, and there was a dance called *piaoguoyue* (Burma music) in southwestern China. Various lion dances were performed in China, Korea, and Japan and influenced each other.

**Arts and Architecture: The West.** The Tang capital of Chang'an was well known in the West. It was called *Khomdan, Khamdan,* or *Kamdan* by the Arabs, *Khoubdan* by the Byzantines, and *Kumdan* by the Syrians. The influence of Manichaeanism may be seen in a Tang bronze mirror decorated in a "lion and grape" design that was popular for a short time before the suppression of foreign religions in 843–845. By the early fourteenth century, Iranian artists had been profoundly influenced by Chinese arts. Persian painters began to paint in the Chinese ink-and-wash style. Later painters in the Near East imitated Chinese paintings of flowers, birds, and animals. Chinese designs of dragons, phoenixes, and unicorns became popular decorations in Persian paintings, buildings, and rugs. Design elements such as the flying goose, the cloud and storm, curved lines, the keyhole, the heart shape, the apple (symbolizing peace), the peach (symbolizing longevity), and the yin-yang symbol also appeared in Persian artworks.

**Arts and Architecture: The East.** During the eighth century, Tang arts and architecture flourished at the Japanese city of Nara. The Horyuji Buddhist temple of Nara, built circa 670, was constructed in the Chinese architectural style of that period. Chinese architectural influence in Japan is also apparent in the Kondo (Golden Hall) of the Toshodaiji, which was founded around 759 by the Chinese monk Ganjin (Jianzhen in Chinese), who went to Japan in 754. The Kondo has the solidity, symmetry, and grandeur of Tang architectural style. As in China, the shape of the heavy roofs and the system of brackets supporting the roofs of the Buddhist temples at Nara contribute greatly to the aesthetics of the building. The Shinto shrines of Heian, Japan, were mostly influenced by Chinese architectural style as well. The great Tang Buddhist bronzes have all been lost, but they are thought to have resembled those in the Nara temples. The most ambitious Nara temple is the Todaiji, which was designed to rival the great Chinese foundations. It contained a remarkable imperial repository of about ten thousand objects, many of them from China. A "Feather Lady" portrayed on a screen loved by a Japanese emperor is identical to the typical opulent female sculpture excavated from Tang tombs. One of the Japanese imperial treasures, *The Imperial Portrait of the Sainted Prince De,* was enormously influenced by Tang figure painting. Song paintings imported by Japan continued to influence Japanese artists. During the thirteenth century the paintings of Fa Chang were exhibited in Japan, and the Japanese called him the "Great Benefactor of Painting." The Jianfosi (Temple of the Healthy Buddha) in Chang'an was influenced by the Indian *sikhara,* or tower of stone. The influence of Indian style may also be seen in the Treasure Pagoda of the Foguang Shizheng (Temple of Buddhist Light) on the Wutaishan (Mountain of Five Terraces)

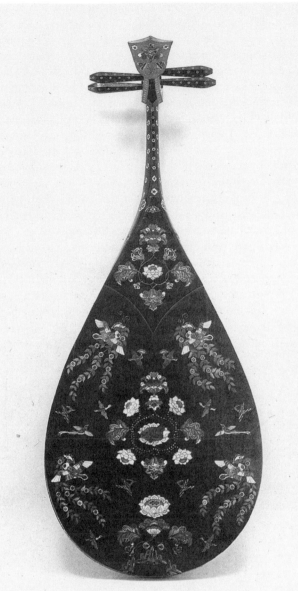

Four-string *pipa,* a type of lute of Iranian origin, circa 700 (from Patricia Buckley Ebrey, *Cambridge Illustrated History of China,* 1996)

in Shanxi Province. Wu Daozi (circa 688 – 758) used a shadow technique in his paintings that Chinese painters learned from Indian artists.

**Ceramics and Textiles.** The shapes and motifs of Tang ceramics reveal strong foreign influences. Chinese stoneware adapted the shape of the Hellenistic amphora. The Tang rhyton (a drinking vessel shaped like an animal or an animal head) was often a copy of an old Persian shape, and many Tang burial figures have a Persian appearance. In 851 *The Story of China and India,* a book in Arabic by an unknown author, probably of Basra, informed its readers about the quality of Chinese pottery. The shape of the Tang circular bottle appeared in the blue-glazed pottery of Parthian Persia and Syria. Fragments of white ware from China have been found in Japan, Korea, Indonesia, Sri Lanka, India, Pakistan,

Iran, Iraq, Syria, and Egypt. Egyptians, Iranians, Iraqis, and Syrians all learned to make Chinese-style porcelain. Chinese phoenix pictures were copied on Persian ceramics. A Japanese scholar, Sanshang Cinan, named the ocean route from China to western Asia the "Porcelain Road." By the Song dynasty Chinese porcelain was exported to more countries, including Vietnam, Cambodia, Thailand, Brunei, Malaysia, the Philippines, Kenya, Sudan, Ethiopia, Somalia, Tanzania, Saudi Arabia, Yemen, and Italy. Among Tang textile products, one called "white brocade of Gaoli" was obviously of Korean origin. During the Song dynasty Chinese silk textile products were widely exported to places such as Japan, Korea, Vietnam, Cambodia, India, Sri Lanka, the Philippines, Malaysia, Indonesia, Iran, Iraq, Yemen, Saudi Arabia, Egypt, Somalia, Tanzania, Morocco, and Europe.

**Language and Literature.** The written language of Japan developed from Chinese characters. In 712 the Japanese book *Kojiki* (Records of Ancient Matters) was written partly in Chinese script and partly in Chinese characters used phonetically. In 720 the Japanese *Nihongi* (Chronicles of Japan) was written in pure Chinese characters. In 751 *Kaifuso* (Fond Recollections of Poetry) collected 120 poems written by Japanese in Chinese over the previous seventy-five years. They mostly resembled copybook exercises of Chinese literary forms. The fame of the renowned Tang-era poet Bai Juyi (772–846) reached Korea and Japan. Foreigners in Chang'an paid large sums of money for copies of his poems. The Japanese emperor Saga (768–842) had Bai's works stored in the imperial secretariat. In Japan, Bai continues to enjoy immense popularity. In Kyoto he is honored during the annual Gion Festival. A shrine dedicated to him is included in the traditional parade, depicting him in a debate with a Buddhist priest. In 905 a Chinese scholar of Japan compiled *Kokinshu* (Ancient and Modern Collection), an anthology of Japanese poems, and in 1020 Izumi Shikibu, a female Japanese writer of Heian, published *Honcho Monzui* (Chinese Prose by Japanese).

Sources:

Conrad Schirokauer, *A Brief History of Chinese and Japanese Civilizations* (San Diego: Harcourt Brace Jovanovich, 1989).

Shen Fuwei, *Zhongxi wenhua jiaoliushi* (Shanghai: Shanghai People's Press, 1988).

Joan Stanley-Baker, *Japanese Art* (London: Thames & Hudson, 1984).

Michael Sullivan, *The Arts of China*, fourth edition, expanded and revised (Berkeley: University of California Press, 1999).

Painting of a scholar relaxing and listening to music, Southern Song dynasty, thirteenth century
(National Palace Museum, Taipei, Taiwan)

# SIGNIFICANT PEOPLE

## BAI JUYI

### 772-846
### POET

**Early Life and Bureaucratic Career.** A native of Weinan, Shanxi Province, Bai Juyi grew up during a period of military chaos and fled from his hometown when he was twelve. He was recognized as a literary prodigy after he wrote his "Grass on an Ancient Plain" at fifteen. He earned his *jinshi* (presented scholar) title by passing the official examinations for the imperial bureaucracy in 800 and was appointed *jiaoshulang* (collator of texts) two years later. In 806 he and his good friend and fellow poet Yuan Zhen wrote seventy-five essays suggesting solutions to social problems. As a result, in 807 Bai was appointed to membership in the prestigious Hanlin Academy in the Tang capital of Chang'an. The following year he was named *zuoshiyi* (commissioner to the left). In 813, however, the prime minister was assassinated, and Bai offended the court with his proposal for how to deal with the incident. As a result, he was sent to provincial posts, including marshal of Jiangzhou in Jiangxi Province (815) and governor of Hangzhou (822) and Suzhou (825).

**Poetry.** Bai was keenly aware of the suffering of common people, and, like Du Fu, he wrote many realistic and poignant poems expressing his sympathy for their plight. In 809 he created a new genre, the *Xinyuefu* (New Music Bureau Ballads), narrative poems dramatizing what he saw and felt about social and political abuses. His best-known poems are two long narrative ballads, *Pipaxing* (The Mandolin Ballad) and *Changhenge* (Song of Lasting Pain). *Changhenge* tells the love story of Tang emperor Xuanzong (ruled 712–756) and his beloved concubine Yang. Bai's poems were widely acclaimed by the common people and were copied on the walls of inns and monasteries. Singing girls were paid high prices to perform his songs. According to one account, Bai often read his poems to an old peasant lady and revised any expression that she could not understand. Bai was also a musician and music critic. He wrote more than one hundred poems describing and commenting on various musical instruments and songs. Late in life, Bai became a devout Buddhist, calling himself *Xiangshan jushi* (Lay Buddhist of the Fragrant Mountain). His influence extended not only to later generations in China but also to Korea and Japan.

Sources:
Bin Ouyang and Xu Shenzhi, *Li Bai, Du Fu, Bai Juyi (Li Bai, Du Fu and Bai Juyi)* (Tainan, Taiwan: Great China Press, 1978).

Chen Youqin, Gong Kechang, and Peng Chongguang, *Bai Juyi jiqi zuopinxuan* (Shanghai: Shanghai Press of Ancient Books, 1998).

## DU FU

### 712-770
### POET

**Life and Career.** Known as the "Sage of Poetry," Du Fu was born into an aristocratic family in Gong County, Henan Province. Given a strict, traditional Confucian education, he wrote his first poems at age seven and was associating with the literati by the time he was fourteen. Du's traditional education made him a gentleman with great integrity and high moral standards while sharpening his appetite for success. After he turned twenty he traveled extensively in China to see life firsthand. When he was thirty-three he met Li Bai, who was already a nationally known poet, and thereafter maintained a strong admiration for his older contemporary. During the 740s and early 750s he held a series of minor government posts. But during the political and military turmoil associated with the An Lushan revolt that threatened the Tang dynasty around 755, he was often jobless and hungry. He eventually died on a tour boat in 770 at age fifty-nine.

**Poetry.** Some 1,400 poems by Du have survived. The few extant poems from his early years are confident and heroic, far different from the pessimistic poems he wrote later. The turning point in his poetry came with "The Ballad of the Army Wagons," the first poem of the Tang era (618–907) that overtly criticized a government policy, in this case conscription. Although still loyal to the Tang government, Du became increasingly aware of the terrible sufferings of the lower class and expressed his concerns for the fate of the nation in "Going Out to the Frontier" and in the groups of poems titled "Three Officers" and "Three Partings." His "Ballad of Beautiful Ladies" and "Washing Weapons" exposed greed and corruption in the highest ranks of the ruling class. Even nature poems such as "Night Thoughts Aboard a Boat" express his disappointment in the failures of Chinese society. Du was also a master of style who had a gift for finding precisely the right word to express his message. He once commented, "I won't have peace even after my death if people do not marvel at my words!"

Sources:

Eva Shan Chou, *Reconsidering Tu Fu: Literary Greatness and Cultural Context* (New York: Cambridge University Press, 1995).

Arthur Cooper, trans., *Li Po and Tu Fu* (Baltimore: Penguin, 1973).

Dorothy Hoobler, Thomas Hoobler, and Victoria Bruck, *Chinese Portraits* (Austin: Raintree/Steck Vaughn, 1992).

# GUAN HANQING

## CIRCA 1213 – CIRCA 1297
### PLAYWRIGHT

**Career.** Known as Yizhaisou (The Old Man Who Studies the Past), Guan Hanqing was one of the earliest playwrights of the Yuan era (1279–1368). A native of Yanjing (now Beijing), he was probably born into a noble family. After he failed to secure an official position as an imperial doctor, he turned his energy to writing and acting, living among the theater people of the urban outdoor entertainment area known as the spontaneous market. His only trip away from Beijing was a visit to Linan (Hangzhou) in the South.

**Writings.** Guan wrote approximately sixty-seven plays, of which eighteen have survived, including *Snow in Midsummer* (also known as *The Wronging of Dou E*), *Rescued by a Coquette*, *The Jade Mirror-Stand*, *The Wife Snatcher*, and *Go with a Single Sword to the Feast*. *Snow in Midsummer* is a classic Chinese tragedy about a virtuous young woman from a humble family who is executed for a crime she did not commit. Her tragic experience moves heaven to redress the wrongs against her. The defiant spirit is one of the main features of Guan's plays, which focus on themes such as love, heroism, and morality. Guan created realistic characters who express themselves in fresh, lively language. He was a master of using dramatic conflict to examine social problems. Still recognized for his contributions to literary history, he was one of the giants of international culture commemorated throughout the world.

Sources:

Wilt Idema and Stephen West, *Chinese Theater 1100–1450: A Source Book* (Wiesbaden: Steiner, 1982).

Zhang Peiheng and Luo Yuming, eds., *Zhongguo wenxueshi* (Shanghai: Fudan University Press, 1996).

# LI BAI

## 701-762
### POET

**Life.** Though he was once believed to have been born in Chengji (Qinan) or in Central Asia, Li is now generally believed to have been born to a wealthy family that settled in Changlong (Jiangyou), Sichuan Province, when he was five. He read widely and mastered swordsmanship as a teenager. Known for his generosity and chivalry, he loved drinking and swordplay. He was also unconventional and ignored the normal path to success through taking the civil examination. Instead, when he was eighteen or nineteen, he went into seclusion with a Daoist recluse, sincerely studied the Daoist religion, and at twenty-three began touring China. Four years later he married the granddaughter of a former prime minister. Eventually the court heard of his poems and invited him to the imperial palace, where Tang emperor Xuanzong (ruled 712–756) welcomed the poet with great honor and offered him a position at the Imperial Academy. Soon, however, the proud and ambitious Li Bai came under attack from envious noblemen. Falling victim to court intrigues, he was allowed to return to his simple previous life. At about this time he met Du Fu, with whom he shared social concerns, and the two poets became good friends. Though living a life away from court politics, Li was still concerned about national affairs. Around 756, he joined the army of Prince Li Lin, who was trying to depose his father. After the prince was defeated, Li Bai was exiled, but he was given amnesty and released, an event that inspired his poem "Early Departure from White Emperor Fortress." By then he was fifty-nine, but he joined the imperial army to suppress the rebels and died of natural causes soon thereafter.

**Poetry.** Among the spectacular poems of the Tang period (618–907), Li Bai's are the most touching, romantic, and optimistic, fully reflecting the spirit of his era. Many Chinese children are still able to recite Li's five-character quatrain "Quiet Night Thought." The vicissitudes of his life developed his individualism and heightened his ability to empathize with every part of society. Though idealism is often identified as the main feature of the Tang poetic style, Li's poems were more idealistic than most. They display his belief in heroism, his hatred of social injustice, and his desire to remove political power from the hands of the aristocracy. Poems such as "Bring On the Wine" and "Drinking Alone Beneath the Moon" are filled with means of blunting individual loneliness and fostering a sense of identity between the individual and the eternal. Expressing his love for and disappointment with life, Li's poems can make a reader want to laugh and cry at the same time.

Sources:

Bin Ouyang and Xu Shenzhi, *Li Bai, Du Fu, Bai Juyi* (Tainan, Taiwan: Great China Press, 1978).

Arthur Cooper, trans., *Li Po and Tu Fu* (Baltimore: Penguin, 1973).

Arthur Waley, *The Poetry and Career of Li Po* (London: Allen & Unwin, 1950).

# LI QINGZHAO

## 1084 - CIRCA 1151
## POET

**A Literary Life.** Known as *Yian jushi* (The Lay Buddhist of Easy Peace), Li Qingzhao was born to talented parents in Licheng (Jinan), Shandong Province. Her father, Li Ge, was a scholar and prose writer, and her mother, the daughter of a noble family, also had literary abilities. Li Qingzhao married the son of a government minister, Zhao Mingcheng, a minor official who was also an antiquarian, a book collector, and a writer of epigrams. They had a happy and literary life together until the Jurchen invasion of 1129. During their escape Li's husband died, and most of her six volumes of poems were destroyed. Only fifty lyrics are extant.

**Lyrics.** Li Qingzhao was good at painting and calligraphy, but her greatest achievement was in lyric writing. She is considered one of the foremost lyric poets, the successor to Su Shi (1037–1101) and the predecessor of Xin Qiji (1140–1207). Li's gift for language enabled her to depict subtle, complex feelings with ruthless honesty. Lyrics such as "Drunk under Flower Shadows," "Spring in Wuling," and "Each Sound Slowly" have been highly acclaimed by generations of readers.

**Sources:**
Lucy Chao Ho, *"More Gracile than Yellow Flowers": The Life and Works of Li Qingzhao* (Hong Kong: Mayfair Press, 1968).

Wang Guangqian, *Li Qingzhao he tadi zuopin* (Taipei, Taiwan: Dafang wenhua shiye gongsi, 1986).

# SU SHI

## 1037-1101
## POET AND ESSAYIST

**Political Career.** Su Shi was born into the family of a humble, self-taught scholar in Sichuan Province. He was influenced by his father, Su Xun (1009–1106), who had managed to secure an official position through diligent study and hard work. When he was twenty-one, Su Shi and his younger brother, Su Che (1039–1112), passed the civil examinations to earn the *jinshi* (presented scholar) title. Su Shi's early political career was promising, but his life soon became filled with difficulties, mainly caused by policy changes. Serving first in a provincial post and then in the capital, Su joined his examiner Ouyang Xiu in opposing the reformist prime minister Wang Anshi. Having chosen the wrong side, Su ended up in jail for a short time.

After his release, although he had been a sincere Confucian, he sought to ease the anxieties of his political career by turning to Daoism and Buddhism. He called himself *Dongpo* (Lay Buddhist of the Eastern Hill). After Wang Anshi's fall from power, Su Shi was recalled to the capital, but he soon offended the new prime minister by opposing his decision to denounce all Wang's reform measures. At his request Su was sent to govern Hangzhou. Thereafter, except for a few brief periods in the capital, he spent most of the remaining years of his life in one provincial post after another.

**Literary Life.** Su Shi and his father and brother, known as the "Three Sus," were are all important prose writers and poets. Though he believed that literature could be a political and moral tool, Su Shi thought literature had more important functions and stressed its artistic, philosophical, and emotional aspects. His prose writings include many excellent essays on historical figures, politics, and nature, including "On Fan Zeng," "On Jia Yi," "On Chao Cuo," "The Investigation of the Mountain Shizhong," and "Red Cliff Rhapsodies." He also wrote nearly twenty-eight hundred poems and about three hundred and fifty lyrics, among them "Inscription on the Wall of the Western Forest," "A Riverside Town," "Water Mode Song," and "Reflections on the Past at the Red Cliff." His style is spontaneous and unrestrained, displaying powerful sentiments and covering a broad range of themes. Su Shi is widely considered the greatest poet of the Song dynasty (960–1279) and one of the "Eight Masters of Tang and Song Prose." He also achieved renown as a painter and calligrapher.

**Sources:**
Chen Guifen, *Qiangu fengliu Su Dongpo (An Eternal Gay Genius Su Dongpo)* (Taipei, Taiwan: Huayan chubanshe, 1996).

Lin Yutang, *The Gay Genius: The Life and Times of Su Tungpo* (New York: John Day, 1947).

# TANG XIANZU

## 1550-1616
## PLAYWRIGHT

**Government Official.** The foremost dramatist of the Ming dynasty (1368–1644), Tang Xianzu was a native of Linchuan in Jiangxi Province. Though he was recognized early for his prodigious learning, for many years he was not allowed to become a *jinshi* (presented scholar) because he refused to make friends with the son of Prime Minister Zhang Juzheng and criticized the emperor and the government. When he was thirty-four, he was finally made a *jinshi* and subsequently served in several low-level posts. The people under his administration loved him for his liberal and compassionate policies. Angry at the heavy taxation imposed on the people, Tang quit government service at the age of forty-eight and spent the rest of his life in seclusion.

**Influential Playwright.** During his final years, Tang wrote *The Purple Flute, The Purple Hairpin* (a revision of *The Purple Flute*), *The Peony Pavilion, The Dream of Nanke,* and *The Dream of Handan*—known collectively as the "Four Dreams of Linchuan." The themes of these plays were the four major elements in Chinese culture and society: chivalry, love, Buddhism, and Daoism. Except for *The Peony Pavilion*—which is known as his masterpiece—Tang's plays are based on tales from the time of the Tang dynasty (618–907). Tang never established a school or literary movement, but the many playwrights who admired and imitated his writing style were called the "School of Linchuan."

Sources:

Huang Zhigang, *Tang Xianzu biannian pingzhuan* (Beijing: Chinese Drama Press, 1992).

Wilt Idema and Stephen West, *Chinese Theater 1100–1450: A Source Book* (Wiesbaden: Steiner, 1982).

Li Zhenyu, *Tang Xianzu* (Shenyang, China: Spring Wind Literature and Arts Press, 1999).

# WANG WEI

## 701-761
### PAINTER, POET, AND CALLIGRAPHER

**Life.** Known as Wei Mojie, after the popular Buddhist saint Vimalakirti, Wang Wei was a native of Taiyuan, Qi County, Shanxi Province. He passed the civil examination to become a *jinshi* (presented scholar) at twenty-one. Before he was thirty, he lived for a while as a recluse on Mount Song, near the eastern capital of Luoyang. Even after taking official positions such as minister to the right and censor, he often spent time alone at a villa in the scenic Chongnan Mountains near Chang'an, where he studied Buddhism. In 756, during the An Lushan revolt against the Tang, he was forced to work for the rebel government, which led to setbacks in his career after the success of imperial forces and further withdrawal from society.

**Poet and Artist.** In his early life Wang wrote many positive and high-spirited poems, but his mood darkened after the An Lushan revolt, and his interest in poetry dramatically declined. His lifelong devotion to Buddhism significantly influenced his creative output. Wang was a great poet, a scholar of Chan (Zen Buddhism), and a master of calligraphy. He also had an excellent command of music and once served as minister of music. The founder of the Southern School of painter-poets, he created the form of the monochromatic landscape painting in ink and wrote about his theory of painting in *Shanshuilun* (*Formulas for Landscape*). His paintings reveal his perceptions of Buddhism and had a major impact on later generations of landscape painters.

Sources:

Marsha L. Wagner, *Wang Wei* (Boston: Twayne, 1981).

Dorothy B. Walmsley, *Wang Wei, The Painter-Poet* (Rutland, Vt.: Tuttle, 1968).

# ZHAO MENGFU

## 1254-1322
### PAINTER, POET, AND CALLIGRAPHER

**Life.** Known as *Songxue daoren* (The Pine and Snow Daoist), Zhao was a native of Wuxing (Huzhou), Zhejiang Province, and a descent of the Song imperial family. As a child he was able to memorize every word he read and improvise essays. He was appointed to an official position at fourteen. During the final years of the Song dynasty, the thirty-three-year-old Zhao took a position at the Hanlin Academy, where he was put in charge of writing a national history. The Yuan government treated him with great honor. Emperor Shizu (Kublai Khan, reigned 1260–1294) called him a "god" and Emperor Renzong (reigned 1311–1320) compared him to Li Bai of the Tang dynasty (618–907) and Su Shi of the Song dynasty (960–1279).

**Renaissance Man.** Zhao was one of the great artists of the Yuan period (1279–1368), talented in poetry, calligraphy, seal making, and music. A pioneer of a new Yuan painting style, he was a master painter of figures, horses, flowers, birds, and especially landscapes. He believed brush strokes in painting should be like those used in calligraphy and criticized the careful, artful style of the Painting Academy. After his death Zhao's writings were collected as *Songxuezhai wenji* (The Literary Collection from the Study of Pine and Snow).

Sources:

He Yanzhe, *Zhongguo huihua shiyao* (Tianjin, China: People's Arts Press, 2000).

Ren Daobin, *Zhao Mengfu xinian* (Zhengzhou, China: Henan People's Press, 1984).

Wang Qisen, *Zhongguo yishu tongshi* (Jiangsu, China: Jiangsu Arts Press, 1999).

# ZHU ZAIYU

## 1536-1616
### MUSICIAN

**Life.** Called *Juqu shanren* (The Mountain Man of Words and Music), Zhu Zaiyu was born in Huaiqing (Qinyang), Henan Province. A son of Ming prince Zhenggong (Zhu Houwan), Zhu Zaiyu was mostly educated by his father and read works by his relatives and ancestors. Around 1550, after his father was imprisoned on false charges and deprived of his royal status, Zhu had to leave the palace. He spent the next nineteen years studying in a simple room. He was later able to inherit his father's imperial title and return to the palace, where he spent the rest of his life studying music, music theory, chronology, and mathematics. His greatest contribution to music theory—as well as acoustics and physics—was the invention of the now-standard twelve equal temperaments, the division of the scale, or octave, into a series of semitones in consonance with each other, which he determined scientifically through accurate mathematical calculations. Zhu's Western admirers include German philosopher-scientist Hermann von Helmholtz (1821–1894), Belgian musical scholar Victor-Charles Mahillon (1841–1924), and British science historian Joseph Needham (1900–1995).

**Sources:**

Chen Wannai, *Zhu Zaiyu yanjiu* (Taipei, Taiwan: The National Palace Museum, 1992).

Dai Nianzu, *Zhu Zaiyu—Mingdai de kexue he yishu juxing* (Beijing: People's Press, 1986).

Xing Zhaoliang, *Zhu Zaiyu pingzhuan* (Nanjing, China: Nanjing University Press, 1998).

# DOCUMENTARY SOURCES

Chen Yang, *Yueshu* (Music Dictionary, 1096–1100) — The first Chinese encyclopedia of music, in 200 volumes; the first 95 volumes comprise a selection of writings on music from before the Qin dynasty (221–206 B.C.E.); the remaining volumes include entries on topics such as twelve temperaments, five tones, musical compositions of past generations, dance music, genre shows, palace-feast music, popular music, foreign music, and various musical instruments.

Dong Qichang (1555–1636), *Huazhi* (The Objective of Painting) — An important theory linking the divergence of the Northern and Southern schools of Chinese landscape painting to two schools of Chan (Zen) Buddhism: the Northern School, which preached gradual enlightenment, and the Southern School, which followed the way of sudden enlightenment; as a result, Dong claimed Northern paintings were academic and precise, depicting expanses of space and suggesting the element of time, while Southern paintings had softer outlines and freer brushwork, depicting misty, impressionistic, seemingly improvised, and symbolic landscapes, which Dong considered superior to those of the Northern School; while often more confusing than convincing, Dong's theory had a profound influence on later painters.

Li Jie (flourished late twelfth century), *Yingzhao fashi* (Building Standards, 1103) — A 34-volume compendium of ancient and current architectural knowledge and building regulations, including standardized measurements, published by the Song government.

*Sanjiao zhuying* (Pearls and Flowers of Three Teachings, late 600s) — A 1,300-volume collection of Tang-era poetry and prose compiled on the orders of Empress Wu (reigned 684–705) by about forty members of the Literati, including Shen Quanqi, Song Zhiwen, Su Weidao, Li Qiao, Cui Rong, and Du Shenyan.

Shen Guo (1032–1096), *Mengxi bitan* (Discussion at Dream Creek) — A comprehensive memoir of contemporary politics, literature, calligraphy, painting, music, astronomy, geography, inventions, and medicine by a Song-dynasty official who held many political, scientific, diplomatic, and military posts between 1063 and 1085, when he retired to Runzhou in Jiangsu Province and built a villa called Dream Creek, where he wrote *Mengxi bitan*.

Sun Guoting (648–703), *Shupu* (Guide to Calligraphy) — A full and profound exposition of the theory and aesthetic appreciation of calligraphy; Sun's well-written study examines calligraphy as a cultural phenomenon and is considered one of the best Tang-era books on Chinese calligraphic theory.

Zhang Haiquan (flourished seventh to eighth centuries), *Shuduan* (Analysis of Calligraphy) — An important Tang-era book on the history and practice of calligraphy; volume one of the three-volume work describes the artistic features and evolution of ten calligraphic styles; volumes two and three analyze the styles of all Chinese calligraphers up to and including Zhang's contemporaries.

Zhu Changwen (1038–1098), *Qinshi* (The History of the Zither, 1233) — The earliest book on an important Chinese instrument, published by the author's grand-nephew Zhu Zhengda; five of the six volumes comprise 162 biographies of zither players since the Tang dynasty; the sixth volume collects eleven essays on the history of the zither and the aesthetics of playing it.

Qianxunta pagoda, circa 850

# COMMUNICATION, TRANSPORTATION, AND EXPLORATION

by GUANGQIU XU

## CONTENTS

*Sidebars and tables are listed in italics.*

**630**
- The first Japanese embassy to the Tang court arrives in China.

**638**
- A Persian emissary arrives in Chang'an, bringing the first news of the rise of Islam to the Chinese.

**641**
- The first Chinese princess given in marriage to the Tibetan royal family arrives in Lhasa. Thereafter, Chinese pilgrims are allowed to go to Buddhist holy places via Tibet and Nepal.

**643**
- A Byzantine delegation arrives in the Tang capital and presents Emperor Taizong with red glass and gold dust.

**674**
- The Tang emperor accepts the Persian prince Firuz as a refugee after Arab armies occupy his hereditary territories.

**700**
- Korea is the first country to which printing spreads from China.

**713**
- Ambassadors of the Caliph arrive in Chang'an to seek Chinese aid, and they are politely received by the Tang emperor.

**716**
- The Japanese monk Gembo starts out with an embassy for Chang'an. He returns to Japan eighteen years later with five thousand Buddhist texts written in Chinese and various objects of piety.

**747**
- The Tibetans start a series of aggressive assaults on the cities of Chinese Turkestan. Tang armies move along the northern arm of the Silk Road in order to cut off the Tibetans and to set up a series of military posts near modern Tashjurgan.

**753**
- Jianzhen, a medical monk from Yangzhou in Gansu, leaves for Japan with four other Chinese monks.

**770**
- One million copies of the Buddhist charm scroll are printed in China on commission from a Japanese empress.

* DENOTES CIRCA DATE

**804**
- Kukai, the eminent founder of Shingon, a Japanese Buddhist sect, travels to China, escorted by Saicho.

**840**
- The Tang emperor decrees that top functionaries in the central government and retired officials be allowed to ride in sedan chairs if they are sick.

**953**
- A complete 130-volume set of the Confucian classics with commentaries is printed by the Chinese National Academy and is the first official publication sold to the public in the world.

**984**
- Qiao Weiyo, assistant commissioner of transport for Huainan, invents the canal pound lock to replace the double slipway.

**1040***
- The commoner Bi Sheng invents effective movable-type printing.

**1107**
- Paper money is printed in three colors in order to prevent counterfeiting.

**1168**
- Admiral Shi Zhengzhi builds a one-hundred-ton warship propelled by a single twelve-bladed wheel.

**1189**
- Construction begins on a segmental arch bridge, later known as the Marco Polo Bridge, just west of Beijing. Completed in 1192, it is 257 yards long and almost 9 yards wide.

**1220**
- Beginning his journey from Shandong, Chang Chun and eighteen disciples traverse Outer Mongolia and the Altai, cross Samarkand, skirt the southern edge of the Hindu Kush, and arrive at Genghis Khan's camp in 1222.

**1221**
- A Daoist monk travels across China to Uliassutai, Urumchi, and on to the Hindu Kush.

**1229**
- The Mongols begin to improve and revive the old steppe route (part of the northern branch of the Silk Road), which connects Mongolia with the lower Volga River valley via Dzungaria and Kazakhstan and eventually the plains of Eastern Europe.

* DENOTES CIRCA DATE

**1245**
- Accompanied by Benedict of Poland, John of Plano Carpini, as the representative of Pope Innocent IV, leaves Lyon for the capital of the Mongol khans. After returning home the next year, he completes a book on his trip, describing the enthronement of Guyug Khan and the manners and customs of the Mongols.

**1253**
- Unsatisfied with the achievements of earlier expeditions, King Louis IX of France and Pope Innocent IV send William of Rubruck to Mongolia in order to establish alliances with the Mongols against the Muslims at the time of the sixth crusade. He crosses the Black Sea and the Crimea and reaches the steppe route.

**1254**
- The famous Venetian merchants Niccolo and Maffeo Polo leave Venice for China.

**1259**
- Chang De, sent by the Khan Mongke on a mission to Persia, begins his journey from Karakorum, crosses the north of the Tian Shan, Samarkand, and Tabriz, and arrives at the Mongol camp of Hulegu.

**1266**
- The Polos leave China, crossing Central Asia again and arriving in Italy through Syria three years later.

**1271**
- The Polos leave for China again, together with Niccolo's son Marco. These three travelers this time pass through the Mongol Khanate of Persia and northern Afghanistan, then follow the Silk Road through the Pamirs and southern Kashgaria, Yarkand, Khotan, and Lob Nor Basin before finally arriving in Kanzhou.
- The Mongols appoint the engineer and mathematician Guo Shoujing to supervise river levels and irrigation in the empire.

**1275**
- Marco Polo travels to Beijing, then called "Dadu."
- The Chinese Nestorian monk Rabban Bar Suma and his disciple Mark embark for the Holy Land.

**1291**
- Italian Franciscan Giovanni di Monte Corvino sails to South China.

**1292**
- Marco Polo, his father, and his uncle board a ship at Quanzhou, leaving for Europe, and return to Venice in 1295.
- The Mongols send a naval expedition to Java.

\* Denotes Circa Date

**1297**
- Wang Chen invents movable wooden type. Within three years the knowledge of this process spreads to eastern Turkestan.

**1314**
- Italian Franciscan Odoric of Pordenone leaves for East Asia. He disembarks at Canton, where he takes another ship to Fuzhou. He then travels to Hangzhou by inland roads and takes the Grand Canal to Beijing.

**1320***
- Small seagoing junks transport approximately 3.5 million catties (more than 200,000 tons) of grain to Dagu, the port on the Bai River closest to the capital of Beijing.

**1325**
- Odoric of Pordenone travels to Beijing again by the sea route, remains there for three years, and returns home by land, crossing the southwest corner of Turkestan.

**1351**
- The Yuan government orders work crews to rechannel one hundred miles of the Yellow River east of Kaifeng. Nearly two hundred thousand laborers recruited from neighboring farm communities work on the canal project for several months.

**1382**
- Ming armies wipe out the last remnants of the Nanxiao rulers, and large-scale settlement of the Yunnan province begins.

**1405**
- The Muslim admiral Zheng He, or Cheng Ho, begins the first of seven expeditions (the others occur in 1407–1409, 1409–1411, 1413–1415, 1417–1419, 1421–1422, and 1431–1433) to various locations in Southeast Asia, the Middle East, and the eastern coast of Africa. The largest of his "Treasure Ships" is 440 feet in length, carries 9 masts, and has a cargo capacity of 2,500 tons and a displacement of 3,100 tons. By contrast, Christopher Columbus's *Santa Maria* is only 117 feet long and has a capacity of 280 tons; the biggest ships of the Spanish Armada are of 1,000 tons capacity.

**1417**
- The Ming government completes a set of improvements on the Grand Canal, including expanding its width, dredging certain channels, and installing a system of locks. The waterway is now slightly more than 1,000 miles long, 50-150 feet wide, and 10-50 feet deep. The canal's water level is sufficiently high to allow the grain ships supplying Beijing to use it year-round.

**1419**
- The Persian king dispatches another ambassador to China.

* DENOTES CIRCA DATE

**1433**
- Zheng He dies soon after his fleet arrives back at Nanking. His death marks an end to government-sponsored maritime expeditions for the next four hundred years.

**1450***
- Under the supervision of Xu Youzhen, a work force of sixty thousand civilians and soldiers repairs broken dikes in western Shandong province that cause floods and interrupt traffic on the Grand Canal. After 550 days of continuous labor, a diversion canal is completed.

**1511**
- The Portuguese capture Malacca, a former ally and base city of Ming naval expeditions.

**1517**
- Portuguese ships reach the southern coast of China.

**1557**
- The Portuguese occupy the island of Macao by enlisting the help of corrupt local Chinese officials.

**1560***
- Over the next twenty years, another series of repairs are made to the Grand Canal and nearby dikes.

**1607**
- Through the use of extensive bribes, Portuguese merchants secure a Chinese prohibition of Dutch trade.

**\* DENOTES CIRCA DATE**

# OVERVIEW

**Natural Barriers.** Communication networks via rivers and mountain passes were scarce in China. While the natural lines of communication that went from east to west were only partly usable, there was an almost total absence of links directly connecting North China and South China. From about the area of Kaifeng, navigation down the Yellow River was seriously thwarted by flooding and constant changes of the river's course. Further upstream, the large rocks located at the Sanmen gorge often hindered the progress of grain-laden barges. Because of heavy silt the Wei River was unserviceable for all ships except shallow-draft vessels. Mountain ranges blocked the path of travelers attempting to transport their merchandise from the Upper Yangzi (Yangtze) River valley to North China. Since the Han dynasty (206 B.C.E.–220 C.E.), the imperial governments had tried to use tributaries of the Han and Wei rivers to establish a link between Chang'an and the Sichuan basin, but such attempts failed and no other regular means of transportation were created.

**Limitations.** The lack of sufficient supply lines to various regions often limited the effective power of central government during the imperial era (617–1644). Densely populated cities sometimes arose far from grain-producing areas or in remote locations chosen for their natural defenses. Imperial governments had the major problem of shipping supplies from the Great Plain of northeastern China, and later from the southern provinces of the Yangzi River valley, to the settlements and military garrisons situated in the Northwest.

**Land Traffic.** Various imperial governments attempted to build roads after the Han dynasty, but their efforts were directed more toward improving central administrative control than enhancing trade and economic growth. The Qin government (221–206 B.C.E.) built a series of roads for their armies, and the Han empire created a postal system so that officials and dispatch riders could travel all over China. (At that time it took about six or seven weeks for the delivery of mail from central China to the military forts along the northwestern frontier.) The Tang (618–907), Yuan (1279–1368), and Ming (1368–1644) courts also had effective postal services.

**Growth of the South.** In the fourth century many Chinese peasants began to migrate to the less-populated South for a variety of reasons. While some wished to avoid northern raiders, famine, and poor soil conditions, others left the North in an attempt to escape taxation and military conscription. The continuation of the migration to the South through the twelfth century not only contributed to the growth of population in the region but also to the expansion of agricultural production in the lower Yangzi valley.

**Importance of the Northeast.** Meanwhile, the old metropolitan regions of the Northwest began to lose their strategic significance. The Liao (916–1115) and Jin (1115–1234) empires rose in the Northeast and gradually extended their hold on Chinese territory. As a result, the Northeast assumed more political importance and the Mongols moved their capital to Beijing by 1272.

**Expansion.** The development of Chinese maritime activities from the eleventh century onward was one of the most important phenomena in the history of Asia. The activity of the ports of Fujian, Zhejiang, and Guangdong was on a much larger scale than that of major European countries. The size of river and oceangoing traffic in the Song (960–1279) and Yuan periods; the Mongol endeavor to invade Japan and Java at the end of the thirteenth century; and the great expeditions of the Ming dynasty in the years of 1405–1433, which sailed as far as the Red Sea and the east coast of Africa, all demonstrated Chinese maritime power.

**Maritime World.** The residents of the coasts of Liaodong, Korea, Shandong, and Japan made important breakthroughs in maritime technology. A type of sail used by boats on Chinese lakes spread as far as the east coast of Africa, while noticeable hull differences distinguished the Chinese ships of Guangdong and Fujian from Arab vessels. Large Chinese high-seas ships appeared toward the tenth or eleventh century. They originated in the communities along the great estuary of the Yangzi River.

**Language.** The written Chinese language played an important role in molding and perpetuating social unity, as well as in shaping and disseminating cultural developments. The influence of written Chinese can be compared with that of Latin, which had been used by European statesmen, clerics, merchants, and intellectuals as the preferred means of international communication until the 1850s. Prior to 617, relatively simple types of characters were used for writings that were engraved or sometimes painted on bones. Complex elaborations, which were not at all standard, became more fashionable when inscriptions, which noted imperial events or acted as title deeds to property, were made on bronze vessels. During the imperial era, wooden or bamboo strips began to be used for preparing governmental records needed by a more complex government. The development of Chinese characters during this time was based on four principles—pictographs (pictorial symbols or signs), ideograms (pictures or symbols used to represent things or ideas but not particular words), logical compounds, and semantic-phonetic compounds.

# TOPICS IN COMMUNICATION, TRANSPORTATION, AND EXPLORATION

### BRIDGE TECHNOLOGY

**Need.** The development of roads and waterways in the imperial era (617–1644) demanded a high level of bridge building. The Chinese constructed different kinds of bridges: timber beam, cantilever timber, suspension, and masonry. In addition, they used the stone arch in many forms: semicircular, horseshoe, elliptical, and segmental.

**Cantilever Type.** Cantilever bridges of timber and stone existed during the early imperial period. This type of bridge is usually made with three spans: the outer two spans are anchored on the shore, while the third is projected out over the channel and supported by cantilever beams on only one side. A good example of a cantilever bridge existed at Lilin in the Hunan province. It crossed the Lu River and had piers twelve feet wide with a span between them of just over fifty-six feet.

**Semicircular Arch Type.** By the seventh century, stone had become the typical material for most important

The Great Stone Bridge spanning the River Chiao Shui, the world's first semicircular arch bridge built by Li Chun in the early seventh century

The Marco Polo Bridge, originally built in 1189

bridges. To solve the problems of building in the sedimentary plain of North China, the Chinese began to develop a lighter and more flexible form of arch. Engineer Li Chun built a semicircular arch bridge in Hebei between 606 and 616, the first of its kind in the world. Named the Great Stone Bridge, it was noteworthy for its four spandrel arches and decorative design. The main arch was composed of 28 parallel lines of 45 massive stones, each approximately one ton in weight and curved in the direction of the span, with a line of thinner slabs on top. Each arch stone was fixed to its neighbors in the direction of the span with two iron clamps. The two pairs of segmental arches in the spandrels not only served to reduce the load of the masonry on the haunches of the arch but also provided an overflow for floodwater. The bridge had a span of 123 feet. Later similar bridges were built with flat segment arches and open spandrels. In these cases the arch stones were relatively flat and shallow, often longer in the direction of the span than in the direction of the center of the curve radius. Therefore, they did not rely on their own heaviness for stability, instead fitting together exactly to shape a thin shell, which passed the load on to the abutments. Mortar was not used in the arch and foundations, and the masonry foundations were often set on wood piles.

**Segmental Arch Type.** During the imperial era, a breakthrough in bridge construction happened when Chinese engineers discovered that a bridge could be built based on a segmental arch rather than the traditional semicircular arch. Segmental arch bridges, using less material, were physically more powerful than ones constructed with semicircular arches. The bridge in the Song era (960–1279) painting *By the River at the Qingming Festival* was a typical segmental arch bridge. It had parallel rows of five round section beams overlapping each other. Five rectangular transverse beams were placed between the arch beams so

that the whole interlaced structure became a rigid flat arch in timber. A layer of dirt covered the boarded deck.

**Marco Polo Bridge.** The greatest segmental arch bridge in China is the well-known Marco Polo Bridge, frequently so called because Polo illustrated it in detail. Located just west of Beijing and constructed in 1189, it is still in use today. The 771-foot-long bridge is composed of a series of 11 segmental arches (each with an average span of 62 feet) extending one after another across the Yongding River.

**Suspension Bridge.** Most of the suspension bridges were in southwestern China, especially in Sichuan and Yunnan provinces, where there are many deep river gorges. The Chinese began to build chain suspension bridges as early as the seventh century, using twisted bamboo cables about four inches thick. (The cables were replaced every year.) One suspension bridge in Sichuan, for example, had ten parallel cables and five more cables on each side, one above the other, shaping the balustrades. The total length of the bridge was about one thousand feet. It consisted of nine unequal spans, the largest of which was about two hundred feet. There were seven intermediate wooden towers and one stone-built tower close to the center of the bridge.

**Transverse Shear Wall.** During the Song dynasty the Chinese developed the transverse shear wall to build more-slender and flexible stone bridges. This solid wall at right angles to the span was set close behind the spring of the arch on both sides of the watercourse, reinforcing the abutment with its relatively deeper foundations. In addition, for purposes of economy, only the sidewalls of the bridges were built of masonry, with the remainder of cheaper materials such as rammed soil. This wall also reduced the effects of unequal settlement between the main foundations and those of the approach.

Sources:

Derk Bodde, *Chinese Thought, Society, and Science: The Intellectual and Social Background of Science and Technology in Pre-Modern China* (Honolulu: University of Hawaii Press, 1991).

James M. Hargett, *On the Road in Twelfth Century China: The Travel Diaries of Fan Chengda (1126-1193)* (Stuttgart: Steiner Verlag Wiesbaden, 1989).

Joseph Needham, *Clerks and Craftsmen in China and the West* (Cambridge: Cambridge University Press, 1970).

## CHINESE MARITIME EXPANSION AND WESTERN NAVIGATORS

**Tang and Overseas Trade.** By the Tang era (618–907) there was extensive sea trade with Japan and Korea. The Japanese and Koreans entered China by way of the mouth of either the Huai or Yangzi (Yangtze) rivers at Hangzhou, thence by canal to the capital, Chang'an. They did not use the Yellow River because it was not navigable in its upper reaches. The ordinary crossing from Japan to China took from five to ten days. Many Buddhist monks and pilgrims also traveled on this route, carrying incense and medicines from China to Japan. In addition to Japan, the Tang court had significant connections with Arab and Persian lands. Hangzhou was the principal port, where thousands of Arab and Persian traders lived.

**Song Maritime Techniques.** Many improvements in seafaring occurred in the Song period. Through experimentation the Song people developed large ships, each with four or six masts, twelve sails, and four decks, capable of carrying about one thousand men. Anchors, rudders, drop-keels, capstans, canvas sails, and watertight compartments had been improved or adopted since the Tang dynasty. Moreover, Song cartography was the most precise and accurate in the world at the time, far surpassing medieval European mapmaking with its religious themes. Song mariners also compiled detailed sounding and current information on the coastlines. More important, the application of the compass, which had been used by geomancers for a long time, to maritime needs made ocean voyages much safer for the Chinese.

**Economic Causes.** Although progress in navigational techniques made marine expansion possible, the development of the mercantile economy really made the difference. Cut off from access to Central Asia and contained in its expansion toward the North and Northwest by the great empires that were rising on its frontiers, the Song empire turned to the sea. Its economic focus shifted toward the trading and maritime regions of the Southeast where the Yangzi (Yangtze) River had extensive tributaries. The sea routes ran from the Abbasid Empire and connected the Persian Gulf with India, Southeast Asia, and the Chinese coast. Japanese, Javanese, and Korean pirates plagued the lanes, but the Song successfully curbed some of their more-damaging raids.

**Yuan Influence.** Although the Mongols were not natural sailors, they nevertheless used sea transport to great effect in developing the spice trade between the Indies and Europe, via Persia and Egypt. Ibn Battuta, a fourteenth-century Muslim traveler from Tangiers, left the southern

## THE SAVAGE WAVES

To honor the expeditions of Zheng He, a text was engraved on a stone tablet in 1432, part of which said:

The Emperor has ordered us, Cheng Ho . . . to make manifest the transforming power of the Imperial virtue and to treat distant people with kindness . . . We have seven times received the commission of ambassadors [and have visited] altogether more than thirty countries large and small. We have traversed immerse water spaces and have beheld huge waves like mountains rising sky-high, and we have set eyes on barbarian regions far way hidden in a blue transparency of light vapors, while our sails loftily unfurled like clouds day and night continued their course, traversing those savage waves as if we were treading a public thoroughfare. . . . We have received the high favor of a gracious commission of our sacred Lord, to carry to the distant barbarians the benefits of his auspicious example. . . .Therefore we have recorded the years and months of the voyages.

Source: J. J. L. Duyvendak, "The True Dates of the Chinese Maritime Expeditions in the Early Fifteenth Century," *T'oung Pao*, 24 (1938): 349–355.

Chinese port of Amoy and sailed south, carrying silk, porcelain, tea, and camphor to the Malay Straits, where he picked up spices for the journey farther west to the Persian Gulf. The profits earned in such commerce encouraged European (primarily Portuguese) trading networks in East Asia in the sixteenth century.

**Motivations of Ming.** Prestige, suzerainty, and trade, rather than territorial acquisition, represented the major motivations of the Ming emperors (1368–1644) for maritime expansion. Between 1405 and 1433 the Ming court dispatched seven major overseas expeditions under Zheng He, which confirmed the military and political assertiveness of the empire and brought tributary envoys to China. In consequence of the fourth voyage, for example, nineteen kingdoms sent tribute including silk, embroideries, various exotic objects, and animals, particularly giraffes.

**Spice Trade.** During the fifteenth century, European traders carried spices from the Syrian and Egyptian ports to the rest of Europe. After the conversion of Persia to Islam halted the trade in that region, the Egyptians used their monopoly to raise prices. As a result, Portugal, Spain, England, France, and Holland all sought other routes.

**Portuguese.** The first Western navigators arrived in China at the beginning of the sixteenth century. In 1511 the Portuguese captured Malacca, the former ally and base city of the Ming expeditions. Within six years Portuguese ships reached the south coast of China, and some of their commanders were sent up to Beijing on a tribute mission. The mission was not a success because the newcomers did not understand their role and behaved disgracefully, at least in Chinese eyes. They were sent off and forbidden to return. Meanwhile the Portuguese, observing the vast

Drawing of a flat-bottomed ocean junk, Song dynasty, 960–1279. The ship has floating rudders for stabilization in high seas (from Louise Levathes, *When China Ruled the Seas,* 1994).

coastline and the absence of effective policing of commerce, decided to establish a colony in China. With the connivance of corrupt local Chinese officials, the Portuguese occupied the island of Macao in 1557 and established factories, warehouses, offices, and living quarters. This event marked the beginning of a new era, which led to the invasion by Western mercantile fleets and to the end of Chinese isolation.

**Ships.** The Portuguese were successful in establishing a colony in China because of their powerful ships. Portuguese vessels were built to perform on long deep-sea voyages. Chinese ships, meanwhile, were smaller, lighter, and designed for short voyages; so were those of Japan. The great ships that Zheng He used were no longer built either by the government or by private merchants. Portuguese ships, however, could be built openly in either government or private yards.

**Dutch.** In the early seventeenth century the Protestant Dutch began to sail into the South China Sea and thereafter had conflicts with the Catholic Portuguese. With bribery the Portuguese secured a Chinese prohibition of Dutch trade in 1607, and the Dutch, like the Japanese and Portuguese before them, promptly turned to smuggling and piracy. They felt free to prey on everyone, Asian and Portuguese, believing that piracy against pagans was not a sin. Since the Dutch did not receive permission to trade or use any islands near the coast as bases, they occupied the large island of Taiwan in 1623 and made it their colony,

although the Portuguese used it earlier and named the island Formosa, which means "beautiful."

**Taiwan.** The island had been incorporated into the Chinese empire during the Tang period. By the early seventeenth century, settlers from the mainland had occupied most of the western fertile plains, confining the native inhabitants, a non-Chinese people, to the eastern mountain chain. Taiwan was supposed to be a prefecture of the province of Fujian. Since the Ming government did not have an effective navy, their control over the province was limited before the Dutch took it over. Pirates of all nationalities had long resorted to this safe refuge. After the Dutch occupied it, order was kept, pirates were excluded, and taxation was lighter than in Ming China. Thereafter, Chinese migration rapidly increased. The Dutch occupation of Taiwan was in many ways the model of the later Dutch empire in Southeast Asia.

Sources:

George H. Dunne, *Generation of Giants: The Story of the Jesuits in China in the Last Decades of the Ming Dynasty* (Notre Dame, Ind.: University of Notre Dame Press, 1962).

C. P. Fitzgerald, *The Southern Expansion of the Chinese People* (London: Barrie & Jenkins, 1972).

Louise Levathes, *When China Ruled the Seas: The Treasure Fleet of the Dragon Throne, 1400-1433* (New York: Simon & Schuster, 1994).

### CHINESE MIGRATION TO SOUTH CHINA

**Lingnan.** Before the Tang dynasty (618–907), the region of the two Lingnan provinces (Guangdong and

Guangxi) was infested with malaria. Few Han Chinese from the North, other than those expelled to the frontiers, crossed the ranges southward. After both the Tang and Song (960–1279) governments developed military agricultural colonies, the migration of northern people into Guangdong increased steadily. Thereafter, Fujian and Chejiang became the cultural centers of the Han Chinese when the Southern Song dynasty (1127–1279) relocated its capital to Hangzhou. After the downfall of the Northern Song (960–1125) dynasty and the occupation of North China by Genghis Khan's powerful armies, the Han Chinese in the Yangzi (Yangtze) River valley migrated south across the Nanling ranges into the Xi River basin. In Ming times (1368–1644) many Han Chinese settled primarily in Lingnan, a favorable climatic region of the subtropical highlands. Beginning in the sixteenth century, the outward migration from southeastern China was directed overseas rather than to Yunnan because of limited overland routes. Nevertheless, both the greater opportunities provided by overseas emigration and the ease and lower cost of transport promoted this movement in the late Ming era.

**Yuan Period.** Before the Yuan dynasty (1279–1368), only about 20 percent of the Yunnan-Gueizhou Plateau was accessible to the Han Chinese. Yunnan was the first of the southern Chinese provinces to be ruled by the Mongols, and they dominated the region for about 130 years. The occupation of Nanchao by the armies of Kublai Khan prompted many Han Chinese immigrants to move to the highland basins—the climatically favorable plateau between the Yangzi gorges and the rift valley of the Red River of Yunnan. During Yuan times the Mongols appointed a Muslim governor in this region, and thereafter many Chinese Muslims moved from northwest China into the Yunnan region. In some locations of Yunnan there were also many settlers from Turkestan.

**Ming Period.** Substantial immigration of the Chinese into Yunnan continued during the Ming dynasty. In 1382, after wiping out the last remnants of the Nanxiao rulers, who had their own government at Dali as vassals of the Mongols, the Ming government promoted the settlement of Yunnan in a planned and large-scale manner. When the first Ming emperor established his government at Nanjing, he forced the former residents of Nanjing to migrate to Yunnan so as to reduce their influence in the capital. Another massive influx of settlers to Yunnan came with the Ming armies. Many troops recruited from South China were sent to Yunnan to put down the local rebellions at the beginning of the Ming dynasty. The Chinese soldiers who were then the main center of Ming power mainly came from the Yangzi province. They later became established as landlords and local nobles in all the major urban centers and key agricultural plains. The policy of sending exiles to a variety of places in Yunnan also arose in Ming times. Among them were some famous persons, including the philosopher Wang Yangming, banished to Gueizhou during the reign of Wuzong (1506–1522). As a

result the number of recently appointed civil servants, merchants, and other transmitters of Han Chinese cultures grew steadily. (In fact, by 1644 Ming culture had spread to about 60-70 percent of China Proper.) The Han Chinese migrants to Yunnan predominantly came from the Yangzhou delta area and to a lesser extent from the Hunan and Nanjing regions. This migration became the exceptional ethnographical contribution of the Ming dynasty in Han Chinese history.

**Impact.** Since the Yuan period, Yunnan had gradually assimilated into Chinese civilization. The Ming dynasty had great impact on Yunnan, particularly on its transportation system. The iron-chain suspension bridges, which spanned the Mekong and Salween rivers, in addition to many lesser rivers in western Yunnan, resulted from the technology introduced by the Han people to Yunnan during the period 1368–1644. The caravan road system, a network of paved pathways crossing ranges and rivers and connecting every major city in the province with other provinces of China, as far as Beijing, was built at that time. Along these roads great slabs of marble, which were eighteen feet in length and five feet wide, were transported in 1405 because the Ming Emperor Yongle was in need of them for constructing the imperial palace at Beijing. Dug out on the high mountain slope at Dali, they were pulled and rolled for hundreds of miles until they could be shipped on rafts on the Hunan River. In addition, Ming builders contributed greatly to many cities of

Yunnan, introducing the Chinese architecture style, such as rectilinear walls and cross streets.

Sources:

C. P. Fitzgerald, *The Southern Expansion of the Chinese People* (London: Barrie & Jenkins, 1972).

Richard von Glahn, *The Country of Streams and Grottoes: Expansion, Settlement, and the Civilizing of the Sichuan Frontier in Song Times* (Cambridge, Mass.: Harvard University Press, 1987).

Herold J. Wiens, *Han Chinese Expansion in South China* (Hamden, Conn.: Shoe String Press, 1967).

## FOREIGN INFLUENCES IN THE TANG DYNASTY

**Capital.** Chang'an, the capital of the Tang dynasty (618–907), was the biggest city in the world at that time, with a population of about two million within its walls and surrounding areas. Chang'an was the heart of the empire, served by a network of roads and canals that connected it to the Silk Road to the west and the Yangzi (Yangtze) River valley to the south. The people of the Tang dynasty knew more about the world than those of the Han dynasty (206 B.C.E.–220 C.E.). Tang people were familiar with regions that had only been known to the Han people by rumor or by occasional and dangerous exploring expeditions. Merchants brought exotic goods from different countries to the markets in Chang'an. Moreover, the city became the meeting place of all kinds of peoples, such as Sogdians, Persians, Arabs, Tibetans, Japanese, Koreans, Turks, Uighurs, Greeks, Kashmiris, and Indians.

**Sogdians.** Persian and Indian influences mixed and equally enriched each other in the whole area extending from Afghanistan to the valley of the Amu Dar'ya (Oxus) River and the oases of the Tarim basin. The most active traders in central Asia and North China came from Samarkand, Meymaneh, Kish, and Bukhara. Their language, Sogdian, an eastern Iranian dialect, was the standard means of communication in Central Asia. Since the commercial route continued from Bukhara to Merv, Balkh, and into China Proper, Sogdian influence was quite extensive, especially in the Chinese art and craftsmanship of the seventh and eighth centuries.

**Byzantines.** The western limit of Tang control was the kingdom of Fulin, the Chinese name for the Byzantine empire in the seventh century. When Emperor Taizong assumed the throne in 643, the Byzantine emperor dispatched a delegation to Chang'an with presents of red glass and gold dust. Between 643 and 719 the Byzantines sent a total of four embassies to China, seeking Tang assistance in wars against the Arabs.

**Persians.** Yazdegerd III, the last Sassanian king of Persia, also appealed to China for assistance against the conquering Muslims. In 638 Yazdegerd sent an embassy to Chang'an, bringing the first news of the rise of Islam to the Chinese. Emperor Taizong refused to provide support on the grounds that his empire, recovering from civil war and Turkish attacks, was in urgent need of peace, and Persia was too far for military expeditions. In 642 the battle of Nahavand decided the destiny of the

Tomb figurine of a Turkish groom, Tang dynasty, 618–907 (from Bradley Smith and Wan-go Weng, *China: A History in Art*, 1973)

Sassanid empire, which fell before the Arab armies. The failure to aid Yazdegerd laid western China open to intrusion, and Muslim embassies entered the Chinese empire in 655.

**Refugees.** After the death of Yazdegerd, his son Prince Firuz fled to Chang'an in 674 through Turkestan. The Tang emperor accepted him as a refugee and still called him "king of Persia." He later became a general of the Imperial Guard, and when he died his son remained in the capital. The Persian refugees were permitted to build temples and to practice the Zoroastrian faith, which thrived among the refugee community for many years.

**Arabs.** From both Persian refugees and Chinese travelers the Tang government soon gained knowledge of the origins of Islam and the country of the Arabs. Arabia was known to the Chinese as "Dashi," which comes

Officials receiving foreign guests; Tang-era tomb painting, circa 711 (Shensi Provincial Museum, Sian)

from the Persian word *Tarzi*, meaning Arab. From 707 to 713 Walid I, a general of the Umayyad Caliphate, conquered Afghanistan, which was then a powerful Buddhist country. The kingdoms of Samarkand, Bokhara, and the confederacy of the western Turks, unable to resist the Arabs' invasion, appealed to the Tang government for help but failed. In 713 the ambassadors of the Caliph arrived in Chang'an and were politely received. However, in 751 Tang forces began fighting against the new Abbasid caliphate, known to the Chinese as the "Black Cloth Arabs." The Muslims defeated the Chinese and wrested Turkestan from their control. The Arabs finally dominated Central Asia, but land travel continued between China and the Middle East in the following centuries.

**Tibetans.** In 747 the Tibetans started a series of aggressive assaults on the cities of Chinese Turkestan. In response the Tang court dispatched a large army to cut off the invaders. It followed the North Road to Kashgar and set up a series of military posts. The army then crossed the Pamirs and penetrated into India as far south as Gilgit.

**Strategic Alliance.** Chinese expansion in the seventh and eighth centuries resulted in extending the influence of Tang culture in many neighboring areas, such as Tibet, Transoxiana, Korea, and Japan. The marriages between Chinese princesses and Turkish and Uighur princes helped introduce Chinese learning into the nomads' societies. After the alliance between the Tang government and the Tibetans was established, the first Chinese princess given in marriage to the Tibetan royal family arrived in Lhasa in 641. Thereafter, the road to Tibet was opened, which allowed Chinese pilgrims to go to the Buddhist holy places via the Tibetan capital and Nepal. Many Chinese monks thereafter made their trips to India in the second half of the seventh century. As a result, the first Buddhist influence infiltrated into Tibet in the second half of the eighth century from China rather than from India.

**Japan.** Chinese influence in Japan was never so broad and intense as in the Tang era. Japan was then barely known to the Chinese people. Jianzhen, a medical monk from Yangzhou in Gansu, left for Japan in 753 with four other Chinese monks and died at Nara in 763. Monk Gembo was one of the most famous Japanese monks who traveled to China to study the laws and to go to Buddhist holy places, such as Chang'an, Luoyang, and Tientaishan in Shanxi. Gembo started out with an embassy for Chang'an in 716 and brought back to Japan five thousand Buddhist texts in Chinese and various objects of piety after eighteen years. Kukai (Kibo Daishi), the eminent founder of the Shingon sect, was in China between 804 and 806, escorted by Saicho (Dengyo Daishi). The monks Jogyo and Engyo traveled to China between 838 and 839. In addition to pilgrimages and embassies, there were also commercial relations. By the end of the Tang period many Chinese ships could be found in Japanese ports.

Sources:

Christopher I. Beckwith, *The Tibetan Empire of Central Asia: A History of the Struggle for Great Power among Tibetans, Turks, Arabs, and Chinese during the Early Middle Ages* (Princeton: Princeton University Press, 1987).

C. P. Fitzgerald, *China: A Short Cultural History* (London: Cresset, 1950).

Ryoichi Hayashi, *The Silk Road and the Shoso-in* (New York: Weatherhill, 1975).

Edwin O. Reischauer, *Ennin's Travels in T'ang China* (New York: Ronald, 1955).

## HORSES AND CARRIAGES

**Horse Raising.** Rough terrain and inadequate pasture lands limited horse raising in ancient China. However, the industry developed steadily in the seventh and eighth centuries. At the beginning of the Tang dynasty (618–907) the government owned a total of about 5,000 horses. Before long, public stud farms were established, soon becoming so successful that by the middle of the seventh century the Tang government had 700,000 horses. This figure fell to 240,000 by 713. Within twelve years government-operated farms had 400,000 horses because of a revival in breeding and purchases from the nomadic people of the steppes. Private breeding developed in North China, especially in eastern Gansu, Shenxi, and Shaanxi, because the government decreed that all militiamen, most of whom belonged to great noble families, should have their own mounts. In the first half of the eighth century, members of the imperial family, high officials, and generals owned herds of horses, oxen, sheep, and camels. A horse market was established in 727 at Yinchuan in northwest China.

**Tibetan Invasion.** In 763 the Tibetans invaded Tang China, and most of the horses on the public stud farms in the Northwest were captured or destroyed. After this point the Tang government had to rely on purchases from private citizens and nomads, and it attempted unsuccessfully in 817–820 to establish state stud farms in the agricultural regions of Shanxi, Henan, and northern Hebei after occupying the lands of the peasants. Since the Tang military depended heavily on cavalry, the late empire was not able to protect its territories against the invasions of the mountaineers and nomads.

**Use of Horses.** In Tang times only government officials or traders who were rich enough to maintain their own stables used horses. For the everyday local distribution of large essen-

Detail from a tenth-century scroll of a party of horsemen (Museum of Fine Arts, Boston)

Handscroll of noblemen riding carriages, circa 1070–1150 (Metropolitan Museum of Art, New York)

tial commodities, transport relied, if not on water, then on the mule or the oxcart. Since the horse had greater prestige than the donkey, all officials were required to ride on horseback. In the Tang dynasty, artisans, merchants, peasants, and Buddhist and Daoist monks could not ride on horseback. In the Yuan era (1279–1368) the families of prostitutes were prohibited from riding on horseback. However, some officials still preferred to ride donkeys to their offices. Regarding this as undignified, Ming Emperor Taizu decreed that the government should provide officials with horses so that the difference between the officials and the commoners could be identified.

**Sedan Chairs.** Sedan chairs were not often used in ancient China. In Tang and Song (960–1279) times the sedan chairs of aristocrats and high ministers were only taken out during ceremonies. For everyday activities, horses were ridden, and even the high-ranking officials, such as the prime minister, had to observe this regulation. In 840 the Tang emperor decreed that all officials in the central government could ride in sedan chairs if they were sick. During the Song dynasty more opportunities arose by which the elite could use this conveyance. In the capital, where the emperor lived, high officials and nobles of the imperial family who were too old to ride horses were allowed to use sedan chairs. This regulation was enforced until the Song court moved to the South. After that point the emperor allowed all officials to ride in sedan chairs because the stone roads in the cities were too slippery for horses. During the Ming dynasty (1368–1644) only officials of the third rank and above could ride in sedan chairs in the capital, while those of the fourth rank and below could ride horses. In the provinces, bureaucrats and military officers of all ranks had to use horses.

**Ordinary People.** In the Tang era the aged mothers and wives of low-ranking officials and traders could ride in a rush-mat-covered vehicle or in a simple bamboo chair without cover or decoration. Ordinary people of the Song period had oxcarts and bamboo chairs, while women used sedan chairs. The commoners of the Yuan dynasty had permission to use sedan chairs if they were old or sick.

**Status.** People belonging to different classes were allowed to ride in sedan chairs, carriages, and on horseback, but the structure, color, and ornamentation of the vehicle or the accessories of the horse varied in line with the status of the rider. In Song times only officials of the third rank and above in the capital and all officials in the provinces could hang a tassel on their horses. In Ming times, however, black tassels could be used by officials and commoners.

**Encounters.** During the imperial era (617–1644), whenever two people of different ranks met, the inferior was required to give way before the superior. When ordinary people saw an aristocrat or official coming, they had to halt and stand at the edge of the road to let him and his attendants pass. Each dynasty had its own laws as to the manner in which a lower official should meet a higher one. Some regulations allowed them to share the same road, some asked the lower official to give way by riding along the side of the road or by halting, and some required them to take an alternative route so as to prevent an encounter. According to Tang, Song, and Ming laws, all violators would be punished with fifty strokes.

**Attendants.** Each government bureaucrat had a set number of attendants according to his rank. The attendants usually rode in front of the official, clearing the way. Wives of the elite had the same privileges as their husbands when they traveled. The commoner was allowed to have one or two servants following behind him. Since silk parasols indicated elite status, ordinary people could not use them and were allowed to carry only rain umbrellas made of oiled paper.

Sources:
Brian E. McKnight, *Village and Bureaucracy in Southern Sung China* (Chicago: University of Chicago Press, 1971).

Yoshinobu Shiba, *Commerce and Society in Sung China* (Ann Arbor: Center for Chinese Studies, University of Michigan, 1970).

Tung-tsu Chu, *Law and Society in Traditional China* (Paris: Mouton, 1961).

## INLAND WATERWAYS AND COASTAL ROUTES

**First Grand Canal.** During the Tang dynasty (618–907) both Chang'an and Luoyang served as capitals of the central government. By that time the problem of supplying the interior was to some extent different from

Illumination of an imperial riverboat, Ming dynasty, 1368–1644 (National Palace Museum, Taipei, Taiwan)

that in the Han era (206 B.C.E.–220 C.E.). With the growth in the Yangzi (Yangtze) River valley, many canals were built to transport grain from the south to the north. Combined into a single system during the Sui empire (589–618), these canals served to link the northern and southern parts of the empire by a route leading from Hangzhou to Kaifeng. Known as the Grand Canal, this system of waterways was supplemented by ancillary routes that carried goods to the Northwest.

**Increased Revenues.** After the unification of the country under the Tang dynasty, movement along internal water routes increased. The opening of the Grand Canal, connecting the basins of the Yellow and Yangzi rivers, marked a new era in communications. It stimulated the growth of water transport in the East and South, greatly influencing agriculture and commerce. By the eighth century, hundreds of thousands of tons of tribute grain were shipped along the canals annually. A coastal route also existed, but it was of little value in solving the problems of transportation, because the central governments were located in the interior. In addition, there was a lack of deepwater vessels. Not until the beginning of the Song dynasty (960–1279) did the Chinese build strong vessels capable of sailing on the high seas.

**Disrepair.** When the Northern Song emperors (960–1125) had their capital at the city of Kaifeng, they continued to use these canals heavily. During the Southern Song dynasty (1127–1279), however, the role of the Grand Canal declined because of the fighting between Song and Jin armies along the Huai River. As a result, the waterway itself fell into disrepair.

**Second Grand Canal.** After occupying China and establishing their capital at Beijing, the Mongols faced the problem of transporting supplies from the South to the North. The Yuan empire tried to solve this difficulty by utilizing a combination of sea routes and inland waterways. Kublai Khan decided to build a new Grand Canal, and as before, this new waterway was intended to connect the North with the Yangzi River via the Huai River valley. The second Grand Canal was directed to the north instead of the northwest so that it crossed the Yellow River itself and arrived at a terminal near Beijing. Some of the stretches of the first canal were repaired for reuse, but overall a new course had to be constructed. This series of waterways, which was completed in 1295, played a significant role in the communication network of China until the introduction of railways in the nineteenth century. However, nature often disrupted the canal system, as when the Yellow River altered its course and damaged the locks. For this reason the Yuan government increasingly relied on the transport of grain by sea.

**Sea Transport.** The huge empire of the Mongols led to a rapid growth in trading. Shipment of tribute rice from South China to the capital at Beijing by sea proved to be quicker and less expensive than by land. As a result, the Yuan court appointed two former salt smugglers and pirates of the Yangzi delta as superintendents of navigation. Ships closely followed the coastline, taking more than two

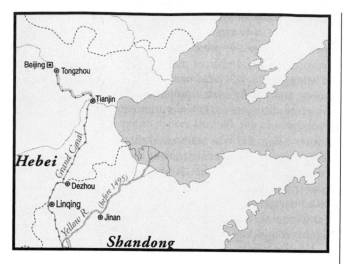

Map showing the course of the Grand Canal during the Ming period (from F. W. Mote, *Imperial China*, 1999)

months to reach Tianjing. The largest seagoing vessels of Yuan had a carrying capacity of 300,000 pounds. Pirates, typhoons, shoals, strong northern winter winds, and southward-flowing currents often caused delays. In order to avoid these problems, ship captains tried to limit their sailing from April to September each year. In 1283 the first shipment of 5.3 million pounds of foodstuffs and goods was made, rising to 76 million pounds in the following year. From 1324 to 1329 the amount shipped annually by sea ranged from 266 million pounds to 465 million pounds.

**Sources:**

C. P. Fitzgerald, *The Southern Expansion of the Chinese People* (London: Barrie & Jenkins, 1972).

*Transport in Transition: The Evolution of Traditional Shipping in China,* translated by Andrew Watson (Ann Arbor: Center for Chinese Studies, University of Michigan, 1972).

Thomas R. Tregear, *A Geography of China* (London: University of London Press, 1965).

## LANGUAGE

**Chinese Han.** Belonging to the Sino-Tibetan language family, Chinese Han is the principal language group of East Asia. Around the tenth century, Modern Chinese developed from Ancient or Middle Chinese. The scholar Sima Guang noted this transition in several studies published in the eleventh century.

**Vernacular.** The letters of Western alphabets simply show distinctions of sound. Although the Chinese characters had the same purpose in their development, the earlier forms were produced to stand for individual material objects or actions, or simple abstract concepts. Vernacular language began to develop in the Tang dynasty (618–907). Partially because of changes of pronunciation in the medieval age, by the late Ming era (1368–1644) it was difficult to identify the correct pronunciation of a given character, which varied in different regions of China, in reference to local dialect. By the late Ming period, hundreds of dialects had developed all over the empire. Several dialect dictionaries appeared, but they were primarily guides to the proper pronunciation of characters found in literary texts. They were quite poor sources for the study of dialectal vocabulary and were not useful in any way in the study of grammar.

**Evaluation.** In the Song dynasty (960–1279) there were a total of 53,525 Chinese characters. The large number of characters and the comparative difficulty of mastering the script discouraged many foreigners from learning the language, which seemed to isolate the Chinese from other civilizations. However, the stability and identity of Chinese writing still served as a means to unify educated people throughout the empire. Although these men communicated in dialects, which were incomprehensible to each other, they were taught to signify their meaning in writing by using the same set of symbols (such as *I, II, III* or *1, 2, 3*

Manual of calligraphy, 687 (National Palace Museum, Taipei, Taiwan)

in Europe) with consistent meanings but changeable pronunciation in different provinces.

**Impact.** During the imperial period (617–1644), Korea, Japan, and Vietnam adopted Chinese writing. In these three countries, Chinese characters became the foundation of the writing system, and classical Chinese became the official written language, similar to the way Latin did in medieval Europe. Over time the inhabitants naturally developed ways of writing their own native languages. They employed Chinese graphs (written or printed representations of basic units of speech such as syllables) to write their own semantic analogues and either borrowed or created new characters.

**Sources:**

Thomas F. Carter, *The Invention of Printing in China and Its Spread Westward,* revised edition by L. C. Goodrich (New York: Ronald, 1955).

Robert A. D. Forrest, *The Chinese Language* (London: Faber & Faber, 1973).

Jerry Norman, *Chinese* (Cambridge & New York: Cambridge University Press, 1988).

Edwin G. Pulleyblank, *Middle Chinese: A Study in Historical Phonology* (Vancouver: University of British Columbia Press, 1984).

## PRINTING

**Origins.** Prior to the Tang dynasty (618–907) the Chinese used steles bearing transcripts and drawings as stamps or blocks to make reproductions of engraved pictures and well-known pieces of calligraphy. The Chinese also used rubbings and seals to produce impressions of written characters, drawings, and religious pictures. Printing developed steadily during the era of the Tang and Five Dynasties (907–960). A new technique was to print from carved woodblocks and create precise reproductions of manuscript pages from ancient texts.

**Woodblock Printing.** Buddhists, realizing the importance of printing for the spread of their faith, were among the first promoters of printing. The earliest printed text in the world was a Buddhist charm scroll printed in China between 704 and 751; one million copies were printed in 770 for a Japanese empress. Reproduced by woodblock printing in 868, the Buddhist *Diamond Sutra*, the first complete printed book in the world, consisted of six sheets of text and one sheet of illustration pasted together to form a sixteen-foot-long scroll. By that time woodblock printing had already been used in the commercial centers and densely populated cities and towns of Sichuan province and southeastern China.

**Coming of Age.** By the end of the Tang dynasty the government regularly printed a newspaper declaring new regulations and appointments. Printing became a prosperous industry in the Song era (960–1279) when government and private printers alike printed specimens of famous art. Printed in 953 by the Chinese National Academy, a complete 130-volume set of the Confucian classics with commentaries was the first official printed publication in the world sold to the public. By that time,

Modern reproduction of movable type invented by Bi Sheng between 1041 and 1048 (Ontario Science Center, Toronto)

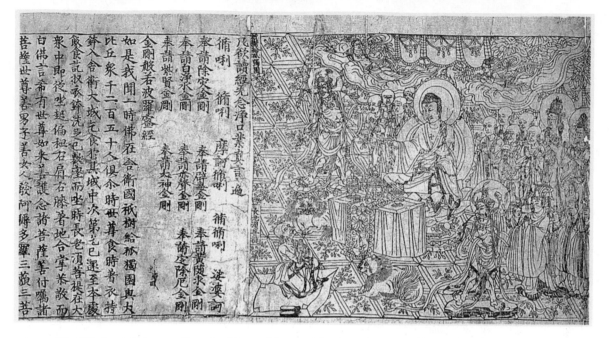

Woodblock print of a page from the *Diamond Sutra,* originally published in 868 (British Library, London)

printing had come of age. Great quantities of certain works were reproduced in millions of copies. Between 972 and 983 the entire Buddhist canon, the *Tripitaka* of 130,000 pages, was reproduced. The set was reprinted twenty times during the Song and Yuan (1279–1368) dynasties from the original woodblocks. More than 400,000 copies of one Buddhist collection from the tenth century still survived in the late Ming period (1368–1644).

**Movable Characters.** The commoner Bi Sheng invented effective movable type between the years 1041 and 1048. The first mention of the invention of movable type in China appeared in 1086 in the famous scientist Shen Gua's *Dream Pool Essays,* a collection of notes mostly on the history of science and technology. Since then, movable type continued to be used from time to time throughout China. A councilor of Kublai Khan's employed it to print books of philosophy. The Mongols utilized pottery, tin, wood, and lead to make this type.

**Use.** By 1300 the Mongols had introduced movable wooden type to eastern Turkestan, known as Turfan. Movable type was much easier to use for the Uighur scripts of Turfan than for the Chinese language. Wang Chen perfected the use of wooden type when printing his classic, the *Treatise on Agriculture,* in 1313. However, owing to the difficult task of handling the huge quantity of movable type required for the most frequently used Chinese characters, woodblock printing remained the ordinary Chinese technique until the seventeenth century.

**Color Printing.** The Chinese invented multicolor printing in the twelfth century. Paper money produced in 1107 was printed in three colors in order to prevent counterfeiting. The money had legends in black, a circle design in vermilion, and a "blue face" in indigo. Two-color printing of texts probably began when an edition of the *Diamond Sutra* was produced in 1340, which used black for the text and red for prayers and pictures. Four-color printing in black, gray, green, and red was also developed. In general, Chinese color-printing techniques used water instead of oily inks to create subtle effects. In the Ming dynasty (1368–1644) multicolor block printing was perfected.

---

## MOISTENED CLAY

Shen Kuo, a great scientist in the eleventh century, mentioned the invention of movable-type printing in his book, *Dream Pool Essays* (1086). He wrote:

As late as the Tang dynasty the production of books by block printing was still practiced on a limited scale. It was not until the time of the Later Tang (923–936) that the government, upon the recommendation of its prime minister Feng Tao, first sponsored the reproduction of the *Five Classics* by block printing. From then on practically all important books were produced by block printing.

During the Ch'ing-li period (1041–1048) a commoner named Pi Sheng first invented the movable type. Each type was made of moistened clay upon which was carved one Chinese character. The portion that formed the character was as thin as the edge of a small coin. The type was then hardened by fire and thus made permanent.

**Source:** Shen Kuow, "Meng-hsi Sketches," in *The Essence of Chinese Civilization,* edited by Dun J. Li (Princeton, N.J.: D. Van Nostrand, 1967).

## TESTING SCHOLARS

Wang Pu, an historian in the tenth century, discussed in his book the role of printing in the spread of classical learning. He wrote:

In the second month of the third year of Ch'ang-hsing (A.D. 932) the First and Second Secretariats petitioned the emperor for the printing of the *Nine Classics,* the test of which would be based upon inscriptions. The Department of Cultural Affairs, ordered by the emperor to be in charge of this undertaking, was to recruit professors and students to collect authentic copies based upon stone inscriptions. Each professor or student was to examine the different versions of a classic in which he specialized, and once the authentic version was determined, duplicate it by hand for as many copies as possible.

The Department of Cultural Affairs was also charged with the responsibility of hiring carvers who would make printing blocks in accordance with the adopted text based upon stone inscription. Copies of the *Nine Classics,* once printed, would be distributed throughout the empire. The imperial order made it clear that anyone who wished to copy any or all of the *Nine Classics* for his own use should copy from the authorized version which was now in printed form. He should not be allowed to use any of the unauthorized versions.

Source: Wang P'u, "The Institutions of the Five Dynasties," in *The Essence of Chinese Civilization,* edited by Dun J. Li (Princeton, N.J.: D. Van Nostrand, 1967).

**Comparison.** Chinese woodblock printing, to some extent, was more advanced in technique than European typography of the fifteenth century. The Chinese experience with seals and stamping and the use of special papers allowed the text being reproduced to appear reversed on the back. In addition, being a fairly inexpensive and flexible procedure, woodblock printing did not need a large capital expenditure.

**Spread.** Korea was the first country to which printing spread from China around the year 700. (Many old printing blocks survive today in South Korea.) Other Asian countries also learned the printing technique from the Chinese. When the Mongols occupied Central Asia, printing spread to Persia and finally to Europe. The first Persian paper money was printed following the Chinese system in Tabriz in 1294. The Persians called paper money "Jiao," the same as the Chinese called it.

Sources:
Thomas F. Carter, *The Invention of Printing in China and Its Spread Westward,* revised edition by L. C. Goodrich (New York: Ronald, 1955).

Robert A. D. Forrest, *The Chinese Language* (London: Faber & Faber, 1973).

Jerry Norman, *Chinese* (Cambridge & New York: Cambridge University Press, 1988).

Denis C. Twitchett, *Printing and Publishing in Medieval China* (New York: Frederic C. Beil, 1983).

**Leeboard.** When sailing into the wind, a tacking ship may experience a lot of leeward drift, which forces the ship to go sideways with little progress forward. To correct this problem the Chinese invented the leeboard in the eighth century. This device was first mentioned in Li Chuan's *Instruction Manual of the White and Dark Planet* (759). The leeboard was a board lowered into the water on the lee side of the ship to apply pressure on the water, stopping drift in that direction and holding the ship erect. Some leeboards would be lowered from a slot in the center of the ship and were therefore called centerboards. The Dutch and Portuguese learned of the leeboard while trading in China, but they did not adopt it until the sixteenth century.

**Paddle-Wheel Warship.** The paddle-wheel warship arose in the Song age (960–1279). Without rudders, it was propelled by a complicated system of paddle wheels on both sides and the stern. Also called the "wheel ship," the paddle wheeler had an average length of three hundred feet and a complement of eight hundred sailors and marines. Such a vessel generated 50 horsepower with an average speed of 3.5 to 4 knots. A fast vessel, it could dart in and out of enemy formations and inflict great damage. However, it was not suited for oceanic voyages because of the strong currents and rough waves. Some paddle-wheel warships even had rammers fitted to their prows. In 1168 Admiral Shi Zhengzhi built a 100-ton warship propelled by a single twelve-bladed wheel. During the Yuan dynasty (1279–1368), however, the use of paddle wheelers declined rapidly as a result of most naval operations occurring on the sea instead of inland waterways.

**Spillway.** Before 984, Chinese boats, which did not have any keels and were almost flat-bottomed, could only move between lower and higher water levels in canals over double slipways. Consequently, a spillway was used to regulate water flow. It extended ramps into the water, and a ship would approach and be fastened to ropes turned by ox-powered capstans. Within two or three minutes the ship would be hauled up the ramp to the higher level and for a moment would balance insecurely in the air. Then it would shoot forward, scudding down the canal at a level several feet higher than it had started. Travelers and sailors had to tie themselves firmly to the boat so as to prevent being thrown about and wounded. The disadvantage of this technique was that boats and their cargoes often sustained severe damage. Many times bandits and corrupt officials would wait for just such moments to loot the vessels and their contents. There is also historical evidence that suggests occasionally boats were brutally handled on purpose or were artificially weakened in order to create "accidents."

**Canal Pound-Lock.** Since grain was the ordinary tax payment throughout imperial China (617–1644), and transportation of it to central repositories and warehouses was the lifeblood of the dynasties, any considerable interruption of this shipping would generate an extremely grave social and political crisis. To eliminate the stealing of grain

Woodcut of a paddle-wheel warship, 1637
(from Norman Kotker, ed., *The Horizon
History of China*, 1969)

grain tribute to the city by canal. As a result they shipped about one-half of the entire annual supplies by sea. As time went on, the need for large boats on the canals was reduced, many smaller vessels came into use, and the pound locks fell into disrepair. While this device became less useful in China, Europeans began to adopt it in 1373.

**Post Stations.** The Tang dynasty (618–907) provided the greatest expansion of waterways, connecting the Yellow River with the Yangzi (Yangtze) and Hangzhou rivers through the Grand Canal. The Tang court also constructed roads along both banks of the canal. These roads and an accompanying network of post stations allowed the government to receive news and send out orders all over the empire rapidly. Elms and willows planted along the sides of the road provided travelers with shade. The post stations, 25 to 30 miles apart, each had 200 horses. The hostelries at the stations had beds with silk coverlets for high-ranking emissaries. On the same roads, there was usually a runner service with stations every three miles. On average, a message could travel up to 300 miles in one day (longer if emergency circumstances warranted night riding and night running).

**Sources:**

Derk Bodde, *Chinese Thought, Society, and Science: The Intellectual and Social Background of Science and Technology in Pre-Modern China* (Honolulu: University of Hawaii Press, 1991).

Joseph Needham, *Clerks and Craftsmen in China and the West* (Cambridge: Cambridge University Press, 1970).

E-tun Sun and Shiou-chuan Sun, trans., *T'ien-kung k'ai-wu: Chinese Technology in the Seventeenth Century* (University Park: Pennsylvania State University Press, 1966).

## TRAVEL IN THE YUAN DYNASTY

**Mongols.** Genghis Khan and his successors united all of Central Asia under one empire. The Mongol rulers took a liberal attitude toward religion, national allegiance, and social customs, and travel within and outside the empire became possible. The establishment of the great Yuan dynasty (1279–1368) and the increase in trade along the Silk Road facilitated the creation of the first direct contacts between China and the West. For the early travelers the most ordinary motivation was commerce, but some had political purposes in seeking allies against the Muslims. Meanwhile, for some travelers, proselytism was the major reason for their trips.

**New Route.** By 1279 the lands of East Asia had been in touch with the Indo-Iranian world via sea lanes and a land route following a group of oases in the Tarim basin. The Mongol expansion in the thirteenth and fourteenth centuries helped to revive the old steppe route, which had connected Mongolia with the lower Volga valley via Dzungaria and Kazakhstan since the New Stone Age (circa 8000 B.C.E.). Beginning in 1229 the Mongols thoroughly reorganized this route, which stretched to the plains of Eastern Europe and extended the Chinese postal relay stations.

**Travelers.** The Mongol territory was traversed by a variety of travelers, such as Muslims of Central Asia and

during canal transport, Qiao Weiyo, assistant commissioner of transport for Huainan, invented in 984 the canal pound-lock. He built two large "hanging gates" at the third dam along the West River near Huaiyin. The 250 feet between the two gates was then covered with a great roof like a hut. After a boat passed the first gate, it closed behind the vessel. The water level in the lock then either rose or fell to match the level of the water toward which the boat was sailing. The other gate then opened and let the boat go through.

**Advantages.** Water levels in an average canal differed by 4 or 5 feet at each lock, and over its entire length a canal could rise more than 100 feet above sea level. (The Grand Canal rose 138 feet above sea level.) However, many canals in China became dry in the summer, and several weeks would have to pass before enough water had been accumulated for flash-gates to be opened in order to let boats enter. The introduction of pound-locks helped to save valuable water resources. Only one lock was used each time, so that the canals, by saving water, could extend the time of their usefulness. More importantly, the previous corrupt practices became limited, and the passage of the ships went on without any obstructions.

**Decline.** The use of pound-lock gates declined because of social changes. After the Mongols moved the capital to Beijing, it was not feasible to transport the whole imperial

the Middle East, Russian Orthodox subjects of the Chagatai, Il-Khan, and Golden Horde empires, subjects of the former Liao and Jin dynasties of North China, and Genoese and Venetian merchants whose trade relationships with Russia and the Near East involved trips to the Far East. In 1219 Yelu Chucai, minister of Genghis Khan, accompanied his master across Turkestan to the West. The next year an envoy of the emperor of North China traveled to Persia and the Hindu Kush to meet Genghis Khan. In 1221 a Daoist monk traveled across China to Uliassutai, Urumchi, and on to the Hindu Kush, ending his travels in 1224. By 1259 imperial messengers made regular trips to Hulagu, then near Baghdad.

**Europeans.** During the Mongol occupation, most Russian princes and grand-dukes were required to travel to Karakorum, the Mongol capital, for their submission and investiture. For this reason, Prince Yaroslav II and Alexander Nevsky crossed the Tarbagatai area in the mid 1200s. Most of these people obviously followed the North Road of the Silk Route. After the Mongol campaigns in Eastern and Central Europe in the thirteenth century, many European prisoners were sent as slaves via the northern route and Turkestan to Karakorum as well as other cities.

**Languages.** Because of the relations between business and administration in the Mongols' political institution, some foreigners even served as officials in the Yuan court. The Mongols began to adapt the Uigur alphabet as the official language of administration in China and to abandon the quadrangular script created by the Tibetan lama 'Phags-pa and adopted in 1269. Persian was the most popular language in commercial circles and on the caravan route connecting Tabriz to Beijing.

**John of Plano Carpini.** The kings and the Popes of Western Europe were determined to dispatch Franciscan missionaries to Karakorum and Beijing in an effort to become allies with the Mongols and to convert them. The first European to China was a Franciscan monk, John of Plano Carpini, sent by Pope Innocent IV. Accompanied by Benedict of Poland, Plano Carpini left Lyon in 1245, traveling from the Tarbagatai via Lake Zaisan to Karakorum. His mission accomplished little, but after his return he wrote an account of the enthronement of Guyug Khan in 1246 and the manners and customs of the Mongols.

**Franciscans.** Unsatisfied with the achievements of earlier expeditions, Louis IX, the king of France, and as Pope Innocent IV tried again in 1253, sending William of Rubruck, a native of Flanders, to Mongolia in order to seek military assistance against the Muslims in the Crusades. He crossed the Black Sea and the Crimea and reached the steppe route. He was interviewed by the Khan Mongke in Karakorum, where he stayed until 1254. Another Franciscan, the Italian Giovanni di Monte Corvino, took a different route. After arriving in Iran, he took ship in 1291 at Hormuz, which was then

the point of departure of the sea routes to East Asia, and landed at Chunzhou in southern China. In 1307 Pope Clement V appointed him Archbishop of Beijing because of his successful mission. The Italian Franciscan, Odoric of Pordenone, left for East Asia in 1314. After visiting Constantinople he crossed the Black Sea and arrived in Iran, where he boarded a ship to India and finally to Guangzhou, where he took another vessel to Fuzhou. After leaving Fuzhou for Hangzhou by the inland roads, he traveled to Beijing by the Grand Canal and stayed there for three years. Returning to Europe through the interior of Asia, he did not arrive in Italy until 1330.

**Venetian Merchants.** In addition to these Catholic missionaries, some merchants of Western Europe also traveled to China. Among them were the famous Venetian merchants Niccolo, Maffeo, and Marco Polo. Marco Polo's father and uncle—Niccolo and Maffeo—left Venice in 1254. After arriving in Constantinople, Niccolo and Maffeo Polo took advantage of the Mongols' relaxed attitude toward trade to travel along the Silk Road to Khanbalik. They continued their journey in 1260 through the Mongol Khanate of southern Russia. From there they made their way to China through Bukhara and Chinese Turkestan. In China, Kublai Khan offered them a pleasant welcome. Before they returned home, the Grand Khan asked them to take a message to the Roman Catholic Church, asking that the Pope send to China one hundred Latin scholars. Leaving China in 1266, the Polos crossed Central Asia again and arrived in Italy in 1269 through Syria. The Roman Catholic Church, however, refused the Khan's request.

**Trip to China.** At the end of 1271 the Polos left for China again, together with Marco. The three this time passed through the Mongol Khanate of Persia and northern Afghanistan, followed the old Silk Road, crossed the Pamirs and southern Kashgaria, Yarkand, Khotan, and Lob Nor Basin, and finally arrived in Kanzhou, called by Marco Polo "Canpchu," a city they identified as a Nestorian community. After staying in the city for one year, they continued their trip to China, visiting the former Tangut capital of Ningxia. In that city they once again discovered a Christian community among the Buddhist population. From there they went into the Ongut country (Suiyuan) and then North China, which Marco Polo, like the Turks of those days, called "Cathay," a word derived from the name of the Qidan people, who dominated the region in the eleventh century. Eventually the travelers arrived at Chandu, the summer palace of Kublai Khan, 160 miles north of Beijing. The Polos there submitted a letter from Pope Gregory X to Kublai Khan. In 1275 Marco Polo went to Beijing, then called "Dadu."

**Homecoming.** Kublai Khan was impressed with Marco Polo and appointed him to a position in the salt tax administration at Yangzhou. Given the task of governing this big trade city, Marco found himself entrusted with a variety of missions by the Yuan court. In 1291 the Polo family decided to go home and were entrusted with the care of a princess intended for the Mongol king of Persia. This time they wanted to return home by water. Early in 1292, Marco Polo, his father, and his uncle boarded a ship at Quanzhou. They visited Vietnam, Java, Malaya, Ceylon, the Malabar coast, Mekran, and the southeast coast of Iran. They arrived at Ormuz in 1294 and returned to Venice the next year, after twenty-five years of living abroad.

**Memoirs.** Taken prisoner by the Genoese, Marco Polo dictated his memoirs in French to Rustichello da Pisa. These memoirs later became a famous book, *Il Milione* (Travels), describing two itineraries in China: one in the West, from Beijing to Yunnan via Shanxi, Shaanxi, and Sichuan; the other in the East, from Beijing to Fujian via Shandong, the lower Yangzi (Yangtze) River, and Zhejiang. Presenting a brief economic survey of North China and South China, this book mentioned navigable waterways and the significance of the Yangzi River, the main artery of Chinese economy. Marco Polo wrote that each year two hundred thousand boats sailed up the river. He also observed the economic significance of the Grand Canal, repaired and completed by Kublai Khan, which made the shipment of rice from the lower Yangzi River to Beijing much easier.

**Friar Odoric.** In 1325 Franciscan Friar Odoric of Pordenone traveled to Beijing by the sea route, remained there for three years, and returned home by land, crossing the southwest corner of Turkestan. He began dictating his memoirs to a fellow monk, but he died before completing it and his story was not published until 1513.

**Travel to the West.** While many foreigners traveled to China in the Mongol era, some Chinese went to the West. They traveled from North China to the Middle East or even to Europe. Among them was the Daoist monk Chang Chun, patriarch of the Zhuan Zhen sect. Genghis Khan ordered him to Afghanistan in 1219. Beginning his journey from Shandong in 1220, Chang Chun and his eighteen disciples traversed Outer Mongolia and the Altai, crossed Samarkand, went around the south of the Hindu Kush, and appeared in 1222 at Genghis Khan's camp in the Kabul area. Leaving Genghis Khan near Tashkent the next year, Chang Chun returned to Beijing and thereafter completed a book on his journey. In 1259 the Khan Mongke sent another Chinese scholar, Chang De, on a mission to Iran. Beginning his journey from Karakorum, he crossed the north of the Tian Shan, Samarkand and Tabriz, and returned home in 1263. Liu Yu left a written record of Chang De's journey titled *Record of a Mission to the West.*

**Nestorian Monks.** Born in Beijing, the Chinese Nestorian monk Rabban Bar Suma and his disciple Mark decided to embark for the Holy Land in 1275. They visited the Nestorian pope in the main city of northwestern Iran, to the south of Tabriz. From the city, Khan Argun sent Suma on a mission to Rome and the kings of France and England. After visiting Constantinople and Rome between 1287 and 1288, he saw the king of England in Gascony and Philip the Fair in Paris. His travel to Rome encouraged Pope Clement III to dispatch Giovanni di Monte Corvino to Beijing.

**Chinese Influence.** The Mongol domination promoted the transmission of certain Chinese techniques in the empire of the Il-Khan. Chinese influence was noticeable in Persian miniatures as well as in Iranian ceramics, music, and architecture of the Mongol age. The introduction in the fourteenth century of playing cards, printed fabrics, and paper money was clearly associated with the emergence of wood engraving in Europe and therefore of printing with movable type.

**Aftermath.** Immediately following the fall of the Yuan dynasty, turmoil ensued and travelers temporarily became rare in western China. In 1419 the Shah Rukh, emperor of Persia, tried to reopen broken communications by dispatching an embassy. The ambassadors reached the Tianshan and followed the Tien Shan Nan Lu on to Turfan, Hami, and Lanzhou. They spent somewhat over one year on their journey. They remained in Beijing five months and started back in May 1422 by crossing the Pamirs, probably along the Silk Road in the vicinity of Kashgar. They reached Heart again on 1 September.

Sources:

Thomas T. Allsen, *Mongol Imperialism: The Policies of the Grand Qan Mongke in China, Russia, and the Islamic Lands* (Berkeley: University of California Press, 1987).

Ch'en Yüan, *Western and Central Asians in China under the Mongols*, translated by Ch'ien Hsing-hai and L. Carrington Goodrich (Berkeley: University of California Press, 1966).

Chih-Ch'ang Li, *The Travels of an Alchemist*, translated by Arthur Waley (London: Routledge, 1931).

Jack Dabbs, *History of the Discovery and Exploration of Chinese Turkestan* (The Hague, Netherlands: Mouton, 1963).

# SIGNIFICANT PEOPLE

## GUO SHOUJING

### 1231-1316
### ENGINEER AND DIRECTOR OF WATERWAYS

**Early Life.** Born in Hebei, Guo Shoujing was a precocious child. At the age of fifteen, coming across a diagram of the "Lotus Clepsydra," he was able to understand at first sight the principle of this time-keeping device. In late 1251, when a bridge was washed away and no trace of its foundations could be identified, Guo Shoujing was put in charge of the restoration project. He first examined the area and located the site of the old bridge. He then cleared away the mud that covered its footings and had the structure rebuilt, thus guaranteeing passage once again. Completed in only forty days, the project needed only four hundred laborers.

**Water Clock.** Sometime around 1260, Guo Shoujing cast a bronze water clock for a local observatory. Completed in 1262, it was subsequently moved to the capital, Beijing. He also built a tower for observing the twenty-eight lunar mansions as well as the larger stars and the constellations.

**Irrigation.** In 1260 Guo Shoujing had a chance to make a comprehensive survey of provincial irrigation systems. Praised for his expertise in waterworks and his unusual intelligence, Guo Shoujing was granted an audience with the emperor. On that occasion the scientist presented six different schemes for improving irrigation and waterways in the region north of the Yellow River. His knowledge greatly impressed the Mongol emperor Kublai Khan, who without delay appointed him superintendent of waterways for the various districts. In 1263 Guo Shoujing received the rank of vice commissioner of waterways, and he was given a silver table.

**Recommendations.** Guo Shoujing became vice director of waterways two years later. On his way to the capital he sailed four days and nights on the Yellow River and conducted the first survey of the upper reaches of the river. He discovered that this particular section was navigable for large cargo boats. After observing many derelict canals, he recommended the old canal be widened and deepened so that it could be used for both navigation and irrigation while safely draining away any excess water. His recommendations were adopted.

**Canals.** In 1272 Guo Shoujing received an appointment as director of waterways. Another large canal was built joining the nearby rivers for irrigation. Kublai Khan ordered all the people from chancellors down to civil servants to form a workforce under Guo Shoujing's supervision. Completed by 1293, the canal greatly improved communications in the area and made it easier to transport foodstuffs into Beijing. For his achievement Guo Shoujing received a cash reward and was assigned to administer the building of another new canal.

**Calendar.** In 1276 Kublai Khan decreed that a new calendar be devised. According to Guo Shoujing, the accuracy of any calendar depended on the accuracy of the observations made by astronomical instruments. He set about to construct seventeen different astronomical instruments. In 1280 the Calendar for Fixing the Seasons was finally completed and formally presented to the court. The khan ordered its formal adoption in the first month in 1281.

**Importance.** Guo Shoujing died in 1316 at the age of eighty-three. In light of his many creative and original contributions, this scholar was regarded as the most outstanding hydrologist and astronomer of the Yuan dynasty (1279–1368) and the last of the great traditional mathematicians in Chinese history.

Sources:
Robert Payne, *The Canal Builders: The Story of Canal Engineers through the Ages* (New York: Macmillan, 1959).

Igor de Rachewiltz, ed., *In the Service of the Khan: Eminent Personalities of the early Mongol-Yuan Period, 1200-1300* (Wiesbaden: Franz Steiner, 1976).

## LI TAO

### 1115-1184
### HISTORIAN

**Early Life.** The son of a classical scholar, Li Tao was fond of learning. From his early childhood he read broadly, not only Confucian classics but also history and books on medicine, agriculture, cosmology, and predictions. Among these works, he was particularly interested in the *I Chang* (Book of Changes).

**Specialization.** History became his area of specialty over other subjects. He committed himself to studying the *Spring and Autumn Annals*. Emphasizing the moral-didactic view of history writing, he believed that the historian should act as an ethical commentator and use the *Spring and Autumn Annals* as a model. While compiling his history, he praised or blamed participants in historical events as a means to encourage the good and warn the evil. He also took compassion on the conduct of the lower classes and paid attention to local events. For this reason, he was considered a positivist historian rather than an active traditionalist.

**Local Official.** In 1132, when he was seventeen years old, he passed the prefectural examination and began to write two historical works, *The Mirror of Both Han Dynasties* and *The Discussion about the Restoration of Righteousness,* both of which contributed to his fame as a moralist historian. He received the Jinshi degree in 1138 and was appointed later as subprefectural registrar of a region. He asked the government, however, for a delay of his assumption of the new office for several years and continued his studies at home. In 1142, when he took the post, he was encouraged by friends to seek a higher position in the central government, but he rejected their suggestions. During this time as a local official he used his energy on academic works, namely the collection and arrangement of historical sources.

**Compiler.** After his father died in 1147, he returned home to observe mourning; three years later he was appointed judge of a prefecture. He then started to compile his life's work, *The Manuscript for the Extension of the Broad Mirror for Helping Government.* In 1162 he was appointed administrator of a prefecture. Five years later he was summoned to the central government and appointed an assistant in the Ministry of War and concurrently an official of the Bureau of Compilation of the Reign History. He became vice director of the Imperial Library and Provisional Secretariat Imperial Reader in 1169, and seven years later assumed the position of director of the Imperial Library, provisional associate compiler of the Bureau of Compilation of Reign History, and associate compiler of the Bureau of Compilation of Veritable Records. He worked on the compilation of the *Reign History of Four Thrones* until his death in 1184.

Sources:
Etienne Balazs and Yves Hervouet, eds., *A Sung Bibliography* (Hong Kong: Chinese University Press, 1978).

Herbert Franke, ed., *Sung Biographies,* 4 volumes (Wiesbaden: Steiner, 1976).

# ZHENG HE (CHENG HO)

## 1371-1433
### COURT EUNUCH AND ADMIRAL

**Zheng He.** Zheng He (Cheng Ho) was born in 1371 in southwestern Yunnan province (north of present-day Laos). His birth name was Ma He because his father had made an overland pilgrimage to Mecca and converted to Islam. Around 1381 Ming armies invaded Yunnan and captured Zheng He. Castrated at the age of thirteen, he became a servant to the Chinese emperor's fourth son, Prince Zhu Di. He held the position of *Sanbao Taijien,* "Grand Eunuch of the Three Jewelries," and became a military officer, instructing the prince in the ways of war and diplomacy.

**First Expedition.** In 1402, when the prince became Emperor Yongle, Zheng He was appointed an admiral, the first such posting for any court eunuch. He took the name *Zheng* officially in 1404 and the next year received command of the "Treasure Ships." (The largest of these vessels was 440 feet in length and had 9 masts.) With 317 ships and nearly 30,000 sailors, Zheng He embarked on a voyage to various ports in Southeast Asia, India, Arabia, and East Africa. The voyage was distinctive in its scope and official sponsorship; the Ming court wanted to assert its power abroad by claiming tributary states as well as to develop commercial networks. In addition to being overall commander, Zheng He, as envoy of the emperor, acted in the capacity of an ambassador. Sailing south along the Chinese coast and then across the South China Sea, the fleet made its immediate base at Malacca.

**Malacca.** The ruler of Malacca greeted the Chinese and paid them tribute. In return the Ming emperor recognized him as king of Malacca. Although he eventually converted to Islam, the first of his line to become Muslim, he remained loyal to China. The Ming empire (1368–1644), like other Chinese dynasties, did not pay attention to the religions that their subjects might profess, provided that they remained loyal to the Chinese emperor.

**Palembang.** From Malacca, Zheng He's fleet proceeded across the straits to Palembang in Sumatra. Long known to the Chinese, this city was a center of Buddhism. When the kingdom of Majapahit declined, a pirate leader from Guangzhou in Guangdong province occupied the city in 1377 with his Chinese followers. After arriving in the port, Zheng He defeated and captured the brigand. This triumph paved the way for safe passage through the straits and increased the prestige of the Ming empire in the region. Afterward, Zheng He appointed a Chinese ruler to the region.

**Calicut.** Zheng He next crossed the eastern Indian Ocean to the major port of Calicut in southern India. The fleet remained there for several months. In 1407 it returned to China, sailing northward and eastward in the summer with the southwest monsoon. (In the winter months, ship captains sailed southward and westward when the northeast monsoon blew. In fact, the monsoon winds help to explain the dates of the six other great voyages and their normal two-year intervals.)

**Second Expedition.** Zheng He began the second expedition in 1407 and returned in 1409. On account of Calicut's delivery of tribute to the Ming court, Zheng He was instructed to extend imperial gifts and greetings to its king and his subordinates. This gesture established the pattern for Chinese dealings with many other native states in the following years. Zheng He also visited Cochin and Ceylon, erecting steles declaring that those two kingdoms and Calicut were vassals of the Ming empire. The fleet returned home with copper, timber, and spices, and the profits earned by the imperial government more than justified the trip.

**Third Expedition.** By the fifteenth century a thriving trade existed in southern Indian cities between Arab merchantmen coming from the West and Chinese ships arriving from the East. During his third expedition (1409–1411) Zheng He sailed to Siam, Malacca, the Malabar coast, and Ceylon. Upon reaching Ceylon, he was faced with strong opposition from King Alagakkonam, who refused to pay tribute to the Ming court and attacked the fleet. Zheng He landed his army and defeated the king, who was captured and sent back to Beijing as a prisoner of war. Thereafter Zheng appointed another ruler who would pay tribute to the Ming empire.

**Fourth Expedition.** On the fourth expedition (1413–1415), after visiting the Indonesian countries and crossing the Indian Ocean, Zheng He reached Calicut and then Hormuz at the entrance to the Persian Gulf. Part of the fleet traveled as far as Aden at the entrance to the Red Sea and the eastern coast of Africa. As a Muslim, Zheng He did not wish to employ military force in the region. He negotiated with great diplomatic skill and eventually nineteen countries sent envoys and tribute payments to the Ming empire. The emperor was so delighted with this achievement that he gave special rewards to all of those who participated in the expedition.

**Other Expeditions.** During the fifth expedition, Zheng He left China in 1417 and visited Hormuz and Aden again as well as present-day Somalia. It returned in 1420 after accomplishing the longest round voyage. On the sixth expedition of 1421–1422, Zheng He's fleet sailed to Sumatra while another fleet went toward East Africa and the Persian Gulf. In the last trip between 1431 and 1433, the Chinese visited Champa, Java, Palembang, Malacca, the Malabar coast, and Hormuz. Some of the ships sailed from Calicut to Jeddah, the port of Mecca, and joined the main fleet again via Aden and the south coast of Arabia. Zheng He himself died soon after his fleet arrived at Nanking in 1433 and was buried near Niushou (Bull's Head Hill) overlooking the shipyards.

**Withdrawal.** The death of Zheng He marked the end of an era in Chinese history. After 1433 the Ming court no longer sent expeditions overseas for several reasons. First, these voyages did not create enough profit to justify their continual occurrence. Second, the eunuch leadership did not win the support of the Confucian officials. When Emperor Chengzu died in 1425, the eunuchs lost an enthusiastic supporter of the emperor, although his successor Xuanzong did send out one last expedition. Third, by 1417 a system of locks in the Grand Canal maintained the water level sufficiently high to allow the grain ships supplying Beijing to use the waterway all through the year. Therefore, the capital no longer had a need to rely on sea transport of food supplies and a large navy became unnecessary. Finally, the Mongol attacks of 1438–1449 forced the Ming government to dispatch troops to the frontier and to use more resources on fort rather than ship construction.

**Significance.** These expeditions helped China to earn a reputation as a powerful political entity. Overseas trade in the form of tribute from various kingdoms increased quickly. The contacts made in the Near East on Zheng's fourth expedition undoubtedly resulted in two embassies to Nanking from Mameluke Egypt, one in the first quarter of the fifteenth century, the other in 1441. The superiority of the Chinese fleet also helped to contribute to the near-complete eradication of Japanese pirates in East Asia. Moreover, Zheng He's expeditions strengthened the old current of trade and Chinese emigration toward the territories of Southeast Asia and the ports of southern India. In fact, Zheng He's triumph in Southeast Asia left such lively reminiscences that he was deified. Temples in his honor were erected and his cult continued in some countries until modern times. Finally, after these expeditions, many geographical works were published, which helped the Chinese identify oceans and faraway lands more accurately. The most famous of these works was the *Treaties on the Barbarian Kingdoms of the Western Oceans*, which was published in 1434.

Sources:

Louise Levathes, *When China Ruled the Seas: The Treasure Fleet of the Dragon Throne 1405–1433* (New York: Simon & Schuster, 1994).

F. W. Mote, *Imperial China, 900–1800* (Cambridge, Mass.: Harvard University Press, 1999).

Shih-shan Henry Tsai, *Perpetual Happiness: The Ming Emperor Yongle* (Seattle: University of Washington Press, 2001).

# DOCUMENTARY SOURCES

*By the River at the Qingming Festival* (circa 960–1279)—A Song-era painting that shows a segmental arch bridge.

Li Chuan, *Instruction Manual of the White and Dark Planet* (759)—Li Chuan describes the leeboard, which was a board lowered into the water on the lee side of a ship, stopping drift in that direction and holding the ship erect.

Li Tao, *The Discussion about the Restoration of Righteousness* (1132); *The Mirror of Both Han Dynasties* (1132); and *The Manuscript for the Extension of the Broad Mirror for Helping Government* (circa 1150)—The major works of a well-respected historian appointed to the directorship of the imperial library. He had a moral approach to history with an emphasis on the lower class and local events.

Liu Yu, *Record of a Mission to the West* (circa 1263)—Describes the travels of the scholar-emissary Chang De to Persia.

Shen Gua, *Dream Pool Essays* (1086)—Contains an early reference to movable type.

*Treaties on the Barbarian Kingdoms of the Western Oceans* (1434)—One of many geographical studies that appeared after the great voyages of the explorer Zheng He.

Wang Zongmu, *Record of Transportation at Sea* (1572)—A treatise on deep-water ships. The book claims that the weather on the first day of each lunar month determined the forecast of the first ten days. On the second day, the author claimed, one could foretell the conditions of the middle ten-day period; on the third day one could predict what kind of weather would prevail during the balance of the month.

Zhou Zhufei, *Answers to Questions about the Regions to the South of the Mountain Ranges* (1178)—The expansion of overseas trade in the Song dynasty (960–1279) resulted in this compilation of works devoted to the description of Southeast Asia and India. Unlike travel accounts written in earlier ages by civil servants or pilgrims, this work has much information on the political system, economic expansion, and social changes.

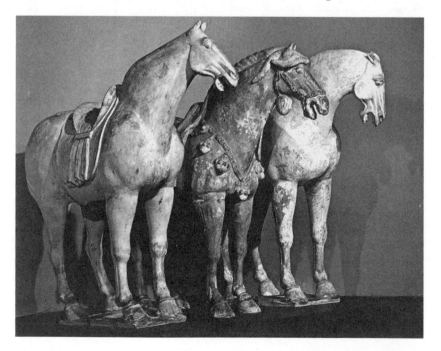

Figurines of horses, Tang dynasty, 618–907 (from Bradley Smith and Wan-go Weng, *China: A History in Art*, 1973)

## CHAPTER FIVE

# SOCIAL CLASS SYSTEM AND THE ECONOMY

by HUPING LING

## CONTENTS

*Sidebars and tables are listed in italics.*

**617**
- General Li Yaun is sent by Emperor Yang to put down a peasant rebellion in Taiyuan, but he turns against the Chinese ruler.

**618**
- Li Yaun declares an end to the Sui dynasty and establishes the Tang dynasty.

**626**
- Li Shimin, later known as the Tang emperor Taizong (Grand Ancestor), captures the Chinese capital, Chang'an, and forces his father to abdicate. During his reign he subjugates the Eastern Turks. He rules China until 649. The Tang rulers continue the "equal field" system of providing equal shares of agricultural land to the taxpaying peasants.

**637-648**
- Taizong undertakes military campaigns to wrest the Tarim Basin from the Western Turks. A military encounter occurs between Tibet, which came under Chinese suzerainty during his reign, and India.

**649**
- Tang emperor Gaozong (High Ancestor), the successor of Taizong, comes to the throne and crushes a coalition of kingdoms—made up of Koguryu (north Korea), Pakche (southwest Korea), and Japan—with assistance from the kingdom of Silla (southeast Korea). Hence, a unified Korea under Silla remains a loyal vassal of the Tang dynasty.

**683**
- Emperor Gaozong dies.

**690-705**
- Empress Wu, who has ruled through several puppet emperors after Gaozong's death, assumes the title for herself. Though denounced as a usurper and condemned by Chinese historians, she is a capable and effective ruler.

**705**
- A palace coup d'état removes Empress Wu.

**712-756**
- Tang emperor Xuangzong (Mysterious Ancestor), who is also known as Minghuang (Brilliant Emperor), comes to the throne. His reign signifies the second flourishing of the dynasty. During Xuangzong's rule, Chief Minister Li Linfu becomes a virtual dictator. Upon the minister's death in 752, Yang Guozhong, a much less capable man and a cousin of the beautiful royal concubine Yang Guifei, takes his place. The dominance of the Yang family in the court causes great discontent among the civil administrators and generals, and this discord eventually ends the brilliance of the dynasty.

* Denotes Circa Date

**755**
- An Lushan, a general of Turkish descent who commanded a Chinese army along the frontier, rebels and forces the court to flee to Sichuan. Along the way, loyal soldiers of Xuangzong force the emperor to have Yang Guifei strangled. Xuangzong then abdicates.

**758**
- The Tang ruler enforces the traditional government monopoly on the sale of salt.

**780**
- Tang emperor Dezong (Brilliant Ancestor) comes to the throne. The Tang government abandons the "equal field" system and adopts the "Double Tax" system, which levies taxes twice a year on the amount of land held by peasant households.

**800***
- Paper money is invented and used by the merchant class. Known as "flying money" because it is issued at one place and can be cashed at another site as if it can "fly" from place to place, it is in fact a draft rather than real currency. A businessman can put his money in the capital and obtain a paper document that he can then exchange for cash in other places. The money is usually backed by copper.

**806**
- Tang emperor Xianzong (Virtuous Ancestor) takes the throne. He is a vigorous ruler who tries to foster institutional renewal and attempts to recover central power.

**812**
- The government takes over the control of paper money and uses it for collecting local taxes and revenues. Exchange certificates redeemable in commodities such as salt and tea are also issued.

**820**
- Xianzong is murdered by the eunuchs, whose influence and power in palace politics grows in the 820s and 830s. An attempted coup against the eunuchs fails in 835.

**840**
- Tang emperor Wuzong (Militant Ancestor) comes to the throne. He is best known for his severe persecution of the Buddhist establishment. During his reign monastic lands and wealth are confiscated, monks and nuns are forced to resume lay life, and slaves and dependents of the Buddhist temples are released.

**884**
- The Huang Chao Rebellion, which has raged for ten years in northern China, finally succeeds in breaking the dynasty. The Tang gives up its attempt to control all of China Proper. The dynasty is virtually destroyed, and an array of regional states is established. A former supporter of Huang Chao later usurps the throne, thus officially ending the dynasty in 907.

*** DENOTES CIRCA DATE**

**907**
- The Five Dynasties and Ten Kingdoms period (also known as Period of Disunity) begins. Usurping generals found the Later Liang (907–923), Later Tang (923–936), Later Jin (936–946), Later Han (946–951), and Later Zhou (951–960) dynasties in brief succession in North China. Meanwhile, in Central and South China, ten states are established by regional commanders. The Five Dynasties and Ten Kingdoms period is characterized by regional militarism and a greater "barbarian" influence in North China.

**947-1125**
- The Liao Empire is established by the Khitan (Qidan) tribes, a branch of the Mongol peoples.

**960**
- General Zhao Kuangyin overthrows the Later Zhou emperor and founds the Song dynasty. Known to history as Emperor Taizu (Grand Progenitor), he succeeds in establishing a lasting dynasty that controls China until 1279. By the time of his death in 976 he rules all of China, except for two states. His success lies primarily in his military reforms that weaken or strip the power of local military commanders. The breakdown of regional militarism, however, also leads to military weakness, which becomes a fatal problem for the dynasty. The Song court also orders new land surveys to correct tax inequities and institute graduated taxes based on the productivity of farms.

**976**
- Song emperor Taizong (Grand Ancestor) begins his reign, which lasts until 997.

**978-979**
- Taizong incorporates the last two independent regional states into the empire.

**1004**
- The Song government agrees to pay the Qidan Liao (a northern-bordering "barbarian" state established by a group of Mongols) an annual sum of three hundred thousand units of silver and silk.

**1023**
- The Song court establishes an office to issue banknotes of various denominations, which are supported by cash deposits. Issued by the government bank, the paper money has on it an announcement to the effect that it is good only for three years. This office is the first governmental reserve bank in the world.

**1038**
- The Tangut tribes of Tibet establish the Xi Xia kingdom in northwestern China, which lasts until 1227.

**1044**
- Unable to confront the Xi Xia militarily, the Song again resorts to appeasement and pays an annual sum to them.

\* Denotes Circa Date

**1067**
- Song emperor Shenzong (Inspired Ancestor) takes the throne.
- Wang Anshi is appointed chief councilor; he initiates a series of economic, military, and educational reforms, which are vigorously opposed by the traditionalists.

**1070***
- Cash payments begin to make up a major portion of imperial tax revenues, and the income garnered from monopolies and commercial taxes exceeds agricultural receipts.

**1085**
- Shenzong dies; the traditionalists regain power and defeat Wang's reforms.

**1100**
- Song emperor Huizong (Excellent Ancestor) comes to the throne.

**1100***
- China has fifty-two large urban prefectures of more than one hundred thousand households each.

**1107**
- Banknotes are printed in at least six different colors.

**1115**
- The Jurchen (Nuzhen) tribes from Manchuria rebel against the Liao and establish the Jin (Golden) Empire. The Song allies with the Jin against the Liao in 1125, hoping to regain sixteen prefectures lost to the Liao two centuries earlier. The Jin destroys the Liao and seizes the Song capital, Kaifeng; captures emperor Huizong; and pursues the Song armies across the Yangzi River in 1126.

**1125**
- Emperor Huizong dies.

**1127**
- Song emperor Gaozong (High Ancestor), a son of Huizong, restores the dynasty in the south, with its capital in Hangzhou, Zhejiang Province. He rules until 1162. The Song empire after 1127 is therefore known as the Southern Song (1127–1279), as opposed to the Northern Song (960–1125).

**1130s**
- General Yue Fei leads the resistance against the Jin armies in an attempt to recapture northern China. A peace faction, led by Qinkuai, controls the court, executes Yue Fei, and signs a treaty with the Jin in 1141. The Song becomes a vassal state of the Jin and agrees to pay an annual sum of three hundred thousand units of silk and silver.

* Denotes Circa Date

**1167**
- Temujin is born. He is given the title *Genghis Khan* (Universal Ruler) at a meeting of the Mongol tribes on the Kerulen River in 1206.

**1200***
- Tax income in cash surpasses that garnered through the collection of grains and textiles; the government begins using silver, gold, and other metals to supplement its copper coinage.

**1211-1215**
- Genghis Khan campaigns against the Jin and destroys its capital south of Beijing; the Jin is forced to move its capital to Kaifeng, in Henan Province.

**1227**
- Genghis Khan's army of about 129,000 men destroys the Xi Xia kingdom.
- Genghis Khan dies. He has, however, established the basis of his Eurasian empire.

**1234**
- The Jin dynasty is ended by the Mongols.

**1260**
- Kublai Khan, a grandson of Genghis, becomes the Great Khan. He adopts the Chinese dynastic name of Yuan (The First Beginning) for his empire in 1271. He also constructs roads and expands the postal-station system to assist in improving domestic commerce.

**1271**
- Marco Polo leaves Venice for China with his father and uncle, who are Venetian merchants.

**1274**
- Kublai Khan dispatches a military expedition against Japan.

**1278**
- Marco Polo begins his service in Kublai Khan's court.

**1279**
- The Song is finally destroyed by the Yuan.
- The Yuan court begins to recall all mediums of exchange and to issue silk notes, a form of paper money backed by bundles of silk. This unified currency circulates throughout the Mongol empire, and by 1294 it is used as far abroad as Persia.

\* Denotes Circa Date

**1281**
- Kublai Khan sends a second, more massive, expedition against Japan. A strong typhoon, referred to by the Japanese as a *Kamikaze* (divine wind), blows the Mongol fleet off course and saves Japan from the invasion; the Khan's fleet also attacks Java (Indonesia) in 1281 and 1292.

**1295**
- Marco Polo returns to Venice. His account of China, in the *Description of the World,* provides the Western world with its first written record of Chinese geography, economic life, and government institutions.

**1300\***
- The Yuan resumes the civil service examination system, which ceased in the north after 1237 and in the south after 1274.

**1340s**
- The Yellow River floods and changes its course, affecting millions of Chinese inhabitants of the region.

**1352**
- The Red Turbans, who wear red headdresses and are mostly followers of the White Lotus Society, a sect of Tian Tai Buddhism, rebel. They believe in the coming of Maitreya, whom they believe will eliminate all suffering and injustice.

**1368**
- The Mongol court flees to Mongolia. Zhu Yuanzhang, known to history as Taizu (Grand Progenitor), establishes the Ming (Brilliant) dynasty with its capital at Nanjing. Zhu joins the Red Turbans, later becomes a military commander, and enjoys the support of the southern gentry, who play a vital role in establishing the new regime. By the end of his reign, in 1398, the Ming control China; dominate the frontier region from Xinjiang to Inner Mongolia, and northern Manchuria; and make Korea, as well as other Central and Southeast Asian nations, tributary states.

**1368-1424**
- The Chinese experience a vigorous military resurgence. After suppressing a plot attributed to his chief minister, Taizu abolishes the Imperial Secretariat, the central administrative organ of past dynasties. Thus, the emperor's rule becomes personal and direct, contributing to Ming despotism. Population registers record an estimated total of 60 million people, who reside on 129 million acres of arable land.

**1375**
- The Ming court creates the "Valuable Note of Great Ming." This banknote is issued in only one denomination for almost two hundred years, during which time it is the legal currency. Because of inflation, its worth is significantly devalued by the end of the Ming era in the mid seventeenth century.

\* DENOTES CIRCA DATE

**1393**
- The Ming government issues a comprehensive body of administrative and criminal laws, known as the "Yongle Dadian" (Grand Law Codes of Yongle).

**1403**
- The emperor Yongle (Perpetual Happiness), the fourth son of Taizu, comes to power after a devastating civil war against his nephew, Taizu's grandson, who had inherited the throne in Nanjing. During his reign Yongle leads five expeditions against the Mongols and incorporates Annam (Vietnam) into the Ming empire.

**1405-1433**
- Seven great maritime expeditions are sent out by imperial order. Led by a Muslim eunuch and admiral named Zheng He, the primary objective is to incorporate Asian states to the south and southeast into the tribute system. The fleets not only visit vast regions of southeastern Asia but also sail to the Indian Ocean, Arabia, and the east coast of Africa. These expeditions exhibit the political and military assertiveness of the Ming dynasty.

**1420**
- Yongle moves the capital to Beijing, which symbolizes the preoccupation of the Ming with its defenses against the Mongols and other Inner Asian "barbarians." He rebuilds the city on a more extensive plan than that of the Mongols. The Early Middle period (1425–1505) of the Ming dynasty enjoys a period of peace, stability, and prosperity.

**1460s-1470s**
- The Chinese military experiences a resurgence in power.

**1487**
- The Chinese begin strengthening and extending the Great Wall.

**1506-1590***
- The Ming dynasty enters a period in which China suffers from inadequate imperial leadership; the Grand Secretariat and the eunuchs wield immense power.

**1512**
- Peasants in the central province of Sichuan revolt against unfair taxation.

**1572**
- Wanli (Ten Thousand Years) begins his reign as emperor. His Chief Grand Secretary, Zhang Juzheng, introduces the Single Whip Reform, a new tax system that combines and simplifies many taxes into monetary payments.

**1592**
- Japan invades Korea. The Ming court fulfills its suzerain duty to Korea by sending troops to attack P'yongyang. They are defeated by the Japanese. The military campaigns against the Japanese drain the resources of the regime.

* DENOTES CIRCA DATE

| | |
|---|---|
| **1600** | • Approximately 150 million people live in China. |
| **1624** | • Wei Zhongxian, a eunuch, takes over the government and persecutes members of the *Donglin* (Eastern Forest) movement, who are mostly dismissed scholar-officials who condemn philosophical eclecticism, factionalism, and the eunuchs' control of government. |
| **1628\*** | • A famine ravages the Shaanxi province. Li Zicheng, an unemployed postal attendant, joins a growing group of bandits, and soon his forces hold much of Hubei, Henan, and Shaanxi. |
| **1630s** | • Zhang Xianzhong, another rebel and Li's major rival, leads raids throughout North China. |
| **1644** | • Li Zicheng seizes Beijing, and the last Ming emperor commits suicide, thus ending the 276-year-long dynasty. Zhang Xianzhong invades Sichuan and sets up a government there. |

\* DENOTES CIRCA DATE

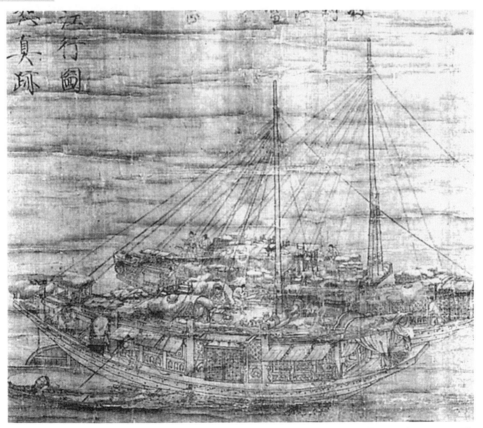

Detail of an illumination of river barges transporting goods; from the hanging scroll *Traveling on the River in Clearing Snow*, circa 975 (National Palace Museum, Taipei, Taiwan)

SOCIAL CLASS SYSTEM AND THE ECONOMY

# OVERVIEW

**Land System.** The large amounts of land concentrated in the hands of the great families contributed to the collapse of the Han dynasty (206 B.C.E.–220 C.E.). Realizing that unequal land ownership was a key cause of dynastic decline, the regimes succeeding the Han nationalized and then distributed land to the taxpaying peasants. In 485 the Northern Wei (386–535) instituted an "equal field" system that assigned uniform amounts of agricultural land to all adult peasants. The Sui dynasty (589–618) continued to practice the equal field system and applied it to the entire country; this policy was further implemented by the Tang dynasty (618–907). In theory, the system depended on the periodic redistribution of land among the taxpaying farmers, but it is questionable whether the policy was ever equitably applied.

**Taxation.** During the Tang dynasty, under the equal field system, a peasant was expected to pay the government three types of taxes: grain; silk or hemp; and corvée (forced) labor. The local government also demanded labor for specified periods. The An Lushan Rebellion (755), however, interrupted the regular collection of the land tax. The loss of revenue resulted in financial difficulties for the government, which in 780 attempted to make up for this reduced income by abandoning the equal field system and adopting the *liang shui fa* (Double Tax system), which levied taxes twice a year on the amount of land held by peasant households. The Song government (960–1279) ordered a new land survey to correct existing inequities in the tax. The Song also eliminated the old system and in its place instituted graduated taxes based on the productivity, rather than the size, of land; they also abolished the corvée. Although the Mongols have been blamed for the destruction of land in northern China, the Yuan (1279–1368) rulers, such as Kublai Khan, supported policies that stimulated agricultural development and land recovery. Kublai Khan also set up a fixed, regular system of taxation. The land tax constituted the major income source of the Ming (1368–1644) government. Based on the Double Tax system, the land tax was collected in the summer and autumn.

**Prosperity.** The Tang dynasty enjoyed unprecedented prosperity. Initially the central government received a stable and ample revenue, much larger proportionally than in any previous dynasty. The Tang period was also known for

its cosmopolitan environment, which attracted thousands of foreign traders, missionaries, and envoys to the capital and port cities. The Song dynasty experienced an economic expansion known as the "commercial revolution," which was chiefly propelled by developments such as improved agricultural technology; the use of the abacus; the invention of gunpowder and new printing techniques; the growth of domestic and foreign trade; and the development of a money economy. During the Yuan dynasty, agricultural incomes declined; however, trade within China and with foreign countries flourished. The Ming economy as a whole experienced growth, as did the size of the population—the Chinese during this period constituted between one-quarter and one-third of all people in the world. Ample supplies of grain, collected as a tax, were transported to the capital by traffic on the Grand Canal. An active domestic trade promoted specialized handicraft production and the development of capitalistic industry.

**Domestic Changes.** The Chinese manufactured silk, paper, and porcelain in the Tang period. As a result of this craft development, domestic trade increased and the cities and towns grew in both size and importance. Traditional official contempt for, and restraints upon, commercialism declined during the late Tang and Song periods. Private marketplaces sprawled far beyond the government markets. Various specialized shops lined the main streets of the cities. After they took control of China, the Mongols, who had viewed barter as indispensable for their pastoral economy, continued to value trade and elevated the social status of merchants. Under Mongol rule the domestic commerce of China developed further; this trend was continued during the Ming period. The development of Beijing and the canal system in southern China stimulated trade between the northern and southern regions of the country. A population shift to the South also contributed to commercial development in southern China.

**Foreign Trade.** As a cosmopolitan nation, China, while under the control of the Tang, welcomed traders from all over the world. Merchants and embassies brought thousands of foreigners to Chang'an, Quanzhou, and Guangzhou (Canton). To a large degree, international trade during this period was in the hands of foreigners, including Persians, Arabs, and Uighurs. Foreign trade also experienced tremendous growth during the Song period. Products from the outside world were carried by caravans that crossed an overland route, well known as the Silk Road. The Chinese traded with merchants from Central Asia, West Asia, and the Mediterranean. Overland trade was supplemented by overseas trade, which grew rapidly during the Song era as a result of improvements in the technology of shipbuilding and navigation. With the development of oceanic commerce, the eastern and southeastern coasts of China became primary regions for international trade and foreign contacts. Foreign trade also flourished during the Yuan dynasty. The trade with Central Asia, the Middle East, and Persia was primarily dominated by Muslim merchants. Among the thousands of foreigners who traveled to the east, Marco Polo, who became one of the most renowned, was the first westerner to leave a written record about China. The Ming government sponsored seven great maritime expeditions, spanning a period from 1405 to 1433. They were led by a Muslim eunuch named Zheng He and were ordered to demonstrate the glory and strength of China and to incorporate southern and southeastern Asian states into the tribute system. Apart from addressing diplomatic and political motives, these voyages also stimulated significant foreign trade.

**Financial Problems and Reforms.** The Tang court survived the An Lushan Rebellion, but it was greatly weakened economically. To help make up for the loss of revenue caused by the interrupted collection of land taxes, the court initiated a policy in 758 to enforce the traditional government monopoly on the sale of salt. In addition, the Tang government in 780 instituted the Double Tax reform, which levied taxes twice a year on the amount of land held by peasant households. This reform signified a far-reaching transition in imperial tax policy. Thereafter, agricultural taxes were assessed on the amount of land held by, rather than the number of people in, the peasant households.

**Economic Reforms.** During the Song dynasty an increased population lowered the agricultural surplus and thus reduced the tax income. As the number of inhabitants rose, each successive generation received smaller farms, therefore affecting the state income because taxes were based proportionally on the size of farms. The concentration of landholdings among the wealthy also reduced income to the state because large landholders often used their connections with the government to evade paying taxes. The Song government, under the leadership of Wang Anshi, tackled these financial problems by introducing reforms such as a government monopoly on trade, lower-interest loans to farmers, and graduated land taxes.

**Prototype Taxation.** During the sixteenth century the Ming government faced many fiscal problems, such as the complexity of the monetary system, the increasing burden of military expenditures, the inadequate salaries of government officials, and the confusion of taxes on land and labor. To solve these problems the government instituted a series of reforms from 1522 to 1619 to simplify the tax structure and secure tax collection. The reforms combined taxes and were known as the Single Whip Reform. It was a prototype of

modern taxation, introducing such principles as the computation of taxes by government offices and cash payments.

**Social Stratification.** Chinese society during the Tang period, as in previous dynasties, was stratified. At the top of the structure was the *Shi* (scholar-official class), members of which derived social prestige and economic wealth not only from family inheritances but also from the academic degrees they earned by passing the civil service examinations and obtaining subsequent official appointments. The *nong* (peasantry), as the primary taxpaying class and the bulk of the population, came next in the social strata. The *gong* (artisan class) was one step below the peasantry on the social ladder, because its members were the secondary taxpayers and producers of society. On the bottom of the social structure was the *shang* (merchant class). Merchants were condemned as social parasites, discriminated against and restricted by imperial policies, and despised by the general public since antiquity. However, the Song transformed China from a highly aristocratic society, common since the early Tang period, into a nearly nonaristocratic and egalitarian society that was defined by a simplified tax system, a growing commercial and money economy, and a more developed civil service examination system. The Mongol rulers, who followed the Song, employed a policy of ethnic discrimination by setting up a strictly enforced hierarchy of social classes—in a descending order of importance, they were the Mongols, *semu ren* (Western and Central Asians), *han ren* (northern Chinese), and *nan ren* (southern Chinese). This rigid discriminatory policy made the Mongols and non-Chinese foreigners the ruling classes over the Chinese. During the Ming dynasty the local landlords, together with government officials, constituted the basic governing structure of society.

**Gentry Class.** The Tang examination system first produced the official-gentry class. The development of a commercial economy and civil service examinations in the Song period further increased the size and prestige of this social bracket. The gentry class depended much less on their agricultural lands and products, as commercial activities became a significant part of their family economy. Many gentry resided in the cities or towns; urban high culture was at the center of their social life. Their economic wealth was translated into political power by the control of government offices, which they acquired through education and meritorious performance on the civil service examinations. Consequently, the gentry class became the backbone of bureaucratic government in China. During the Ming period the gentry performed administrative responsibilities without obtaining official appointments. They helped collect taxes and raise funds for local public works; maintained Confucian culture by establishing and sponsoring schools and temples; organized charitable institutions for orphans, widows, and the disabled; provided relief during natural disasters; and even formed a militia to defend their wealth and the community. These administrative, cultural, and social activities were encouraged and recognized by the government.

# TOPICS IN SOCIAL CLASS SYSTEM AND THE ECONOMY

## MING DYNASTY (1368-1644): THE ECONOMY

**Population Growth.** The economy during the Ming dynasty, as a whole, experienced growth, and the population of China expanded greatly. The Chinese constituted between one-quarter and one-third of the world's population during the Ming period. A census undertaken in 1393 recorded a population of at least 60,545,812. The figure more than doubled to about 150,000,000 by 1600. This increase was a result of combined factors. First, the long period of peace established by the Ming government encouraged population growth. Second, China suffered no nationwide epidemics. Third, the vast lands of China provided people with a safeguard against natural disasters, warfare, and social unrest. Internal migrations from distressed areas to more-prosperous regions mitigated large-scale human suffering, thus offsetting the consequences of natural calamities and social disturbances. In addition to population growth, there was a continuous shift of people

Woodcut of a flat-bottomed river barge carrying grain to the capital city of Beijing, Ming dynasty, 1368–1644
(from Louise Levathes, *When China Ruled the Seas*, 1994)

During the imperial era the population of the southern provinces of Guangdong and Guangxi (collectively known as Lingnan) increased as peasants migrated into the region from North China and elsewhere. Significant growth occurred especially in the Ming era (1368–1644) because of long periods of relative peace and economic prosperity.

| Year | Households (Thousands) |
|------|------------------------|
| 742  | 300  |
| 1080 | 750  |
| 1200 | 1250 |
| 1290 | 800  |
| 1391 | 750  |
| 1600 | 1850 |
| 1661 | 1750 |

**Source:** Robert B. Marks, *Tigers, Rice, Silk, and Silt: Environment and Economy in Late Imperial South China* (Cambridge: Cambridge University Press, 1998), p. 85.

to the lower Yangzi region and areas even farther south, such as *Lingnan*, which primarily included the Guangdong and Guangxi provinces.

**Trade Development.** During the Ming period domestic trade was further developed. The establishment of Beijing and the construction of a canal system in the south stimulated trade between northern and southern China. The southerly population shift also contributed to commercial development in that region. Merchants from Jiangxi province, for example, exported porcelains, silk, tea, salt, and other local products. The expansion of trade in turn promoted specialized handicraft production and the development of early capitalistic industry. Jindezheng in Jiangxi province became the center of Chinese porcelain production; pottery from this region was in high demand for its beauty and quality. It was made from a special clay, called *gaoling* (a hydrous silicate of alumina), that was found in a nearby hill. The Songjiang region near Shanghai was the center of cotton textile production; its products were transported everywhere in the country. Some textile shops hired more than twenty workers. These laborers, and the mass production of textiles, have inspired academic debate on whether incipient capitalism appeared in China before modern times. In the commercial centers, especially Beijing, regional guilds—usually sponsored by officials and merchants from the same geographical area to provide

Ming-era woodcut showing the production of copper coins, 1637 (from Arnold Toynbee, *Half the World*, 1973)

mutual aid for its members while they traveled far from home—were established.

*Li-Jia* System. The land tax constituted the major income source for the Ming government. Based on the Double Tax system, this tax was collected in the summer and autumn. The summer tax (grain) was collected in the eighth lunar month; the autumn tax (husked rice) was collected in the second month after the harvest. To ensure proper tax collection and to maintain peace and order at the local level, the Ming government established the *li-jia* system. 110 households were grouped into a *li*, which was divided into ten *jia* of 10 households each. Family heads from the additional 10 households, usually comprising local notables, each served as the *lizhang* (heads of *li*) for one year in a ten-year rotation and was responsible for collecting and delivering the summer and autumn taxes. The *li* were normally structured along existing natural villages and neighborhoods. In cases in which the villages were too small, several communities were combined to make a *li*. Otherwise, larger villages and towns were divided into several *li*.

Sources:

Wm. Theodore de Bary, *Self and Society in Ming Thought* (New York: Columbia University Press, 1970).

John K. Fairbank and others, *East Asia: Tradition and Transformation* (Boston: Houghton Mifflin, 1973).

Ray Huang, *1587, A Year of No Significance: The Ming Dynasty in Decline* (New Haven: Yale University Press, 1981).

Charles O. Hucker, *The Ming Dynasty: Its Origins and Evolving Institutions* (Ann Arbor: Center for Chinese Studies, University of Michigan, 1978).

Robert B. Marks, *Tigers, Rice, Silk, and Silt: Environment and Economy in Late Imperial South China* (Cambridge & New York: Cambridge University Press, 1997).

F. W. Mote, *Imperial China, 900–1800* (Cambridge, Mass.: Harvard University Press, 1999).

Mote and Denis Twitchett, eds., *The Cambridge History of China*, volume 7, *The Ming Dynasty, 1368–1644, Part 1* (Cambridge & New York: Cambridge University Press, 1988).

Witold Rodzinski, *A History of China*, 2 volumes (Oxford & New York: Pergamon, 1979, 1983).

Shih-shan Henry Tsai, *Perpetual Happiness: The Ming Emperor Yongle* (Seattle: University of Washington Press, 2001).

## MING DYNASTY (1368-1644): FOREIGN TRADE

Tribute System. Over time the Chinese government developed a mechanism known as the "tribute system" to deal with the outside world. Under this system a tribute state accepted its vassal status to the Chinese and was required to exchange envoys and gifts, monitor foreign trade, and handle diplomatic relations. Scholars such as John K. Fairbank have argued that rather than being "an aggressive imperialism," the tribute system was "a defensive expression of culturalism." To maintain relations with China, a foreign country had to accept Chinese terms and recognize the supremacy of Chinese civilization and its emperors. Although an asymmetric relationship developed between China and the tribute state, the latter still benefited in terms of increased trade (in the form of gift

Manuscript page describing a giraffe sent to the Emperor Yung Lo as tribute, early fifteenth century (from Norman Kotker, ed., *The Horizon History of China*, 1969)

exchanges), cultural inspiration, and military protection from the Chinese government in times of need.

Maritime Expeditions. One of the major means undertaken in expanding foreign contacts during the Ming dynasty was a series of seven great maritime expeditions, spanning from 1405 to 1433, led by a Muslim eunuch named Zheng He (Cheng Ho). The first expedition was manned by 28,000 sailors onboard 62 or 63 large ships and 255 smaller vessels. The succeeding voyages were similar in scale; they reached not only the southeastern Asian nations but also the Indian coast, the Persian Gulf, and the east coast of Africa. These unprecedented voyages reveal the advanced development of Chinese shipbuilding and navigational skills. Zheng He's fleets included ships of more

Reconstruction of a treasure ship in the fleet of Zheng He (from Louise Levathes, *When China Ruled the Seas*, 1994)

than one hundred meters in length, with four decks and a dozen watertight compartments. These huge ships were powered by sails hung from multiple masts. Guided by compasses, navigators used accurate sailing directions.

**Expeditionary Importance.** The initial purposes of these imperial expeditions were to demonstrate the glory and strength of the Ming government and to incorporate the southern and southeastern Asian states into the tribute system. These voyages successfully displayed the military and political vitality of the regime and brought many foreign envoys to the Chinese court. In addition to the traditional tributary states of Vietnam and Siam, about fifty more states were brought into the system. Apart from the diplomatic and political motives, these voyages also served to stimulate significant foreign trade. Ships carried Chinese silk, textiles, chinaware, and copper coins to areas of Asia that had desired these commodities for centuries. In return, exotic objects and animals were imported from these foreign lands. The animals greatly amused the emperor and court officials. For example, giraffes brought to Beijing particularly delighted the ruler. Although the court did not initiate the expeditions for their commercial benefits, these voyages attracted more attention from people of different lands to Chinese products.

**Ming Anticommercialism.** Scholars have speculated about the causes behind the sudden termination of these voyages. One obvious reason was the great cost, because they were undertaken when the Ming dynasty was still campaigning against the Mongols and building Beijing. Another widely accepted reason focuses on the leadership of the venture. The fact that the voyages were led by a court eunuch antagonized Chinese scholar-officials, who generally opposed the encroachment of Chinese power and influence by such men. The most profound force against the maritime expeditions, however, lay in the traditional anticommercialism of the Chinese, which became Ming official policy. The agrarian economy in China dictated that the Ming government receive more revenues from land taxes than from trade. The dominance of neo-Confucian orthodoxy in the Ming period fortified official contempt of commerce. Furthermore, the defense strategy of the government prioritized Mongols as the chief enemy, and, consequently, the government focused its defense on the northwestern frontier rather than on the southeastern coasts.

Sources:
Wm. Theodore de Bary, *Self and Society in Ming Thought* (New York: Columbia University Press, 1970).

John K. Fairbank and others, *East Asia: Tradition and Transformation* (Boston: Houghton Mifflin, 1973).

Ray Huang, *1587, A Year of No Significance: The Ming Dynasty in Decline* (New Haven: Yale University Press, 1981).

Charles O. Hucker, *The Ming Dynasty: Its Origins and Evolving Institutions* (Ann Arbor: Center for Chinese Studies, University of Michigan, 1978).

Robert B. Marks, *Tigers, Rice, Silk, and Silt: Environment and Economy in Late Imperial South China* (Cambridge & New York: Cambridge University Press, 1997).

F. W. Mote, *Imperial China, 900–1800* (Cambridge, Mass.: Harvard University Press, 1999).

Mote and Denis Twitchett, eds., *The Cambridge History of China*, volume 7, *The Ming Dynasty, 1368–1644, Part 1* (Cambridge & New York: Cambridge University Press, 1988).

Witold Rodzinski, *A History of China*, 2 volumes (Oxford & New York: Pergamon, 1979, 1983).

Shih-shan Henry Tsai, *Perpetual Happiness: The Ming Emperor Yongle* (Seattle: University of Washington Press, 2001).

## MING DYNASTY (1368-1644): THE SINGLE-WHIP REFORM

**Causes of Reform.** During the sixteenth century the Ming government faced several fiscal problems, one of which was the inadequacy of the monetary system. To supplement the shortage of copper coins, the government introduced unminted silver in tax transactions. When con-

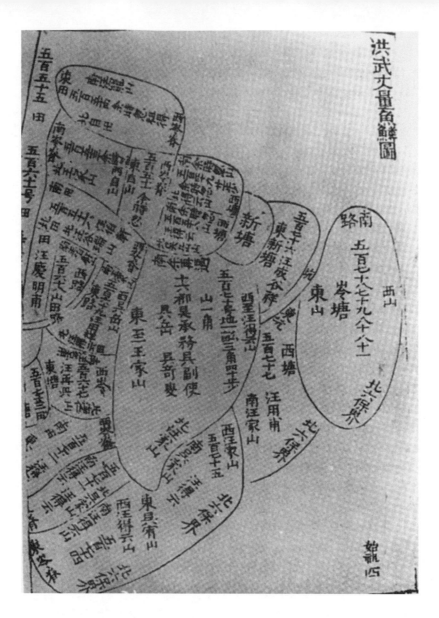

Ming map used in the assessment of taxes and showing contiguous landholdings, 1581 (Museum of Chinese History, Beijing)

verting commodities into silver, surcharges were often imposed on the peasants. In addition to this monetary problem, the increasing burden of military expenditures proved onerous. Ming armies were largely supported by the land tax, and a substantial portion of the government revenue was allocated for military expenses. The third problem was the inadequacy of government officials' salaries, which were paid in grain. These payments were often converted into commodities at a low exchange rate when government funds were insufficient. The shrinkage of the salaries affected morale and encouraged corruption. The biggest problem, however, was the confusion and complexity of taxes on land and labor. The tax was assessed according to the classification of the land, which was reevaluated around every ten years. This system was maintained by local wealthy household heads who therefore were able to avoid their responsibilities by falsifying land records, a problem compounded by the complexity of taxes and labor services. Eventually, these problems negatively affected the peasants.

**Single-Whip Reform.** To solve these fiscal problems, the Ming government, from 1522 to 1619, undertook a series of reforms to simplify the tax structure and to secure tax collection. Many taxes were combined and simplified into monetary payments, a reform known as the *yi tiao bian* (combining many items into one) or Single Whip Reform. The Chief Grant Secretary, Zhang Juzheng, was the engineer of these reforms. His first major measure simplified land classifications from around one hundred different rates to only two or three rates. The second measure combined land taxes from thirty or forty types into two or three. Third, both land and labor taxes were computed into one tax to be paid in silver. Finally, the government established uniform tax collection dates to reduce the possibility of tax fraud and evasion.

**Significance of Reform.** These reforms were a prototype of modern taxation practices. Its principles, such as computation of taxes by government officials and use of cash payments, are employed in current tax structures. The assessment of taxes was based on the budgetary needs of the state, and therefore it assured a reliable income to run the government. Silver could be used to pay government officials and hire laborers. Peasants were also freed from the trouble of transporting grain to the government granaries, instead paying their taxes directly to collecting agencies at the local level.

Sources:

Wm. Theodore de Bary, *Self and Society in Ming Thought* (New York: Columbia University Press, 1970).

John K. Fairbank and others, *East Asia: Tradition and Transformation* (Boston: Houghton Mifflin, 1973).

Ray Huang, *1587, A Year of No Significance: The Ming Dynasty in Decline* (New Haven: Yale University Press, 1981).

Charles O. Hucker, *The Ming Dynasty: Its Origins and Evolving Institutions* (Ann Arbor: Center for Chinese Studies, University of Michigan, 1978).

Robert B. Marks, *Tigers, Rice, Silk, and Silt: Environment and Economy in Late Imperial South China* (Cambridge & New York: Cambridge University Press, 1997).

F. W. Mote, *Imperial China, 900–1800* (Cambridge, Mass.: Harvard University Press, 1999).

Mote and Denis Twitchett, eds., *The Cambridge History of China,* volume 7, *The Ming Dynasty, 1368–1644, Part 1* (Cambridge & New York: Cambridge University Press, 1988).

Witold Rodzinski, *A History of China,* 2 volumes (Oxford & New York: Pergamon, 1979, 1983).

Shih-shan Henry Tsai, *Perpetual Happiness: The Ming Emperor Yongle* (Seattle: University of Washington Press, 2001).

## MING DYNASTY (1368–1644): SOCIAL STRUCTURE

**Examination System.** The recovery of Chinese rule over the country during the Ming period (1368–1644) led to the reinstitution of the civil service examination system, which used three levels of examinations. Preliminary examinations were held at the county level to select and grant qualified scholars a degree called *xiucai* (flowering talent). This degree honored a scholar's intellectual achievements and included him in the privileged class of the gentry, who were exempted from labor service and corporal punishments. *Xiucai* holders could further enter the second level of examinations, held at the provincial capitals every three years. During the several-day-long tests the candidates were confined in rows of tiny cells at the examination field to write essays on Confucian classics. Less than 1 percent of the candidates passed the examination, earned a degree called *ju ren* (recommended men), and were allowed to proceed to a third level of triennial metropolitan examinations held at the capital, Beijing. Successful candidates who obtained the highest academic title, *jinshi* (presented scholar), could take the final examination at the court, presided over by the emperor himself, which then determined the official ranking and government post of the *jinshi* holders.

**Merits and Defects.** The civil service examination system in the Ming period was strictly regulated to prevent possible defaults and partiality. Names of candidates were concealed, and sometimes the candidates' papers were copied to ensure anonymity. Provincial examiners were dispatched from the capital. The examinations were managed by the Minister of

## GENTLEMANLY BEHAVIOR

Lu Kun, governor of Jiangxi during the Ming dynasty (1368–1644), defined the code of gentlemen in his book, *Groanings*. The following are some of his suggestions:

He should hide a large portion of whatever goodness he might have and thus cultivate his "ethical profoundness." Likewise he should conceal to a great extent the shortcomings of others and thus enlarge his "magnanimity." Patience is essential to planning, and a peaceful mind is a prerequisite to the management of affairs. Modesty is the most important item in the preservation of one's life, and tolerance and forgiveness should be the basic attitude towards others. To cultivate his mind, a gentleman should not be unduly concerned with such things as affluence or poverty, life or death, constancy or change.

Every event has its reality, every word its abode of beatitude, and every object the reason that sustains its existence. Likewise there are ways that make man a man; the purpose of education is to learn these ways. A gentleman learns them whenever and wherever he is, constantly and tirelessly. He will not cease to learn until he knows them all and knows them well.

**Source:** Lu Kun, *Groanings,* in *The Essence of Chinese Civilization,* edited by Dun J. Li (Princeton, N.J.: Van Nostrand, 1967).

Rites, rather than the Minister of Personnel, who supervised government officials. Overall, officials selected through this system had mastered the Confucian classics. This universal training helped to foster a unified bureaucracy that strengthened the centralization of government. Meritocracy also provided hope, though slim, to millions of Chinese men, who normally would not otherwise have had a chance to advance and be part of officialdom. Yet, the civil service examinations, centered as they were around Confucian classics, favored candidates whose training was through book learning and not practical application. The lengthy period of preparation also meant that only wealthy students could afford to prepare for these exams.

**Gentry Class.** Chinese degree-holders of all ranks have been known as *shen shi* (officials and scholars). The English term "gentry" has been used to define this class. In the context of Chinese society, however, the meaning of gentry was broadened to include both office-degree holders and landlords, from whom the degree holders often originated. These men were entrusted with the responsibilities of maintaining order and peace; they were the unofficial extension of the government at the local level. Therefore, both office holders and landlords were perceived as the privileged gentry class.

**Gentry Characteristics.** The gentry class formed the backbone of Chinese Confucian government. This class thus performed administrative responsibilities without official appointment. They helped collect taxes and raise

Detail from a handscroll of candidates after taking civil service examinations, mid sixteenth century
(National Palace Museum, Taipei, Taiwan)

funds for local public works, such as building and repairing dikes and roads; handled local disputes over property or conflicts that were the result of individual personalities; maintained Confucian culture by establishing and sponsoring local schools and temples; organized charitable institutions for orphans, widows, and disabled people; provided relief during natural disasters; and formed a militia to defend their wealth and the community. These administrative, cultural, and social activities were encouraged and recognized by the government. Official recognition, together with economic privileges, gave the gentry influence, prestige, and power over the bulk of the population—small landowners and tenant farmers. While most of the gentry restrained themselves with Confucian virtues and morals, a great many also abused their power and influence and became local despots who exploited and squeezed the local people. These actions deepened the social conflict between landlord and tenant classes and at times even incited social upheaval.

Sources:

Wm. Theodore de Bary, *Self and Society in Ming Thought* (New York: Columbia University Press, 1970).

John K. Fairbank and others, *East Asia: Tradition and Transformation* (Boston: Houghton Mifflin, 1973).

Ray Huang, *1587, A Year of No Significance: The Ming Dynasty in Decline* (New Haven: Yale University Press, 1981).

Charles O. Hucker, *The Ming Dynasty: Its Origins and Evolving Institutions* (Ann Arbor: Center for Chinese Studies, University of Michigan, 1978).

Robert B. Marks, *Tigers, Rice, Silk, and Silt: Environment and Economy in Late Imperial South China* (Cambridge & New York: Cambridge University Press, 1997).

F. W. Mote, *Imperial China, 900–1800* (Cambridge, Mass.: Harvard University Press, 1999).

Mote and Denis Twitchett, eds., *The Cambridge History of China*, volume 7, *The Ming Dynasty, 1368–1644, Part 1* (Cambridge & New York: Cambridge University Press, 1988).

Witold Rodzinski, *A History of China*, 2 volumes (Oxford & New York: Pergamon, 1979–1983).

Shih-shan Henry Tsai, *Perpetual Happiness: The Ming Emperor Yongle* (Seattle: University of Washington Press, 2001).

Italian missionary Matteo Ricci, who was in China from 1583 to 1610, observed carefully the social lives of the Chinese. The following excerpt is from his journal.

When relatives of friends pay a visit, the host is expected to return the visit, and a definite and detailed ceremony accompanies their custom of visiting. The one who is calling presents a little folder in which his name is written and which may contain a few words of address depending upon the rank of the visitor or of the host. . . . These folders or booklets consist of about a dozen pages of white paper and are about a palm and a half in length, oblong in shape, with a two-inch strip of red paper down the middle of the cover . . . one must have at least twenty different kinds on hand for different functions, marked with appropriate titles. . . . Men of high station in life are never seen walking in the streets. They are carried about enclosed in sedan chairs and cannot be seen by passers-by, unless they leave the front curtain open. . . . Carriages and wagons are prohibited by law. . . . People here travel more by boat than we in the West, and their boats are more ornate and more commodious than ours. . . . Sometimes they give sumptuous dinners aboard their yachts and make a pleasure cruise of it on the lake or along the river.

Source: Matteo Ricci, *China in the Sixteenth Century: The Journals of Matthew Ricci, 1583–1610*, translated by Louis J. Gallagher (New York: Random House, 1953), pp. 61–62, 80–81.

## SONG DYNASTY (960–1279): COMMERCIAL REVOLUTION

**Economic Expansion.** While the Song dynasty (960–1279) was characterized by financial problems and military weakness, it also experienced an economic expansion so great that it was referred to as the "commercial revolution" by scholars. The economic upturn was chiefly propelled by improved agricultural technologies; the use of the abacus, gunpowder, and new printing techniques; the growth of domestic and foreign trade; and the development of a money economy.

**Technological Development.** A great increase in agricultural productivity occurred during the Song era. In southern China the double cropping of rice was made possible by the introduction of a new strain of rice, which matured more quickly than local plants, from Champa in southern Vietnam. Several major water-control projects were undertaken that significantly improved the irrigation of rice paddy fields. In addition, more commercialized crops were introduced into farming. For instance, the growth of tea plants on the hillsides and the cultivation of cotton not only contributed to the income of growers but also diversified the agricultural resources of the country.

**Other Advances.** Meanwhile, other technological developments took place during the Song dynasty. Traditional techniques in silk weaving, porcelain making, and lacquer production were further developed. By the later Song dynasty the Chinese began to use the abacus, which became the primary calculating device for East Asian people until the twentieth century. Chinese scholars also learned how to use gunpowder in explosives, which was especially important in mining practices. Among all the technological developments, printing was the most significant advance. Printing technology evolved from an earlier technique of stone rubbing, which produced a block print with white characters on a black background by adhering a moist sheet to the stone and rubbing the surface with lamp soot. By the eleventh century the Chinese had learned to arrange movable carved characters on a woodblock, thus inventing the technique whose principles are still applicable to modern printing technology.

**Domestic Trade.** Historically, Chinese governments of the various dynasties despised merchants and instituted government restrictions on commercial activities. This contempt and restraint on commercialism, however, was broken during the late Tang and Song periods. Private marketplaces sprawled far beyond the traditional government markets. Various specialized urban shops lined the main streets and tempted undecided buyers and pedestrians who crowded the busy avenues. The development of private trade advanced to such a degree that merchants were

The city of Kaifeng (K'ai-feng), Henan Province, served as the capital of the Northern Song dynasty (960–1125). Kaifeng's importance as a trade center grew rapidly. The following is a description of activities there:

K'ai-feng was the marketplace for its immediate population, for places in the market area of which it was the center, and for more distant places in North or South China or foreign countries. Beyond the things produced or made in K'ai-feng or its satellite cities, it consumed or exported (sometimes after processing) many products or commodities from elsewhere. The first Sung emperors had fostered the textile industries, resettling workers from Szechwan and the Yangtze delta. The iron and steel industries of the K'ai-feng market area for the first time replaced small-scale and more or less seasonal operations with highly organized enterprises dependent on more sophisticated techniques, great investments in equipment, and large numbers of workers. The industries were developed both by the government and by private iron masters with extensive capital resources. K'ai-feng workshops of many kinds, of course, produced articles of luxury for the imperial family, high officials, and wealthy businessmen or other residents, and such special products naturally figured in the export trade. Tea from the south was an important item for re-export.

Source: E. A. Kracke Jr., "Sung K'ai-feng: Pragmatic Metropolis and Formalistic Capital," in *Crisis and Prosperity in Sung China*, edited by John Winthrop Haeger (Tucson: University of Arizona Press, 1975), pp. 51–52.

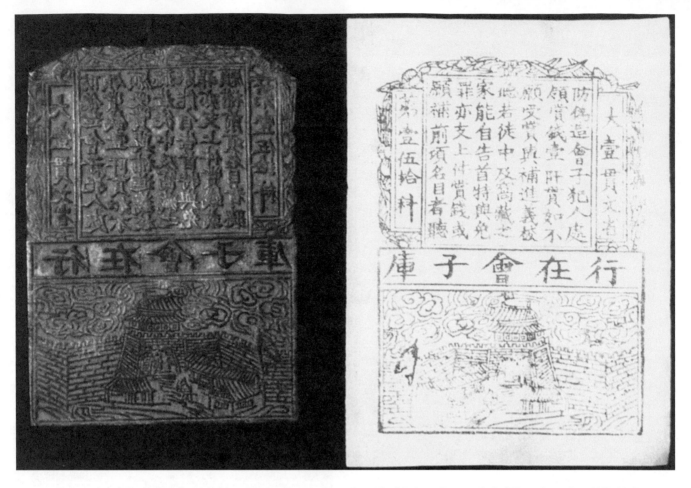

Copper plate for printing money (left) and an imprint on paper, from the Southern Song capital of Hangzhou, circa 1127–1279 (Ontario Science Center, Toronto)

divided into two categories: wholesalers and retailers. The *zuogu* (large wholesalers or brokers) accumulated vast quantities of farm produce and manufactured goods in their warehouses for later sale to retailers, who ranged from *xingshang zoufan* (petty traveling peddlers) and local shop owners to large-scale proprietors with networks of branch shops in different cities. The specialization of private trade and the increase in the volume of exchange caused *hang* (trade guilds), organizations of traders who set prices and protected their members from competition, to become necessary. The most important guilds included merchants who sold such basic commodities as salt, grain, tea, or silk.

**Growth of Foreign Trade.** In addition to domestic barter, foreign trade during the Song period experienced tremendous growth. Trade with the outside world was first conducted overland, starting as early as the Han dynasty (206 B.C.E.–220 C.E.), when the Chinese started trading with merchants from Central Asia, West Asia, and the Mediterranean region. Merchants traveled across the Silk Road, a series of routes that ran from Kazakhstan to Chang'an, across the Sinkiang and Gobi deserts. Neighboring tribal states to the north and northwest had long cultivated a taste for such products as silk and tea, and there was a steady demand for Chinese goods. Continuous failures of military operations against the Liao, Xi

Xia, and Jin made the Song lose land and millions of people to their nomadic neighbors. These expatriates further increased the demand for Chinese commodities. Commercial trade and profit made it possible for the Song government to pay huge appeasements to their enemies and to buy horses from the steppe for the defense of China against the "barbarians."

**Overseas Trade.** During the Song period overland trade was supplemented by overseas efforts. Although trade by sea with India and the Middle East had existed since the late Han period, maritime trade grew rapidly during the Song era. Improvements in the technology of shipbuilding and navigation assisted overseas commercial activities. Chinese vessels now utilized sails, oars, and transverse watertight bulkheads (to prevent ships from sinking). The Chinese also used the compass to help navigate their ships. With the development of oceanic commerce, the eastern and southeastern coasts of China became primary regions for international trade and foreign contacts, which significantly reduced the importance of the northwestern frontier. The latter region gradually sank to the status of a backward hinterland. A few large ports along the southern coast and on the lower Yangzi River were developed and the government established custom houses to collect duties. Chuanzhou, in particular, with its convenient access to the tea-

and porcelain-producing regions of China, emerged as the leading port city.

**Nature of Foreign Trade.** The development of maritime trade is a good indication of Chinese prosperity and demonstrates the leading role China played in the economic life of the world. China mostly exported manufactured goods; its silk fabrics and porcelain products were appreciated worldwide. Chinese books, prints, and art objects were in great demand in Korea and Japan. Chinese copper coins were shipped to the east and to southeastern Asian countries. China in return mainly imported raw materials, such as horses and hides from Inner Asia, as well as spices, gems, ivory, and other luxury items from southern and southeastern Asia.

**Foreign Traders.** The trade with neighboring Korea and Japan was dominated by Korean merchants, while Iranians and Arabs controlled much of the trade with southern and western Asia. Foreign traders lived under their own customary laws, in designated quarters in the Chinese cities, a practice similar to the extraterritorial nature of modern times, but without its humiliating and insulting undertones to Chinese pride and sovereignty. Traders from west Asia, for instance, brought Islam with them and built mosques in their communities. These quarters served as home to thousands of foreigners in Guangzhou and Yanzhou, a major industrial and commercial center on the lower Yangzi.

**Money Economy.** During the late Tang and Song periods, China experienced a great expansion of its money economy. Chinese copper coins came into use as early as the eastern Zhou period (771 B.C.E.–256 B.C.E.), but only now did this currency play an indispensable role in government finances and in the daily lives of Chinese citizens. By the end of the first century of the Song dynasty, cash began to comprise a significant portion of imperial tax revenues, and the income from government monopolies and commercial taxes exceeded agricultural taxes. During the Southern Song era (1127–1279) the tax income in cash surpassed that of its grain and textile revenues. Previously, taxes were largely collected in the form of agricultural products. The wider use of money increased the demand for copper coinage. To ease the pressure on this currency, the Song government incorporated gold and silver into its monetary system. The most important advance, however, was the development of paper money. Since copper coins were too cumbersome and bulky for long-distance commercial transactions, various paper credits and monies were invented for such activities. One type of paper money, called "flying cash," was used to pay for goods bought from distant regions and could be reimbursed at the Chinese capital. The development of a money economy during the Song period reached a level far ahead of the rest of the world.

**Urban Centers.** Commercial development of the Song period made the urbanization of China inevitable. By the twelfth century China had fifty-two large urban prefectures with more than one hundred thousand households each. In these urban centers culture was sophisticated and diversi-fied, and life was exciting and luxurious. Amusement quarters dominated city life; one could indulge in the many liquor and tea stores, in restaurants featuring specialized cuisines, and in houses furnished with female entertainers and prostitutes. City dwellers could also be amused by puppet shows, acrobats, storytellers, jugglers, and other entertainments. As the highly diversified urban life glittered, its dark side also began to show at this time. Urban poverty and pauperism emerged. Private charitable organizations, sponsored by local notables, rose to take care of the misfortunate ones and thus became a tradition largely responsible for social welfare in China.

Sources:

John K. Fairbank and others, *East Asia: Tradition and Transformation* (Boston: Houghton Mifflin, 1973).

Herbert Franke and Denis Twitchett, eds., *The Cambridge History of China*, volume 6, *Alien Regimes and Border States, 907–1368* (Cambridge & New York: Cambridge University Press, 1994).

F. W. Mote, *Imperial China, 900–1800* (Cambridge, Mass.: Harvard University Press, 1999).

Witold Rodzinski, *A History of China*, 2 volumes (Oxford & New York: Pergamon, 1979–1983).

John Winthrop Haeger, ed., *Crisis and Prosperity in Sung China* (Tucson: University of Arizona Press, 1975).

## SONG DYNASTY (960–1279): ECONOMIC PROBLEMS

**Economic Problems.** Although the Song (960–1279) enjoyed more prosperity than any previous dynasty, the problems of the degeneration of imperial leaders and fiscal difficulties associated with the dynastic cycle resurfaced by the end of the eleventh century. During the first six decades of the dynasty, government revenues increased to 150,850,000 units (each unit was approximately equivalent to a string of one thousand coins) in 1021. The government income, however, soon declined by almost 25 percent.

**Causes.** Scholars have attributed the Song economic problems to several causes. First, in the beginning of the dynasty there was a period of population increase as the leaders more vigorously and effectively maintained relative peace and stability. This increase lowered the agricultural surplus and thus reduced the taxable income. Second, the growing number of people meant that each succeeding generation received less land to farm, which affected the tax since it was based on the size of farms. Revenues were further decreased as land was concentrated in the hands of large landholders, who often used their connections with government officials in order to evade paying taxes. Third, Song military expenditures consumed the largest part of government revenues. The Song constantly faced the threat of invasion from the Inner Asian tribes, which were located along the border in the north and northwest. Yet, the army proved to be the weakest military of all the major dynasties as a result of the Song founder's policy of curtailing regional militarism. To reduce the power of regional military commanders, the Song emperor Taizu replaced them with civil officials and placed the military under the control of the central government. This policy successfully helped establish a lasting dynasty, but it also contributed to the

Paper money made from the bark of a mulberry tree, Song dynasty, 960–1279 (from Robert E. Murowchick, *Cradles of Civilization: China*, 1994)

weakness of the military. Mercenaries used by the Song army were not only ineffective but costly, compared to the inexpensive Tang militia system. To compensate for this military inefficiency, the government increased the size of its force, causing huge expenditures. By 1041 the Song army fielded 1,259,000 men and cost nearly 80 percent of the budget to maintain. In addition to the enormous expenditure to operate its army, the Song government was forced to appease its enemies financially.

**Sources:**

John K. Fairbank and others, *East Asia: Tradition and Transformation* (Boston: Houghton Mifflin, 1973).

Herbert Franke and Denis Twitchett, eds., *The Cambridge History of China*, volume 6, *Alien Regimes and Border States, 907–1368* (Cambridge & New York: Cambridge University Press, 1994).

F. W. Mote, *Imperial China, 900–1800* (Cambridge, Mass.: Harvard University Press, 1999).

Witold Rodzinski, *A History of China*, 2 volumes (Oxford & New York: Pergamon, 1979–1983).

John Winthrop Haeger, ed., *Crisis and Prosperity in Sung China* (Tucson: University of Arizona Press, 1975).

## SONG DYNASTY (960-1279): TRANSFORMATION OF SOCIAL STRUCTURE

**Gentry Class.** Commercial development during the Song dynasty (960–1279) brought profound social and cultural changes. China was transformed from a highly aristocratic society of the early Tang period (618–907) into the nearly "nonaristocratic and more egalitarian society" of the Song era. A variety of factors contributed to this change. First, a simplified tax system implemented since the late Tang era made it difficult for the great aristocratic families to evade paying taxes. Second, a growing commercial and money economy made it impossible for the aristocratic estates to stand alone as self-sufficient economic units. Third, the more-developed civil service examination system provided the country with leadership based not on hereditary wealth but on individual talent. Consequently, the aristocracy merged into a much broader social bracket of the gentry (landowners in the Western world) class.

Handscroll illumination of a peddler, circa 1190–1230 (Palace Museum, Beijing)

**Characteristics.** Different from the old aristocracy, the gentry class depended much less on their agricultural land and products; commercial activities became a significant part of their family economy. In many cases the landowners were found to have come from merchant origins and often remained engaged in commercial trade. Along the same line, the daily life of the gentry class was often separated from the countryside and from the lands they owned. Many of the gentry resided in the cities or towns. The high culture of urban life was the center of their social world. Furthermore, their economic wealth could be translated into political power, which they acquired through advanced education and accomplishment in the civil service examinations (which gained for them government offices). Thus, on the surface, the gentry class seemed to obtain political prominence more from their intellectual achievements than from their economic wealth. Consequently, the gentry became a reputable social group and the backbone of bureaucratic governments throughout Chinese history.

**Decline of Women's Position.** While the lives of rich men, often part of the gentry class, were greatly improved by commercial development during the Song period, women's social conditions drastically declined at the same time. The deterioration of women's positions may have been associated with urban development. During this period the institution of concubinage grew. Social restrictions on the remarriage of widows were also strengthened. The custom of footbinding, a practice believed to have started among palace dancers during the Tang era, was also introduced among upper-class women. The concentration of the upper class in the cities reduced the importance of women in family economic activities and may have contributed to the wider practice of footbinding. A girl's feet were tightly wrapped until all the toes, except the big toe, were bent under the arch. This triangle-shaped "lily-foot," about half the size of a normal foot, crippled women for life, effectively confining them within the boundaries of the home.

Sources:

John K. Fairbank and others, *East Asia: Tradition and Transformation* (Boston: Houghton Mifflin, 1973).

Herbert Franke and Denis Twitchett, eds., *The Cambridge History of China*, volume 6, *Alien Regimes and Border States, 907–1368* (Cambridge & New York: Cambridge University Press, 1994).

F. W. Mote, *Imperial China, 900–1800* (Cambridge, Mass.: Harvard University Press, 1999).

Witold Rodzinski, *A History of China,* 2 volumes (Oxford & New York: Pergamon, 1979–1983).

John Winthrop Haeger, ed., *Crisis and Prosperity in Sung China* (Tucson: University of Arizona Press, 1975).

## SONG DYNASTY (960–1279): WANG ANSHI REFORM

**Financial Problems.** Heavy financial burdens forced the Song (960–1279) government to reduce the salaries of its functionaries. Inadequate salaries may have contributed to corruption among the bureaucrats and factionalism in the government. The bureaucratic factions were deeply divided on all major issues of policy, which severely affected the efficiency of the governing machine. The young emperor Shengzong (Inspired Ancestor), who reigned from 1067 to 1085, came to the throne determined to tackle these financial problems. In 1067 he appointed Wang Anshi as his chief councilor, who initiated a series of economic, military, and educational reforms.

**Reforms.** On the economic front, Wang Anshi first installed the central economic manipulation policy, which had been known in the Han dynasty (206 B.C.E.–220 C.E.) as the "leveling" system. Under this policy the government bought specialized products from one region and sold them in other regions in order to stabilize prices and use the profits. This measure helped increase government revenues, but it conflicted with the interests of the larger interstate merchants. Second, Wang provided government loans to peasants at a 20 or 30 percent interest rates, a comparably low figure. Some private moneylenders charged rates as high as 70 percent. This new policy helped poor farmers to maintain themselves, but it hurt the profits of the private moneylenders. It also reduced the dependency of the poorer farmers on their wealthier landlord neighbors. Third, Wang ordered a survey in order to correct existing inequities in the land tax. He eliminated the old system and in its place instituted a graduated scale of taxes based on the productivity of land rather than on the size of acreage.

Drawing of an agricultural scene with rice fields, Song dynasty, 960–1279 (Palace Museum, Beijing)

He also abolished corvée service and commuted it into a monetary tax.

**Military Reforms.** Wang Anshi revived the collective responsibility system called *bao-jia*, which organized the peasant households into groups of *bao* (tens) and *jia* (hundreds) to maintain local peace and order. The *bao-jia* system also provided the government with a trained and armed militia, maintained at local expense, to assist the central army. Wang furthermore created a system that increased the breeding of horses for military use and assigned the stock to families in North China. The recipients in turn provided cavalry militia during wartime.

**Educational Reforms.** Wang Anshi increased the number of government schools to reduce the influence of the *shuyuan* (private academies), which had dominated academic training. The most important reform was related to drastic changes in the civil service examination system. Wang advocated more testing on practical problems and administrative skills than on a student's knowledge of classical literature. He also suggested that the prefectural supervisory offices be turned into formal teaching institutions, and he redesigned the National Academy to function as a real school.

**Opposition to Reform.** Wang's reform measures were highly controversial. While many of his reforms—such as the graduated tax, low-interest government loans, and price regulation—protected average farmers and increased tax revenues, they also hurt the interests of different social groups, particularly the large landlords, moneylenders, and merchants. His reforms of the civil service examinations antagonized most bureaucrats, whose privileges in education and official recruitment were threatened. Opposition forces vehemently attacked Wang, who lost his power upon the death of Shanzong in 1085. When the traditionalists returned to power, they overturned Wang's measures, thus nullifying whatever economic and military benefits the reforms had brought in.

Sources:
John K. Fairbank and others, *East Asia: Tradition and Transformation* (Boston: Houghton Mifflin, 1973).

Herbert Franke and Denis Twitchett, eds., *The Cambridge History of China*, volume 6, *Alien Regimes and Border States, 907–1368* (Cambridge & New York: Cambridge University Press, 1994).

F. W. Mote, *Imperial China, 900–1800* (Cambridge, Mass.: Harvard University Press, 1999).

Witold Rodzinski, *A History of China*, 2 volumes (Oxford & New York: Pergamon, 1979, 1983).

John Winthrop Haeger, ed., *Crisis and Prosperity in Sung China* (Tucson: University of Arizona Press, 1975).

## TANG DYNASTY (618-907): CRAFTS AND TRADE DEVELOPMENT

**Crafts and Domestic Trade.** Silk, paper, and porcelain were manufactured during the Tang dynasty. The Chinese were known for the high quality of their manufactured goods. Craft guilds appeared in many towns where crafts-

Silver bottle, Tang dynasty, 618–907 (Shaanxi Provincial Museum, China)

men were concentrated. As a result of this industrial development, domestic trade increased. Improved transportation, as well as a new postal system that connected the capital with the outlying districts, also stimulated domestic trade.

**Urban Development.** Along with the growth in domestic trade, the cities and towns grew both in size and importance. Chang'an, the capital, was the focal point of the highly centralized state power and economic wealth. The city was organized in a checkerboard fashion with straight and wide north-south and east-west avenues that divided the city into 110 blocks. Chang'an had an estimated population of more than one million people. Other significant cities involved in trade, such as Loyang and Guangzhou (Canton), also experienced similar growth. Many provincial capitals had populations of more than one hundred thousand people.

**International Trade.** China was a cosmopolitan nation. The Tang welcomed traders from all over the world. Trade and diplomacy brought thousands of foreigners to Chang'an, Quanzhou, and Guangzhou. To a large degree, international trade during the Tang period was dominated by foreigners, especially the Persians, Arabs, and Uighurs. Foreign contacts brought many new agricultural products and inventions to China. Tea, for instance, was introduced from Southeast Asia, first as a medicine and a stimulant for meditation. During the Tang dynasty it was more widely served as a drink. The consumption of tea eventually spread to Europe, and tea became the most popular beverage in the world. Chairs were also introduced from the West; they gradually replaced traditional sitting pads and mats.

**Foreign Settlements.** One sign of the close contact with the outside world was the presence of large numbers of foreigners in China. Generally, there were three types of foreigners in the country during the Tang period: envoys, clerics, and merchants. Most foreigners came to China overland by caravan or overseas in large merchant ships that sailed across the Indian Ocean and China Seas. Guangzhou, a wealthy port city with a population of two hundred thousand, attracted many foreigners, who settled in the special quarter, an area set aside south of the Pearl River. They were monitored by a specially designated elder, and they enjoyed some extraterritorial privileges. However, foreign traders also encountered some restrictions. They were, for example, forbidden to wear Chinese costumes, to live in Chinese residential areas, and to intermarry with the Chinese. Furthermore, they were hardly free agents. International trade from the Chinese side was monopolized by the government. The "Commissioner for Commercial Argosies" in Guangzhou had controlled the government monopoly ever since the Han dynasty (206 B.C.E.–220 C.E.) in order to prevent smuggling and speculation by the great merchants. This practice, though it protected Chinese interests, frustrated many foreign merchants.

Ceramic model of a caravan traveler from central Asia, Tang dynasty, 618–907 (from Robert E. Murowchick, *Cradles of Civilization: China*, 1994)

## THE FOREIGN QUARTER IN CANTON

An historian describes some of the activities of foreigners who lived in Canton:

Many of these visitors settled in the foreign quarter of Canton, which by imperial sanction was set aside south of the river for the convenience of the many persons of diverse race and nationality who chose to remain in Canton to do business or to wait for favorable winds. They were ruled by a specially designated elder, and enjoyed some extraterritorial privileges. Here citizens of the civilized nations, such as the Arabs and Singhalese, rubbed elbows with less cultured merchants, such as the "White *Man*-barbarians and the Red *Man*-barbarians." Here the orthodox, such as the Indian Buddhists in their own monasteries, whose pools were adorned with perfumed blue lotuses, were to be found close to the heterodox, such as the Shi'ah Muslims, who had fled persecution in Khurasan to erect their own mosque in the Far East. Here, in short, foreigners of every complexion, and Chinese of every province, summoned by the noon drum, thronged the great market, plotted in the warehouses, and haggled in the shops, and each day were dispersed by the sunset drum to return to their respective quarters or, on some occasions, to chaffer loudly in their outlandish accents in the night markets.

Source: Edward H. Schafer, *The Golden Peaches of Samarkand: A Study of T'ang Exotics* (Berkeley: University of California Press, 1963), p. 15.

**Foreign Culture.** In addition to obtaining foreign products, contacts with the outside world also introduced new religions to China. Zoroastrianism (or Mazdaism), the fire-worshiping religion of Persia, arrived in China by the sixth century. Manichaeism and the Nestorian branch of Christianity also reached Tang China by the seventh century. These religions, however, were eliminated under the persecutions of 841–845. Yet, two other foreign religions survived this purge. Judaism was practiced in some small communities and is still present in modern times. The observance of Islam grew steadily, attracting millions of followers, and often became the breeding ground for popular revolts.

Sources:
Woodbridge Bingham, *The Founding of the T'ang Dynasty: The Fall of Sui and Rise of T'ang, a Preliminary Survey* (Baltimore: Waverly, 1941).

John K. Fairbank and others, *East Asia: Tradition and Transformation* (Boston: Houghton Mifflin, 1973).

Herbert Franke and Denis Twitchett, eds., *The Cambridge History of China*, volume 6, *Alien Regimes and Border States, 907–1368* (Cambridge & New York: Cambridge University Press, 1994).

Witold Rodzinski, *A History of China*, 2 volumes (Oxford & New York: Pergamon, 1979, 1983).

Arthur F. Wright and Twitchett, eds., *Perspectives on the Tang* (New Haven: Yale University Press, 1973).

## TANG DYNASTY (618-907): DOUBLE TAX SYSTEM

**Financial Policy.** Although the Tang court survived the An Lushan Rebellion (755)—a revolt led by a Mongol general who captured the capital and installed himself as the new emperor, but who was assassinated in 757—it was greatly weakened politically as well as economically. The government was divided into quarreling factions. The eunuchs rose in power and competed with the bureaucrats for the control of, and influence on, court politics. The rebellion also interrupted the regular collection of the land tax. The loss of revenue resulted in financial difficulties for the government, which had expanded during Xuangzong's reign in both size and expenditures. To make up for this reduction in revenues, the court initiated a policy in 758 to enforce the traditional government monopoly on the sale of salt. A commissioner of salt and iron was appointed to oversee the implementation of this policy. Regional offices were established to make sure that only licensed producers could sell salt; they then resold the salt, now highly taxed, to the merchants. The higher cost was passed on to consumers. The policy worked well and provided a significant supplement to the land tax; a few years after the establishment of the monopoly, salt taxes provided more than 50 percent of the total cash revenue for the government.

**Double Tax System.** In 780, Dezong (Brilliant Ancestor) came to the throne. A vigorous ruler, who served until 805, Dezong was determined to reorganize the government in order to stop the decline of the dynasty. He installed capable men, who were loyal to him, as his chief ministers. Yang Yen, a well-known financial officer, was the most prominent individual among the men Dezong put into office. Under Yang Yen's leadership the Tang government abandoned the "equal field" system and adopted the *liang shui fa* ("Double Tax" system), which levied taxes twice a year on the amount of land held by the peasant households. To be specific, the Double Tax system replaced the old head tax and introduced a more equitable system, which was based on the assessment of land cultivated by the farming families. Meanwhile, the reform also curtailed the power of the eunuchs, who had controlled palace revenues. This policy assured that state revenues would be received by the government treasury. The Double Tax reform proved to be a success. The tax income collected in 780 alone surpassed the total revenue from all sources in the previous year.

**Significance.** This reform signified a far-reaching transition in imperial tax policy. Thereafter, agricultural taxation was assessed according to the amount of land one owned, rather than on the number of people in the household. This change lifted government concern about the development of private holdings, as they no longer reduced revenues to the state. On the contrary, these individual properties now helped increase the tax income.

Sources:
Woodbridge Bingham, *The Founding of the T'ang Dynasty: The Fall of Sui and Rise of T'ang, a Preliminary Survey* (Baltimore: Waverly, 1941).

John K. Fairbank and others, *East Asia: Tradition and Transformation* (Boston: Houghton Mifflin, 1973).

Herbert Franke and Denis Twitchett, eds., *The Cambridge History of China*, volume 6, *Alien Regimes and Border States, 907–1368* (Cambridge & New York: Cambridge University Press, 1994).

Witold Rodzinski, *A History of China*, 2 volumes (Oxford & New York: Pergamon, 1979–1983).

Arthur F. Wright and Twitchett, eds., *Perspectives on the Tang* (New Haven: Yale University Press, 1973).

## TANG DYNASTY (618-907): "EQUAL FIELD" SYSTEM AND TAXES

**Before the Tang.** Large landholdings were controlled by the great families in the later Han dynasty (206 B.C.E.–220 C.E.). This concentration of land contributed to the collapse of the regime. Realizing that uneven land distribution was a key cause of dynastic decline, regimes that followed the Han implemented policies to solve this problem. One solution was to nationalize land and then distribute it to the taxpaying peasantry. The government of the Northern Wei (386–535) first tackled this problem in 485, when it instituted an "equal field" system, which assigned agricultural lands in equal amounts to all adult peasants. Upon the death of a peasant or the passing of the age limit at around sixty, the land was to be returned to the government. The equal field system, though it was only applied to free peasants, helped slow down the flow of land and peasants into the protection of the great families and stabilized the financial situation of the central government. The Sui dynasty (589–618) continued to practice this system and applied it to the entire country. They forced the great families to become part of the system by assigning their holdings as "rank lands," parcels that were not to exceed the maximum amount of 1,370 acres for the highest rank.

**Categories.** During the Tang dynasty the equal field system was further implemented. Land was generally divided into four categories. First, the rank lands, similar to those adopted by the Sui dynasty, were assigned to the great families. Second, "official lands" were granted to government functionaries; these parcels varied in size according to the specific government office that the recipient held. The third category, "official fields," were used to support the organs of local government. The bulk of land, the fourth level, was divided equally among male peasants between the ages of eighteen and fifty-nine, with each man receiving about 13.7 acres. Only about one-fifth of the land could be permanently owned as "mulberry" land, on which were grown mulberry trees for feeding silkworms, or other tree crops.

**Taxes.** Supported by the equal field land, a peasant in return paid the government taxes of three types—2 piculs of grain, 20 feet of silk or hemp, and twenty days per year of corvée labor for the central government, as well as other periods of labor for the local government. (A picul was the equivalent of roughly 133 pounds.)

The corvée could be paid with textiles or money. In addition, peasants who were selected to provide military service were exempted from other taxes and levies. To ensure that the system worked effectively, the Tang government carried out, fairly systematically, a census and land register throughout the country. Remaining records of these land surveys indicate that specific categories of land were allotted to individual taxpayers. The equal field system worked well, to a large degree, for about a century; the taxes collected through this system supported the Tang government during a brilliant period in Chinese imperial history.

**System in Practice.** In theory the equal field system depended on the periodic redistribution of land among the taxpaying farmers. It is, however, questionable that the land was ever equitably redistributed. A long period of peace resulted in population growth that surpassed the increase of natural resources, thus upsetting the population-to-land ratio. Moreover, most of the land tilled by the peasants was registered as permanent possessions. Meanwhile, imperial grants of property further reduced the total quantity of land available for redistribution. After a century and a half in operation, the system began to break down.

**Revenue.** The equal field system resulted in significant agricultural production; vast amounts of fallow land were brought under cultivation. During the early Tang period the central government received stable and ample revenue, much larger proportionally than in any previous dynasty. According to one government record the tax income of the central government amounted to more than 52 million silver units. In addition, government also utilized the free labor and military service provided by the taxpaying peasantry.

**Reasons.** The economic prosperity enjoyed by the Tang dynasty was the result of several factors. First, advances in agricultural technology helped increase productivity. Irrigation systems were improved, and better seeds and fertilizers were used. Second, the administration, at least during the early period of the dynasty, was effective. The country was centralized and divided into a uniform system of *tao* (provinces), *zhou* (prefectures), and *xian* (districts). The bureaucracy was staffed by officials who were selected through the merit-based civil service examination system. Third, the great population growth in the Yangzi Valley contributed to prosperity. The primary breadbasket of the country did not stay long in the dry millet- and wheat-producing lands of the North China Plain, but shifted to the wet rice paddies of the lower Yangzi region. Fourth, the Great Canal, constructed during the Sui dynasty (589–618), provided an efficient transportation system that linked the agriculturally rich south with the capital and the frontier areas in the north.

Sources:

Woodbridge Bingham, *The Founding of the T'ang Dynasty: The Fall of Sui and Rise of T'ang, a Preliminary Survey* (Baltimore: Waverly, 1941).

John K. Fairbank and others, *East Asia: Tradition and Transformation* (Boston: Houghton Mifflin, 1973).

Herbert Franke and Denis Twitchett, eds., *The Cambridge History of China*, volume 6, *Alien Regimes and Border States, 907–1368* (Cambridge & New York: Cambridge University Press, 1994).

Witold Rodzinski, *A History of China*, 2 volumes (Oxford & New York: Pergamon, 1979, 1983).

Arthur F. Wright and Twitchett, eds., *Perspectives on the Tang* (New Haven: Yale University Press, 1973).

## TANG DYNASTY (618-907): SOCIAL ORGANIZATIONS

**Social Stratification.** Chinese society was stratified during the Tang dynasty, as it had been in previous dynasties. The *shi* (scholar-official class), which derived its social prestige and economic wealth not only from family inheritances but also from the academic degrees earned by men who passed the civil service examinations and obtained subsequent official appointments, was the top stratum of society. The *nong* (peasantry), which was the primary taxpaying body and bulk of the Chinese population, came next in the social strata. Occupying the level just below that of the *nong* were the *gong* (artisans). They were

Figurine of a Persian trader carrying a wineskin, Tang dynasty, 618–907 (Seattle Art Museum)

the secondary taxpayers and producers of goods. On the bottom of the social structure was the *shang* (merchant class), whose members were condemned as social parasites. Discriminated against and restricted by imperial policies, they had been despised by the general public since ancient times. In reality, however, there were many cases throughout Chinese history in which great merchants not only enjoyed extravagant lifestyles but also were accepted into government service and the imperial court.

**Examinations and the Scholar-Officials.** The Tang dynasty continued the system of government schools and examinations of the previous dynasty. Specialized national schools were established in the capital. In addition, many prefectures and districts also ran official institutions to help talented students prepare for the examinations. The Ministry of Rites held examinations for students from the government schools and for nominees sent by local governments. There were two chief academic degrees: the *xiucai* (flowering talent) for current political issues, and the *jinshi* (presented scholar) for letters. The latter was the most prestigious degree and the primary passage to officialdom. Prior to being awarded a government appointment, those men who succeeded in obtaining the *jinshi* title had to enter a second series of examinations administered by the Ministry of Personnel. Applicants were tested and judged both on their written answers and on their physical appearance and verbal eloquence. The Tang examination system helped create a bureaucracy of merit that selected, by and large, the most talented men to run its government machine. Furthermore, the examination system fostered an intellectually unified nation, since those men who desired the degree and the subsequent imperial appointment had to acquire the same classical education. The system, however, was weighted overall in favor of the rich and powerful. Only those boys who were supported by wealthy families could sustain the lengthy education and preparation necessary for passing the examinations.

Sources:
Woodbridge Bingham, *The Founding of the T'ang Dynasty: The Fall of Sui and Rise of T'ang, a Preliminary Survey* (Baltimore: Waverly, 1941).

John K. Fairbank and others, *East Asia: Tradition and Transformation* (Boston: Houghton Mifflin, 1973).

Herbert Franke and Denis Twitchett, eds., *The Cambridge History of China*, volume 6, *Alien Regimes and Border States, 907–1368* (Cambridge & New York: Cambridge University Press, 1994).

Witold Rodzinski, *A History of China*, 2 volumes (Oxford & New York: Pergamon, 1979, 1983).

Arthur F. Wright and Twitchett, eds., *Perspectives on the Tang* (New Haven: Yale University Press, 1973).

## YUAN DYNASTY (1279–1368): CHINA AND THE INNER ASIAN PEOPLES

**Life on the Steppe.** Unlike the Chinese Han (206 B.C.E.–220 C.E.) people, who lived in a settled, agrarian economy, the lives of the Inner Asian peoples of the steppe evolved around a pastoral economy. The nomadic tribal peoples depended on

Manuscript page of caravan travelers, fourteenth century (National Palace Museum, Taipei, Taiwan)

sheep and horses for their livelihood. These people ate mutton and drank horse milk; were clothed in sheepskins and slept in felt tents; and used dried animal dung for fuel. They rode horses when tending their herds, moving the animals from pasture to pasture, and fighting their enemies. They only needed to contact agricultural people when they traded for salt, tea, grain, textiles, and metals. They migrated on a seasonal basis, herding in the open plains in summer and in sheltered mountain valleys in winter. The migrant nature of life made it hard for these nomads to accumulate wealth, and therefore they always needed trade and territorial expansion. When the Chinese government was strong and effective, it confronted these "barbarians" and chased them out of the frontier areas, whereas, when the dynasty was weak, the horse-riding nomads invaded, looted the agricultural Chinese, and took their lands as pastures.

**Liao Dynasty.** The Khitan (Qidan) tribes, a group of Mongols from the steppe, established the Liao dynasty (947–1125) in northern China. The territory of the Liao included the agricultural areas in northern China and southern Manchuria, grasslands in western Manchuria and Mongolia, and the forested valleys of eastern and northern Manchuria. The Khitan people lived a semiagricultural life and operated a seminomadic economy. They grew crops, raised pigs, and kept horses and camels. By 907 the Khitan formed a tribal confederation, and the chieftain declared himself an emperor. By 947 the Khitan empire expanded to include sixteen prefectures in northern China, and it adopted the Chinese dynastic title of the Liao dynasty. The Khitan Liao incorporated a Chinese-style government and examination system.

**Xi Xia Kingdom.** While the Liao dynasty existed in northern China, the Tanguts, a Tibetan people, established a kingdom, called Xi Xia (1038–1227), in northwestern China (approximately in present Gansu province). The Tanguts had a semi-oasis economy. They irrigated arid lands to grow their crops, herded sheep, and traded with the Chinese and Central Asian peoples. In 1038 the Tangut leader declared himself the emperor of Xi Xia. Like the Liao dynasty, the Xi Xia kingdom adopted the Chinese government structure and educational system but made Buddhism its state religion.

**Jin Dynasty.** The Jurchen (Nuzhen) tribes, a Tungusic-speaking people from northern Manchuria, were Khitan vassals. In 1115 a capable Jurchen leader unified the tribes and declared himself emperor. The Jurchens named their dynasty the Jin (Golden, 1122–1234) after a river in Manchuria. The Jin invaded the Song lands, captured their capital in 1126, and pushed the royal court to the south of the Hui River, thus occupying the entire northern part of China. Like the Khitans and Tanguts, the Jurchen tribes also experienced a significant level of sinification. They established their main capital in Yanjing, the site of modern Beijing, and modeled their bureaucratic state after China. The Jurchen rulers studied Confucian classics and patronized Chinese art. Interracial marriages between the Chinese and Jurchens were allowed by the government. With the settled lifestyle, the Jurchen chariot men gradually became tenant farmers. In 1215, pushed by the Mongols, the Jin moved their capital from Yanjing to Kaifeng in Henan Province. In 1234 the Mongols finally eliminated the Jin dynasty.

Sources:

John K. Fairbank and others, *East Asia: Tradition and Transformation* (Boston: Houghton Mifflin, 1973).

Herbert Franke and Denis Twitchett, eds., *The Cambridge History of China*, volume 6, *Alien Regimes and Border States, 907–1368* (Cambridge & New York: Cambridge University Press, 1994).

John D. Langlois Jr., ed., *China under Mongol Rule* (Princeton: Princeton University Press, 1981).

F. W. Mote, *Imperial China, 900–1800* (Cambridge, Mass.: Harvard University Press, 1999).

Witold Rodzinski, *A History of China*, 2 volumes (Oxford & New York: Pergamon, 1979, 1983).

Morris Rossabi, *Khubilai Khan: His Life and Times* (Berkeley: University of California Press, 1988).

## PROSPEROUS MERCHANTS

Under the Yuan, both domestic and foreign merchants prospered. Here is a portion from Marco Polo's famous account of China:

And in each of these suburbs or districts for perhaps a mile distant from the city are many and fine factories in which stay and lodge the merchants and the traveling foreigners, of whom there are many from all parts to bring things as presents to the lord and to sell to the court, and all other men who come there for their business, who come there in very great quantity, between [those who come] for the court of the lord (and wherever he holds his court the people come there from every side for various reasons) and for this that the town is in so good a market that the merchants and the other men come here for their business. And to each kind of people one factory is set apart, as if one said one for the Lombards, another for the Germans, and another for the French. Moreover I tell you that there are as beautiful houses and as beautiful palaces in the suburbs as in the town, except those of the great lord . . . And again you may know quite truly that. I believe there is not a place in the world to which so many merchants come and that dearer things and of greater value and more strange come into this town of Cambaluc from all sides than into any city of the world, and greater quantity of all things, and I will tell you what. First of all [I shall tell] you that all the dear things that come from Indie, these are precious stones and pearls, and silk and all the spicery, and all other dear things, are brought to this town. And again all the beautiful things and all the dear which are in the province of Catai and from Mangi and from all other provinces round about are brought there also. And this happens because everyone from everywhere brings there for the lord who lives there and for his court and for the city which is so great and for the ladies and for the barons . . . come to this town and greater quantities than into any town in the world, and more goods are sold and bought there than in any other city, so that so much of everything comes there that it is without end. For you may know in truth that among the rest, almost each day in the year there come into this town more than a thousand carts loaded with silk alone, for many cloths of gold and of silk are made there and many other things.

Source: Marco Polo, *The Description of the World*, translated by A. C. Moule and Paul Pelliot (London: Routledge, 1938), pp. 235–237.

Drawing of a village craftsman constructing a barrel, Yuan dynasty, 1279–1368 (National Palace Museum, Taipei, Taiwan)

## YUAN DYNASTY (1279–1368): THE ECONOMY

**Agricultural Policies.** As the first nomadic conquerors to rule over China, the Mongols have been blamed by traditional historians for the damage to and destruction of the agriculture-based Chinese economy during the Yuan period. The more recent, revisionist studies, however, suggest that the Mongol rulers encouraged agriculture. In 1261 Kublai Khan established an Office for the Stimulation of Agriculture and named eight officials to start programs to improve the agricultural economy. Kublai Khan also initiated policies to help recover land in northern China, which had been damaged by warfare for half a century. These relief measures included tax remissions and emergency grain provisions for farmers. To protect agriculture Kublai Khan issued an edict to prohibit the nomads' herds from roaming in the farmlands. Kublai Khan and his advisers also founded the state-sponsored rural organization called *she*, which organized fifty households under the direction of village leaders. The primary goal of the *she* was to stimulate agricultural production and encourage land reclamation. In addition, Kublai Khan established a fixed, regular system of taxation.

**Commercial Policies.** Merchants prospered during the Yuan dynasty. Traditionally, they were perceived as parasites of society, and previous Chinese dynasties imposed restrictions on the larger merchants. Within the social hierarchy, merchants were ranked at the bottom, below not only the gentry-scholars but also the farmers and artisans. The Mongols, on the contrary, had viewed trade as indispensable for their pastoral economy. After they conquered China, the Mongols continued to value trade, and they elevated the social status of merchants. Domestic commerce soon developed. To promote this trade Kublai Khan enforced the use of paper money throughout China and devised three types of this currency. Kublai Khan also promoted the construction of roads and expanded the postal-station sys-

Crate of ceramic bowls excavated from a Mongol ship that sank off the coast of Korea in 1323 (from Patricia Buckley Ebrey, *Cambridge Illustrated History of China*, 1996)

tem to assist in the development of commerce. The postal stations, which had existed as early as the Tang dynasty (618–907) for the transmission and delivery of official mails, now also served as hostels for traveling merchants.

**Foreign Trade.** Foreign trade flourished under the Yuan dynasty. The overland trade to Central Asia, the Middle East, and Persia was primarily dominated by Muslim merchants. They imported horses, camels, rugs, medicines, and spices. Chinese textiles, chinaware, lacquerware, and other items were exported. The overseas trade also continued to deliver goods to the southeastern port cities of Quanzhou and Fuzhou, where Chinese silk, porcelain, and copper coins were traded for gems, rhinoceros horns, medicines, carpets, and spices. The Yuan rulers required foreign traders to convert their metal coins into Chinese paper currency. This policy helped the court to share in the profits of foreign trade.

**Marco Polo.** Among the thousands of foreign merchants to visit China, Marco Polo was the most

renowned. He was the first westerner to leave a written record about China. Born into a merchant family in Venice, Marco Polo was fascinated by the stories of China told by his father, Niccolo, and uncle Maffeo, who had traveled to China to trade. In 1271 he left home for China with his father and uncle; they arrived in China four years later. He served in Kublai Khan's court for seventeen years and returned home in 1295. His *Description of the World* was a vivid account of the geography, economy, and government system of China. He wrote about the use of coal, the salt trade, and the local customs of Yangzhou, where he claimed he had served as governor for three years. He also wrote about his many conversations with Kublai Khan, and he described the Chinese ruler as "neither too small nor too large," with black eyes and a prominent nose. Although disbelieved by his contemporaries, his account of China was widely read, and it inspired generations of adventurers.

Sources:
John K. Fairbank and others, *East Asia: Tradition and Transformation* (Boston: Houghton Mifflin, 1973).

Herbert Franke and Denis Twitchett, eds., *The Cambridge History of China*, volume 6, *Alien Regimes and Border States, 907–1368* (Cambridge & New York: Cambridge University Press, 1994).

John D. Langlois Jr., ed., *China under Mongol Rule* (Princeton: Princeton University Press, 1981).

F. W. Mote, *Imperial China, 900–1800* (Cambridge, Mass.: Harvard University Press, 1999).

Witold Rodzinski, *A History of China*, 2 volumes (Oxford & New York: Pergamon, 1979, 1983).

Morris Rossabi, *Khubilai Khan: His Life and Times* (Berkeley: University of California Press, 1988).

## YUAN DYNASTY (1279-1368): THE RISE OF THE MONGOLS

**Mongol Life.** Like the other Inner Asian peoples, the Mongols followed a pattern of seasonal migration. They lived in felt tents, ate mutton, practiced polygamy, and worshiped the hearth. Their basic social and political units were the patriarchal clans, which further formed tribes bound by blood relationships. Conflicts among tribes over women and territory often resulted in warfare, and the losers consequently became subordinates of the victors. Mongol soldiers were known for their mobility and military prowess. The Mongol cavalry consisted of excellent riders. It was reported they could stay on their saddles constantly for about ten days and nights. In battle the Mongol warriors encircled and harried their enemies, and they then used their heavy bows to kill them. They also utilized tactics of psychological warfare, such as terrorizing their opponents. Their military superiority gave them an edge in fighting against other Inner Asian tribes and the Chinese.

**Genghis Khan.** In 1167 a Mongol boy was born and given the name Temujin. Although of aristocratic origin, Temujin lost his father when he was young, and he subsequently led a hard life. The young Temujin first rebelled against his own lord, then slowly subjugated one tribe after another. Finally, in 1206, the Mongol tribes held a great meeting on the bank of Kerulen River, and Temujin was granted the title of *Genghis Khan*, meaning "universal ruler." The power of Genghis Khan was first based on the social organization of Mongols, beginning with the families, then the clans, and then the tribes. Second, the military organization of Genghis Khan proved effective. The Mongol army was organized in units of tens, hundreds, and thousands and was led by aristocratic leaders. In 1227 the Mongol army numbered about 129,000 men, more than 10 percent of the total population. In addition, Mongol military tactics—including encirclement, espionage, and terror—further enhanced their power. In 1215 Genghis destroyed the Jin capital. Before his death in 1227, Genghis eliminated the Xi Xia kingdom, thus establishing the basis of a Eurasian empire.

**Kublai Khan.** The conquest of the Southern Song (1127–1279) was completed under Genghis's grandson, Kublai Khan. He became Great Khan in 1260 and made Beijing his winter capital in 1264. In 1271 he adopted the Chinese dynastic name of Yuan (The First Beginning). In 1279 the Mongol forces finally destroyed the Southern Song court, bringing the entire area of China under Mongol rule. The Mongol leaders, however, continued warfare against other countries. In 1274 and 1281 Kublai Khan's forces attacked Japan. Both expeditions

Illumination of Genghis Khan and Mongol horsemen pursuing enemy forces, thirteenth century (Bibliothèque Nationale, Paris)

failed; the Mongols planned a third assault, but they never carried it out. Mongol forces also organized military campaigns against Vietnam and Burma. In 1281 and 1291 the Mongol fleet attacked Java. These military campaigns expanded Chinese territory and brought local rulers into tribute relationships with China.

**Preserving Identity.** Kublai Khan was determined to rule all of China. After the conquest of the Southern Song, the Mongols faced the same problem as previous non-Chinese conquerors—how to rule such a vast land and yet not be inundated by Chinese culture. Previous khans had lived among their herds and in their tents. Kublai Khan spent most of his time in Beijing or in the summer capital at Shandu in Inner Mongolia. He was recorded in the histories as Shizu (Grand Ancestor) following Chinese tradition. Kublai Khan was also careful to preserve Mongol identity. He took only Mongol women into his palace and prohibited Mongols from marrying Chinese. Kublai Khan managed to strike a balance during his thirty-four-year rule as leader of the Yuan.

**Sources:**

John K. Fairbank and others, *East Asia: Tradition and Transformation* (Boston: Houghton Mifflin, 1973).

Herbert Franke and Denis Twitchett, eds., *The Cambridge History of China*, volume 6, *Alien Regimes and Border States, 907–1368* (Cambridge & New York: Cambridge University Press, 1994).

John D. Langlois Jr., ed., *China under Mongol Rule* (Princeton: Princeton University Press, 1981).

F. W. Mote, *Imperial China, 900–1800* (Cambridge, Mass.: Harvard University Press, 1999).

Witold Rodzinski, *A History of China*, 2 volumes (Oxford & New York: Pergamon, 1979, 1983).

Morris Rossabi, *Khubilai Khan: His Life and Times* (Berkeley: University of California Press, 1988).

## YUAN DYNASTY (1279-1368): SOCIETY UNDER MONGOL RULE

**Hierarchy of Social Classes.** Although the Mongols had established Yuan dynasty rule over all of China, their conquest was not completed without difficulty. Chinese in both northern and southern China organized resistance movements against Mongol control and employed guerilla warfare, or individuals refused to collaborate with their conquerors. Facing hostility from the Chinese, Mongol leaders employed a policy of ethnic discrimination by setting up a strictly enforced hierarchy of social classes, ordered in descending level of importance: from the Mongols, *semu ren* (Western and Central Asians), *han ren* (northern Chinese), to the *nan ren* (southern Chinese). During the Yuan period many foreigners, especially Muslims from Central and West Asia, were employed by the Mongol court as advisers, civil officials, military officers, financial managers, tutors, translators, physicians, astronomers, and skilled craftsmen. These non-Chinese foreigners, or *semu ren*, were ranked second in society. The Chinese from northern China, since they had capitulated earlier and were therefore more accustomed to Mongol rule, were ranked below the non-Chinese collaborators, but above citizens from southern China, who were the most defiant against their new rulers. This rigid discriminatory policy made the Mongols and non-Chinese foreigners the ruling classes over the Chinese. This practice served at least two purposes. First, it enabled the Mongols and foreigners to extort resources from China. Second, it was meant to hurt psychologically the national pride of the Chinese people. Furthermore, the Mongols utilized the ancient ruling technique of "divide and rule" by differentiating between the northern and southern Chinese. This deliberate racial and ethnic discrimination, combined with traditional Chinese despotism, made the Yuan dynasty the darkest age in imperial Chinese history.

**Confucian Scholars.** While the Yuan court practiced racial discrimination and class oppression, it also tried to soften the hostility of the Chinese, especially from Confucian scholars. Kublai Khan issued orders to protect Confucian temples, and he restored Confucianism as the official philosophy. He also exempted Confucian scholars from taxation and encouraged them to serve in his court. Overall, however, Chinese scholars were largely used only as bureaucratic clerks and few rose to prominent positions. Mongol rulers abolished the civil service

Illumination of tribute bearers, fourteenth century (Avery Brundage Collection, University of Illinois at Urbana-Champaign)

examination system and did not revive it until 1315. Confucian scholars also resented the Mongols for their patronage of foreign religions. Nestorian churches and Islamic mosques—along with various Buddhist, Daoist, and Confucian temples—were exempted from taxation. The flourishing of various religions was clearly a backlash against the Song school of neo-Confucianism.

**Sources:**

John K. Fairbank and others, *East Asia: Tradition and Transformation* (Boston: Houghton Mifflin, 1973).

Herbert Franke and Denis Twitchett, eds., *The Cambridge History of China,* volume 6, *Alien Regimes and Border States, 907–1368* (Cambridge & New York: Cambridge University Press, 1994).

John D. Langlois Jr., ed., *China under Mongol Rule* (Princeton: Princeton University Press, 1981).

F. W. Mote, *Imperial China, 900–1800* (Cambridge, Mass.: Harvard University Press, 1999).

Witold Rodzinski, *A History of China,* 2 volumes (Oxford & New York: Pergamon, 1979, 1983).

Morris Rossabi, *Khubilai Khan: His Life and Times* (Berkeley: University of California Press, 1988).

# SIGNIFICANT PEOPLE

## HAI RUI

### 1513-1587

### GOVERNMENT OFFICIAL

**Early Life.** Hai Rui was a native of the capital of Hainan Island. His grandfather was a magistrate in Fujian. When he was three years old, Hai Rui lost his father. His mother trained him to read the classics and took care of his education. At school, where he remained for some twenty years, he was famous for his good conduct and earned the admiration of his fellow students. About 1546, his mother asked him to divorce his first wife, who then sued him for the return of her dowry. To evade a court trial and publicity, he borrowed money to pay her.

**Official.** In 1549 he earned a juren degree after passing the examination. A year later, when traveling to Beijing to take the higher examination, he submitted a memorial to the Ming court on the pacification in the central highlands of Hainan. In 1553, after failing the metropolitan examination for the second time, Hai was appointed as instructor of the district school of Nanping, Fujian. After arriving there in 1554, he encouraged his students to study Confucianism, stressing self-cultivation for the achievement of firm integrity and strict observation of regulations. He also preached public-mindedness and thrift as the basics of incorruptibility. He finally had a chance to prove that he practiced what he preached when he was appointed to be magistrate of a city in Zhejiang in 1558. On coming to office he declared to his subordinates, clerks, students, and elders that he would firmly observe the law and promote the general welfare.

**Prison.** By reexamination of the land, Hai made a more fair distribution of the tax burden based on landholding, known as the Single Whip system. He attacked corrupt practices, constructed the city wall, opposed unlawful demands by superiors, and brought his clerks under control. He himself lived a plain life, even planting his own garden vegetables. The people worshiped Hai, but some of his supervisors hated him. In 1562, soon after Hai published a collection of public papers, he was appointed as magistrate to a city in Jiangxi, where he served for a couple of years. Called to Beijing, he was appointed as a secretary in the Ministry of Revenue. He found fault with the emperor for his search for longevity, for his ridiculous involvement in Daoist ceremonies in the court, and for his eccentric ways of building houses on the palace grounds. Angered by this criticism, in 1566 the emperor sent Hai to prison. Interrogated about his motives, Hai almost died of the tortures used to extract a confession. He was compelled to divulge the names of possible conspirators.

**Restoration.** Early in 1567, a few days after the emperor died, Hai was set free from prison and restored to his former rank. Later, he was promoted to transmission commissioner of Nanjing. In 1569 he accepted the appointment of governor with headquarters at Suzhou, and at the same time as chief inspector of grain and storage. Once more, when he came to office, he declared that he would eliminate all corrupt practices.

**Retirement.** When Hai compelled some big landowners to return some land to their original owners, these powerful landlords plotted his removal. In 1570 a censor accused Hai of protecting the evildoers and hurting the landlords. He was forced to retire. During the fifteen years of retirement, Hai built up a large library but lived plainly in a humble house on his small plot of land.

**Man of the People.** In 1585 Hai was appointed assistant head of the Ministry of Censorate in Nanjing. Almost immediately after his arrival at Nanjing, he was promoted to vice minister of the Ministry of Personnel and for about a month as acting minister. Again he affronted the administrators by preventing any official from charging the local people for expenses not specified by law. His policy obviously delighted the people and increased his popularity. In 1586 Hai was appointed as censor-in-chief in Nanjing. Once more his insistence on the letter of the law incited some officials to plot for his removal. He died in office a year later. When his body was carried from Nanjing to the river, hundreds of thousands of people participated in the funeral procession.

**Evaluation.** Throughout the Ming Empire, Hai's bravery in speaking the truth produced admiration and sympathy. The Ming government, recognizing Hai's strength of character, gave him the posthumous name, "Loyal and Incorruptible." Admirers bought prints of his portrait to worship at home, and shrines were built at the places where he had held office. Hai was also honored in legend and folk literature in the following centuries.

Sources:

L. Carrington Goodrich and Fang Chaoying, eds., *Dictionary of Ming Biography* (New York: Columbia University Press, 1976).

F. W. Mote, *Imperial China, 900–1800* (Cambridge, Mass.: Harvard University Press, 1999).

# MARCO POLO

## 1254-1324
### EXPLORER, MERCHANT, AND AUTHOR

**Childhood.** Marco Polo was born into a noble family and grew up in Venice (although his place of birth is uncertain). He was reared with the traditional education for Italian boys—trained in the classics and theology. He knew French as well as Italian and was interested in "the ways of people and interesting plants and animals." When Marco was six years old, Niccolo and Maffeo, his father and uncle, respectively, traveled to Cathay (China) and met Kublai Khan. They left China with good relations and the intention to return. When the Polo brothers returned to Venice, Marco was fifteen years old, and his mother had passed away. Two years later, when he was seventeen, Marco left home with his father and uncle and accompanied them on their return trip to China.

**Explorer.** With his father and uncle, Marco traveled along the Silk Road into western Asia. The three men made it through to China across a route farther north than had previously been taken by the brothers. All along the way Marco recorded what he observed in each place that they visited. Three and a half years after leaving Venice, and 5,600 miles later, the small party finally reached the original capital of Kublai Khan at Shandu (then the summer residence). For twenty-four years Marco traveled and explored the vast regions of Central Asia, China, and South Asia.

**Service in the Khan's Court.** Marco met and later became a confidant to Kublai Khan. He served on the Khan's court for the remainder of the time he was in China. In 1277 the Khan appointed him as an official of the Privy Council. He was also named as a tax inspector for three years in Yangzhou, a city on the Grand Canal, northeast of Nanjing. Marco's service to the Khan gave him the ability to travel to Burma, India, and other places throughout China, which also allowed him to become "a gifted linguist and master of four languages." In his book Marco described Kublai Khan's capital, ceremonies, hunting practices, and public assistance in great detail. He also included a description of the rise of the Yuan dynasty (1279–1368). Compared to the grandeur of Chinese civilization, Marco felt that everything in Europe was on a much smaller scale. He discovered that China had been using paper currency and coal for years, both new concepts to him. He wrote of a communication system that was established throughout the khan's territory. He was impressed by the extreme wealth of the dynasty, including its strong economy, iron production that well exceeded that of Europe, and the abundance of salt produced from the land. Overall, he concluded that China was a land of prosperity that could not be compared with any European country at the time. In 1295, after living seventeen years in China, the Polos returned home.

**The Book.** Three years after his return, Venice was engaged in a war against its rival city of Genoa. Marco Polo was captured during the fighting and was incarcerated in a Genoese prison for a year. While in prison he met a writer of romances and told him about his travels to China, which became known as *Description of the World* or *The Travels of Marco Polo*. Though his stories were met with disbelief, the book inspired generations of adventurers, including Christopher Columbus. Marco Polo died at the age of seventy at his home in Venice.

Sources:

John Larner, *Marco Polo and the Discovery of the World* (New Haven: Yale University Press, 1999).

"Marco Polo and His Travels," Internet website, <http://www.silk-road.com/artl/marcopolo.shtml>.

Morris Rossabi, *Khubilai Khan: His Life and Times* (Berkeley: University of California Press, 1988).

# TAN GAOZU LI YUAN

## 566-635
### EMPEROR

**Sui General.** The Sui Dynasty (589–618) was falling apart under Emperor Yang (Sui Yang Di), who ruled from 604 to 617. During the first decade of the seventh century many Chinese staged rebellions against the dynasty. Tan

Gaozu Li Yuan, a military governor of Taiyuan under the Sui in northern China, was sent by Emperor Yang in 617 to fight and control a peasant rebellion that had arisen in the province.

**Founding the Dynasty.** Under the persuasion of his son, Li Shimin, Li Yuan instead took this opportunity to challenge the rule of the emperor. He traveled throughout the country to raise troops. Soon after this recruitment trip, Li Yuan and thirty thousand soldiers headed for Chang'an, the capital of the Sui dynasty. They crossed the Yellow River and arrived at Guan Zhong, where their army was increased by two hundred thousand people who were involved in the peasant rebellions. In Chang'an, Li Yuan's daughter gathered ten thousand more soldiers—called "the army of women"—to help fight with her father. In the end Li Yuan's army won the struggle and Chang'an was conquered, thereby affording him the right to become the new emperor.

**Emperor.** After the assassination of Emperor Yang's son in 618, Li Yuan declared an official end to the Sui dynasty and installed himself as emperor, thus beginning the Tang dynasty (618–907). One of his first acts was to abolish laws declared by the Sui dynasty. He ruled until 626, when his son forced his abdication from the throne. After eight years of fighting under his rule, the country was reunified. The Tang was a dynasty of economic wealth, cultural growth, and military expansion. The post-humous title *Tang Gaozu* (High Progenitor) was added to Li Yuan's name after his death in acknowledgment of his contribution to the dynasty.

**Sources:**
Woodbridge Bingham, *The Founding of the T'ang Dynasty: The Fall of Sui and Rise of T'ang, a Preliminary Survey* (Baltimore: Waverly, 1941).

Witold Rodzinski, *A History of China,* 2 volumes (Oxford & New York: Pergamon, 1979, 1983).

Pan Yihong, *Son of Heaven and Heavenly Qaghan: Sui-Tang China and Its Neighbors* (Bellingham: Center for East Asian Studies, Western Washington University, 1997).

# WANG ANSHI

## 1021-1086

### POET AND STATESMAN

**Confucian Ideals.** Wang Anshi was a writer, poet, and statesman. His educational background in the Confucian beliefs and experience in literature aided him in composing his reforms. He believed that the empire should unite in a manner similar to the ways practiced by the ancient kings. Ten years before Wang's promotion to the position of Grand Councillor, he traveled to the capital, Kaifeng, to deliver a speech that has come to be called the "Ten Thousand Word Memorial," in which he stated his philosophy of how China should be run. Although he believed that the key to operating a successful government was to exhibit Confucian ideals, he saw that China needed to have capa-

ble rulers who promoted these ideals for the overall betterment of the country.

**Reformer.** Wang served from 1069 to 1076 as Grand Councillor under Emperor Shenzong, who reigned from 1068 to 1085. During Wang's lifetime barbarians continuously invaded China and made many demands upon the country, which placed stress on its leaders. He worked to make compromises with these enemies, and, as a result, a period of new reforms was established. He helped to introduce many political, social, economic, and educational changes in the structure of China. Some of the changes he implemented, which were known as "Wang Anshi Reforms," were: ending tax immunities for large landowners, abolishing forced labor on public works in favor of cash payment of taxes, and establishing a state monopoly in buying and selling goods. These initiatives undermined the power of the large landholders. Wang also helped rearrange the political system, strengthen the military system, and channel excess money to the areas where it was needed. He established a new educational system in which local authorities operated schools, which all candidates for civil service examinations were expected to attend.

**Life after Reforms.** Wang's reforms were deliberately sabotaged by rival civil servants. Some critics claimed he was destroying the traditional social structure, while others did not like the forced uniformity. Still others felt the reforms were being pushed too rapidly. He was compelled to resign in 1076, and he spent the remaining years of his life writing poetry and scholarly works. He died in 1086, a few months after the death of Emperor Shenzong.

**Source:**
John Winthrop Haeger, ed., *Crisis and Prosperity in Sung China* (Tucson: University of Arizona Press, 1975).

James T. C. Liu, *Reform in Sung China: Wang An-shih (1021–1086) and His New Policies* (Cambridge, Mass.: Harvard University Press, 1959).

F. W. Mote, *Imperial China, 900–1800* (Cambridge, Mass.: Harvard University Press, 1999).

# YAN SHI

## 1182-1240

### POWERFUL OVERLORD

**Early Life.** Born in 1182, the youngest son of a farmer in western Shandong, Yan Shi did not have the family background necessary for a successful political career under usual conditions. He had a nice appearance and an attentive mind but little formal education. He was brave, kind, and friendly. Because of his excessive spirit, he was repeatedly in severe trouble and was jailed for a variety of reasons. He was, however, able to break out of jail with the assistance of his young followers. In his early life Yan Shi was a hooligan by normal criteria.

**Opportunity.** The chance for Yan Shi to climb from the world of ruffian to bureaucrat came when much of northern China was invaded by the Mongols. Instead of demolishing only the border defenses of the Jin dynasty, as they had done in preceding years, Mongol troops launched a considerable campaign, sweeping across Shandong and Shanxi, as well as Hebei. One consequence of this invasion and the later withdrawal of the Mongol army was increased militarism all over the country. For self-protection armed bands of different sizes and political affiliations were created by members of locally famous families and individual strongmen. Yan Shi was among those militia leaders who were enlisted by the government. After the Mongols retreated from Shandong in 1213, he was appointed as a centurion in his native district. As an officer in the Jin army, Yan Shi had the chance to show his military talent, and he quickly extended his influence with the rise of Song (960–1279) power in northern China. In early 1220, when an envoy went to North China, Yan Shi formally confirmed his allegiance to the Song, bringing with him nine prefectures in western Shandong, southeastern Hebei, and northern Henan.

**Submission.** Yan Shi was soon disappointed with his announced alliance because Song forces in North China did not receive extensive assistance from the royal court. As a result, when the Mongol army invaded Shandong again in 1220 and Yan Shi realized that they would eventually occupy all of China, he lost no time in offering his surrender. Greatly benefiting the Mongols and hurting the Song, his surrender gave the Mongols not only the largest number of households (three hundred thousand) ever given up by a defector but also a vast territory that paved the way for their attack on the capital. Because of this contribution the Mongols granted him the Chinese honorific title of Gold and Purple Great Officer of Eminent Dignity and assigned him as chief of the Regional Presidential Council of West Shandong.

**Powerful Overlord.** In subsequent years Yan Shi was among the few high-ranking Chinese generals whose mission was to deal with the Jin and Song empires in eastern China. After more than ten years of cooperation with the Mongols, Yan Shi was appointed chief civil administrator of West Shandong. His domain, including twenty cities, was one of the largest territories occupied by an overlord in northern China. Other than controlling the land and people, Yan Shi commanded a large army.

**Aid to People.** Yan Shi was not only a strong militarist but also distinguished himself by his efforts to alleviate misery produced by the war. He saved many lives and aided the local populations by discouraging the Mongol commanders from killing tens of thousands of people. He not only prohibited his own soldiers from murdering people but also paid ransoms for civilians detained by other forces. He saved many lives by giving food to starving refugees, who were either sent back to their homes or resettled as farmers.

**Reforms.** Aside from helping the civilian population at large, Yan Shi made a particular effort to aid displaced intellectuals and officials of the Jin dynasty, many of whom he appointed to his government. With so many intellectuals available, Yan Shi staffed his court with competent men. With the help of this civilian staff, Yan Shi was able to accomplish several important administrative, fiscal, and educational reforms. Managerially, he improved the integrity and efficiency of officials. Economically and financially, Yan Shi reduced taxes as well as promoted agriculture. His most noteworthy contribution was the revitalization of education and culture. For example, a well-endowed prefectural school had been founded during the Northern Song and Jin periods, but it was destroyed in 1213 when the Mongols first devastated the area. Yan Shi rebuilt the institution in 1236, as well as other schools, where pupils studied rites and music that were generally regarded as the core of Confucian education. As one of the strongest overlords in northern China, Yan Shi was a foremost promoter of Chinese culture in an age of chaos during the twelfth and thirteenth centuries.

Sources:

Richard L. Davis, *Wind against the Mountain: The Crisis of Politics and Culture in Thirteenth-century China* (Cambridge, Mass.: Harvard University Press, 1996).

Herbert Franke, ed., *Sung Biographies,* four volumes (Wiesbaden: Steiner, 1976).

Igor de Rachewiltz and others, eds., *In the Service of the Khan: Eminent Personalities of the Early Mongol-Yuan Period (1200–1300)* (Wiesbaden: Harassowitz, 1993).

# YANG HUAN

## 1186-1255
### SCHOLAR

**Early Life.** Born in 1186, Yang Huan was the descendant of a wealthy landlord who had settled in a village in northern China. Huan began studying the classics under the guidance of his mother, a moral and educated woman, who sold her jewelry to buy a library for the family. She had a great impact on her children, especially Huan. In 1200 he took the prefectural examination for the first time and passed it. His name was at the top of the list of winning candidates. His talent caught the notice of the authorities, and two years later the local government employed him as an accountant in the prefectural office. Huan worked industriously; his supervisor was impressed by his talents and excellent work and encouraged him to further his studies under a local Confucian scholar. Three years of working as an accountant gave Yang many experiences in the management of fiscal affairs, which was helpful when he later served the Mongols.

**Official.** In the fall of 1205 Huan took the department test at Chang'an; he passed and then took the palace examination in the Jin capital (modern Beijing) in 1206. There were 1,200 participants, but only 28 passed; Huan was one of the unsuccessful candidates. In 1220 he returned to Chang'an to make another attempt to pass the palace examination, but he failed again. In 1238 he retook the test with many younger students from his locality, after the Mongols restored the civil service examination. He topped the list of candidates in two subjects and was ranked first of the 4,030 students to have passed all levels of examinations.

He was first appointed a member of the examining commission and then made the chief inspection commissioner of the Henan Tax-collection Bureau, a new department established after the collapse of the Jin state on the model of the fiscal and administrative office created in northern China by the Mongols. He suggested that the authorities proceed steadily and carefully to restore the economic health of the province. His program received a warm response and support from the Yuan court (1279–1368). Huan served in this position for twelve years until he resigned in 1251.

**Scholar.** During his service in the administration of Henan, Huan continued teaching. After returning home he built a pavilion and committed himself to studying and writing essays and poetry. He completed most of his writing in these last two years of his life. After a short sickness Huan died in 1255 at his place of birth. His literary accomplishments could be more easily evaluated in the area of historical scholarship through his two most important works, in which he tried to cope with the tough issue of the legitimacy of the many empires in Chinese history, according to the principle of the legitimate line of succession. He also wrote commentaries on the *Four Books,* emphasizing the significance of true learning for all candidates to administrative service, rather than the demand for celebrity and profits. He also composed treatises criticizing the removal of the classical Confucian tradition of the Tang intellectuals and Song (960–1279) neo-Confucianists from the schools.

Sources:

Richard L. Davis, *Wind against the Mountain: The Crisis of Politics and Culture in Thirteenth-century China* (Cambridge, Mass.: Harvard University Press, 1996).

Herbert Franke, ed., *Sung Biographies,* four volumes (Wiesbaden: Steiner, 1976).

Igor de Rachewiltz and others, eds., *In the Service of the Khan: Eminent Personalities of the Early Mongol-Yuan Period (1200–1300)* (Wiesbaden: Harassowitz, 1993).

# ZHANG JUZHENG

## 1525-1582

### SCHOLAR, POET, AND REFORMER

**Reformer.** Zhang Juzheng was a Confucian scholar who was proficient in poetry and prose. He was a leading reformer in the Ming dynasty (1368–1644). Although many of his reforms succeeded, he did not seek the support of the people or the bureaucracy, which caused his changes to fail after he died. Yet, as a leader, he helped bring the Ming dynasty to its peak.

**Reforms.** Zhang Juzheng served as Chief Grand Secretary from 1572 to 1582 under Emperor Wanli, whose reign started in 1573 and ended in 1620. Zhang was a tutor for Wanli during his childhood. This position allowed Zhang to influence the young ruler, who became emperor at the age of ten, and to help establish himself as a prime minister. Because of this prominent position, Zhang was unable to make reforms directly, but he was able to spread his ideas through his influence on several leaders and his control over imperial documents. He reviewed several accounts, recorded his observations and ideas, and implemented the changes he thought needed to be made in order to make the empire stronger. His policies included: a stricter tax-collection system, a program making it difficult for individuals to escape paying their taxes, and severe punishment for tax evaders. He also set up a treasury system that helped the country retain excess money, which was used to strengthen the army. He is credited with ending many special privileges formerly held by wealthy landholders, and he reclaimed for the state many lands that were not being taxed.

**Contributions.** During Zhang's time of influence the military grew stronger and Mongol enemies were forced to present themselves before the emperor. This event was seen as a great achievement for Zhang, accomplished in part because of his strict control over the flow of money in state coffers. Zhang's influence over the emperor was also seen in the ruler's theory of frugality, which was subsequently spread throughout the empire. The strictness with which the emperor carried out these measures led to resentment against Zhang, who died while trying to implement additional reforms. After Zhang's death Emperor Wanli's management of state affairs became less responsible, and the country fell back into a period of ineffective control managed by the eunuchs.

Sources:

Ray Huang, "The Ming Fiscal Administration," in *The Cambridge History of China*, volume 8, *The Ming Dynasty, 1368–1644, Part 2,* edited by Denis Twitchett and Frederick W. Mote (Cambridge & New York: Cambridge University Press, 1988), pp. 106–171.

Charles O. Hucker, *The Ming Dynasty: Its Origins and Evolving Institutions* (Ann Arbor: Center for Chinese Studies, University of Michigan, 1978).

# DOCUMENTARY SOURCES

Bangzhan Chen, *Songshi jishi benmo* (Record of the History of the Song, circa 1620)—An official history of the Song dynasty (960–1279).

Chen, *Yuanshi jishi benmo* (Record of the History of the Yuan, circa 1620)—An official history of the Yuan dynasty (1279–1368).

Guang Sima, *Zizhi Tongjian* (A Comprehensive Mirror for Aid in Government, 1084)—The most comprehensive Chinese history from the Zhou dynasty (771 B.C.E.–256 B.C.E.) to the Song dynasty.

Lian Sung and others, *Yuan Shi* (Yuan Dynastic History)—A complete history of the Yuan dynasty (1279–1368).

Marco Polo, *Divisament dou monde* (The Description of the World, 1298)—The first vivid account of the geography, economy, and government of China by a European. The book was written while the author was incarcerated in a Genoese prison.

Matteo Ricci, *De Christiana expeditione apud Sinas suscepta ab Societate Jesu* (1615)—A record of Ricci's twenty-seven years in China and a rich source on the government, culture, and geography of China. Originally translated into Latin by Nicolao Trigautio, and later translated into English as *China in the Sixteenth Century: The Journals of Matthew Ricci, 1583–1610*, by Louis J. Gallagher.

Ming Taizu, *Ming Taizu Shilu* (Ming Taizu Veritable Record, circa 1390)—the speeches, decrees, events, and documents relating to the Ming founding emperor, Taizu.

Shi Naian and Luo Guanzhong, *Shui Hu Zhuan* (Outlaws of the Marsh, circa 1300)—An historical novel based on folk legends about a peasant rebellion in the Shandong province during the late Northern Song dynasty (960–1125). The rebels fought against what they viewed as corrupt government, and the novel reveals much about crime and punishment during the imperial era.

Wei Yingwu, *Poems* (circa 790)—A minor official, Wei Yingwu wrote poems that revealed much about the economic and social tensions of the era, especially after the An Lushan rebellion.

Xie Zhaozhe, *Wu za zu* (Five Assorted Offerings, circa 1610)—Written by a government official in the Zhenjiang and Shandong provinces, this volume contains anecdotes, descriptions, and comments on the province in which he was stationed.

Zhang Juzheng, *Di jian tu shuo* (The Emperor's Mirror, 1573)—A compendium of annotated anecdotes about previous Chinese emperors that was created for the young emperor Wanli.

## CHAPTER SIX

# POLITICS, LAW, AND THE MILITARY

by GUANGQIU XU

## CONTENTS

*Sidebars and tables are listed in italics.*

**617**
- Sui emperor Yangdi unsuccessfully attacks the Turks. This failed military campaign seriously depletes the state coffers, and as a result Yangdi requires taxes to be paid years in advance. When the peasants revolt, he appoints the general Li Yuan to crush the insurrection.

**618**
- After ordering the assassination of the Sui emperor at Yangzhou, Li Yuan founds the Tang dynasty in Chang'an.

**626**
- In what is known as the Xuanwu Gate Incident, Li Yuan's second son, Li Shimin, kills his brothers and forces his father to abdicate.

**630**
- A Tang army defeats the eastern Turks.
- The first Japanese embassy is established in Chang'an.

**638**
- Sassanid Persia establishes an embassy in Chang'an.

**641**
- The Tang empire expands its influence westward, dominating the Silk Road.

**645**
- After fifteen years of military campaigning, the Chinese control Central Asia.

**649**
- The emperor Taizong dies, and Gaozong succeeds to the throne.

**655**
- Beginning in 644, Tang forces invade Koguryo (Korea) by land and sea in order to help the kingdom of Silla, but they are defeated.

**657**
- The Chinese and Uighurs (a Turkic people originally from present-day Mongolia and eastern Turkestan) are defeated by the western Turks.

**661**
- The Tang empire establishes puppet governments in Kashmir, Bokhara, the Amu-Darya River valley, and on the borders of eastern Iran.

* DENOTES CIRCA DATE

**663**
- Tang forces defeat the Japanese.

**668**
- After two years of fighting, the Tang dynasty defeats the kingdoms of Kogaryo and Paekche, which come to be under Chinese control. Meanwhile the kingdom of Silla unifies southern Korea.

**680**
- Tibetans raid northwestern China and Central Asia.

**684**
- The empress Wu comes to power and six years later establishes the new dynasty of the Zhou (690–705).

**692**
- The Tang court develops the recruitment of civil servants by examination and establishes a governor-general of Central Asia at Kucha.

**694**
- The Chinese defeat the Tibetans and Turks.

**705**
- The empress Wu is removed by her high-ranking officials, and the Tang dynasty is restored in the person of the son she had deposed earlier, Zhongzong.

**712**
- The emperor Xuangzong succeeds to the throne, ending a power struggle during which the nominal emperors, Zhongzong and Ruizong, were forced to share power with the corrupt empress Wei and the formidable Taiping princes.

**733**
- The number of imperial civil servants is 17,680, and that of the locally recruited government staff is 57,416.

**742**
- The emperor Xuangzong takes various measures against Buddhism in favor of Daoism. In addition, the emperor adopts a new reigning title, *Tianbao* (Heavenly Treasures), with Daoist connotations, to symbolize the changed nature of his divine mandate to rule.
- The Tang court appoints ten imperial commissioners to defend the frontiers.
- An Lushan commands Tang armies in southern Manchuria, Shandong, Shanxi, and Hebei.

\* Denotes Circa Date

**751**
- Beginning in 745 Tang military forces launch attacks against Arabs in Transoxiania. Although the Chinese win victories south of Lake Balkhash, they are defeated near Alma Ata on the river Talas.

**755**
- A political clash develops between the Mongol general An Lushan and the government minister Yang Guozhong. After invading Hebei, An Lushan quickly progresses south and occupies Luoyang, where he proclaims himself emperor of a new Xia dynasty.

**756**
- After the death of his concubine Yang Guifei, Emperor Xuanzong abdicates. An Lushan occupies the capital and declares himself emperor.

**757**
- The revolt is suppressed, and An Lushan is assassinated. During An Lushan's rebellion millions of people die, while millions more flee to the South.

**762**
- The Uighurs occupy Chang'an and massacre many inhabitants.

**781**
- The emperor Dezong attempts to unify the country by force but fails because many provincial warlords resist the power of the central government.

**787**
- The Tang government reaches a peace agreement with the Tibetans and then forms an alliance with the Uighurs against the Tibetans.

**821**
- A Sino-Tibetan treaty is concluded in Chang'an, recognizing the independence of Tibet and its occupation of Gansu.

**826**
- A clan of eunuchs puts the emperor Wenzong in power.

**884**
- Huang Chao's rebellion comes to an end after ten years of fighting against the Tang government.

**902**
- The Wu Kingdom is formed at Guangling, marking the beginning of the Ten Kingdoms, a group of predominantly southern rulers.

\* DENOTES CIRCA DATE

**907**
- The Tang dynasty, which lasted for three hundred years, comes to an end, and the Later Liang dynasty is founded at Kaifeng, marking the beginning of the Five Dynasties.

**916**
- The Liao dynasty, the Turco-Mongol kingdom of the Khitans (Qidans), is founded in eastern Mongolia and Manchuria. Beijing becomes the capital.

**960**
- Fearing an invasion from the North, the palace guards of the Later Zhou revolt and place their commander Zhao Kuangyin on the throne. He founds the Northern Song dynasty, with its capital at Kaifeng. The period of the Five Dynasties ends.

**979**
- The era of the Ten Kingdoms comes to an end.

**986**
- The Khitans defeat the Northern Song dynasty and expand their influence in Manchuria.

**1004**
- The Northern Song empire and the Khitans reach a peace agreement, requiring the Song court to pay a heavy annual tribute in silk and silver. The tribute is increased in 1042.

**1040**
- War begins between the Northern Song dynasty and the Xi Xia empire. At the end of the conflict in 1044, the Song court agrees to pay the Xia dynasty a heavy annual tribute in silks, silver, and tea.

**1067**
- Chinese reformer Wang Anshi begins a campaign to suppress widespread corruption in the government and the army. The following year the new fiscal, administrative, and military laws of Wang are implemented.

**1085**
- The conservative Sima Guang is called upon to govern, and he begins to repeal the New Laws of Wang Anshi; both men die the next year.

**1094**
- Reformers are recalled from exile.

**1115**
- The Jurchens from Manchuria, with the help of the Song court, overthrow the Khitan Liao, their former masters, and establish the Jin dynasty.

\* Denotes Circa Date

**1125**
- The last army of the Khitan Liao is defeated.

**1127**
- Fearing Jin attacks, the Song court takes refuge south of the Yangzi, marking the beginning of the Southern Song dynasty. Emperor Gaozong moves the capital to Hangzhou in 1132.

**1142**
- The Southern Song dynasty concludes a peace treaty with the Jin dynasty. The Chinese accept vassal status, relinquish all lands north of the Jinling Mountains and the Huai River, and pay annual tribute to the Jurchens.

**1206**
- Temüjin, known as Genghis Khan (Universal Ruler), comes to power in Mongolia.

**1234**
- The Mongols occupy the city of Kaifeng, destroying the Jin dynasty.

**1279**
- Kublai Khan suppresses the last Song resistance, and the whole of China is under the control of the Yuan (First) dynasty.

**1281**
- The Mongols invade Japan.

**1328-1333**
- Four successive Mongol emperors take the throne as rival factions vie for control of the Yuan empire.

**1346**
- Peasant revolts flare up as famine strikes several provinces.

**1368**
- Zhu Yuanzhang establishes the Ming (Radiance) dynasty.

**1402**
- After a long period of civil war, Zhu Di, the uncle of the second Ming emperor Jianwen, seizes the throne and takes Nanjing, marking the beginning of the Yongle era.

**1420**
- The Yongle emperor moves his main capital to the former Yuan capital Dadu, renaming it Beijing (Northern Capital), in an effort to defend China against Mongol invasion. Nanjing becomes the second capital.

\* DENOTES CIRCA DATE

**1424** • The emperor Yongle, who seized the throne twenty-two years earlier, dies. His reign is regarded as a "second founding" of the Ming dynasty.

**1449** • The Mongols defeat the Chinese in Shanxi and take the emperor prisoner.

**1487** • The emperor Hongzhi orders the strengthening of the Great Wall, a defensive structure in northern China begun in the third century B.C.E., to prevent another Mongol invasion.

**1512** • Peasants in the central province of Sichuan revolt against taxes.

**1520** • A Portuguese ambassador comes to Beijing.

**1550** • The Mongols besiege Beijing for a week.

**1555** • Japanese pirates attack Hangzhou and surround Nanjing.

**1557** • The Portuguese build a trading post at Macao.

**1563** • Ming generals suppress Japanese piracy along the South China coast.

**1583** • The Burmese invade Yunnan province.

**1598** • Ming armies repel a Japanese invasion of Korea.

**1615** • A three-year conflict between court eunuchs and the Donglin party (composed of scholars and former government officials) begins.

**1624** • The powerful eunuch Wei Zhongxian establishes a dictatorship in the Ming court.

\* DENOTES CIRCA DATE

**1625**
• The members of the Donglin movement are persecuted.

**1629**
• Private academies throughout the empire are suppressed because they have become centers of opposition to the dominance of the eunuchs and their agents in the late Ming empire.

**1636**
• The Manchus in northeastern China adopt the Chinese dynastic name Qing for their new state.

**1644**
• Rebels under Li Zicheng occupy Beijing, where the Ming emperor commits suicide. Manchu forces then drive the rebels out of Beijing, marking the end of the Ming dynasty.

* DENOTES CIRCA DATE

Detail of a painting of Mongol cavalry fighting the Chinese, sixteenth century (British Museum, London)

# OVERVIEW

**Dynastic Changes.** Chinese history from 617 to 1644 can be divided into several major dynastic periods. The Tang dynasty (618–907) marked significant military and administrative achievements in Chinese history. When the dynasty collapsed in the early tenth century, China became divided: the Northern area was ruled by the Five Dynasties (907–960) and the Southern region was controlled by the Ten Kingdoms (902–979). The Song dynasty (960–1279) gradually incorporated all the independent states into its empire and restored centralized government, although it had to contend with the rival Liao dynasty of the Khitans, or Qidans (916–1115), and the Jin dynasty of the Jurchens, or Ruzhens (1115–1234). The Mongols began to sweep out of the steppes in 1210, and by 1279 they dominated the whole of China. Their dynasty, the Yuan, ruled until 1368, and the subsequent Ming dynasty (1368–1644) succeeded in unifying the whole country under Chinese rule for the first time in four hundred years. In 1644, when the last Ming emperor hanged himself, Qing troops from Manchuria attacked the city of Beijing in June and established the Qing, or Manchu, dynasty (1644–1911).

**Government Administration.** Beginning in the Tang dynasty several significant innovations were launched in the spheres of administration and governmental operations. The strong centralization of authority in the throne was the most important feature in the development of administrative organization. It was achieved by structural changes both in the central government itself and in the relations between the capital city of Chang'an and the local provinces. Newly appointed officials provided a counterweight to the influence of advisers (eunuchs and generals) and also to the arbitrary power of the emperors. The political system made further progress in the following centuries. The Song central government was basically organized along Tang lines, comprising a secretariat and a chancellery. The same continuity was evident in Song regional governments, and the Mongols created an administrative organization basically similar to those governments. The Yuan central government comprised a secretariat-chancellery headed by two chancellors, a bureau of military affairs, and a censorate. The Mongols kept all high offices and important positions for themselves only and filled lower-level posts with Chinese. Since the Ming emperors abandoned the office of chancellor, the branch secretariats consisted of three separate agencies: a civil administration, military commission, and surveillance office. From the tenth to seventeenth centuries, structural changes in regional administration were more plentiful and significant than in the central government. The basic administrative unit was the prefecture, which was responsible for many of the functions of the central government.

**Absolutism.** Accepting the doctrine of the Mandate of Heaven, the Chinese emperors were always ensured to be absolutist in theory. The situations of rulers were in general markedly different, especially under the native dynasties (Tang, Song, and Ming). Supported by tribal or clan leaders who had independent power bases, the foreign rulers (Khitans, Jurchens, and Mongols) by and large were chieftains. Separated from all other persons by a social gap, the Song and Ming emperors were complete autocrats whose authority was unchallenged by anyone in theory and in law. The clearest symbol of this change was the strict rule that developed around one's appearance before the emperors. In Tang times, grand councilors usually sat together with their emperor to discuss state affairs; in the Song era, officials stood at attention in the imperial presence. At the Ming court, officials were required to kneel before an emperor who looked down on them from a throne on an elevated platform. Adopting a barbarous Mongol custom, the Ming emperors even had officials flogged in open court. In this despotic exercise the victim, whatever his rank or prestige, was held flat on the floor with all court officials in attendance. Ming rulers also used their imperial bodyguard, a totalitarian secret police without any legal restraints, to spy on, arrest, imprison, and torture all subversives.

**Personnel Administration.** Although the early Tang government was staffed mainly on the basis of family and other connections, it began to create an elaborate examination system in order to recruit ordinary people to enter the government. The system of civil service examinations came into its own in the Song period and remained the most prestigious means of government recruitment. The Song dynasty revised the examinations to test the candidate's practical knowledge of government and problems of administration. From 960 onward experiments were carried out to build a civil service based on merit. These prestigious personnel-recruitment procedures continued until the Qing dynasty, but the Liao, Jin, and Yuan rulers naturally allowed only their own ethnic groups to dominate their governments in spite of the examination-recruitment tradition. During the Yuan dynasty the civil service examinations were revived after 1315. This system favored the Mongols and their non-Chinese allies, because they took only simplified examinations and they occupied 30 percent of all government posts. In the Ming dynasty the examinations were revised in order to promote conformity, making those who had earned examination degrees the most honored members of officialdom. Therefore, officials with other backgrounds could not expect to attain high office. The long-established practices of granting men official status on the basis of recommendations, inheritance privileges, and graduation from the national university began to disappear from Song to Ming. However, in times of fiscal crises, dynasties still allowed the purchase of some official posts.

**The Armies.** The core of the Tang armies in the seventh century was aristocrats who served in the best corps—the imperial guards and the palace troops. To maintain its frontier forces, the empire had to recruit from friendly alien tribes and rely on permanent frontier armies of mercenaries. The development of such armies under circuit controllers resulted in the devastating rebellion of An Lushan in 755–763 and led to regional warlordism in the hinterland in the late Tang era. Meanwhile, the palace armies controlled by the eunuchs rose to prominence in the capital, setting the stage for eunuch domination of the Tang court. The Song rulers were interested in state defense, inventing new military machines, increasing the strength of armies, creating a navy at the time of the Jurchen invasion (1115), and devoting most of national resources to the wars. The Song emperors also tried to maintain and assert the absolute supremacy of the civil authority over the military. The Mongol army was a superb force in terms of overall direction, organization, and the toughness and ability of its individual fighting men. The Ming regime restored the glories of Tang times by creating strong armies, especially by sending great fleets as far as the East Coast of Africa to seek tributes.

**Laws.** To win the support of people suffering under the harsh punishment of the last years of the Sui dynasty (589–618), the first Tang emperor, after his occupation of the Sui capital in 617, proclaimed a fundamental law in twelve articles restricting the death penalty to murder, robbery, desertion from the army, and treason. This law was replaced by a code founded upon the Sui code of 583. The Tang code published in 619 included only fifty-three articles, but the one published five years later comprised more than five hundred articles divided into twelve sections. It served as a model not only for later Chinese codes but also for the laws of Japan, Annam, and other countries. The Tang code dealt with both criminal and administrative concerns and consisted of primary and secondary laws. Although the first Song emperor followed tradition in establishing a commission to undertake a revision of the laws, the Song code copied the Tang code virtually without any modification and only inserted edicts or other rules that had come into force since 737 but had never been incorporated. The Mongolian occupation of China resulted in a break in legal tradition, particularly in the failure of the Mongolian dynasty to make a penal code of the kind that had appeared under Tang and Song. The Chinese laws, after an initial setback, continued to develop, and the Ming dynasty became more interested in the law than were the earlier dynasties. The first Ming emperor reverted to the traditional pre-Yuan pattern of codification and particularly looked to the Tang code as his model. At the same time he seemed to counter what was regarded as the laxity of the Yuan court in terms of punishment. The Ming legal code was not completed until 1397.

# TOPICS IN POLITICS, LAW, AND THE MILITARY

## ADMINISTRATIVE STRUCTURE

**Tang Central Government.** The central government of the Tang dynasty (618–907) had four main sections: Department of State Affairs, which performed the essential tasks of administration and included six ministries (personnel, revenue, rites, war, justice, and public works); Imperial Chancellery, which acted as a center for the transmission of imperial edicts; Imperial Grand Secretariat, which was responsible for the drafting of official decrees; and the Council of State, which comprised the emperor, great dignitaries, and the civil chiefs of the six ministries. There were also several services with more limited functions, the most important of which was the censorate, a separate branch of government. It acted as an inspector general of the administration, hearing complaints from the general public and preventing officials from engaging in corruption, extortion, and fraud.

**Song Central Government.** Many features of Tang administration were revived in a modified form in the Song dynasty (960–1279). The office of prime minister developed in the 1080s when reformer Wang Anshi made the two heads of the Department of State Affairs concurrently the secretariat and the chancellery. These two officers formulated and reviewed policies before presenting them to the emperor for approval. After being approved, the policies were implemented by the Department of State Affairs (comprised of six ministries). The heads of the chancellery and secretariat were recognized as the chief ministers. Kept separate from civil affairs, the Bureau of Military Affairs reported directly to the emperor only. The Song censorate remained independent, but its power and staff were greatly reduced. It was not allowed to send touring censorial inspectors throughout the empire as it did in Tang times.

**Yuan Central Government.** The Jin dynasty (1115–1234) in North China reorganized its central government by abolishing the secretariat and chancellery. The Yuan dynasty (1279–1368) followed the Jin precedent but changed the name of the remaining unified general administration agency from Department of State Affairs to Secretariat. Thus the Council of State was replaced

Painting of Song emperor Huizong with advisers, circa 1102 (Palace Museum, Beijing)

## DYNASTIES AND KINGDOMS OF IMPERIAL CHINA

| NAME | DATES OF RULE | REGION | CAPITAL |
|------|---------------|--------|---------|
| Tang | 618–907 | China Proper | Chang'an |
| Five Dynasties | 907–960 | | |
| 1) Later Liang | 907–923 | North | Kaifeng |
| 2) Later Tang | 923–936 | North | Luoyang |
| 3) Later Jin | 936–946 | North | Bian |
| 4) Later Han | 947–950 | North | Bian |
| 5) Later Zhou | 951–960 | North | Bian |
| Ten Kingdoms | 902–979 | | |
| 1) Wu | 902–937 | East | Guangling and Jinling |
| 2) Southern Tang | 937–975 | Southeast | Xidu |
| 3) Former Shu | 907–925 | Central | Chengdu |
| 4) Later Shu | 935–965 | Central | Chengdu |
| 5) Southern Han | 917–971 | South | Canton |
| 6) Chu | 927–951 | South | Changsha |
| 7) Wu-Yue | 907–978 | East | Xifu |
| 8) Min | 909–945 | Southeast | Changle |
| 9) Nanping/Jingnan | 924–963 | Central | Jiangling |
| 10) Northern Han | 951–979 | North | Taiyuan |
| *Northern Song | 960–1125 | North | Kaifeng |
| **Southern Song | 1127–1279 | South | Hangzhou |
| Yuan (Mongols) | 1279–1368 | China Proper | Beijing |
| Ming | 1368–1644 | China Proper | Nanjing; Beijing after 1403 |

*with the Liao empire of the Khitans (Qidans) on the northern border

**with the Jin empire of the Jurchens (Ruzhens) in northern China

Sources: John K. Fairbank and Merle Goldman, *China: A New History* (Cambridge, Mass. & London: Belknap Press of Harvard University Press, 1992).

F. W. Mote, *Imperial China, 900–1800* (Cambridge, Mass. & London: Harvard University Press, 1999).

David C. Wright, *The History of China* (Westport, Conn. & London: Greenwood Press, 2001).

with two senior secretariat officials who became grand councillors. They presided over the Tang-style six ministries that carried out routine administrative business, a powerful and independent Bureau of Military Affairs, and a Censorate, which was more concerned with the surveillance of officials than with receiving complaints about them. The Censorate staffed with Mongols was larger than that of the Tang dynasty.

**Ming Central Government.** The Ming dynasty (1368–1644) originally copied the Yuan government, making only name changes. The Office of Grand Secretariat was expanded in the fifteenth century because few emperors were able to supervise so many agencies effectively. This group of administrative aides was given concurrent status as ministers or vice-ministers. However, grand secretaries never managed to rise to chief councillor status, and they became focal points of recurrent factional controversies.

Many emperors ignored them and other officials vilified them. Since the close cooperation between grand secretaries and palace eunuchs was essential for effective administrative function in the times of the more reclusive and inattentive emperors, the consequent lack of stable coordination in the court was an important reason for the decline of the Ming dynasty.

**Prefectures.** The Tang empire began the practice of dividing the empire into prefectures, or districts, known as *zhou*. (Special prefectures were designated as *fu*.) They varied in size according to the density of their population. The central government appointed prefects of the imperial civil service to administer these districts.

**Circuit.** Tang emperors also introduced the circuit, a new level of government to oversee the prefectures. Fearing regional independence, the early Song emperors temporarily repealed this agency and established direct lines of

Detail of a silk painting of a Song official and an attendant, Song dynasty, 960–1279 (Musee Guimet, Paris)

communication between prefectures and the six ministries in the capital. Yet, the later Song court realized the importance of intermediary-level coordination, and it began to send circuit intendants as short-term regional representatives of the central government. Thus fiscal intendants, judicial intendants, military intendants, and intendants of transportation and monopolies were assigned to different groups of contiguous prefectures. However, no circuit intendant or combination of intendants had a chance to become independent as Tang regional governors had done at the expense of the central government's power. When the Song dynasty was creating these overlapping, functionally differentiated intendancies, the Liao dynasty (916–1115) was dividing its northern empire into five regions, each supervised by a "capital" in direct contact with all its prefectures. The Jin dynasty, in Liao fashion, formed six capitals in its northern empire and further created nineteen supervisory circuits of the prefectures. The circuit anticipated the provincial administration of the Ming imperial period.

**Proto-Provinces.** The Mongols created the most complex system of intermediary-level agencies in Chinese history. Yuan prefectures were divided among 185 supervisory regions, which were further grouped into 12 protoprovinces. The metropolitan censorate established two branch censorates, one in the West and the other in the South, which supervised the branch secretariats. Twenty-four regional surveillance offices were established to oversee lower-level agencies, and six geographic jurisdictions under the Bureau

of Military Affairs were set up to supervise the military garrisons. Thus the Yuan empire was subdivided into three different kinds of provinces—12 for general administration; 3 for censorial surveillance; and 6 for military control.

**Provinces.** Not until Ming times did provinces begin to appear. In 1421 the Ming emperor divided China into 13 provinces. Three agencies—Provincial Administration Office, Provincial Surveillance Office, and Regional Military Commission—had supervisory responsibility over each province. Later the Ming government set up two levels of higher supervisory offices. Every province came to have a grand coordinator, and large regions comprising two or more provinces earned more prestigious coordinators known as supreme commanders. These coordinators and supreme commanders were civil officials, but they were also in charge of regional military affairs. This system of provincial-level government remained in place for many centuries with little change.

**Subcounty Organization.** Below the formal structure of local government, the people themselves came to bear administrative responsibilities. During the Song period and even under the Mongols, rural villages were required to organize themselves so that local leaders could be chosen to keep order, maintain peace, arbitrate disputes between families, sustain irrigation systems, organize small-scale construction projects, provide local militiamen when needed, and assess, collect, and deliver taxes. Such village leaders, whether a council of elders or a wealthy landlord, received no payment from the state. In Ming times a new system known as the Lijia system began to be created throughout the empire, under which families were grouped into tens and hundreds for local self-governance. This sub-county organization was especially effective in informing the peasants about the laws and educating them with the Confucian value system espoused by the state. Each village community had regular monthly meetings, during which they were taught about Confucianism or listened to the recitation of imperial decrees requiring them to be filial and obedient to parents, to respect superiors, to be in harmony with neighbors, to teach their children, and to do nothing harmful to others. This organization helped to bring order-liness of life to the peasants in the country.

**Sources:**

Etienne Balazs, *Chinese Civilization and Bureaucracy* (New Haven, Conn.: Yale University Press, 1964).

Wolfran Eberhard, *History of China* (London: Routledge & Kegan Paul, 1977).

Denis Twitchett and John Fairbank, eds., *The Cambridge History of China*, volumes 1, 7, and 10 (Cambridge: Cambridge University Press, 1978–1995).

## THE GOLDEN AGE OF TANG

**Establishment.** The Tang dynasty (618–907) is regarded as one of the two golden ages in China's history (the other is the Han dynasty of 206 B.C.E.–220 C.E.), in which Chinese civilization was at its highest and most powerful. The Tang empire emerged from the disintegration of the Sui dynasty (589–618). Its founder, General Li Yuan, was a member of a northern aristocratic family. Appointed to quell a peasant revolt, Li Yuan instead negotiated with the Turks, promising them riches and his vassalage. In 617 Li began to rebel, and within only one year he occupied the capital city of Chang'an, where he declared the founding of the Tang dynasty. He was later given the posthumous title of *Gaozu*. He took another six years to conquer the whole country.

**Reign.** Supported by the same northern aristocratic clans that had backed the Sui dynasty, Gaozu initially continued Sui practices in government administration and maintained the existing legal and taxation systems. The first few years of the Tang dynasty were a time of internal consolidation. After all resistance had been crushed, Gaozu began to reorganize the administration. The empire thereafter was divided into ten big regions, which were directly controlled by inspectors of administration, finance, and justice. Gaozu also did much work in the fields of law, agriculture, tax, and education.

**Xuanwu Gate Incident.** Gaozu's regime ended suddenly in 626. Li Shimin, the emperor's second son, who helped his father rise to power, was a bitter rival of his elder brother, the heir to the emperor. Li had played a major part in the campaigns to consolidate Tang control and won considerable success as a military commander. With support from the military, Li Shimin plotted to carry out a coup to become emperor. After killing the crown prince and another brother, Li forced his father to abdicate. The

## FINANCIAL CRISIS

**B**y the middle of the Tang dynasty (618–907) the system of equalized landholding administered by the ruler had seriously deteriorated. As a result the government found difficulty in collecting taxes and there was less revenue for the state. In the eighth century Yang Yen, a high-ranking official, expressed concerns over the growing financial crisis in a memorial to the Tang emperor:

When the dynastic laws were first formulated there was the land tax, the labor tax on able-bodied men, and the cloth tax on households. But enforcement of the law was lax; people migrated or died, and landed property changed hands. The poor rose and the rich fell. The Board of Revenue year after year presented out-of-date figures to the court. Those who were sent to guard the frontiers were exempted from land tax and labor tax for six years, after which they returned from service.

Source: *Hsin Tang Shu* (New Tang History), in *Sources of Chinese Tradition*, edited by William Theodore de Bary (New York: Columbia University Press, 1960).

event, known as the Xuanwu Gate Incident, resulted in the succession of Li Shimin, then known as Taizong.

**Military Campaigns.** The Tang dynasty began its expansion in Asia in 630. After the defeat of the Turks, Tang armies extended their influence to central Asia between 630 and 645. In 648 the emperor organized an expedition (which included Nepalese and Tibetan troops) in order to extend Tang influence to the little kingdom of Magadha in northeastern India. By 660 Tang armies had conquered the whole of Northeastern China—Manchuria and almost the entire Korean peninsula. Tang expansion from Korea to Iran and from the Ili valley to central Vietnam was the most important movement in the political history of Asia in the seventh century. The success of military campaigns resulted from remarkable military and administrative organization, quick-moving cavalry forces, efficient horse breeding, and the establishment of military colonies for the provisioning of Tang armies in Central Asia.

**Rise of An Lushan.** By the eighth century the frontier was divided into nine districts, each headed by a military governor. At the beginning this system worked well because the military governors came from aristocratic backgrounds and had close relationships with the bureaucracy. Some governors enhanced their own reputations by waging successful frontier campaigns. The central government, however, began to appoint non-Chinese governors in the 740s on the grounds that they were better soldiers and had no political ambitions. This new policy gave An Lushan, whose father was a Sogdian and whose mother was a Turk, an opportunity to rise to prominence. In 742 he was given the key military governorship of Pinglu in Northeast China, where the powerful families nurtured some antipa-

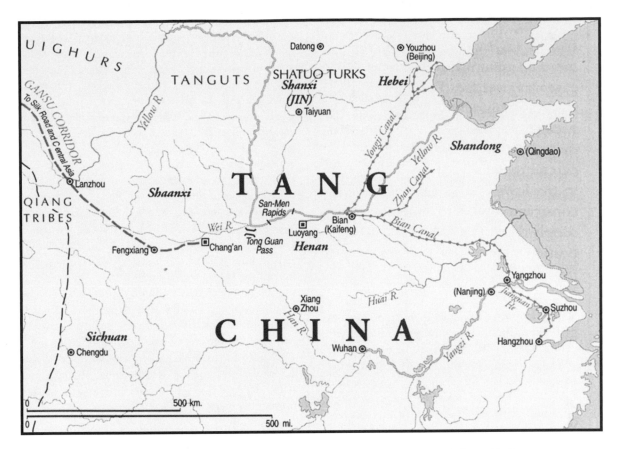

Map of China during the Tang dynasty, 618–907 (from F. W. Mote, *Imperial China*, 1999)

thy toward the aristocracy of Chang'an. An Lushan's military success ingratiated him with the emperor Xuanzong.

**Court Intrigue.** The immediate causes of An Lushan's rebellion (755–763) related to the situation at court and the military arrangements on the frontier. In the 740s Xuanzong had increasingly left the conduct of government to Li Linfu while first immersing himself in a search for personal enlightenment and then becoming infatuated with his concubine, Yang Guifei. (Although Yang Guifei had some powerful personal connections, she came from a family of modest standing; her father was a minor official in Sichuan.) After gaining her emperor's favor, Yang Guifei obtained various court posts for her relatives, including her second cousin Yang Guozhong, who became a law officer working for Li Linfu. In 746 Li Linfu began a series of bloody purges directed against his critics, and Yang Guozhong used this opportunity to advance the interests of the Yang family. From 749 onward, Yang Guozhong began to intrigue against Li Linfu himself, who later died in 752. After Li's death, Yang Guozhong, who held the military governorship of Sichuan, took his place and became the most powerful figure at court. Rivalry also developed with An Lushan when Yang Guozhong tried to alienate him from the emperor.

**Revolt.** Realizing that he was in danger, An Lushan began to revolt in 755 with 160,000 troops in the northeast. He soon occupied both Chang'an and Luoyang and declared the establishment of a new dynasty. For the next 8 years the country was in a civil war. After Yang Guozhong failed to recapture Luoyang, the emperor was forced to abandon Chang'an and flee north. During the flight, the commander of the emperor's escort killed Yang Guozhong on the grounds that he was responsible for the catastrophe. The commander then demanded the death of Yang Guifei; with immense grief Xuanzong ordered her execution. The emperor then fled to Chengdu in the southwest and later that year abdicated in favor of his son, who had gone to the northwest to mobilize military forces. An Lushan was assassinated by his son in 757, but the rebellion did not collapse. Led first by another general, Shi Siming, and then by his son, the rebellion continued until 762. Xuanzong's grandson, the Emperor Daizong, succeeded to the throne in 762 and thereafter defeated the remaining rebels with the help of Uighurs and Tibetans. In 763 the court was able to move back from Sichuan to the capital.

**Turning Point.** Although the rebellion was eventually defeated and the Tang empire survived for another 150 years, the dynasty never recovered its former authority or glory. The rebellion had several immediate and long-term consequences. Some regions of the country became depopulated, while others suffered severe economic and social crisis. The state's financial system collapsed. The northeast of the empire became independent, while some regions were controlled by military governors. The fall of the capital deeply shocked the Tang aristocracy and forced many of them to migrate to the south. The violence of the rebellion had a profound impact on the minds of some writers, who thereafter concentrated their studies on the lessons of history. The involvement of the frontier armies in a civil war incited the Tibetans to attack the empire, and in 763 they briefly occupied Chang'an. Although they retreated later, their attacks continued in the following years. By that time the Tang empire was no longer an expanding power, having difficulty defending its frontiers. An Lushan's rebellion, which shook the Tang empire to its foundations, has been identified as one of the great turning points in the history of the Chinese world. The crisis seemed to speed up changes. Foreign relations, economic policies, societal developments, and intellectual life all changed rapidly from the crisis of 755-763.

**Restoration.** Tang rulers began to rebuild after the rebellion. The central and regional governments continued to function, and reforms of the administrative systems and a new frontier policy were introduced. The central government lost much of its power to regional governors, and the Tang dynasty became highly decentralized. The emperor Xianzong, who ruled from 805 to 820, decided to use force to regain control of those provinces that had in effect become autonomous. In 806 he sent a punitive expedition to Sichuan, defeating the general who had usurped the command there and replacing him with a new governor who was willing to accept central government order. Xianzong thereafter retained control of the central provinces but was not successful in the northeast. In the meantime he carried out reforms to reduce provincial autonomy by imposing more taxes on the wealthy Yangzi regions. Since the rebellion had completely damaged the Tang frontier strategy, the regime abandoned the system of military colonies and therefore lost the pasture lands from which it had obtained its supply of war horses to Tibet. Since Tang rulers had to purchase expensive horses from the Uighur empire, Emperor Dezong concluded a formal alliance with the Uighurs against the Tibetans. This alliance continued to be the cornerstone of Tang frontier policy until the Uighurs disintegrated in 840.

**Signs of Decline.** The Tang dynasty began to decline after 820 when a series of young emperors were unable to assert their authority over the courts. In its last fifty years the Tang dynasty was further weakened by divided loyalties in the central government, by mistrust between officials in the capital and the military commanders in the frontier, and by mismanagement, corruption, and incompetence. In the meantime bandit gangs became a refuge for the desperately poor and dislocated people. They organized themselves into confederations and progressed from raiding to rebellion. The number of civil disturbances increased each year, and the government was unable to suppress all of them. When another emperor named Xuanzong came to the throne in 846, he tried to reform the grain transport system and the salt monopoly, but he ignored the most serious problems: the growth of large landed estates, chronic fiscal problems, and a deteriorating situation on the frontiers.

**Renewed Civil Strife.** The fall of the dynasty came about because of a rising tide of revolts. The first wave of rebellions occurred in the lower Yangzi in the 850s, but the government crushed them. In the 860s, when the state of Nanzhao in southeast China attacked Annam, the Tang armies forced the Nanzhao to retreat. This military campaign exhausted the Chinese treasury, which prompted a wave of mutinies. Headed by Pang Xun, some rebels pillaged the lower Yangzi region. In 874 another disastrous rebellion broke out in the area between the Yellow and Huai Rivers because this area had been overtaxed and had suffered from a succession of floods and droughts. The most serious uprising was led by Wang Xianzhi. After Wang was killed in 878, Huang Chao led the rebellion, making a dramatic sweep south. He occupied Guangzhou in 879, killing many foreign as well as Chinese inhabitants in the city. He then returned to the lower Yangzi, where he should have been defeated and captured but he escaped. In 880 he occupied Chang'an, forcing the emperor to flee to Chengdu, and established a new dynasty. Yet, he failed to win public support and establish an effective government. The Tang forces rallied with the assistance of the Shatuo Turks, defeated the rebels, and killed Huang Chao in 884. After this insurrection, China was greatly weakened and thoroughly divided.

**Shatuo Turks.** After Huang's rebellion, the survival of the Tang court depended on the support of foreigners who inhabited the northern borderlands. The Shatuo Turks were the most important among these foreign peoples because their intervention on behalf of the Tang government rescued it from collapse several times and enabled the dynasty to survive the Huang Chao rebellion. In 905 the Shatuo Turks established an alliance with a Mongolian people called the Khitans. During the period of the Five Dynasties (907–960) the Shatuo Turks established a new dynasty, the Later Tang (923–936), which, as its name implies, tried to rule in the Tang tradition but did not last for a long time.

**Imperial Commissioners.** The men who directly contributed to the downfall of the Tang court were the imperial commissioners in command of military regions. These individuals, members of the aristocracy or the scholarly class, were the administrative staff in the military regions. They chose their own successors while the Tang court only approved their choices. After 900, each independent region assumed either the name of *dynasty* or *kingdom,* while each leader usurped the title of *emperor.* The only difference between the Five Dynasties of the North and the Ten Kingdoms (902–979) of the South was that the five northern governments in the capital areas controlled a more extensive territory and claimed to be the true successors of the Tang dynasty. The founding of these ten small independent kingdoms caused a breakup of the Tang regime.

**Demise.** By the beginning of the tenth century, non-Chinese forces occupied a large part of the Tang empire in the North, military governors had seized power in the East, and independent states were formed in much

Detail of the hanging scroll *Emperor Ming Huang's Journey to Shu;* Song-era copy of the
eighth-century original (National Palace Museum, Taipei, Taiwan)

of Central and South China. The final demise of the powerful Tang dynasty occurred in 907 when military governor Zhu Wen extended his control over a large part of North China, deposed the last Tang emperor, and established the Later Liang dynasty (907–923), the first of the Five Dynasties. This event marked the end of the hereditary high aristocracy that had dominated the imperial government for a long time, and ended a period of Chinese martial vigor and self-assertion in relation to its nomadic and seminomadic neighbors.

**Sources:**

Charles Hartman, *Han Yu and the Tang Search for Unity* (Princeton, N.J.: Princeton University Press, 1986).

Edwin Reischauer, *The Background of the Rebellion of An Lu-shan* (London: Oxford University Press, 1955).

Denis Twitchett, *Financial Administration under the T'ang Dynasty* (Princeton, N.J.: Princeton University Press, 1988).

Twitchett and Arthur F. Wright, eds., *Perspectives on the Tang* (New Haven: Yale University Press, 1973).

## GOVERNMENT PERSONNEL

**System of Sponsorship.** To find suitable candidates for public service, the Tang court created a system of sponsorship allowing certain senior officials to nominate family members for governmental appointment. This method of recruitment was justified by a saying of Confucius: "Raise to office those of virtue and talent whom you know." The sponsorship system emphasized character, and the official had to guarantee the candidate's ability when nominating him.

**Song Personnel Administration.** Personnel administration in the Song dynasty (960–1279) generally developed in the patterns created during the Tang dynasty (618–907). The Tang requirement of sponsorship inevitably favored the influential families. To recruit the right type of personnel for the bureaucracy, the Song court tried to make the system of personnel administration more open by building state-supported schools in the prefectures, by abolishing the monopoly on entrance to the national university (which sons of officials had enjoyed since Tang times), and by giving competitive prelimi-

nary examinations at the prefectural level. Obviously, the examination system had the potential to produce more clever candidates than the system of sponsorship.

**Reform of Examinations.** The system of civil service examinations was the most prestigious means of government recruitment. The Tang court created a system of annual examinations, which led to the award of a variety of degrees to a small number of successful candidates. The Song court modified the system by incorporating prefectural examinations, establishing quotas to determine how many candidates should pass at the prefectural level, and providing provisions for impartiality. For example, to prevent a reader from recognizing the author of any paper by his calligraphy, all papers of candidates were identified only by number and were copied by clerks before being submitted for grading. Success in the examination was difficult, requiring a thorough command of the classics. Candidates had to identify well-known lines, the most obscure passages, and even sequences of characters. Competition was rough, and preparing for and taking the examinations became a way of life for many persons in Song times.

**New Schools.** Schools supported by the state had existed since the Tang dynasty, both in the capital and in the prefectures, but provisioning for them was limited. To improve educational facilities, Song local officials began to build new schools and to provide them with a set of the Confucian classics, which were available in print at that time. At the capital, the Imperial University, which had originally been reserved for children of officials, was opened to prefectural candidates.

**Ming School System.** Since the founder of the Ming dynasty (1368–1644) did not inherit from the Yuan dynasty (1279–1368) a pool of experienced and reputable officials, he depended primarily on recommendations to staff his government. Much more successfully than his Song predecessors, he set up a state-supported school in every city and county and set a quota of state-supported students for each school. From these schools, some honor students, known as tribute stu-

Painting of Yang Shih-chi, Yang Jung, and Yang Pu, three brothers who were advisers to Ming emperors, fifteenth century (National Palace Museum, Taipei, Taiwan)

dents, were summoned to the capital to continue their studies. While studying as national university students, they continued to work as apprentice officials. After finishing their studies, they were appointed as regular officials. Since the examination-recruitment system was renewed in the fifteenth century, the degree-holders produced by this system, as during the Song period, once again became the bureaucratic elite. By that time the national university had an enrollment of ten thousand students, many of whom wanted to have a prestigious examination degree before direct appointment as regular officials. In the meantime private academies spread throughout the empire and played an important role in supplementing the state school system, expanding the supply of educated men and promoting widespread literacy. Obviously, the Ming dynasty created China's most extensive system of public education to produce men worthy of official appointment.

**Cultivated Talents.** In the Ming examination system, the potential degree holder had to pass three major examinations in order to take a final Song-style palace examination. Provincial education intendants conducted the first examination, a basic certification test, at regular intervals. The intendants certified candidates as competent students known as *xiucai* (cultivated talents). *Xiucai* were entitled to wear distinctive caps and sashes and were exempted from state labor service. They generally served as tutors in rich families and naturally became community leaders. However, they were subject to periodic reexamination and could be deprived of their status, privileges, and prestige if they did not sustain their scholastic competence or behaved improperly.

**Elevated Men.** All *xiucai* were eligible to take provincial examinations given every third year at the provincial capitals in three daylong sessions. This provincial examination required a general understanding of the classics and history, the capability to link classical precepts and historical precedents to general philosophical principles or particular political issues, and proficiency in literary composition. Those who passed this examination became *juren* (elevated men) and were entitled to more honors and privileges. Their status was permanent, and they could be appointed as lower-level officials.

**Presented Scholars.** All *juren* were eligible to take the metropolitan examination on similar subject matter at the national capital; the test was conducted a few months after the provincial examination. Successful candidates became *Jinshi* (presented scholars), and the subsequent palace examination served to rank them. The highest-ranking *Jinshi* were appointed to the Hanlin Academy (national academy) and were expected to rise eventually into the Grand Secretariat. They were highly praised as national heroes, similar to sports figures in the present-day United States. Other new *Jinshi* would be appointed to county magistracies or posts of provincial governments when vacancies occurred.

**Intense Competition.** The examination in Ming times was more competitive than in Song times. The number of provincial *juren* degrees awarded each examination year was about 1,200, and *Jinshi* degrees were approximately 120 per exami-

Statue of a civil official at the tomb of Emperor Yongle, Beijing, fifteenth century

nation. In other words, less than 10 percent of *xiucai* became *juren*, and less than 10 percent of *juren* advanced to *Jinshi*.

**Quotas System.** The Song examination system, without any prescribed geographical quotas, produced a less representative civil service than the recommendation system of Tang, because there were more scholars in the southeast than in other regions. When restoring examinations in 1315, the Yuan government attempted to maintain regional balance by setting limits on the number of candidates from each province who would take the metropolitan examination in any year. Ethnic considerations also encouraged the Yuan government to create equal quotas for four categories of examination candidates: Mongols; central Asians; northern Chinese; and southern Chinese, who comprised perhaps 75 percent of the total population of Yuan. With limits on the number of *juren* degrees that could be awarded in each province at any one time, southerners became disproportionately successful in the metropolitan examinations. For example, southerners took all the *Jinshi* degrees in 1397. Irritated by this situation, the emperor Taizu, a northerner, executed the chief examiner for favoritism, repealed all the new degrees, and chose a list of northern graduates. Thereafter, examiners were more careful, but grading standards still favored southerners. In the 1420s, for example, strict objectivity was abolished in favor of a regional quotas system. As a result, southern candidates were allowed to take only 55 percent of *Jinshi* degrees in each examination, westerners 10 percent, and northerners 35 percent.

**Eight-Legged Essay.** In the late Ming period the intellectual quality of examination graduates decreased. In the examination, candidates had to use only classical explanations approved by the Zhu Xi school of neo-Confucianism; abnormal interpretations of the classics were regarded as unorthodox. Because of this requirement, free thought was suppressed. In addition, a standard rhetorical form known as the "eight-legged essay" was required. Test essays were written in an eight-part structure. Examiners considered the form of essay more important than the content of it. As a result, students became more interested in the rhetorical structure of an essay than any ideas it contained. Handbooks on the writing of eight-legged essays became popular. Later, the examiners even graded answers mainly on the basis of calligraphy, not paying attention to intellectual content or rhetorical form. As a result, the quality of the examination degenerated.

Sources:

Charles Hucker, *China's Imperial Past: Introduction to Chinese History and Culture* (Stanford, Cal.: Stanford University Press, 1975).

Thomas H. C. Lee, *Government Education and Examination in Sung China* (Hong Kong: Chinese University of Hong Kong, 1985).

## IMPERIAL LAWS

**Tang Code.** Based on the northern Zhou Code of 564, the legal code of the Tang dynasty (618–907) was first compiled in 624 and frequently modified in the following decades. The code was revised in 637 with a decrease in the number of offenses entailing death or exile. The most important change was the integration of an authoritative commentary in 653. This commentary not only provided clarification of the highly elliptical articles of the code but also introduced further rules not in the original text. The final redaction of the code in 737 dealt with both criminal and administrative concerns, including primary laws. The final format of the Tang code included 502 articles organized into 12 books: 1) general principles and regulations; 2) laws concerning the passing into or through prohibited areas (imperial court, town gates, city walls, frontier garrisons, and so forth); 3) offenses committed by officials in the exercise of their duties; 4) statutes relating to ordinary families (land, taxation, marriage, and so forth); 5) laws concerning state property; 6) laws relating to the maintaining of armies; 7) offenses against individuals and against property; 8) offenses committed in the course of argument; 9) falsification and counterfeiting; 10) various laws of special natures; 11) laws concerning guilty individuals; and 12) laws relating to the management of justice.

Detail of the scroll *Ten Kings of Hell* showing corporal punishment, Tang dynasty, 618–907 (British Museum, London)

## THE YUAN CODE

The Mongol legal code had strict provisions concerning the fate of criminals and captives, as is seen in the following decree:

After a bandit has surrendered himself to the government, the government official who accepts his surrender shall under no circumstances accept as gifts captured men and women. . . . If these people do not have any relatives and have consequently no place to go, the official should match them as husbands and wives so that they can establish their own households. All people who have been detained by bandits are to be set free.

A government official in charge of barbarian affairs who willfully marries a confiscated woman under his custody will receive eighty-seven blows by a wooden stick and be dismissed from his office. The woman in question will receive forty-seven blows by the same instrument.

Source: *Yuan Shi* (History of Yuan), in *The Essences of Chinese Civilization*, edited by Dun J. Li (Princeton, N.J.: D. Van Nostrand, 1967).

**Song Code.** The Song dynasty (960–1279) adopted the Tang code, including some statutes that were out-of-date even during the earlier dynasty. One of these antiquated articles concerned the system of land tenure. Under this statute, land granted with certain conditions to families by the emperor could not be sold. In both the Tang and Song times, land granted by the state was in fact bought and sold by families, but the Song code still included the regulations forbidding such alienations. Therefore, the Song code in this respect adopted rules that had not been applied for many decades.

**Taihe Lu.** Before the Mongol conquest of China, the strength of the native Chinese legal tradition was clearly apparent. When the Song empire lost control of the northern provinces to a nomadic people who founded the Jin dynasty (1115–1234), the invaders adopted a law code known as the *Taihe Lu,* modeled after that of the Tang court. The Mongols who overthrew the Jin dynasty and established their empire in North China began to implement the *Taihe Lu* until Kublai Khan abolished it in 1271.

**Chiyuan Xinge.** After the repeal of the *Taihe Lu,* Mongolian customary laws represented the major elements of official statutes until 1291. In that year the emperor bowed to pressure and agreed to issue an important collection of laws known as the *Chiyuan Xinge,* applicable to the Chinese people. Although arranged systematically according to subject matter, the *Chiyuan Xinge* was not a penal code because many of its rules did not prescribe punishment for offenses. Encouraged by Chinese scholars, the Yuan court later issued several important codifications of legal material, combining administrative with penal measures, but they did not follow the format of either the Tang or Song penal codes. The Mongols adopted the Chinese laws and changed them to comply with their needs. Discrimination was obvious in their laws. A Chinese, for example, was prohibited from retaliating if assaulted by a Mongol. The Mongols were allowed to possess arms while the Chinese were not. Legal cases involving both Mongols and Chinese were dealt with in special courts where Mongols did have some advantages.

**Great Ming Ordinance.** The *Daming Ling* (Great Ming Ordinance) issued in 1368 contained both administrative and penal rules in 145 articles, providing a clear and simple statement of the law to guide people. An important feature of this ordinance was the classification of government responsibilities. The Ming dynasty (1368–1644) did not issue the first regular penal code until 1374.

**Ming Legal Code.** In 1397 the *Daming Lu* (Ming Legal Code) was issued, following the Tang code in its division of the material. Of its 606 articles only 31 were new; the rest were taken directly from the Tang code or from other legislation. Similar to the *Daming Ling,* the Ming Legal Code was arranged by subject matter according to the divisions of governmental authority represented by the six ministries or boards. The first part was the general principles section, followed by six main specific-offense sections. The section on administrative law included the rules specifying punishments for breach of duty by officials. The section of civil law consisted of the rules on family, marriage, land, taxes, loans, and public markets. The section of ritual law had the penal rules concerning sacrifices and ceremonies. The section of military law contained the rules on royal palaces, imperial guards, the frontier, horses and cattle, and postal services. The section on penal law covered offenses against individuals, such as killing, physical injury, insult, property damage, theft, sexual assaults, and violations committed by those responsible for maintaining justice. Finally, the section on public works primarily dealt with construction and the management of rivers.

**Five Punishments.** Various forms of punishment existed in imperial China. Both the Tang code and the Song code used the Five Punishments. Initially enumerated in 653, the five punishments included: 1) Beating with a light stick (five degrees: ten to fifty blows); 2) Beating with a heavy stick (five degrees: sixty to one hundred blows); 3) Penal Servitude (five degrees: one to three years); 4) Life exile (three degrees: at distances of two hundred to three thousand *li* [three *li* = one mile]); and 5) Death (two degrees: strangulation and decapitation).

**Penal Servitude.** Penal servitude included hard labor for the offender and removal from his place of origin to another area for a fixed term of years. In Ming times, persons sentenced to penal servitude were sent from the province of their conviction to another province, where they worked in the iron or salt industries. Each person was forced to smelt four pounds of iron or to produce, through boiling, the same amount of salt every day. The condemned were not sent from their own province to another province randomly; for each province of origin there was a specific counterpart province to which persons were sent.

A magistrate's court; painting from the inside lid of a seal-box, circa 1600 (British Museum, London)

**Military Exile.** Military exile began to be clearly discernible from ordinary exile in Song times. It was further elaborated in Yuan times and came to be clearly systematized as a major punishment during the Ming dynasty. Originally, military exile was primarily a substitute for ordinary exile in the case of officers or soldiers who committed crimes, consisting of lifetime military service at some distant frontier garrison or military colony. Later, unauthorized sellers of salt, dishonest recipients of land or grain, instigators of false accusations, unregistered citizens, and many civilians underwent military exile. As a result, such punishment became prevalent for all criminals, and its scope was expanded to include service at army posts along the frontiers. More than ten varieties of military exile were listed in the 1585 edition of the Ming Code.

**Discrimination in Punishment.** In the Yuan penal code the most severe punishments were reserved for the Chinese. For example, only the Chinese were to be tattooed for the crime of theft. Mongols and Semu were tried according to Mongol law, while the Chinese were tried according to Chinese law. A Chinese who murdered a Mongol would be sentenced to death and had to pay the funeral expenses, while a Mongol who killed a Chinese was punished by a mere fine.

Sources:
Derk Bodde, *Law in Imperial China* (Cambridge, Mass.: Harvard University Press, 1967).

Hok-lam Chan, *Legitimation in Imperial China: Discussion under the Jurchen-chin Dynasty (1115–1234)* (Seattle: University of Washington Press, 1984).

Paul Heng-chao Chen, *Chinese Legal Tradition under the Mongols: The Code of 1291 as Reconstructed* (Princeton, N.J.: Princeton University Press, 1979).

Wallace Johnson, trans., *The Tang Code,* volume 1: *General Principles* (Princeton, N.J.: Princeton University Press, 1979).

Brian E. McKnight, *Law and Order in Sung China* (Cambridge: Cambridge University Press, 1992).

## THE MILITARY ORGANIZATION

**Fubing System.** In the middle of the sixth century a new *fubing* (militia) system was created. Every family with more than 2 sons had to send 1 man for permanent service in *fu* (garrisons) located throughout the empire. The militiamen themselves, rather than their families, had an exemption from taxes and other labor levies. The state provided their essential needs, but the garrisons were required to become self-sufficient by farming state-assigned lands in intervals between military activities. The system, consisting of a series of militias, each of 800 to 1,200 men, continued to exist in Tang times (618–907), but it was not based on universal conscription for short terms. This type of service was highly respected, and well-to-do families tried to get officer positions for their sons. Young men were chosen at the age of twenty-one on the basis of their physical fitness and respectable family backgrounds. There were about six hundred garrisons clustered in the Tang capital and scattered along the northern frontier. Militiamen remained on duty until they retired at sixty years of age. In rotation, groups of militiamen were sent to the capital for a month of service. In another rotation, the garrisons dispatched men to serve for three years in the frontier units. They also sent contingents to join in special military campaigns in times of war.

**Imperial Guard.** The core of Tang armies in the seventh century was aristocratic; the great families in North China provided the best troops. Their men served in the elite corps—the imperial guards (palace troops). Their nomad background and the prolonged influence of the steppe culture in North China had an impact on these aristocrats' taste for military affairs and their love of horses. The imperial guards were concentrated around the capital, and their essential tasks were to protect the empire against invasions from the borderlands and to defend the imperial court against local rebellions. They also provided an escort for the emperor when he traveled outside the palace.

**Northern Army.** In addition to the imperial guards, there was a standing army at the capital—the Northern Army, which served as the emperor's personal force. It was established by the Tang court during the rebellion against the Sui dynasty (589–618) and was replenished with sons of the aristocracy. The Northern Army, a permanent body of professionals, came to have the greatest military prestige and was the core of battle strength for the Tang empire.

**Frontier Armies.** Tang frontier armies had two different roles: they were either expeditionary troops of cavalry or garrisons responsible for holding the lines of defense and centers of communication. The troops quartered in the provinces represented only a small fraction of the total Tang forces since the imperial court did not rely on the army to maintain peace in regional areas.

**Song Army.** The army of the Song dynasty (960–1279) comprised mainly professionals, and the best troops were

Detail of a scroll depicting a Ming warship under full sail, 1598 (from Bradley Smith and Wan-go Weng, *China: A History in Art*, 1973)

Painting by Li Zanhau of a Khitan nobleman with his horse, circa tenth century (National Palace Museum, Taipei, Taiwan)

stationed around the capital under leaders directly controlled by the emperor. Contingents from the palace troops were rotated out to frontier defense units for three-year tours. Frontier commanders thus did not have any opportunity to build personal followings among their troops. In addition, soldiers in and around the capital often outnumbered the combined frontier forces. Less-capable soldiers were assigned to small garrisons that were scattered throughout the empire under the control of military intendants. Conscripted militiamen often supplemented regional units. Both the Northern Song dynasty (960–1125) and the Southern Song dynasty (1127–1279) each fielded about one million troops. The cost of maintaining this army was so enormous that it exhausted Song financial resources. Song armies were well equipped with armor and weapons because of the development of the iron and steel industry, and they occasionally fought well against invading Khitans, Jurchens, and Mongols. By the twelfth-century Song armies had effectively used fire bombs and tank-like carts sheathed in iron armor against the invaders.

**Reform.** After the Song armies (including various contingents of former nomads and mountaineers) participated in the campaigns of 963–979, the empire had difficulties recruiting any efficient auxiliaries, and military expenditure absorbed most of the state budget, causing economic depression. Thereafter, reformer Wang Anshi began to carry out military reforms between 1068 and 1085 in an effort to build an efficient army as well as reduce military costs. He restored the universal militia obligations of former dynasties and created special frontier units. He formed the *baojia* registration system to make household groups provide and provision conscripts. This system was organized on the basis of households, each *jia* being made up of ten households, and each *bao* of ten *jia*. The *baojia* draftees, however, refused to serve in other frontier garrisons, and the professionals refused to introduce draftees into the palace guards. Wang's military reform program failed.

**Navy.** After retreating to the Yangzi valley between 1126 and 1127, the Song court began to develop a substantial navy with bases on the great rivers and on the coast. At that time the Song navy began to use boats with paddles actuated by a crank or by a system of connecting rods, some of which had as many as twenty-five paddle wheels. The Song navy employed these boats in battles against the Jurchen in 1130 and 1161. This kind of fast boat in fact appeared as early as the eighth century, while the European paddleboats did not develop until 1543.

**New Techniques.** From the eleventh century to the thirteenth century, remarkable progress occurred in military techniques, which changed the nature of warfare and had great impact on the world. In recruitment, for example, certain objective principles of selection were adopted. Soldiers were recruited after a series of tests of physical ability, such as running, jumping, and shooting, and the taller and stronger individuals were sent to the crack units. Special units equipped with incendiary weapons, crossbows, and catapults were formed. The theory and technology of siege warfare also developed considerably.

**Yuan Army.** The army of the Yuan dynasty (1279–1368) was a superb force in terms of organization and the toughness and ability of its soldiers. Mongol soldiers lived in the saddle, and they could even sleep on horseback. Their horses were so strong that they could endure extremes of climate and find food in winter by digging it out from under the snow or stripping bark from trees. The Mongols were excellent at planning and carrying out their operations, and rapid movement, precise coordination, and superb tactical discipline made them formidable combatants. The Mongols broke up the tribal organization of the Khitans and Jurchens into a more centralized hierarchy. These military units, known as hundreds, thousands, and ten thousands, were stationed throughout the empire and were supported primarily from the produce of confiscated lands cultivated by slaves. As in Song times, the largest and most reliable armies concentrated in the capital as palace guards. The elite force known as the *kesig* was a large imperial bodyguard. The *kesig* was divided into four units that served in daily rotation as palace attendants. Consisting of sons of Mongol aristocrats, it was virtually above the law. It also played a disruptive governmental role similar to that of palace eunuchs in the Song dynasties. Of the Yuan armies, Mongol tribesmen were the most privileged, and other auxiliary units, in descending order of prestige and privilege, were Central Asians, northern Chinese, and southern Chinese. Service in all the regular Yuan armies was hereditary. The civilians were called on to provide militiamen for limited local police duty, but they were prohibited from owning weapons of any sort or engaging in military training. Since the iron and steel industry had decreased from its high level of development during the Song dynasty, Yuan military technology fell back to the bow-and-arrow stage.

**Weisuo System.** The founder of the Ming dynasty (1368–1644) built a strong military by combining some elements of the Yuan system with others, such as the *fubing* militia system. He concentrated most of his garrisons around the capital and along the northern frontier and located other garrisons at strategic places throughout the country. Each garrison was allotted a tract of government-owned land known as *tuntian* (military colony), where the soldiers were required to work in shifts to provide for their own food. The basic garrison unit was a *wei* (guard) of about five thousand men; *wei* were subdivided into *so* (battalions or companies). Soldiers and officers of *wei* and *so* were required to participate periodically in special training at the capital. Soldiers of the garrisons along the northern frontier guarded the Great Wall fortifications, and those of other garrisons guarded coastal forts. All soldiers were on rotational deployment from their garrisons, under the leadership of tactical commanders directed by regional commanders. In large-scale military campaigns, soldiers were gathered from *wei* and *so* throughout the country into unplanned tactical units directed by military officers specially sent from the central government. This division of authority between garrison and tactical commanders was to prevent regional military officers from declaring independence.

**Problems.** The *weisuo* system was designed to reduce the military cost to the public and to make the Ming army more efficient. Desertion, however, became a serious problem, and it was hard for the government to replace deserters and battlefield casualties, according to prescribed hereditary principles. In addition, few garrisons produced enough food, especially in the poor farming regions along the frontiers where large forces were located. After the fifteenth century, the imperial government began to provide annual financial support, and these subsidies increased year by year. Even with these subsidies the strength and fighting ability of the *weisuo* standing army continued to decline. Supplemented by local militiamen and by conscripts from the general population,

the military rolls swelled to a total of four million men in the late Ming era, but they were inadequately equipped, poorly trained, and erratically fed and clothed.

**Sources:**

Hsiao Ch'i-ching, *The Military Establishment of the Yuan Dynasty* (Cambridge, Mass.: Harvard University Press, 1978).

James B. Parsons, *The Peasant Rebellions of the Late Ming Dynasty* (Tucson: University of Arizona Press, 1970).

Morris Rossabi, *The Jurchens in the Yuan and Ming* (Ithaca, N.Y.: Cornell University Press, 1982).

## MING ABSOLUTISM

**Absolutist Trend.** The political structure of the Song dynasty (960–1279) was based on the coexistence of independent departments and a system of checks and balances. Political decisions were the topic of discussions in which conflicting opinions could be freely expressed. An absolutist trend, however, began to appear in Song times and

Tomb sculpture of a soldier, Beijing,
Ming dynasty, 1368–1644

Painting showing procession of Ming emperor Wu-tsung, sixteenth century (National Palace Museum Collection, Taipei, Taiwan)

advanced further under the Mongols. By the early Ming era (1368–1644) all power had become concentrated in the hands of the emperor. The unchecked growth of imperial power in the late fourteenth century was regarded as the political character of Ming times. The reason for this trend was that the Ming empire was established by a peasant who felt an instinctive mistrust of scholars, which forced him to control directly the government and the civil service.

**Authoritarianism.** In 1380 Emperor Hongwu cancelled the post of grand secretariat and assumed direct control of the six ministries (public administration, finance, rites, armies, justice, and public works). He also created a General Direction of the Five Armies so that he could better control the military. The tendency to centralization and authoritarianism continued into the late Ming era.

**Great Purges.** Fearing that he would lose power, Emperor Hongwu began to persecute those who had helped him to gain the imperial throne. He accused his old friend and loyal follower, Hu Weiyong, of planning a revolt and communicating with the Mongols and Japanese. A great trial began in 1380 with more than fifteen thousand people involved in the case. Hu was found guilty and put to death. After Hu's execution, Hongwu concentrated more authority in his own hands. Another purge took place in 1385 when several officials were accused of committing crimes of high treason. By that time Hongwu had become

so sensitive that he even regarded certain written characters as criticism of his person and his origins, and many intellectuals were persecuted.

**Court Eunuchs.** Another characteristic of Ming absolutism was the political power of court eunuchs. Most of the eunuchs were lower-class northerners and were entirely dependent on imperial favor. Castrated males, eunuchs were trusted by the emperors. They commanded the palace guard, checked the tributes presented by the provinces and foreign countries, served in the court as the emperor's personal secretaries, traveled to tributary states as the emperor's personal envoys, and managed the imperial workshops. Enriched by their supervision of trade and foreign relations, they were thus at the source of military power and commercial wealth. Having exceptional access to the emperor, they could exert great influence on emperors who distrusted the legitimate representatives of the imperial government in the provinces. The autocratic tendencies of the Ming regime made the rise of powerful and devoted servants inevitable.

**Eunuch Dictators.** The importance of eunuchs resulted in some of them becoming dictators. They controlled the whole administration and appointed and promoted officials in the central government and in the provinces. Becoming the center of power, they began to abuse their authority. Liu Jin, chief of imperial staff, was an example of eunuch misuse of power. Coming to the throne as a minor in 1506, Liu Jin was blatantly corrupt and oppressive. His excesses created many enemies who accused him of plotting to kill the emperor, for which crime he was put to death. The last and most infamous eunuch dictator was Wei Zhongxian, who rose to power during the period of the Tianqi emperor (1621–1627). Trusted by the emperor, he abused his power by using spies and secret police to instigate a reign of terror.

**Surveillance System.** A surveillance system supported the absolutist framework. Emperor Hongwu maintained an elaborate secret operation by using spies and security guards who carried out the major purges of his reign. In 1382 he formed the Brocaded Guards, a sort of political police that watched the activities of high officials. Later, Emperor Yungle created the Men of the Eastern Esplanade, which succeeded the Brocaded Guards and were under the control of the eunuchs. Created in the years 1465–1487, the Red Horsemen of the Western Esplanade, acting as secret envoys and spies on behalf of the eunuchs, took advantage of their unlimited and secret powers to blackmail and intimidate the populace.

Sources:

Julia Ching and Willard G. Oxtoby, eds., *Discovering China: European Interpretations in the Enlightenment* (Rochester, N.Y.: University of Rochester Press, 1992).

William Theodore de Bary, *The Liberal Tradition in China* (New York: Columbia University Press, 1983).

Charles Hucker, ed., *Chinese Government in Ming Times: Seven Studies* (New York: Columbia University Press, 1969).

## MING DECLINE AND COLLAPSE

**Mongol Offensive.** The Mongol attacks on China between 1483 and 1489 signaled the end of Chinese expansion in the North. Beginning in 1540 the Mongols were making good progress toward unification, posing a serious threat to the Ming dynasty (1368–1644). The Jiajing emperor had to deal with the rise of a new Mongol empire under Altan Khan, who raided Chinese territory in an effort to get supplies for his campaigns against his enemies. In 1550 the Mongolian army beleaguered Beijing for three days and looted the surrounding areas. In 1552 Altan Khan occupied part of Shanxi province. To extend his influence in Central Asia, he invaded Qinghai in 1559 and Tibet in 1570. The Ming court attempted to bribe the Mongols and to strengthen the Great Wall, but these raids continued until Altan Khan reached a temporary peace agreement with the Chinese in 1572. The Mongols, however, continued to threaten Ming's northern borders until a new threat from the Manchus in the seventeenth century. Mongolian raids on the Ming empire indicated a decline in that dynasty's military power.

**Japanese Piracy.** Beginning in the 1540s, the Ming empire confronted another grave danger: the attacks of Japanese pirates, known as *wokou*. Japanese traders and pirates appeared along the southeast coast of China and built their bases in 1550 on the coast of Zhejiang province, threatening the whole region. In 1554, the Japanese raiders

Scroll depicting Ming military officers conferring with an army commander, late sixteenth century (from Bradley Smith and Wan-go Weng, *China: A History in Art*, 1973)

attacked Songjiang, the center of the cotton industry, and killed the magistrate. Large-scale raids from the sea by Japanese pirates revealed the inadequacy of the coastal defenses and the ineffectiveness of the Ming regular army. Thereafter, Qi Jiguang, an unconventional Chinese commander, trained a volunteer force and used firearms as well as traditional weapons to resist the attacks of the Japanese pirates. Peace was not restored until the Ming court lifted the ban in 1567 on Chinese participation in overseas trade. Ming failure to maintain frontier policies further exposed the weaknesses of the dynasty.

**Incompetent Emperors.** In the late Ming dynasty there was a lack of able emperors. The Jiajing emperor, becoming obsessed with Daoism and the search for the elixirs of immortality, withdrew from the active supervision of the government for many years. His search for eternal life led to his death by poisoning in 1566. Between 1589 and 1615 Emperor Shenzong did not hold a single general audience, and from 1590 to 1620 he conducted only a few personal interviews with grand secretaries. The eunuch dictator Wei Zhongxian rose to power during the reign of the incompetent Tianqi emperor (1621–1627). Although the following Chongzhen emperor, a man who was active and well-intentioned, tried to carry out reforms to save the empire, he was hampered by the service of untrustworthy officials and lacked a consistent policy.

**Power of the Gentry.** The gentry came to believe that the competition for examination success had become more severe and the risks associated with a bureaucratic career had increased. This view brought about a change in their orientation: from a state-centered vision of gentry life, which stressed engagement with worldly affairs, to a Buddhism-centered philosophy, which implied withdrawal from public life. In addition the gentry grew more abusive in their local power by removing many of their fields from the tax rolls. Large landlords were able to find tax shelters through various manipulations, and only small peasants remained to pay taxes. The increasing power of the local gentry weakened the authority of the central government, and the delicate balance between the central government and the local elite was upset.

**Donglin Movement.** In the late sixteenth century several private academies were founded, where scholars and former officials complained about the decline of Confucian standards and the political immorality of the dynasty. In 1577 the scholars criticized Grand Secretary Zhang Juzheng for failing to observe the period of mourning after his father's death. As a result Zhang ordered a personnel evaluation, which resulted in discharging some officials from the government. Dismissed officials then joined the academies, the most famous being the Donglin academy. Donglin sympathizers were kept out of government until 1620. In 1621, when the new emperor came to the throne, eunuch Wei Zhongxian was put in charge of the imperial tombs. The members of the Donglin returned to power at the beginning of the Tianqi era, but their influence did not last for a long time. Wei organized a network of accom-

## EARTHQUAKE!

The Chinese regarded earthquakes and other natural catastrophes as signs of Heaven's anger. Many times people interpreted them as warnings of other things to come. In 1626, eighteen years before the Ming empire collapsed, a strong earthquake hit the area around Beijing. The following is a description of the event:

When the . . . partisans [palace eunuchs] were secretly plotting in the palace, there was a sudden earthquake. A roof ornament over the place where they were sitting fell without any apparent reason and two eunuchs were crushed to death. In a moment there was a sound like thunder rising from the northwest. It shook heaven and earth, and black clouds flowed over confusedly. Peoples' dwellings were destroyed to such an extent that for several miles nothing remained.

The reason why the earth growls is that throughout the empire troops arise to attack one another, and that palace women and eunuchs have brought great disorder.

Source: Donald F. Lach and Carol Flaumenhaft, eds., *Asia on the Eve of Europe's Expansion* (Englewood Cliffs, N.J.: Prentice-Hall, 1965).

plices and soon controlled the whole administration. From 1625 until the death of Tianqi, there was a terrible repression of the seven hundred members and supporters of the Donglin, many of whom were sentenced to death. The academies that served as centers for the opposition were closed. The serious conflict between civil intellectuals and the eunuchs at court in the crisis of 1625–1627 had a profound negative impact on late Ming government. This Donglin movement represented the interests of a landowning class resentful of the Ming court, and factionalism deriving from the Donglin movement further weakened the Ming central government.

**Financial Crisis.** The late imperial court spent much money. The military campaigns against the Japanese from 1595 to 1598 and the Koreans from 1593 to 1598 exhausted the empire's treasury. The numbers of the imperial nobility increased from generation to generation so fast that by the end of the Ming dynasty the government had difficulty paying allowances to these aristocrats. The allowances paid to relatives of the imperial family also contributed to the financial deficit. To maintain a healthy financial situation, the Ming court raised commercial taxes by building custom posts on the Yangzi and the Grand Canal and levied heavy taxes on the peasantry. The new taxes and duties provoked anger and discontent, which was aggravated by the poor economy and the dismissal of state employees, and finally resulted in insurrections (1627–1644).

**Peasant Discontent.** A peasant rebellion precipitated the collapse of the dynasty. The rebellion began in 1628 in

Detail of a scroll showing Japanese troops defending a fort from Ming attack, 1598
(from Bradley Smith and Wan-go Weng, *China: A History in Art*, 1973)

northern Shaanxi and then spread throughout the empire. As revolts grew in size and strength, they progressed from disorganized raiding to more ambitious political objectives. The Ming court put down the largest insurrection, but the survivors scattered. At that time there were two powerful rebellions, one led by Zhang Xianzhong in Sichuan, the other led by Li Zicheng in central China. Li Zicheng's troops successfully seized Beijing on 24 April 1644 and forced the Ming emperor to commit suicide. Li, however, proved unable to found a new dynasty because he had never won the support of the scholar-official elite.

**Manchu Invasion.** The Jianzhou Jurchen were living in the vicinity of the Changbai mountains and founded the Manchu state under the leadership of Nurhaci. In 1599 the entire Jurchen population were organized into "banners." Groups of three hundred households formed one company, and fifty companies composed one banner. The four initial banners eventually increased to eight Manchu banners and eight Chinese banners. As a tribute state ruler, Nurhaci continued to send gifts to Beijing until 1609. However, when he became powerful enough, he began to defy the Chinese empire. In 1616 he declared himself emperor of the Late Jin. By the end of 1621 Nurhaci completely controlled the whole of Liaodong in Manchuria. Nurhaci established his capital at Shengyuan in 1625 but died the next year. The new ruler, Abahai, then began to invade the Ming empire. In 1629, in a spectacular raid, Abahai successfully crossed the walls of Beijing. Seven years later Abahai changed the dynastic name of *Jin* to *Qing*, signifying "clear" or "pure." In 1643 Abahai died, and his five-year-old son inherited the throne, assisted by the new emperor's uncle Dorgon. The Manchurians never gave up their dream to occupy all of China and continued to attack it. When the Ming general Wu Sangui, who controlled access to Beijing, decided to cooperate with the Manchus, the Qing troops quickly occupied Beijing in June 1644, driving Li Zicheng's troops out of North China. When the last Ming emperor hanged himself, the Ming dynasty collapsed.

**Sources:**

Ray Huang, *1587, a Year of No Significance: The Ming Dynasty in Decline* (New Haven: Yale University Press, 1981).

Charles O. Hucker, *The Ming Dynasty: Its Origins and Evolving Institutions* (Ann Arbor: University of Michigan Press, 1978).

Hucker, *The Traditional Chinese State in Ming Times (1368–1644)* (Tucson: University of Arizona Press, 1961).

James B. Parsons, *The Peasant Rebellion of the Late Ming Dynasty* (Tucson: University of Arizona Press, 1970).

## MING MILITARY EXPANSION AND POLITICAL REFORMS

**Early Ming Army.** The first Ming emperor, Hongwu, maintained much of the Mongol military structure, under which the Ming army was commanded by a hereditary officer class. The early Ming armed forces mainly derived from Hongwu's followers and the bands who surrendered to him during the military campaigns when Hongwu promised that their units would be kept unbroken and their leaders' commands would be made hereditary. At that time, Hongwu's army officials were also rewarded with noble titles and ranked higher than other military and civil officials.

**Military Colony System.** The founding father of the Ming tried to transform the Ming army into a kind of autonomous organization, whose members and income were to be provided by their families with a special statute—the armed families, who settled on the lands of military colonies. For each ten soldiers, three were to be assigned to military tasks and seven to agricultural work on the lands of military colonies. Their families had to support the army. The greatest concentration of military colonies was located in the capital area, on the northern frontier, and in Southwest China. Therefore, a living, autonomous organism spread all over the Ming empire, and the armies acquired in time a sort of regional specialization.

**Offensives.** The Turkic conqueror Tamerlane posed the most significant threat to Ming power. After occupying a vast Central Asian empire, Tamerlane began to invade China in 1404, but he died en route the next year. Meanwhile the Urianghad and Jurchen tribes on the Northeastern frontier were disunited, and they were forced to recognize Chinese rule. In the West, the Tatar and Oirat tribes in Mongolia still presented a danger to the Ming dynasty (1368–1644). Emperor Yongle launched five expeditions in person against them between 1410 and 1424, winning great victories. Because of these successful military campaigns, the Ming government occupied Manchuria up to the mouth of the Amur River and then appointed a governor-general there. In the South, Yongle's armies put down the tribal resistance and then moved against Annam, which was an independent state in Tang times, sending tributes to the imperial emperors annually. A powerful Ming army of 200,000 men invaded Dai Viet in North Vietnam in 1406 and overthrew the Kingdom of the Tran. The Ming annexation of the Red River basin and central Vietnam was not without resistance. An independence movement began in 1418 and finally drove out the Chinese in 1427.

**Transfer of the Capital.** Yongle made a significant decision to transfer the capital from Nanjing to Beijing. The main reason for the move was to permit closer control over the military forces in the North. Another reason for this decision was the strategic importance of the Beijing area for the control both of eastern Mongolia and of the northeastern territories. The transfer of the capital seemed to reflect Yongle's desire to expand the Chinese empire toward the steppe zone and Manchuria. It was his ambition to reassume in Asia the dominant position held by the Yuan empire between the end of the thirteenth century and the middle of the fourteenth century. The construction of the new capital began in 1406 and involved the obtaining of large quantities of timber and bricks and the deployment of many thousands of laborers

Portrait of Ming Emperor Yongle, who launched offensives against Mongolia and Annam and transferred the capital to Beijing, fifteenth century (National Palace Museum, Taipei, Taiwan)

and artisans. The city walls and the major palace buildings were not completed until 1417.

**Hai Rui's Reforms.** Inequality in taxation, which not only reduced the government's revenue but also hurt small peasants, encouraged the reformers to introduce a new tax system. Hai Rui was one of these reformers who had a reputation for uprightness, courage, and concern for the ordinary people. As a magistrate he reexamined the land in order to make taxes more equitable. He hated corruption and tried to wipe it out effectively while leading a life of exemplary frugality. After submitting a scathing memorial that accused the emperor of neglecting his duty and spending too much time in religious ceremonies, he was sent to prison, tortured, and condemned to death by strangulation. Saved by the emperor, he was released from prison and returned to his office but was forced to resign later when he offended powerful landlords again by ordering them to return lands they occupied illegally. After his death in 1587 the people idealized him as the perfect official.

**Zhang Juzheng.** A Confucian legalist, Zhang Juzheng was a different kind of reformer. He believed that strong and strict government was ultimately for the people's benefit, and efficiency and control were the hallmarks of his policy. He started a project to repair the Grand Canal, reformed the courier system, designed rules to strengthen central control over local officers, and decreased the number of officials. Moreover, he made an effort to reduce eunuch influence in the six ministries, to prohibit censors from abusing their authority, and to reform the provincial schools.

**Examination Reform.** One of Zhang Juzheng's major achievements was the reform of examination. Zhang was unhappy when the emperor Taizu favored an essay form composed of eight rigidly stipulated sections, known as the "eight-legged essay." Evaluation of papers on the basis of form rather than content was becoming a new trend in the civil service examination. This situation helped the examination readers to grade papers more easily but threatened to turn the examinations into mechanical exercises. Serving as an examiner in 1571, Zhang required the questions to emphasize current problems and the answers to be graded on content. To carry out his examination reform, he went too far, closing private academies in 1579, although the decree banning academies did little permanent damage to these schools.

**Financial Reform.** To maintain healthy government finances, Zhang directed an all-China land survey and introduced the "single whip method of taxation," which was previously tried in some provinces, providing for the consolidation of tax obligations into a single annual bill. This new taxation replaced the Two Tax System that had been in place since the Tang dynasty (618–907). Implementation of the new taxes remained incomplete, however. His other important financial reform was the use of silver as the value base for tax assessment, and thereafter the silver *tael* (ounce) remained the standard monetary unit until the twentieth century. Because of these successful fiscal reforms, the sound economy at the time enabled the Ming government to maintain heavy military expenditures, resist Mongol invasions between 1550 and 1570, and sustain military preparedness. The government's fiscal health at that time also indicated the economic strength of Ming.

Sources:

Albert Chan, *The Glory and Fall of the Ming Dynasty* (Norman: University of Oklahoma Press, 1982).

John W. Dardess, *Confucianism and Autocracy: Professional Elites in the Founding of the Ming Dynasty* (Berkeley: University of California Press, 1983).

Edward Dreyer, *Early Ming China: A Political History, 1355–1435* (Stanford, Cal.: Stanford University Press, 1982).

Edward Farmer, *Early Ming Government: The Evolution of Dual Capitals* (Cambridge, Mass.: Harvard University Press, 1976).

## THE MONGOLS

**Conquest.** The Mongols were pastoral nomads who lived in a tribal society in Mongolia in the eleventh century. Superb horsemen and warriors, they frequently came into conflict with the Tatars, their neighbors to the West. When the Mongols began to develop an ethnic consciousness, Temüjin exploited this political situation. In 1206 he claimed the title *Genghis Khan* (meaning "Universal Ruler"

or "Khan from Ocean to Ocean") and began to invade China in 1211. He died in 1227 during the campaign, and thereafter the Mongol Empire was divided between his sons and grandson. Kublai Khan, Genghis Khan's grandson, becoming Great Khan in 1260, transferred the capital to Beijing in 1264 and adopted in 1271 a Chinese name, *Yuan*, as the title of his dynasty. When the last Song loyalists were defeated at sea in 1279, the Mongols became the first nomadic conquerors to rule all of China.

**Adaptation.** Under the influence of the Chinese, the Mongols carried out less-harsh policies toward the conquered people and began to adopt certain institutions of Chinese origin. Yelu Chucai, a descendant of the Khitan aristocracy, was the major designer of the Mongols' conversion to Chinese administrative methods. He worked hard to fashion a centralized administration along Chinese lines but achieved only partial success. He divided China into large-scale and loosely controlled military commands that later evolved into the large provinces in the Ming dynasty (1368–1644). He freed Chinese scholars from captivity and appointed them as tutors to Mongol nobles. In 1229 postal relays were created for the first time, a system of property taxes was set up, and public granaries were built. Seven years later paper money was first issued, and translation offices were established in order to produce Mongol versions of the Chinese classics and official histories of the preceding dynasties. Meanwhile, Kublai Khan personally developed the pattern of Mongol rule over China, retaining many superficial characteristics of the Song administration, such as the secretariat and the six ministries and the traditional division between the civil, military, and censorial branches of government. He also incorporated Chinese court ceremonial and Confucian rites into his government.

**Distrust.** Although the Mongols adopted native institutions, they still did not trust former Chinese officials; a significant number of Muslims, many of whom came from Central Asia, occupied important government positions. Directing the state financial administration from 1262 until his death in 1282, the Muslim Ahmad played a prominent role in Kublai Khan's reign. The Mongols occupied all posts of command, and the administration of the finances was given to men from the Islamic areas of Central Asia and the Middle East. Assisted by Mongol military detachments, Muslim merchants, grouped in associations, practically established a monopoly in the profitable business of collecting taxes.

**Military Campaigns.** Kublai Khan's ambitions were not confined to China proper. He launched two military campaigns against Japan in 1274 and 1281, but both failed. By sending his fleets to invade Java in 1281 and 1292, he forced the natives into ritual submission but failed to expand the Yuan empire's territory. In the meantime Kublai Khan and his successors concentrated on securing Mongolia. Despite their success on China's inner Asian frontier, the Mongols failed to dominate Central Asia.

**Collapse.** The reasons for the collapse of the Yuan dynasty were many and were mutually related to each other:

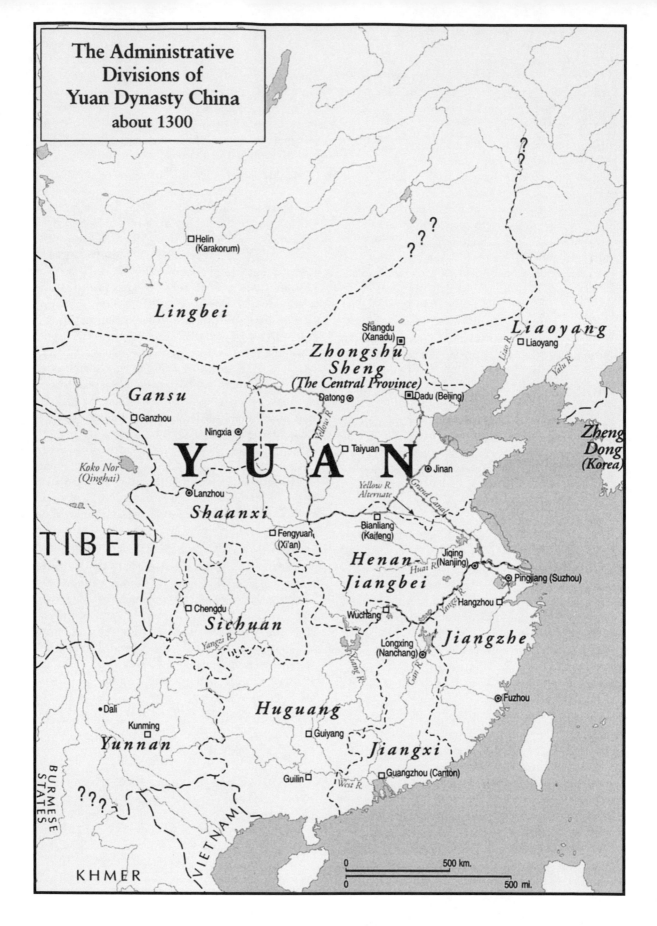

Helin
(Karakorum)

*Lingbei*

Shangdu
(Xanadu)

*Liaoyang*
□ Liaoyang

*Zhongshu
Sheng
(The Central Province)*

*Gansu*

□ Ganzhou

Datong ◉
◻ Dadu (Beijing)

Ningxia ◉

**Y U A N**

Taiyuan

*Zheng
Dong
(Korea)*

*Koko Nor
(Qinghai)*

◉ Jinan

*Yellow R.
Alternate*

◉ Lanzhou

*Shaanxi*

**TIBET**

□ Fengyuan
(Xi'an)

□ Bianliang
(Kaifeng)

*Henan-
Jiangbei*

Jiqing
(Nanjing) ◉

◉ Pingjiang (Suzhou)

*Huai R.*

□ Chengdu

Wuchang ◻

Hangzhou

*Sichuan*

*Yangzi R.*

Longxing
(Nanchang) ◉

*Jiangzhe*

• Dali

Kunming
□

*Huguang*

◉ Fuzhou

*Yunnan*

□ Guiyang

*Jiangxi*

**B
U
R
M
E
S
E
S
T
A
T
E
S**

Guilin □

Guangzhou (Canton)

**K H M E R**

**V
I
E
T
N
A
M**

*West R.*

| 0 | | 500 km. |
| 0 | | 500 mi. |

Map of China Proper at the height of the Mongol Empire (from F. W. Mote, *Imperial China*, 1999)

بادراطیعت درنیک از نوم موجب کاتک شنه پودد ترکنه نالنکری از نول لز سنا از اتول لز سنا ذا از حدود طا کدد طال زنه وان زتکر فراخای را
ارانان نان کرمخته الجی زبتنا ذبودند کهراند اتیان برنشد و اتشکرا ننا وردنده باتان بمزطالد و راحبا مع
کددنند

Illumination of the Mongol army besieging Cheng-tu, circa thirteenth century (Bibliothèque Nationale, Paris)

disorder in the government; greed of the Mongol and Muslim officials; skyrocketing inflation; corruption of the Tibetan monks who controlled all of the Chinese clergy and interfered in political affairs; the growing poverty of the peasantry; and rebellions in many provinces.

**Military Weakness.** After the conquest of China, the Mongols divided all the military forces into four parts: the Mongol army; associated nomadic army; Chinese and Qidan army from North China; and the Chinese army from the South. The first three armies were given lands and slaves. They were exempted from taxation and were required to be self-sustaining. This military system was created to repress internal disturbances. Since many slaves ran away, Mongol households could not cultivate their lands. In the 1290s there was impoverishment and a decline in military standards. By the 1340s many Mongol military households became poor and the garrison system began to collapse.

**Government Weakness.** Since the Mongols lacked a tradition of orderly succession to the throne, the Yuan dynasty had begun to weaken by the fourteenth century. In only forty years after Kublai Khan's death, several emperors came to the throne through violent means. Rul-

ers succeeded each other rapidly in the midst of internal troubles, plots, and usurpations. There were four emperors between the years 1320 and 1329 alone. Great ministers and high officials were the masters in the capital, and local authorities, who became more and more corrupt, acted as they wanted.

**Chancellor Bayan.** The Yuan court did not revive the civil service examinations based on the Confucian classics and the commentaries of Zhu Xi until 1315. Although a major concession to the Chinese scholars, the examinations favored the Mongols and their non-Chinese allies because they were given simplified versions. Therefore, some Chinese had to use foreign names. The Mongols occupied 30 percent of all government posts at that time. In 1335 Chancellor Bayan obtained an imperial decree to cancel the examinations and thereby became the enemy of the Chinese scholars, who regarded the reinstitution of the examinations both as a step toward the normalization of government and as an opportunity for personal advancement. Although examinations were restored in 1342, they did not regain the prominence Chinese scholars had enjoyed in the Song times, and the examinations did not become the major method of government recruitment. The Chinese were also

Kublai Khan with a hunting party; detail of a painting attributed to Liu Kuan-tao, circa thirteenth century (National Palace Museum, Taipei, Taiwan)

disappointed with the Yuan policy of military supremacy over civilian authority.

**Yellow River Problem.** The Yellow River broke through its dikes, flooded, and began to change its course in the 1340s. One part of the river flowed North to the Shandong Peninsula, while another branch emptied into the Grand Canal. This change resulted in great dislocation and suffering for the inhabitants of the affected areas and threatened the economic survival of the court by interrupting shipments of grain from the South to Beijing. The central government had to reestablish control over the river or over the sea route. In doing so, under the direction of a Chinese engineer, the dynasty employed 150,000 civilians and 20,000 troops. The Yellow River problem was solved, but the cost was high, exhausting the state financial resources. The consequence was great inflation, which added its toll to the hardship of the peasants already suffering from government exactions.

**Downfall.** Along with the flooding of the Yellow River, other crises emerged in the 1340s. Peasant revolts flared up in the countryside, and pirates threatened the shipment of grain to the capital by sea. In 1351 the emperor called upon Toghto, an experienced professional who had previously served as chancellor. After returning to office, Toghto carried out new policies to increase revenue, control the floods, and put down the rebels. He at first was successful in handling the situation. He began a great project, employing thousands of peasants as laborers, to reopen the Grand Canal, which had silted up. Yet, his project aroused a new and greater rebellion. In 1355, under pressure from Chancellor Toghto's opponents, the

emperor removed him, and his dismissal marked the end of the Yuan dynasty. Thereafter, the emperor controlled only the capital and the surrounding regions, while other parts of the empire were held by independent commanders. As the insurrection grew, a civil war broke out among the Yuan supporters. In 1368 the court fled to Manchuria, and the Yuan dynasty finally collapsed.

**White Lotus Society.** The deteriorating situation incited people to look for religious salvation. Although the imperial government forbade and persecuted secret societies, they continued to spring up. Some of these organizations were more obviously religious than political in their aims. The White Lotus Society, a sect dedicated to the worship of the Buddha Amitabha, was founded in the twelfth century. The teachings of the White Lotus Society appealed to many people placing their faith in the coming of Maitreya (Mi-le), the redemptive Bodhisattva, who would end all suffering and injustice in society. Led by someone who claimed descent from the Song imperial line, the society attracted the miserable: dismissed clerks, laborers from the Yellow River project, peddlers, outlaws, the idle, and the displaced, who believed in the imminent restoration of the Song dynasty (960–1279). It also appealed to many poor peasants who hated to pay heavy taxes or to carry out compulsory labor.

**Red Turbans.** Another important secret organization was the Red Turbans, so called for the headdress adopted by its members. These people once revolted during the Song period and turned to open rebellion again in 1352. The Yuan court, under Toghto's leadership, was determined to put down this challenge, but the Red Turbans evaded the

Mongol armies and established a special base in Sichuan, an isolated province that had a tradition of semi-independence.

**Debate.** Traditional interpretations of the downfall of the Yuan dynasty emphasize the persistent Chinese hatred of the Mongols who failed to modify their rule to meet Chinese expectations. It was therefore only a matter of time until a combination of dynastic decline and rebellion would bring an end to the dynasty. In recent years scholars proposed a rather different explanation: a series of disastrous events occurring between the 1350s and 1360s ruined the empire, even though, under Kublai Khan and his immediate successors, the Mongols devised an effective and acceptable means of ruling the Chinese. In other words, Mongol rule might have lasted much longer without these events.

Sources:

Hsiao Ch'i-ching, *The Military Establishment of the Yuan Dynasty* (Cambridge, Mass.: Harvard University Press, 1978).

Elizabeth Endicott-West, *Mongolian Rule in China: Local Administration In the Yuan Dynasty* (Cambridge, Mass.: Harvard University Press, 1989).

Herbert Franke, *China Under Mongol Rule* (Aldershot, U.K.: Variorum, 1994).

## SONG POLITICAL REFORMS

**Overview.** Zhao Kuanyin, known as the Emperor Taizu, founded the Song dynasty (960–1279) by reunifying North China. By his death in 976 he had already laid down the foundations of one of the most famous dynasties in Chinese history, and all of China, apart from two independent kingdoms, had been under his control. The Northern Song dynasty (960–1125) had its capital in Kaifeng on the Grand Canal, a city more readily supplied from the South than Chang'an or Luoyang.

**Fan Zhongyan.** In the early Song era, scholars and officials advocated reforms to deal with the perceived problems. During the reign of the Renzong emperor (1023–1063),

Fan Zhongyan proposed a ten-point program of reforms, including policies to improve the efficiency of the government, raise the standard of the examinations, increase agricultural yields, and reduce the demands on the people for labor service. Of these proposals, however, only some educational reforms were carried out, such as the creation of a national school system and the introduction of anonymity for examination candidates.

**Ouyang Xiu.** Another reformer was the eleventh-century writer Ouyang Xiu, who urged bringing Song society closer to the ideal Confucian society of the past. He even incited able men to establish a reform committee. He

Painting of a Song official on horseback, 1296 (Palace Museum, Beijing)

Song-era portrait of Emperor Taizu, the general who founded the Song dynasty (National Palace Museum, Taipei, Taiwan)

understood that the organization of an opposition was unacceptable in politics but justified his suggestions on the grounds that his supporters would be men of principle while their opponents would be men motivated mainly by profit.

**Wang Anshi.** Wang Anshi was China's most famous reformer in the eleventh century. Holding several official positions in the local governments, he presented to Emperor Renzong in 1058 a document known as the *Ten Thousand Word Memorial.* In it he expressed anxiety about the current situation of the Song empire and advocated a series of conventional Confucian measures to remedy the situation, in particular by putting more able officers in the state government. He made an important proposal that men be placed in positions for which they were qualified, an idea opposite to the Confucianism that an official should be a man of wide general learning. He also suggested that the emperor himself only oversee the government and support the reform. Emperor Renzong ignored Wang's proposals, but when Emperor Shenzong (1068–1085) came to the throne, he appointed Wang his chief minister, a post he occupied until 1085.

**New Laws.** Wang began a reform program, known as the New Laws, affecting the economy and taxation, security and military affairs, and the administration. Identifying a shortage of revenue as one of the main weaknesses of the state, he suggested several important measures in which revenue might be increased. His measures were intended to help the ordinary people. Thereafter, the government offered farmers low-interest loans in order to enable them to escape the exploitation of moneylenders. Since many moneylenders were landlords, this policy was also meant to reduce the concentration of landholding and the evasion of taxation. Hating the extravagance of the rich landlords, Wang threatened to adopt a new policy to limit the manufacture and sale of luxury commodities. The military reforms were to reduce the cost of the imperial army. As a result, Wang renewed the *baojia* system, the age-old system of collective security. Groups of ten households were responsible for local security and for a supply of men to be trained as a militia. With regard to the administration reform, he intended to promote candidates of good character. His emphasis in the examination

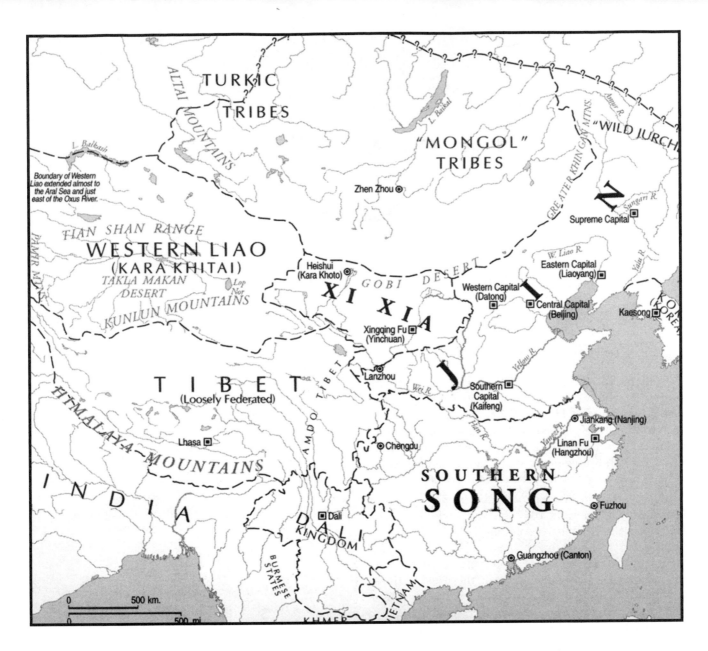

Map of China during the Song dynasty, 960–1279 (from F. W. Mote, *Imperial China*, 1999)

was the exposition of the Confucian classics, rather than the exercise of literary skills. To achieve this end, Wang himself composed commentaries on the classics.

**Conservative Reaction.** Although Wang's proposals fell within the Song tradition of pragmatic reform, conservative scholars began to attack him. The scholar Sima Guang resigned in protest against the reforms, claiming that the New Laws were to satisfy Wang's own ambitions and to oppress the poor. Sima Guang's attack on Wang Anshi seriously damaged the reformer's reputation among Confucian scholars. In 1076 Wang was forced to leave the office, and several of the New Laws were abolished.

**Revival.** Ten years later, after the death of the Shenzong emperor, the new Zhezong emperor (1086–1101) appointed Cai Jing, Wang's son-in-law, to office, and Cai Jing remained in power under the Huizong emperor (1101–1126). There was a partial revival of the reform program under Huizong, but it never recovered its former support.

**Public Welfare.** A public welfare system existed during the Song era. Using the charitable foundations created by the Buddhist monasteries in the seventh century as models, Song officials established orphanages, hospices, hospitals, dispensaries, public cemeteries, and reserve granaries.

**Sources:**
John W. Haeger, ed., *Crisis and Prosperity in Sung China* (Tucson: University of Arizona Press, 1975).

Edward A. Kracke, *Civil Service in Sung China: 960–1067* (Cambridge, Mass.: Harvard University Press, 1953).

James T. C. Liu, *China Turning Inward: Intellectual—Political Change in Early Twelfth Century* (Cambridge, Mass.: Harvard University Press, 1988).

Brian E. McKnight, *Law and Order in Sung China* (Cambridge: Cambridge University Press, 1992).

# SIGNIFICANT PEOPLE

## CHENG HAO

### 1032-1085
### BUREAUCRAT AND PHILOSOPHER

**Student.** In his early life, Cheng Hao traveled with his father, who was a magistrate, to various counties in Jiangxi, Anhui, and Henan. When he was only fifteen years old, Cheng studied with a Zhou Duni, famous philosopher of the time. In 1052 he went with his father to the capital, Kaifeng, and studied at the Grand Academy. In that year, Cheng gained the *Jinshi* degree.

**Official.** Cheng was appointed as keeper of records (assistant magistrate) in 1059. He was a wise judge and an effective official in preventing a famine, checking floods, and rehabilitating prisoners. He helped eliminate bureaucratic red tape, from time to time taking direct action before going through the usual chain of command. Sick people had to have certificates before obtaining food; he expedited the process by keeping rice in reserve for ready delivery without waiting for the presentation of certification. He reformed the tax on land and constructed dikes. When people were scared by the rumor of a dragon demon, he had the reptile caught to eliminate the superstition that it was a monster; when he saw people using sharp-pointed sticks to kill birds, he broke the sticks into pieces as a way of protest. In 1065 he was made magistrate of a county in Shanxi. He strengthened the local militia, made rich families sell their rice at low prices when it was needed, and called for conscription of men into the military according to family size. He organized community societies and invited elders to talk with him.

**Magistrate.** He built schools, dismissed unqualified teachers, personally edited texts for children while visiting schools, and encouraged moral education. His three years in the county made his subjects look on him as if he were their parent. The civilizing effect of his administration was so considerable that a little more than a decade later the county had produced hundreds of Confucian scholars.

**Censor.** In 1067 Cheng went to the capital as assistant staff author. In 1069 he was appointed commissioner of irrigation, and later in the year, at the recommendation of the censor in chief, he was promoted to undersecretary of the heir-apparent in the secretariat and interim investigating censor at large. Even the emperor had heard of his reputation and called him to an audience several times. During his months spent at the capital, Cheng submitted many suggestions in which he emphasized the Confucian way of government and the clear difference between a sage ruler and a tyrant. He proposed ten measures on teachers, government organization and functions, land boundaries, community relations, the reference of scholars, military service, food supply, condition of the people, natural resources, and rankings and ceremonies. Though not put into operation, these recommendations boosted his political fame and posed a strong challenge to the political establishment. In response to a request from the emperor, he recommended dozens of people for government positions, naming his uncle and his brother in the first line. He strongly opposed Wang Anshi's radical reforms, which included developing greater government revenue, increasing the size of the military, and expanding government participation in commerce and agriculture. In his discussion with the emperor, Cheng stressed the Confucian doctrine of sincerity and humanity and would not even talk about profit or success. This stance indirectly attacked the utilitarianism espoused by Wang Anshi.

**Demotion.** The conflict between the two men became open and bitter, and in 1070, after Cheng had been at the court for 263 days, he was demoted to the position of a signatory officer at the service of a regional commandant. In 1078 he was appointed a county magistrate in Henan. When he was in office, he equalized taxes and the price of rice, as well as restored order and peace. His father and brother were with him for several months. In 1080 his political enemies finally had him dismissed. Thereafter, for five years, he lived in poverty and devoted himself to the advancement of Confucian doctrines.

Philosopher. For a period of almost a decade he turned to Daoism and Buddhism, but he eventually returned to Confucianism. A man of warm and peaceful character, he fascinated ordinary people as well as great scholars. One of his students, who traveled with him for three decades, said that Cheng never showed any anger nor even uttered a harsh expression. His clarification of Confucian doctrine was so profound and his influence so significant that he was called Master *Mingdao* (illuminating the way). He was the first person to represent the authentic spread of the Way of the Sages. The highest honor came to him in 1235 when he was posthumously named the Earl of Henan by the imperial court and a sacrifice to him was ordered in the Confucian temple. He established the idealistic wing of Neo-Confucian thought and regarded *li* (principle) as the basic law of existence, particularly emphasizing the principle of nature. He strongly regarded the idea of production and reproduction as the chief characteristic of the universe and identified the spirit of life in all things. To him, this creativity was *Jen* (humanity, love), which removed all distinctions between the self and the other and combined Heaven, Earth, and man as one. All these ideas became cardinal principles in Neo-Confucianism that profoundly influenced the institutional development of the family during the Song dynasty.

Sources:
Carson Chang, *Development of Neo-Confucian Thought*, 2 volumes (New York: Bookman, 1957–1962).

Herbert Franke, ed., *Sung Biographies* (Wiesbaden: Steiner, 1976).

Frederick W. Mote, *Intellectual Foundations of China* (New York: Knopf, 1971).

# GENGHIS KHAN

## CIRCA 1167-1227
### FOUNDER OF THE MONGOL EMPIRE

Tribal Leader. The origins of the great Mongol leader Genghis Khan are obscure. Originally called Temüjin, he was the son of a Mongolian tribal chieftain poisoned by the Tatars. Forced into exile, he spent several years wandering, and during this time he developed a following and claimed the leadership of his tribe. Many who knew Temüjin found him to be quite charismatic and ruthless, a young man with strong leadership skills, great determination, and courage. He steadily defeated rival clans and tribes, and, at a great meeting of the Mongol tribes held in 1206, he became Genghis Khan, meaning "Universal Ruler." He claimed to be Heaven's chosen instrument and declared that those against him were in defiance of Heaven's will. As the supreme ruler he organized the Mongols into a keen fighting force and began military campaigns to conquer other territories to enlarge his empire.

Army. Clans and tribes represented the basic units of Mongol social organization, but at a higher level Mongols were bound together by loyalty to the Great Khan and by a law code first issued in 1206 and later enlarged. The Great Khan organized his army on a decimal system in units of tens, hundreds, and thousands. An elite corps of 10,000 men formed its core, and during campaigns the army had nearly 130,000 men in addition to an almost equal number of non-Mongol soldiers. Superb horsemen, the Mongols had a reputation for ferociousness and destructiveness, and the use of terror greatly aided them in their conquests.

Campaigns. In 1210 Genghis Khan invaded the Xi Xia kingdom, making it a tribute state and cutting China's trade routes to the Northwest. Five years later he captured Yanjing, the capital of the Jin dynasty (1115–1234), and sacked ninety other towns before turning westward to occupy Bokhara and Samarkand. For the moment he began to employ Chinese and Qidan officials and sent Mukhali, one of his most loyal generals, to govern the Chinese territory he had conquered. In 1226 he launched another campaign against the Xi Xia kingdom but died the next year. By the time of his death, he set up a great Mongol empire in Central Asia and dispatched military expeditions as far east as Russia. His headquarters remained in Mongolia, where Karakorum served as the capital, although it did not have any city walls or permanent buildings until 1235.

Aftermath. The death of Genghis Khan did not stop Mongol conquests. His sons divided the kingdom into four khanates: Persia, South Russia, Central Asia, and China. In 1231 the Mongols crossed the Yalu River to invade Korea and continued their advance in North China, taking the capital city, Luoyang, in 1234. In the same year they completely destroyed the Jin dynasty. However, it was not until 1279 that Kublai Khan, the Great Khan's grandson, completed the Mongol conquest of China and established the Yuan dynasty (1279–1368).

Sources:
Herbert Franke, *China under Mongol Rule* (Brookfield, Vt.: Variorum, 1994).

Adam T. Kessler, *Empire Beyond the Great Wall: The Heritage of Genghis Khan* (Los Angeles: Natural History Museum of Los Angeles County, 1993).

John Langois, ed., *China under Mongol Rule* (Princeton: Princeton University Press, 1981).

R. P. Lister, *Genghis Khan* (New York: Stein & Day, 1969).

Paul Ratchnevsky, *Genghis Khan: His Life and Legacy*, translated by Thomas N. Haining (Oxford: Blackwell, 1992).

Morris Rossabi, *Khubilai Khan: His Life and Times* (Berkeley: University of California Press, 1988).

# LI SHIMIN (TAIZONG)

## 598-649
### FOUNDER OF THE TANG DYNASTY

**Great Monarch.** Li Shimin, or Taizong, has been regarded as one of the greatest monarchs in Chinese history, though he obtained the throne by murdering his brother and forcing his father, also named Taizong, to resign. The founder of the Tang dynasty (618–907), Li employed a succession of capable ministers, who came to epitomize the ideal relationship between an emperor and his advisers. Conserving many characteristics of his father's government, he took a personal interest in the careers of regional officials and dispatched commissioners to check on the quality of their work.

**Imperial Clan.** Li employed some persons in the court from areas other than his native Northwest, but his government remained in the hands of aristocrats of the Northeast, identified as semibarbarians. During his administration the distance between the emperor and the ordinary people began to increase. An example of this tendency was Li's attempt to create the superiority of the imperial line above that of the four categories of clans, the leading families of the Northeast. He ordered a genealogy to be compiled in order to define the importance of various families throughout the empire, and later he rejected the first draft of the document in an effort to downgrade one of the great Hebei lineages. In 638 a revised national genealogy was issued, which showed the Li clan in a preeminent position.

**Foreign Wars.** In foreign affairs Li pursued a strong, expansive, and aggressive policy, beginning an extraordinary expansion of Chinese power into Central Asia. With the assistance of the Eastern Turks, Li successfully split the western Turks and restored Chinese influence in the Western regions as the Han dynasty (206 B.C.E.–220 C.E.) did. The military campaigns of 647 reduced the western Turks to vassals of the Tang court and advanced the empire to the borders of Persia. At the same time Li sent punitive expeditions against Korea, which had once been part of the Han empire and now was a tributary of the Tang. The Koguryo throne was overthrown in 640, and the new ruler came to pose a threat to the kingdom of Silla in southern Korea, Tang's faithful tributary. The threat of a unified Korea encouraged Li to take action, and in 645 he invaded Koguryo. The expedition made slow progress and had to be withdrawn because of severe winter weather. A similar campaign failed in Korea in 646. Li planned to launch an even larger campaign in 649, but he died before it could be realized. Ultimately Li pushed Chinese power farther West than had the Han dynasty and with Tang power expanded to the Pamirs Mountains (in present-day Tajikistan), trade flourished.

**Religious Life.** Li, like those emperors of the Sui dynasty (589–618), relied on religion to legitimize his reign. In 629 he ordered the construction of seven monasteries where prayers would be offered for the souls of soldiers killed in combat. Later he passed measures to control corruption in the Buddhist church. In 637 he issued an edict criticizing the prominent position that Buddhism had occupied and ordered that Daoist clergy would take priority over Buddhist clergy. In the same year a legal code was promulgated, which included a section regulating the Buddhist monks and restricting their participation in secular affairs. He was careful not to isolate the Buddhists, but like his predecessors he tried to keep the Buddhist establishment under control. Since the Tang emperors claimed descent from Lao Zi, founder of Daoism, Li also favored that religion. For example, he ordered Xuanzang, a famous Buddhist, to translate the Daoists' *Daodejing* into Sanskrit to benefit the Indian Buddhists. This text was included in the civil service examinations, which was a major stronghold of Confucian influence. In contrast to earlier dynasties, Li emphasized few rites centered on his own ancestors and was fond of more-public rituals performed by the emperor for the good of all.

**Education.** Li created a system of state schools and colleges, one of which was reserved for children of the imperial family and high-ranking officials. Many students came to Chang'an to study, and the state sponsored a variety of scholarly projects, particularly the writing of the histories of the empire, which served to legitimize the succession of the Tang dynasty. Examinations were held regularly. The great majority of officials continued to come from the great clans, but those who had passed one of the literary examinations could occupy the highest positions.

**Last Years.** In his last years Li was disappointed with his sons and heirs. The crown prince became so obsessed with nomadic ways that he lived in a yurt and later was deposed. The emperor's favorite son was too deeply involved in machinations over the succession to be trusted. In the end the succession went to a weak young prince who, after Li's death, became Emperor Gaozong.

Sources:

John Fairbank and Edwin O. Reischauer, *East Asia: Tradition and Transformation* (Boston: Houghton Mifflin, 1989).

C. P. Fitzgerald, *Son of Heaven: A Biography of Li Shih-min, Founder of the Tang Dynasty* (Cambridge: Cambridge University Press, 1933).

## QI JIGUANG

### 1528-1588
### MILITARY OFFICER

**Military Life.** Born to a traditional military family in Shandong, Qi Jiguang received a well-rounded education in the Confucian classics and literature in addition to the military arts. After assuming his father's rank in 1544, Qi Jiguang performed his duties well. One of his assignments was to take a Shandong detachment yearly to defend the Great Wall north of Beijing. He did this five times between 1548 and 1552. In 1549, after taking the military examinations, he received the military *Juren* in Shandong in 1549 but failed to pass the higher examination in Beijing a year later. As a result, he remained in the capital to perform some duty during that time when the Mongols broke through the Great Wall and reached the suburbs of Beijing. He participated in the defense of the city, and submitted a plan to fight the Mongols on the frontier.

**Coastal Defense.** Appointed as an acting assistant commissioner of the Shandong regional military commission in 1553, Qi was in charge of coastal defenses. Two years later, he was transferred to the Zhejiang commission in charge of the military farms. During that time the raids of Japanese pirates along the Zhejiang coast increased, and selected military offices were dispatched to the province to reinforce the local military organization with tactical commands. In 1556, Qi was appointed as assistant commander in charge of defending the area.

**Mandarin Duck Formation.** From the bitter experience of the Japanese pirates' assault, Qi created a plan to train volunteers to defeat the invaders. His plan was approved by the supreme commander in 1557, and three thousand men from that area received military training. One of his innovations in the training program was the tactical formation known as the "Mandarin duck," which was composed of basic units of twelve men each (one leader, two shield men, two soldiers with short bamboo lances, four soldiers with long bamboo lances, two fork men, and one cook). They advanced in that order or in two five-man columns dividing the weapons equally. Qi established the harsh regulation that all soldiers acted to protect the leader from being injured. If the leader lost his life during a battle that ended in defeat, any survivor in his unit was to be put to death. Thus, each soldier was trained in the spirit of win or die.

**Tactics.** During that time weapons were designed particularly to fight Japanese longbowmen and swordsmen renowned for their prowess. In Qi's tactics, the shield was to take care of the arrows, and the bamboo lance, with its bushy branches intact, could slow down the attack and entangle the swordsman, making it possible for the other lancers to kill him. Since the Japanese swordsmen were terrifying combatants, Qi recommended five-to-one odds, organizing four basic units to a platoon, four platoons to a company, and three companies to a battalion of about six hundred men. A few muskets were assigned to each company and a battery of cannon to each battalion.

**Victories.** In 1562 Qi led a relief expedition to Fujian against the Japanese pirates; after several victories, Qi returned to Zhejiang. Next year Qi was appointed vice-commander on the north Fujian coast, and at the end of 1563 he was transferred to Fujian, becoming area commander for the coasts of Zhejiang and Fujian. By 1567 Qi and his forces had cleared the Fujian coast of the Japanese pirates.

**Reasons for Success.** Qi's success against the pirates resulted from not only his selection and training of troops but also his defense plans and his close collaboration with civil authorities. During that time, there was a debate among military leaders on whether to meet the Japanese on water or on land. Because it was difficult to move men overland and there were not enough troops to deploy along the coast, some thought it was wise to meet the brigands on the sea. On the water, others argued, the pirates were in their element and at their best. Qi preferred to meet them on the land and set up a three-tiered defense system, which needed an early warning system on the islands off the coast of Fujian. This system proved successful in defeating the Japanese pirates.

**Northern Frontier.** A major reexamination of the defense of the northern frontier was under way at Beijing when the Mongols began to pose a threat to the capital. Recommended as a successful trainer of troops, Qi was appointed vice commander of the firearms division of the Capital Army in 1567 (his father held the post before him). In 1570 he was named junior commissioner-in-chief and became senior commissioner-in-chief, the highest military rank in the empire in 1574. He retired in 1585 and died several years later.

Sources:
L. Carrington Goodrich and Fang Chaoying, eds., *Dictionary of Ming Biography* (New York: Columbia University Press, 1976).

Albert Chan, *The Glory and Fall of the Ming Dynasty* (Norman: University of Oklahoma Press, 1982).

Charles O. Hucker, *The Ming Dynasty: Its Origins and Evolving Institutions* (Ann Arbor: University of Michigan Press, 1978).

## ZHU YUANZHANG

### 1328-1398
### FIRST EMPEROR OF THE MING DYNASTY

**Early Life.** Zhu Yuanzhang was born in Fengyang, an area under the influence of the White Lotus Society. Anticipating the coming of the future Buddha and the establishment of a "pure land," the White Lotus sect appealed to peasants. In 1351 the Yuan court enlisted thousands of men to work on rerouting the Yellow River, which incited the Red Turban rebellion. In just one year the revolt had swept through the Yangzi Valley and had restricted the Yuan army to Nanjing and the other major cities in the region. This turmoil had great impact on Zhu Yuanzhang. After the death of his parents in the famine of 1344, Zhu Yuanzhang first took refuge in a Buddhist temple, then became a beggar and finally a soldier. In 1352 he joined a Red Turban band under the leadership of Guo Zixing, which was active near Fengyang. In only one year Zhu Yuanzhang had enlisted twenty-four men from his native area and had married Guo Zixing's adopted daughter. In the next two years the imperial forces put down much of the rebel activity.

**Opportunity.** In January 1355 the insurrection flared up again. The leader of the northern Red Turbans claimed descent from the Song dynasty (960–1279) and declared himself emperor. By 1360 the Yuan empire (1279–1368) had totally lost control of the Yangzi valley, where several regional leaders had their own independent bases. In this situation, Zhu Yuanzhang was given an opportunity to rise to power.

**Rising.** Zhu Yuanzhang's military ability and skill in creating tactical alliances contributed to his victory. As his influence grew he heeded the advice of Confucian advisers and gained a reputation for taking care of ordinary people. By 1355 he had built a base camp and had organized an army. He took over Nanjing in 1356. When his forces occupied a town he created a new civil government staffed by scholar-officials, some of whom had previously served the Yuan government. He appointed officials to oversee the repair of river defenses and to promote the development of agriculture. Meanwhile, he slowly severed his relationship with Red Turban ideology and with the northern Red Turban dynasty, which collapsed in 1367. In these and other ways he demonstrated his eagerness to acquire the qualities associated with a Chinese emperor. In January 1368, defeating his main opponents and believing that the Mongols could not offer any resistance, he announced the founding of the Ming (Radiance) dynasty (1368–1644) and assumed the title of *Hongwu*.

**Reign.** Hongwu's first task was to control the rest of China, sending a military expedition to the north to force the Mongols from their capital, Dadu. After occupying the city, Hongwu renamed it Beiping, meaning "the north is pacified." Although Hongwu attempted to restore the practices of the Tang (618–907) and Song dynasties at the beginning of his reign, he actually sustained most of the features of the Yuan empire. He retained much of their military structure; the army continued to be treated as an occupational class commanded by hereditary officials. The same principles were used in early Ming government administration. Throughout his reign, claiming to take care of the welfare of his subjects, Hongwu ruled as a thorough autocrat. After his death he was buried in the suburbs of Nanjing.

Sources:

Edward Farmer, *Early Ming Government: The Evolution of Dual Capitals* (Cambridge, Mass.: Harvard University Press, 1976).

Carrington Goodrich and Fang Chaoying, eds., *Dictionary of Ming Biography, 1368–1644* (New York: Columbia University Press, 1976).

Ann Paluden, *The Imperial Ming Tombs* (New Haven: Yale University Press, 1981).

Romeyn Taylor, trans., *The Basic Annals of Ming T'ai-tsu* (San Francisco: Chinese Materials Center, 1975).

# DOCUMENTARY SOURCES

Sima Guang, *Complete Mirror of the Image of Government* (1084)—This book, a general history of China between 403 B.C.E. and 959 C.E., was the biggest and most famous of the historical works of the eleventh century. It took the author twelve years to write it. Sima Guang not only used a variety of sources, including literary works and inscriptions, but he also critically analyzed them.

Cheng Qiao, *Tongzhi* (Encyclopedia, 1162)—A collection of monographs dealing with the genealogy of great families, philosophy, phonetics, historical geography, botany, zoology, bibliography, archaeology, and other fields. This book was in use until the late eighteenth century. Scornful of the book learning of the literati and interested in the natural sciences, Cheng Qiao was a thinker admired by the intellectuals of his age.

Ouyang Xiu, *Xintangshu* (New History of the Tang Dynasty, 1060) and *Xin Wudai Shi* (New History of the Five Dynasties, 1070)—Implicit judgments on the period of chaos and partition between the end of the Tang dynasty (618–907) and the coming of the Song dynasty (960–1279). These moralizing trends, the stress laid on the problems of dynastic legitimacy, and the search for a moral meaning in history were typical of the Song times and in harmony with the new trends being adopted by Chinese philosophy.

Liu Zhiji, *Generality on History* (710)—Liu Zhiji heralded the scholars of the Song dynasty (960–1279) in his rejection of any irrational interpretation of the past, in his opinion of the necessity for books on cities and clans, and in his desire to analyze only human factors in history. *Generality on History* was one of the first works of this kind in the world, and it indicated a new trend in historiography that continued to develop into the eleventh century.

Qi Jiguang, *A New Treatise on Disciplined Service* (1560)—The successful training methods of Qi Jiguang, a famous military officer in the Ming dynasty (1368–1644), who organized an army to fight Japanese pirates. His methods included how to recruit his men chiefly from places near the area of conflict on the coast, to hire them with the help of the local magistrates, and to pay them well. His training methods proved very successful in defeating the Japanese pirates.

Zeng Kongliang, *General Principles of the Classic on War* (1044)—A treatise on the military art that details new kinds of weapons and novelties, including the mention of a paraffin flamethrower with a mechanism consisting of a double-acting piston that made it possible to produce a continuous jet of flame. It also describes troops equipped with incendiary weapons, sappers, and catapult personnel.

Detail of the handscroll *The Imperial Sedan Chair* depicting Emperor Taizong receiving a Tibetan envoy; Song dynasty, 960–1279 (Palace Museum, Beijing)

Detail of scroll showing military officers, Song dynasty, twelfth century (National Palace Museum Collection, Taipei, Taiwan)

## CHAPTER SEVEN

# LEISURE, RECREATION, AND DAILY LIFE

by GUANGQIU XU

## CONTENTS

*Sidebars and tables are listed in italics.*

**617\***

- Tea becomes a popular drink during the Tang dynasty (618–907), although it originated somewhere along the Burma-India border and was most likely introduced into China by Buddhist monks well before this period.

- Dragon-boat racing becomes a widespread recreation on the Yangzi (Yangtze) River and the West River in South China.

**620\***

- Influenced by central Asians, the Tang people begin to abandon their tradition of sitting on floor mats and accept the foreign habit of sitting on chairs and stools.

**626**

- Hair buns are being combed higher; hairstyles increase in number and become more complex.

**630\***

- The Tang court establishes a series of martial arts examinations and contests.

**640\***

- Tea Masters begin to appear in the Tang dynasty. They are responsible for buying teas, procuring pure tea water, and preparing tea for the family and guests. It is a sign of great prestige for the rich family to have a Tea Master on the household staff.

**660\***

- The curtained hat, a kind of bamboo headpiece with high top and broad brim, begins to appear and gradually replaces the covering kerchief.

**674**

- The Tang emperor decrees that purple, scarlet, green, and blue are to be worn only by officials with rank, while officials without rank and the masses are prohibited from using these colors because many unauthorized people are wearing them under their outer garments. Lower level officials and commoners are permitted to wear only yellow and white.

**700\***

- *Weiqi*, a board game known in the West by the Japanese name *go*, begins to appear and becomes a popular recreation in the following centuries.

**710\***

- The Tartat hat is fashionable, but in the following decades women opt for switch buns, called false buns.

- Clothing styles change when women no longer apply red powder to their faces; instead, they use only black ointment for their lips.

**715**

- The emperor builds a forty-five-meter structure laden with fifty thousand lanterns for the pleasure of the inhabitants of the capital.

\* DENOTES CIRCA DATE

**732**
- The Tang court orders that mothers or wives of officials dress according to the rank of their sons or husbands; women associated with men of higher than the fifth rank are allowed to wear mauve—those higher than the ninth rank can wear crimson.

**790***
- The design of turbans begins to change when the ear flaps, either round or broad, stick up a little, looking like stiff wings. This type of headgear is called the Stiff-Flapped turban.

**800***
- The Chinese invent paper playing cards.

**890***
- High hair buns are often decorated with different kinds of flowers.

**900***
- The turban becomes used purely as a hat by the end of the Tang dynasty.
- Li Ye flies a kite with a small section of bamboo fastened to it by a silk ribbon, and his kite creates a musical or whistling sound because of the vibration of the wind on the ribbon. Kites are thereafter named *fengzheng* (aeolian harps).

**938**
- Jurchen government leaders decree that officials of certain ranks may, as a sign of special respect, display lances before their gates.

**960***
- Teahouses begin to appear and become popular throughout China by the end of the Song dynasty (960–1279). They become social, entertainment, and cultural centers.
- Two types of handmade fans—flat and folding—begin to appear in China.

**970***
- The turban becomes the chief headgear of men. Civil officials and military officers, even the emperor, generally wear turbans when attending sacrificial rituals and significant court sessions.
- The Chinese begin to use high tables for eating, writing, painting, and praying at home and in temples.

**1000***
- Regional cuisines have been well developed by the time the Chinese support regional restaurants in capital cities. Sichuan cooking is distinguished from other styles by its spiciness and the use of mountain products and herbs. Cantonese cooking also appears in the capitals.

**1061**
- The *Illustrated Basic Herbal,* which illustrates and describes hundreds of foods, is published.

* DENOTES CIRCA DATE

**1100\***
- Li Jie completes a manual for palace-style building, *Yingzao Fashi* (Building Principles), which codifies the standards required for constructing wood-frame dwellings.

**1120\***
- After the rule of the Northern Song (960–1125), the styles of skirts change. The width of most skirts increase more than six fold and ruffles are employed.

**1140\***
- By the reign of the Southern Song (1127–1279), wrapping turbans become popular, and high-ranking officials at the imperial courts enjoy wearing them.

**1250\***
- Tea production is becoming an intensely commercialized agribusiness, completely different from peasant subsistence farming, toward the end of the Song dynasty, because monopolistic government control of tea production increases significantly, and the cult of the teahouse develops along with other refined arts of life.

**1280\***
- Mooncakes begin to appear at the Moon Festival. Stamped on top with pictures of the Moon Goddess, Chang E, or with favorable Chinese characters, mooncakes are buns filled with a sweet paste made of lotus or watermelon seeds or red dates, which stand for the fertility of the season.

**1330**
- Imperial physicians present to the emperor a monograph, *Essentials of Dietetics,* including entries on antelope, bears, various deer, tigers, leopards, marmots, swans, pheasants, cranes, and many other wild animals and birds. Although some of these animals are used for medicinal purposes, most of them are regarded as food.

**1360\***
- The folding fan becomes the main style of fan used by artists, intellectuals, and scholars, who frequently draw flowers and write poems on fans for their colleagues.

**1368\***
- The Ming government organizes contests to promote the expansion of the martial arts.

**1368-1399**
- During the reign of Emperor Taizu, ordinary people can neither have designs on their boots nor decorate them with gold thread.

**1370\***
- Chen Wangtin develops the martial art of *taijiquan,* also known as Supreme Pole Boxing; it combines graceful moves with spiritual meditation.

\* DENOTES CIRCA DATE

**1379**
- The Ming court (1368–1644) decrees that common people, government runners, merchants, physicians, and diviners can wear only leather boots, while officials, their fathers, brothers, paternal uncles, brothers' sons, and sons-in-law can wear satin boots.

**1380***
- The lion dance becomes popular among villagers in Guangdong province to scare away wildlife that has killed many people and domesticated animals.

**1393**
- The Ming government codifies a new set of costume rules to encourage people to undertake the extensive reform of dress, bringing about the reinstatement of clothing worn during the Tang and Song dynasties.

**1397**
- The Ming declares that no matter how wealthy a commoner is nor how many houses he holds, no hall can surpass in width three *jian*, a space between two support beams in a row.

**1500***
- Mahjong based on tarot cards is introduced to China from Europe and soon becomes a popular recreation in the Ming dynasty.

**1506-1521**
- During the reign of Emperor Wuzong, merchants, officials with rank, servants, prostitutes, actors, and all "mean" people are forbidden to wear sable.

**1522-1567**
- Women's hairstyles become more varied during the reign of Emperor Jiajing.

**1530**
- The ground-nut (peanut) is mentioned for the first time in Chinese books.

**1555**
- Mentioned for the first time by books in Honan, maize is high yielding and easy to grow even in hilly and poor soil, and its cultivation spreads rapidly in Ming China.

**1594**
- The Fujian governor encourages people to eat sweet potatoes, which were introduced to China in the later half of the sixteenth century, for famine relief; these tubers become an important food source for poor families.

**1630***
- By the end of the Ming dynasty, switches (hair extensions) have become more varied and popular.

* Denotes Circa Date

# OVERVIEW

**Foodstuffs.** The old reliable foodstuffs—millet, rice, pork, beans, chicken, plums, spring onions, and bamboo shoots—remained popular in Tang times (618–907). Wheat vastly increased in importance, too. When the Tang dynasty came to power and war-like Turkish nomads of the steppes became allies of the new empire, more-refined foods were adopted from foreign lands. Little cakes fried in oil became particularly popular. Recipes for these cakes may have come from India. Wine was imported from the Tarim River basin, kohlrabi (cabbage) was imported from Europe by way of the Silk Road, and pistachio nuts were brought from Persia. By Song times (960–1279), rice became more essential, reaching its modern level of importance as the great staple of China; while wheat was more common in the south, flour was becoming a vital food too. The poor in South China, unable to find money to buy rice, used flour as their staple. Flour was most often made into noodles, still a common food of rich and poor alike in South China. Sugar, which began to be used during the Song period, was more available during the Ming era (1368–1644) because of new processing technology and a subsequent increase in acreage devoted to cane cultivation.

**Consumption Patterns and Tastes.** By the start of the Song dynasty, Chinese agriculture and food styles were firmly established; food production became more balanced and scientific. The increase in food available during the Song to Yuan or Mongol (1279–1368) periods was essential because Chinese agricultural methods and productivity would not improve dramatically again until the twentieth century. By the end of the Ming period, food consumption patterns and tastes were relatively established. Seventy percent of grain consumed was rice, while the rest was wheat. Sugar, oil, and tea all reached an importance similar to that of modern times. Diversified and specialized farming of fruits and vegetables was extensive, but it was most prevalent in areas with good land and excellent infrastructure, especially the Yangzi valley and southern China. In Ming times new food products from the Americas began to be distributed in the provinces by three main routes: shipped through southeastern coastal ports; brought across land routes through southeast Asia into Yunnan; or transported by the traditional silk route from Persia and Turkey. The most significant crops introduced into China were maize, sweet potatoes, peanuts, and potatoes.

**Cuisine.** Song-era cooks benefitted from both the agricultural and commercial revolutions; they enjoyed, especially in the two capitals, a new abundance, which most likely made city inhabitants the best-fed population in world history at that time. Material abundance contributed to the development and modification of attitudes about food. The elite and middle classes produced some of the greatest cuisine, not only for the Chinese but also for people around the world. Tang food was not complicated, but by the late Song period a complex cuisine with regional specialties was well developed. The rise of local bourgeoisie populations was partially responsible for the introduction of new recipes. Beginning with simple tribal cooking, such as that of the historic Mongol tribes, the Song people developed quite complicated cuisines, based on familiar ingredients but utilizing intricate processing that came to characterize Chinese culinary art. Imperial tastes remained more expensive, but royal recipes were less innovative than those of the merchants and local gentry. Song food was spiced with local and imported condiments, particularly ginger, cassia, brown pepper, nutmegs, and a variety of Indian and Near Eastern perfumed fruits and seeds. During the Yuan period the Chinese appeared to have been little attracted to Mongol cuisine. In the Ming dynasty people began to restore Song cuisine styles.

**Tea Culture.** Tea, called the oil of Chinese civilization, is a bridge between peoples. Tea, which originated somewhere in the Burma-India border kingdoms, was most likely introduced to China by Buddhist monks. Tea arrived well before the seventh century and became the most popular drink in the following centuries throughout the country. During the Tang dynasty more people enjoyed tea, which became a major example of the importance of westward influence at that time. Beginning in the Han dynasty (206 B.C.E.–220 C.E.), a host offered a cup of welcoming tea to a guest. By the Tang dynasty, hosts served "Greeting Tea" to every visitor, a custom already widespread during the Song Dynasty, when Chinese tea manners were formalized. The Tang invented the position of Tea Master, but the Song created the teahouse. After the first teahouses became successful, they grew rapidly to rival taverns in number. By the end of the Song dynasty, teahouses were spread throughout the country even to small distant villages and had become an important gathering place in Chinese daily life. The Mongol occupation was a vital moment in China and in the history of tea. During their short rule the use of loose tea, created by the Song, became more popular, setting the stage for its prevalence in Ming times. The greatest Ming contribution to tea drinking was the introduction of flower-scented teas. With plentiful, cheap flowers available, Ming people made scented teas that the middle classes could afford.

**Housing.** A remarkable continuity of form and layout is characteristic of Chinese dwellings from earliest times through the late imperial period. No conspicuous innovations in material or building techniques interrupted the evolutionary process and no striking differences emerged between monumental and more-plebeian buildings. For both types of structures, earth and wood rather than stone were the principal building materials, even when alternatives were readily available. Convention and sumptuary regulations influenced size and proportion, establishing scale and refinement of decoration as the principal means of differentiation. Flexibility, guided by a sense of precedence related to patterns of human relationships, generally ordered the utilization of interior space. Chinese houses emphasized convention rather than novelty. From the Tang to Ming dynasties, the government regulated the size, number of rooms, design, and ornamentation of houses for the aristocracy, officials, and commoners. The number of *jian*, the space between two support beams in a row, was regulated in every dynasty.

**Dress and Costumes.** The Tang dynasty was the wealthiest period in Chinese history. Chang'an, the capital, was the political, economic, and cultural center of the empire. About seventy foreign states had relations with the Tang during different periods. Inhabitants of Chang'an included Uygurs, Tibetans, Nanzhaos, Japanese, Koreans, Persians, and Arabians. People often traveled to and from such countries as Vietnam, India, and the East Roman Empire, and Chang'an thus distributed Chinese culture to other parts of the world. All the national minorities and foreign envoys who crowded the streets of Chang'an contributed something of their cultures to China. As a result, painting, carving, music, and dance of the Tang incorporated foreign skills and styles. The Tang court adopted every exotic form, whether it be types of hats or clothing. Tang costumes became more charming and beautiful. The styles of women's costumes, for example, reached an unparalleled level. At the beginning of the Yuan dynasty, the Mongolians, with an undeveloped economy and nomadic cultures, emphasized the simplicity of their clothing. However, influenced by the Han people of the Central Plains, they also became more splendidly dressed and developed a comprehensive system for costumes. After the establishment of the Ming dynasty, emperors abandoned the rules and regulations for costumes created by the Yuan dynasty. Following the custom of the Han people, the Ming undertook extensive reform of dress, reinstating costumes worn during the Tang and Song dynasties. This restoration started in 1393 when new rules were codified. Dress was also a main indication of social status. Official garments differed in design and color in proportion to rank. They were worn at the imperial court and in the course of official duties, at wedding rituals and sacrifices, and at less formal family gatherings. When officials retired or resigned, they were permitted to retain their official garments, and a corpse could be clothed at interment according to the rank of the deceased. Some colors were set aside for official garments, while others were designated for use by ordinary people. Within these categories preference differed from dynasty to dynasty, but when the line of separation was identified, it had to be obeyed.

**Games.** The Chinese were tremendously fond of games during the medieval ages. *Bo* was a game of dice played by two persons with 6 black and 6 white pieces each on a board of 12 squares. *Shupu*, a more complicated version of *bo* invented in the fourth century, was played by five people using 20 pieces of 5 different colors and 5 marked bamboo sticks on a board divided into 3 sections of 120 squares each. Another similar game called *shuangliu* became popular in the Song era (960-1279), and spread to Japan. This game, similar to backgammon, was played by two persons using 16 pieces each and 2 dice on a board divided into 8 sections. *Yi*, played by two persons, had 120 black or white pieces each on boards with 17 rows of 17 squares. Also known as *weiqi* or *go* (Japanese name), the goal of this game was to encircle as many pieces of the opponent as possible. *Xiangqi* (Chinese chess) was more complex. It was played by two persons using 16 red or black pieces each on a board divided into two parts of 32 squares each.

**Dice and Dominoes.** The Chinese also liked to play games with dice and dominoes. *Majiang* was played by four persons with 136 tiles marked by suits of symbols while *tianjiu* (dominoes) was composed of 32 pieces. Beginning in the Tang dynasty (618-907), some games were played with *yezi* (cards). In addition, the Chinese were famous for their puzzles, such as *qiqiaoban*, which became known as Tangram in Europe, and *jiulianhuan*, a complex ring game. Games of chance, such as guessing the victors of national examinations or the names of famous historical persons were favored by the Chinese, too.

**Other Leisure Activities.** Children's game and toys included shuttlecock, flying the kite, windmills, self-righting dolls, and an assortment of dolls made of clay, wood, or straw. In games of competition, there was cockfighting, bullfighting, and cricketfighting. People also engaged in rowing or tug-of-war competitions. During medieval times the Chinese also enjoyed the martial arts. They embraced techniques based on spiritual training close to yoga, such as *taiji*. They also developed a style of fighting without weapons, such as the forms created by the monks of Shaolin in Tang times. In the thirteenth century the Mongols developed wrestling.

# TOPICS IN LEISURE, RECREATION, AND DAILY LIFE

### CITY LIFE IN TANG

**The Capital.** The emperors of the Sui dynasty (589–618) built Chang'an as a political statement, and those of the Tang dynasty (618–907) rebuilt and enlarged it for the same reason. By the early Tang period Chang'an was large, with outer walls stretching about six miles along the east-west axis and five and a half miles along the north-south axis. These walls, five yards high, were covered with bricks and formed a perfect rectangle around the city. The emperor's palace, surrounded by a square wall, was located at the center of the city, with the market to the north and both the temple to the imperial ancestors and shrine of the earth to the south. The emperor and imperial family lived in the palace, which was not open to the public.

**Regulated City.** Chang'an was a planned and highly regulated city. Internal walls divided the city into more than one hundred smaller quarters, mainly for safety reasons. Each quarter had gates that operated according to curfew. Gates were opened in the morning and closed and locked at night. Soldiers on horseback patrolled the streets and people had to remain indoors. City government sustained a complex system of drum towers that proclaimed the time. Local officials, in order to collect taxes and recruit soldiers, forced the residents to register in each quarter.

**Government Offices.** South of the palace were offices of the imperial government, including buildings that held the meetings of six boards: revenue, civil appointment, rites, works, punishments, and war. The emperor met with the chiefs of these six boards to discuss significant state affairs. Other departments were responsible for official correspondence and documents.

**Foreigners.** The center of the foreign quarter was the Western Market, where a large non-Chinese population, about one-third of the city total, lived. China had about one million foreign residents, half of whom lived inside Chang'an. These foreigners built their own institutions dedicated to the religions practiced in their homelands. Persian-speaking businessmen worshiped at temples devoted to faiths they brought with them from Iran. They sacrificed live animals at Zoroastrian fire altars and sang hymns about the power of light triumphing over that of darkness at Manichaean temples. Travelers from Syria practiced Nestorianism, their form of Christianity, believing that Christ had two different characteristics: the human from his mother, Mary, and the divine from his father, the Lord.

**Merchants.** Since Chang'an was located at the end of the Silk Road, many merchants in the city were involved in this lucrative trade, bringing exotic goods all the way from Persia and India eastward and from Japan westward. These merchants were richer than those who worked with their hands. Many people envied their wealth, even though it created prosperity in Chang'an. Sumptuary laws, however, limited the size and types of decoration of houses, though merchants had ways to circumvent these laws. Government officials not only policed their lifestyles but also forced merchants to operate their businesses in only two markets under strict supervision. In addition, officials were especially suspicious of all merchants involved in long-distance trade. Regarding them as potentials spies, officials maintained strict surveillance over traders as they traveled from one city to the next. Travel documents were inspected at every checkpoint, and the ownership of all animals and slaves in the caravans was scrutinized.

**Markets.** The two markets in Chang'an were large, each covering about one kilometer square, and were located at the confluence of two transportation systems—the imperial roads and canals. The markets opened only at noon and closed at dusk. The Western Market specialized in foreign goods, while the Eastern Market focused on locally produced items such as salt, tea, silks, precious metals or jewels, slaves, grain, timber, and horses.

**Silk.** Silk was an essential good during the Tang dynasty, although the secret of making it had already proliferated beyond the borders. In Tang times silk served different functions; it was a currency equivalent in value to silver bars and copper coins, and most peasants paid some of their taxes with bolts of silk. The material, however, continued to be used for fashioning clothes, often ornamented with elaborate foreign drawings, worn by wealthy people.

**Market Supervisor.** The imperial government tightly controlled commerce and trade in Chang'an. Two market directors enforced government rules. These supervisors could penalize traders for any offense against public order, and they were responsible for checking weights and measures and the quality of goods on sale. Since there was a chronic shortage of bronze coins (made out of copper, lead, and tin), bolts of silk served as the main currency, sometimes supplemented by silver coins brought from Iran. Thus, market officials also regulated the quality of money in circulation. Their main task was to prevent unfair trading practices such as cornering the market on commodities and deceiving buyers. Every ten days they issued new prices for three grades of each basic good. Sellers of livestock, slaves, or land had to apply to their offices for a certificate of sale. Therefore, traders endured a high level of government control.

**City Inhabitants.** The life of common people in the city was simple. They ate basic meals, often only twice each day. Most families shared one or two rooms. The poor were frequently forced to pawn their possessions, on which they made installment payments every two months. When families were pressed for funds, they generally pawned clothing or bolts of silk, but sometimes they offered carpets or copper mirrors.

**Work.** Many people were employed in such menial jobs as maintaining shops, working on gardens, cleaning streets, feeding horses, and peddling goods. When they fell ill, they received medicine from Buddhist clinics, although many commoners who lived outside of the capital did not have this service.

**Prostitution.** City officials regulated houses of prostitution, which were located in the eastern market. Prostitutes, who had been deserted by their husbands or parents or had been abducted, worked for women whom they called their fictive mothers. These madams taught the prostitutes to sing, dance, and play drinking games. Limited to this district, these prostitutes could leave only if their customers posted a bond. Men could pay additional money to gain the exclusive services of an individual woman.

**Relocation.** Insufficient grain supplies created another problem for the common people in the city. In the seventh century repeated canal blockages compelled the emperor to move the capital from Chang'an to Luoyang, a city in the east, located on a better section of the canal system. This relocation burdened commoners in the city, especially working people, because they had to do the carting of materials over a longer distance.

**Taxation.** As the life of urban inhabitants was highly regulated, so too was it for people living in rural areas. The Tang court set up a common and uniform system of household registration, land distribution, taxation, martial conscription, and labor service. Theoretically, a peasant in the northwest, where there was a shortage of good land, was

---

## ORDINARY PEOPLE IN TANG

**B**o Juyi, a great poet in the later Tang period (618–907), paid close attention to the misery of the poor. Here is one of his poems.

An old charcoal seller

Cuts firewood, burns coal by the southern mountain.

His face, all covered with dust and ash, the color of smoke,

The hair at his temples is gray, his ten fingers black.

The money he makes selling coal, what is it for?

To put clothes on his back and food in his mouth.

The rags on his poor body are thin and threadbare;

Distressed at the low price of coal, he hopes for colder weather.

Night comes, an inch of snow has fallen on the city,

In the morning, he rides his cart along the icy ruts,

His ox weary, he hungry, and the sun already high.

In the mud by the south gate, outside the market, he stops to rest.

All of a sudden, two dashing riders appear;

An imperial envoy, garbed in yellow (his attendant in white),

Holding an official dispatch, he reads a proclamation.

Then turns the cart around, curses the ox, and leads it north.

One cartload of coal—a thousand or more catties!

No use appealing to the official spiriting the cart away:

Half a length of red lace, a slip of damask

Dropped on the ox—is payment in full!

**Source:** Po Chü-yi, "An Old Charcoal Seller," in *Sunflower Splendor: Three Thousand Years of Chinese Poetry*, edited by Wu-chi Liu and Irving Yucheng Lo (Bloomington: Indiana University Press, 1975), pp. 206–207.

---

entitled to the same allocation of property to support his family as a peasant in southern China, where there was much more land. Peasants were required to pay the same taxes and perform similar military and labor obligations—twenty days of service each year. Officials performed inspections to calculate all members of a household and to find out which young men had come of age and were qualified for military and labor obligations. They also classified the elderly and the crippled, who qualified for different degrees of tax immunity. On the basis of information contained in these registers, officials divided the population into nine grades that defined each man's level of taxation and labor service. Many people, including the imperial family and all their relatives, were exempt from paying taxes. Monks and nuns, recorded on separate household registers, paid no taxes and performed no labor service.

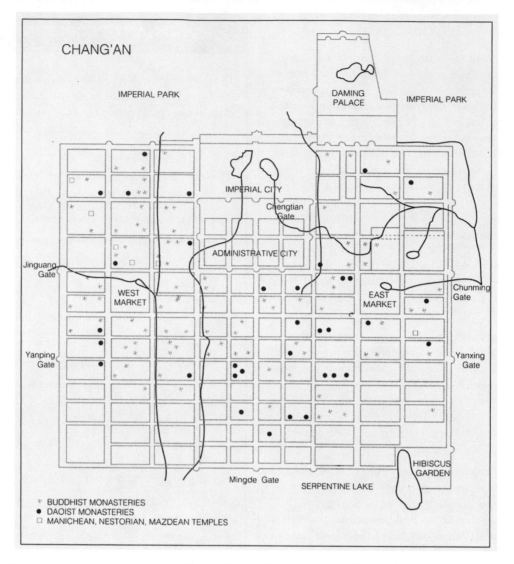

CHANG'AN

IMPERIAL PARK

DAMING PALACE

IMPERIAL PARK

IMPERIAL CITY

Chengtian Gate

ADMINISTRATIVE CITY

Jinguang Gate

WEST MARKET

EAST MARKET

Chunming Gate

Yanping Gate

Yanxing Gate

Mingde Gate    SERPENTINE LAKE

HIBISCUS GARDEN

⚛ BUDDHIST MONASTERIES
● DAOIST MONASTERIES
☐ MANICHEAN, NESTORIAN, MAZDEAN TEMPLES

Diagram of the Tang capital city (from Patricia Buckley Ebrey, *Cambridge Illustrated History of China,* 1996)

Merchants who owned no land paid few taxes because commercial taxes were extremely light. Many people fabricated personal information, so government registers showed too few people and too little occupied land throughout the empire. A constant lack of funds resulting from these inefficiencies plagued the Tang dynasty.

**Celebrations.** The lunar New Year signaled the coming of spring and the time of grand celebration. On the fifteenth day of January the lantern festival was celebrated. On this day commoners did not have to go to work and had a chance to eat meat, the only time each year they were able to do so. For the rest of the year they ate wheat and millet gruel, supplemented by vegetables. They visited their relatives in the city or went out of town to worship at temples. In 715 the emperor built a 45-meter-high structure laden with fifty thousand lanterns for the pleasure of the inhabitants of Chang'an.

**Sources:**
Hugh R. Clark, *Community, Trade, and Networks: Southern Fujian Province from the Third to the Thirteenth Century* (Cambridge & New York: Cambridge University Press, 1991).

Patricia Buckley Ebrey, *The Aristocratic Families of Early Imperial China: A Case Study of the Po-ling Tsui Family* (Cambridge & New York: Cambridge University Press, 1978).

John Curtis Perry and Bardwell L. Smith, eds., *Essays on T'ang Society: The Interplays of Social, Political and Economic Forces* (Leiden: Brill, 1976).

Edward H. Schafer, *The Vermilion Bird: T'ang Images of the South* (Berkeley: University of California Press, 1967).

Denis Crispin Twitchett, *Financial Administration under T'ang Dynasty* (Cambridge: Cambridge University Press, 1963).

Arthur F. Wright and Twitchett, eds., *Perspectives on the T'ang* (New Haven: Yale University Press, 1973).

## CLOTHING AND SOCIAL STATUS

**Official Colors.** From the Tang (618–907) to Song (960–1279) dynasties purple, scarlet, green, and blue were kept exclusively for use by officials with rank, while all others were prohibited from using them. In 674 the emperor issued a decree to enforce this policy because many unauthorized people were wearing these colors under their outer garments. In the early Tang period officials without rank and commoners were permitted to wear only yellow and white; in later years ordinary folk were permitted to wear black. In Ming times (1368–1644) males were allowed to wear garments of various colors except yellow. Females were permitted to wear purple, green, peach, and other light colors, except scarlet, blue black, or yellow. Their formal clothing might be dyed purple.

**Lower Classes.** Customarily regarded as inferior to commoners, merchants had the colors of their clothing regulated from time to time. Since slaves, servants, actors, prostitutes, and government runners were considered humble and were not on the same level as commoners, their dress was distinguished from all others. In Tang times male and female slaves wore yellow and white dresses, but female slaves could also wear blue and green outfits. In Yuan times (1279–1368) prostitutes wore black-purple clothes and males in their families bound their heads with blue scarves. In Ming times actors wore green scarves; musicians only wore bright green, pink, jade, peach, and tea-brown, with red or green belts; and singing girls wore black vests. Government runners in the early days wore black robes, which were later colored light blue.

**Materials.** The fabric in one's clothing differed in accordance with one's social status. Brocade or embroidery, and all varieties of fine silk, were worn only by certain persons. In Tang times only highly ranked officials were permitted to wear fine silks; ordinary people and slaves wore coarse silks and wool. Government runners were allowed to wear only coarse silks. During the Ming dynasty commoners were permitted to wear plain gauze silks but not brocade. The use of gold embroidery and shiny materials was severely regulated; those who violated the regulations were penalized, and the offending garment was confiscated. Among the four classes of common people only farmers could wear coarse silks, gauze, and cotton. Merchants wore only coarse silks and cotton. Moreover, if a member of an agricultural family was a merchant, no one in that family could wear ordinary silk or gauze. Buddhist and Daoist monks in Ming times were permitted to wear only coarse silk and cotton.

**Furs and Hats.** During Ming times, merchants, officials without rank, servants, prostitutes, actors, and all people of lower class were prohibited from wearing sable. Hats also were regulated. In Yuan times common people were not permitted to ornament their hats with gold or jade. During the Ming dynasty, officials without rank and commoners were not permitted to wear hats with buttons on top, and all ornaments had to be of crystal or sandalwood. Cap rings could not be made of gold, jade, agate, coral, or amber.

**Shoes and Boots.** During the Tang dynasty women in the families of officials without rank and ordinary people were not permitted to wear boots or shoes of certain colors. In Yuan times the commoners were not permitted to have designs on their boots. In early Ming the lower classes could neither have designs on their boots nor embellish them with gold thread. In 1379 the Ming court decreed that common people, government runners, merchants,

Minister Jiang Shunfu (1453–1504), wearing the first-rank civil badge depicting cranes (Nanjing Museum, Nanjing)

physicians, and diviners could wear only leather boots, while officials, their fathers, brothers, paternal uncles, brothers' sons, and sons-in-law could wear satin boots.

**Jewelry.** From the Tang to Ming dynasties common people were not permitted to wear jewelry of jade, gold, or silver. In Tang days commoners could wear only copper and iron. In Song times officials with rank could put jade, gold, silver, or rhinoceros horn on their belts, while common people, artisans, and merchants could use only copper, iron, or black jade for embellishment. Differences were also identified in minor items of decoration. In Yuan and Ming times officials of the first, second, and third ranks were permitted to have fine gauze curtains ornamented with gold flower designs; those of the sixth rank and below were permitted to use plain fine gauze; ordinary people were allowed coarse silk. In Ming times officials of the first through fifth ranks could have their mattresses and comforters made of fine hempen cloth, brocade, or embroidery; those from the sixth to ninth ranks were permitted fine silk gauze, ordinary silk, or coarse silk; and common people could use only ordinary silk, coarse silk, or lower-grade cloth.

**Women.** A woman's social standing depended on the status of her father before marriage and on that of her husband or son after marriage. The mother or wife of an official was given the right to wear certain garments, which varied according to the rank of the husband or son, at weddings and other occasions. Dresses and ornaments of these women were distinguishable from those of lesser-ranked wives. In 732 the Tang court ordered that mothers or wives of officials could dress in line with the rank of their husbands or sons; those higher than the fifth rank were allowed to wear mauve, those higher than the ninth rank crimson. In Yuan times the mothers and wives of officials of the first, second, and third ranks could wear gold dresses; fourth- and fifth-ranked women could use gold vests; and sixth-, seventh-, eighth-, and ninth-level women could wear spangled-gold vests. Common women were not allowed to wear such clothing.

**Limitations.** In Tang through Yuan times only mothers and wives of officials with rank were permitted to wear gold, pearls, and jade. Women commoners, no matter how rich their family, were banned from wearing them. In Song times lower-class women were prohibited from embellishing their dresses with spangled gold, splashed gold, or pearls. Yuan women of the sixth rank could wear gold ornaments but could only use pearls for earrings. Ordinary women were allowed chrysoprase hairpins, gold hairpins, and earrings of gold or pearls; all other embellishments had to be of silver. In Ming times the mothers and wives of officials of the first and second ranks could put on gold, pearls, chrysoprase, and jade; those of the third and fourth ranks gold, pearls, and chrysoprase; of the fifth rank gold and chrysoprase; from the sixth rank down gold-washed silver and pearls. Ordinary women could wear head adornments of gold, pearl earrings and silver bracelets. Any other embellishment made of valuable stones or pearls was confiscated.

**Utensils.** Only the imperial family could use gold and jade utensils. In Song times only officials of third rank and above, and members of the imperial and consort families, could use utensils with gold corners. Officials of the first, second, and third ranks could use tea or wine utensils made of gold or jade. Those of the fourth and fifth ranks could use only gold cups. Those of the sixth rank and below could use only gold-plated cups. Ordinary people were allowed wine pots and cups made of silver. In the Ming dynasty dukes, marquises, and officials of the first and second ranks used wine pots and cups made of gold, while all other utensils were made of silver. Officials of the third, fourth, and fifth ranks used gold cups, but silver was used on their wine utensils. Those of the sixth rank and below used wine utensils made of silver. Ordinary people used wine pots made of tin and cups made of silver, with all other utensils made of porcelain or lacquer. In Ming times ordinary people and Buddhist and Daoist monks were prohibited from using gold-decorated furniture and gold or silver wine utensils.

Sources:

Valery M. Garrett, *Chinese Clothing: An Illustrated Guide* (Hong Kong & New York: Oxford University Press, 1994).

Tung-tsu Chu, *Law and Society in Traditional China* (Paris: Mouton, 1961).

Zhou Xun and Gao Chunming, *5000 Years of Chinese Costumes* (San Francisco: China Books and Periodicals, 1987; Hong Kong: Commercial Press, 1987).

## CLOTHING FOR MEN

**Turbans.** Men's costumes during the Tang dynasty (618–907) were composed largely of turbans, gauze hats, and robes with round collars. The turban was made of silk. Unlike kerchiefs the four corners of the turban were deliberately cut into ribbon forms, two of which were tied at the back of the head so that they hung free, while the other two were first folded upward and then tied together at the top of the head. Therefore this headdress was named the upfolded turban. After the mid-Tang period designs of turbans underwent additional changes. The flaps, either round or broad, when stuck up looked like stiff wings, hence this design was called the Stiff-Flapped turban. By the end of the Tang dynasty the turban had evolved differently from the kerchief category, becoming a hat. The gauze hat, worn by Confucian scholars and solitary persons, was the common headdress for such events as imperial court congregations, hearings in the law courts, and formal banquets and receptions. Although the design differed according to the tastes of the wearer, people paid greater attention to new and unique patterns.

**Song Cap.** The Tang turban became the principal headgear worn by the Song dynasty. From the emperor down to civil officials and military officers, turbans were usually worn, except for participation in sacrificial rituals or significant court gatherings, where coronets were required. The most famous characteristic of the Song turban, which actually had developed into a cap, with two "legs"—filled with supporting wire, string, or bamboo strips, mounted with satin and gauze, and bent into various shapes—which were called straight, curved, or crossed according to their design. The first type was customarily used by emperors and officials; the second and third were worn by staff, assorted public servants and couriers, and musicians, who were of low social status. Covered with gauze, the turban initially had a rattan lining; a coat of paint was applied to the gauze to resist deterioration. The rattan lining was later eliminated, once it was discovered that the painted gauze was strong enough, and the cap was afterward called the paint-and-gauze turban. Tang turbans were normally made of black gauze, while those of the Song were not restricted to that color. At special events, such as weddings and banquets, bright colors were acceptable. Some turbans had gold silk threads, which were made into a variety of designs and attached on top.

**Wrapped Turban.** As turbans changed into caps worn by all civil and military officers, common people no longer wore them. Scholars and students gradually returned to wearing the wrapped turban, as they considered it extremely elegant. Called the scholar's wrapper, this type of headdress had a high crown and short brim. There were also other wrapping turbans, such as scholar Chen's wrapper, vale wrapper, high scholar wrapper, and uncontrolled wrapper. By the Southern Song dynasty (960–1125) the wrapping turban became so common that even high officials wore them. As a result, people slowly forgot the rules governing the coronet.

**Yuan Headgear.** During the Yuan dynasty (1279–1368) headgear for Chinese officials was almost the same as the turban, similar to those worn during the Song dynasty. The upturned turban was worn by the staff and servants and

Man's dragon robe, seventeenth century (Hong Kong Museum of Art)

was made of lacquered gauze with two tails stretching out on either side. Worn by gentlemen and scholars, such turbans followed the Tang type, their two tails slanting down behind the head to create a "/ \" shape. Common people wore turbans according to their individual tastes. Many Mongolian men wore ridged hats made of rattan strips, while some preferred bamboo hats. They wore their hair in plaits in different patterns; split it in the middle of the crown to create a cross; shaved the back of the head; trimmed the bangs in the front into different forms, such as square, pointed, or peach-like; or let their hair hang unaffectedly over the brow, plaited on either side of the cross and fastened into a ring that reached the shoulders.

**Ming Turban.** During the Ming dynasty (1368–1644) turban designs largely were the black gauze cap, net turban, quadrangular flat-topped turban cap, and six-in-one cap. Officials usually wore black gauze caps during routine court gatherings. Officials wore turbans when presenting reports or showing gratitude to the emperor. The shape of the turban was like those worn during Song times, but it featured ends that were stretched apart like straight rulers. Knitted of good black thread, horsetail, and palm thread, the net turban was a sort of hood that bound hair buns. A net turban not only maintained one's hair in place, but also

it indicated a man's age. Net turbans were customarily worn underneath coronets, although they could be used individually. The quadrangular flat-topped turban cap, made mostly of black satin, was the normal cap for bureaucrats and intellectuals and was so named because of its right angles at the four corners. Worn customarily by ordinary people, the six-in-one cap, frequently called small circular skullcap, was a patchwork of six caps of gauze. Several other styles of caps were displayed during Ming times, such as the tall scholar's turban, fidelity coronet, and sun-shading cap.

**The Robe.** Sporting a round collar, the robe was the main style of men's costumes in Tang times. Ordinary people and officials often wore robes as casual dress, but not during sacrificial rituals. Most robes were made of fabrics woven with veiled-pattern designs and in different colors to demonstrate the rank of the wearer. In the lower half of the robe there was generally a horizontal band. This kind of apparel was called the band robe and it continued to be the official dress of scholars through the Song dynasty.

**Boots.** In the days of Tang, men frequently wore boots, formerly part of the Tartar gear. Later, not only military officials but also civil officials and even ordinary people were permitted to wear them, though there were different types of

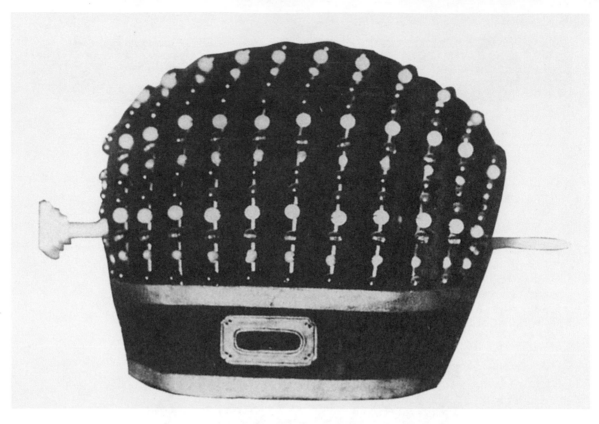

Black silk hat decorated with gold thread, jade beads, and a jade hairpin, from the tomb of the Wanli emperor, Ming dynasty, 1368–1644 (Museum of Dingling)

boots. Although prior to this period one had to wear shoes when entering the imperial court, in the Tang dynasty boots were also tolerated.

**Simplicity.** The growth of idealist philosophy in the Song dynasty influenced the lifestyle of the people, whose opinions of aesthetics changed noticeably. In paintings, for instance, simplicity and delicacy were appreciated; inks and light colors were favored. The desire for simplicity was even more obviously revealed in clothing and related adornment, when people opposed too much display in dress. Therefore, clothing of the Song dynasty was rather moderate and conservative, with fewer differences and quieter colors, expressing a sentiment of simplicity and unaffectedness.

**Official Dress.** In Song times government officials wore mostly robes with round collars, except for sacrificial rites. These robes were of various colors—such as purple, crimson, red, blue, or green—to show rank and status. Although regulations concerning the proper styles and colors were created in the Tang dynasty, the Song government continued them. Officials of the sixth rank and above could have robes of purple or crimson with gold and silver fish-pockets—originally used to hold a "fish tally," an adornment made of copper used to identify rank—hung around their waists. This three-inch-long ornament was carved with Chinese characters; afterward it became a badge to indicate rank, and it was cut into halves. One half was kept in the imperial court and the other piece in the local government. At the time of promotion the two halves had to be presented as proof of existing rank. The pass used for entering or leaving palace or city gates was also fish shaped. Since a fish's eyes are open day and night, they were believed to stand for continuous watchfulness, which explains the significance of the shape of passes. According to the regulations of the Tang dynasty, all officials above the fifth rank were granted fish pockets to hold their tallies. Although the Song court no longer used the fish tally, the fish pocket was not abandoned and was still regarded as a great honor when worn. When officials of lower ranks were sent on uncommon missions, such as diplomatic ones, they were required to borrow special robes before departing, which were called borrowed purple or borrowed crimson.

**Yuan Robes.** The robe was the principal costume in Yuan times. Officials wore muslin robes similar to the Han model, with loose sleeves, round collar, and buttons on the left-hand side; the body length generally was long enough to touch the toes. Various colors were used to indicate different ranks. Single-color clothes ranks, with respective specifications, were used by the emperor and aristocrats at court feasts. Made of a special brocade, these clothes had a plentiful diversity of designs, each with its own adornments. For example, there were twenty-six different designs for the emperor alone and more than twenty styles for civil and military officers. In everyday life both aristocrats and common people wore tight-sleeved gowns; less frequently they wore short-sleeved over-jackets, as were favored by servants and entourages. Mongol men wore cuffs that were taut and under the robe over-trousers, which had neither waist nor crotch but were basically trouser-legs fastened to the belt.

**Ming Officials.** Clothing for men in Ming times indicated a restoration of traditional characteristics, and the gown became popular for men. Court garments for officials employed traditional rules, which called for the wearing of coronets or caps and formal costumes. In significant sacrificial rituals all civil and military officers, no matter their rank, were obligated to wear coronets or caps with their formal attire. Ranks were distinguished by the number of strips mounted and type of ribbon fastened on the strap. When participating in routine court meetings, an official normally wore his ordinary civic costume, which usually was composed of a black gauze cap, circular-collared upper garment, and leather belt. The early Ming government decreed that officials had to wear the over-gown as their ordinary dress, decorated with embroidered square patches that featured birds for civil officials and animals for military officers. Different designs were created for all nine official ranks as an index of hierarchical status.

**Civic Costumes.** Costumes and trimmings for men of other social classes were identified during the Ming dynasty. Government servants wore lacquered cloth coronets decorated with peacock feathers and knitted girdles of red cloths round their waists. Policemen of lower rank wore small caps, blue clothes with outer waistcoats of red cloth, and blue knitted girdles. Wealthy businessmen wore dresses of silk, satin, or gauze; they cautiously avoided being excessively obvious by confining the colors to blue or black. Yet, they adorned their collars with white gauze or satin to single themselves out from servants and government administrators.

**Masses.** The formal dress for common people during the Ming period could only be made of coarse purple cloth; gold embroidery was forbidden. Gowns could only be in such light colors as purple, green, and pink. Under no circumstances were commoners allowed to wear crimson, reddish blue, or yellow. These regulations were enforced without any major changes during the Ming dynasty.

**Footwear.** Officials usually wore boots or closed toe shoes, called court shoes, while scholars and pupils often wore black double-vamp shoes. Most ordinary people wore normal shoes; in the southern regions they preferred straw sandals. Since the climate in northern China was cold, commoners wore leather boots with erect stitches. Women who had bound feet wore bow shoes with tall soles made of camphor wood. The shoes had external wooden soles, decorated with perfumed leaves, lotus seeds, or lotus flowers. Shoes with internal soles were named interior tall soles or Daoist priest's coronets.

Sources:

Tung-tsu Chu, *Law and Society in Traditional China* (Paris: Mouton, 1961).

Richard L. Davis, *Court and Family in Sung China, 960–1279: Bureaucratic Success and Kinship Fortunes for the Shih of Ming-chou* (Durham, N.C.: Duke University Press, 1986).

Zhou Xun and Gao Chunming, *5000 Years of Chinese Costumes* (San Francisco: China Books and Periodicals, 1987; Hong Kong: Commercial Press, 1987).

## CLOTHING FOR WOMEN

**Covering Kerchief.** Women's headdresses went through several phases of development, from the kerchief, which covered the whole body, to the comparatively revealing curtained hat and Tartar hat that became popular later. The covering kerchief was made of thin transparent silk gauze, a style initially worn by men and women of the western national minorities. In the Tang dynasty (618–907) men became less interested in this fashion, and women continued to wear it only when they traveled far from home and were afraid of being seen by men on the road.

**Tang Curtained Hat.** During the reign of Tang emperor Gaozong the use of the curtained hat became popular and slowly surpassed the covering kerchief. Also called the mat hat, the curtained hat was a sort of bamboo headdress with tall top and broad brim. Around the brim, either on two sides or at front and back, a piece of net-like curtain hung down the neck. In later modifications the curtain was replaced by a black silk kerchief that wrapped the two sides of the head so that the entire face was uncovered.

**Tartar Hat.** The Tartar hat, originally used in western China, was usually made of brocade and black sheep's wool. The top of the hat was narrowed and covered with a pattern of flowers; some hats were inserted with jewelry.

**Tang Hairstyles.** Tang women wore buns of many types that were decorated with various sorts of embellishments, such as gold and bright green hairpins, together with combs made of rhinoceros horn. In early Tang, hair beautification was quite simple, but during the reign of Emperor Taizong the buns became taller and increased in number. During the earlier years of the reign of Emperor Xuanzong the Tartar hat was fashionable, but in late Tang many women chose switch buns, called false buns, and high buns were often ornamented with various kinds of flowers.

**Facial Appearance.** Women of the Tang dynasty valued facial appearance, and the application of powders or rouge was popular. Some women's foreheads were painted dark yellow; dark blue was adopted to paint eyebrows in different styles. There were dozens of methods to paint the eyebrows; colorful decorations—made of specks of gold, silver, and bright green feathers—were often placed between the brows. Some women painted their cheeks with designs, such as a moon or coin, and applied rouge to their lips. However, during the reign of Emperor Xuanzong costumes were altered, and women did not apply red powder to their faces. They used only a black salve for their lips and made their eyebrows look like Chinese characters.

**Tang Jackets and Skirts.** The primary costume for women in early Tang times was the small-sleeved short jacket and long skirt with waist fastened under the armpit. After the mid-Tang period, sleeves became bigger and collars had various shapes: round, square, and slanting straight. Some collars were worn without undergarments to cover the bosom. Skirts were similar to those worn in previous dynasties, but the texture, colors, and designs, as well as embellishments, were different. The hundred-bird feather skirt was somewhat popular among aristocratic women, but the garnet skirt was more frequently worn by commoners until the Ming dynasty (1368–1644).

**Tang Upper Garments.** Apart from robes and jackets, Tang women also wore a kind of upper garment, named half-covered arm. Only maids of honor wore this item at first, but later on it became a fashion among commoners. Yet, in stricter families women were not allowed to be dressed in this kind of garment. As a result, its attractiveness dropped after midway in the Tang period, and a system of capes emerged to replace it. The imperial court ordered that ordinary people should put on shawls before and capes after marriage.

**Song Styles.** Hairstyles for women of the Song dynasty were similar to those of the Tang, and the high bun was the most popular design. Women's buns were frequently more than one foot in height, and some young women's buns were combed into a heavenward design. Switches were usually used to make this type of bun. Women of wealthy families generally had hairpins and combs—made into the shapes of flowers, birds, phoenixes, or butterflies—that were pinned on top of the buns.

**Song Coronet Combs.** The coronet comb was another kind of headgear in vogue during Song times. It was a high ornamental wreath or band made of painted yarn, gold, silver, pearls, or jade, with two loose-hanging patches hanging over the shoulders, and a long comb of white horn set on top. Since these combs were almost one foot long and were heavy with ornaments, the wearer had to turn her head to one side when entering a carriage or going through a door. This type of coronet was popular in the northern Song dynasty.

Sleeveless court vest belonging to Empress Dowager Li, made for her fiftieth birthday in 1595
(Asian Art Museum of San Francisco)

Blouse and dress worn by a noble woman, Ming dynasty, 1368–1644 (from Valery Garrett, *Chinese Clothing,* 1994)

**Song Pin Flowers.** It was popular in Song times to pin flowers on the coronet. Inheriting the fashion of the Tang, Song women created artificial flowers, such as peach, apricot, lotus, chrysanthemum, and plum. Some even combined different flowers and mounted them on the coronet. This custom was not restricted to women. The emperor and high-ranking officials also wore flowers as ornamentation on their headgear on important occasions.

**Song Head Covers.** When Song women left home, they wore a head cover, most probably a derivation of the turban. Women also wore this type of headdress on their marriage day to cover their faces. The representative of the bridegroom's family raised the veil softly to expose the "flowery face." This custom continued in the Ming dynasty.

**Song Upper Garments.** Song women's upper garments were composed of coat, blouse, loose-sleeved dress, over-dress, short-sleeved jacket, and vest, which were often of muted, mixed colors, such as light blue, whitish purple, silver grey, and bluish white. Lower-class women usually wore jackets. Coats were worn in wintry weather and blouses in summer. The blouses were generally made of silk or satin. The over-dress was commonly worn by women in the Song dynasty, such as the empress, emperor's concubines, servants, attendants, slave actresses, and musicians. Men wore them, too, but customarily within the official dress. The short-sleeved upper garment and waistcoat (without sleeves) were basically the same for commoners.

**Song Skirts.** The lower garment skirts were usually made of strong colors such as green, blue, white, and apricot-yellow. Skirt styles in Song times were inherited from preceding dynasties, including the crimson skirt, double butterfly skirt, and embroidered satin skirt. Noble women had their skirts dyed in tulip juice; when worn they produced a flow of perfume, which was extremely attractive. After the Northern Song period skirt style underwent some minor changes. The width of most skirts, for example, was enhanced more than six-fold and sported ruffles in the middle, historically named one-hundred-folds or one-thousand-folds. Such skirts were worn with a silk belt tied around the waist and a ring of ribbon sagging.

**Song Shoes.** Song women rarely wore boots because they were not compatible for bound feet. Consequently they wore footwear made of satin or silk and embroidered with various patterns, such as embellished, brocade, phoenix, and gold-thread shoes.

**Yuan Styles.** The robe was the leading item of clothing for Mongolian women and was customarily buttoned on the left-hand side. Upper-class Mongolian women often wore hats, whereas Chinese women generally combed their hair into buns.

**Ming Hairstyles.** In the early Ming period women's hairstyles were similar to those of the Song and Yuan dynasties, but they became increasingly diverse. Among them was the peacock bun, with the hair combed flat and circular with expensive stones pinned on top in a flowery pattern. Some women combed their hair tall, laced it with gold and silver thread, and then embellished it with pearls and hard, deep-green precious stones. Seen from a distance, this type of hairstyle was similar to a man's gauze cap. Some women copied a well-liked Han style known as the dropping-from-the-horse bun, in which the hair was coiled upward and laced so that it swayed at the back of the head. The switch bun was made on a ring fixed firmly with iron wire in a style widespread in former times. The drum, false hair one and a half times as tall as normal, was fixed firmly on top with hairpins. There were various styles of switches; noted ones included the hat bun, idler bun, pair-of-soaring-swallows bun, and the bun that loosened on contacting the pillow. Some buns were ready-to-wear and available in jewelry shops and continued to be fashionable in the late Ming dynasty.

**Ming Hair Clasps.** In Ming times young women wore hair clasps, initially constructed of palm fiber, which was formed into a net to hold the hair. Clasps made of yarn and satin became popular later. The clasp form changed frequently and gradually narrowed. By late Ming times these decorations had been transformed into narrow strips fastened onto the foreheads, named the marten-cover-on-brow and the fish-woman's tie.

**Ming Commoners.** Clothing for ordinary women in Ming times comprised primarily gowns, coats, rosy capes, over-dresses (with or without sleeves), and skirts. These designs were similar to those of the Tang and Song dynasties, although they were somewhat modified.

**Ming Elite.** Mothers and wives of officials observed strict rules for their dress. There were two major types of clothing: formal and informal. Titled women wore formal dresses when meeting with the empress; getting together with uncles, aunts, or husbands; or going to sacrificial rituals. The outfit consisted of the phoenix coronet, pink cloak, loose-sleeved shirt, and over-garment. During the Ming government special rules were established for substance, color, prototype, and size in order to forbid certain classes from wearing clothes that did not match their rank. For instance, a loose-sleeved shirt could only be pink, and a sleeveless embroidered cloak or over-dress could only be blue-black. Size was also given for each part of the formal dress. Informal clothes of titled women included a long coat and long skirt. Since rules for informal clothes were

Painted wooden figurine showing women's dress, excavated from the tomb of a Chinese official, Xinjiang province, Tang dynasty, 618–907 (Chinese Historical Museum, Beijing)

less severe, women could wear all sorts of gauze, satin, or silk; border ornamentations, however, were fixed.

**Fans.** The Chinese used fans to stimulate the fire in a home to keep it burning or to drive away insects. As time went on, fans were created in different shapes. In the Song dynasty (960–1279) there were two types of fans made by hand: the flat fan and folding fan. The flat fan was invented in the Han dynasty (206 B.C.E.–220 C.E.) and was made by attaching

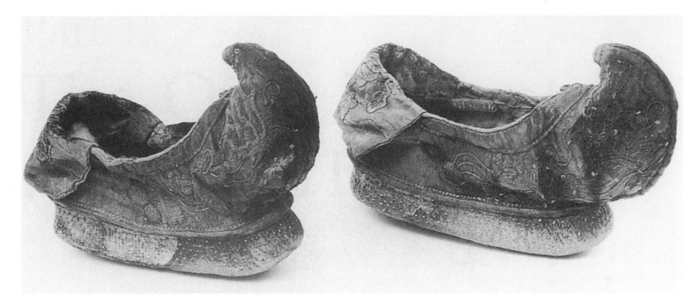

Shoes with embroidered uppers and stitched soles made for bound feet, Ming dynasty, 1368–1644 (from Valery Garrett, *Chinese Clothing*, 1994)

pieces of paper or silk to wooden handles. The folding fan, created in Japan in the seventh century, arrived in China via Korea in the eleventh century and was made from small strips or ribs of bamboo or sandalwood that were attached. After the eleventh century many Chinese artists ornamented flat and folding fans with bird-and-flower paintings, embroidery, and calligraphic inscriptions or poems. The Chinese even mounted and framed the painted pieces of silks or papers for fans as pictures for exhibition, instead of attaching them to handles. The artists frequently carved scenes into the wooden frames. The Chinese also made expensive fans from feathers or woven bamboo, dried grasses, palm leaves, or wheat straw. By the Ming dynasty, the folding fan had become the main style used by artists, intellectuals, and scholars. On average a man's fan usually had twenty or twenty-four ribs and a woman's fan thirty or more.

**Jade.** The Chinese regarded jade as the most precious material, believing that it had supernatural healing qualities because it was so hard and seemed eternal. Its intensity and fineness were linked to the qualities of intelligence, decency, power, immortality, and integrity. Since it was too hard to be carved or cut exactly, jade had to be worn down by using an abrasive and water. Only diamond drills were capable of drilling holes in the gemstone. This time-consuming, careful process for carving jade no doubt enhanced its value. During the age of imperial China (618-1644) many well-off Chinese began to use such jade implements as hairpins, earrings, belt hooks, and lucky charms. Some bowls, plates, cups, and chopsticks, were also made from jade. It was also used to make containers and rests for brushes, table screens, and signature seals as well as figures of plants, humans, animals, and fruits. Even the emperors held jade scepters as sign of their supremacy. As the gemstone produced an enjoyable musical sound when hit, pieces of it in different shapes were suspended on frames to create musical instruments. Many religious statues were carved in this material, especially Buddhist deities, *guanyin* (the goddess of mercy) with bowl-shaped lotus flowers

(the Buddhist emblem of purity), and the Eight Immortals (eight superhuman figures representing good fortune in the Daoism).

**Sources:**
Donald Altschiller, ed., *China at the Crossroad* (New York: H. W. Wilson, 1994).

Arthur Cotterell, *China: A Cultural History* (New York: New American Library, 1988).

Tung-tsu Chu, *Law and Society in Traditional China* (Paris: Mouton, 1961).

Richard L. Davis, *Court and Family in Sung China, 960–1279: Bureaucratic Success and Kinship Fortunes for the Shih of Ming-chou* (Durham, N.C.: Duke University Press, 1986).

Brian Hook, ed., *The Cambridge Encyclopedia of China* (Cambridge: Cambridge University Press, 1991).

Dorothy Perkins, *Encyclopedia of China: The Essential Reference to China, Its History and Culture* (New York: Facts on File, 1999).

Howard Wechsler, *Offerings of Jade and Silk* (New Haven & London: Yale University Press, 1985).

Zhou Xun and Gao Chunming, *5000 Years of Chinese Costumes* (San Francisco: China Books and Periodicals, 1987; Hong Kong: Commercial Press, 1987).

## FOOD

**Rice.** During the Tang dynasty (618–907) millet was the staple food in northern China, while a variety of rices became popular in the south. The introduction of double-cropping (planting twice a year) of rice in southern regions was the most significant change in Chinese food and agriculture. Thereafter, people had sufficient food to support themselves, which encouraged immigrants to settle in these newly secured lands. Although some Chinese had moved south since the Han dynasty (206 B.C.E.–220 C.E.), the region did not experience large-scale settlement until the Tang dynasty. For this reason, unlike northerners who called themselves the Han, the Cantonese in the South spoke of themselves as people of Tang. In the deep South, the regional diet was based on rice and tubers. Yams and taro, regarded as uncivilized food, became major staples for the local people, while rice became the universal preferred

Mural showing scholars at a banquet, Tang dynasty, 618–907 (from Patricia Buckley Ebrey,
*Cambridge Illustrated History of China*, 1996)

food for the Chinese from that time on. During the Song period various grades of rice appeared, with wealthy individuals favoring the more-expensive white polished rices.

**Wheat.** In the North, where both wheat and millet were grown, the use of crop rotation continued to expand. New milling methods more easily produced flour from wheat. Millet was the daily staff; wheat was a luxury food. Wheat was cooked into dumplings and noodles; small breads, covered with sesame seeds and baked in the sides of large ovens, were popular in Tang times. People also liked to eat wheat-flour cakes of various kinds. (Noodles, or spaghetti, are usually considered a Chinese invention, although no one knows for certain. They were first consumed in China in the Han dynasty, 206 B.C.E–220 C.E.)

**Dairy.** The Chinese were never intensely fond of milk products, but in Tang times powerful Central Asian influences meant that dairy foods were more widely consumed. Since the royal family was of part-Turkic background, cream, yogurt, cheese, curds, and butter were popular. Consumption of dairy products peaked in China at this time. Dairy foods were still widespread and popular in the Northern Song period (960–1125), but in later Song, people in the south became less interested in these products. After the Song court moved to the southeast, Central Asian power was weakened in the country, and the northern dynasties were regarded as enemies. Thus, dairy products came to be a symbol of the barbarian and enemy.

**Yuan's Dairy Food.** In Yuan times (1279–1368) Central Asian foods were again favored. The Mongols enjoyed cream, butter, and all kinds of milk products. Mare's milk was of great daily and ritual significance. When Yunnan province in southwest China was occupied by the Mongols, yogurt was introduced and became popular among other ethnic groups. Central Asian foods, such as grape wine and wheat products, were in demand.

**Fish.** An important source of protein came from fish, which were plentiful in the lakes and rivers; prepared raw fish was considered a major luxury. Freshwater fish were usually accessible because most major inland cities were located near rivers. While ordinary Chinese were unfamiliar with saltwater fish, freshwater fish dishes became universal and were often prepared for special occasions. The consumption of fish began to outpace that of chicken during the Tang dynasty, and by the Song period chicken had almost vanished from the Chinese diet. Not only did fish become more significant as a food, but also all water creatures became culturally important and intensely loved. Fish raising was an industry in the Southern Song period.

**Sushi and Meats.** The golden age of Chinese sushi manufacturing occurred during the reign of the Southern Song (1127–1279). Sushi was made of rice, vinegar, oil, raw fish, and meats. The meats were usually cooked. Initially, pork was a sign of wealth or luxury; most peasants ate chicken only a few times a year. Sheep, goats, and even donkeys were also eaten. People ate beef, but they often had a sense of disgrace while eating it because of the impact of Indian religions on China. Poultry—such as chickens, ducks, geese, quail, pheasants, and game birds—was plentiful. Swans were rarely seen from the Yuan period onward.

**Fat-Tailed Sheep.** Mongols consumed heavily the fat and connective tissue of the buttocks of the fat-tailed sheep, a variety that appeared in Central Asia and was often used to pull small carts. When cooked, the meat took on a rubbery texture. The fat had a special flavor, stronger but more enjoyable than mutton; it was probably the favorite food in Central Asia. Boiled mutton was almost certainly the chief food besides grains. Mongol recipes were strongly influenced by Arabic-Persian or Turkic cooking, while Chinese traditions were most visible in their preparation of vegetables.

**Game.** Antelope, bear, deer, tiger, leopard, marmot, both tundra swans, pheasants, cranes, and many other wild animals and birds were standard Mongol fare. Some animals, such as the tiger and leopard, were hunted for medicinal purpose only, but most were regarded as food.

**Vegetables and Nuts.** Buddhism resulted in extensive vegetarianism and the development of an assortment of products that were substituted for meat. Song people ate such vegetables as cabbages, onions, garlic, spinach, turnips, radishes, cucumbers, gourds, eggplants, cresses, carrots, and many others, particularly domestic and wild greens. Pine nuts, almonds, chestnuts, and walnuts were also popular.

**Sweet Potatoes.** By the end of the Ming period New World foods became well known to the Chinese. Presented by the Spanish and Portuguese, these crops were spread principally from Manila by returning Chinese merchants. Macau was one of the most important ports of entry, while some plants appear to have been carried across the mountains from India. Sweet potatoes were the most significant borrowing, coming into China in the second half of the sixteenth century. Brought by the Spanish from Mexico, they may have first appeared in Manila. Some scholars believe they were brought overland from India to Yunnan. In China they were called the golden tuber or white tuber.

**Maize.** The Portuguese found that maize grew much better in a tropical environment than any other crops they had planted. Introduced into China when Europeans reached East Asia, maize may also have come into the empire by sea routes or overland from Yunnan. Highly productive and easy to grow even in hilly and poor land, maize plants spread quickly all over China, although the Chinese did not mention it in their records until 1538.

**Tou Fu.** Bean curd, called Tou Fu (tofu), was invented in the late Tang period, but it was not widely used until the early Song period. Buddhists had long sought substitutes for meat and dairy foods. They put sea salt into bean milk to preserve it, and the resulting coagulation was a delicious food, which became more and more popular.

Drawing of laborers processing sea salt, Ming dynasty, 1368–1644 (from Arnold Toynbee, *Half the World*, 1973)

Painted scroll showing the various stages of rice production, Yuan dynasty, 1279–1368
(Smithsonian Institution, Washington, D.C.)

**Sweets.** Dates, cardamom, galangal, citrus, cassia, banana, litchi, and other fruits were among the important crops grown in the South. Iced and brought to the Tang court by couriers, litchis and other subtropical fruits were considered great delicacies and were enjoyed by the emperors. Popular fruits included pears, apples, mulberries, jujubes, persimmons, Chinese quinces, tangerines, mandarin oranges, apricots, haws, arbutus, peaches, plums, pomegranates, and coconuts. Fruits were often dried or candied with white sugar, which became more obtainable. Sugar was used to preserve foods and make all kinds of sweetmeats and candies, including little models of humans, animals, birds, flowers, and fruits.

**New World Crops.** Tobacco and several minor food crops were also brought into China by the Spanish in the sixteenth century. Several such crops grown in South China were the tomato, guava, and pomegranate. Introduced from the New World, they were typical of the Latin American plants that Iberians chose and distributed extensively. At the same time the Chile pepper was well-received throughout most of south and east Asia. In Ming China it became fashionable to use this spice, particularly in Hunanese cooking. By the end of the Ming dynasty New World food crops were significant even in distant regions of China.

**Salt.** The Song government controlled the distribution of salt, but officials were somewhat lax about enforcing regulations in the early days. After the control was strengthened, merchants were licensed under increasingly severe limitations on the trade in salt, and the government gathered much revenue. Salt was produced from seawater; the crystals took shape when the water evaporated. They were

then purified and boiled down. In another method ashes were scattered on the fields before flooding, thus capturing the natural salts crystallizing on the plants. These methods were of profound importance to the Chinese diet because they preserved in the salt such trace minerals as potassium, iodine, magnesium, manganese, copper, and irons present in seawater and plant ash. The latter was especially wealthy in potassium. The plant-ash method also helped maintain an individual's sodium-potassium balance. The heavy consumption of salt was healthier for the Song than for Westerners because the Chinese plant-based diet was so high in potassium. In western China, however, salt was produced from wells and therefore not as rich in trace minerals.

**Tribal Foods.** People living during the Song period (960–1279) became more dependent on rice, but people in areas controlled by the northern dynasties continued to depend on millet. Other northern grains appeared in some quantity. Buckwheat was not present among the Mongols in Central Asia, although it was important in China and grew well in dry and cold areas. Mongolian and Jurchen peoples habitually lived the life of hunting, herding, fishing, and small-scale farming. Hunting was regarded as significant in keeping men in fighting shape. Liao emperors took pleasure in their fishing trips. Dairy products, soured or fermented, were the most important animal products eaten by the Jurchen and Mongols. Yogurt, sour cream, cheese, and other products were made from the milk of many animals, but sheep's milk was the most essential and was consumed in huge quantities. In addition, they had fruit trees, such as apple, and gathered mulberries, jujubes, wild onions, and leeks. They also had a variety of melons, including a unique Persian variety. Tribal peoples consumed as much meat as they could, but their animals were too important for use in dairy products and transportation to be killed unless under special circumstances. Nevertheless, the herds, through selection and natural deaths, provided a supply of meat for most commoners, except for the poorest tribesmen. Additionally, marmots and birds were part of the diet.

**Dishes.** The Song people ate a considerable variety of dishes. At a single banquet there might be more than two hundred different dishes, ranging from ordinary rice to fruits and sweetmeats. Soups, pies, dumplings, noodles, and snacks were popular. The small pastries were more diverse, frequently bigger, and more substantial than modern counterparts. There was a great variety of cakes. Restaurants became famous for specific dishes. Breakfasts in the towns and cities were composed of tripe, steamed hotcakes, and fried puff-pastry shreds. Light lunches, often purchased from street peddlers, included sweet congee and other cakes. Blood soup, tripe soup, and other soups were plentiful. In the capital, special restaurants served local foods, prepared both hot or cold.

**Regional Cuisine.** Different cuisines were popular in the capital city since people supported regional restaurants. Northern cuisine was based on meats, dairy products, and dry-grown grains, while southern cuisine used rice and aquatic foods. Southwestern cooking was well known for its spiciness and use of mountain products and herbs. Regional restaurants often served homesick immigrants. Residents enjoyed minced meat and noodles with fish and shrimp common to Yangzhou or the spicy food of Sichuan.

**Cookbooks.** Tang was the golden age of China, famous for its unparalleled poetry and arts. In the development of Chinese culinary arts, however, the period was not particularly significant. The first Chinese cookbooks and nutrition textbooks were published at this time. Recipes were included in encyclopedias, which described hundreds of different foods. The invention of printing during the Song period made medical works and recipe books available to ordinary people. The Song emphasized the relationships between health and diet and published many recipe books of medical inspiration. Certainly, much of the amplification and variety of Song cuisine was owed to medicine. The Chinese word *fang* was both a medical and culinary phrase.

**Religious Impact.** In Song times Daoists began to withdraw from their diets the five grains, meat, and other supposed contaminants. Buddhist abandonment of meat, onions, and garlic had an important impact on Chinese cuisine. Special restaurants and temple cafeterias catered to these congregations and became popular when inhabitants were looking for a variety of foods.

**Imperial Diet.** The imperial court enjoyed the most luxuries, operating the largest grocery store and dining hall in the world. The imperial kitchen staff reached 9,462 workers in the mid fifteenth century, but decreased to 7,874 in the sixteenth century. More than 200,000 animals were sacrificed each year, including 160 pigs, 250 sheep, 40 young bullocks, 18,900 swine, 17,900 sheep, 32,040 geese, and 137,900 chickens.

Sources:
E. N. Anderson, *The Food of China* (New Haven: Yale University Press, 1988).

K. C. Chang, ed., *Food in Chinese Culture: Anthropological and Historical Perspectives* (New Haven: Yale University Press, 1977).

Frederick J. Simoons, *Food in China: A Cultural and Historical Inquiry* (Boca Raton, Fla.: CRC Press, 1991).

Reay Tannahill, *Food in History* (New York: Stein & Day, 1973).

## HOUSING

**Villas.** In Tang times (618–907) country villas contained multiple courtyards surrounded by lavishly furnished buildings that held splendid ornaments. They sometimes had gardens that contained mock mountains and pools. Those buildings, using modular systems of construction, indicated that wood-frame construction had completely developed by the tenth century.

**The Great House.** Two-story buildings became popular in Tang times. Both the main central structure and side

Detail of a village house from the scroll *Odes to the State of Pin,* thirteenth century (Metropolitan Museum of Art, New York)

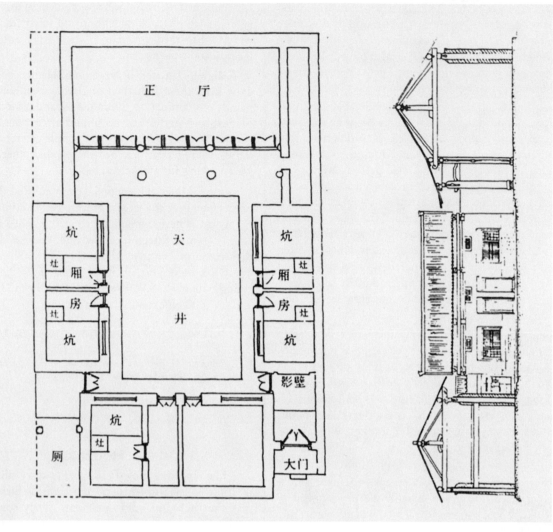

Plans of the oldest standing dwelling in Beijing, showing characteristics of a Ming-style residence
(from Ronald Knapp, *China's Old Dwellings*, 2000)

wings had second stories. Inside the house there were delightful murals, modern-looking chairs and tables, large free-standing screens with landscapes painted on them, and a big wood-framed and paneled settee or bed on which several people could sit or lie down simultaneously.

**Song Hotels.** There were various kinds of houses in the cities of the Song dynasty (960–1279), many of which were moderately simple structures containing small suburban restaurants or wineshops. Most hotels had two stories, and the upper levels had rooms that opened to a balcony. The decorative structure of bamboo over the hotel entrance served as a kind of advertisement or signboard.

**Ming Dwellings.** In Ming times (1368–1644) the fully developed dwellings of the wealthy, such as palace and temple buildings, included a range of common attributes because comprehensive sumptuary policies directed the size and ornamental decoration according to the owner's rank and status. Peasants, even as they became wealthier, were prevented from building large dwellings except in regions far from imperial power. Since the Tang dynasty ordinary

people were lawfully allowed only to build houses that did not exceed three bays. There were many different types of two-story dwellings in compact villages and towns. They generally did not exceed three bays in width and included only small backyards instead of substantial interior courtyards. Exterior walls were whitewashed without ornamentation; ornately engraved wood adorned ceilings, roof barriers, and upper windows. In each of these dwellings a major hall, serving ritual purposes, was located at the center of the rear section. Flanked by living space, the main hall held the ancestral belongings of the occupants. Bedrooms were located on the better-ventilated second floor.

**Clay Model.** The clay house of the Ming dynasty was similar to those constructed during the Han dynasty (206 B.C.E.–220 C.E.). It featured a series of courtyards flanked and faced by separated halls, which were subdivided into smaller rooms. The high-pitched roof, supported by columns and covered with tiles, was similar to that of the Han house. The major entrance was protected by a spirit screen placed on the inside, and a wall was erected outside to block any view of the inner courtyard. Another function of the spirit screen was to prohibit evil spirits from crossing the threshold. According to Chinese demonology, devils can only travel in a straight line, therefore this device was an ideal protection against their invasion of the home.

**Multifamily House.** The clay-type house had been used without any changes for many centuries because it was entirely adapted to the social circumstances of Chinese life. A Chinese home was expected to be a common dwelling place of a big family, and each son occupied a separate smaller courtyard within the big house. As a result, all Ming houses were designed in the same mode, from the small country farm or humble town dwelling of the common people, with only one courtyard, to the gigantic and roomy palaces. Courtyard units often proliferated and expanded until the house arrived at imperial size.

**Single-Family House.** In Ming times some two-story houses in small towns, or isolated in open ground outside the villages, were not huge. They were not built for large families, the houses belonging generally to merchants who were prosperous but not wealthy and sometimes to petty officials. They were intended for single families because the sons of such businessmen left to trade and no longer lived with their parents. Since sumptuary laws restricted their size and decoration, with some exceptions, the frontage was restricted to three bays; red was forbidden to be used on outside doors and windows and even on inside columns.

**Details of the House.** Most houses faced south or southwest, but rarely southeast, in part to avoid southerly wind currents and to obtain winter sunlight. Privacy was strictly kept. Therefore, these two-story houses were rather ordinary and compact, with extremely shallow courtyards, blank walls, and without windows on the outside. Only the entry door was decorative on the outside; ornamentation was lavished on the interior balustrades, windows, attic, ceilings, and roof timbers. Exterior walls were made of brick, rendered and whitewashed, but the structure was normally made of timber. Occasionally, the outside wall was a totally self-supporting two-story-high screen. The roof had its own corbelled and tiled coping. Courtyards were paved with stone while interior floors were laid with brick. Columns, which had small curvature and downward taper, were set in engraved stone bases. The wooden stairways also rested on stone bases at ground-floor level. Upper floors were of wood boarding on rafters, sphere shaped or rectangular, carried by the major beams. In some houses there were boarded suspended ceilings, tinted with rather elegant designs in pale colors, and the rafters were painted in similar colors. More customarily, the beams, rafters, and boarding were left visible from the ground-floor rooms, and on upper floors the beams and roof members were elaborately engraved. The panel walls on the open side, where not closed by a screen wall, were all made of wood. Some ground floors were open to the courtyard, while others contained doors and screens with simple wooden boardings or plastered panels.

**Regulation.** In Tang times officials of the third rank and above could not have a hall of more than five *jian* (the

Late-tenth-century mural from Tun-huang showing an enclosure with two-story buildings

The Daxiongbao Hall of the Fengguo-si, built in 1020

space between two beams), and a front gate of more than three *jian;* officials of the fourth and fifth ranks could not have a hall of more than five *jian* and a front gate of more than three *jian.* By Ming times a duke could own a front hall of five or seven *jian* with two side rooms, a center hall of seven *jian,* a back hall of seven *jian,* and a front gate of three *jian;* officials of the first and the second ranks could possess a hall of seven *jian* with a front gate of three *jian;* officials of the third, fourth, and fifth ranks could have a hall of five *jian* and a front gate of three *jian;* officials of the sixth, seventh, eighth, and ninth ranks could possess a hall of three *jian* and a front gate of one *jian.* In all dynasties, an ordinary person's house could contain only three *jian* with a front gate of one *jian.* Hence, no matter how rich a common person might be or how many houses he might own, according to the edict of 1397, the hall in any one of them could not surpass three *jian.*

**Animal Designs.** During the Tang dynasty only officials could use tiles with animal designs; officials of the fifth rank or higher could put a bird's head knocker on their gate. In the Yuan period (1279–1368) a commoner who ornamented his roof ridge with animal-figured tiles was given thirty-seven strokes. In Ming times officials of the fifth rank and above could use animal-figured tiles on their roofs. Ming dukes and marquises could have gold-colored gates with animal-head tin knockers. First- and second-rank officials could own green oil-painted gates with animal-head tin knockers; third-, fourth-, and fifth-rank officials could have black oil-painted gates with animal-head tin knockers; and all the sixth-, seventh-, eighth- and ninth-rank officials could obtain only black gates with iron knockers.

**Lances.** In some dynasties lances were also used as an index of rank. In Tang times an official of the third rank and above could display from ten to sixteen lances before his gate. In Sung times lances were displayed before a gov-

ernor's office. The government of the Jin dynasty (936–947) decreed in 938 that officials of certain ranks might, as signs of special respect, display lances before their gates. Apparently, a bystander could identify the status of a homeowner by simply studying the decoration.

**Supports.** Beams and rafters under the eaves could be decorated with colored paintings only in the houses of ranking officials. In Ming times dukes and marquises could paint them in a variety of colors; officials of the first through fifth ranks were allowed to use blue and green; officials of the sixth through ninth ranks were permitted earth-yellow. In each dynasty commoners were forbidden to paint their beams.

**Interior Furniture.** In early times the Chinese sat cross-legged on the floor while eminent persons sat on platforms covered with mats. During the Tang dynasty they began to adopt the Central Asian practice of sitting on chairs and stools; one kind of chair during this era was even named *huchuang* (barbarian couch). Prominent persons were permitted to sit on armchairs with round or square backs; subordinate persons sat on chairs without arms; and the peasants used stools or barrel seats. The armchairs of military officials were covered with furs, such as tiger skins, while civilian officials' chairs had lavish textiles, such as silk brocade. In the Song dynasty the Chinese began to use high tables for eating, writing, painting, and praying at home and in temples. People put long, narrow, formal side tables against the centers of walls to show flower arrangements and porcelain objects. Some used a type of square dining table, made of varnished or lacquered wood, for wedding, birthday, and funeral banquets. Rather than using desks, the Song people wrote and drew on a large flat table, known as a "painting table." By the early Ming dynasty, Chinese furniture-making attained its highest point. Hardwood furniture in simple form, made with the best woods, such as red sandal and mahogany, were solid and fine grain with glossy surfaces. Workers used wood-working tools with carbonized iron parts, which were particularly effective for hardwood processing. Without any glue or metal nails, they used only different types of miter and mortise-and-tenon joints to produce furniture so as to make the pieces strong and easy to dismantle and reassemble. Floating tongue-and-groove panels allowed the pieces of wood to shrink and enlarge to avoid cracking when the temperature changed. In Ming times high-ranking officials and well-off merchants living in Suzhou, Yangzhou, and the capital city of Beijing built huge houses and gardens with beautiful furniture inside.

**Sources:**

Andrew Boyd, *Chinese Architecture and Town Planning, 1500 B.C.–A.D. 1911* (Chicago: University of Chicago Press, 1962).

C. P. Fitzgerald, *China: A Short Cultural History,* edited by C. G. Seligman (London: Cresset Press, 1935).

Brian Hook, ed., *The Cambridge Encyclopedia of China* (Cambridge University Press, 1991).

Henry Inn, *Chinese Houses and Gardens,* edited by Shao Chang Lee (Honolulu: Fong's Inn Limited, 1940).

Ronald G. Knapp, *China's Traditional Rural Architecture: A Cultural Geography of the Common House* (Honolulu: University of Hawaii Press, 1986).

Sterling Seagrave, *The Song Dynasty* (New York: Harper & Row, 1985).

Laurence Sickman and Alexander Soper, *The Art and Architecture of China* (Baltimore: Penguin, 1956).

Robert Temple, *The Genius of China: 3,000 Years of Science, Discovery and Invention* (New York: Simon & Schuster, 1986).

## RECREATION AND LEISURE ACTIVITIES

**Kites.** Known as "paper birds," Chinese kites began to appear in the fifth century B.C.E. They were made of frames of thin pieces of wood or bamboo that were bound together and coated with brilliantly painted paper. In the sixth century C.E. besieged cities flew kites to send military signals for help. Some people flew kites in order to draw fevers out of patients, believing that kites had healing powers. Li Ye flew a kite in the tenth century C.E. and attached a piece of bamboo to it with a silk ribbon. The vibration of the wind on the ribbon made a whistling sound, and kites thereafter were called *fengzheng* (aeolian harps). Kites of various types of shapes and colors were made; the most popular shapes were human and mythical figures, flowers, birds, fish, worms, bats, dragonflies, and others. Kites were divided into two types, according to the method they were made. The frame of a "soft wing" kite could be disassembled so that it could be put in a box. A "hard wing" kite was made with the body, head, and wings in one piece and was covered with thick paper or silk fabric so that it could fly in strong winds. The city of Weifang in Shandong became a well-known center of kite making and flying in Ming times (1368–1644).

**Popular Board Game.** *Weiqi* or *go* was first played in India about four thousand years ago. In the Tang era (618–907) the modern form of the game began to appear. *Weiqi* was played on a square board with 19 horizontal and 19 vertical lines dividing it into 361 small squares. It was played by only two players, one having 180 white markers

Ceramic model of musicians riding a camel, 723
(Chinese Historical Museum, Beijing)

or "stones" and the other having 181 black ones. The black player went first. The goal of the game was to place enough stones on the board to occupy more squares than the opponent. *Weiqi* is still a popular recreation in China today.

**Mahjong.** The game mahjong became popular in Ming times and is played by four people using dice and 136 tiles. The aim of this game is to gain a perfect hand: 4 sets of 3 tiles each and an identical pair, called mahjong. The Chinese word *majiang* literally stands for "house sparrow," because when the players are shuffling the tiles, they create a bird-like sound. Mahjong came from a card game named *ma tiao*, which was based on tarot cards and transmitted to China from Europe in the sixteenth century. Although the rules of mahjong were complicated and difficult to follow, both men and women in every social class enjoyed playing it.

**Playing Cards.** Playing cards were made from thick, hard papers and ornamented with numbers and pictures and used to play various games. The Chinese were the first to invent paper playing cards as early as in the ninth century. The Song scholar Ouyang Xiu later claimed that the use of paper playing cards resulted in the change of book design from paper rolls to paper sheets and pages. Playing cards were printed with woodcut blocks and frequently colored by hand. The cards were usually two inches long and one inch wide. Made of thick paper, more durable than those of today but harder to shuffle. The ordinary designs for the backs were drawn of fic-

Ball players, painting on silk, twelfth century (National Palace Museum, Taipei, Taiwan)

tional characters by famous artists. Designs often depicted figures from the famous Chinese book, *Shuihuzhuan* (The Water Margin), a collection of stories and plays of the Northern Song dynasty (960–1125). This form of entertainment spread to Europe from China through Arab merchants and travelers such as Marco Polo. Playing cards did not appear in Europe until 1377, when the Germans and Spanish began to use them.

**Lion Dance.** By the Song dynasty (960–1279) the lion dance had been developed. Initially, soldiers used the dance to frighten enemy horses and elephants on the battlefield. During the Ming dynasty lion dances became common after villagers in Guangdong province performed them to scare away wild animals. Lion dances were performed at such festivals as the New Year celebration. One lion dancer acted as the lion's body and was covered with long, yellow fur while another dancer in the front held the costumed head. Both dancers performed gymnastic actions to the sounds of loud drums and gongs. Sometimes they could climb up on a big ball and roll it with their feet.

**Martial Arts.** Martial arts originated from early farming tools and hunting techniques. During the Tang dynasty the imperial court created a program of choosing military officials through martial arts examinations and contests. In the Song period the central administration set up regulations for open competitions, and during the Ming era the government organized contests to promote the expansion of the martial arts. Meanwhile, a diversity of martial arts techniques contributed to the development of different schools. Schools of South China, known as *nanquan*, stressed hand techniques, whereas schools in North China accentuated kicking. When the "soft" technique, named *taijiquan*, began to develop, martial arts started to shift from physical battles to concerns with enhancing health and longevity.

**Supreme Pole Boxing.** *Taijiquan* stands for "Supreme Pole Boxing." *Tai* represents "supreme," while *Ji* implies "polarity" in the sense of *yin* and *yang*. *Quan* signifies the fist and is translated as boxing or fighting. During the Ming dynasty Chen Wangtin, a famous martial arts master and army general who lived in Henan Province in central China, developed *taijiquan* by bringing together the traditional techniques of boxing and deep natural breathing. *Taijiquan* was a slow, curving movement of the arms, head, torso, and legs, calling for harmonization of all sections of the body and attention of the mind. These graceful movements adopted artistic gestures used in Chinese operas and acrobatics. The soft and yielding quality of this exercise, a form of spiritual meditation, helped a person gain strength. Ming people began to practice *taijiquan* because this movement was useful in improving the performance of the body's circulatory, respiratory, and metabolic systems.

**Sources:**

Scott Morton, *China: Its History and Culture* (New York: McGraw-Hill, 1995).

Dorothy Perkins, *Encyclopedia of China: The Essential Reference to China, Its History and Culture* (New York: Facts on File, 1999).

Colin A Ronan, *The Shorter Science and Civilization in China: An Abridgement of Joseph Needham's Original Text* (Cambridge: Cambridge University Press, 1978).

## TEA CULTURE

**Trade.** Since ancient times the Chinese have appreciated the speedy, well-built horses raised by people called barbarians, who lived outside the Great Wall and who enjoyed Chinese teas, together with silk, porcelain, and other products. During trade these people did not want to accept any bills of exchange issued by the Tang government (618–907) or paper money invented by the Song court (960–1279) as payment. Tea bricks, used in trading with Tibet, had been one of the first international monies; tea was among the goods used to pay for foreign horses. This trade became so significant that the influential Horse and Tea Commission, a government agency, was created especially to control it. A monopoly was held by the Chinese empire over the tea trade, which continued in the following centuries; the Chinese also developed new tea flavorings to please their barbarian customers.

**Contest.** In Song times homes were normally halls of meditative silence. When friends came for tea, it was a joyous, noisy occasion with animated conversation, gossip, jokes, and laughter. The Song people loved tea parties. Parlor games were popular during this dynasty, and teatime was the perfect time for playing them. One of the most popular luxurious games of the upper classes was Ta Cha, or Tea Contest. Although Tang people invented this game, the Song revived and played it with a passion. During the Tea Contest an arbitrator was first designated, then each participator in turn prepared an unnamed tea of his choice with pure water brought from special springs. The goal of the game was for each player to guess where the different teas had been grown; winners obtained costly prizes offered by the host. The finding of an unknown tea or tea-water source was a guarantee of social achievement in addition to a good opportunity for showing one's wealth.

**Customs Spread.** Tea customs in the Song period were widespread throughout the empire. When a visitor arrived, he passed through a gate into the house compound and slowly walked along a stone path, taking time to view a beautiful garden. He continued in to the south-facing entrance hall of the mansion, where many servants busily removed his fur-trimmed outer clothes and straightened his long gown. He was then accompanied at a leisurely pace to the honor hall. A courteous host, informed by his servants of the visitor's arrival, stood in the hall to welcome the guest. (If a person came to the hall without prior notice, he could be put off by the servants saying, "Master does not have any time today, please come another day and he'll invite you to tea.") Host and guest bowed to each other, rather than shaking hands, in front of the tea table, which symbolized Chinese hospitality.

**Table.** Song tea tables were taller than modern coffee tables and similar in height to dining tables. Large enough to seat four to six people comfortably, rectangular tea tables varied in style and price, from the intricately carved, ornately decorated lacquered tea tables of the aristocracy to the ordinary bamboo tea tables of the poor. After bowing in greeting, the host and guest seated themselves on opposite sides of the tea table. In northern China during cold winters, however, people liked to sit on cushioned, heated beds made of brick. Custom called for the host to present tea when everyone had been seated.

**Master.** The Song people were among the most knowledgeable tea drinkers in Chinese history. Since they spent huge amounts of money buying quality teas, they did not waste it and prepared it seriously. Rich families hired a permanent Tea Master, who was in charge of buying good teas, obtaining pure tea water, and preparing tea for the family and guests. It was prestigous to employ a Tea Master on the household staff. Since many merchant families could not afford a full-time Tea Master, they hired Traveling Tea Masters, most of whom were former monks. No matter who made the tea, nor the financial situation of the host, all guests felt honored, and teacups were always put before each person deferentially with two hands. Teacups were not to be more than four-fifths full. A host often provided guests with salted nuts and seeds, sweetmeats, or fruit, but no host was required to serve any food.

**Servant Boys.** Since tea was important in the daily life of the Chinese, tea servants were important members of every mansion's family. Tea boys collected water, oversaw its boiling, and prepared and gave hot towels to guests so they could freshen up and wash their hands. Tea maids gauged the tea leaves, supplied finger foods, and cared for the teapots and teacups. Since separation of the sexes was characteristic of daily life in dynastic China, dinner parties, tea parties, and other social congregations were segregated along gender lines. Gentlemen hosted men-only parties. Ladies were restricted to women's areas. This severe separation of the sexes did not, however, apply to tea servants, who were allowed to go to any quarters of large mansions. Tea boys were the only male servants permitted to go into the women's quarters, and they were often paid by the master to spy on the women's activities. Since the system worked both ways, smart tea boys often earned good money through undercover work.

**Teacups.** Song teacups did not have handles; when boiled tea was poured into them, the sides became hot and could not be touched. When the teacups were only four-fifths full, however, the rim remained a little cool and could be grasped with

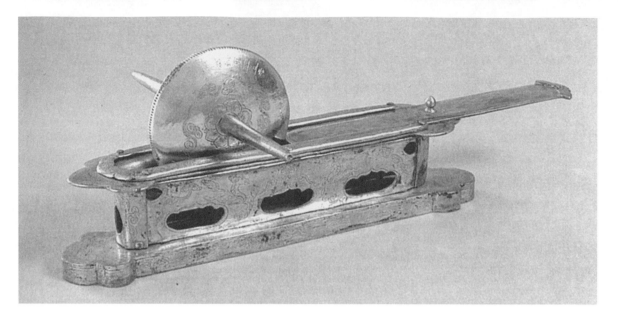

Silver tea grinder dated 869 (from Patricia Buckley Ebrey, *Cambridge Illustrated History of China*, 1996)

the index finger and thumb in a crab grasp. In this manner, people could drink hot tea without burning either their lips or fingers and, more important, people could hold the teacup tightly to prevent spilling any liquid.

**Finger Guard.** The deft Chinese, who used chopsticks to eat, did not have any problem mastering the crab grasp, but rich mandarins, who wore finger guards, had difficulties in handling teacups. Women's feet were bound at birth to show that they did not need to work and to make them more attractive; wealthy men tried to make their fingernails grow for similar reasons. Frequently, these fingernails might grow as long as six inches in length. Because these long nails were particularly fragile, people had to wear scabbard-like fingerguards made of gold or silver and coated with valuable jewels. As the hands moved, the fingerguards touched each other, making a continuous clicking sound.

**Guest Leaving.** Before a guest's departure, a host usually served a final, simple, symbolic cup of tea. This demonstration of good manners implied that the guest's company was so enjoyable that it was a pity he could not stay longer. However, a polite guest understood his host's implication and did not drink any of this tea. When the guest stood up and was ready to leave, he politely said to the host, "Thank you very much for the tea," although he had not drunk any.

**Language.** A perfect example of both the impact and reputation of tea on the Chinese language is the emotional comparison of good deeds to "handing out tea on a hot day." Acquaintances even welcomed each other by asking "Have you already drunk tea?" instead of "How are you?" The Song people often said, "It's as welcome as a teahouse fire!" This aphorism alludes to the fire burning for tea water in every teahouse, which was a nice place to be on chilly days. References to tea were ubiquitous in the speech of the Song people, who used tea for estimating the amount of time it took to accomplish a task. "It occurred in less time than it takes to drink a cup of tea" became the

customary way of saying "rapidly." A man who was looking for his friend in a teahouse might be told, "He left the time it takes to drink a cup of tea," which meant "He has just left." "As big as a tea kettle" and "the size of a teacup" were employed by Song people to describe volume measures in the same way European and American cooks use cup and spoon measures.

**Names.** In Song times custom dictated the serving of tea as a sign of good manners, and each tea bore a name that indicated its proper use. Instead of using the flowery names of teas, simple terms for politeness were employed. The first welcoming cup of tea presented to a guest was called "Greeting Tea." Tea served to Buddha was named "Sacrificial Tea." New neighbors often received a welcoming gift of tea and tidbits called the "Enjoyment at New Neighbors Tea."

**Cult.** Tea, traded under tight government control, was still a luxury in Song times, and its use had not become essential in poor households by the end of the dynasty. The cult of tea expanded greatly, however, in company with other refined arts of life. Tea production became more commercialized at the end of the Song empire.

**Mongols.** Long before their occupation of China the Mongols had enjoyed drinking tea. Their only wealth was tied to the ownership of horses. As early as the Tang Dynasty, Mongols exchanged horses for Chinese goods and tea. When loose tea emerged in the Song Dynasty to replace solid ball and cake tea, Mongols were perhaps the first people to adopt it. Although the original taste was hardly pleasant, it did not discourage the Mongols from drinking a kind of tea (milk tea) called barbarian drink, which the Chinese could never have endured. The Mongols boiled mare's milk to pasteurize it and put in the tea leaves simultaneously to make a drink that satisfied their love for both flavors.

**Flower-Scented Tea.** The Ming people (1368–1644) had great passion for flowers; irrespective of shape or color, they were appreciated. The Ming flower cult had a great impact on improvements made to teas, and for the first time flower-scented teas appeared. Although they were invented at least as early as the Tang Dynasty, scented teas were made with prohibitively expensive essential oils and were actually reserved as Imperial Tribute Teas. The intelligent Ming people hit upon the fresh idea of scenting tea with plentiful, cheap flowers.

**Servant's Tea.** Good scented teas are a gracious combination of smell and taste, which is their typical characteristic. Because of this unusual duality, scenting can either increase or mask the taste of tea. Scenting was so often used to disguise the taste of inferior teas that the upper classes of the late Ming Dynasty scorned the practice, calling jasmine tea "servant's tea."

**Commoner's Tea.** Before the creation of the tea bag several centuries ago, Ming drinkers prepared tea by infusing whole leaves, a technique known to most Western tea drinkers. The drinkers put tea leaves into a porcelain teapot the same size as a large apple. The small size of this pot represented the high price of tea. After boiling water was poured into the pot, the leaves were infused for the time it took to inhale and exhale three times, and then the tea was poured through a sieve made of bamboo into the china cups to warm them. After a few minutes the tea was poured back into the teapot, where the leaves were again infused for the same length of time as before. After the leaves had been adequately infused, the tea was ready to drink. The teapot was never supposed to be refilled more than two times, although in poor families the leaves were infused several times. Simply prepared Ming-style tea became commoner's tea, and Tea Masters of the Tang dynasty were no longer needed.

**Arrangements and Treats.** In Ming times beautiful, craftily arranged flowers always dignified tea tables; in addition, a great assortment of sweets was served. Since the Ming people liked sugar, sweet foods began to replace salty foods on tea tables. For the first time the Ming people dunked finger foods into their cups of tea, setting a model Europeans would copy with special tea biscuits. Sweet pastries and candied fruit were dunked in hot tea to sweeten it, but many Ming did not think this sugaring proved sufficient and usually added yellow lump sugar. Dates were the most common addition to green tea, immediately scenting and sugaring it nicely. It was a sign of respect to put a few luxurious dates in a guest's china cup.

Sources:

John C. Evans, *Tea in China: The History of China's National Drink* (New York: Greenwood Press, 1992).

Morris Rossabi, *Khubilai Khan: His Life and Times* (Berkeley: University of California Press, 1988).

Shiba Yoshinobu, *Commerce and Society in Sung China*, translated by Mark Elvin (Ann Arbor: University of Michigan Press, 1970).

## TEAHOUSES

**Public Accommodations.** In Song times (960–1279) many teahouses were established. After people went into a teahouse and chose their seats at a tea table, a waiter immediately asked: "What kind of tea would you like, Sir?" Customers requested steeped tea; spicy, sugared ginger tea; or other teas. Beverages, such as sour plum drinks, spring water, and warm wine, were also served. On each table there was a bowl of salted pine nuts, walnuts, or melon seeds, which were free to customers because eating them resulted in a thirst that promoted the purchase of more drinks.

**Delicious Food.** Every teahouse served snacks and light meals. The prices of such food varied depending on the culinary talents of each cook, but generally teahouse food was outstanding, the most delicate and tasty food in Song China. A hundred different dishes, such as piping-hot bowls of noodles, meat, and fish; hot steamed buns; date pudding; and a variety of imaginative pastries were provided by the teahouse.

**Business and Social Center.** People might spend the whole day in the teahouse, which functioned as both a business and social center. Teahouses were well known as places where people could relax and have a wonderful time. Friends met in a favorite teahouse, spending many hours chatting or playing dice, dominoes, Chinese checkers, or chess. Traders met customers at the tea table and discussed business over steaming cups of tea. Fortune-tellers, marriage brokers, and dentists were frequent clients of large teahouses and often ran their own businesses there. Criminals liked to meet in teahouses when the owner let them rent a private room in the back of the building for conducting illegal deals. Teahouse owners were paid a lot of money by criminals, especially if they informed them of the coming of the police in time for them to escape.

**Unofficial Bank.** Most teahouse owners always had plenty of cash on hand, and they functioned as unofficial bankers to guarantee gamblers' bets; provide loans at usurious interest rates for wedding dowries, to purchase a house,

Ceramic teapot with lid, Liao and Northern Song dynasties, 960–1125 (Institute of Cultural Relics, Shijiazhuang, Hebei Province)

Glazed teacup and stand, Song dynasty, 960–1279
(Hong Kong Museum of Art)

innumerable rapidly changing characters and emotions.
Teahouse storytellers did not become rich but earned
enough money to support their families, and a few of them
became well known.

**Street Stories.** Many teahouse storytellers not only
worked for teahouses but also developed their own businesses in the street. They first bought some tea, a kettle, a
small stove, a few pieces of charcoal, and several cups and
then found a place on a busy street where there was enough
room for people to gather. The storytellers then encouraged the people to listen to unbelievable tales for the price
of a cup of tea.

**Topics of Interest.** Any topic that interested people or
captured the imagination provided a worthy story for a
teahouse tale, and many stories told in Song teahouses continue to be told in modern China. Song literature was written in the street dialect that best expressed the universality
of human sentiment. Song short stories, epics, and dramas
were similar to modern ones, making people laugh, cry,
love, hate, and feel anger and injustice just as modern
entertainments do.

**Drama.** Theater was another fashionable passion in
Song-era China, and plays performed in teahouses provided entertainment. Tragedy, comedy, and scenes of daily
life were common dramatic themes; favorite characters
were the irritating wife, bribed policeman, bad official,
immoral monk, suspicious criminal, corrupt tax collector,
and stupid scholar. Teahouse dramas were often divided
into two parts because during the first act noisy spectators
often did not pay attention to the actors, so after a short
break the audience would calm down to watch the second
act, which all patrons knew to be the best part of the
drama. Most teahouses could be changed into theaters by
setting a stage at one end of the room. Since audiences
were interested primarily in dialogue, there was no scenery,
curtain, or costuming. Most actors wore their own street
clothes to perform a play.

**Actors.** Teahouse actors, as well as storytellers, were
self-employed professionals working for established circuits. They stayed at one teahouse for a while and then
moved to another place; often they worked several
teahouses in the same big city or traveled to other cities in
order to attract larger audiences. A good actor could play
more than one hundred different roles, although most were
character parts, performing the dialogue extemporaneously
rather than reciting it from memory.

**Problems.** Conflict concerning tea was always regarded
as a serious matter. Its seriousness is exposed in the prov-
erb, "Murder can be pardoned, but affront over tea never."
Voices raised in anger and occasional scuffles were part of
teahouse life, although there were almost certainly fewer
arguments in Song teahouses than in modern restaurants.
Teahouse customers were usually satisfied with the drink,
food, service, and entertainment they found there, but dis-
contented patrons sometimes might threaten the owner by

or to open up a new shop; or to give financial support to
business deals, such as trading in tea, valuable metals, or
real estate.

**Generosity.** When customers were leaving the teahouse,
they usually said, "Charge the tea," no matter what they
had eaten or drunk. An arrogant businessman might shout,
"Charge his tea to me!" generously paying for another's
food and drink to show that he was wealthy.

**Credit.** Since teahouse owners often had close relationships with the criminal underground and could hire money
collectors, they extended credit to loyal customers. They
might also give credit to new customers after a regular customer had vouched for them. It would be an insult to a
steady customer if the teahouse owner rejected credit under
this situation.

**Entertainment.** In Song times teahouses also functioned as entertainment and cultural centers, especially in
smaller communities. Almost every teahouse employed
gifted storytellers to attract audiences, and many entertainers enjoyed the same standing as their counterparts in
Medieval Europe. Teahouse storytellers' memories were
unusual, and most of them could remember more than
three hundred stories. In addition, like actors, some gifted
and famous storytellers could change their voices across a
wide scale while adapting their facial expressions to mimic

saying, "Don't make me mad or I'll wreck your place and turn it ass over teakettle."

Sources:

John C. Evans, *Tea in China: The History of China's National Drink* (New York: Greenwood Press, 1992).

Morris Rossabi, *Khubilai Khan: His Life and Times* (Berkeley: University of California Press, 1988).

Shiba Yoshinobu, *Commerce and Society in Sung China*, translated by Mark Elvin (Ann Arbor: University of Michigan Press, 1970).

## VILLAGE LIFE IN MING

**Villages.** During Ming times (1368–1644) about 90 percent of the Chinese still lived in villages, most of which had about fifty families. Villages were usually smaller in the north than in the south. Few Chinese lived in single families on isolated farms. Villages were real communities, small gathering places for group activity.

**Intervillage Marriage.** Villagers' lives were not confined to their local streets and the nearby fields where they worked. Villages acted within a large system of social interaction. Generally, villagers had only one surname. People who had the same surnames were considered kin, if often very remote. To avoid incest taboos, married women in such villages had to have different surnames from their spouses, and therefore came from a different village, under a system operated by law and by custom. For this reason men sought wives from other villages, and as a result, there were close relations among different villages.

**Intervillage Activities.** Trade was also significant in intervillage activities, although there was a move from barter to money transactions in many areas of China during mid-Ming times. Small villages might not have any permanent stores or shops but would have a market that conducted business on a regular schedule, usually for one or more days. When a village was too small to support regular market, its people walked to nearby villages on their market days as buyers or sellers, or only as sightseers looking for excitement and enjoyment. Peddlers walked through a region with their wares, gossip, and news. Large villages and towns had scheduled markets that met as often as every other day, while some communities had permanent stores. Large villages in more prosperous regions had central streets with both a marketplace and some permanent stores, craftsmen's shops with storefronts, and booths where doctors, fortune-tellers, barbers, letter writers, and other individuals provided services.

**Entertainment.** Most ordinary Chinese spent their time on work and little time on entertainment. The simple pleasures focused on holiday meals with special food at home or at religious events held at temples and shrines. At tea shops the men of farming and crafts households got together for refreshments, chats, and business discussions. In prosperous cities there were inns, restaurants, brothels, and entertainments of many kinds. People gathered together to listen to professional storytellers, while actors and acrobats presented their skills on temporary portable stages or in the courtyards of temples. Most villagers had chances to watch performances of touring theater troupes at least once a year. Buddhist monasteries hosted annual regional fairs that attracted buyers from long distances. Rural life during Ming times was bustling and, at times, exuberant with activity.

**Family Religious Duty.** Most villages had small votive shrines and temples. Monks and nuns traveled extensively, providing links to the outside. They often promoted village group pilgrimages to religious sites such as well-known temples. These several-day-long journeys became joyous holidays as well as spiritual experiences. Most villages had schools that were established on temple premises. Since many Chinese worshiped their ancestors, the home, not a temple or shrine shared with the community, was the site of a family's primary religious duties. They performed rituals of veneration at home on the first and fifteenth days of the lunar month, on birthdays, and on special occasions. The eldest male heir or a near-kin surrogate conducted the ceremonies at home and at family tombs in the spring. Although Buddhist and Daoist religious observances and ceremonies of local cults were colorful and popular, they

## THE TEN DISCIPLINES OF THE HUNG SOCIETY

Secret societies existed in China since ancient times, but their activity and numbers increased after the barbarians invaded the Song empire (960–1279). The Hung Society, one of the active secret societies in south, west, and central China during the Ming period (1368–1644), was mainly political, though with a religious coloring. The following are the ten disciplines of the secret society.

It is not permitted to injure or destroy a fellow Brother [that is, in the Society's secret language, be disrespectful to him].

It is not permitted to curse or scold parents.

It is not permitted to stir up a lamp or put out a light [stir up trouble].

It is not permitted to oppress others because of one's superiority.

It is not permitted to deceive Heaven and cross the river [cheat people].

It is not permitted to skim off the fat and leave the soup [take the best for oneself].

It is not permitted to be inhumane and unrighteous.

It is not permitted to pick the red and take what is submerged in water [take illegal fees or compensation].

It is not permitted to struggle to go ahead when walking with others [push ahead for personal glory].

It is not permitted to usurp any position in the Society.

**Source:** William Theodore de Bary and others, eds., *Sources of Chinese Tradition* (New York: Columbia University Press, 1960), pp. 658–659.

Drawing of villagers engaged in rice processing, sixteenth century (Bibliothèque Nationale, Paris)

took precedence over family religious duties. Among popular religions, sectarian lines were indistinct or absent, especially at lower levels of society where the differences among Buddhism, Daoism, and local cults were unclear.

**Nationwide Holidays.** In all villages most people in Ming times observed the three big holidays of the year: the lunar New Year, the Festival of Dragon Boat, and the mid-autumn festival. Holidays were observed differently in various regions, but these three holidays were celebrated nationwide. The solar-lunar calendar marked the annual round of seasons and festivals.

**New Year Festival.** *Xin Nian* (new year), the most important holiday among Chinese all over the world, is celebrated in late January or early February, in accordance with the traditional Chinese lunar calendar, and continues for fifteen days. It was said that in ancient times a wild beast called *nian* devoured many people in a village in the last part of every winter. One year the peasants frightened the beast away by beating gongs and drums and bursting firecrackers. These activities later celebrated the arrival of spring and the start of a new cycle all through imperial China (618–1644). During the New Year people respectfully visited elders and went to see relatives, wrote poems, hung red strips of paper, and enjoyed banquets with many dishes. Special food with emblematic significance was served. Abalone, for instance, was a symbol of abundance;

bean sprouts, black seaweed, soybeans, and pork stood for wealth; dumplings represented union and enjoyment; oysters predicted good business; and carp, a large fish, implied success. Special foods were also put on the altar to the family's ancestors, such as ground nuts and lotus seeds, which signified children and permanence; lichees, which meant success; and longan, a sweet, round fruit, signified harmony and delight. During festival holidays people also presented brilliantly colored woodcuts in the popular art tradition that illustrated happy children, good crops, and folk heroes; held lion dances; and fired strings of loud firecrackers to dismiss evil spirits. Before the New Year people tried to pay off old debts and cautiously cleaned their homes for the festival, considering that one week before the New Year festival the Kitchen God would go to Heaven to report what had happened on Earth during the year. The New Year festival ended with the Lantern Festival on the fifteenth day, the first full moon of the first lunar month.

**Dragon Boat Festival.** The Chinese developed the Dragon Boat Festival from an ancient ceremony held to propitiate the dragon just before the rainy season began in the sixth month, believing that the dragon would control the rivers and bring more rain. At the Dragon Boat Festival people ate *zongzi*, sweet rice balls wrapped in bamboo or lotus leaves. They also carried out races in long, narrow boats with carved wooden dragon heads on

## NAMES OF THE SEASONS

| Western Date | Period |
|---|---|
| 5 February | Spring Starts |
| 19 February | Rain Waters |
| 5 March | Stirring Insects |
| 20 March | Vernal Equinox |
| 5 April | Clear and Brilliant |
| 20 April | Grain Rains |
| 5 May | Summer Starts |
| 21 May | Grain Fills |
| 6 June | Grain Forms Ears |
| 21 June | Summer Solstice |
| 7 July | Slight Hot |
| 23 July | Great Hot |
| 7 August | Autumn Starts |
| 23 August | Limit of Hot |
| 8 September | White Dew |
| 23 September | Autumnal Equinox |
| 8 October | Cold Dew |
| 23 October | Hoar Frost Goes Down |
| 7 November | Winter Starts |
| 22 November | Tiny Snow |
| 7 December | Severe Snow |
| 21 December | Winter Solstice |
| 6 January | Slight Cold |
| 21 January | Harsh Cold |

their prows. Each boat had from eight to fifteen pairs of rowers, and viewers on the river banks applauded the teams. Dragon-boat racing turned out to be widespread during the Tang dynasty in the Yangzi (Yangtze) River and the West River valleys in South China.

**Autumn Moon Festival.** The Autumn Moon Festival was a celebration to honor the harvest moon on the fifteenth day of the eighth month in the lunar calendar. Adults went out at night to view the full moon, drink rice wine, and produce poems while children held lanterns made of bamboo frames and colorfully ornamented papers. People presented mirrors as gifts to represent brilliance and wisdom. In the Yuan dynasty (1279–1368) mooncakes filled with sweet paste began to appear at the Moon Festival. One year in the 1350s a peasant named Zhu Yuanzhang put secret messages in mooncakes and passed them to the villagers on the day of the Autumn Moon Festival in order to encourage them to revolt against Mongol rule. In the following year Zhu was successful in overthrowing the Mongols and establishing the Ming dynasty. Mooncakes are eaten at present-day Moon Festivals in China.

**Twenty-Four Seasons.** The yearly calendar was based on the journey of the sun, determined by its solstices and equinoxes, while the stages of the moon provided the number of days for each month. The passage of the seasons was divided into a sequence of twenty-four fortnightly periods, each named for a seasonal phenomenon of importance to the timetable observed by the Chinese. Peasants and urban dwellers observed the calendar, to which they turned to mark events that added excitement to their otherwise mundane lives.

Sources:

Hilary J. Beattie, *Land and Lineage in China: A Study of T'ung-ch'eng County, Anhwei, in the Ming and Ch'ing Dynasties* (Cambridge & New York: Cambridge University Press, 1979).

Timothy Brook, *Praying for Power: Buddhism and the Formation of Gentry Society in Late-Ming China* (Cambridge, Mass.: Harvard University Press, 1993).

John Fairbank, *China: A New History* (Cambridge, Mass.: Harvard University Press, 1992).

Ray Huang, *China: A Macro History* (Armonk, N. Y.: M.E. Sharpe, 1990).

Michael Loewe, *Imperial China: The Historical Background in the Modern Age* (London: Allen & Unwin, 1966).

F. W. Mote, *Imperial China, 900–1800* (Cambridge, Mass.: Harvard University Press, 1999).

Dorothy Perkins, *Encyclopedia of China: The Essential Reference to China, Its History and Culture* (New York: Facts on File, 1999).

# SIGNIFICANT PEOPLE

## LU YU

### CIRCA 733-804
### AUTHOR AND AUTHORITY ON TEA

**Foundling.** According to legend Lu Yu was born in Hunan province in southeastern China during the Tang dynasty (618–907) and was left as an infant to be raised by the Zen Buddhist monk Ji-Ji of the Dragon Cloud Monastery. As a child he worked around the monastery at menial chores, including preparing tea for his elders, but later he chose not to join the priesthood (although some scholars believe he actually served a period as a monk). When he was old enough to leave the grounds, he took to the road as a traveling storyteller and clown. Thirsty for more knowledge, and with the help of a benevolent patron, Yu obtained access to Chinese books and mastered them.

**Tea Specialist.** Tea merchants, eager for someone to compile information about the cultivation and use of tea, selected Yu to write a book on the product. He traveled throughout the country sampling waters and teas, and was renowned for his ability to distinguish the locations from where different waters were drawn. He produced and presented to his patrons the *Cha jing* (*Tea Memoir*, or *Tea Scripture*). In this book, which was not published until circa 780, he established the groundwork for the development of proper tea service, which later evolved into the Tea Ceremony. He detailed the characteristics of tea plants, harvesting methods, and the equipment needed for the proper presentation of the finished drink. His code covered everything from the proper metals for pots to measuring and straining the tea, and to cleaning utensils. He became famous throughout China, earning even the patronage of the emperor.

**Returned To Roots.** For Yu, tea was "a way of aiding men to return to their sources, a moment in the rhythm of the day when prince and peasant shared the same thoughts." Yu was treated as a prince and even a saint; the fame and admiration, however, wore heavily on him, and he retired from public life to a monastery to meditate and write. Allegedly he wrote nine additional books, but none have survived. Considered the father of Chinese tea culture, Yu died in 804.

Sources:

Kit Chow and Ione Kramer, *All the Tea in China* (San Francisco: China Books, 1990).

John C. Evans, *Tea in China: The History of China's National Drink* (New York: Greenwood Press, 1992).

William H. Ukers, *All About Tea*, volume 1 (New York: The Tea and Coffee Trade Journal Company, 1935), pp. 10–22.

Lu Yu, *The Classic of Tea*, translated by Francis Ross Carpenter (Boston: Little, Brown, 1974).

## WAN GUIFEI

### 1430-1487
### IMPERIAL CONSORT

**Early Life.** Wan Guifei was born in Shandong; her father was a government clerk. At only three years old she was selected to go to the palace to serve Empress Sun. She became the empress's preferred servant and was appointed to the entourage of her grandson, Zhu Jianshen, who was born in 1447. When he rose to the throne in 1464, she had already been his most frequent companion for some time. This status stimulated the envy of the recently installed Empress Wu, who had the Lady Wan whipped. In this struggle for power Empress Wu was defeated, losing her title after only thirty-two days and being replaced by Empress Wan.

**Unchallenged Power.** After this triumph Lady Wan gained unchallenged power within the palace for many years. In 1466 she produced a boy and was granted the title Huang Guifei, a rank immediately below that of the empress. Although the boy died a year later, she continued to have power as actual empress. She sometimes put on military attire, indicating maleness, which most likely showed her supremacy over the emperor and the eunuchs. During the first twelve years of his reign the emperor spent most of his time in her room. In 1468 the emperor's special attention to her became the topic of several memorials by courtiers who warned and urged him to pay attention to other women in order to provide his ancestors with a male heir. For ten years Lady Wan allegedly took action to ensure that any pregnancy in the palace would result in a miscarriage.

**Corruption.** During that time Lady Wan's attention was also oriented toward commercial activities, such as trading in pearls and other treasures, transactions in the salt monopoly, sale of patents for the Daoist and Buddhist priesthood, and the inappropriate award of minor official ranks directly by imperial order. She was also in charge of the eunuch office, which served as a kind of holding company supervising a store in Beijing and agents in the regions. Since the court was then in financial crisis, perhaps the emperor conspired with Lady Wan in raising funds to meet the expenses of the palace. In 1466 he decreased the salaries of officials in the capital in order to solve the financial problems. In the following years the eunuchs squeezed a large amount of money from the empire to help meet the emperor's expenses. Without doubt, Lady Wan and her family also profited from these transactions. Her brothers became hereditary officers in the Embroidered-Uniform guard, the secret police of the emperor. Wan Tong, one of her brothers, held the rank of an assistant regional military commissioner and accepted bribes from officials who sought favor.

**Aftermath.** Lady Wan died in 1487, only eight months before the emperor passed away. Immediately after his death two censors brought a variety of charges against the eunuchs who had served Lady Wan and other officials who gained promotion or appointment through them. Some were quickly found guilty; some were exiled; and others were either cashiered or reduced in rank. Her brothers were dishonored. Later they were forced to return to the state the land and gifts obtained during her period of influence.

**Sources:**
Victoria Cass, *Dangerous Women: Warriors, Grannies, and Geishas of the Ming* (Lanham, Md.: Rowman & Littlefield, 1999).

L. Carrington Goodrich, ed., *Dictionary of Ming Biography, 1368–1644: The Ming Biographical History Project of the Association for Asian Studies* (New York: Columbia University Press, 1976).

Charles O. Hucker, *The Ming Dynasty: Its Origins and Evolving Institutions* (Ann Arbor: University of Michigan Press, 1978).

# ZHU KEROU (CHU K'O-JOU)

## FLOURISHED 1127-1161
## WEAVER AND EMBROIDERER

**Tapestries.** Elaborate, detailed embroidery formed a major part of the fabric used to make robes worn by members of the royal family and wealthy individuals in China. It was also used to make other items such as purses, boots, jackets, vests, book covers, and coats. Some of the more-elaborate items of clothing might take several artisans more than a year to complete. This skill was further developed in the creation of silk tapestries (*kesi*, or carved silk), which were often used in clothing or for decorative purposes; the sewing was so fine that it more closely resembled paintings. Embroidery shops were run by the government of the Song dynasty (960–1279). Most young women, particularly of the wealthier families, were taught embroidery, and a master of this practical art form was Zhu Kerou, who was born in Sungchiang, Kiangsu province. She lived and worked primarily during the Southern Song dynasty (1127–1279).

**Pieces.** Although most embroidery and elaborate robes—possibly more than 99 percent of the total produced—were destroyed over time, some individual signed pieces still exist. One such masterpiece is Zhu's *Camellias*. She appears to have concentrated on natural themes, preferring to depict flowers, insects, and animals. The *Pied Wagtail* shows two delicate white butterflies hovering above the bird, and the *Pied Wagtail on a Blossoming Polygonum* depicts the bird eyeing a potential insect lunch; different birds appear in several of her existing works, most of which are held in the National Palace Museum in Taipei.

**Sources:**
James C. Y. Watt and Anne E. Wardwell, *When Silk Was Gold: Central Asian and Chinese Textiles* (New York: Metropolitan Museum of Art, 1997).

Zhao Feng, "Art of Silk and Art on Silk in China," in *China: 5000 Years*, edited by Howard Rogers (New York: Guggenheim Museum Publications, 1998), pp. 98–102.

Zhao, *Treasures in Silk: An Illustrated History of Chinese Textiles* (Hong Kong: Edith Cheung, 1999).

# DOCUMENTARY SOURCES

Cao Zhao, *Ge Gu Yao Lun* (The Essential Criteria of Antiquities, 1388)—A treatise on Chinese connoisseurship, covering such things as the use of red sandalwood for furniture and frames to mount paintings and scrolls, and the proper use and manufacture of inkstones.

Gao Lian (Kao Lien), *Zunsheng Bajian* (or *Tsun-sheng Pa Chien*) (Eight Discourses on the Art of Living, circa 1591)—Commentaries on Chinese connoisseurship.

Hao Jing, *An Unofficial Commentary on the Spring and Autumn Annals* (1265)—A work by this famous scholar of the Yuan dynasty (1279–1368) who, without reference on hand, reproduced the work from memory, added a commentary of his own, divided the text into paragraphs and sentences, wrote notes on pronunciation and meaning, and established an order of priority among the three existing commentaries.

Li Jie (Lie Chieh), *Yingzao Fashi* (Treatise on Architectural Methods, 1069)—A government treatise on proper building techniques, codes, and dimensions of houses, as well as for other forms of woodwork.

Lu Ban, *Lu Ban Jing* (Classic of Lu Ban, circa 1400s)—A manual for carpenters by a master; the work examines building materials, ways to measure, construction techniques, and the life of the craftsman; it also transmits knowledge of traditional Chinese woodworking in fashioning furniture.

Lu Yu, *Cha jing* (*Tea Memoir*, 780)—The first comprehensive compilation of knowledge of tea cultivation, preparation, and presentation by the man considered the "father" of tea drinking in China.

Wen Zhenheng, *Zhangwu zhi Jiaozhu* (Treatise on Superfluous Things, circa 1618)—Commentaries on elite Chinese connoisseurship and interior design; contains information on such things as furniture, rock-crystal carvings, and incense burners.

*Ziren Yizhi* (Traditions of the Joiner's Craft, 1264)—A treatise on woodworking and furniture making.

# THE FAMILY
# AND SOCIAL TRENDS

by JIELI LI

*Sidebars and tables are listed in italics.*

**620\***

- Beginning in the Tang period, Chinese surnames are well established to be either a badge of family dignity or lineage identity.

- The Tang administration reestablishes the old *bao-jia* household system, in which peasants are grouped in social units, each consisting of five families to be collectively responsible for paying taxes, punishing crimes committed by individuals within that unit, and obtaining help from state agencies.

**624**

- The Tang Code is first compiled to formalize the administrative and criminal procedures of state regulations, which include aspects of family life and marriage. The code is revised several times in later years.

**630\***

- Under the reign of Taizong (Li Shimin) the Tang dynasty is at the zenith of its power and prestige. It is an era characterized by economic prosperity, population growth, and political stability. From this period on, the Chinese family transforms from a conjugal structure to stem and extended structures.

- The imperial court decrees that the appropriate marriage age for males is twenty and for females is fifteen; the marriage age is later reduced to fifteen for males and thirteen for females.

**640**

- In early Tang times a relatively small number of noble families, called *Wang Zu,* are preeminent in social and political life, but this trend has declined since midway in the Tang period.

**659**

- The imperial government revises the national genealogy, with a new list increasing the number of important families from 235 to 2,287. This transition shifts social rule from the old aristocratic families to a new scholar-elite class.

**660-680\***

- Under the reign of Tang Gaozhong the empire makes more contacts with the outside world. The country is covered by an international commercial network, as foreign merchants arrive by both land and sea. Social life is thus greatly enriched by the diversity of culture and ethnicity, and the capital, Chang'an, becomes a bustling center of international trade and cultural exchange. Tang society is generally open and tolerant of diversity.

**690-701**

- Under the reign of Empress Wu, women enjoy greater freedom in many aspects of social life.

\* DENOTES CIRCA DATE

**713-755**

- Confucianism and Taoism regain favor in Tang society.

**733**

- The number of imperial civil servants rises to 17,680, and the number of locally recruited staff to 57,416.

**737**

- The Tang Code is finalized; it includes 502 articles in 12 volumes, one of which is the first systematic regulation of family and marriage in Chinese imperial history.

**770***

- Systematic efforts are made to formalize the civil service examination system to select government officials.
- Marriages no longer solely emphasize family status and wealth.

**793**

- The state imposes a tea tax, similar to one already placed on salt, because the trade is thriving and tea is becoming popular. People chew tea leaves, which contain refreshing properties despite the bitter taste, and in some regions tea probably serves as a substitute for wine.

**804**

- Lu Yu writes a book giving a detailed analysis of the origin of tea, methods of growing and preparing it, and proper utensils used to serve and consume it. The book is said to make drinking tea a fashion among educated and cultured social circles and also contributes to the popularity of porcelain products for tea. Lu Yu classifies items in terms of their quality in making tea tasteful.

**843**

- The Tang imperial court issues a decree banning Buddhist practices, which also prohibits any foreign religions. In the following years 4,600 Buddhist temples, as well as 40,000 shrines and monasteries, are secularized; all statues are required to be melted down and delivered to the government. This period also marks the decline of the Tang dynasty.

**960***

- Beginning in the Song dynasty, moral teachings are fully integrated into rules used to govern family life.

**970***

- The imperial government issues a legal code punishing wives who leave their husbands without their mates' consent.

**980***

- Chastity is held as the highest virtue of women. This philosophical outlook is largely promoted by the Chen (yi)-Zhu (xi) doctrines.

***DENOTES CIRCA DATE**

**990\***
- As the outlook on female morality becomes increasingly stringent, footbinding as an imperial court fashion is elevated as a convenient way to ensure the separation of the sexes and to prevent women from leaving the confines of the home.

**1000\***
- Ouyang Xiu and Su Xun, Song scholar-officials, advocate a clan organization that they believe will facilitate moral teachings and societal stability. "Kin-clans" or "Sib-organizations" emerge as popular social units among the gentry class. Families are held together by shared genealogies; clans own their land and establish regulations for clan affairs.

**1050\***
- Neo-Confucianism becomes popular. Its chief representatives are Cheng Hao, Cheng Yi, and Zhu Xi. The last makes a significant contribution to the transition of the familial institution from *Jia* (family) to *Jia Zhu* (kin-clan), in which ancestral worship becomes a common practice.

**1100\***
- Civil service examinations are highly developed, which creates greater social mobility. Personal achievement, rather than family status, is emphasized in determining an individual's merit.

**1100**
- The market economy of capitalism is highly visible, particularly in urban life. Kaifeng, the Northern Song capital, reaches a population of 1.4 million (in comparison ancient Rome at its highest had 1 million people).

**1130\***
- The plum-flower wine tune begins to be played in teahouses. Often young men gather in teahouses to practice singing or playing musical instruments; to give an amateur performance is called "getting posted."

**1200**
- The population of Hangzhou, capital of the Southern Song, reaches approximately 2.5 million, making it the largest city of the world at the time.

**1279-1368**
- Chinese family structure during the Yuan (Mongol) dynasty remains basically the same as during the Song dynasty. Nevertheless, increased intermarriage adds more diversity to marriage customs. Unlike the Song, the Mongols impose less-strict regulations on marriage and frown upon footbinding. One conspicuous change, however, is the decline of the kin-organization.

**1290\***
- Beginning in the Yuan dynasty, the imperial government requires paperwork—an agreement signed by either the matchmaker or wedding officiant—as proof of a valid marriage; it is probably the only period in which such written agreements are used.

**\* Denotes Circa Date**

**1300\***

- The practice of footbinding is gradually transmitted from northern areas to central and southern China among the ethnic Chinese communities.

**1340**

- The imperial government realizes the importance of the civil service examination and opens it to both Mongol and Chinese applicants. Some of the sociocultural systems developed during the Tang and Song periods gradually prevail under Mongol rule in the following decades.

**1370\***

- The Ming imperial court restores many Song practices lost during the Yuan dynasty. The "kin-organization" and "ancestral hall" are revived and reinforced. Ming society is repressive to women as the cult of chastity and footbinding become the social requirements of women's virtues.

**\* DENOTES CIRCA DATE**

Palace women bathing children; detail from a fan mounted as an album leaf, circa thirteenth century
(Smithsonian Institution, Washington, D.C.)

**THE FAMILY AND SOCIAL TRENDS**

# OVERVIEW

**Family Institution.** Significant, but gradual, changes in family institutions occurred during the imperial period of China. Family/kinship systems were in a state of flux—one of constant transformation and confusion—for a millennium prior to the Tang dynasty (618–907), whereupon they became stabilized. The key changes that occurred from the Tang dynasty through the Song (960–1279) and Yuan dynasties (1279–1368) until the Ming dynasty (1368–1644) eventually led to the firm establishment of what is viewed as the core structure of the Chinese family. Traditional families could be classified as three distinctive types: the small conjugal family, the medium stem family, or the large extended family. The first type averaged five or six people—including a man, his wife, and their unmarried children—living under one roof. The second type consisted of two conjugal units, with an average of ten people, living together as the "stem" of the family tree. The third example, which usually represented well-to-do families, contained several conjugal units, including members from as many as four generations, all of whom were connected along the paternal line of descent and lived in the same household complex.

**Familial Evolution.** The evolutionary development of the Chinese family in the imperial era can be traced through four essential components—*Jia* (family), *Zu* (kin-clan), *Zong* (genealogy), and *Ci* (ancestral hall)—from which family composition, descent, authority, filial piety, and various social customs were derived. Prior to the Han dynasty (206 B.C.E.–220 C.E.) the Chinese family was mainly characterized by a simple nuclear system that constituted a small, self-sustaining economic unit. Yet, from the late Han period to the Tang dynasty, there was a conspicuous transition from a simple conjugal structure to stem and extended structures. By Song times *Zu*, *Zong*, and *Ci* were absorbed into and became an integral part of *Jia*. In the dynasties following the Song, particularly the Ming, *Zu* and *Ci* became firmly established as an indispensable part of the family institution. By most accounts the family, along with the institution of marriage, constituted the foundation of imperial Chinese society and played key roles in transmitting societal values and norms and exercising the mechanism of social control, thereby sustaining long-term dynastic stability.

**Marriage.** The development of the marriage institution in imperial China was closely tied to familial patrilineality, filial piety, and patriarchy. From the Tang dynasty onward, key features of marriage included rules that were based on a strong concept of patrilineal descent. For instance, one could not marry patrilineal kin, a rule that was eventually extended to include all people of the same surname. Regulations also governed polygamy: a man could have multiple wives, although his first wife had the most legitimate status in the family; the number of concubines a man could have was not limited. Generally, there were two critical transitional periods in the evolution of marriage practices. From the Han to the Tang periods marriages emphasized family status. A critical change occurred during the Tang period, when many laws and regulations of marriage were formulated and enforced. The Tang formalized the Chinese legal system through codification. The Tang Code consisted of 502 articles covering major legal issues in society. One article, titled "Families and Marriage," established specific rules for family and marriage affairs. With the exception of the Yuan period, it became standard practice for later dynasties to refer to the structure and content of the Tang Code to establish rules for marriage. Another critical transition occurred from the Song period to the Ming era, when the state increased its regulation of love and marriage. The "cult of chastity" and "cult of widow" were two typical examples of social regulations that were pushed to the extreme during the Ming dynasty. Another obvious change was an increase in intermarriage among people of different ethnic/racial backgrounds, a common trend during the Yuan dynasty because of territorial expansion undertaken by the Mongol rulers.

**Gentry Society.** The dynamics of a money economy (such as printed currency), which emerged in the Tang dynasty, accumulated over the years and eventually turned into a commercial revolution during the Song period. This revolution released to the open market those commoners who had been clients of the aristocratic estates. As a result, the opportunity for people to seek fame and wealth by either attending the civil service examination or engaging in merchant business increased. Trade promoted the growth of towns and cities, where urban cultures started taking shape. A new political order, called the gentry class, emerged and became the social base of local politics, upon which the imperial courts relied. In general, this class consisted of the families of scholars, bureaucrats, and merchants or combinations of the three groups. This gentry society differed from Western feudalist society, which was dominated by a landlord class. Chinese society was controlled by men whose status depended on academic degrees obtained through rigorous civil service examinations rather than on the economic resources they owned. Elite family status could be preserved only by producing several generations of degree-holders and scholar-officials. Because of the high turnover of government offices, scholar-officials usually enriched themselves as much as they could during their careers and then returned to their hometowns to become *Yuan Wai* (retired officials). Using these fortunes, they invested in property and businesses, thereby becoming landlords. This group played an indispensable role in the development of clan organizations and built a harmonious relationship between local communities and the imperial government. Under the influence of neo-Confucianism in the Northern Song period (960–1125) a new patrilineal worship system ended the tradition of "no ancestral temple for commoners"; ancestor worship thereafter became one of the pillars of Chinese culture.

**Sex Life.** Historians of imperial China have noticed a fundamental difference between the Tang and Song periods, particularly in terms of public attitudes toward sex. Tang society had less-strident restrictions on the sexual freedoms of women. Premarital sex (loss of virginity), divorce, and remarriage were not considered as significant (or shameful to the family) as they would be in later dynasties. Educated and articulate women enjoyed more freedom because they were often seen as desirable companions at social occasions. There was less societal demand for women's chastity. Women remarried fairly frequently, either after divorce from—or the death of—their first husbands. There were often two, and sometimes three, recorded marriages of women in the imperial clan. For example, twenty-three Tang princesses remarried once and four were married three times. Even Han Yu, the most respected Tang scholar, allowed his daughter to marry twice. In addition, Tang courtesans wrote direct and frank revelations about their feelings in verse, showing that their intellectual development was unhindered. By the Song dynasty, however, there was a great shift away from the liberal attitudes toward sex. While remarriage was still commonplace, several noted Chinese scholars took a dim view of feminine liberty and intellectual freedom; they claimed that a woman of virtue should be a conventional lady of little talent. The cult of chastity, not commonly practiced in Tang times, and concubinage became much more common. This trend was reinforced during the Ming dynasty; the cult of chastity and cult of widow became popularized through the endorsement of the imperial government. Footbinding, a practice believed to have started during the Song dynasty, was another cruel social regulation. Bound feet were believed to reduce sexual indulgences because binding made it difficult for women to walk.

**Sexual Orientation.** Tang mores toward prostitution were relaxed and courtesans could be seen at court. Tang society also tolerated homosexual behavior on the part of men and women. By the Song dynasty, however, Chinese society became more repressive toward individuals who were not heterosexual, as clan organizations gained in strength.

**Home Life.** While home life varied from one region to another during the different dynasties, social customs followed a similar cultural heritage and interactive pattern. Common home life usually included the performing of ceremonial rites for a variety of purposes, mainly in observing ancestral worship, child rearing, weddings, and funerals. The patterns of such customs were regularized without significant alteration after the Song dynasty, and some traditions are still prevalent in modern Chinese society. Family rites varied in practice and could be either generally or meticulously observed. The Miu family instructions, from the Guangdong province in the Ming dynasty, serve as a good example. They highlight how to observe major rites stipulated according to the *Zhu Zi Jia Li* (Book of Family Rites), written by Zhu Xi of the Song dynasty. Some of his instructions include: "the ancestral temple should be prepared in advance for the seasonal sacrifices, and the ceremonies performed at dawn"; "sacrifices at the graves should be made on Tomb-Sweeping Day and at the Autumn Festival"; and "established customs should be followed in deciding how much wine and meat should be used, how much different kinds of sacrificial offerings should be presented and how much of the yearly budget should be spent on the sacrifices." For funeral services "one should make an effort to acquire solid and long-lasting objects to be placed in the coffin; but one need not worry as much about the tomb itself, which can be constructed according to one's means." Mourners were further advised that "when attending a funeral service, one should bring only incense and paper money, never hand-towels, fruit, or wine, and should stay for only one cup of tea." The Miu instructions also included advice on other essentials of home life. For instance, "Marriage arrangements should not be made final by the presenting of betrothal gifts until the boy and girl have both reached thirteen." For child education the book counseled that, "on reaching five, a boy should be taught to recite the primers and not be allowed to show arrogance or laziness. On reaching six, a girl should be taught Admonitions for Women and not be allowed to venture out of her chamber. If children are frequently given snacks and playfully entertained, their nature will be spoiled and they will grow up to be unruly and bad. This can be prevented if caught at an early age." For entertaining visitors, the book advised, "When inviting a guest to dinner, one should serve not more than five dishes or more than two soups. Wine and rice should also be served in the right proportion."

**Folk Festivals.** Throughout the long imperial period, several major festivals prevailed; most of these traditions have survived and continue up to the present. Festivals became a vital part of popular culture. They often served to enliven the monotony of social life and on many occasions strengthened community identity. The Chinese lunar calendar was used to determine the dates for most commemorative events and festivals. The year was divided into twenty-four *Jie* (sectional seasons): Beginning of Spring, Rain Water, Waking Thunder, Spring Equinox, Brightness, Corn Rain, Beginning of Summer, Small Grain Full, Grain Full, Summer Solstice, Slight Heat, Great Heat, Beginning of Autumn, Withdrawal of Heat, White Dew, Autumn Equinox, Cold Dew, Landing of Frost, Beginning of Winter, Small Snow, Big Snow, Winter Solstice, Slight Cold, and Great Cold. Revolving around the four seasons were eight popular folk festivals celebrated in most regions of China: New Year's Festival, Kitchen God Worshiping, Lantern Festival, *Qing Ming* (Tomb-sweeping) Festival, Dragon Boat Race, Festival of "Cow Boy" and "Weaving Girl" Union, Ghost Festival, and Mid-Autumn Festival.

# TOPICS IN THE FAMILY AND SOCIAL TRENDS

### ANCESTOR WORSHIP

**Lineage Clans.** The term *Zongfa* refers to the "descent-line" system of categorizing the shrines from the *Zong* (recent ancestors) to the *Tiao* (remote ancestors). The *Zongzu* (lineage clans) were organized along the lines of patrilineal kinsmen, who were honored by such shrines. The *Zongzu* were groups of people who had the same surname and shared the same descent line; they were organized along the generation-age hierarchy. The veneration of ancestors had a long tradition dating back to antiquity, as described in the *Zhu Zi Jia Li* (Book of Family Rites): "'The way of humanity is to treat the kin in the way appropriate to kin. Because the kin are treated in the way appropriate to kin, the ancestors are venerated. Because the ancestors are venerated, the descent-line is respected. Because the descent-line is respected, the lineage is united."

**Descent Lines.** The association of ancestral worship with the continuity of descent lines became the bonding force of *Zongzu* in China up to the present time. However, prior to the Han dynasty (206 B.C.E.–220 C.E.), the right to ritualize ancestral worship had been considered a right of distinction, a privilege reserved only for the rulers and nobility; ordinary people were not permitted to install shrines for their ancestors. After the Han dynasty the hereditary dominance of the nobility declined and so did their privileged rights for erecting ancestral shrines. The obvious change took place during the Song dynasty (960–1279) when neo-Confucian scholars strongly advocated removing the status barrier between commoners and aristocrats for conducting ancestral rites. For example, Chen Yi argued that "the great-great-grandfather falls within the mourning grades, so it would be extremely wrong not to worship him in sacrificial rites. From the son of Heaven down to the common people, there should be no distinctions in the mourning grades." This demand was justified by "righteousness." Another eminent Song scholar, Zhu Xi, even elaborated on how an ancestral hall should be designed in a common household. He wrote in *Zhu Zi Jia Li:* "When a man starts building a house, his first task should always be setting up an offering hall to the east of the main chamber of his house. Four altars should be installed to hold the ancestral tablets of his ancestors." The flourishing of ancestral shrines during the Song period established a common family practice throughout society. This change paved the way for the thriving of *Zongzu* in succeeding dynasties such as the Ming (1368–1644) and Qing (1644–1912).

**Specifying Lineage.** Further development was made in the Ming dynasty in terms of the specifications of ancestral lines. In the Song dynasty an ancestral hall was commonly used to hold the tablets of five generations, as stipulated clearly in Zhu Xi's *Zhu Zi Jia Li*. When the time came, each generation was required to add the most recent ancestor by removing the tablet of the fifth generation previous. During the Ming dynasty, when lineage organizations were getting stronger, the need to trace the roots and unite kinsmen broke through the limitation of ritualized worship of only five generations. The emergence of dedicated shrines to distant ancestors in the ancestral hall or temple became a social phenomenon, greatly strengthening the organizational power of kinship clans. From the mid-Ming period onward the installation of altars to distant ancestors became standard family prac-

Drawing of imperial family members offering libations before the altar of the family shrine, circa 1085
(Metropolitan Museum of Art, New York)

The following passage is a detailed depiction of a sacrificial ceremony held at the ancestral graveyard of one kinship clan during the festival of *Qing Ming*.

After all things are in readiness, the whole party stands until the director gives the word. He first cries with a loud voice, "Let the official persons take their places"; this is immediately done and the ceremonies proceed.

Director: "Strike up the softer music." Here the smaller instruments begin to play.

Director: "Kneel." The priest then kneels in a central place fronting the grave, and behind him, arranged in order, the aged and honorable, the children and grandchildren all kneel down.

Director: "Present the incense." Here stewards take three sticks of incense, and present them to the priest. He arises, makes a bow towards the grave, and then plants one of the sticks in an incense vase in front of the tombstone. The same form is repeated a second and a third time.

Director: "Rise up." Here the priest and party stand up.

Director: "Kneel." Again the priest and all the people kneel.

Director: "Knock head." Here all bending forward and leaning on their hands, knock their foreheads against the ground.

Director: "Again knock head." This is forthwith done.

Director: "Knock head a third time." This is also done. Then he calls out: "Rise up, Kneel, Knock head," till the three kneelings and the nine knockings are completed. And all this is done in the same manner as the highest act of homage is paid to the emperor, or of worship to the supreme powers, heaven and earth. This being ended, the ceremonies proceed.

Director: "Fall prostrate." This is done by touching the ground with knees, hands and forehead.

Director: "Read a prayer." Here the reader approaches the front of the tomb holding in his hands a piece of white paper on which is written one of the sacrificial forms of the prayer. He read: "... I Lin Kwang, the second son of the third generation, presume to come before the grave of my ancestor, Lin Kung. Revolving years have brought again the season of Spring. Cherishing sentiments of veneration, I look up and sweep your tomb. Prostrate, I pray that you will come and be present; that you will grant to your posterity, that they may be prosperous and illustrious; at this season of genial showers and gentle breezes, I desire to recompense the root of my existence, and exert myself sincerely. Always grant your safe protection. My trust is in your divine spirit. Reverently I present the fivefold sacrifice of a pig, a fowl, a duck, a goose, and a fish; also, an offering of five plates of fruit; with oblations of spirituous liquors; earnestly entreating that you will come and view them. With the most attentive respect, this annunciation is presented on high."

Director: "Offer up the gold and precious things." Here one of the stewards presents gilt papers to the priest, and he, bowing towards the grave, lays them down before it.

Director: "Strike up the grand music." Here gongs, drums, trumpets and flutes are beaten and blown to make as great a noise as possible.

Director: "Burn the gold, and silver, and precious things." Here all the young men and children burn the gilt papers, fire off firecrackers....

Such is the sum of a grand sacrifice.... But to many the best part of the ceremony is to come, which is the feast upon the sacrifice. The roast pigs, rice, fowls, fish, fruits and liquors are carried back to the ancestral hall."

Source: Leon E. Stover, *The Cultural Ecology of Chinese Civilization: Peasants and Elites in the Last of the Agrarian States* (New York: PICA Press, 1974), pp. 207–208.

tice; it became more popular during the succeeding Qing dynasty, when the power of the kinship organization reached its peak as the result of distant ancestral worship that effectively bound kinsmen together. As it turned out, the kinship clans played a significant role in the social control of local communities.

**Two Cults.** Ancestor worship ceremonies played an integral part in the Chinese family and kinship systems. There were two cults for ancestor worship. In the family cult, worship was given to immediate ancestors who had passed away in the past five or six generations. The family altar held wooden tablets carved with the names of those people; in some regions a list of names was written on a sheet of paper. The altar was the center of all household worship rituals that took place in designated times of the year. Associated with the family cult was the lineage cult, which focused on generalized ancestors that could be traced back dozens of generations. Particu-larly in southern parts of China, a visible symbol of the lineage cult was an ancestral hall, a temple-like building with a large chamber and beautiful decorations. Standing on a huge altar were rows of carved wooden tablets, bearing the full names, titles, and wives' surnames of past generations, around which the rituals of filial respect were usually carried out under the leadership of men aged sixty-one years or older in the kin-group.

**Social Role.** The lineage cult played a significant social role in village life. The lineage elders often assumed considerable moral authority that directed the values and norms of kinship as an integrated community, because the elders were believed to serve as the living link between the deceased and younger generations. In addition, a lineage ancestral hall was a center of socialization for a kin-group; social gatherings and public services often took place there. For example, a marriage became legitimate only after a newlywed male showed respect before the ancestral altar. In doing so, the

Album painting of a family giving thanks before a shrine, circa 1644 (British Museum, London)

descent line, as well as spiritual communication between living and dead, could continue without disruption.

**Customs.** Two customs that originated in the Tang and Song dynasties, and prevailed thereafter, became a standard practice of ancestor worship in the Chinese family. One was the ceremony held at the grave site, and the other was the rite performed before the ancestral tablets at home. The principal occasion each year for grave visiting was during the Qing Ming Festival, sometimes known as the "Grave-Sweeping Festival," when it was the duty of the living to clean up grave sites—weeding, sweeping, repainting, and repairing. Sacrifices were made to the ancestors, who were worshiped by the whole family, and the ceremonial foods were eaten afterward at a picnic held beside the graves. Yet another ceremony was held at home, where an "ancestor tablet" was placed in a position of prominence; it was a permanent presence, and the ancestors were considered to be watching over their descendants. The ancestor tablet could take several forms. The most common was a narrow wooden block, about one foot in height, sunk into a wooden base. The name, generation number, and attainments of the ancestor were written or carved on the front. Every day, tea and incense would be offered to the ancestors, and an eternal light of some kind was often kept burning before the altar to ensure that the ancestors were constantly borne in mind.

**Worship Days.** On the first and fifteenth days of each lunar month the ancestors would be given offerings of food, fruit, or money in addition to tea and incense. During the lunar New Year the ancestors were provided even more elaborate offerings; on the anniversaries of their birth dates and/or death dates they were again remembered. Any event of importance to the household was reported to the ancestors, and they ritually partook of all special foods that were prepared by the family for weddings, the month-long feast for a newborn, or other ceremonies and festivals. They were a significant part of everyday life. Daily worship was usually undertaken by women, falling as it did within the home, the women's sphere. On the most important occasions, however, such as New Year or on an ancestor's birth date, it was more likely that men, particularly the male head of the family, would officiate. There were no monk-priests present, as the ancestors could be worshiped only by their own descendants, and simple rites required no great ritual expertise.

**Rites.** Designated festivals were observed twice a year—the autumn rites for the distant ancestors and spring rites for the founding generation of the family. During the Song dynasty, spring rites were practiced at the ancestral grave-yard, as kinsmen paid a special visit to "sweep ancestral graves." The spring ancestral rites usually occurred in the first week of April and were called *Qing Ming*. The autumn rites in some regions gradually changed and eventually fell on the Lunar New Year. This festival was also the time for family members and kin-relatives, far and near, to gather together. Rites were usually practiced in the households or in the ancestral halls. The procedures were basically the same. A memorial speech was followed by offerings of burning incense, lit candles, and sacrificial food as symbolic ways to contact the spirits of the ancestors. Foods offered at the shrine table included a whole roasted pig, gourmet dishes, rice, steamed bread, and rice wine. Those in attendance then lined up by generation-age order to *Kow Tou* (kneel and bow) before the ancestral tablets. The rites ended with the reading aloud of ancestral mottos of family instructions, which were passed down through the generations. Etiquette in the ancestral hall called for the utmost solemnity and respect; everyone was required to dress properly to show piety. No one was allowed to come and go at will or to stand without proper manners while the rites were proceeding.

**Commensal Feast.** After the rites were completed, a commensal feast was held for all attending members to share the sacrificial food. In some regions only a limited number of those in attendance were eligible to eat the sacrificial food—usually only those individuals older than fifty years of age and men with academic degrees and official ranks. The rationale behind this exclusiveness was that old age indicated longevity and prosperity, while degrees and government rankings were symbols of achievement and success. These people, therefore, added to the honor of the family tradition, thus making ancestors proud of them up in Heaven. There was another practical reason to offer such privileges to selected members: they were major sources of donations to defray the expenses of these yearly ceremonies. For some wealthy families the ancestral ritual ceremonies were often followed by kin-group meetings where family matters were discussed and future plans made. Attending the ancestral rites each year was considered a family obligation, but at the same time it was a great honor for all male adults. Most family rules forbade women to attend the ancestral rites. In some cases, if a woman was found at the scene, not only did she have to leave immediately, but her husband or adult son was also flogged forty times as punishment for not having good supervision over

her. Women were permitted in some regions to attend the ancestral rites merely for service purposes. Ancestral rites were also the time to punish misbehaving family members. It was an ultimate disgrace for male adults to be excluded from attending the ancestral rites.

**Social Role.** Ancestral rites played a crucial role in promoting family cohesion. Naturally, they were memorial services for family members to keep past generations in their thoughts and prayers. It was a popular belief in China that the spirits of human beings had a postmortem existence and that the departed spirits of ancestors were able to interfere in the affairs of the living. It was a committed duty of the living to keep communicating with ancestral spirits through these rites so as to be blessed for continued peace or prosperity of the family. Keeping the ancestral rites alive served the purpose of maintaining the family tradition of showing respect for living elders.

Sources:

Patricia Buckley Ebrey, ed., *Chinese Civilization and Society: A Sourcebook* (New York: Free Press, 1981).

Hui-Chen Wang, *The Traditional Chinese Clan Rules* (Locust Valley, N.Y.: Association for Asian Studies, Augustin, 1959).

H. P. Wilkinson, *The Family in Classical China* (Shanghai: Kelly & Walsh, 1926).

## CHILD-REARING CEREMONIES

**Birth.** The birth of a child was clearly of great importance to the family in ancient China. Every year, between the eleventh and fifteenth days of the first and eighth months in the Chinese lunar year, the temples of *Song Zi Guan Ying* (child-giving goddess) were crowded, especially by married young women who were eager to have children. They went there to procure special, symbolic, paper shoes blessed by the goddess. These shoes were lined up on a table and surrounded by burning incense and candles. After offering incense and candles before the image of *Song Zi Guan Ying*, while simultaneously making pledges of returning the favor if the goddess would aid her in bearing a child (her first choice was always a male), a woman picked a pair of shoes supposedly belonging to her and took them home. She would place the shoes in a special place in her room for worshiping, as if they were connected with the goddess. She would pray in front of the shoes on the first and fifteenth day of each month until she became pregnant. After the child was born, the temple from which the shoes were obtained would be thanked with offerings.

**Paper Flowers.** In some regions married women went to a temple to pick up paper flowers instead of shoes from the goddess and then placed them in a paper vase at home. During the year a woman eager to have children made as many trips as possible to obtain these flowers, which were believed to be blessed, and burned them after a certain ceremony was performed by a sorceress or sorcerer. It was said that this custom was based on the popular belief that bearing a child would have much similarity to rearing a flower in a vase, and therefore repeating this ceremony made one's wish a reality.

Detail of the scroll *Learning at School* depicting pupils playing a prank on a sleeping instructor, Ming dynasty, 1368–1644 (Metropolitan Museum of Art, New York)

**Pregnancy.** Once pregnant, a woman's prenatal care started early. There were several rituals expected to be practiced during a pregnancy. She should live separate from her husband until after the birth of the child. While sleeping, she should lie on her back; while sitting or standing, her body should be in an upright position, with her weight evenly distributed. She should not laugh loudly. She should not eat spicy or bad-flavored food, nor anything that was not cut properly. To eat improperly prepared food was thought to give a careless disposition to the child, as it was an indication of a careless disposition on the part of the mother. For a similar reason she should not sit down on a mat that was awry but first should turn it square. Her eyes should not see bad colors, ugly sights, or obscene pictures. She should hear no obscene sounds, nor should she gossip or listen to improper conversations. She should be careful of her language. She should read good poetry, tell nice stories, and, when about to retire at night, call in blind storytellers and listen to beautiful tales so that, while sleeping, her mind might dwell upon lovely things. All the months of her pregnancy she must be watchful of things by which her mind was affected and keep a strict guard upon her temper. If she was affected by good things, the child would be good; if by bad things, the child would be bad. If she was careful to obey these rules, her child would be born physically, mentally, and morally in perfect condition.

**Ceremony.** Toward the end of the pregnancy a priest from a nearby temple would be hired to perform a special ceremony to drive away any evil spirits, so that the woman would be safe during childbirth. In some regions, for example, in the southern part of China, such a ceremony was carried out meticulously: "a table is spread with eight or ten plates of food, with incense, candles, flowers, and mock-money. A priest recites the classics appropriate to the occasion. Ten or twenty pieces of a kind of grass cut up about an inch long, and several likenesses of the crab, cut out of common paper, are put into the censer and burned. Or sometimes several live crabs, after being used in the ceremony, are taken and turned out into the street. It is thought that these will greatly aid in frightening those bad spirits or propitiate their good will, so that they will not dare to come into the room at the time of childbirth." At the end of the ceremony the ashes of the incense were collected and wrapped up in a piece of red paper to be stored until thirty days after childbirth. The purpose was to deter evil spirits from coming back to disturb the mother and newborn baby.

**Child Delivery.** At the time of childbirth, in case of difficult labor there would be another ceremony performed to drive away any evil spirit that prevented the child from coming into the world. A priest again was invited to perform the ceremony by arranging on a table three cups of wine, a plate containing five different kinds of fruit, together with lit incense and candles. "After the priest has mumbled over some unintelligible jargon or formula, attended with thumping on the table, for about half an hour, he produces three yellow paper charms, two or three inches wide, and a foot or more long; one of these is to be stuck over the door of the bedroom or on the bed-curtain, one is to be worn on the head of the sick woman, and the ashes of the other, mixed with hot water, is to be given to her to drink." When the delivery took more than the usual time, another emergency ceremony was performed at the bedside of the groaning expectant mother. Her family members performed a special show in which a paper figure of the "child-giving goddess" was maneuvered to dance around in the room and over to the body of the suffering woman and then returned to dancing again. It was believed that the goddess would help relieve suffering and make labor go easily. If the delivery was successful after its use, a thanksgiving ceremony would be given in praise of the divine power of the goddess.

**First Celebration.** Celebrations that were most intimately connected with the family had to do with birthdays and the lives of children. On the third day after a child was born, it was given its first bath, performed often by the midwife. Special female friends of the family would be invited to witness the ceremony. Immediately after the bath most families observed an important custom by "binding baby's wrists," in hopes that it would help the baby to grow up well behaved and to live a prosperous adult life. Some families bound ancient coins around each wrist with a red cotton cord; others put a loose red string in the shape of a ring around the wrist; and still others decorated the wrists with a string of miniature silver toys. The baby carried them for up to a whole year, depending on local customs.

**Second Celebration.** The second celebration in the life of a child was when the family performed the custom of "shaving the child's head" when it was a month old. Many parents, after the shaving, purposefully let the hair grow only on the front part of the head. A boy's hair was shaved regularly, but with a small portion of hair always left on the top of his head, a style he wore until he was sixteen years old. Such a hairdo was believed to be conducive to the health of a boy. Others explained that doing so helped protect the child's soft spot on the skull. Girls were allowed to grow a patch of hair on both sides of the head.

Painting titled *Children Playing in the Palace Garden*, circa 1200–1400 (Metropolitan Museum of Art, New York)

**First Feast.** The head of the child was often shaved before the guests arrived; some families performed the shaving in front of the ancestral tablets. A feast was prepared by the parents for the guests, who often came with presents such as lacquered boxes in which were placed cakes in the form of the peach of longevity; or round cakes with the character for "long life" stamped or written in red ink; or vermicelli, which when cooked appeared in long strings, indicative of the guests' wish that the child have a long life. The maternal grandmother of the child was always expected to bring or send gifts of clothing or special food on this day.

**Second Feast.** When the child was one year old, the family gave another feast. Friends and relatives gathered and brought presents for the child. Before the feast commenced, a large platter was placed on a table, usually set before the ancestral tablets. On the platter lay several items,

Detail of a painting of a court lady playing with two children, early twelfth century (from Wen C. Fong, *Beyond Representation*, 1992)

such as money scales, a pair of shears, a foot measure, a brass mirror, brush pen, ink stone, abacus, and one or two books. The child, usually dressed in new garments, was allowed to see these items and to make a selection. The first thing it took in its hand was supposed to indicate the profession or calling it would follow. If the child chose a brush pen, ink stone, or book, it would be a scholar; if an abacus, a merchant or banker; or any kind of tool, a tradesman. The tradition was said to originate from a legendary story from the Song dynasty (960–1279): on the first anniversary of his birthday a boy was asked to make a selection of objects spread on a bamboo sieve. His first picks were two miniature military weapons in one hand and two small sacrificial vessels in the other hand. His second pick was a seal. After these selections the boy showed no interest in other things on the sieve. As it turned out, he became chancellor of the empire. Since then, the ceremony became a common custom for families to observe on the celebration of children's first anniversary. A different set of objects would be placed on the platter for females—scissors, a thimble, or other things that would be appropriate to indicate the scope of a girl's life.

**Lucky Stars.** Those families that had a sick or physically weak child performed a ceremony called "worshiping lucky stars," which were said to exist in the sky in both the northern and southern heavens. Stars in the northern heavens represented the god of longevity; stars in the southern heavens represented the god of fortune. In folk belief, worshiping lucky stars brought benefits—life and fortune—to sickly children. This ceremony was frequently performed on the fourteenth or fifteenth day of the eighth month in the Chinese lunar year, or alternatively on the child's birth-

day. The origin of this custom was based on a legendary story about how a boy changed his predestined fate: Once upon a time there was a young man who wandered into a street and ran into an old fortune-teller named Kuan-lo, who sized up the young man, saying, "You are a fine boy, but unfortunately, your life is to be so short." The young man then asked how long his life was to be, and Kuan-lo told him that he was to die at the age of nineteen. This prediction really frightened the young man because he was near that age. In a panic he asked the fortune-teller what he could do to avoid his bad fortune. Kuan-lo instructed him to carry a plate of preserved venison and a bottle of wine to the top of a certain mountain, where he would find two old men playing chess. He was told to place the venison and wine by the side of the men without saying a word and then wait patiently until they had finished the game. The young man followed Kuan-lo's instructions and climbed to the top of the mountain. He saw two mysterious men playing chess. Quietly he placed the food and drink next to the chess table and waited patiently until the two men finished the game. Then the young man walked over and offered them food and drink. Having eaten the offerings, the two men turned to the young man and asked how they could help him. The young man told them the story and begged them to save him from dying young. The men took out a book of records and after a careful examination found that the young man was indeed almost finished with his life. To save his life, they took a pen and changed the figure nineteen to ninety-nine with a single stroke on the record. The Chinese worshiped these two mysterious men, whom they believed were lucky stars that came from the northern and southern heavens, and who could change the course of an individual's life. On the day of this ceremony some families fashioned a table layout, presented in the format of seven stars in the heavens, which they filled generously with food. Sometimes a Daoist priest would be hired to do some praise chanting for one family by another.

**Schooling.** When the child was old enough to begin to study, the calendar and soothsayers were consulted, and a lucky day was selected for entering a school. Children usually went to the family or village school or to a private tutoring studio. Some regional customs required a boy on the first day of school to bring two small candles, a few sticks of incense, and a small amount of mock money. Then he would bow, while burning these articles, in front of a paper with some titles of Confucius written on it. This simple ceremony was called "entering school" or "worshiping the sage." Some regional customs also required a boy to worship both Confucius and his own ancestors. After doing so, the child entered school, where his teacher selected a name to replace his *Nai Min* (milk name), which had been given to him by his mother. The classic book *Li Ji* (Canon of Rites) laid out the basic procedures of training children that became the primary mode of education in traditional China. According to the *Li Ji*, when a child was able to eat without assistance, parents should teach him or her to use the right hand. When they were able to speak,

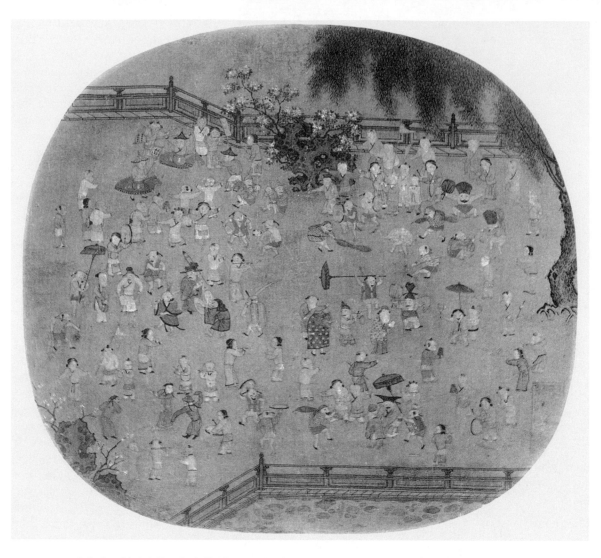

Painting titled *A Hundred Children at Play,* Song dynasty, 960–1279 (Cleveland Museum of Art)

parents should train boys to be confident and clear in response, whereas girls learned to be submissive and soft in voice. At the age of six, children learned how to identify numbers and the names of cardinal points. At seven, boys and girls were not allowed to play on the same mat or eat together. At eight, they learned how to behave properly both inside and outside of the home by following their elders. At nine, children were taught to acquaint themselves with the cycles of months and years.

Sources:

Isaac Taylor Headland, *Home Life in China* (New York: Macmillan, 1914).

Thomas H. C. Lee, *Education in Traditional China: A History* (Leiden & Boston: E. J. Brill, 2000).

Leon E. Stover, *The Cultural Ecology of Chinese Civilization: Peasants and Elites in the Last of the Agrarian States* (New York: Pica Press, 1974).

## CONTACT WITH THE WEST

**Exchanges.** Direct contact between China and the West came during the Han dynasty (206 B.C.E.–220 C.E.), when its military thrust reached the Tarim Basin, and the Chinese established garrisons there. Some historians argue that it was from the reign of Xiao Wu Di that trade between East and West, through caravan traffic over rugged desert roads, came into being. It was said that many new things were introduced to China, such as grape wine and lucerne (alfalfa). Chives, cucumbers, sesame, coriander, and many other products followed. In exchange, silk, oranges, peonies, azaleas, and many other items found their way to the West.

**Contacts.** By the early eighth century, Tang China reached its golden age, and its power and prestige promoted extensive contacts with the outside world during the imperial period. The Chinese monk Xuanzang traveled across Central Asia and India for fifteen years and returned with the knowledge of different religions and cultures that attracted the Tang imperial court. Of the greatest importance for the spiritual history of China was the importation of Buddhism, which has since exerted everlasting impact on the lives of the Chinese people. The Tang capital, Chang'an, was the largest cosmopolitan city in the world and was the terminus of the Silk Road, over which merchants from Eurasian countries traveled and traded. Thus, Chang'an became a multicultural city in which world religions and cultures met.

**Foreign Influences.** China in Tang times was more open to the outside world than at any other time in the imperial era until the mid nineteenth century. On the streets of Chang'an, goods from distant regions—horses, jewels, musical instruments, food, wines, and arts—flourished. Foreign fashions in hairstyles and clothing were often copied, and foreign amusements, such as polo, became favorite pastimes of the elite class. Caravans that came from Central Asia fascinated the Tang people so much that representations of camels and their non-Han grooms appeared on pottery. In addition, various designs of silver cups, plates, ewers, and other small objects showed the great influence of Persian innovations and techniques. The Tang people's lives were enriched by new musical instruments and tunes from India, Iran, and Central Asia. Allegedly these items transformed Han Chinese music, which had mostly been performed by a single instrument. The "upside-down larynx," or falsetto singing, replaced the conventional Chinese style of singing, making Tang music distinctive.

**Temples.** Among the imported sports such as polo and soccer, there was another popular activity during the second half of the seventh century. This activity became part of the celebration for the coming of winter and required that onlookers shower naked dancing youths with cold water. In Tang times foreign influence had such an impact that the practice of sitting on floor mats was replaced by the use of stools and chairs. In Chang'an were found Buddhist temples, Jewish synagogues, Islamic mosques, and even Nestorian Christian chapels (the latter faith was condemned as heresy in the West in 431 C.E.). The Japanese and Koreans greatly admired Tang civilization. The Japanese modeled their capital city after Chang'an. The Japanese tea ceremony and the formal kimono dress were inspired by Chinese fashions in the Tang period. Chinese literature and poetry reached their height and spread across the borders to Eastern and Southeast Asian countries. For example, the earliest literature in both Korea and Japan was mostly written in Chinese.

**Changes.** Historians noticed some fundamental changes in China as the country transformed from an outward-looking society in the Tang era to an inward-looking society in the Song period (960–1279). This shift reflected a turning away from foreign cultures and arts, which were often labeled "barbarian." In the Yuan dynasty (1279–1368) contact with the West revived because of excessive territorial expansion, but the cultural impact was limited because the Yuan remained in power for less than one hundred years. Moreover, the Mongol conquerors of China seldom fully trusted Chinese officials and appointed Mongolian or Central Asian commissars to supervise them and keep close tabs on their activities. The Mongols also canceled the Chinese civil service examinations for most of the Yuan dynasty. The Ming (1368–1644) reinstituted the examination system and developed it to its full extent.

Sources:

Wolfram Eberhard, *A History of China*, translated by E. W. Dickes (Berkeley: University of California Press, 1950; London: Routledge & Kegan Paul, 1950).

Shen Fuwei, *Cultural Flow between China and Outside World throughout History* (Beijing: Foreign Language Press, 1996).

David Curtis Wright, *The History of China* (Westport, Conn.: Greenwood Press, 2001).

## THE CULT OF CHASTITY

**Chastity.** During the Song dynasty (960–1279) chastity was held as the highest virtue of women. This philosophical outlook was largely promoted by the Chenq (yi)-Zhu (xi) doctrines, which proposed that for a woman to lose her virtue was worse than starving to death. Such a high social demand on women became the moral base for the "cult of chastity," which turned into a social trend. Neo-Confucian moral ethics discouraged a widow from remarrying, and in most regions her remarriage was considered adultery, because chastity required a woman to remain forever a wife to her husband, even after his death. When a widow was allowed to remarry, she was stripped of the privileges she once had with her former husband's family. For example, she had no right to take with her the family property and could not retain her place in the genealogy of the late husband's kin-group.

**Widowhood.** The "cult of widow" was pushed to its zenith in Ming times (1368–1644). By custom, widows were expected to dress in white, black, or blue outfits. An old saying referred to a man who took a widow as his bride as "marrying the wearer of a white skirt." It was considered a disgrace to a family for one of its sons to marry a widow, and equally shameful for a widow to remarry. Even if a man of modest means chose to marry a widow because of the small betrothal expense, she was not allowed to ride in the red bridal chair to the residence of her intended husband. She was carried

Detail of the painting *Admonitions of the Instructress to the Court Ladies*, circa seventh century (British Museum, London)

Detail of a scroll depicting an emperor berating a court lady, circa seventh century (British Museum, London)

instead on a black-covered bridal chair. Under this tremendous social pressure most widows chose not to remarry, because they did not want to bring shame to both their own dignity and the honor of their husband's families. The stigma of widowhood was carried to such an extreme that a girl who had been betrothed, but her husband-to-be died before their formal wedding, would often be turned down for new engagements by families of potential suitors because she was labeled "a girl of bad luck." Sometimes a girl under such circumstances chose to take her own life rather than live unmarried—her coffin would thus be buried alongside that of her betrothed. A woman who chose to die rather than lose her virtue by remarrying was highly praised. Halls of chastity were established in their honor and their names were recorded in books such as *Nei Xun* (Advice from Palace), *Nu Xue* (Ethics of Women), *Nu Er Jing* (Principles of Women), and *Gu Jing Lie Nu Zhuan* (Stories of Chaste Women from the Past to the Present).

**Song Tradition.** In the Ming dynasty the imperial state went to great lengths to sponsor the cult of chastity, a tradition inherited from the Song dynasty and held as the ultimate moral identity for what was considered a decent woman. Virginity was a critical part of virtue for unmarried young women. A popular book at the time, *Za Shi Mi Zhong* (Tracking Down the Mysteries), taught men how to check on a woman to find out whether she was a virgin. Furthermore, state laws allowed the village-based family clans to enforce their own customary laws to punish "immoral women" by a variety of

means, ranging from humiliating them to putting them to death (hanging or drowning were popular methods).

**Virtuous Women.** Incense and candles were burned in the local temples on the first and fifteenth day of each month to honor "virtuous and filial" women. Honorary tablets were installed to commemorate women who had devoted their lives to filial piety for their parents and husbands. In some regions huge slabs of black stone or granite were erected by the sides of main streets; inscriptions were carved on the crosspieces in praise of select women's chastity and filial piety. These stones were often placed under the special permission and sponsorship of the imperial court. In some communities chaste and filial widows, when they reached the age of fifty, were eligible to have their names carved on tablets in praise of their long-term devotion (not seeking to remarry). In Ming times, because of massive involvement by the state, the social demand for women's chastity escalated to such an extreme level that many widows took their own lives in order to be granted such honors. By way of comparison, as shown in historical documents, the women of chastity officially recorded in the *Song Shi* (History of Song Dynasty) were 55 in total; the number of documented chaste women increased dramatically, from 187 in the *Yuan Shi* (History of Yuan Dynasty) to more than 10,000 in the *Ming Shi* (History of Ming Dynasty).

Sources:
Rubie S. Watson and Patricia Buckley Ebrey, eds., *Marriage and Inequality in Chinese Society* (Berkeley: University of California Press, 1991).
Ruikai Zhu, *Zhongguo Hun Yin Jia Ting Shi*, translated as *History of the Family and Marriage in China* (Shanghai: Xueling Press, 1999).

## FAMILY AUTHORITY

**Father.** *Xiao* (Filial Piety) and *Li* (Rites) were two pillars of patriarchy in ancient China. *Li* stipulated that the highest rank and respect be awarded to the *Jia Zhang* (family head, or father); *Xiao* was the beginning of *Li* and was used to ensure the proper ordering of the family. With few exceptions, laws in the Tang (618–907), Song (960–1279), and Ming (1368–1644) dynasties proclaimed that all family property belonged to the father. The concept of *Jia Zhang* was deeply ingrained in traditional Chinese familial culture. As the family head the father had the highest authority, which required total obedience from other family members because he was seen as their superior. In a similar vein, broadly defined, the head of the clan was also authorized to play the role of *Jia Zhang* in relation to his kinsmen in the larger community.

**Power.** The *Jia Zhang* could use any means (even death) to penalize a disobedient child or family member without fear of being held accountable by state laws. After the Tang dynasty almost all imperial family laws favored patriarchy, particularly those regulations made during the Song and Ming times. During the Song dynasty the theoretical patriarchal system was laid out by Zhu Xi in the *Zhu Zi Jia Li* (Book of Family Rites). He proposed that "everyone in the family owes complete obedience to Jia Zhang (the family head)." The effort of the state to popularize ancestral halls and rites reinforced familial stratification. The rapid growth of the *Zu* (kin-clan) in Song times put various communities under the total control of the *Jia Zhang*. In a kin-clan, power was concentrated in a few male elders, called *Zu Zhang*, who presided over community affairs. For kinsmen the ancestral temple in the village was their court, and clan regulations were laws by which they complied.

**Customary Laws.** The rise of kin-clan power occurred when Chinese customary law—an informal legal system in which most communities were given a high degree of autonomy in exercising control over local affairs—came into being. As long as these rules did not conflict with the interests of the state, the local clans, villages, and guilds were allowed to settle minor legal disputes among their members. Customary law was most evident in the realms of the family and marriage. Clan elders and parents were entrusted to decide matters of marriage, divorce, and succession on behalf of their juniors. They also had the final say in settling disputes; informal hearings were usually set up in the family compound or at the ancestral temple, and disciplinary actions were carried out according to customary rules. Similarly, customary law was applied to the informal settlement of disputes in the guilds or other businesses. The heads of guilds were entrusted with the responsibility of exercising discretionary power to redress damages, grievances, and abuses among their members. State courts handled only those complicated and serious cases that the family and guild heads found impossible to resolve.

**The State.** The authority of the *Jia Zhang* and that of the *Guo Jia* (the state, as viewed as a family head) were closely associated. If a father was regarded as the *Jia Zhang* of the house, so too was the state seen in relation

Pottery figurines of women doing kitchen chores, Tang dynasty, 618–907 (National Palace Museum, Taipei, Taiwan)

Detail of a scroll showing children paying respect to their father, twelfth century
(National Palace Museum, Taipei, Taiwan)

to broader society and the emperor in relation to all his subjects. During the Tang and Song dynasties, laws imposed the responsibility of the family head on family affairs and compelled his loyalty to the state and to the emperor. Both dynasties demanded that family heads assist the government in house registration, taxation, and the draft of soldiers; state laws also outlined the punishments for those who failed to do so.

**Sources:**
William Theodore de Bary and others, *Sources of Chinese Tradition* (New York: Columbia University Press, 1960).

Maurice Freedman, *Chinese Lineage and Society: Fukien and Kwangtung* (London: Athlone Press, 1966; New York: Humanities Press, 1966).

H. P. Wilkinson, *The Family in Classical China* (Shanghai: Kelly & Walsh, 1926).

## FAMILY AND CHILD EDUCATION

**Training Children.** Starting from the age of ten, boys and girls were expected to take different paths in life. A boy usually was sent to a master/tutor's house to learn classical literature as well as proper manners. At thirteen he was instructed in music, in how to recite the classics, and in carrying out the gentle-man's rites. At the same time he was taught archery and chariot driving. At twenty he was "capped" in order to be permitted to attend to various filial and fraternal duties and to assume social responsibility as an adult. At the age of ten a girl was forbidden to leave the home; for a girl of a well-to-do family, her mother or father sometimes hired a governess to teach her woman's work. She was instructed in the arts of gentle speech and obedience, how to weave silks and fashion ribbons, and how to assist in setting up stands and dishes for various family ceremonies. At fifteen she was endowed with a hairpin that signified that she was allowed to marry and become a wife through the betrothal rites. Though there was variety in child rearing during the long span of imperial Chinese history, all customs shared the similar pattern of training children for socially defined functions and the duties of adulthood.

**Grandfather's Instructions.** In Tang times (618–907) Confucian social ethics were taught in elementary education primers. In the "Family Instructions of the Grandfather," regarding the proper behavior of both young men and women, it was written:

When his father goes out to walk
The son must follow behind.
If on the road he meets a senior
He puts his feet together and joins his hands.
In front of a senior
He does not spit on the ground.

The moral teaching of women's behavior was also covered:

A bride serves her husband
Just as she served her father.
Her voice should not be heard
Nor her body or shadow seen.
With her husband's father and elder brothers
She has no conversation.

**Commitment.** Parents were held accountable for neglect of their children's educations, especially in upholding filial piety. It was a social obligation for parents to give their young children training in proper social behavior that honored the generation-age order until such conditioning became habit. For example, children were expected to know that it was improper to reach for food before their elders were served during meals. It was imperative that youngsters receive a good upbringing and that parents share responsibility for such training. It is thus not difficult to understand why parents in traditional Chinese society often accepted social blame and stigma when their children were found guilty of misconduct. From this perspective, mutual obligations for both the parents and children underscored the significance of filial piety. On the one hand, it was the parents' commitment to rear their children to be fully aware of social obligations. On the other hand, it was the children's responsibility to fulfill those obligations when they grew up. In doing so, both the parents and children observed their socially defined roles so that the family could be maintained in good order and harmony.

**Zhang Family.** One case, often cited in the classical literature on family relationships, regards the Zhang family in the Tang dynasty. When the emperor heard that the Zhang family had lived together for nine generations in succession, he was amazed about this unusual solidarity and continuity, and he asked the head of the clan to offer the secrets of family politics. Without uttering a word in reply, the family head took a piece of paper and on it wrote the word *Ren* one hundred times. *Ren* in English translation means "patience," "toleration," or "conciliation."

**Education.** The family was the arena where formal education started under the close supervision of the parents or guardians. Because a man's prospects hinged upon his becoming a literati, which helped him gain entry to high social status, the education of sons was a priority of Chinese families, especially the well-to-do. Generally, private schooling was the major educational avenue to success in imperial Chinese society. Wealthy families could afford to hire private tutors for their male

Detail of Chen Hongshou's painting, *Lady Zuan Wenjun Giving Instructions on the Classics,* 1638 (Cleveland Museum of Art)

children, while boys of poor families attended clan-financed schools that provided free education.

**Elite Competition.** Education was an essential part of Chinese family values. This fact had much to do with the tradition of Chinese education being open to all talented individuals regardless of social status; this system can be traced back to Confucius's teachings during the Zhou dynasty (771–256 B.C.E.) and was developed in successive dynasties. During the Han dynasty (206 B.C.E.–220 C.E.) the Grand Academy of Education was established, and students took examinations to compete for entry into government service. By the Tang dynasty the educational system was elevated to higher official status as the *Guo Zi Jian* (State Academy Directorate), one of five state directorates. The *Guo Zi Jian* encompassed six schools, enrolling as many as 2,210 students through a highly competitive selection process designed to prepare them for the metropolitan examinations. The best students were awarded the most prestigious degree, the *Jinshi*, which guaranteed access to appointments in the imperial government—the key to upward social mobility. Many eminent statesmen and literary figures in Chinese imperial history were holders of the *Jinshi*.

**Elementary Education.** The Song dynasty was more of a meritocracy than an aristocracy, because it expanded the civil service examination system and made official careers available to men of talent, regardless of their

Masters Chen and Tung established a firm schedule for their students during the late Song dynasty (960–1279). This excerpt indicates that children's education was strongly influenced by neo-Confucian teachings, a tendency that continued until the end of the imperial period in China.

SCHOOL REGULATIONS ESTABLISHED BY MASTER CH'ENG AND TUNG:

All students of this school must observe closely the following regulations.

1. *Ceremonies held on the 1st and 15th of every month.* At daybreak, the student on duty for that day will sound his clappers. At the first round of the clappers, you should rise, wash your face, comb your hair, and put on proper clothing. By the second round of the clappers, you should be dressed either in ceremonial robes or in summer robes and gather in the main hall. The teachers will then lead you to the image of Confucius, to which you will bow twice. After the incense has been lit, you will make two more bows. . . .

2. *Daily salutations held in the morning and in the evening.* On ordinary days, the student on duty sounds the clappers as described above. At the second round of the clappers you will enter the hall and line up to wait for the teachers to come out. Then the teachers and you bow to each other with hands folded in front. Next, you divide into two groups and bow to each other, after which you begin your daily studies. . . .

3. *Daily behavior.* You should have a defined living area. When in a group you will be seated according to your ages. When sitting, you must straighten your backs and sit squarely in the chair. You should not squat, lean to one side, cross your legs, or dangle your feet. At night, you should always wait for the elders to go to bed first. After they are in bed, you should keep quiet. Also, you should not sleep during the day.

4. *Gait and posture.* You should walk slowly. When standing, keep your hands folded in front. Never walk or stand in front of an elder. Never turn your back on those who are your superiors in age or status. Do not step on doorsills. Do not limp. Do not lean on anything.

5. *Looking and listening.* Do not gape. Do not eavesdrop.

6. *Discourse.* Statements should always be verifiable. Keep your promises. Your manners should be serious. Do not be boisterous or playful. Do not gossip about your neighbors. Do not engage in conversations about vulgar matters.

7. *Appearance.* Be dignified and serious. Do not be disobedient. Do not be rough or rude. Do not be vicious or proud. Do not reveal your joy or anger.

8. *Attire.* Do not wear unusual or extravagant clothing. Yet do not go to the other extreme and appear in clothes that are ragged, dirty, or in bad taste. Even in your private quarters you should never expose your body or take off your cap. Even in the hottest days of summer you should not take off your socks or shoes at will.

9. *Eating.* Do not fill yourself. Do not seek fancy foods. Eat at regular hours. Do not be discontent with coarse fare. Never drink unless on a holiday or unless you are ordered to do so by your elders. Never drink more than three cups or get drunk.

10. *Travel.* Unless you are called upon by your elders, ordered to run errands by your teachers, or faced by a personal emergency, you are not allowed to leave the campus at will. Before your departure and after your return you should report to your teacher. You must not change your reported destination, and you must return by the set time.

11. *Reading.* You should concentrate on your book and keep a dignified appearance. You should count the number of times you read an assigned piece. If, upon completion of the assigned number, you still have not memorized the piece, you should continue until you are able to recite it. On the other hand, if you have memorized the piece quickly, you should still go on to complete the assigned number of readings. . . .

12. *Writing.* Do not scribble. Do not write slanted or sloppy characters.

13. *Keep your desk tidy.* The assigned seats should be kept in order. Your study area should be simple but tidy. All book chests and clothing trunks should be locked up carefully.

14. *Keep the lecture halls and private rooms clean.* Each day one student is on duty. After sounding the second round of the clappers, he should sprinkle water on the floor of the lecture hall. Then, after an appropriate wait, he should sweep the floor and wipe the desks. The other cleaning jobs should be assigned to the pages. Whenever there is cleaning to be done, they should be ordered to do it, regardless of the time of the day.

15. *Terms of address.* You should address those who are twice your age as "elder," those who are ten years older than you as "old brothers," and those who are about your age by their polite names. Never address one another as "you." The same rules should be followed in letter writing.

16. *Visits.* The following rules should be observed when a guest requests to visit the school. After the teacher is seated and the student on duty has sounded the clappers, all students, properly dressed, enter the lecture hall. After the morning salutation, the students remain standing; only when the teacher orders them to retire may they leave. If the guest should wish to speak to a student privately, he should, after seeing the teacher, approach the student at his seat. If the student finds the visitor incompatible, he is not obliged to be congenial.

17. *Recreation.* There are rules for the playing of musical instruments, for archery, as well as for other games. You should seek recreation only at the right time. Gambling and chess games are lowly pastimes and should be avoided by our students.

18. *Servants.* Select those who are prudent, honest, and hardworking. Treat them with dignity and forbearance. When they make mistakes, scold them or report to the teacher. If they do not improve after being punished, report to the teacher to have them discharged. A student should not expel his page at will.

If you can follow the above regulations closely, you are approaching the true realm of virtue.

**Source:** Patricia Buckley Ebrey, ed., *Chinese Civilization and Society: A Sourcebook* (New York: Free Press, 1981), pp. 114–116.

family backgrounds. Chinese elementary education became systematic in terms of the standardized curriculum adopted by schools of various kinds. This curriculum included three primers: *San Zi Jing* (Trimetrical Classic), *Qian Zi Wen* (Thousand Character Classic), and *Bai Jia Xing* (Book of Hundred Surnames). These classic books provided the basic vocabulary of approximately two thousand characters for beginners, before they moved up to formal education that required the mastery of the *Wu Jing* (Five Classics). The *Wu Jing* was a corpus of moral and literary texts formulated in earlier dynasties and formalized in Tang times. The first classic was the *Book of Changes*, followed in order by the *Book of Documents*, the *Book of Odes*, *Record of Rituals*, and *Spring and Autumn Annals*. Two more texts were later added to this collection of Confucian classics: the *Lun Yu* (Analects) and Mencius's *Men Zi* (Mencius). In the Song period (960–1279) four Confucian texts received special attention in the curriculum—the *Lun Yu*, *Men Zi*, *Daxue* (Great Learning), and the *Zhongyong* (Doctrine of the Mean).

**Examination.** The improvement of printing in the Song dynasty encouraged a great expansion of the education system. The Song basically followed the pattern established by the State Academy Directorate of the Tang Dynasty but also set up official schools at the provincial and prefectural levels. Many community and charity schools also appeared at the local level. The Yuan (1279–1368) and Ming (1368–1644) dynasties continued this tradition, but the Ming fully revived the functions of the State Academy Directorate, which became an important channel for men entering official service. In comparison with previous dynasties, the Ming was more open to the general public participating in the civil service examinations. According to research data, between 1371 and 1610 more than half of the students who took the examinations were from families in which no ancestor for three generations had held any academic degree, while only 8 percent came from a family that produced literati in the previous three generations.

**Academic Degree.** For Chinese parents the academic degrees that their sons earned through the Chinese education system not only brought the family fame and wealth but more importantly provided the incentive to carry on this family tradition. For a young man there were two happiest moments in his life. One was the first night spent with his bride in the bridal chamber after the wedding ceremony; the other was when he saw his name posted on the golden list of *Jinshi* holders.

Sources:

Patricia Buckley Ebrey and James L. Watson, eds., *Kinship Organization in Late Imperial China, 1000–1940* (Berkeley: University of California Press, 1986).

Weiming Shi, *Yuan Dai Shen Huo* (Social History of the Yuan Dynasty) (Beijing: Chinese Social Sciences Academy Press, 1996).

Sing Ging Su, *The Chinese Family System* (New York: International Press, 1922).

## FAMILY COMPOSITION

**Extended Structure.** During the Tang dynasty (618–907) there was a conspicuous transition from a simple family structure to stem and extended structures. The reasons compelling family members from several generations to live together were primarily economic, political, and social. First, the progress of agrarian development required greater cooperation among a large family unit for it to be able to accumulate sufficient capital and labor to achieve maximum economic benefits. Second, the prevalence of Confucianism, in conjunction with Buddhism, emphasized filial piety, especially by Tang times. For example, co-residing families with members from five generations were applauded in society, whereas a married son, living apart from his parents, was condemned. Families of ten or twenty individuals became a common phenomenon in the Tang dynasty and even more popular in Song times (960–1279). This trend continued without much change during the Yuan (1279–1368) period, though it was somewhat weakened by Mongol laws that were more flexible, and into the Ming (1368–1644) dynasty. Third, increased state power intervened in the family institution. The Tang and Song imperial governments issued laws to ensure that sons cared for their aged parents, a policy that directly pushed the further development of stem and extended family structures.

**Prosperous Family.** Stem and extended structures also helped boost the social distinction of a large and prosperous family, especially when kinsmen attained high social prestige that brought the kin-clan enduring honor. Before the Tang period, however, only the noble class had a distinctive family-clan organization, called the *Shi*, and its lineage, called *Zong*, bound the whole kinship system through primogeniture. This organization eventually gave way to a new social order in which all the sons received equal inheritance rights. Clan organizations no longer revolved around primogeniture but were established according to social prestige and political power. As a result, several powerful family clans, generally called *Wang Zu* (eminent family-clan), dominated local regions and enjoyed close association with the imperial courts, which provided them with special privileges in taxation and civil service appointments. Five *Wang Zu* survived the Han (206 B.C.E.–220 C.E.) and Sui (589–618) dynasties and became powerful social groups, but the "big five" families drastically declined during the Tang period, when the imperial court abolished many privileges once enjoyed by these clans.

**New System.** Yet, Tang China was still an aristocratic society. In elite circles, genealogies continued to be much discussed, and eminent forebears were looked upon as a source of pride and admiration; members of the most-prestigious families still largely married among themselves, giving coherence and visibility to the highest stratum of the elite. Early in the Tang dynasty the emperors tried to undermine the prestige of aristocratic pedigrees and to assert that high office carried more honor than having notable ancestors. In addition, during classical times, ancestral rites were performed only by royal and aristocratic families, but in the Tang dynasty these ceremonies were spread beyond the elite to common families. These changes exerted a tremendous impact on the evolution

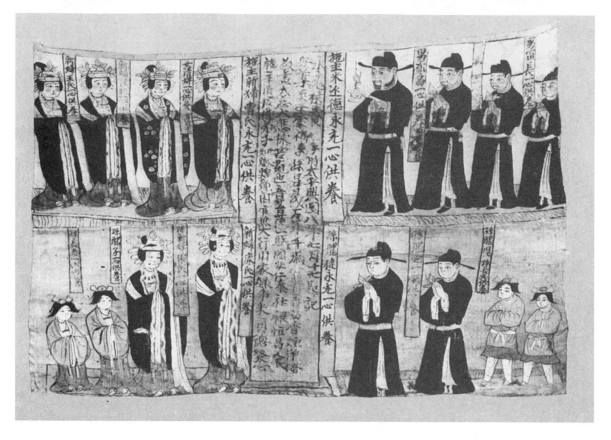

Detail of a painting on silk of a Chinese family, circa 985 (British Museum, London)

of the Chinese family, which in time transformed from a privileged clan united for political interests into an economic and social organization centered on the performance of ancestral rites. This system became widespread in the Song dynasty and was firmly established in the Ming dynasty.

**Influential Thinker.** Song philosopher and scholar Zhu Xi—who advocated neo-Confucianism—laid the moral as well as structural foundation for the family institution; his influence can still be seen in contemporary Chinese society. He recommended that people consult the *Four Books,* which embodied the fundamentals of Confucianism. They were Confucius's *Lun Yu* (Analects), *Zhongyong* (Doctrine of the Mean), and *Daxue* (Great Learning), as well as Mencius's *Book of Confucius Disciple.* To maintain family stability, Zhu Xi introduced an institution called *Xiangyue* (Community Compact), which involved regular assemblies to facilitate communication among local residents. He also advocated a hierarchy of authority; five age grades, with rules for the conduct of all family members; the celebration of major rituals, with corresponding dress codes; and many other detailed instructions for managing family affairs. Zhu Xi saw these practices as essential to balance the relationship between the state and the family.

**Sources:**
Maurice Freeman, ed., *Family and Kinship in Chinese Society* (Stanford, Cal.: Stanford University Press, 1970).

Olga Lang, *Chinese Family and Society* (New Haven: Yale University Press, 1946 / London: Cumberlege, 1946).

Ruikai Zhu, *Zhongguo Hun Yin Jia Ting Shi,* translated as *History of the Family and Marriage in China* (Shanghai: Xueling Press, 1999).

## FAMILY ETHICS: FILIAL PIETY

**Relations.** *Xiao* (filial piety) in China derived from the doctrines of Confucianism. The *Zhongyong* (Doctrine of the Mean) arranged the fundamental human relations according to an ordering of superior/inferior relationships, or *Wu Lun:* "There are five universally applicable principles, . . . that of the relationships between ruler and minister, that of father and son, of husband and wife, of elder and younger brother, and of friend and friend." The essence of *Xiao* existed in the age and gender hierarchy of the family, starting with the father-son relationship and then extending by analogy to other social relationships. The aim was the orderly running of the family and through it, of the state. *Xiao* always went hand in hand with ancestor worship and was the cornerstone of family ethics. The duty of a man was first to his parents and only secondly to the state, but the two were inseparable in principle because, according to Confucianism, "a man who respected parental authority would respect the law and one who accepted filial responsibility would honor his social obligations." Therefore, the virtue of filial piety was more than just passive obedience: it was a personal commitment to the well-being of one's parents. A man's loyalty to his parents, according to Confucian principles, took precedence over his love for his wife. The rationale was that parents were like Heaven and Earth to their children because they gave them their bodies and souls and reared them to be mature human beings. It was therefore

Drawing from the *Book of Filial Piety* showing children paying respect to their parents, Song dynasty, 960–1279
(National Palace Museum, Taipei, Taiwan)

a moral duty for children to show appreciation and respect in return.

**Proper Behavior.** The proper behaviors of filial piety by children were to please and support their parents whenever they needed them, to remain pious toward parents unconditionally, to share responsibilities with brothers to provide for aging parents, to bury deceased parents properly, and to perform ancestral rites for their spirits thereafter. The key point of filial piety was to satisfy the wishes of the parents—while they were alive and after they had died. The installation of the ancestral hall indicated that filial responsibility extended beyond the lifetime of the parents; any neglect of burials or indifference to worship was disrespectful to the spirits and was considered a serious offense to moral ethics. In the Ming dynasty (1368–1644) it was a serious offense for a state employee not to announce the death of a parent and then to retire to mourn for the statu-

tory period of more than two years. Thus, *Xiao* manifested itself in the ultimate duties of offspring to provide for and attend to the daily needs of their parents, to obey their commands, to take good care of them while they were ill, to arrange proper funerals when they passed away, to visit their grave sites at regular intervals, and to remember them through memorial services. This tradition was consistently upheld and reinforced through the performance of rites.

**Five Virtues.** Because *Xiao* ran deep in people's psyches, it affected many social institutions. For example, in the period preceding the Tang dynasty, the imperial government often tolerated the concealment of crime among family members. Except in the case of treason, a son was absolved from the responsibility of reporting any crime committed by his father. A son who reported such an offense was punished by the state, because he was condemned as being unfilial for betraying his parent. The Tang dynasty not only continued this tolerance

Detail of a drawing of a younger brother bowing to an elder sibling; from the *Book of Filial Piety,* circa 1085 (Metropolitan Museum of Art, New York)

**Moral Principle.** Imperial Chinese rules of family/kinship varied from one community to another, but they shared some characteristics: they all placed an emphasis on moral principles or Confucian concepts, translating them into the norms of personal conduct in daily life. Violations of these norms were usually met with group disapproval, ranging from gossip and ridicule to punishment and exclusion. However, the rule of family/kinship gave priority to moral persuasion rather than to physical punishment, unless the latter penalty became absolutely necessary. Moral persuasion started when a person was young and continued through lifelong socialization.

**Six Elements.** With an emphasis placed on the hierarchy of generations and ages, moral persuasion comprised six elements: showing filial piety to one's parents; respecting one's elders; staying in agreement with the common interests of the community; taking responsibility for teaching and disciplining one's children and grandchildren; attending properly to one's vocation; and committing no conduct forbidden by law. It is worth noting that these basic principles were largely in agreement with those upheld by state laws. For example, the offense of filial impiety was generally punishable without immunity, and the offender was flogged forty times. During the Song dynasty moral instructions were fully integrated into the rules of the family, which established a common practice of virtue for all kinsmen. By this standard it was a father's duty to discipline his sons; an elder brother's duty to offer good advice to his younger brothers and to take care of their widows and orphans; a kinsman's duty to give relief to fellow members in distress; and all kinsmen's duty to help settle disputes in order to reach harmony. In doing so, it was believed, Heaven, or the Way of the Nature, could reach its balance and in turn be a blessing for both individuals and families.

**Punitive Power.** While having a strong moral character—stressing many ethical values of personal integrity—family/kinship rules traditionally contained enormous punitive power to control the deviant behavior of clan members. Yet, with increased centralized state power as of the third century B.C.E., this power was largely limited by the legal system. Nevertheless, the state still recognized that the kinship group had a certain degree of autonomous authority to handle minor cases among its members, because it was believed that punitive power was a logical extension of the family's moral disciplinary functions. There was a clear line of demarcation, however, in terms of judiciary power between the government and kinship clan. Cases involving the violation of ethical values—such as a family feud, children's harmful acts toward parents, and adultery—were generally handled by the family/kinship clan, and the offenders were judged and punished (usually by flogging) at the ancestral hall. Cases involving serious offenses such as murder, treason, and intergroup brutality fell under government jurisdiction, and the offenders were turned over to the courts for trial and punishment.

but also extended it to include a broader circle of family members, such as parents-in-law, brothers-in-law, and even nephews. For example, Tang and Song laws even protected the family concealment of crime by stipulating that those who betrayed parents or grandparents should be put to death. In the Ming and Qing dynasties, however, new laws dropped the death penalty for those who betrayed their parents. This change did not mean that society had de-emphasized *Xiao.* Actually, *Xiao* was broadened to define the five virtues of a person's behavior. They were: *Li*—politeness in complying with all hierarchical orders and rites; *Ren*—humanity or benevolence in all activities; *Yi*—justice or righteousness that one should have in performing *Li; Zhi*—wisdom and knowledge of performing appropriate behavior; and *Xin*—sincerity and honesty in performing *Li.* It is interesting to note that, while state laws usually tolerated children who concealed the crimes of their parents, kin-clan laws often punished individuals who failed to reveal a parent's offense and rewarded those who reported it. Some scholars point out that this balance between state and customary laws was the key to the long-term dynastic stability of imperial China.

**Sources:**
Maurice Freeman, ed., *Family and Kinship in Chinese Society* (Stanford, Cal.: Stanford University Press, 1970).

Hui-Chen Wang, *The Traditional Chinese Clan Rules* (Locust Valley, N.Y.: Association for Asian Studies, Augustin, 1959).

Ruikai Zhu, *Zhongguo Hun Yin Jia Ting Shi,* translated as *History of the Family and Marriage in China* (Shanghai: Xueling Press, 1999).

Detail of a scroll showing a court scene in which an adulteress (lower right) is being whipped, Song dynasty, 960–1279 (from Norman Kotker, ed., *The Horizon History of China*, 1969)

**Punishment.** Each kin-clan maintained a record of family instructions that spelled out the dos and don'ts of carrying out punishments. The judiciary power of the government was weak below the county level, and some kinship clans avoided turning serious cases over to the government for trials; instead, they imposed the death penalty on "guilty" members who they considered had brought shame upon the ancestors. Such decisions were made by the head of the clan, but the opinions of elder members carried much weight. It is interesting to note that punishment was not always confined to an individual offender but was often extended to one's family, which was held responsible for the misbehavior of the offender. For example, a father who overlooked his son's crime or a husband who allowed his wife to commit misconduct would also be punished, though not at the same level as the offender. In some cases a son was even liable for the misconduct of his widowed mother. Punishment in the family/kinship rules varied in terms of degree, ranging from an oral reprimand or monetary fine to corporal punishment, including expulsion and even death (often in the form of forced suicide). Expulsion from the family/kinship was considered to be the most severe penalty, which also meant that the offender would be excluded from the genealogy of the kin-clan and all privileges associated with such status. This punishment

was the most humiliating experience for any group member in a close-knit community, for one's name would not be carved on a posthumous tablet placed in the ancestral shrine and his descendants would not be allowed to enter the ancestral hall.

**Sources:**

Werner Eichhorn, *Kulturgeschichte Chinas*, translated as *Chinese Civilization: An Introduction*, by Janet Seligman (New York: Praeger, 1969).

James T. C. Liu and Wei-Ming Tu, eds., *Traditional China* (Englewood Cliffs, N.J.: Prentice-Hall, 1970).

Michael Loewe, *Imperial China: The Historical Background to the Modern Age* (New York: Praeger, 1966).

## FAMILY NOMENCLATURE

**Branches.** From the Tang dynasty (618–907) until the end of the Ming dynasty (1368–1644) family nomenclature became more standardized with the efforts of successive imperial governments. By the Qing dynasty (1644–1912) the system of naming family relations, which had developed over three thousand years, was formally recorded and explained in the *Grand Dictionary of Kang Xi*. A family tree is composed of several branches, with one trunk as the central point from which paternal and maternal kin deviate. Though regional variations of naming existed, in Mandarin (standard) Chinese, the character for father is *Fu*. The characters for grandfather are *Zhu Fu* and for grandmother, *Zhu Mu*. The character *Wai* is added to refer to one's mother's father, called *Wai Zhu Fu*, or mother's mother, *Wei Zhu Mu*. The characters for great-grandfather are *Zhen Zhu Fu*. Those for great-great-grandfather are *Gao Zhu Fu*. Distant ancestors are called *Yuan Zhu*. The paternal uncle, or one's father's elder brother, is designated *Bo*, and a father's younger brother is *Shu*. For deferential purposes the character *Fu* is often added to the characters for elder and younger paternal uncles, therefore called *Bo Fu* or *Shu Fu* respectively. In a broad sense the character *Fu* means head, or family head. Giving such a title to paternal brothers indicates their significant status in the family patriarchy.

**Parents' Brothers and Sisters.** One's mother's brother, a maternal uncle, is called *Jiu*. Similarly, the character *Fu* can be added to *Jiu* to indicate respect for the closest relation to one's mother, and for the same generation of one's own father. The character for one's father's sister is *Gu*, often called *Gu Ma*, and the mother's sister is *Yi*, or often *Yi Ma*. The character *Ma* (mother) carried the same meaning as *Mu*, explicitly indicating one's close relations with both paternal and maternal sisters, who commonly assumed the role of second mother under certain circumstances.

**Siblings.** The character denoting one's elder brother is *Xiong* and a younger brother is *Di*. The characters *Zi* (or alternatively *Jie)* and *Mei* are used to refer to one's elder sister and younger sister, respectively. The character *Tang*, meaning "internal," refers to one's cousins on paternal lines, and the character *Biao*, meaning "external," refers to one's cousins on maternal lines. Thus, sons of one's father's brother are designated as *Tang Xiong* for the eldest and *Tang Di* for the youngest; their sisters are accordingly called *Tang Jie* for the eldest and *Tang Mei* for the youngest. For

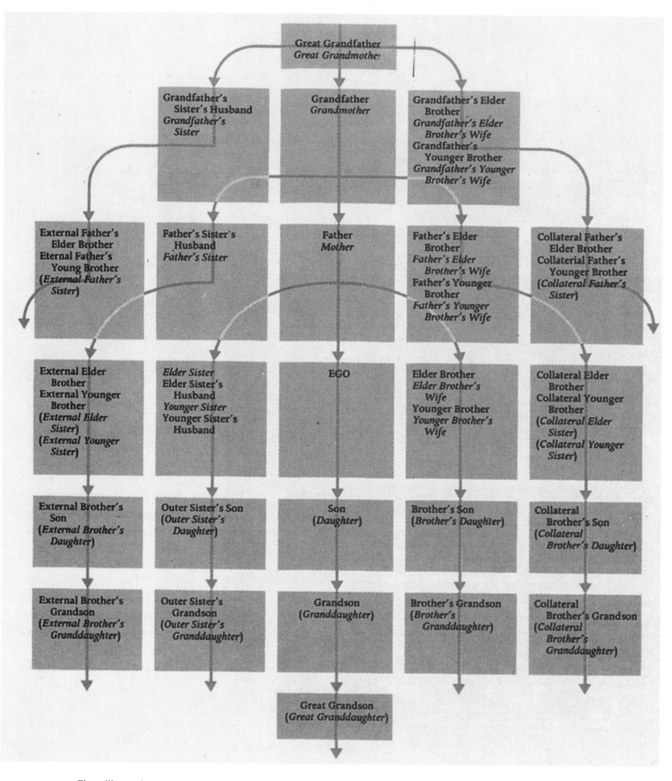

Chart illustrating family relationships (from Caroline Blunden and Mark Elvin, *Cultural Atlas of China,* 1983)

Detail from a scroll showing a family gathering, Ming dynasty, 1368–1644 (Metropolitan Museum of Art, New York)

cousins from one's father's sisters, the characters *Biao Xiong* are used for the elder male cousin and *Biao Di* for the younger male cousin. In similar manner, *Biao Jie* are used for the elder female cousin and *Biao Mei* for the younger female cousin. The character *Biao* also denotes one's relationships with cousins from the mother's brothers and sisters, and the usage is similar to the one for cousins from the father's sisters. In some regions the character *Gu* is added prior to *Biao* to distinguish cousins of paternal lines from those of maternal lines.

**Other Characters.** There are other characters used to indicate family relations. A stepfather is referred to as *Ji Fu* and a stepmother as *Ji Mu*. An adopting mother is addressed as *Yang Mu*, a woman who raises a child to adulthood. A milk mother, or wet nurse, is called *Ru Mu* or *Ru Ma*. Also in traditional China there was a formal name for a father's concubine, *Shu Mu* (secondary mother), as addressed by sons of the legal wife (first wife) or by sons of other concubines.

**Strict Classification.** The significance of family nomenclature in imperial China was in its strict classification of generation-gender patriarchy. The paternal male lineage enjoyed exclusive privileges, as was evident in all family rites, whereas the maternal-side members were generally considered "outsiders" because they did not carry the family surname. From the Ming dynasty onward, with the revitalization of kinship organizations after the Yuan dynasty, the clan or sib-group prevailed. In a clan society, "clan-elder-brother-father," a literal translation of *Zhu Bo Fu*, was ele-

vated to a position equal to one's own father, because *Zhu Bo Fu* was the elder agnatic grandson of one's father's great-grandfather, being of the same line of descent, from one's own great-grandfather.

Sources:
Hugh D. R. Baker, *Chinese Family and Kinship* (New York: Columbia University Press, 1979).

Paul S. Ropp, ed., *Heritage of China: Contemporary Perspectives on Chinese Civilization* (Berkeley: University of California Press, 1990).

H. P. Wilkinson, *The Family in Classical China* (Shanghai: Kelly & Walsh, 1926).

## FAMILY PATRILINEAGE

**Patriarchy.** The family, whether large or small, was patrilineal and patriarchal in imperial China. Maternal relatives, and the family of one's mother, were never closely bound to the primary kinship unit. Only paternal relatives were recognized as members of the kin-group and were able to participate in all rituals honoring common ancestors. The most important parts of Chinese family life were the use of patrilineal surnames, the worship of patrilineal ancestors, and the organization of kinship based on a common patrilineal descent. The ancestral cult was intimately tied to the kinship organization.

**Surnames.** Names that the Chinese use are diverse and complex. Chinese surnames were well established after the Tang period as either a badge of family dignity or of lineage identity. It is alleged that about five thousand years ago the earliest family names were given by Huang Ti to his twelve sons. From these cognomens derived additional clan and family names. The *Bai Jia Xing* (Book of Hundred Surnames), a Song-era primer, listed only one hundred names, but in reality there were well more than this figure. In Tang times there was a popular fashion of having a *Hao* (sobriquet), especially among members of literary and elite circles. A person acquired a *Hao*, usually designated by himself or conferred upon him by an elderly or respected person, later in life.

**Ancestors.** In the classical era, however, commoners often did not have family names. Even the names of aristocrats were highly confusing. The real beginning of the system of patrilineal surnames appeared after the unification of the country by Qin Shi Huang, the first imperial emperor of China, and his efforts to register the entire population. Surnames came to be considered an identification of kinship, making it easy for everyone (particularly males) to identify with a patrilineal descent line and to consider themselves part of a "continuum of descent." The family with the most direct descent from a common ancestor claimed the political and ritual leadership of the clan. The obligation to observe ancestral rites also led to the need to secure male heirs. The Mencius Doctrine, claiming that "the worst of unfilial acts was a failure to have descendants," laid the foundation for patrilineal ancestral rites. Yet, in early classical periods these rites were reserved for the privileged class. By law the emperor had seven ancestral temples; a lord had five, an official three, a scholar one, but a commoner had none.

**Aristocracy.** The aristocracy, controlled by a few great families of nobility, or *Wang Zhu,* declined in political and social influence during the Tang dynasty. Their remaining power dissipated during the Song dynasty, when the imperial government took measures to break the aristocracy by reducing the great estates into smaller holdings divided among multiple owners. During the Tang dynasty the rewards of passing the civil service examination prevailed over the use of the aristocratic family names in determining government appointments.

**Kin-based Village.** In Song times the patrilineal kinship organization became more systemized because of the impact of the *Zhu Zi Jia Li* (Book of Family Rites), which introduced to commoners the designs of ancestral halls, protocols of ancestral worship, responsibilities of the family head, and steps to record the family history. The significance of the *Zhu Zi Jia Li* was that it changed the tradition that ancestral rites were confined only to royal and pedigreed families, thus making the practice of ancestor worship available to any family, regardless of its social rank. Since families that shared the same ancestors were grouped into clans, they tended to live in the same geographical area. Kin-based villages prevailed during the Ming dynasty; if the kin-clan was extended, it usually only spread to adjacent villages.

**Kinship.** Ouyang Xiu and Su Xun, Song scholar-officials, believed that if kinship organizations were able to uphold ethical teachings, they would give an added

Drawing from the *Book of Filial Piety* of a young couple (top right) entertaining the husband's parents, circa 1085 (Metropolitan Museum of Art, New York)

degree of social stability. Kinship, as an organizational form of the extended family structure, became a well-established institution that held kinsmen together through the practice of ancestor worship. Every kin-group had its own *Jia Pu* (record of family genealogy), which had been a tradition among families of pedigree in early classical periods. During the Song dynasty, recording the family genealogy became a social trend. The obvious purpose of keeping a family genealogy was to facilitate the worshiping of ancestors. Yet, the function of *Jia Pu* went well beyond ancestor worship; it was widely used by the imperial government as a document of reference or verification in selecting candidates for official appointments. It also served as a symbol of social distinction, especially when a family produced several high achievers either as distinguished scholars or high-ranking imperial officials.

**Affinities.** Kinship organizations played a pivotal part in social relations. To a great extent, community-based kinship organizations were the cornerstone of social stability in imperial China. First, the group was united by a natural affinity of blood relations. Ancestral rites reminded everyone that they were descendants of a common ancestor and that they shared the responsibility for maintaining family honor and dignity. Second, the group handled self-protection and mutual assistance. Kinsmen were organized for the common interests of their group to ensure security and economic needs. Wealthy families provided property or assistance for philanthropic purposes and children's education, especially for poor families in the kin-group. Third, the group disciplined deviant members. Every village was self-governing and had no officials. The kinship organization assumed collective legal responsibility for its members; the state allowed a certain autonomy to be exercised by family leaders and at the same time took from them the severest cases, such as murder, for punishment under state laws.

Sources:

Hugh D. R. Baker, *Chinese Family and Kinship* (New York: Columbia University Press, 1979).

Han-Yi Feng, *The Chinese Kinship System* (Cambridge, Mass.: Harvard University Press, 1967).

Zhenman Zheng, *Ming Qing Fujian jia zu zu zhi yu she hui bian qian,* translated as *Family Lineage Organization and Social Change in Ming and Qing Fujian,* by Michael Szonyi and others (Honolulu: University of Hawaii Press, 2001).

## FOOTBINDING

**Origins.** The worst manifestation of the subjugation of women in imperial China was the custom of footbinding. This practice emerged during the periods of the "five dynasties" (907–960) and the early Song dynasty (960–1279).

Imperial-era woodcut of Yao Niang, favorite concubine of Tang emperor Li Yu, binding her feet (from Wang Ping, *Aching for Beauty*, 2000)

Small feet had been esteemed in China since antiquity, but before the tenth century there was no evidence indicating that small, bound feet were popular. Available evidence for the Tang period (618–907) weighs heavily against footbinding. Women depicted in eighth- and ninth-century paintings were robust and vigorous physical types without the slightest hint of needing support or of walking with a hobbled gait. Primary references make it clear that Tang ladies were encouraged to engage in many athletic events requiring strenuous physical exertion—such as horseback riding, polo, and ball games—that were much better suited for a natural-footed participant. Polo and ball games were also popular among palace ladies, which would not have been so if tiny feet had already become an imperial harem vogue.

**Control.** During the Song dynasty, when the outlook on female morality became increasingly stringent, footbinding as an imperial court fashion came to be elevated as a convenient way to ensure the separation of sexes and to prevent women from leaving the confines of the home. Thus, a chaste wife had to stay in the house and was not to be seen in the fields or streets. At the same time, bound feet indicated economic status. A man who had a wife with bound feet proved to the community that he was wealthy enough to feed her and did not need her help in the fields or in the shop. It was said that the philosopher Zhu Xi, a moral proponent of chastity in Song times, was part of the initial effort to enforce footbinding for women. When he served as governor in Chang Prefecture, Fujian, he noted that women there tended to be unchaste and to indulge in lewdness. He therefore ordered that all women's feet be bound to an excessive degree, causing them to be hampered in moving about. He believed that footbinding would help change their immoral habits, because it was so inconvenient for them to get about that their chances for indulging sexually were greatly lessened. However, footbinding was not yet commonplace during the Song period, even among upper-class families. The famed poetess Li Qing Zhao, for instance, was not bound-footed.

**Yuan Period.** Footbinding was gradually transmitted from the northern areas to central and southern China among the ethnic Chinese communities during Mongol rule. A Yuan dynasty (1279–1368) treatise justified footbinding because it guaranteed feminine chastity. A Chinese manual for instructing women similarly pointed out that the purpose in binding feet was not to make them more attractive but to prevent women from easily being able to leave their quarters. There are two possible explanations for the spread of footbinding: the Chinese emphasized it in order to draw a clearer cultural distinction between themselves and their large-footed conquerors, or the Mongols encouraged it to weaken the Chinese by impairing the health of their women.

**Ming Period.** Footbinding was more stringently enforced during the Ming dynasty (1368–1644) than in any dynasty before it, and the custom received official and popular sanction. As a consequence, footbinding became a prerequisite to a proper marriage and received its due share of attention in society. Young ladies, especially those from respected families, had their feet deformed by tight binding from an early

Modern reproductions of imperial-era footbinding materials: rolls of binding cloth; jar of medicinal foot powder; bamboo cage for fuming binding cloth; scissors; and box of fragrant foot powder (Bata Shoe Museum, Toronto, Canada)

age. Women without small feet were thought never to be able to achieve the standard of feminine beauty or ever to be able to marry a man of social standing. The painful process started when girls had their feet tightly wrapped in bandages, which gradually broke the arch and pushed the toes and heel to grow toward one another; the process was completed when girls reached their late teens. Chinese literature is full of bitter stories about mothers who wept as they forcefully wrapped their screaming daughters' feet. Ming poets, novelists, and diarists frequently referred to bound feet as "the golden lotus" and praised their dainty beauty. It was widely believed at the time that binding the foot resulted in a heavier thigh and that a woman's genital region tightened and became better developed. During the Yuan and Ming dynasties men made a love fetish of the tiny foot; small shoes became symbols of passionate love and an integral part of drinking games. Nevertheless, footbinding was rarely practiced by the Hakka of the south or by most other ethnic minorities in traditional China.

**Sources:**

Dorothy Ko, *Every Step a Lotus: Shoes for Bound Feet* (Berkeley: University of California Press, 2001).

Howard S. Levy, *Chinese Footbinding: The History of a Curious Erotic Custom* (New York: Rawls, 1966).

Wang Ping, *Aching for Beauty: Footbinding in China* (Minneapolis: University of Minnesota Press, 2000).

## FUNERAL CEREMONIES

**Endings.** Death, along with birth and marriage, is recognized as one of the three major events in the course of an individual's life. In China since classical times the rites for funerals were observed with no less importance than those for birth and marriage. Mourning rites were formalized in the Zhou dynasty (771–256 B.C.E.), but they became more elaborate and were popularized, along with the development of the kinship system, in the Tang dynasty (618–907). Mourning rites exemplified differentiation and generational stratification of the kinship system, characterized by an exogamous *Zhong Zu* (clan organization). At funerals such generation-age hierarchy showed up in the differences of mourning costumes and in the degrees of grief one was expected to express.

**Dressing.** The dead were dressed according to their social status. At the ceremony of "slighter dressing" of the dead, an embroidered sheet was used for a ruler's body; for that of a ranking official, white silk; and for that of a scholar, black silk. At the "fuller dressing" ceremony each of the deceased had two sheets. A ruler had one hundred suits of clothes buried with him; a ranking official, fifty; and a scholar, thirty. The walls of the longest, or outermost, coffin of a deceased ruler were eight inches thick; the next coffin was six inches thick;

Wood coffin of Zhang Kuangzheng with Siddham and Chinese words painted on the sides and lid, Liao dynasty, 916–1115 (Institute of Cultural Relics, Shijiazhaung, Hebei Province)

and the innermost coffin was four inches thick. The outer shell of a ruler's coffin was made of pine; a ranking official, cypress; and a student, various kinds of wood. The coffin for an official of the highest grade was eight inches thick and the inner one was six inches; for an official of the lowest grade, the dimensions were six and four inches; the coffin of a scholar was six inches thick. A coffin for a common person was only four inches thick.

**Contributions.** According to the *Li Ji* (Canon of Rites), contributions were made at the time of a funeral and were usually divided into three kinds. Contributions for the dead were called "shrouds," including such things as sheets and clothes, or were called "gifts," such as "spiritual vessels." The value of these contributions depended on the rank, wealth, or intimacy of the contributor. Contributions for the mourner, called "helps," were usually in the form of money or other gifts. Contributions for both the dead and mourner, for instance, could be silk, carriages, horses, sheep, or other items. These gifts were used both for the obsequies and for financial assistance to the family.

**Mourning Categories.** There were *Wu Fu* (Five Mourning Grades), categories of mourning garments and periods that kin of differing relationships with the dead

were expected to observe. The deepest mourning was observed in a lineal direction for the longest time for the closest kin, such as one's father and mother; slightly less-deep mourning was observed for paternal grandparents, and so on, until the least severe mourning was observed for paternal great-great-grandparents (whom few people could ever have lived to mourn). The mourning prescriptions worked similarly in a lateral direction, so that deeper mourning was observed for one's brother than for one's first cousin, and the least deep mourning for one's third cousin. Accordingly, mourning periods were divided into three years, one year, nine months, five months, and three months. The longest period was reserved for the nearest kin. The rationale behind such classifications was given in the *Li Ji:* "Why is it that the mourning period for the nearest kin is one year? Because the interaction of heaven and earth has run its round; and the four seasons have gone through their changes. All things between heaven and earth begin their processes anew. The rules of mourning are intended to resemble them. . . . Why should there be three years mourning (for parents)? The reason is to make it more impressive by doubling the period, so that it embraces two round years. . . . Then why have the mourning of nine months? The reason is to prevent excessive grief."

Table with offerings, from the tomb of Zhang Wenzao, Liao dynasty, 916–1115
(Institute of Cultural Relics, Shijiazhaung, Hebei Province)

**Special Offerings.** The funeral rite was treated as an essential contact between two worlds, for people believed that the afterlife was an extension of present life and that the souls of the dead remained with the family. To take care of the deceased, surviving family members offered special food and incense and burned "spirit money" to transmit life's necessities to their loved ones in the other world. Though there was a personal, sentimental side to the remembrance of the dead, the most important implications of funeral rites were social and ethical, because they were intimately related to the social demands for filial piety. To be filial to a parent while living was easy, but one's genuine affection should be best shown when the parent was dead, and hence exhibited in one's proper treatment of the parent's burial. This practice therefore became a ritual prop to reinforce family unity.

Sources:

Norman Kutcher, *Mourning in Late Imperial China: Filial Piety and the State* (New York: Cambridge University Press, 1999).

Yongzhou Qin, *Zhongguo She Hui Feng Shu Shi* (History of Chinese Social Customs) (Shangdong, China: Shangdong People's Press, 2000).

Shuang Ren, *Tang Dai Li Zhi Yan Jiu* (The Rites of the Tang Dynasty) (Changchun, China: Northeast University Press, 1999).

## LOVE AND MARRIAGE: SOCIAL REGULATIONS

**Multiple Marriage.** In imperial China a man was allowed to have only one wife, but he could have multiple concubines. Such a polygamous institution prevailed not only among the wealthy and powerful but also in ordinary families. An official wedding ceremony sealed the union between a man and his wife, and laws established by the Tang dynasty (618–907) prohibited bigamy, yet the same man was allowed to possess other women as concubines. Because of this legal difference, there was a huge stratification in social standing among the wife and the concubines in terms of status and privileges within the family. Concubines were called the *Xia Qi* (second wife), *Xiao Qi* (minor wife), or *Ce Shi* (companion).

**Sons.** The desire for male children to perpetuate the family name and to have descendants to burn incense before the ancestral tablets after one's death had an immense influence on people's minds. By the established social customs a man whose first wife was childless could marry a second wife, but only with the consent of his first wife. In the family hierarchy, the secondary wife, even if she bore children, was lower in status than the first wife, to whom she must

By all accounts divorce was a privilege of the husband and was referred to as *Xiu Qi* (dismissing a wife). Legally a woman could not divorce her husband; the idea of a wife doing so, for whatever reason, was considered absurd and preposterous. Socially, divorce was shameful for a woman but not for a man. A man's commitment to his parents carried more weight than that to his wife. It became highly justifiable that a man divorce a wife who disrespected his parents and disrupted the family harmony. Chen Yi, an eminent scholar-official of the Song dynasty (960–1279), discusses the ethics of divorce with his students in the following passage:

Someone asked, "Is it proper to divorce a wife?"

[Ch'eng I] answered, "When a wife is not worthy, there is no harm in divorcing her. For instance, [Confucius' grandson] Tzu-su once divorced his wife. The current custom is to look on divorce as something ugly, so people are reluctant to engage in it. The ancients were different. Wives who were not good were sent away. It is just that people today make this into a big thing and bear it silently without revealing it. Sometimes there is some hidden sin, which is handled quietly, or even tolerated, which just fosters wrongdoing and thus obviously is bad. Cultivating the self and disciplining the family are the most urgent tasks for men. Best is to first cultivate oneself and then discipline one's family.

[The disciple] also said, "What about the cases among the ancients of divorcing wives hastily for something not very bad like scolding the dog in front of one's mother-in-law, or serving a pear that wasn't ripe?"

[Ch'eng I] answered, "This was the way the ancients practiced generosity. In ancient times if someone severed a friendship, he did not say anything bad [about the former friend], and a gentleman could not bear to expel his wife for a great sin, so sent her away for a minor fault. Consider the one who scolded the dog in front of [her husband's] mother. There was nothing so serious in this incident, but some other day there [must have been] a major reason, so [the husband] used this pretext to divorce her."

Someone asked, "If she was expelled for this petty reason, how could there have been no objections? What about the fact that outsiders would not have been able to tell who was right and who was not?"

[Ch'eng I] replied, "She would know her own faults. If she can correct them herself, fine. Why must other people know? Those with insight will understand. Anyone who must expose his wife's wrongdoing is simply a shallow fellow. A gentleman is not like this. Most people when they talk try to make the other party look wrong and themselves look right. Gentlemen have a forgiving attitude."

Someone commented, "There is an old saying, 'In divorcing a wife, make it so she can remarry; in severing a friendship, make it so he can make new friends.' Is this the idea?"

[Ch'eng I] said, "Yes."

**Source:** Patricia Buckley Ebrey, *The Inner Quarters: Marriage and the Lives of Chinese Women in the Song Period* (Berkeley: University of California Press, 1993), pp. 257–258.

submit under all circumstances. The secondary wife's inferior position showed in her wedding ceremony, in which she was not allowed to worship "heaven and earth" together with her husband, which was an essential part of the marriage ceremony of the first, or primary, wife.

**Concubines.** In Tang times, except for the emperor himself, laws determined the number of concubines that a government official could possess. Officials of first rank could have ten concubines; eight, six, four, and three concubines were permitted to officials of second to fifth ranks, respectively. Economic prosperity in Tang times also made it common for well-to-do men to have one wife and one concubine. For some wealthy families the masters of the house also kept several "singing" or "dancing" women for their entertainment, whose status in the family was lower than concubines but higher than female housemaids. These women suffered from constant physical and emotional abuse by their masters. Yet, *Tang Lu Shu Yi* (Tang Laws) protected such privileges of the masters and were lenient in assessing penalties. Masters often went unpunished, or were slightly punished, if they raped or killed their entertainment women or maids.

**Marriage Law.** Males and females of the same family name were customarily forbidden to intermarry. Cousins who did not share the same ancestral name could marry but usually only in cases of the children of sisters on the maternal side. One important passage in Tang marriage law clearly prohibited bigamy and marriages among close kinship members as well as between brothers and sisters with the same mother but different fathers. These rules were adopted by following dynasties, fostering a strong taboo in late imperial China. Tang marriage law was indicative of gender discrimination in the marriage relationship. A widow could be punished if she remarried before the conclusion of the designated mourning period after the death of her husband, but a man who decided to remarry during the mourning period of his wife's death could do so unpunished. Women who injured their husbands received much heavier punishments than husbands did for abusing their wives.

**Validity of Marriage.** Tang law made clear that betrothal gifts served as the social acceptance of marriage. Drawn from the classic *Li Ji* (Canon of Rites), which stated that "without receipt of the betrothal gifts there is no contact and no affinity," these rules stated that, once these presents were received, the girl's family could be prosecuted if it broke off the engagement. Presenting and accepting gifts was essential to the betrothal ceremony; one was not married legally without some token transfer of objects from the groom's family to the bride's family. By contrast, the validity of marriage did not depend on the bride's bringing anything to the marriage. Nor were objects she brought to her new home termed gifts; they were simply her possessions. During the Song dynasty (960–1279), as in Tang times, betrothal gifts continued to be considered proof of a valid marriage. In the Yuan dynasty (1279–1368), however, the imperial government required paperwork—an agreement signed by either the matchmaker or marriage officiant—to verify a valid marriage. This period was probably the only time in imperial Chinese history that such written proof of marriage was required. One possible explanation for this change is that, because of the territorial expansion of this era, interethnic marriages became more common, and the written agreement therefore served as a means to minimize cultural misunderstandings. Yet, in the Ming dynasty (1368–1644) and thereafter, again no paperwork was required to certify a marriage.

**Marriage Age.** The first official attempt to regulate marriage ages for males and females occurred during the Tang dynasty. During the reign of Taizong the imperial court declared that the appropriate marriage age for males was twenty; for females it was fifteen. The marriage age was later reduced to fifteen for males and thirteen for females. Fluctuations in the acceptable marriage age were mainly caused by societal needs. Tang efforts to regulate marriages had an enduring impact on the stability of the family institution, and the same policy was adopted by later dynasties and continued through imperial Chinese history. For instance, Song marriage laws prohibited bigamy for both men and women and punished violators; men were still, however, allowed to keep concubines, which was not considered a crime. One conspicuous change during the Song dynasty was that marriage regulations became more formalized with the codification of basic legal procedures.

**Arranged Marriage.** By law as well as by custom, arranged marriage was the principal form of sexual union throughout the history of imperial China. A marriage set up through a matchmaker, with the consent of the parents (or guardians if one's parents had died), was by law unchallengeable. Custom led to the popular belief, which ran deep in people's psyches, that one's fate determined the match. It was thought that Heaven decided who was to be one's husband or wife and that the match was made by a "red silk thread"—the heavenly power beyond human comprehension.

**Victims.** From a sociological perspective the prevalence and persistence of arranged marriages was a derivation of the patriarchal family institution, which controlled unions between young males and females and limited their freedom for mate selection. Those who suffered most from the institution were females. They became victims of an unequal patriarchal system characterized by polygamy. Wealthy merchants, landlords, scholars, and officials commonly kept concubines or second wives of lower social origins in addition to their primary wife, who usually came from a social status similar to her husband's. For families of moderate incomes a secondary wife was acquired only if the first wife was found to be infertile some years after marriage. Poorer men simply could not afford to have more than one wife. Lower-class families often supplied girls when parents could not afford to marry off their daughters and were instead forced to sell them to wealthy families. These girls, who often worked as housemaids, were at the bottom of familial stratification and lived a life of blood and tears. They were often economically exploited and physically abused by their masters.

**Child Brides.** Two extreme forms of arranged marriage existed from the Song era. One was the "Child Bride"—a situation in which parents arranged a marriage for their child even before she reached the prime age. Child brides came to be customary in lower-class families. The popularity of the child-bride arrangement was caused by several social factors. First, for a husband's family, spending a small amount of money to buy a daughter-in-law-to-be guaranteed a marriage for their son and at the same time added a helping hand to family chores. For a wife's family, marrying their daughter early saved them from having to accumulate a dowry, which could become a heavy financial burden.

**Death Wedding Custom.** The other extreme form of arranged marriage was known as the "Death Wedding"—a situation in which a man and woman were to be married, but either individual died before the ceremony, and the survivor was encouraged (or pressured) to kill himself or herself in order to be buried alongside the intended spouse as if they had been married. Women more often than men were forced to sacrifice their lives in such a manner. Arranged marriages, such as the child bride and death wedding, continued to be practiced well into the Qing dynasty (1644–1912).

**Early Betrothal.** The "Little Bride" was another popular custom of arranged marriage in many regions of China. A young girl, often from a poor family, was betrothed at an extremely young age. She was given away or sold to her future in-laws when she was one or two years old. A matchmaker was employed to arrange a formal engagement, as if the boy and girl were advanced in age. Then the girl was taken to the boy's home to be brought up together with her future husband. While growing up the girl was treated as slave labor until she was eventually married to the man. On the wedding day no red bridal chair was used, because she had already become a member of her husband's family.

**Four Virtues.** Being a woman (and a wife) in imperial China was not easy, because she was compelled to comply with "three subordinations" and "four virtues" as advised in the classics of Confucianism. An ideal wife was expected to be subordinate to her father before her marriage, subordi-

Section of a tomb mural with a husband and wife at a table and servants in attendance, Baisha, Henan Province, Song dynasty, 960–1279

nate to her husband after marriage, and subordinate to her son after he took over the household by succeeding his father. The four virtues were: serving parents-in-law and husband with fidelity; bringing up children with love and attending to household chores with industriousness and thrift; being polite and soft in speech and never saying more than was necessary; and keeping good deference and demeanor. "When a good wife sits, she sits gracefully without crossing her knees; when she stands, she stands without planting her feet wide apart." It was considered proper for the husband to set the pace and for the wife to follow. The wife's duty was to assist her husband and never to rule over him, because, according to Confucian doctrine, a family dominated by the wife would inevitably decline. The most popular classic instructions for women's ethics were the *Nu Jie* (Book of Women's Fidelity) and *Nu Run Yu* (Book of Women's Ethics). The former consists of eighteen chapters covering the essentials of women's behavior from girlhood to motherhood. The latter has twelve chapters that instruct

women about fidelity and obedience to their husbands and about taking care of households and educating their children. A wife's failure to live up to these expectations often led to divorce.

**Seven Reasons.** The Song imperial government issued a legal code, based on prevailing ethics, that punished a wife who left her husband without his agreement. A husband, however, could expel or sell his wife for any of seven socially and legally acceptable reasons. They were: mistreatment of parents-in-law; the inability to bear children, which was thought to be unfilial—Confucius claimed that "There are three ways of being unfilial and of these not begetting descendants is the most serious"; adultery; excessive jealousy, including preventing a husband from having a concubine; complaining (to the extent that family stability was threatened); theft; and having a virulent disease (such as leprosy). In most cases a husband did not have to go to any government service to be granted a divorce; he simply went to his wife's parents' house to present a document of

## MARRIAGE

The following story has been repeated for hundreds of years, to deliver a cultural message among the Chinese: that the engagement of parties in marriage is unalterable by fate.

In the time of the Tang dynasty, Ui-ko was once a guest in the city of Sung. He observed an old man by the light of the moon reading a book, who addressed him thus: "this is the register of the engagements in marriage for all the places under the heavens." He also said to him, "In my pocket I have red cords, with which I tie the feet of those who are to become husband and wife. When this cord had been tied, though the parties are of unfriendly families, or of different nations, it is impossible to change their destiny. Your future wife," said the old man, "is the child of the old woman who sells vegetables in yonder shop at the north." In a few days Ui-ko went to see her, and found the old woman had in her arms a girl about a year old, and exceedingly ugly. He hired a man, who went and (as he supposed) killed the girl. Fourteen years afterward, in the country of Siong-chiu, was a prefect whose family name was Mo, surnamed Tai, who gave Ui-ko in marriage a girl who he affirmed was his own daughter. She was very beautiful. On her eyebrow she always wore an artificial flower. Ui-ko constantly asking her why she wore the flower, she at length said, "I am the daughter of the prefect's brother. My father died in the city of Sung when I was but an infant. My nurse was an old woman who sold vegetables. One day she took me with her out into the streets, when a robber struck me. The scar of the wound is still left on my eyebrow."

Source: Justus Doolittle, *Social Life of the Chinese*, volume 1 (New York: Harper, 1865), pp. 68–69.

Sources:

Patricia Buckley Ebrey, *The Inner Quarters: Marriage and the Lives of Chinese Women in the Song Period* (Berkeley: University of California Press, 1993).

Paul S. Ropp, ed., *Heritage of China: Contemporary Perspectives on Chinese Civilization* (Berkeley: University of California Press, 1990).

Hui-chen Wang, *The Traditional Chinese Clan Rules* (Locust Valley, N.Y.: Augustin, 1959).

## MATE SELECTION AND MARRIAGE

**Matrimony.** Following the Han dynasty (206 B.C.E.– 220 C.E.), Chinese society developed in distinctly aristocratic directions. Family status and dowries were two determining factors of the institution of marriage during the Tang dynasty (618–907). A relatively small number of families were preeminent in social and political life. People also celebrated the top-ranking families of the aristocracy, or *Wang Zhu* (esteemed families), in preceding dynasties. Even when descendants of these families were poor and of low political rank, they were esteemed for their pedigree of the past. In elite marriages, family status and pedigree became the basic criteria for the selection of a potential spouse.

Late-sixteenth-century woodcut of the farewell scene in the Yuan play *The Lute Story*, Ming dynasty, circa 1573–1620 (Palace Museum, Beijing)

divorce, and the procedure was complete. The husband's decision, however, usually required the approval of his parents or elders in the kin-clan.

**Dismissed.** A dismissed wife was sent back to her birth home, which was considered a great disgrace to her parents. Similarly, a divorce reflected shame upon a husband's family, and therefore a husband would usually do everything possible to keep his wife under his control rather than dismiss her. As a result, long-term oppression and humiliation often led a married woman to attempt suicide; suicidal behavior was even more common among women who served as second wives or concubines. A husband who divorced his wife at his will, or without so-called legitimate reasons, was often condemned by public opinion and might even be punished by the imperial courts. A popular historical tale features the ungrateful Chen Shi-Mei, a government official who was punished for deserting his wife, who had helped him before he was honored with an official appointment after passing the civil service examination and who also had served Chen's parents well until they died.

Painting of two young lovers being secretly united by the family maid, Ming dynasty, 1368–1644 (Smithsonian Institution, Washington, D.C.)

**Finance.** Marriage in imperial China normally involved some financial outlay by both the husband's and wife's families and therefore caused some redistribution of wealth. Starting from the Han dynasty, but being well established throughout China by the Tang dynasty, the status of a man's family could be established by the value of gifts given to the family of the bride, who normally prepared a dowry for her as well. Moreover, along with the admiration for aristocratic pedigrees came an inflation in the value of the betrothal gifts the highest-ranking families could expect to receive when they married off their daughters. During this period betrothal gifts could include fields and animals.

**Individual Talent.** Sometime in the second half of the Tang dynasty, along with systematic efforts by the state to formalize the civil service examination system, marriages that had solely emphasized family status and financial standing were gradually replaced by ones that focused on an individual's talent. Thereafter, this quality, rather than family status, carried more weight in mate selection, although the latter criterion remained an important consideration to some families. In a relatively open society such as

Tang China, not only was a man's intelligence appreciated in society, but a woman's talents also attracted educated men, though women were barred from taking the civil service examinations.

**Transition.** A further decline of marriages arranged by family status occurred during the Song dynasty (960–1279). There was a social trend that "where you come from is no longer the basis of official appointment, neither your family status is for match-making in marriage." If a girl was a descendant of an esteemed family but was poor, she might not be able to marry in her prime. It became possible, however, for wealthy merchant families, though not having glorious aristocratic roots, to marry their children into noble houses and to attract men who passed the civil service examinations in the top group as their sons-in-law. Many high-ranking Song officials married their daughters to talented young officials who came from modest family backgrounds. Two factors contributed to this transition: an improved agrarian economy that helped produce more wealth and thus reduced the economic gaps among social groups and, on the other hand, an open, merit-based civil service examination system that allowed men of lower social class to obtain governmental positions. A story recorded in the *Song Shi Zhuoxing Zhuan* (History of the Song Dynasty) indicates that in Northern Song times (960–1125) a young man named Liu was engaged to a girl from a poor family. After Liu obtained the *Jinshi*, the highest degree awarded in the national civil service examination, he changed his social status overnight. The girl's parents asked Liu to break the engagement with their daughter because they thought she no longer matched his status, but he refused to do so and married the girl.

**Dowries.** While the family pedigree stopped being a top priority in determining a suitable partner in Song times, marriage practices changed again when society demanded that a bride's family provide a sizable dowry. Those families that presented large dowries became socially admired, a trend not seen in previous dynasties, when the groom's family was largely responsible for providing gifts. Prior to this time, a bride's family was not obliged to present gifts to the groom's family, although the bride would be sent with clothes and personal items such as jewelry packed in cases, and she could be supplied with female attendants who might serve as her maids or her husband's concubines (especially in unions between aristocratic families). There were many stories about both upper- and lower-class families that searched for daughters-in-law who could bring larger dowries. In upper-class marriages, however, this motivation was by no means a simple economic need; it also came with political connotations. Marriages sealed with transfers of wealth and property brought prestige and connections. It became a distinctive tradition that tangible wealth and intangible benefits of honor and connections worked well together in elite marriages.

**Sources:**
Patricia Buckley Ebrey and James L. Watson, eds., *Kinship Organization in Late Imperial China, 1000–1940* (Berkeley: University of California Press, 1986).

Maurice Freedman, *Rites and Duties, Or Chinese Marriage: An Inaugural Lecture Delivered 26 January 1967* (London: London School of Economics, Bell, 1967).

Rubie S. Watson and Ebrey, eds., *Marriage and Inequality in Chinese Society* (Berkeley: University of California Press, 1991).

## POPULAR FESTIVALS

**New Year.** During the latter years of imperial Chinese history, the most important family gathering was the New Year festival, a time when the whole family joined in celebration. During this festive season, families celebrated their prosperity and prayed for continued success. The New Year was also a time for paying respects to the ancestors and the God of Wealth.

**Party.** The celebration of the New Year started early in the morning of the first day of the lunar year. For most families the kin-clan gathered and celebrated the five parts of the holiday ceremony. Individuals were expected to make sacrificial offerings to heaven and earth; to worship the god or goddess belonging to the family tradition; to worship deceased ancestors; to prostrate themselves before living parents and grandparents (it was the time parents and grandparents offered small change, or "blessed money," to their children or grandchildren); and to visit each other upon the invitation to feasts or to exchange gifts among relatives and friends. All these activities took place in the name of *Bai Nian* (New Year's greetings), which constituted an indispensable part of socialization, important not only for common people but also for government officials who wanted to keep close ties to one another.

**Entertainment.** Feasts and fireworks characterized the first day of the New Year. Homes were hung with special woodblock prints depicting various scenes, such as of a prosperous household, of the God of Wealth and his assistants hauling carts of gold and silver into the family courtyard, or of a bevy of young boys collecting strings of coins from ever bearing money trees. In general, however, the first half of the month was filled with a variety of entertainments, such as the dragon dance, music presentations, and operas, usually sponsored by wealthy families in local communities. Many customs have been retained and continue even in modern times. The traditional New Year celebration is now called the "Spring Festival," because China officially adopted the Western calendar in 1949. Like many other countries, China now celebrates New Year's Day on 1 January.

**Demon Hunter.** The legend of Zhong Kui contributed to another custom in imperial Chinese society. It was related to the culture of ghosts, in which vengeful spirits could be merciless toward those who did not serve them properly. Only Zhong Kui, a human exorcist, could subdue or expel them. According to Patricia Buckley Ebrey, editor of *Chinese Civilization and Society: A Sourcebook* (1981), the legend originated in a Tang story:

> Emperor Xuanzong encountered first a small demon who stole his favorite concubine's embroidered perfume bag and his own jade flute and then a large demon who came to the

## GHOST FESTIVAL

On the fifteenth day of the seventh month after a person's death there was another important festival called the "Ghost Festival," which is said to have originated in the Tang dynasty. The following is a summary of the story of Mulian [Mu-lien]:

> Since the death of his parents, Mu-lien (Maudgalyayana) has become a monk and has therefore given up his lay name of Lo-pu. Thanks to his good religious life he has attained to the grade of *arbat* and, "supported by the power of the Buddha," he comes at last to the hall of heaven. From here he begins to look round for his parents but finds only his father; of his mother there is no sign. In tears, he asks the Buddha after her and learns that, as a result of unpardonable misdeeds (which she need not necessarily have committed herself) she has been condemned to hell. He at once prepares to seek her there. But he cannot find her in any of the more supportable purgatories. Finally, however, Mu-lien learns from a guardian of the lowest and most terrible hell that she may well be there and he induces him to call out her name through the various tiers. At this very moment the mother is having eighteen iron nails driven through her body and dares not open her mouth lest yet more unpleasant treatment befall her. But a servant of hell recognizes her and asks why she does not announce her presence, since her son, the monk, Mu-lien, is asking for her. She answers that she has no son of this name or calling. Thereupon Mu-lien explains that during her life-time, when he was a layman, his name was Lo-pu. At this she recognizes her son and he leads her out of the lowest hell. But they advance no further than the region of the hunger-spirits (*preta*). There the mother is plagued by a terrible hunger which cannot be satisfied, for all food is changed to flames and all liquor to pus before her eyes. So Mu-lien asks the Buddha for advice and learns that on the fifteenth day of the seventh month on the occasion of the Ullambana festival arranged for the hunger-spirits his mother will receive a meal. Shortly after this the mother is re-born as a black dog. Mu-lien then also returns to the human world and at last finds his mother by a pagoda in the capital. He now recites Buddhist sutras without intermission for seven days and seven nights and accumulates such great merit thereby that his mother is restored to human form. The dog's coat is hung as a memento on a tree near the pagoda. At last Mu-lien brings his mother into the presence of the Buddha, who absolves her of all the sins of previous existences.

**Source:** Werner Eichhorn, *Kulturgeschichte Chinas*, translated as *Chinese Civilization: An Introduction*, by Janet Seligman (New York: Praeger, 1969), pp. 225–226.

emperor's aid by not only catching the small demon but gouging out his eyes and eating them. When Xuanzong questioned this helpful demon, the demon introduced himself as Zhong Kui, a man who had committed suicide by dashing his head against the palace steps decades earlier on learning that he had failed the palace examination. In

Detail of a handscroll showing a Dragon Boat Festival, Yuan dynasty, 1279–1368 (Palace Museum, Beijing)

gratitude for the posthumous honors the Tang emperor had then bestowed on him, Zhong Kui had vowed to rid the world of mischievous demons.

In many regions of China, people posted a portrait of Zhong Kui on their doors, especially on New Year's day, in hopes of getting his assistance in expelling unwanted ghosts who had invaded their households during the year. Often in those posters, Zhong Kui was depicted as a menacing figure with a dark face, wearing an official's robe and hat.

**Kitchen God.** On the morning of the fourth day of the New Year, people performed a ceremony called "receiving the gods." People believed that it was the time when many family gods descended from heaven to carry out their duties on earth. Kitchen God worshiping was the most important custom practiced at home. A shrine was placed above the stove for the Lord of the Kitchen, who also served as the household guardian angel. The shrine was a kind of altar with a paper representation of the divine figure, with an incense burner on a tiny table at its base. It was commonly believed that the Kitchen God made a trip to Heaven a week before the end of the lunar year to report the family finances of the past year; he came back on the lunar New Year to guard the family for the next year. To send him off to Heaven in a speedy way, people placed a representation of the god in a paper sedan chair and burned it on a tiny altar of twigs outside the front door. To welcome him back, people hung a new portrait of the Kitchen God over the stove at dawn on New Year's day and placed a cup of wine and bowls of uncooked food, as well as fruit, under the portrait. In some regions a newlywed couple was required to practice the "coming out of room" ceremony; they were led into the kitchen to worship the Lord of the Kitchen. They performed *Kow Tou* (kneel and bow) to a picture representing the divinity, which was placed above a small table on which incense and candles were lighted. It was believed that paying early and respectful attention to the divinity would keep the family well supplied with food in the year to come. There were other ceremonies, "keeping company with the gods," performed in local temples, which were

soaked in the smoke of burning incense during the days prior to the fifteenth day of the first month.

**Lantern Festival.** On the fifteenth day of the first month the Day of Lanterns was observed. Houses and streets were decorated with all types of lanterns, mostly made of bright red paper. Some were cubical; some were shaped as balls; others were circular, square, or oblong; and some resembled different kinds of animals. Chinese characters were often written on the lanterns; the messages carried the owners' wishes for happiness, wealth, and longevity. The holiday was an occasion of public gathering, when people walked the streets to see the display of colorful lanterns. It was also the evening when young women, usually secluded at home, were allowed by custom to join the crowd. According to historical records, in Tang times the streets were thronged with cheering crowds as "the din of drums filled the heavens, the glare of torches lit up the earth. Many people wore animal masks and men dressed up as women. Singing girls and jugglers went about in fantastic attire."

**Day of Lanterns.** In the Song dynasty (960–1279) many love poems described the passions of both young men and women who fell in love at first sight on the evening of the Day of Lanterns. In some regions people celebrated the festival with feasts entertaining family members and relatives. They "ate taro under the lanterns," a custom that was believed to make people become "bright-eyed" and "clear-sighted" throughout the year. The Day of Lanterns also served as a tradition of literary amusement. Puzzles and riddles were usually written on the lanterns displayed at certain public attractions. People who got the correct answers to the riddles were awarded prizes on the spot.

**Lunar Festival.** The *Qing Ming* Festival was usually observed in the latter part of the second month or the first part of the third month of the Chinese lunar year. In the Western calendar it usually occurred early in April. People visited the graves of their ancestors and presented offerings before them. They swept or tidied up the tombs of their ancestors by removing tall grasses or weeds that grew upon

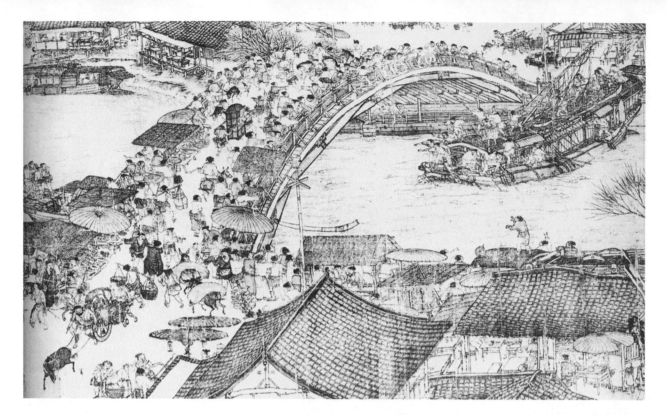

Detail of the scroll *Going on the River* at the *Qing Ming* Festival, depicting the Northern Song capital of Kaifeng, 1111–1126 (Palace Museum, Beijing)

them. "Sweeping tombs" meant more than just cleaning work; it indicated that the dead had living descendants to carry the "family's incense and candles" from one generation to the next—a sign of prosperity and continuity. By custom, a postsacrificial ceremony was observed for the kin to eat the offerings, because it was believed that the spirits consumed the essentials of the food and wine, and that living descendants then had to finish what was left behind. It was a ritual of sharing with the spirits of the ancestors.

**Water Fun**. The Dragon Boat Race was one of the most popular seasonal festivals. It took place on the fifth day of the fifth month of the lunar year, sometime in June according to the Western calendar. This occasion brought great amusement for both old and young when they watched or joined in racing the dragon boats on a river or lake. These boats were specially designed; they were long and slender in proportion to their width, having an elevated bow resembling a dragon's head with an open mouth. Each boat could hold ten to fifteen people; one man sat on the head of the dragon, waving a flag directing the rowers, while another stood at the end of the boat beating a large drum. The competition was merely an entertainment rather than a pure sport, and the award for winning the race was more symbolic for its honor than for the value of the prize. The festival of the Dragon Boat Race originated in the Zhou dynasty (771–256 B.C.E.) but prevailed throughout imperial Chinese history, and it continues into the present time. It is said that the festival started as the commemoration of a poet and politician named Chu Yuan, who drowned himself as a protest against corrupt imperial politics that barred him from carrying out reforms to save his country—the state of Chu. The boat race originally was a search to recover his body. Gradually the boat race became a customary festival that people observed every year in hopes of averting misfortunes. At the end of the race, as described in a witness account by Yang Szu-chang of the Ming dynasty (1368–1644), "the boats carry sacrificial animals, wine, and paper coins and row straight downstream, where the animals and wine are cast into the water, the paper coins are burned, and spells are recited. The purpose of these acts is to make pestilence and premature death flow away with the water. . . . In the evening when the boats return, the people take the water in the boats, mix it with various grasses, and use it to wash their bodies. This is said to prevent bad luck and is a kind of purification."

**Cow Boy and Weaving Girl.** On the seventh day of the seventh month there was a major festival, celebrated in many regions, called "the meeting of a cow boy and a weaving girl on the milky way." It was based on a legendary story that two stars, one representing a "cow boy," or a young male, and the other "a weaving girl," or young female, met at the "silver river," or the Milky Way. The festival was usually observed by unmarried females who celebrated it by lighting incense, in hopes of finding a real love and having a good marriage. Some regional customs required an unmarried girl to thread a needle in the dark or under a table in order to prove her sewing skills. Success was considered a good omen of a happy and peaceful marriage in the future.

**Ghost Festival.** On the fifteenth day of the seventh month another important festival was celebrated. The Ghost Festival, said to have originated in the Tang dynasty, was based on the popular legend of Mulian, who risked his life and endured countless sufferings in a journey to the netherworld to save his mother. The morally edifying aspects of the story became a source of the festival, which spawned an important social event observed in later dynasties. On this day Buddhists and non-Buddhists alike, from well-to-do families to illiterate commoners, put out food in order to feed hungry ghosts suffering in the netherworld. The Japanese monk Ennin, who spent many years in China (838–847), described this festival. He wrote that the forty-odd monasteries in the city of Yangzhou competed with each other to make unusual candles, cakes, and artificial flowers to offer in front of Buddha. "Everyone in the city goes around to the monasteries and performs adoration during this most flourishing festival." In some regions the Ghost Festival was alternatively called "the middle of the seventh month," in which family members burned paper clothing and mock paper money for their deceased ancestors in front of the ancestral tablets. It was believed that such observances would provide the dead with clothing and money they might need in the other world in the middle of the year.

**Mid-Autumn Festival.** On the fifteenth day of the eighth month the Mid-Autumn Festival was celebrated. Like the New Year festival, it was a time of family gatherings. According to the Chinese reckoning, the middle of autumn was thought to be a propitious season of harvest, which brought fruitfulness and joyfulness. People worshiped a full moon, which was believed to occur on this date. The custom also included making various kinds of cakes, always in the shape of the moon. People ate these "moon cakes" in the moonlight as a kind of offering to "reward" or "appreciate" the moon—a silver palace where the goddess Chang Er and her man, Wu Gang, were believed to live in peace and harmony. Many poets in the Tang, Song, Yuan, and Ming dynasties extolled the purity of moonlight and used it as a metaphor for love and nostalgia. In popular belief this special moonlight carried greetings, such as a person's wish, across thousands of miles to his or her loved ones.

Sources:

William Theodore de Bary and others, *Sources of Chinese Tradition* (New York: Columbia University Press, 1960).

Li-Ch'eng Kuo, *Chung-Kuo Min Su Shih Hua* (Tales of Chinese Folk Customs) (Taiwan: Hankuang Press, 1983).

Leon E. Stover, *The Cultural Ecology of Chinese Civilization: Peasants and Elites in the Last of the Agrarian States* (New York: PICA Press, 1974).

## SEX LIFE

**Love.** Literature on free love in the Tang dynasty (618–907) was incomparable in terms of its quantity to that published during other times in the imperial period of China. In addition to many poems, there were several popular novels on the subject, such as the "Story of Ying Ying," about a lady of upper-class origin who engaged in a romantic and premarital affair with a poor man name Zhang Zhen, and the "Story of Fei Yan," which praised the courage of a young woman who fought for the right to love the man she chose. Fei Yan, a concubine of a rich man, had an affair with that young man. The story ends tragically with Fei Yan committing suicide rather than surrendering to social pressure. Tang literature also touched boldly on human sexuality. *Tian Di Yin Yang Da Jiao Huan* (A Happy Intercourse Between Yin and Yang on Heaven and Earth) was probably the most graphic story written in prose; it included a detailed description of genital organs, sexual intercourse, and orgasm.

**Medical Care.** Sex health care constituted an important part of Tang medical literature. The most important book was *Qian Jing Fang Yao* (A Thousand Valued Prescriptions) by Sun Shi Mao. Drawing from the doctrines of Daoism and imported Indian Buddhism, *Qian Jing Fang Yao* associated sex life with health care, proposing proper sexual habits and skills for both men and women, especially for men. According to the book, a proper sex life was essential for the good health and longevity of men. It even stipulated the proper place, time, position, and duration that a man should have while engaging in sexual intercourse with a woman, because all these factors were believed to be important to keeping his *Qi* (energy) in good balance. Sun Shi Mao even suggested that men who were older than forty years should refrain from sex because this period was when a man's *Qi* was in decline and uncontrolled sex escalated its downhill trajectory. In another book, *Yu Fang Mi Jue* (Secrets of Sex Life), Zhang Ding Zhi proposed that a proper sex life could also help prevent and even cure a variety of illnesses caused by improper intercourse.

**Freedom.** During the Tang period, women enjoyed more freedom in social life. They were not only allowed to play folk sports similar to present-day polo and soccer but could also hunt together with men. Women's voluntary social clubs or societies also thrived; members attended regular meetings and gave mutual assistance. This social phenomenon indicates that the strict family doctrines of the Confucians were no longer a dominant force in every sector of society and that women were able to enjoy some life of their own outside the family circle.

**Beautification.** Women in the Tang era were more liberal in dress, hairstyles, and facial makeup compared to women during the Song (960–1279), Yuan (1279–1368), and Ming (1368–1644) periods. They were depicted in colorful, light, and sexy clothes in the classic paintings of the Tang period. Women were allowed to pursue beauty in a variety of ways, including using seventeen popular fashions of lip beautification. They freely expressed their physical charms and femininity. Fairly large numbers of women, presumably for the first time, earned a living by working as singers, dancers, and performers in large cities. Women often made public appearances outside the "inner chambers" and attended various festivities along with men. According to historical documentation, "Unseemly abuse (of the authorities) was received as rare fun and common obscenity as wit. The inmates of the inner and outer chambers (i.e.,

Detail of the scroll *The Joys of Forbidden Love,* Ming dynasty, 1368–1644 (from *Dreams of Spring,* 1997)

women and men) looked on together and did not remain separated from one another."

**Homosexual Societies.** Homosexuality was tolerated in Tang society for females and males. *Xiang Huo Xiong Di* (Brothers of Burning Joss-Stick) and *Han Lu Ying Xiong* (Heroes of Dry Land) were two popular societies for male homosexuals. Together with female prostitutes, male prostitutes thrived in the Tang capital, Chang'an, and they were seen openly in the imperial court as well as in the streets.

**Song Women.** The Song dynasty was more repressive on both men and women, particularly the latter. The concept of womanly virtues was pushed to the extreme. Whereas women in the Tang dynasty were relatively free to divorce or remarry, women in the Song period lost such freedoms; remarried women were considered sinful and immoral. It thus came as no surprise that princesses in the Song imperial courts, except one in an early period, did not seek remarriage, a sharp contrast to the Tang imperial courts. There were many other customary rules that restricted women's freedom and secluded

them from the public. For example, women were not allowed to sit with male relatives at the same table during family feasts at ceremonial celebrations. In other cases a married woman was not allowed to sit with her father-in-law or brothers-in-law at meals. Women, whether married or unmarried, were advised to shun public life, such as visits to temples and attendance at festivals. They were also discouraged from socializing with individuals considered to be of bad moral influence—such as female fortune-tellers, nuns, matchmakers, sorceresses, midwives, and remarried women—who were likely to spread indecent gossip so as to be harmful to family harmony.

Sources:

R. H. van Gaelic, *Erotic Colour Prints of the Ming Period: With an Essay on Chinese Sex Life from the Han to the Ch'ing dynasty, B.C. 206–A.D. 1644,* translated by Yang Quan as *Mi Xi Tu Kao: Fu Lun Han Dai Zhi Qing Dai Di Zhongguo Xing Sheng Huo, Gong Yuan Qian 206 Nian—Kung Yüan 1644 Nien* (Guangdong, China: Guangdong People's Press, 1992).

Paul Rakita Goldin, *The Culture of Sex in Ancient China* (Honolulu: University of Hawaii Press, 2002).

Ta-lin Liu, *Chung-kuo Ku Tai Hsing Wen Hua,* translated as *The Sex Culture of China* (Ningxia, China: Ningxia People's Press, 1994).

Detail of a scroll showing a man seducing a woman;
from the erotic novel *Rouputuan*, Ming dynasty,
1368–1644 (from *Dreams of Spring*, 1997)

## WEDDING CUSTOMS

**Marriage.** From the Zhou dynasty (771–256 B.C.E.) proceeding to the Tang period (618–907), the marriage institution evolved into a complex structure that was passed down to later dynasties without much alteration. Yet, those gradually established rules and customs laid the foundation for marriage laws set down under Tang rule. Parental consent remained the first marriage requirement, in which the father had final decisional power according to the law. If the parents were dead, the intention of marriage had to be reported to their spirits in the ancestral hall and at a shrine at home. Marriage also was required to be arranged through a go-between, who made the proposals to the two households. A marriage made without such a medium was often considered incomplete and to a large extent illegitimate. Another important custom prohibited marriage between persons of the same surname. The reason for this prohibition was the belief that people with the same surname were likely to be of similar origin, thus blood related, and therefore the family with a consanguineous marriage would produce few children and would not thrive. In some regions marriage between people of the same surname was condemned as an act of incest. Other taboos included marrying the widow of a deceased brother, marrying a fiancée of an elder brother, and marrying a female who had a history of elopement. All such marriages were believed to bring disgrace to the family and should be nullified.

**Quality.** In choosing a mate for their child, many parents' foremost concern was the social standing of the other family. Many parents preferred that the other family have a good reputation. Equally important was the personal quality of the young man or woman. In most cases the integrity and ability of a young man were valued more than family wealth. This tendency became most obvious starting with the Song dynasty (960–1279). The desired qualities for a bride were her virtues, one of the most important of which was her obedience to her future husband and parents-in-law. Her beauty was only a secondary priority, because general opinion held that a beautiful girl could not make a good wife and that she was more likely to have a loose morality and to cause trouble.

**Six Rites.** There were six rites that originated in classical times and were performed only in elite marriages prior to the Han dynasty (206 B.C.E.–220 C.E.), but in the Tang dynasty they became a common practice in the marriages of ordinary people. The six rites enjoyed legal status as part of marital law in the Tang, Song, and Ming Codes and became an established custom in imperial China. For a man to properly marry a woman the rites had to be performed in their correct order. The first rite was "giving choice." After the marriage proposal was made, along with an accompanying gift, a lady's family was, usually through a go-between, given the choice to accept the proposal. If they did so, the process could proceed. The second rite was "inquiring into the lady's name and birthday," to ensure that the bride-to-be did not bear the same surname or have any blood relative in common. The first and second rites were usually completed at the same time. The third rite was "giving the lucky result" of divination—usually performed in a religious way, to ensure that the marriage union was a balanced match, according to astrology. The fourth rite was "giving engagement" presents to the lady's family. The fifth rite was "inquiring about the date" of the wedding. This step often involved consulting the lunar calendar and selecting a lucky day. Finally, the sixth rite was the groom's "personal receiving" of his bride from her parents.

**Preparations.** Usually on the day prior to the wedding, the bride had her hair done in the fashion of a married woman and selected her dress. The bride's parents invited female relatives for a farewell party for their daughter. The bride was then required to proceed by kneeling down to her parents, grandparents, uncles, and aunts; she would also light scented incense before the ancestral altar for her last worship there. On the wedding day the bride got on a bridal sedan, dispatched to her residence by the bridegroom, and she was carried to her future husband's house, usually accompanied by a band and a group of attendants holding red lanterns or shooting off firecrackers. When the bridal sedan was carried into the house of the bridegroom, the bride, whose face was covered by a thick veil, was led into the reception room. In some regions a woman who had borne children, particularly males, was the first person to greet the bride and lead her inside. The implication of this act was to bring good luck to the bride in childbearing.

**New Family.** The next major step of the wedding was for the bride and bridegroom to "worship heaven and earth." They were guided to kneel down and bow to the family's religious totems, then to the groom's parents, to his ancestral tablets, and sometimes to a representation of the emperor-in-reign. *Kow Tou* (kneel and bow) always proceeded in an even number (two or four times) rather than an odd number (one or three times), because odd numbers were, and still are, regarded in some regions as inauspicious on a wedding day. Finally, after other minor procedures, the couple was led into the bridal chamber to consummate the union. Only then did the groom remove the bride's head covering. Often it was the first time ever that the husband or wife saw each other's facial features. The custom of covering the bride's face with a thick red veil on the wedding day is said to have originated in the Tang dynasty as a way to add some mystique, because prior to the wedding a prospective bride and groom were rarely even acquainted. Once their names were known to each other, etiquette demanded that they avoid contact until the wedding. This custom later turned out to be an effective way to assist in arranged marriages and to regulate romance between young men and women. In some regions another popular wedding custom was to spread soybeans and peanuts on the marriage bed, in hopes that the couple would add more offspring to the family.

Sources:

Richard Gunde, *Culture and Customs of China* (Westport, Conn.: Greenwood Press, 2002).

Li-Ch'eng Kuo, *Chung-Kuo Min Su Shih Hua* (Tales of Chinese Folk Customs) (Taiwan: Hankuang Press, 1983).

Yongzhou Qin, *Zhongguo She Hui Feng Shu Shi* (History of Chinese Social Customs) (Shangdong, China: Shangdong People's Press, 2000).

Painting of a family, Ming dynasty, 1368–1644
(Metropolitan Museum of Art, New York)

# SIGNIFICANT PEOPLE

## EMPRESS WU (WU ZHAO)

### 627-705

### FIRST FEMALE MONARCH

**Rise to Power.** Empress Wu, or Wu Zhao, challenged the patriarchal system by advocating women's intellectual development and sexual freedom. Born to a newly emerging merchant family in the Northeast, Wu Zhao had been a concubine of Li Shimin, or Taizong, founder of the Tang dynasty (618–907). In defiance of convention Emperor Gaozong started an affair with her, and she bore him a son in 652. She then began to plot against Gaozong's consort, Empress Wang, incriminating the empress in the death of Wu's infant daughter. By 655 she had consolidated her position after her son inherited the throne. Wu disposed of her enemies, first the former empress and then the high-ranking officials, who had strongly opposed her rise.

**New Capital.** To consolidate her power, in 657 Wu designated Luoyang as a second capital. By transferring the normal seat of the court from Chang'an to Luoyang, she was able to escape the control of the great families of the northwestern aristocracy, which played an important role in the rise of the Tang dynasty. Favoring the power base in the Northeast, the royal family finally moved to Luoyang in 683. Economic considerations also played a role in this relocation. The area around Chang'an could not produce the amount of food required to feed the court and garrisons, and the transportation of grain up the Yellow River, traversing the Sanmen rapids, was exceptionally expensive. Luoyang was favorably located on the last stop of the river routes from the South, which greatly reduced the cost of shipping grains from the Southeast to the imperial capital.

**Empress Dowager.** When Gaozong suffered a stroke in 660, the empress made herself the ruler. Gaozong's third son succeeded to the throne in 683 after his death, but Empress Wu became the empress dowager in a few months, after forcing the young emperor to abdicate.

**Reign of Terror.** After rising to power, Wu tried to remove from power the representatives of the northwestern aristocracy, who had controlled the government from the beginning of the dynasty through the medium of the imperial chancellery. In 684 Li Jingye led a revolt of those northwestern families who had been disgraced and exiled to the Yangzi Valley. After suppressing this revolt, the empress dowager began to purge her opponents at court. She ordered the executions of several hundred of these aristocrats and of many members of the imperial family of Li. She founded a secret police and conducted a reign of terror, justifying the mass executions on the grounds that discrimination against a woman's open exercise of power forced her to use terror to defend her authority.

**Zhou Dynasty.** Removing the legitimate heir, she took the name of *Emperor Zetian* and founded the Zhou dynasty in 690, becoming the first and only female emperor in Chinese history. Her usurpation marked a significant social revolution, the rise of a new class, which the empress tried to use in her struggle against the traditionalist, northwest nobility. Empress Wu proved to be a wise monarch, and in her reign of twenty years she continued many policies and practices of her predecessors.

**Buddhists' Support.** Wu Zhao embarked on religious life as a nun in a convent after Li Shimin's death in 649. Before coming to power, she was presented with three petitions containing sixty thousand names and urging her to ascend to the throne, which suggested that she had some popular support. To legitimize her position, Empress Wu turned mainly to Buddhism, proclaiming herself an incarnation of Maitreya (Mi-le), the Buddhist savior.

**Patronage of Buddhism.** During her reign she ordered the erection of temples in every province to explain the *Dayunjing,* which predicted the emergence of a female world ruler seven hundred years after the passing of the Buddha. Her patronage of Buddhism also expanded to other temples and sects, and much work was done on the cave temples at Longmen on her orders. She particularly supported Huayan Buddhism, which regarded Vairocana Buddha as the center of the world, much as Empress Wu wished to be the center of political power. Unlike her predecessors she was fond of the Buddhist community, which led her to build at great expense the Mingtang, or Hall of Light. It was used for religious rites supervised by her lover Xue Huaiyi. When he fell out of favor, he burned the building to the ground. Thereafter the empress favored Confucianism.

**Examination System.** Under Wu's rule the government was expanded, and many of the new positions were filled through the examination system. To recruit a new class of administrators through competition, the examinations that had played only a secondary role in the recruitment and promotion of civil servants in Han times (206 B.C.E.–220 C.E.) had been organized in a systematic way by the year 669. This institution became a political weapon in the hands of Empress Wu when she usurped the throne in 690. Although this system opened government positions to a wider group than ever before, in the final stages of the process candidates continued to be judged on their appearance and speech. These criteria no doubt favored the aristocratic families. Since candidates normally tried to win favor with an examiner prior to the tests, some could use their family connections to send samples of their verse in an effort to impress the men who held the keys to government positions. In the reign of Empress Wu, persons who entered government through the examinations were able for the first time to occupy the highest positions, even that of chief minister. Nevertheless, court intrigues still greatly influenced the recruiting of civil servants.

**Territorial Expansion.** Under the administration of Empress Wu, Tang territory expanded through constant fighting with other peoples, particularly the Tibetans. In 605 the Qidan, who lived in Manchuria in the marginal areas between the open steppe and settled areas, invaded the Tang empire and gained a dramatic victory over Wu's armies near the site of modern Beijing. Meanwhile, the Turks invaded Gansu, and the Tibetans posed a threat to Chinese possessions in Central Asia. The empress responded with both diplomacy and force, concluding a marriage alliance with the Turks and defeating the Qidan in battle. On the Korean peninsula Empress Wu supported the unification movement under the state of Silla. Although she was not able to control the newly unified state, relations continued to be friendly during her reign.

**Abdication.** In her last years Wu lost influence, although she remained energetic and cruel. Her extravagant construction projects and expensive frontier campaigns had exhausted the treasury, which led to a financial crisis. From 697 onward she found it so difficult to win support that she attempted to return the throne to her son Zhongzong. Her courtiers, however, hatched a plot and afterward forced her to abdicate in 705; she died later that year. While Confucian historians condemned her usurpation, extravagance, and scandal, Wu Zhao has been credited for providing strong leadership and ruling during an age of relative peace and prosperity.

**Sources:**

Woodbridge Bingham, *The Founding of the T'ang Dynasty: The Fall of Sui and Rise of T'ang, a Preliminary Survey* (New York: Octagon, 1975).

R. W. L. Guisso, *Wu Tse-t'en and the Politics of Legitimation in T'ang China* (Bellingham: Western Washington University, 1978).

Edward Schafer, *The Divine Women: Dragon Ladies and Rain Maidens in T'ang Literature* (Berkeley: University of California Press, 1973).

# ZHU XI

## 1130-1200
### SCHOLAR

**Early Life.** Zhu Xi was one of the most important scholars of the Song dynasty (960–1279). He was a prolific writer, and he helped to clarify the institutional development of the family and women's social life in *Zhu Zi Jia Li* (Book of Family Rites). Born into a literary family in Fujian province, Zhu Xi was the son of a district magistrate. At the age of eighteen he won his *Jinshi* degree and thereafter spent most of his life in a succession of government positions. Some positions required much activity, which helped him to improve his administrative ability; others were less demanding, such as serving as a temple guardian, which gave him plentiful leisure time for learning, writing, and teaching. Following his extensive philosophic and literary pursuits, he taught many pupils who gathered about him.

**Court Official.** He was offered several official positions in the central government, but he turned them down with moralizing arrogance. However, in 1194 he accepted the position as adviser to a new emperor, Ningzong. Normally backing the "war party" that advocated hard opposition against pressures from the Jurchens of northern China, Zhu constantly accused his opponents, who controlled the Southern Song (1127–1279) government at that time, of do-nothing policies. After less than two months of service, he was forced to retire by partisan enemies embroiled in a court intrigue. Many other scholars were also removed from government positions. After suffering from a temporary, undeserved disgrace from 1197 to 1199, he was restored to honorable status as a retired official.

**Achievements.** Like many other neo-Confucians, Zhu was enthralled by Buddhism and Daoism in his youth; later, when he was about thirty years old, he finally gave them up in favor of Confucianism. He was thoroughly won over to the doctrines of the Chen brothers (Chen Hao and Chen Yi). Subsequently, Zhu produced many works philosophically attacking both Buddhism and Daoism. He criticized the four major classics, interpreted the writings of the famous philosopher Zhou Duni, edited the works of the Chen brothers, clarified the *Yi Jing* (Classic of Changes), and abridged a general Chinese history in which he evaluated historical events in line with his philosophical values.

He taught a large number of disciples, primarily at the White Deer Grotto Academy, which he established in Jiangxi province. When he was fifty, he had won celebrity and reputation as an intellectual.

**True Way School.** Zhu Xi synthesized Song philosophers' thoughts into a single doctrine, and his ideas became known as neo-Confucianism. To the metaphysical ideas of the Northern Song philosophers, Zhu added a revitalized stress on the *Dao* (The Way) that all individuals should endeavor to follow, calling for greater self-nurturing and an intense understanding of the Confucian classics. Because of Zhu's emphasis on the *Dao*, his teaching became known as the True Way School, which fascinated many of his pious disciples who adopted old ceremonies, traditional fashions, and strict manners in order to distinguish themselves from the career-minded Confucian civil servants. In 1195, almost immediately after Han Tuozhou became chief minister, the True Way School was denounced as untrue and a subversive philosophy that distracted men from the original teachings of Confucius and Mencius at a time when the neo-Confucian movement was dominated by this school. Zhu was exiled. However, the prohibition was soon revoked, and, following Han Tuozhou's death, the True Way School steadily became mainstream state doctrine. As the Mongols in North China began to accept traditional Confucianism, the Southern Song turned to the True Way School.

**Author.** The best known presentation of Zhu's ideas was a compact book called *Jinsi lu* (Mirror Image of Things at Hand), which he compiled during 1175 and 1176 with the assistance of a friend. It was a handbook of the principles of the True Way School, designed to serve beginning students as a springboard to the Four Books. It is indisputably the most prominent single work of philosophy created in China between the Song and Ming (1368–1644) dynasties.

**New Method.** Zhu, whose role in the growth of neo-Confucianism is often compared to that of St. Thomas Aquinas in European Christianity, was a brilliant philosopher, a productive intellectual, a stimulating educator and debater, and an unwilling bureaucrat. Zhu synthesized different ideas that found expression in the intellectual agitation of the eleventh century. He applied to the Four Books a new method, clarifying the classics. He replaced the phrase-by-phrase interpretation practiced since the second century with philosophical comments that revealed the great significance of the text.

**Synthesizer.** He combined the ideas of the intellectual forerunners into a single system and was considered to be the greatest synthesizer in Chinese philosophy. His prolific writings and commentaries on the classics brought the rationalistic school to full maturity and created a form of Confucianism that remains orthodox.

**Official Recognition.** The new philosophy, neo-Confucianism, obtained its classic formulation from Zhu, but the *Jinsi lu* and other works were not accepted as orthodox in his times and were not officially adopted until the mid thirteenth century. Of the Four Classics, considered repositories of fundamental truth, only the *Analects* was generally respected by all Confucians. The other three works—*Mencius*, *Da Xue* (Great Leaning), and *Zhong Yong* (The Doctrine of the Mean)—were subjects of much debate in Song times.

**Impact.** Neo-Confucianism was not generally recognized in Zhu's lifetime. Conservative scholars resisted his ideas and aggressively accused him of being a turncoat; some opponents even insisted that he be sentenced to death. Zhu's standing kept growing after his death from dysentery in 1200, and prior to the collapse of the Southern Song his classical explanation of Confucianism was used in the civil service examinations. The Yuan and Ming governments declared Zhu's interpretations as the only accurate explanation of Confucianism and made them the standard for teaching and the civil service examination. His ideas crystallized into orthodoxy in the Ming dynasty (1368–1644) and were as admired as those put forth in Europe by the philosopher Aristotle. Zhu was posthumously ennobled as a duke, and beginning in 1241 his tablet was placed in Confucian temples.

Sources:

Wang-tsit Chan, ed., *Chu Hsi and Neo-Confucianism* (Honolulu: University of Hawaii Press, 1986).

Chan, *Chu Hsi: New Studies* (Honolulu: University of Hawaii Press, 1989).

Patricia Buckley Ebrey, trans., *Chu Hsi's Family Rituals: A Twelfth-Century Chinese Manual for the Performance of Cappings, Weddings, Funerals, and Ancestral Rites* (Princeton: Princeton University Press, 1991).

Hoyt Cleveland Tillman, *Confucian Discourse and Chu Hsi's Ascendancy* (Honolulu: University of Hawaii Press, 1992).

# DOCUMENTARY SOURCES

Ban Zhao, *Admonitions for Women* (circa 45–116)—A guide to proper etiquette for women, written by this eminent female Confucian scholar.

Li Boyan, *Beiji Shu* (circa seventh century)—Using sources assembled by his father, who was an official under the Northern Jin and Northern Zhou, Li Boyan wrote this work about the political, economic, and social development of these kingdoms in the seventh century.

Liu Yin, *Sishu Jiyi Jingyao* (1330)—This book comprised the masters' teachings as they were recorded by his students. The collection is huge, totaling several million characters, far too large to serve as a practical reference for most students. In addition, many entries did not precisely represent the master's authoritative views.

Peng Zhao, *Inscription on Reconstruction of the Ancestral Shrine of the Li of the Baited* (1489)—This book argues that during the Ming dynasty (1368–1644), when lineage organizations were getting stronger, the need to trace family roots and unite more kinsmen broke the limitations of sacrificing only to ancestors of five generations. The emergence of dedicated shrines to distant ancestors in the ancestral hall or temple became a social phenomenon, greatly strengthening the organizational power of kinship clans.

Sima Guang, *Zizhi Tongjian* (A Comprehensive Mirror for Aid in Government, eleventh century)—A treatise by a famous historian of the Song dynasty (960–1279), it is a study of nearly the whole of Chinese history, from the earliest beginning to the Tang dynasty (618–907). Sima Guang claimed that an accurate description of the past could teach moral and practical lessons for the present.

Song Ruoxin, *Analects for Women* (circa 618–907)—A Tang-era primer on proper standards of behavior for women, written by a female scholar for her daughter. The existing text may not be the actual words of the contributing author, which might have been recast later in the form of four-word rhymes.

Wang Yinglin, *San Zi Jing* (The Trimetrical Classic, circa 1250)—A primer, allegedly written by this Confucian scholar for young Chinese children, which distills the essentials of Confucian thought by presenting the concepts in couplets of three syllables.

# RELIGION
# AND PHILOSOPHY

by GUANGQIU XU

## CONTENTS

*Sidebars and tables are listed in italics.*

**621** • Daoist priest Fu Yi claims that Buddhist communities are becoming a burden on the state; he encourages the Tang court to break up the Buddhist clergy and put their monasteries to better use.

**629** • Buddhist monk Xuan Zang leaves Chang'an for India. He travels overland across Central Asia.

**630** • Tang emperor Taizong decrees that temples in honor of Confucius are to be set up in all districts and that intellectuals must offer sacrifices in their capacities as government officials.

**631** • The Gospels are transported to Chang'an by the Nestorians, followers of a branch of the Christian faith that is based in Syria and Persia.

**635** • Nestorian missionary Olopen (known as Jiang Jiao) arrives in China and labors to translate the Scriptures into Chinese.

**645** • Buddhist monk Xuan Zang returns from India to Chang'an.

**647** • Taizong decrees that tablets honoring twenty-two worthies are to be placed in the Confucian temples, and as a consequence, he transforms these shrines into Halls of Celebrity.

**671** • Yi Jing begins a pilgrimage to India by boarding an Italian merchant ship. He leaves India in 685 and comes back by sea to China in 695.

**694** • Manichaeanism, a religion practiced in Persia, first appears in China, but it is not until the early eighth century that the Uighurs are converted to this faith and it becomes more widespread among the Chinese.

**700** • Cantonese monk Huineng founds the southern branch of the Chan Buddhism school, which soon surpasses the northern branch in popularity. Huineng is recognized as the sixth Patriarch of China.

**716-719** • Subhakarasimha and Vajrabodhi, Indian masters of Tantric Buddhism, arrive in China.

\* DENOTES CIRCA DATE

**720**
- Ten images of a seated Confucius are placed in the main hall of temples dedicated to him. His cult is so closely associated with the divinities, such as the city gods, that he is soon seen as a god himself.

**729**
- A census is taken by the government to ensure that each prefecture has only one Buddhist monastery and thirty monks.

**742**
- The first Muslim mosque is constructed in China; many more mosques are built in the following years.

**756**
- Buddhist master and translator Bukong (Amoghavajra) returns to Chang'an from Ceylon and begins translating many Tantric texts.

**766–779**
- Manichaean shrines are built at Jingzhou in Hebei, Yangzhou, Nanking, and even as far south as Shaoxing in Zhejiang, where many Chinese are converted to this faith.

**781**
- A Nestorian stela is erected in Chang'an, and Nestorianism, known as *Qinjiao* (Luminous Religion), is gradually adopted by the Chinese.

**819**
- After a request is made by the Emperor Xianzong, the finger bone of Buddha is brought to Chang'an for worship. Confucian scholars actively campaign against Buddhism. Han Yu, an orthodox member of the literati and a notorious anti-Buddhist scholar, is ordered into exile by the emperor.

**836**
- Tang emperor Wenzong issues a decree prohibiting the Chinese from having any relations with "people of color," a term that denotes foreigners such as the Iranians, Sogdians, Arabs, Malays, Indians, and Sumatrans.

**842–845**
- Emperor Wuzong takes decisive action against Buddhism, issuing the proscriptive decree that charges the faith—seen as a foreign religion—with bringing about the moral and economic decline of the empire. The great suppression of Buddhism, as well as other foreign religions, begins.

**843**
- The Tang emperor confiscates Manichaean properties, burns their manuscripts, and destroys their temples and images.

\* DENOTES CIRCA DATE

**955**
- The Northern Zhou dynasty (951–960), in order to make coins, confiscates and melts precious metals from Buddhist shrines.

**966**
- The Tang court organizes the last great pilgrimage to the West, in which more than 150 monks participate; only a small number of the monks that reach India, by a route along the Central Asian oases, are able to return to China in 976.

**972-983**
- The original version of the Buddhist *Tripitaka* is printed. It is republished frequently.

**1019**
- Supported by the Song rulers, the collection of the Daoist *Tripitaka* is completed and printed. Although republished frequently, it is not accepted throughout China as widely as the Buddhist canon.

**1047**
- A group of Buddhists expecting the arrival of Maitreya (Buddha of Love, or the "future" Buddha) revolt in Beizhou in Hobei. Led by a soldier, Wangzi, the revolt is crushed by the central government.

**1067**
- The sale of certificates to men desiring to become monks is approved by the government. The government also sells certificates for higher positions within the temples.

**1176**
- The philosopher Zhu Xi's *Jinsi lu* (Mirror Image of Things at Hand) is completed. It is a handbook on the principles of the True Way School of Confucionism, the most prominent single work of philosophy created in China during the Song dynasty.

**1194**
- Zhu Xi takes a position as an adviser to the new emperor, Ningzong.

**1195**
- Zhu Xi's True Way School is denounced as untrue learning; he is forced to resign from his position in the central government as the result of a court conspiracy.

**1199**
- Zhu Xi is restored to honorable status as a retired official. He dies the following year.

**1223**
- Genghis Khan, who respects the Daoist priest Qiu Chuji, makes him patriarch of all religious orders in the Mongol empire and authorizes the Daoists to answer all religious questions.

* DENOTES CIRCA DATE

**1241**
- Zhu Xi's tablet is first placed in the Confucian temples.

**1242**
- A monk, Haiyun, convinces the Mongol emperor to transfer his religious preference to the Chan school of Buddhism. This faith holds a dominant position in Chinese society and its influence increases within the Mongol empire in the following decades.

**1246**
- A Franciscan monk, representing the Christian order dedicated to poverty and faith that was founded by St. Francis of Assisi in 1209, arrives at the court of the Khan at Karakorum.

**1253**
- French king Louis IX sends Franciscan friar William of Rubrouck to investigate the potential for Christian expansion in Asia.
- The Tibetan lama (Lamaist monk) 'Phags-pa arrives in Beijing; he invents an alphabetic script for the Mongolian language in 1260.

**1274**
- The Yuan ruler appoints a Muslim governor in China.

**1277**
- The Mongols begin to trust the Tibetan monk Yanglian Zhenjia; the government favors Lamaism.

**1280**
- Yuan ruler Kublai Khan establishes an office in charge of monitoring the activities of Christians.

**1281**
- Kublai Khan orders that Daoist excesses be restricted and launches a more efficient persecution against members of that faith.

**1285**
- A Tibetan (or Tangut) lama named Yang, who is in charge of Buddhist teaching south of the Yangzi River, angers many Confucians by breaking open the tombs of the Song royal family and taking the treasures to restore Buddhist shrines.

**1291**
- Liu Yin, a distinguished scholar, turns down an offer to become an academician at the Imperial Academy. His refusal to commit himself to public service is regarded as an example of Confucian eremitism, a departure of Confucian intellectuals from worldly affairs as a protest against the Mongol regime.

\* DENOTES CIRCA DATE

**1300**
- John of Montecorvino (Giovanni da Montecorvino), the first Roman Catholic priest to visit China (1294), is permitted to construct a church in Beijing. By 1305 he has converted about six thousand persons to Catholicism.

**1309**
- The Yuan court, which continues to favor Lamaism, issues an edict that anyone caught beating a lama will have his hand cut off; an offender will lose his tongue for verbally affronting a lama.

**1313**
- With the money donated by a wealthy Arab, Roman Catholics build a church in the great port of Chuanzhou (Zayton), which has a close trade relationship with the Persian Gulf. This church will be turned into a cathedral with a friary attached; other churches are later constructed in the city.

**1340**
- After the fall of Chancellor Bayan the Yuan government restores the examination system, which is now offered not only to the Chinese but also to Mongol applicants. As a result Confucianism recovers some of its ideological supremacy.

**1418**
- The emperor declares that only twenty Buddhist and Daoist clergy can be ordained in a district.

**1484**
- Widespread corruption in the sale of monk certificates increases within the Buddhist temples.

**1506**
- After offending an authoritarian eunuch, the philosopher Wang Yangming is sent to prison and later exiled to Guizhou. He dies in 1529.

**1530**
- The use of images of Confucius in the temples is forbidden; they are replaced with tablets. Simultaneously, the term "Confucius temple" is replaced by "Confucius hall."

**1552**
- Francis Xavier, a Spanish priest and the first Jesuit missionary to travel to Japan (1549), dies while attempting to gain access to Guangzhou in southern China.

**1583**
- Italian Jesuit missionary Matteo Ricci arrives in Guangdong; he travels to Suzhou, Nanchang, and Nanjing in the following years.

\* DENOTES CIRCA DATE

**1588**
- Li Zhi, a radical Confucian official who espoused unorthodox ideas, turns out to be a Buddhist monk. Two years later the local nobles organize a crowd that flattens the temple where Li is staying.

**1589**
- Ricci builds a church but uses a Chinese architectural design. He realizes that priests of any kind are associated with the reviled Buddhists, hence he takes on the clothes, behavior, and learning of a Confucian scholar.

**1595**
- Ricci and his missionary fellows move their activities north to the Yangzi valley.

**1600**
- Xu Guangqi, one of the first scholars to communicate with the Jesuit missionaries, meets Ricci in Nanjing; he is later baptized and christened as Paul by Jean de Rocha.

**1601**
- Ricci obtains oral authorization to establish a mission in the capital; his missionaries enter Beijing in January.

**1602**
- Li Zhi commits suicide.
- A Portuguese missionary, Benedict de Goaes, leaves India to find out whether Marco Polo's Cathay is really China. He arrives in Gansu in 1605, but he dies the next year.

**1604**
- A group of moderate Chen-Zhu conservatives founds the Donglin Academy at Wuxi near Shanghai in an effort to resist the moral decay and political corruption of the country.

**1621**
- Baptized and christened Michael in 1612, Yang Tingyun, a high-ranking Chinese official, publishes an essay extolling the advantages of Christianity over Buddhism.

**1639**
- One of the first anti-Christian essays in China, the *Poxiechi* (Compilation of Disproved Heresies), appears.

\* DENOTES CIRCA DATE

RELIGION AND PHILOSOPHY

# OVERVIEW

**Important Role.** From the Tang dynasty (618–907) to the Ming period (1368–1644), several religions and philosophies played important roles in justifying political power, establishing administrative authority, upholding peace and order, maintaining civil values, inspiring faith in the government, and raising public morale in times of crisis. Although the Tang government employed Confucian forms and learning, the rulers often favored Daoism. Chinese Buddhism reached its peak during the Tang era. Buddhist monasteries thrived throughout the empire and fulfilled significant social roles; outstanding monks formulated new doctrines and developed innovative teaching methods. Buddhism prevailed as the major spiritual, intellectual, and aesthetic influence, but the family ethic and political ideology of Confucianism never totally disappeared during the golden age of Chinese Buddhism. In the ninth century, intellectual interest began to move away from Buddhism and return to Confucianism. Influenced greatly by both Daoism and Buddhism, scholars launched the neo-Confucianism movement, a new belief system that was profoundly different from earlier Confucianism.

**Song Dynasty.** The Song empire (960–1279), which succeeded the Tang dynasty after a fifty-year interval of chaos known as the Five Dynasties (907–959), was politically far weaker than its predecessor. In 1127, while under attack by the formidable Mongols, the Song court was forced to abandon North China entirely and shift its capital to Hangzhou in the south. This event marks the division (1125–1127) between Northern and Southern Song periods. Zhu Xi, the greatest synthesizer of Chinese thought, helped to develop neo-Confucianism, known as rationalism, which became the major orthodoxy after his death (1200) until late in the Ming period. Chan and Pure Land Buddhism, as well as Daoism, thrived, but neo-Confucianism was especially attractive to scholars.

**Yuan Dynasty.** During the Yuan dynasty (1279–1368) China fell for the first time under the rule of the Mongols, who produced little of philosophical interest. Mongol toleration of foreigners, however, was extended to their religions; Nestorians, Muslims, Christians, and Jews entered the country and established churches. Daoism was particularly favored during this period, but the competition for official patronage was finally won by proponents of Tibetan Buddhism (Lamaism).

**Ming Dynasty.** The Chinese succeeded in driving out the Mongols and established the Ming dynasty. It was a prosperous and reasonably stable period, but culturally less creative than the Tang and Song dynasties. In the field of thought the rationalism of Zhu Xi remained dominant, but a school of idealism within neo-Confucianism started in the Song period with Zhu's contemporary, Lu Jiuyuan, and reached its peak with the teachings of Wang Yangming. They argued that the mind itself is above distinctions of good and evil, an ideology with a strong Buddhist flavor and compatible with Daoist ideas. The tendency to combine Confucianism, Buddhism, and Daoism attracted many intellectuals.

**Three Major Religions.** Confucianism, Buddhism, and Daoism were the three major religions practiced in China during the imperial period (618–1644). Both Confucianism and Daoism were developed by the Chinese, while Buddhism was brought into China from India. Although the two faiths had much in common, Confucianism stressed the patriarchal extended family and the performance of worship to dead ancestors, while Daoism fascinated many Chinese because of its stress on personal freedom and harmony with nature.

**Daoism.** The founder of Daoism was Lao Zi, who lived in the sixth century B.C.E. and who is credited with writing the most significant Daoist text, the *Daodejing*. The second principal Daoist philosopher was Zhuangzi, who created a collection of Daoist writings known as the *Zhuangzi*, one of the greatest literary and philosophical books. *Dao* means "way," "path," or "road." Daoists do not believe in any particular trail to be followed, but only in the invisible reality lying behind appearances. They emphasize *wuwei* (doing nothing) and *ziran* (being spontaneous). The best kind of government is one that governs the least and with the least effort. The perfect ruler is an intelligent man who is in harmony with the *Dao* so that his subjects will not be ruled. The *Dao* is everlasting, never-ending, fixed, independent, meaningless, voiceless, shapeless, and cannot be seen as an object.

**Deities and Rituals.** Daoism embraces many popular Chinese gods, the most famous of which are the Jade Emperor (the monarch of Heaven); the Eight Immortals (human beings who gained immortality by means of hard work in meditating, carrying out good deeds, and making sacrifices; they were not worshiped in temples, but their pictures and symbols were used in murals and wall carvings to symbolize longevity and immortality); Xiwangmu (Royal Lady of the Western Paradise, the heavenly land where everyone goes after death); and Mazipo (Queen of Paradise and Sacred Mother, who is worshiped particularly by seamen and fishermen). To earn their daily living, priests perform rituals for individuals, the most discernible part of Daoism, and are called upon to bring prosperity to communities, eliminate illness, avoid misfortune caused by mystical forces, and pray for the dead at funerals.

**Daoist Movement.** After Emperor Gaozu, founding father of the Tang empire (618–917), declared that Lao Zi was his ancestor, he constructed an ancestral shrine at the site where Lao Zi was allegedly born. Emperor Xuanzong, an enthusiastic sponsor of Chinese arts and scholarship, obtained a diploma verifying his comprehension of Daoist philosophy. In 741 he introduced a new national civil service examination in which Daoist—rather than Confucian—texts were included. In 742 he decreed that the major Daoist books had the same standing as traditional Confucian classics. Consequently, the practice of Daoism was resolutely established through government support. Since the Daoists were also interested in methods of achieving immortality, they concentrated on alchemy in an attempt to discover an exemption from death. By the Song dynasty the alchemical procedures of refining were transformed into a physiological quest to invent an immortality-related substance for the human body. In addition, greatly inspired by the Daoist respect for nature, landscape painting, known as "mountains and water," was well developed and continued to be the leading artistic style up to modern times. Daoism was not limited to the Han ethnic Chinese. The Jurchens, who founded the Jin dynasty (1115–1234) in northern China, developed several new Daoist sects. After expelling the Jurchens, the Mongol leader Genghis Khan, who was interested in this religion, employed a Daoist priest in his government as a political consultant and in the hope of obtaining immortality. To reward the priest, Genghis Khan decreed in 1223 that all Daoists were exempted from taxation. Mongol leader Kublai Khan, who established the Yuan dynasty (1279–1368), had close relations with the head of the Daoist religion in southern China and allowed Daoists to have more influence in his administration. In 1281, however, Kublai Khan began to persecute Daoists and decreed the burning of all Daoist literature after they lost a great debate at court with Buddhist leaders. During the imperial period Daoism coexisted with Confucianism, but it never supplanted Confucianism as the official philosophy.

**Confucianism.** The philosophy that recognizes Confucius as its founder and provided the social and political ideas that dominated China for more than two thousand years is called Confucianism. Confucius believed that anyone could become good, not by birth, but by means of acquiring five virtues: kindness, rectitude, politeness, intelligence, and credibility. These five virtues became essential to Confucianism. During the Song dynasty Confucianism was revived and was known as the neo-Confucianism movement. Members of this school looked back to the philosophy of Confucius and its leading place as the ideology of imperial government, but they also adopted both Buddhist and Daoist concepts to highlight the spiritual characteristics of Confucian thought. This movement was typified by a reconfirmation and renaissance of classical Confucian ethics, a promotion of political and social reforms, a new historical awareness, and a heightened perception of the political function of government and its ethical responsibilities.

**Role and Growth.** During the Tang dynasty Confucius was idolized as a deity. In 630 Emperor Taizong decreed that a Confucian temple would be set up in every province and country throughout the empire. By 647 these temples became national shrines to Confucius and to those government administrators whose learning had added greatly to Confucianism. The Confucian temple became a type of national hall of fame where the tablets of men who had exceptional literary accomplishments were set after their deaths. Emperor Xuanzong also created the Hanlin Academy as an assembly of intellectuals who could help the emperors and imperial regimes by composing diplomatic letters and government documents. During the Ming dynasty the intellectuals of the Hanlin Academy became the principal body in imperial administration. In 1530 the Ming government decreed that the custom of placing images of Confucius and other worthies in the temples was prohibited, although tablets were permitted.

**Buddhism.** Buddhism was divided into two main branches: Hinayana, which was introduced to Southeast Asia; and Mahayana, which was introduced to China. Mahayana Buddhism was brought into China from northeastern India around the first century. During the imperial Chinese era four major sects of Mahayana Buddhism existed: the Tiantai, Flower Garden, Pure Land, and Chan. Believers in Tiantai argued that all human beings could gain enlightenment if they had faith in the everlasting transcendent Buddha, who came to the world to liberate all people from suffering. The Flower Garden sect instructed its followers that all things were produced by the Mind. People could become released from pain by having a tranquil mind and removing from their thoughts extreme passions and false thinking. The Pure Land sect claimed that everybody was capable of achieving salvation through faith; it attracted many lay people and became the most popular sect in China. The Chan sect asserted that enlightenment could be attained through meditation, self-contemplation, and intuition rather than through study of the scriptures. Tibetans developed their own sect of Buddhism, known as Lamaism. Lama stood for a privileged religious master, and the Dalai Lama became the spiritual and secular leader of Tibet. Lamaism was first brought into the Mongol court in the thirteenth century, but it obtained wholehearted support from Kublai Khan, who made the Tibetan Grand lama 'Phags-pa his spiritual tutor. During the Ming dynasty, since Buddhism did not appeal to many intellectuals, it, along with Daoism, attracted followers mainly from the lower classes.

**Temples.** Buddhist temples were established in an architectural style similar to Confucian and Daoist temples. They varied from small buildings to huge compounds that were constructed around several courtyards. The main hall included a table with a beautiful sculpture of a seated deity and an altar that included such apparatus as was needed for performing religious rites. Assistant deities were arranged to the right and left of the highest deity. Worshipers entered a temple at any time to worship the deity as well as to obtain suggestions for personal difficulties or to help them make life choices. They might burn several sticks of incense and put them in the brazier on the altar, bend down, and put fake paper money on the fire. Divination

obtained the deity's answer. Many Buddhist temples and monasteries were constructed in the tranquil countryside, beside lakes or rivers, or in the mountains.

**Development.** During the early Tang period Buddhism attained its peak of development in China. Empress Wu sponsored Buddhism in order to legitimize her supremacy. Although the Tang court reinforced the Confucian-based imperial administration, Buddhism coexisted with Confucianism and Daoism as the "Three Teachings." Confucianism was closely associated with family rites, scholarship, and officialdom; Daoism with therapeutic and farming practices; and Buddhism with memorial performances. Although there were severe persecutions between 842 and 845 all over the empire, Buddhism could not be eradicated because it had comprehensively penetrated society. At that time the government controlled the church by bringing the monks under the jurisdiction of the secular legal system and assigning laymen to supervise their activities. In the Song era, Confucianism continued to be powerful, but Confucians began to accept Buddhist theoretical ideas.

# TOPICS IN RELIGION AND PHILOSOPHY

## BUDDHISM IN EARLY TANG

**Brilliant Center.** The early Tang period (618–907) was a brilliant era in which Buddhist monasteries thrived. They became cultural centers for both laymen and adherents, and they fulfilled many important social roles. Scholarly monks—who specialized in such arts as poetry, painting, and calligraphy—studied Buddhist philosophy, practiced techniques of concentration, and debated points of doctrine with priests in monasteries or mountain hermitages. By the eighth century Buddhism was widely accepted and recognized as the dominant faith throughout the Tang empire. The principles of Buddhism were respected and its spiritual truths were unchallenged; the faith had a significant impact on the lives of all people and communities. Buddhism, the universal religion for most Asian people, not only formed an integral part of society and politics at that time, but the Chinese branch of the faith also became a sort of second home for Japanese and Korean adherents. Chinese Buddhism enjoyed a high reputation for its relics, traditions, sanctuaries, pilgrimage sites, and memorable masters.

**Roots.** Buddhism is based on the teachings of Siddhartha Gautama (Buddha), a member of a royal house in what is now known as Nepal. He lived and taught during the sixth and fifth centuries B.C.E. He rejected his privileged life and wandered in search of spiritual enlightenment, allegedly achieving this state of mind after a long period of meditation when he was thirty-five years old. His doctrines (the Sutra) became popular, and after his death a faith built upon his teachings spread orally throughout India and Central Asia, eventually reaching China and other areas of Asia. In the first century B.C.E. the Sutras were recorded on palm leaves, known as the *Tripitaka*. Buddha taught that suffering was the normal state of man and was caused by unchecked desires. Only by controlling these desires, by following a prescribed series of actions, could one relieve this suffering. One had to know oneself; had to avoid thoughts of sensuality, ill will, or cruelty; had to eschew lies, slander, and frivolous conversation; had to be self-controlled and upright in one's actions; had to avoid work that included trading in slaves, alcohol, poisons, weapons, and meats (all considered harmful occupations);

Seventy-meter-tall sculpture of Buddha, hewn from rock at Leshan in Sichuan province, eighth century

had to try to lead a good and helpful life; had to be aware of how one's actions affected oneself and others; and had to develop through meditation a calm and concentrated mind. One's past actions (karma) determined one's future circumstances, especially in the process of rebirth (reincarnation) after one's death.

**Imperial Favors.** Emperor Taizong tried not to alienate the Buddhists; however, like his predecessors, he took measures to keep the Buddhist establishment under his control. When Emperor Gaozong, who came to power in 649, attempted to restrict the number of monks, regulate the monasteries, and have monks pay obeisance to the state, the monks argued successfully that this policy went against their vows and that any emperor who forced them to do so would destroy his own chance for salvation and bring disaster to the empire. In the end the emperor gave up his reform plan. To legitimize her rule, Empress Wu, who assumed power in 684, turned mostly to Buddhism, declaring herself an incarnation of Maitreya (Buddha of Love, or "future" Buddha, who was believed to be the last Buddha to come to Earth to teach) and ordering temples set up in every province to explain the Sutra, the *Dayunjing*. Adopting harsher policies than his predecessors, Emperor Xuanzong, who reigned until he was forced to abdicate in 756, refused to grant Buddhism any imperial favors in the construction of monasteries, mass ordination of monks, or involvement in ceremonies. He tried, however, to reinforce the connection between the monasteries and the imperial institution by calling on monks to celebrate the emperor's birthday and to install images of Buddha in the likeness of the ruler.

**Growth of Sects.** Early in the Tang dynasty the Buddhist canon became more Chinese and several sects appeared. Their growth exemplified the inner vigor of the faith. Eight sects emerged between 581 and 755, but four enjoyed only temporary or limited success. The remaining sects had a significant impact on China. Outstanding Chinese monks, with sufficient self-confidence to make their own formulations of doctrine, expanded Buddhist teaching in new ways. The blossoming of a typically Chinese Buddhism inspired various novelties in the field of explaining the doctrines. Chinese Buddhist beliefs thereafter spread to Japan; contributions to the faith were imported to China from India and other countries, and a substantial number of new traditions enriched Buddhism.

**Tiantai School.** Taking its name from a sacred mountain in Zhejiang in southeastern China, the Tiantai school, founded by the monk Zhiyi, enjoyed the greatest official support under the Tang rulers. This school enlarged doctrinal and metaphysical Buddhist beliefs, combining elements of various doctrines and practices. An entirely Chinese endeavor, the school offered a doctrine of universal salvation through intellectual inquiry and sought to combine the scholarly traditions of the south with those of northern pietism and meditation. The complete truth for the Tiantai school, which was found in the *Lotus Sutra* (Lotus of the True Law), became extremely influential in east Asia and inspired many artistic representations. Tiantai doctrine

contained three truths: that all phenomena were empty; that people, however, existed temporarily; and that they were above emptiness and temporariness. These three truths all engaged and required each other.

**Huayan School.** The Huayan, or Flower Garden, School was generously supported by Empress Wu. Its third Patriarch, Fazang, categorized the various Buddhist sects into "vehicles" and claimed that the Huayan doctrine united all that was precious in each. This school taught the doctrine of emptiness and the interplay of all phenomena, but its contention that all phenomena arise at the same time in reciprocal causation was novel. Huayan Buddhists were more interested in doctrinal nuances than were the Tiantai Buddhists.

**Pure Land School.** The Jingtu, or Pure Land, sect—which derived its name from a concept of a Western paradise (Western Pure Land) or "Ultimate Bliss"—followed the sutras of Amituofo (Buddha of Infinite Light). The Pure Land movement started in the Jiangxi hills, some three hundred miles up the Yangzi River. Claiming that salvation came through faith rather than through good works, this school maintained that the believer could reach a state of grace by the frequent repetition of Amituofo's name. In other words, if this special practice was done with wholehearted sincerity, the believer would gain rebirth in the Pure Land. Drawing from a long Mahayana tradition (a branch of Buddhism that sought a broader faith by accepting gradations of a Buddha's life), this school emphasized faith as the means for gaining rebirth in paradise. The philosophy of salvation by faith was often coupled with the idea that this path was the appropriate means to achieve spirituality during a corrupt age. Many Chinese were attracted to this sect. The faith also inspired the Japanese master, Shinran, who emphasized practice more than doctrine.

**Chanism.** The Meditation School, known as Chan, was created by an Indian master who arrived at the court of the Northern Wei in 520. He stressed the significance of contemplation; his teaching later included elements of Daoism (a mystical philosophy founded in the sixth century B.C.E. in which one worked in harmony with nature). In the eighth century Chan Buddhism was divided into two major schools founded by chief disciples of Hongren, the fifth Chinese Patriarch. Shenxiu (who died in 706) founded the northern school, while Huineng (who died in 713) organized the southern school. Believing in gradual enlightenment, the northern branch of Chan emphasized sitting in silent meditation. Accepting the notion of sudden enlightenment, the southern branch emphasized instinct rather than intellect. Huineng, a semibarbarian Cantonese monk, stressed also contemplation. Meditation was seen as the way for one to pierce through the world of illusion and to obtain enlightenment. This school recognized that the nature of Buddha was within oneself. Meditation was only one of many practices adopted by other schools. The Chan school rejected all other techniques, such as the performance of meritorious deeds or the study of scriptures. Hostile to all systems, dogmas, scriptures, and rites, Huineng held that illumination came in a sudden flash, although only after long probing. The southern school soon surpassed the northern branch in popularity. Huineng was later recognized as the sixth Patriarch, the true successor of Hongren. All the later influential groups in Chanism arose from the disciples of Huineng.

**Pilgrimages.** The greatest pilgrims and translators in Chinese Buddhist history lived during the Tang dynasty. The two most famous pilgrims of the seventh century were Xuan Zang and Yi Jing. Leaving China secretly in 629, Xuan Zang traveled overland to India to gather Buddhist manuscripts; he returned to Chang'an in 645. Yi Jing boarded a merchant ship in 671 to travel to India. He left in 685 and returned by sea to China in 695. Empress Wu welcomed him. He later published two famous historical books, one dealing with the kingdoms of Buddhism in India and Southeast Asia, and the other including information on Chinese pilgrims who traveled to Buddhist countries in the seventh century. When the Central Asian routes were closed because of the invasion of Tibetans and Arabs, the number of Buddhist communities in China decreased. In addition, because of the great persecution of 842–845 there was a decline of pilgrimages to India. The Tang government organized a big pilgrimage in 966, however, in which more than 150 monks participated; only a small number of them reached India, after traveling by a route that stopped at major Central Asian oases, and few were able to return to China in 976.

**Japanese Pilgrim.** Many Japanese monks traveled to China to study with the great masters of the law and to visit the most famous Buddhist centers and holy sites. Ennin was one of these religious students, and he arrived during the great oppression of the Buddhist faith (842–845). Ennin was not the first Japanese monk to seek religious instruction in China, but his diary provides important information on Sino-Japanese relations and the type of contacts that could be made at this time. As a result of his travels and learning, Ennin's work caused significant development of Buddhism in Japan.

**Social Roles.** Buddhism played a considerable role in Tang society. In the countryside, Buddhist temples performed important economic functions: they operated mills and oil presses; maintained vaults for the safe deposit of valuables; and managed other banking services, such as serving as pawnbrokers. Some temples provided medical care and entertainment; others invested most of their wealth in art; and still others owned large amounts of land cultivated by their servants. Monks also profited from their close relationships with wealthy nobles who sought to evade taxation by registering their land under the name of a temple.

**Tantrism.** In Tang times an obscure form of Buddhism known as Tantrism was introduced into China and came to have a great influence in the country. Based on magic and mysticism, Tantrism was best known in a purified form as being connected with symbolical speculations. It prevailed noticeably in India after the middle of the seventh century, then spread to Ceylon and Southeast Asia, and finally into China and Tibet. Chinese translations of Tantric texts increased in the eighth century after two Indian masters—Subhakarasimha and Vajrabodhi—arrived in China in 716 and 719, respectively. Particularly important was the work of the famous master and translator, Bukong (Amoghavajra), after he returned to China following a five-year visit to his homeland. Born in Ceylon, Bukong spent his youth in China. From 756 until his death in 774 Bukong translated many Tantric texts while he lived in Chang'an, and he gained enormous influence within the Tang government. Tantrism, the last contribution of Indian Buddhism to China, brought about great changes that set the Tang world onto new paths and resulted in the decline of the large monastic communities.

**Sources:**

Kenneth K. S. Chen, *Buddhism in China: A Historical Survey* (Princeton: Princeton University Press, 1964).

Chen, *The Chinese Transformation of Buddhism* (Princeton: Princeton University Press, 1973).

Arthur F. Wright, *Buddhism in Chinese History* (Stanford, Cal.: Stanford University Press, 1959).

Erik Zurcher, *The Buddhist Conquest of China: The Spread and Adaptation of Buddhism in Early Medieval China* (Leiden, the Netherlands: E. J. Brill, 1959).

## BUDDHISM IN LATE TANG

**Imperial Patronage.** The An Lushan rebellion (755) during the Tang period (618–907) had a disastrous impact on the Buddhist establishment, bringing about the devastation of many temples and the loss of important collections of documents. After this period of upheaval, Buddhism at first received increased patronage from the rulers. Convinced that the Tang court owed its survival to Buddhism, Emperor Daizong, who came to the throne in 762, began to provide government aid to build monasteries and he authorized the ordination of thousands of monks. He showed his personal devoutness by revering Buddhist relics and by providing vegetarian banquets for the clergy. In the 780s his successor, Dezong, was more cautious in his sponsorship of Buddhism, but he too became a great patron of the monastic temples and of Buddhist scholarship.

**Criticism.** The expansion of the temples brought about criticism from opponents of Buddhism. As early as 621 the Daoist priest Fu Yi denounced Buddhist communities, claiming that they were becoming a burden on the state. He encouraged the government to disband the clergy and put monasteries to better use. During the reign of Dezong, Peng Yan, a Confucian official in the Bureau of Records, suggested to the emperor that he abolish the monasteries—because of abuses caused by the ignorance of the clergy—and regain lost tax revenues. Peng estimated that the yearly expense of supplying a Buddhist monk with food and clothing equaled the taxes paid by five peasants.

**Scholar Protest.** When the Emperor Xianzong ordered that the finger bone of Buddha be brought to Chang'an in 819 so that he could worship it, Confucian scholars began

In the year 845 the Tang emperor Wuzong denounced Buddhism as a foreign and unwanted doctrine.

It was only from the Han and Wei on that the religion of idols gradually came into prominence. So in the latter age it has transmitted its strange ways, instilling its infection with every opportunity, spreading like a luxuriant vine, until it has poisoned the customs of our nation; gradually, and before anyone was aware, it beguiled and confounded men's minds so that the multitude have been increasingly led astray. It has spread to the hills and plains of all the nine provinces and through the walls and towers of our two capitals. Each day finds its monks and followers growing more numerous and its temples more lofty. It wears out the strength of the people with constructions of earth and wood, pilfers their wealth for ornaments of gold and precious objects, causes men to abandon their lords and parents for the company of teachers, and severs man and wife with its monastic decrees. In destroying law and injuring mankind indeed nothing surpasses this doctrine!

Now if even one man fails to work the fields, someone must go hungry; if one woman does not tend her silkworms, someone will go cold. At present there are an inestimable number of monks and nuns in the empire, each of them waiting for the farmers to feed him and the silkworms to clothe him, while the public temples and private chapels have reached boundless numbers, all with soaring towers and elegant ornamentation sufficient to outshine the imperial palace itself. . . .

Source: William Theodore de Bary and others, ed., *Sources of Chinese Tradition* (New York: Columbia University Press, 1960), pp. 435–436.

a campaign against Buddhism. The greatest Chinese prose writer since the Han dynasty (206 B.C.E.–220 C.E.), Han Yu, an orthodox member of the literati and a notorious anti-Buddhist Confucian scholar, submitted a memorial to the emperor. He stated that he was surprised Xianzong was promoting Buddhism by greeting the relic. Proclaiming that Buddha was a barbarian who did not speak the Chinese language and who wore clothes of a different fashion, he condemned the scenes of mass hysteria that accompanied the transfer of the relic. Angered by this attack on Buddhism, the emperor initially threatened to sentence the author to death but thereafter ordered him to go into exile in the far south.

**Political Motive.** The court eunuchs—uneducated, superstitious, and avaricious devotees of Buddha—had played an important role in the emperor's decision to support Buddhism. To restrain the power of these eunuchs, Li Deyu, the authoritarian chief minister and a committed Confucian who came to hate the excesses of popular Buddhism, encouraged the emperor to change his policy toward the faith, although he did not express the outrage voiced by Han Yu.

**Financial Difficulty.** The most forceful reason for the government decision to reduce official support for Buddhism was financial. After An Lushan's rebellion the Tang empire was in financial crisis and lacked copper for coins. This severe scarcity resulted from the use of copper in casting images, bells, and chimes for the Buddhist temples, which held most of the Chinese stock of valuable metals in the form of objects of piety, instruments, and statues. In addition, because of their tax exemption, Buddhist temples became wealthy, while at the same time state revenues were greatly reduced.

**Imperial Decrees.** In 836 Emperor Wenzong issued a decree prohibiting the Chinese from having any relations with "people of color"—a term that denoted such foreigners as Iranians, Sogdians (from Central Asia), Arabs, Malays, Indians, and Sumatrans. Emperor Wuzong, who took power in 840, vigorously committed himself to Daoism and hated the sight of Buddhist monks. As a result, he took decisive action and issued in 845 the proscriptive decree that charged Buddhism, a foreign religion, with bringing about the moral and economic decline of the brief southern dynasties—the Jin, Song, Liang, and Chen. The great suppression of Buddhism and other foreign religions began under Wuzong's rule.

**Great Suppression.** The most radical campaign against Buddhism started in 842. At the beginning authorities aimed only to purge the Buddhist priesthood of uneducated monks and hypocrites. The government, however, then began to confiscate private possessions of the *bonzes* (monks) and banned Buddhist ceremonies in official worship. Finally, the court made a general inventory of sacred property owned by the temples and forced Buddhists to surrender their estates, slaves, money, and metals. The government demanded that all monks and nuns under the age of forty be secularized. Thereafter, some 4,600 monasteries, temples, and shrines were ruined or converted into public buildings; 250,000 Buddhist monks and nuns were laicized and registered as taxable; 150,000 dependants of monasteries, who enjoyed exemptions from both taxation and forced labor for the government, were put on the census lists; several million acres of land were confiscated; and 40,000 small places of worship were knocked down or rehabilitated for other uses. The emperor preserved only a few official temples that were maintained by a small number of monks. Religions of Iranian (Persian) origin—such as Mazdaism (Zoroastrianism), Manichaeanism, and Nestorianism—suffered a more radical fate: they were totally banned and their monks, a few thousand, were laicized.

**Restoration.** These radical measures greatly damaged Buddhism in Tang China. Since the country was as extensive in size as the whole of medieval Europe, however, Emperor Wuzong's prohibitions were probably not fully enforced, except in the capital, Chang'an. Everywhere, even among officials responsible for implementing the decrees, there was quiet opposition that made it possible in some distant regions to save the monks and their places of worship. When the successor to the emperor Wuzong inherited the throne, he tried to relieve the severity of the measures by permitting many defrocked monks and nuns to return to religious life and by ordering the restoration of certain temples. As a consequence, the power of Buddhist communities was preserved and strengthened in the tenth century in some regions, such as the kingdom of Min in Fujian and elsewhere in southern China.

**Aftermath.** Since the end of the eighth century, Chinese Buddhism had been cut off from the great religious centers of India, which had been its source of inspiration for more than five hundred years. Chinese Buddhists could not go to the holy places; the faith itself was endangered on the borders of India and Iran by the expansion of Islam. Only the Chan Buddhist sect remained active in China at the end of the Tang age. Furthermore, translations of Indian texts became less common in China after the great translators and commentators died off.

Sources:

Wing-Tsit Chan, trans., *A Source Book in Chinese Philosophy* (Princeton: Princeton University Press, 1975).

Christian Jochim, *Chinese Religions: A Cultural Perspective* (Englewood Cliffs, N.J.: Prentice-Hall, 1986).

W. Pachow, *Chinese Buddhism: Aspects of Interaction and Reinterpretation* (Washington, D.C.: University Press of America, 1980).

Laurence G. Thompson, *Chinese Religion: An Introduction* (Belmont, Cal.: Dickenson, 1969).

## CULT OF CONFUCIANISM

**State Cult.** Beginning in the Song dynasty (960–1279), there was a reassertion of the classical Confucian religion centered on the supremacy of Heaven and the position of the ruler as the true son of Heaven. This state cult, based upon a reexplanation of traditional Confucianism by neo-Confucian intellectuals, who had been greatly influenced by the beliefs of Buddhism, continued as the official religion for the following dynasties, with the exception of a short period of Mongol rule (1279–1368) when Buddhist influence dominated the government.

**Rituals.** Since state rituals were performed for the benefit of all people, the emperor himself, assisted by his high-ranking officials, performed the state sacrifices. At the same time, regional and local officials performed lesser sacrifices in their prefectures and counties.

**State Ritual.** The emperors recognized the existence of Confucianism, Daoism, and Buddhism, but they tried to keep an eye on all public religious activities. Since emperors and their officials had to contribute crucially to the well-being of the empire, which was believed to be the entire civilized world, they asserted that a harmonious relationship should be upheld among Heaven, Earth, and man. This relationship could be maintained undamaged only if the emperor performed as the son of Heaven with deep respect and with careful attention to the details of the

Portico of the temple of Confucius, Beijing, early seventeenth century

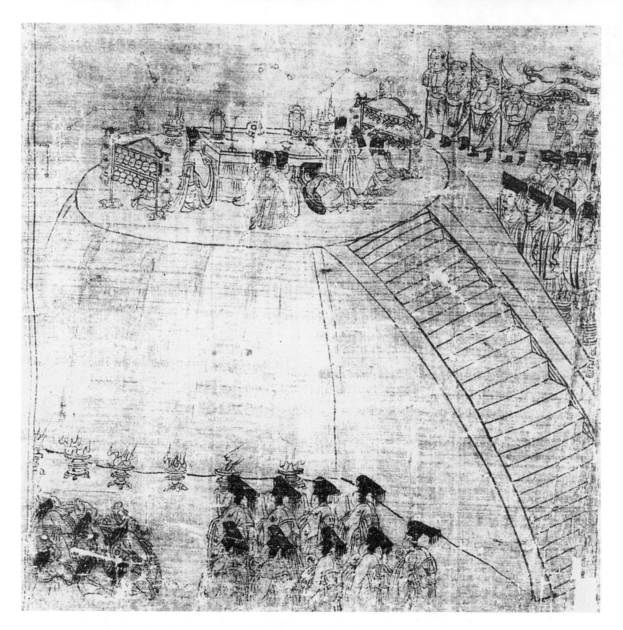

Illumination of an emperor and his chief adviser kneeling before an altar, circa 1041–1106
(Metropolitan Museum of Art, New York)

sacred and sacrificial rituals, which were said to have originated in ancient times. And only the emperor, as a unique man, could perform those highly religious functions.

**Ceremonies.** Since the ceremonies of the state cult were many and complicated, they not only required much of the ruler's time and attention but also demanded the founding of one of the most significant departments of the government, the *Li Bu* (Ministry of Rites). There were three classes of ceremonies. The first was performed by the emperor himself—the worship of Heaven, Earth, the emperor's ancestors, and the gods of soil and grain. The second class was the middle sacrifices made for the worship of sun and moon, the emperors and great men of former dynasties, the patron of agriculture, the patroness of silkworms, and the many spirits of land and sky. The last class covered the lesser sacrifices, comprising some thirty smaller

ceremonies, in which the emperor did not participate personally. There were sacrifices to minor gods, such as patrons of medicine, water, writing, mountains, lakes, rivers, winters, glacial stars, and cities. Most spirits represented in imperial sacrifices were also worshiped on a lesser scale by administrators on the emperor's behalf in special shrines throughout the provinces, prefectures, and counties.

**National Worship.** The highest act of national worship, vital to the imperial cult, was the great yearly sacrifice to *Shangdi* (Supreme God) performed at the altar of Heaven during the winter solstice. It was held on an open altar in the early hours before sunrise in the light of burning torches. The altar, made of shiny white marble, was located in a park south of the ancient city walls. This area featured three circular terraces of remarkable simplicity.

## CONFUCIAN REVITALIZATION

The famous historian Ouyan Xiu was one of several scholars who advocated the revitalization of Confucianism and condemned Buddhism.

Tung Chung-shu was concerned at this and retired to devote himself to the practice of Confucianism, for he knew that when the way of Confucius was made clear, the other schools would cease. This is the effect of practicing what is fundamental in order to overcome Buddhism.

These days a tall warrior clad in armor and bearing a spear may surpass in bravery a great army, yet when he sees the Buddha he bows low and when he hears the doctrines of the Buddha he is sincerely awed and persuaded. Why? Because though he is indeed strong and full of vigor, in his heart he is confused and has nothing to cling to. But when a scholar who is small and frail and afraid to advance hears the doctrines of Buddhism his righteousness is revealed at once in his countenance, and not only does he not bow and submit, but he longs to rush upon them and destroy them. Why? It is simply because he is enlightened in learning and burns with a belief in rites and righteousness, and in his heart he possesses something which can conquer these doctrines. Thus rites and righteousness are the fundamental things whereby Buddhism may be defeated. If a single scholar who understands rites and righteousness can keep from submitting to these doctrines, then we have but to make the whole world understand rites and righteousness and these doctrines will, as a natural consequence, be wiped out.

Source: William Theodore de Bary and others, ed., *Sources of Chinese Tradition* (New York: Columbia University Press, 1960), p. 445.

---

Everything was first prepared with great care under the supervision of the Ministry of Rites, and officials and prayers were submitted to the emperor for his endorsement several days before the ceremony. A three-day fast and vigil was compulsory for the emperor, princes, and officials who were scheduled to participate in the ceremony. The ruler observed the third day of the vigil in the Hall of Self-denial, located close to the great altar. After observing the altar and holy tablets in nearby temples and examining the sacrifices to see whether they had any imperfections, the emperor purified himself and then went to the great altar.

**Local Ceremony.** Religious responsibilities of local officials were many and difficult. At certain times of the year a city magistrate had to visit places of worship of different public divinities and there perform somber acts of worship. In times of catastrophe—such as drought, famine, or plague—he had the duty of finding where local gods had been affronted and of inaugurating suitable ceremonies for their placation. Comprehension of rituals and sacrifices was part of the scholarly equipment of a local official.

**Worship of Confucius.** On the whole, the scholar class followed Confucianism, a philosophy adopted in schools as well. While each family sacrificed and prayed to the spirits of its ancestors, and each guild paid annual reverence to its patron god, scholars honored Confucius in the temples because he was deemed to be the source of all Chinese education and wisdom. Just as veneration was paid to Confucius as the great master, respect was paid to his pupils and to all celebrated intellectuals of the past whose teachings had made a distinguished contribution to learning and morality.

**Halls of Celebrity.** In 630 the Tang emperor Taizong decreed that temples in honor of Confucius be set up in all districts and that intellectuals offer sacrifices in their capacities as government officials. In 647 he put the tablets of twenty-two worthies in these sites for the first time and converted these temples into Halls of Celebrity. Confucius was represented in these early days by images. After 720 ten additional images of a seated Confucius were put in the main halls of temples, while pictures of Confucius's seventy disciples and the worthies were painted on the walls. Up to the Ming dynasty (1368–1644) the cult of Confucius was treated as if the city-gods were divinities, and Confucius was seen as a god himself. To many rationalistic scholars, this idolization of Confucius constantly clashed with those who recognized him as merely mortal, albeit the greatest of human beings. It was not until 1530 that the more rationalistic attitude prevailed; the images were forbidden to remain in the Confucian temples and were replaced by tablets. Simultaneously, the term "temple" was replaced by "hall."

**Significance.** When the Jesuit mission was in Beijing (1601), the missionary Matteo Ricci contended that worship paid to Confucius was not different from that shown to ancestors. He claimed that there was no trace of worship and no superstition because the respect shown was only to identify him as a great man. The imperial governments promoted the cult of Confucius in an effort to bolster public morality and to maintain the power and authority of the intellectuals who remained throughout Chinese history as principal members of the bureaucracy.

Sources:

Carson Chang, *Development of Neo-Confucian Thought,* 2 volumes (New York: Bookman, 1957, 1962).

Thomas A. Metzger, *Escape from Predicament: Neo-Confucianism and China's Evolving Political Culture* (New York: Columbia University Press, 1977).

D. Howard Smith, *Chinese Religions* (New York: Holt, Rinehart & Winston, 1968).

## DAOISM AND BUDDHISM

**Origins.** Daoism originally had a political dimension, but later it became focused on natural harmony rather than on social harmony, the purview of Confucianism. To the Daoists, social harmony follows from a return of man to harmony with nature and its fundamental reality. The first great Daoist classic, the *Daodejing,* appeared in the third

*The Three Teachings*, a painting of the founders of Buddhism (Buddha), Confucianism (Confucius), and Daoism (Lao Zi), Ming dynasty, 1368–1644 (Nelson-Atkins Gallery of Art, Kansas City)

century, and the philosophy continued to develop in the following centuries.

**Daoism in Tang.** When Li Shimin established the Tang dynasty (618–907), the Daoists proposed that he was a descendant of Lao Zi, the founder of Daoism, who possessed the same surname "Li." Daoists won Li Shimin's support even though he favored Buddhism. Many emperors of the Tang dynasty became active patrons of Daoism, granting titles and dignities to Lao Zi. Emperor Xuanzong decreed that a Daoist temple should be built in every city and that every aristocratic family should have a copy of the *Daodejing.* During his reign the *Daodejing* and *Zhuang Zi,* the other classic Daoist text, were recognized as suitable books to be studied for the civil service examinations.

When Wuzong came to the throne in 840, he soon came under the influence of the Daoist monks and alchemists. Encouraged by these advisers, Wuzong started a powerful campaign against all "foreign religions," especially Buddhism. The pattern of Daoist religion was by that time fully established, and few essential changes occurred in subsequent centuries.

**Texts.** During the Song dynasty the "Jade Emperor" became so popular that he was regarded as the supreme Daoist divinity, and his image began to occupy a central place in the main hall of Daoist monasteries. Supported by the Song rulers, the collection of Daoist doctrines was completed, catalogued in the tenth century, and printed in 1019. According to Daoist doctrine, a person's virtues and sins were regularly reported to Heaven, and a person's life was significantly shortened by sin. By performing many good actions, a man not only would extend his life span but also would become immortal.

**Monks.** There were approximately eighty-six Daoist sects during the Song period, but their priests were divided into two major sects. Those individuals who searched for "perfect realization" had to withdraw from the world and stress hygiene techniques, meditation, severe asceticism, and physical exercises. These monks lived a celibate life, refrained from using alcohol, and practiced vegetarianism. Followers of the other sect, the Celestial Masters of the Dragon and Tiger Mountain, did not live in monasteries but performed religious ceremonies, sold charms, told fortunes, and showed magical arts in cities and villages. They married and passed on their offices and arts to their children. Since they claimed that they could control evil spirits, superstitious people sometimes asked them for help in cases of illness or bad luck.

**Pan-Buddhist Movement.** Of the many Buddhist sects that endured, the popular Pure Land and meditative Chan schools prevailed, but both were disunited. Pure Land monasteries and related lay societies spread their doctrines of salvation by faith without any hierarchical cooperation; each large monastery was the head office of an independent subsection. Chan followers had bigger temples, but they, unlike the Pure Land devotees, often lived inconspicuously among the common public, each monastery with a small number of adherents. Doctrinal dissimilarity among Buddhists hardly ever incited hostilities. A pan-Buddhist unification campaign began in the Song period and grew powerful. One of the most distinguished pan-Buddhist campaigners was the Ming monk Zhuhuang, who encouraged the growth of lay Buddhist organizations and was one of the early Chinese Buddhist writers of pamphlets disapproving of Christianity.

**Lack of Unity.** Daoism was not as organized as Buddhism. The most typical practitioner was a secluded village priest, similar to a local sage. Daoism never had any unification campaigns like those of the pan-Buddhist movement, though the leader of the Zhang family of Jiangxi province remained the commonly recognized "pope" of Daoism during Ming (1368–1644) times.

**Sanjiao.** Beginning in the Song period, a major tendency in popular religion was eclecticism—an integration of Buddhist, Daoist, and Confucian basics into one system known as *Sanjiao* (Three Religions). The Chinese began to perform *Sanjiao* practices extensively, and by the Ming dynasty this eclecticism was advocated as its own philosophy, particularly by the sixteenth century. The government denounced *Sanjiao* as dissent, but its exercise dominated popular religion until the late Ming era. People refused to regard it as improper to respect state-supported ceremonies and to perform ancestor worship at home in line with Confucian traditions, while also practicing Daoism and Buddhism in their religious exercises at local shrines and temples.

**Shrines.** The images of Confucius, Lao Zi, and Buddha could be seen in *Sanjiao* shrines, which were frequently looked after on an inherited basis by uneducated beggars who seemed mainly to favor Daoist beliefs, although their religious affiliations are hard to assess. Such shrines won the support of communities, officials, and private individuals. At the local level Daoism and Buddhism were not remarkably hostile to each other, and Confucian officials accepted them as well as *Sanjiao*. Both Buddhists and Daoists published and spoke from treatises promoting sanitation, friendly collaboration, personal ethics, and other behavior that the government also promoted.

**State Control.** Daoism and Buddhism were subject to more-coherent government management under the Song and Ming dynasties than during earlier empires. There were no extensive campaigns against these religions, such as Buddhism suffered in the 840s; but during the Song, Yuan (1279–1368), and Ming dynasties, non-Chinese as well as Chinese took over the ordination of all monks as a state affair and attempted to restrict the assets and authority of religious establishments. In the eleventh century the Northern Song (960–1125) court, urgently needing new revenue, began the comprehensive open sale of ordination certificates, setting an example for following governments. This activity was one of the causes of the continual deterioration in monastic morale, self-control, and reputation.

**Registries.** The Yuan and Ming courts put all monks under the disciplinary control of the Daoist and Buddhist Registries—government offices founded at the national, prefectural, and county levels—which were run by religious notables responsible for supervising their fellow priests. Controls on the clergy were not executed harshly because church institutions were not considered a threat to the empire.

**Imperial Patrons.** The most liberal imperial patrons of religion were the Mongols. Genghis Khan especially admired Daoism. Refusing to serve in the court, the Buddhist Liu Pingzhong had a great impact on Genghis's grandson, Kublai Khan, when he governed China. Kublai showered particular favors on the shamanistic Tibetan version of Buddhism known as Lamaism, in part for diplomatic reasons. He and his successors gave the lamas greater prestige and immunities than any other

Painting of disciples of Buddha giving alms to beggars, twelfth century (Museum of Fine Arts, Boston)

religious order, alien or native, had been given in Chinese history. Thereafter, Chinese Confucian scholars, as well as Daoist and Buddhist leaders, criticized the Yuan emperors, who permitted lamas to abuse their privileges and exemptions. Ming emperors dealt politely with prominent Tibetan lamas but gave them no particular privileges in China.

**Combination.** With the rise of neo-Confucianism, both Daoism and Buddhism declined, gradually lost much of their uniqueness, and were combined in a disjointed mass of peasant ideas and activities in which the worth of a god or his priestly agents was determined by the results attained. Academically, Daoism and Buddhism contributed primarily to neo-Confucianism. Neither doctrine created important new philosophers or works, while both imitated Confucian learning in some degree and expanded their traditions of canonical study. The original version of the Buddhist *Tripitaka,* printed between 972 and 983, was republished frequently. Daoist canonical writings, known as the Daoist *Tripitaka,* were first printed under the sponsorship of the Song government in 1019 and were later republished, though not as frequently as the Buddhist canon. Educated monks took part in the philosophical debates that enlivened Chinese academic life from the Song dynasty to the Ming dynasty, and many scholar-officials who were regarded as loyal Confucians studied Buddhist and Daoist learning with admiration. Regarded as independent philosophical traditions, however, neither Daoism nor Buddhism was a significant intellectual movement from the Song period onward.

**Continued Importance.** Both Buddhism and Daoism suffered the loss of philosophical strength and inspiration because a revitalized, modified Confucianism went determinedly to the forefront of academic life, but they remained important features of Chinese society until late in the Ming dynasty. Their monastic organizations stayed alive, albeit with reduced status, while individual priests frequently enjoyed great social admiration and, infrequently, political power. Chinese people looked to the monks to provide charms, drugs, predictions, ways to prolong life, and comfort they needed in their daily lives. Daoism retained a good grip on the Chinese: people practiced a vegetarian culture, encouraged mutual support in religious life, and practiced such activities as meditation, study, and good works. Daoism also gained strength among secret peasant societies, which gave religious sanction to radical activities during times of turmoil. Like Daoism, Buddhism continued to have a great impact on Chinese architecture, art, music, medicine, and literature.

Sources:

Judith M. Boltz, *A Survey of Taoist Literature: Tenth to Seventh Centuries* (Berkeley: Institute for East Asian Studies and Center for Chinese Studies, University of California, Berkeley, 1987).

Max Kaltenmark, *Lao Tzu and Taoism,* translated by Roger Greaves (Stanford, Cal.: Stanford University Press, 1969).

John Lagerwey, *Taoist Ritual in Chinese Society and History* (New York: Macmillan / London: Collier-Macmillan, 1987).

Henri Maspero, *Taoism and Chinese Religion,* translated by Frank A. Kierman Jr. (Amherst: University of Massachusetts Press, 1981).

Kristofer Schipper, *The Taoist Body* (Berkeley: University of California Press, 1993).

## JESUIT MISSION

**Early Contact.** To Europeans the sixteenth century was an age of conquerors and of the Counter-Reformation. Ignatius Loyola founded the Jesuit order in 1534, principally in an effort to convert pagans to Christianity. Francis Xavier, a Spanish Jesuit, arrived in western Japan in 1549 and marched on Kyoto. The Jesuit mission, led by Xavier, began to go to China in the late sixteenth century. Xavier died near Guangzhou in south China in 1552. In the following decades, through the knowledge and enthusiasm of Jesuit missionaries, the Christian Church was resolutely reestablished in China during the Ming dynasty (1326–1644). Their achievements resulted in the arrival of Dominican, Franciscan, and other Christian missionaries in almost all the Chinese provinces.

**Macao.** Immediately after establishing the Ming dynasty, Emperor Zhu Yuanzhang and his successors closed the Chinese door to foreigners, and there was almost no relationship between China and the West for the next 150 years. At the beginning of the sixteenth century Portuguese merchants came into view at the mouth of the West River in southern China. Since piracy was prevalent at that time, the Ming government, considering all foreigners pirates and adventurers, prohibited them from living on the mainland, but they were allowed to construct provisional houses on an island at the mouth of the river and to live there each summer in order to carry on a profitable trade with the natives. Since they proved useful in repelling pirates who infected the area, they were finally permitted to establish a more permanent village at Macao, to the west of the West River estuary. Thereafter, Macao became the missionaries' main base for their activities in East Asia, as well as a large and prosperous trading post for the profitable trade with China and Japan.

**First Efforts.** Following the traders, Jesuit missionaries soon played a dominant role reestablishing the Christian church in China. Dominicans, Franciscans, and Augustinians (who came mainly from the Philippines, a Spanish colony) made the first efforts to break open the door to Christian influence. Missionaries penetrated China by traveling the sea route to southern China rather than along the overland Central Asian trade routes as they had in the Tang (618–907) and Song (960–1279) times.

**Rivalry.** A rivalry developed between Spanish and Portuguese missionaries. The Spanish had succeeded in spreading Christianity to the Philippines where many Chinese resided. With the assistance of Chinese converts the Spanish made several attempts to penetrate into China. The aforementioned rivalry, as well as antagonism from merchants who were afraid that missionary activity would cause the abolishment of their hard-won trade concessions with Ming authorities, frustrated the first missionary efforts.

**Success.** While all of his predecessors had failed, the Italian Jesuit Matteo Ricci succeeded through persistence and adaptation. Ricci's enthusiasm, determination, and learning opened the way for the founding of a Christian mission on the mainland. With diplomacy and perseverance he gradually won the companionship of scholars and magistrates. Dressing in a Buddhist monk's robe, which was the custom of missionaries in Japan and the Philippines, was not working in China. Ricci realized that he had to adopt Confucian dress and manners and study the classical culture of China in order to win over the highly educated Chinese scholars. With assistance from scholars and

Facade of St. Paul's Church at Macao, built by the Jesuits at the beginning of the seventeenth century

officials, he entered Guangdong in 1583 and went on to Suzhou in 1589, Nanchang, the capital of Jiangxi, in 1595, and later to Nanjing.

**Beijing.** Ricci, who became friends with the Chinese literati, increasingly extended Christian influence, but he realized that unless he won recognition from the emperor, he could not establish a permanent mission in China. Therefore, Ricci endeavored to obtain permission for himself and his colleagues to reside in Beijing. Despite strong opposition he finally got oral authorization to live in the capital, and he entered Beijing on 4 January 1601. Gradually, he and his colleagues obtained a reputation for scholarship, won over several famous scholars, converted many Chinese, and founded a Christian church.

**Evangelization.** Step by step, Ricci was successful in defining a method of evangelization that highlighted the similarities between Chinese classical traditions and Christianity; he supported negative views against Buddhism, Daoism, and popular beliefs; and he pleased scholars with the science, technology, and arts of the West. The missionaries also tried to impress the Chinese with mechanical curiosities such as clocks. Due to their scientific and technical knowledge Jesuits were appreciated at court and among high-ranking civil officials. The services they provided to rulers—as mathematicians, astronomers, cartographers, interpreters, painters, and musicians—allowed Jesuits to keep their positions in the central government.

**Spread of Evangelization.** The first Jesuit missions were established along the road that Ricci followed from Macao to Beijing, including major cities in the Guangdong, Jiangxi, Jiangsu, and Hebei provinces. They thereafter spread to most provinces by the end of the Ming dynasty but were more plentiful in the lower Yangzi River area and in Fujian, where the Dominicans and Franciscans were also active. Several missionaries arrived in China by the Burma Road or through Central Asia, such as the Portuguese brother of Goez (Benedict de Goaes), who departed from Agra, the capital of the Mogul dynasty, in 1602 to find out whether Marco Polo's Cathay was really China. Goez traveled through Kabul, Samarkand, and the oases of the Tarim basin and finally arrived in Gansu in 1605.

**Curiosity.** Undoubtedly, Chinese reactions to the Jesuit missions varied. In the countryside missionaries aroused curiosity about their strange manners and practices. For example, the funeral of a Christian attracted a large crowd and incited astonishment. The missionaries looked like a variety of Buddhist priests; Christianity was able to take root in the countryside partially through a sort of syncretism between Christian beliefs and Chinese traditions. Thus, several themes of Buddhist and Daoist hagiography appeared in the biography of Father Etienne Faber, a missionary in Shanxi in the latter part of the Ming period. Faber was believed to be able to ward off attacks by man-eating animals; to heal the sick; to defend against an invasion of grasshoppers by spraying them with sacred water; to exorcize haunted houses; and to predict the accurate date of

Painting of Jesuit missionary Matteo
Ricci, late seventeenth century
(Chiesa del Gesu, Rome)

his own death. It was said that his corpse did not decompose, his tomb was spared by a flooded river, and that after his death he was changed into the god of the local soil.

**Converts.** Jesuits were able to gain impressive results with some scholars. The most famous intellectuals who converted to Christianity were the "three pillars of the evangelization." Born in Shanghai, Xu Guangqi, who won his *jinshi* degree in 1604, was one of the first men to communicate with the Jesuit missionaries. Hired as a tutor by a wealthy family of Shaozhou, he first met Father Lazarro Cattaneo, then Matteo Ricci, in Nanjing in 1600. Baptized and christened as Paul by another missionary, Jean de Rocha, Xu Guangqi lived in Beijing between 1604 and 1607 and there received training from Ricci. After his death a small church was constructed close to his home in the suburbs of Shanghai.

**Yang Tingyun.** Also a scholar and civil servant, Yang Tingyun, born in Hangzhou, was a censor at Beijing in 1600. He was in charge of transportation on the Grand Canal and management of the Suzhou region. Interested in Chan Buddhism during a period of retirement at Hangzhou in 1609, he met Cattaneo and then Father Nicolas Trigault in 1611. Converted by them to Christianity, he was baptized and christened Michael in 1612. He established *Shengshui Hui* (Association of the Holy Water) and wrote a book on Christian doctrine. In 1615 he wrote assorted essays on the sciences, geography, European philosophy, and Christianity; in 1621 he published an essay in which he tried to show the advantages of Christianity over

Buddhism. In 1621, the year he passed away, Yang constructed a Christian church in the city of Hangzhou.

**Defense of Christianity.** Li Zhizao, also a native of Hangzhou, met Ricci shortly after he arrived in China. Fascinated by geographical questions, Li studied Western sciences and cartography. He received training from Ricci between 1604 and 1610, and he translated various scientific and religious books. Going back to Hangzhou in 1611, he requested that Fathers Cattaneo, Fernandez, and Trigault give sermons in the city. During the first "persecution" of Christians in 1616 and the second one in 1622, Li defended the Christians of Hangzhou. In 1625 he wrote a note on a Nestorian stela (an inscribed pillar), identifying Nestorianism with Christianity. Trusted by both Xu Guangqi and Father Longobardo, Li created a new calendar in 1629, a year before his death.

**Difficult Dialogue.** By presenting the excellence and supremacy of the sciences and inventions of Europe, the missionaries believed that they were also demonstrating the superiority of Christianity. Aside from a small number of literati and high-ranking civil officials in close contact with the Jesuits, who were convinced of the relationship between the ancient Chinese traditions and Christianity, most Confucian scholars were antagonistic to the foreign faith. They thought the growth of Christian communities among ordinary people interrupted public order, and they regarded Christianity as full of overgenerous and conflicting ideas. Missionaries found it difficult to explain clearly the central ideas of their faith to persons with dissimilar ideas about the world and religion. The Chinese had a different approach to religion that required total faithfulness and implied the reality of truth. The Chinese were not familiar with inspiration because their essential concept was that of an immanent order simultaneously cosmic and human, natural and social. Thus, dialogue between Christians and Chinese included deep disagreements.

**Criticism.** Christians in China were blamed for damaging morals, demolishing statues and sanctuaries belonging to the Chinese cult, and harming society. Beginning in the early seventeenth century, Confucians published these criticisms in brochures that attracted many readers. One of the first anti-Christian essays was the *Poxiechi* (Compilation of Disproved Heresies), published in 1639. Chinese intellectuals who were antagonistic to missionaries negatively regarded Christianity as a combination of Buddhism and Islam, or other religions.

**Consequence.** Jesuits in Beijing made themselves so helpful to the Ming ruler that, despite strong resistance and short periods of persecution, they survived to strengthen their mission. They gained permission to construct churches in several cities throughout the provinces. More appeasing attitudes of the Ming court in the early decades of the seventeenth century helped Dominicans and Franciscans to establish missions in southern China, but their methods frequently proved embarrassing to the Jesuits. Their rude manners, alien customs, and prejudiced attitude toward native beliefs incited the distrust, abhorrence, and scorn of many Chinese. In addition, Jesuit efforts were damaged by the Pope, who declined to authorize their moderation of Catholic doctrine or their tolerance of some Confucian rituals so as to avoid affronting potential converts. As a result, with the collapse of the great Ming empire many priests and Chinese converts disappeared. However, their records became a significant source of knowledge about China in the West and contributed to the European Enlightenment.

Sources:

Jacques Gernet, *China and the Christian Impact: A Conflict of Cultures*, translated by Janet Lloyd (Cambridge & New York: Cambridge University Press, 1985).

Kenneth Scott Latourette, *A History of Christian Missions in China* (London: Society for Promoting Christian Knowledge / New York: Macmillan, 1929).

A. C. Moule, *Christians in China before the Year 1550* (London: Society for Promoting Christian Knowledge / New York: Macmillan, 1930).

## LOCAL DEITIES AND WORTHY MEN OF SONG

**Popular Gods.** The expanding markets in Song times (960–1279) had great impact on the worship of popular gods. In addition to supporting Buddhist and Daoist monasteries, each district in Song China had a group of temples devoted to local gods. Many of these deities had been human beings who came to be adored in their native districts after their deaths. Nature divinities—including tree, mountain, and river gods—were also worshiped. These gods achieved miracles suitable to the agricultural society from which they sprang. Local people prayed to them in order to bring or stop rain, to hold off drought and locusts, and to defend them from disease, food shortages, and the dangers of childbirth.

**Seeking Help.** Lay people could confer with a host of religious specialists, who might in some cases be affiliated with Buddhism and Daoism. They could pray directly to deities for help while they were in search of some person, or god with the power to perform miracles, which they called *Ling* (efficiency). For example, if someone, whether human or divine, could cure an ill person or make it rain, then people would seek their help irrespective of their religious affiliation.

**Good Luck Charms.** Merchants and traders who traveled to buy and sell goods often carried their gods with them. Worshiping a Six Dynasty hero, for instance, some merchants grew lotus pods and roots that they sold at market, and they credited their god with sending rain that swept locusts away from their precious lotuses. Traders also credited their gods with keeping them safe, even when traveling far from home on business.

**Shrines to the Local Worthy.** During the Song dynasty temples to popular deities were not the only religious institutions located in the countryside, although their numbers were expanding. Alongside these temples were shrines, frequently situated in schools or Confucian academies, that were dedicated to worthy men. Unlike the gods, these men were honored for having accomplished good deeds in life, and they had no divine powers. Most had been noted statesmen, bureaucrats, generals, or writers. They were native residents, whose memories the community attempted to keep alive by setting up a tablet in a shrine to them. Many had been highly moral local officials. The shrines, sites of worship, and memorial halls were established to encourage people to imitate the achievements of these dead notables. From time to time students and teachers came to these shrines to offer incense and foodstuffs as an expression of respect for the privileged dead.

**Shrines to the National Worthy.** While the temples of popular deities and shrines to worthy men were of local character, some were constructed in communities with no direct relations to the deified men. The honored individuals had not been born in, had not served as officials in, and had never even visited these communities. Temples of this sort, for example, were constructed all over south China to honor three well-known philosophers: Zhou Dunyi, Cheng Yi, and Cheng Hao.

Sources:

Valerie Hansen, *The Open Empire: A History of China to 1600* (New York: Norton, 2000).

Robert P. Hymes, *Statesmen and Gentlemen: The Elite of Fu-chou, Chiang-hsi, in Northern and Southern Sung* (Cambridge & New York: Cambridge University Press, 1986).

Brian E. McKnight, *Village and Bureaucracy in Southern Sung China* (Chicago: University of Chicago Press, 1971).

## MING THOUGHT

**Social Roles.** Ming-era (1368–1644) intellectuals had to deal with the problems of living a Confucian lifestyle in a world that remained obstinately un-Confucian. In spite of official state support for Confucianism, the Ming government and society were far from the Confucian ideal. In

---

### TO BE A SAGE

Wang Yangming, the most famous philosopher of the Ming dynasty (1368–1644), believed that it was possible for everyone to become a sage.

The highest good is the ultimate principle of manifesting character and loving people. The nature endowed in us by Heaven is pure and perfect. The fact that it is intelligent, clear, and not obscured is evidence of the emanation and revelation of the highest good. . . . how can anyone who does not watch over himself carefully when alone, and who has no refinement and singleness of mind, attain to such a state of perfection? Later generations fail to realize that the highest good is inherent in their own minds, but each in accordance with his own ideas gropes for it outside the mind, believing that every event and every object has its own definite principle. For this reason the law of right and wrong is obscured; the mind becomes concerned with fragmentary and isolated details, the desires of man become rampant and the principle of Heaven is at an end.

**Source:** William Theodore de Bary and others, ed., *Sources of Chinese Tradition* (New York: Columbia University Press, 1960), pp. 573–574.

---

Daoist tablet used during ritual audiences with deities,
Ming dynasty, 1368–1644 (Staatliches Museum für
Volkerkunde, Munich)

addition, Ming intellectuals had to redefine the role of educated scholar-officials in society, because the development of trade created new wealth, a new source of power, and in effect, a new value system. Simultaneously, the increase of literacy weakened the monopoly on classical ideas and culture, as well as the position of classically educated persons. Finally, in a post-classical era, the only way a scholar could play a personal role was by specialization, which indicated a departure from the traditional goal of broader knowledge. To identify their personal and social roles, intellectuals were forced to question their own nature—it became a quest for intelligence and learning.

**Wang Yangming.** Believing that principle alone existed, Wang Yangming identified human nature with the "mind heart." Everyone had an inner goodness and an inborn ability to know good. Self-perfection enlarged this capacity to the greatest extent. Everyone could reach perfection because every person had the ability of a sage. Individuals might differ in their abilities in quantity, but their qualities were similar, just as the gold in a small coin was not inferior to that in a large one. External sources of doctrinal influence, including classical learning and lectures of sages, had only a minor, subordinate function. The truth was in the mind. It remained whole, because the mind and principle were universal.

**New Schools.** Some of Wang Yangming's supporters and students led courageous, but quite conservative, lives of public service, self-perfection, and teaching; other scholars, however, developed more-extreme ideas. Thus, he claimed that the mind was beyond the distinctions of good and bad, an idea with strong Buddhist sentiments and consistent with Daoist ideas. The trend to merge Confucianism, Buddhism, and Daoism appealed to Ming thinkers. Wang Yangming's teaching created the basis for the growth of philosophical schools in the sixteenth century, though they exhibited many differences. These schools comprised several dozens, sometimes hundreds, of students who followed one of many masters. The manner of educational conversation and the multiplicity of centers of study—complete with libraries—were features of intellectual life during the sixteenth century. Some people saw in this growth of schools a disturbing sign of division; the universal harmony of minds was endangered by intense deviation, which especially troubled the most respected traditions.

**School of Taichou.** One school was noted for its stress on impulsiveness and its denunciation of social restraints. Its basic theory was that no attempt was needed to gain innate knowledge, which was displayed in every man. Known as the school of Taichou, it was established by a self-educated former salt worker, Wang Gen, and Wang Ji, who liberally used Buddhist and Daoist terms and mastered Daoist skills of controlling one's breathing.

**Radicals.** In their personal conduct, in addition to their teachings, the most radical supporters of Wang Yangming extended the restrictions of Confucianism beyond the limits accepted by the Ming court. He Xinyin,

Daoist hanging scroll of the pantheon of gods, Ming dynasty, 1368–1644 (Nelson-Atkins Museum of Art, Kansas City)

**Revival.** Even after Buddhism triumphed as the major religious, scholastic, and aesthetic influence in the Tang dynasty (618–907), the family ethic and political ideology of Confucianism never completely disappeared. During the Song dynasty (960–1279) Chan and Pure Land Buddhism, as well as Daoism, thrived, but Confucianism was particularly appealing to a new generation of intellectuals. This revival of interest, known as neo-Confucianism, gave meaning to the life of the individual, developed an ideology to uphold state and society, and created a philosophy that presented a convincing structure for understanding the world. Neo-Confucianism regarded the world as an organic whole that constituted a system in which each aspect of life reinforced the others, both in theory and in practice.

**Old Roots.** Confucianism, the philosophy based on the teachings of the sixth and fifth century B.C.E. teacher and reformer Kong Zi (K'ung Ch'iu, Confucius), permeated Chinese society. A secular state religion, the main purpose of its ethical and moral teachings was to produce educated, well-mannered, virtuous men. People were considered good from birth; environment played a heavy role in determining one's character. A man who accepted Confucianism had to strive for knowledge and to set a good example; he was expected to be sincere, benevolent, and obedient to his superiors (especially his parents); and he was to be honest, just, and kind. A Confucian observed rites of passage (coming to adulthood, marriage), was responsible for the members of his family, and carried out feasts and celebrations in honor of the ancestors. The system was patriarchal and hierarchal; the head of the family (or the state, in the case of the emperor) was expected to lead by example.

**Background.** The renewal of Confucianism resulted from a nationalist reaction that followed the An Lushan Rebellion (755) and from a movement that advocated a return to the ancient ways of doing things. Han Yu, a famous Confucian scholar, advocated that it was necessary to adopt traditional Chinese sources; he believed that the classics, deserted since the acceptance of Buddhism, included a hidden philosophy that, once understood and utilized, would make it possible to guarantee social harmony and public order. In addition, Song thinkers expressed their desires for systematization—the search for a total interpretation of the universe that could be substituted for the clarifications provided by Buddhist religion and philosophy.

**Reaction.** The revival of Confucianism in Song times was a chauvinistic reaction to alien influences on Chinese politics and thought. Confucianism for many centuries was dominated by the examination-recruited civil servants who attempted to apply the principles they learned from ancient writings to the realm of practical governance. These thinkers believed that they could answer the stunning metaphysical questions with which Buddhism and Daoism had long been preoccupied. They contended that they could find these answers by restudying classical Confucian texts and

a bold protector of free conversation in the academies, was so dedicated to all humankind that he revolted against the family as a restraining, self-centered, exclusive institution. His nontraditional ideas and troublesome personal behavior ultimately helped land him in jail, where he was beaten to death.

**Syncretism.** A significant movement in the late Ming period was toward syncretism in both religious thought and scholarly writing. For example, Jiao Hong exceeded earlier thinkers who had regarded Confucianism, Buddhism, and Daoism as independent and balancing. He, however, regarded the three teachings as a single entity, so that each could assist the others.

**Sources:**

Alison Harley Black, *Man and Nature in the Philosophical Thought of Wang Fu-chih* (Seattle: University of Washington Press, 1989).

Julia Ching, *To Acquire Wisdom: The Way of Wang Yang-ming* (New York: Columbia University Press, 1976).

Kung-Chuan Hsiao, *A History of Chinese Political Thought,* translated by F. W. Mote (Princeton: Princeton University Press, 1979).

Feng Yu-lan, *A History of Chinese Philosophy,* second edition, translated by Derk Bodde (Princeton: Princeton University Press, 1952–1953).

by using traditional Chinese ideas for the proper organization of state, society, and individual lifestyles.

**Criticism.** The effort by differing sects to create opposing metaphysical outlooks, which was clearly obvious in Chinese Buddhism, was the most important factor in sparking the rise of neo-Confucianism. Some Chinese philosophers had been extremely critical of Buddhist ideas ever since they were introduced to China. They attacked the emphasis on overcoming suffering and death, which to Confucians looked like little more than selfish dodging. The monastic aspect of Buddhism, which involved the renunciation of family and society, seemed foolish because it was undoubtedly impracticable that human beings could ever escape these responsibilities. They were also critical of the Buddhist belief that all things were empty of reality. To Chinese scholars this concept was contradictory. The Buddhists considered all things, such as food and clothing, as unreal, but they had to depend on them. Perhaps the deepest difference between Chinese philosophers and Buddhist schools was that Confucian scholars stressed social and moral reality as fundamental, while the Buddhists concentrated on consciousness and metaphysical reality. Given these differences, the emergence of neo-Confucianism was not difficult to understand. This new movement was an attempt by Chinese thinkers to offset Buddhism with a more broad and superior philosophy.

**Major Philosophers.** The neo-Confucianism movement began with Han Yu, but a comprehensive and definitive formulation of his philosophy was not completed until the School of Reason was promoted by the Chen brothers (Chen Hao and Chen Yi) and the great synthesis of Zhu Xi was accomplished, both achieved during Song times. The School of Mind, which leaned in the direction of idealism, was later created by the philosophers Lu Jiuyuan and Wang Yangming.

**New Truths.** Neo-Confucianism was not a reassertion of ancient Confucian political and moral values supported by cosmological and metaphysical ideas adapted from Buddhism and Daoism. New truths were produced from old learning, which philosophically undercut otherworldly Buddhism and unworldly Daoism and gave vibrant life to the positivist, optimistic canons that human fulfillment would be found in life as people knew it and that everyone had the potential of realizing such fulfillment. Thus, like the revival of classical learning experienced centuries later in Europe, neo-Confucianism during the Song period refreshed almost all facets of life, initiating a transformation that greatly influenced changes that distinguished China in the later dynasties. Neo-Confucianism took several forms: a revival of classical scholarship, new accomplishments in historical learning, a fresh departure in speculative thought, and a more-serious devotion to Confucian principles.

**Historiography.** Confucianism had always stressed the study of history, and the revival brought a renewed interest in historiography. Exceptional among the new generation of historians was Sima Guang, who looked to the classics

for counseling. He had confidence and vision to do what no scholar had attempted since the Han dynasty (206 B.C.E.–220 C.E.)—to study the whole of Chinese history rather than confining himself to a single dynasty. Believing that an accurate account of the past could teach moral and practical lessons to the present, he wrote *Zizhi Tongjian* (A Comprehensive Mirror for Governance). Distinguished from traditional histories, it included discussions of the inconsistencies he found in the sources and his motive for choosing one version of events over another.

**Schools.** Confucianism also stressed "right" understanding of the past as a guide to good life and preparation for service to the empire. This belief implied a commitment to education. Confucius himself became a teacher when he failed to win the support of a ruler in putting his reform concepts into practice. As a result, during the period of neo-Confucian revival, new institutions were built: government schools in the Northern Song (960–1125) period and private academies in the Southern Song (1127–1279) period. Famous among Southern Song schools was the White Deer Grotto Academy, which was administrated for a time by the philosopher Zhu Xi. It was primarily through the private academies that neo-Confucian philosophy attracted many scholars.

**Dedicated Educators.** Students at the White Deer Grotto Academy were exposed to a heavy combination of moral exhortation and learning so that they would become both virtuous and well educated. Like other dedicated educators, the committed Confucian scholars encouraged their students to forget such careerist considerations as passing examinations and to give attention to the serious business of self-improvement. The guidance of a teacher was believed to be extremely significant if a student was to become truly educated.

*Jinsi Lu.* To help those students who lived in distant places and without easy access to teachers, Zhu Xi and his friend Lu Zuqian compiled an anthology of Song Confucianism for self-study. This work had a great impact on China as well as on both Korea and Japan. Based on the writings of four Northern Song philosophers, who came to be considered the founders of neo-Confucian philosophy, the book *Jinsi Lu* (Mirror Image of Things at Hand) dealt with matters of practical concern ranging from guidance on how to take care of a family to advice on when to accept or to reject a political offer. It also covered political institutions and individual behavior; the goal of a man, the book claimed, was to seek self-perfection.

**New Form of Writing.** Song-era neo-Confucianism, given the general designation of *Daoxue* (Study of the Way), was an extremely scholarly and academic movement that gained its strength in the state schools and, particularly, in the private academies. Its major philosophical principles were found in annotations that successive intellectuals appended to the traditional classics, which concentrated on philosophical explanations rather than on philosophical clarifications as was common for pre-Song commentaries. The neo-Confucians also began to use a

Painting of the Dragon King, ruler of the water world, surrounded by a bodyguard of water deities,
Song dynasty, 960–1279 (Museum of Fine Arts, Boston)

new form of writing, preferred by the Chan Buddhists: extensive reports produced by pupils on their teachers' discussions, teachings, and debates. These works were called minutes of conversations. The reason for this new development was that the neo-Confucians, enthusiastic educators and debaters, actively communicated with one another, and some of their ideas were best expressed in their preserved letters.

**Four Books.** Like Han Yu, the Song-era neo-Confucians were interested in the works of the third and fourth century B.C.E. philosopher Mencius (Meng-tzu), whom they regarded as the final transmitter of the authentic way of Confucius. They were also attached to several works that were marginal to original Confucianism: the *Zhou Li* (Zhou Rituals), a source of utopian political thought; the *Yi Jing* (Classic of Changes), a book of divination; and two sections in the *Li Ji* (Book of Rites)—the *Da Xue* (Great Leaning), an article on self-cultivation and the ordering of family and society, and the *Zhong Yong* (Doctrine of the Mean), which dealt with how man and his actions might result in harmony with the universe. Song neo-Confucians later raised the *Da Xue* and the *Zhong Yong,* together with Confucius's *Lunyu* (Analects) and the *Mencius* (a collection of Mencius's writings), to a special status as the "Four Books," the core of their teaching and philosophical scholarship. These works became the basic textbooks for primary education.

**Comparison.** Neo-Confucians were successful in persuading scholars that the universe detectable to the senses was real, not illusory as Buddhists asserted, and that human beings achieved fulfillment by sincere involvement in society, not by standing distant from it, as the Daoists were inclined to do. They looked down on Buddhist assurances of spiritual salvation and Daoist claims of physical immortality. They argued that the human cycle from birth to death was normal and good, and they emphasized social and political reforms in the world and individualistic self-cultivation in this life.

**Two Trends.** After the governmental reform movements in the early Song period, neo-Confucian emphasis on practical effort and efficient government gave way to speculative aspects that expanded gradually in the Northern Song period and finally, in the twelfth century, became the best-known element of the movement. By that time two philosophical trends emerged as irreconcilable neo-Confucian mainstreams. One, known as *Li Xue* (Study of Principles), or Chen-Zhu school, was frequently featured as dualistic and rationalistic; the other, known as *Xin Xue* (Study of the Mind), or Lu Wang school, was typified as monistic (belief in one principle) and idealistic. As neo-Confucianism continued to develop, passing through several stages with changing emphases, the early Song reformist enthusiasm came to be subordinated in Ming times (1368–1644) to an intense stress on personal self-cultivation.

**Cosmology.** Several Song philosophers developed a common base of cosmology that greatly influenced all neo-Confucian philosophical assumptions. Adapted to concepts found in the ancient *Yi Jing* (Book of Changes), their cosmology came from extremely developed traditions of Buddhist and neo-Daoist metaphysics. Borrowed from the analysis of the third-century neo-Daoist Wang Pi, much of the cosmology came from obscure diagrams created by a Daoist monk in the tenth century. The neo-Confucian cosmology was shaped by the students of the *Yijing.* Zhou Duni, of Hunan province, who held several minor official posts in the south, used the *Yijing,* the Five Elements, and the concepts of *yin* (the feminine, passive principle) and *yang* (the masculine, aggressive principle) to identify the "Supreme Ultimate," the principle matter from which all beings were derived. Zhang Zai, an official of the Shaanxi province, who was ousted from the government for opposing Wang Anshi's reforms and who later devoted himself to private teaching, suggested that the entire universe was composed of a single primal substance, referred to as *qi.*

**Supreme Ultimate.** The neo-Confucian cosmology presented by Zhou Duni was a complex representation of linked circles, called the diagram of the Supreme Ultimate, which was an aggregation of perfect abstract forms or principles. The material world came into being by a process similar to the coagulation of matter, which changed into a formless basic stuff, out of which individual things appeared. The driving power in this process was provided by the interaction between the indivisible cosmic forces, *yang* and *yin.* The Five Elements—fire, water, earth, wood, and metal—were regarded as basic forces. Things were what they were (men, mountains, trees, cats, and rocks, for example) because of the abstract form, or *li* (principle), which united with and shaped *qi* (matter). Thus, the concept of the Supreme Ultimate, or Great Ultimate, became key in the Chen-Zhu school of neo-Confucianism.

**Opposites.** Song scholars, like earlier Chinese philosophers, found it pleasant and productive to think in terms of balancing opposites (interacting polarities), such as inner and outer, substance and function, and knowledge and action. Perhaps they were interested in this mode of thought because it enabled them to observe differences without doing violence to what they recognized as an ultimate organic unity. According to the neo-Confucians, the Supreme Ultimate was the universal reality and underscored all existence. Principle or reason existed in all activity, through which it generated *yang.* After reaching its limit, activity became tranquil, and through tranquility the Supreme Ultimate generated *yin.* When tranquility reached its limit, activity started, the one producing the other as its opposite. Through the interaction between *yin* and *yang* the five elements came into being and the ten thousand things in the universe were created. The Song-era neo-Confucians were interested in the idea of the reversal of opposites created by Daoist thought, but they were primarily focused on the conceptual pair *li* and *qi.*

**Part of the System.** *Li* was usually translated as a principle or a network of principles. Each individual *li* was part of the entire system; nothing could exist if there was

**B**elow is an extract from the diary of the Jesuit missionary Matteo Ricci, who stayed in China from 1583 until his death in Beijing in 1610.

Individually, the Chinese do not choose this sect; they rather imbibe the doctrine of it in the study of letters. No one who attains honors in the study of letters or who even undertakes the study would belong to any other sect. Confucius is their Prince of Philosophers, and according to them, it was he who discovered the art of philosophy. They do not believe in idol worship. In fact they have no idols. They do, however, believe in one deity who preserves and governs all things on earth. Other spirits they admit, but these are of less restricted domination and receive only minor honors. The real Literati teach nothing relative to the time, the manner, or the author of the creation of the world. We use the word real, or true, because there are some of them, less celebrated, who interpret dreams, but not much faith is placed in them as they deal mostly with trifles and improbable things. Their law contains a doctrine of reward for good done and of punishment for evil, but they seem to limit it to the present life and to apply it to the evil-doer and to his descendants, according to their merits. The ancients scarcely seem to doubt about the immortality of the soul, because, for a long time after a death, they make frequent reference to the departed as dwelling in heaven. They say nothing, however, about punishment for the wicked in hell. The more Literati teach that the soul ceases to exist when the body does, or a short time after it. They, therefore, make no mention of heaven or hell. To some of them this seems to be rather a severe punishment and so this school teaches that only the souls of the just survive. They say that the soul of a man is strengthened by

virtue and solidified to endure, and since this is not true of the wicked, their souls vanish, like thin smoke, immediately after leaving the body.

The doctrine most commonly held among the Literati at present seems to me to have been taken from the sect of idols, as promulgated about five centuries ago. This doctrine asserts that the entire universe is composed of a common substance; that the creator of the universe is one in a continuous body, a corpus continuum as it were, together with heaven and earth, men and beasts, trees and plants, and the four elements, and that each individual thing is a member of this body. From this unity of substance they reason to the love that should unite the individual constituents and also that man can become like unto God because he is created one with God. This philosophy we endeavor to refute, not only from reason but also from the testimony of their own ancient philosophers to whom they are indebted for all the philosophy they have.

Although the Literati, as they are called, do recognize one supreme deity, they erect no temples in his honor. No special places are assigned for his worship, consequently no priests or ministers are designated to direct that worship. We do not find any special rites to be observed by all, or precepts to be followed, nor any supreme authority to explain or promulgate laws or to punish violations of laws pertaining to a supreme being. Neither are there any public or private prayers or hymns to be said or sung in honor of a supreme deity. The duty of sacrifice and the rites of worship for this supreme being belong to the imperial majesty alone.

**Source:** Matteo Ricci, *China in the Sixteenth Century: The Journals of Matthew Ricci, 1583–1610*, translated by Louis J. Gallagher (New York: Random House, 1953), pp. 94–95.

no *li* for it. This concept applied as much to the field of human behavior as it did to the physical world. The *li* for fatherhood had the same status as the *li* for mountains. No difference was made between the former, which was defined in moral terms, and the latter, into which value judgments did not enter because the world of moral action and that of physical objects was held to be one and the same. Both were understandable and both were equally natural. For common people the way to gain perfection was by grasping the *li*.

**Essential Force.** *Qi* was characterized as the essential force and matter of which man and the world were made. It was regarded as energy that occupied space. In its most refined form, *qi* appeared as a kind of rarefied ether, but when it was condensed, it turned into solid metal or rock. In his cosmology Zhu Xi imagined the world as a sphere in constant rotation, so that the heavier *qi* was held in the center by the centripetal force of motion. The *qi* becomes progressively lighter and thinner as one moves away from the center. This con-

cept clarified why, for instance, air at a high altitude was thinner than that at sea level.

**Harmony.** The Supreme Ultimate, creating all things and deciding their functions, was a combination of *qi* and *li*. The nature of things was the consequence of what they were and how they worked. When *qi* and *li* were in balance, things were in order and there was a grand harmony. The Supreme Ultimate stood for a harmony of *qi* and *li*, and therefore order was the law of the universe. Asserting that the Supreme Ultimate was the principle of universal goodness, Zhu Xi transformed his pervasive metaphysics into the groundwork for a social and moral philosophy.

**Ethical System.** Neo-Confucians of the Chen-Zhu school created an ethical system that was based on Daoist-influenced cosmology. This school realized that an individual's fundamental identity, or *li*, was inseparably connected with the Supreme Ultimate. The original perfection of one's *li* was tarnished by the embodiment of *li* in matter, or *qi*, just as the reflections of a mirror were dulled by an out-

Painting of scholars studying the yin-yang symbol, early seventeenth century
(British Museum, London)

side layer of dust. Therefore, neo-Confucians advocated dusting off one's mirror in the same manner that Mencius had earlier promoted the idea to restore one's "lost" child's mind. Becoming a wise person, which was the fulfillment sought by neo-Confucians generally, was achieved by realizing one's essential identity and opposing the selfish aspirations and other unworthy desires that arose from one's *qi*. The wise person did not become eternal, spiritually or physically. When he died, he went to a well-deserved rest.

**Meditation.** In order to become sages, neo-Confucians were absorbed in Chan Buddhist–like meditation in an effort to withdraw temporarily from the bustle of daily life to focus on the cultivation of an attitude of earnestness or genuineness. Some adherents advocated experiencing sudden enlightenment in the Buddhist manner. Prescribed in the ancient text *Da Xue* (Great Leaning), the method of self-cultivation used by neo-Confucians was to put right the mind by making one's intentions sincere, by expanding one's knowledge, and by exploring matters. For the

neo-Confucians, especially the students of the Chen-Zhu school, to investigate things meant to study rationally and objectively the *li* and other worldly phenomena, which would come to expand contact with the collection of all *li*—the Supreme Ultimate.

**Chen Brothers.** The ideas of early neo-Confucian cosmology continued to be developed by Chen Hao and Chen Yi, who spent most of their lives in Luoyang and Kaifeng. They emphasized the unity of the human mind with the universe. After studying intensively both Buddhist and Daoist ideas, they combined *Yi Jing* cosmology with ancient Confucian ethical teachings, and thereafter neo-Confucianism began to be developed into a full-scale philosophical system. There were no significant philosophical differences between the Chen brothers, but the ideas of Chen Yi were transmitted through a chain of teacher-pupil relationships to Zhu Xi, who synthesized and expanded them into a system known as the Li Xue school, while the ideologies of Chen Hao gradually became a rival system known as the Xin Xue school, led by Zhu Xi's contemporary Lu Jiuyuan and developed more fully in the sixteenth century by Wang Yangming.

**Influences.** In Song times neo-Confucianism, which was not a monolithic philosophy, absorbed some ideas from Daoism and Buddhism, although they were at the same time attacked by the neo-Confucians. Even the most devoted Confucian was not resistant to the attractions of Chan Buddhism. Therefore, Daoism and Buddhism greatly influenced Song philosophers who sought to weaken Buddhism and Daoism by developing a more sophisticated philosophy of their own.

**Opponents.** In the energetic intellectualism of Southern Song times neo-Confucians faced challenges from anti-intellectualism in the central government. Encountering many philosophical opponents, Zhu Xi often debated with them publicly at his White Deer Grotto Academy and elsewhere. Among his opponents was Chen Liang, a Chekiang pragmatist, who argued for practical activism in government service, although he had a disastrous political career—he was imprisoned three times—and had not won his *jinshi* degree until the year before his death. Chen asserted that material reality was the only reality and that metaphysical speculation about the Supreme Ultimate was impossible and extravagant. Another opponent was Lu Jiuyuan, who wrote little and as a result had little impact on the philosophic trends of his own time but later founded the Xin Xue school.

**Northern Confucianism.** While the Li Xue and Xin Xue schools competed in the Southern Song period, Chinese intellectuals who served the Jurchen Jin state (1115–1234) in northern China continued to practice traditional Confucianism, typified by earnest personal morality and a serious awareness of public obligations. Conservative Confucians in the north came under Mongol control long before the Southern Song fell to the invaders; they were the only Confucians who enjoyed some respect in the early periods of Yuan rule (1279–1368) over China. To many conservatives the whole neo-Confucian movement looked like an unfortunate deviation among unstable, excessively exhausted southerners who were stained by Buddhist and Daoist metaphysics. Since Zhu Xi's writings were a scholarly challenge that could not be ignored, his ideas penetrated into northern China, and his Li Xue school soon dominated the private academies in Yuan times.

**Yuan Period.** To the Yuan rulers the Li Xue school, an appealing and comfortable version of Confucianism, discouraged extreme political activism, recognized external standards of value and authority, and encouraged zealous self-cultivation through serious study of the instructions and precedents of the past. It seemed moderate, if not conservative, and authoritarian enough to serve as an ideological support for absolute monarchy. On the contrary, the assertive individualism inherent in the Xin Xue school—such as the worldliness of Buddhism and the unworldly, anti-establishment tradition of Daoism—was to the Yuan emperors an unappealing, even dangerous, alternative.

Therefore, Yuan rulers and intellectuals disregarded Lu Jiuyuan's doctrines for many years while Chen-Zhu doctrines won universal admiration and official state support.

**Practicality.** Intellectual life in the early Ming period was not favorable to unorthodox ideologies. After many years of alien invasions, followed by the civil wars of the late Yuan years, an enormous expenditure of energy was put into military, governmental, and social reconstruction; only restricted pragmatism was acceptable. Furthermore, the form of government founded by absolutist Ming rulers promoted conservatism. The dominant practicality of the early Ming era, however, redirected the interests of intellectuals away from the cosmological metaphysics of the Chen-Zhu school, and the terrible conditions of government service also induced many sensitive scholars to live simple, rural lives at home and to dedicate themselves to self-evaluation and self-cultivation.

**Chen Xianzhang.** The most respected philosopher of the first half of the Ming dynasty was Chen Xianzhang. Although he gained celebrity as a living sage, who rejected many offers based on his reputation, he decided to spend his life studying and teaching in his remote home province, Guangdong. Challenging Zhu Xi modestly on many points, Chen imagined the universe in entirely naturalistic terms, lectured on the significance of naturalness and quiescence, and absorbed himself in meditation of quiet-sitting. He did not openly accept the beliefs of Lu Jiuyuan, but his ideologies contributed directly to the later full development of the Xin Xue school of Wang Yangming, the greatest of the latter neo-Confucian philosophers.

**Attacks on Confucius.** In the late Ming period some second-generation followers of Wang Yangming publicly stated that every person was his own judge of right and wrong, that every desire should be translated instinctively into action, and that the streets were full of wise men. They offered democratic, tolerant doctrines to large, excited gatherings in the towns and cities. Among these scholars was Li Zhi, a Confucian official in Fujian province, who later became a Chan Buddhist. As a freethinker Li totally rejected Confucius and the classics as the standard of right and wrong, asserting instead the ready-made perfection of one's child-mind and regarding egotism and profits as valuable motives. He accused traditional Confucians of being unquestioning job seekers; passionately defended and studied the popular, conversational literature that openly scorned traditional Confucianism; promoted marriage by free choice; and proclaimed that Confucianism, Buddhism, and Daoism were of equal truth and value. As a government official Li was sometimes engaged in working in Buddhist temples.

**Donglin Academy.** As Li Zhi's teachings became accepted, traditional Confucians became more worried about Wang Yangming's left-wing pupils. Arrested finally as an exponent of an unorthodox opinion, Li Zhi killed himself in prison in 1602 before his trial. Thereafter, a group of moderate Chen-Zhu conservatives founded the

Donglin Academy at Wuxi near Shanghai in 1604 in an effort to resist the moral decay and political corruption that came, they believed, from the philosophical misrepresentation of the Wang Yangming school. Although the Donglin Party was put down by the government in the 1620s, Wang's extremism was effectively dishonored and vanished when the Manchus overthrew the Ming empire. Wang's own teachings were not concealed, but Chen-Zhu orthodoxy remained the mainstream of Chinese philosophy in the early Qing dynasty (1644–1912).

**Sources:**

William Theodore de Bary, *Neo-Confucian Orthodoxy and the Learning of the Mind-and-Heart* (New York: Columbia University Press, 1981).

John B. Henderson, *The Development and Decline of Chinese Cosmology* (New York: Columbia University Press, 1984).

John M. Koller, *Oriental Philosophies* (New York: Scribners, 1970).

Thomas A. Metzger, *Escape from Predicament: Neo-Confucianism and China's Evolving Political Culture* (New York: Columbia University Press, 1977).

## NESTORIAN AND FRANCISCAN MISSIONS

**Foreign Missions.** Christian missionaries from the West began to enter China in the seventh century to preach and spread their faith, build churches, and convert the Chinese. Although they increased their influence slowly, they were finally expelled from China because of changes in political circumstances, as well as the antagonism and fear stimulated by a religion that never adjusted to certain essential Chinese attitudes and practices. The Chinese generally looked upon Christianity as "foreign," and though its indirect influence in China was substantial, it never at any time appealed to any significant portion of the population. Both Buddhism and Islam were more successful than Christianity in China.

**Nestorian Church.** Nestorianism, a branch of Christianity practiced primarily in Syria by followers who had splintered off from the Eastern Orthodox Church, was introduced into China in 635 by Olopen (known as Jiang

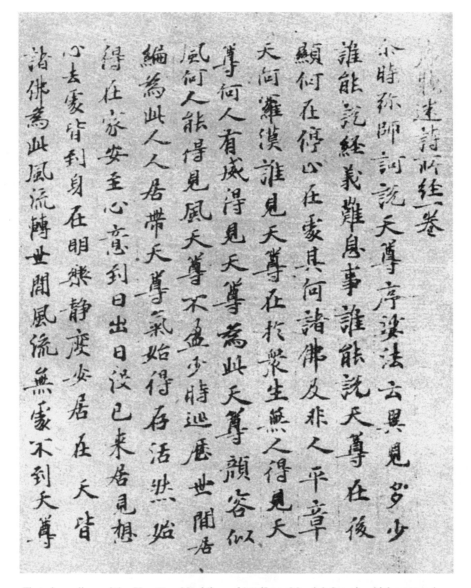

First eleven lines of the *Hsu-t'ing Mi-shih-so-ching* (Jesus Messiah Sutra), which summarizes Christian precepts for daily living, circa 635–638 (P. Y. Saeki, *The Nestorian Documents and Relics in China*, 1951)

Jiao), a monk from *Da Qin* (Syria). The Tang emperor Taizong welcomed him and asked him to build a church and monastery in the capital and to translate his religious books into Chinese. In addition, he and his followers were authorized to spread their faith. By the time a stela was erected in the year 781, Nestorianism, known as *Qinjiao* (Luminous Religion), had won many believers and the support of some of the most prominent people, including the supreme commander of the army and chief ministers of state, who spent much money on restoration of churches and support of monks and priests. During the reign of Gaozong, the son and successor of Taizong, churches were constructed in many major cities, and for a moment Christianity looked like it would flourish throughout the empire.

**Nestorian Influence.** In the early Tang period (618–907) there was substantial cooperation between Buddhists and Nestorians, and in fact, the latter helped to introduce Buddhism into the early Tang dynasty. The Nestorians, however, suffered from many obstacles placed by, and persecution from, their Buddhist competitors. The Nestorian church, along with other "foreign" religions, was attacked during the great persecution of 842–845, and it was not until the thirteenth century that Christians were again allowed overtly to practice their religion in China. Nestorian missionaries were successful in converting many people in Central Asia—such as Uighurs, Kirghiz, Khitans, Keraits, Naimans, and Alans. After Mongol troops finally occupied China, during the reign of Kublai Khan, great movements of population throughout the empire resulted in the settlement of many Christians in China. The French Franciscan friar William of Rubrouck, who was sent to investigate the potential for Christian expansion in Asia, visited the court of the great Mangu Khan at Karakorum in 1253 and claimed that there were Nestorians in fifteen Chinese cities, as well as one bishop. It was said that there were thirty thousand Nestorians living in China during the Yuan dynasty (1279–1368). With the downfall of the Mongol empire, the toleration of Christians in Ming-era (1368–1644) China came to an end, and the Nestorian church vanished.

**Destruction.** Several factors, in addition to the chauvinism of the Ming rulers, were responsible for the total demolition of the Nestorian church. The faith in Western and Central Asia was nearly eliminated by the expansion of Islam and the esoteric Buddhism known as Tantrism. The Chinese, as well, could not easily identify the major differences between Nestorian and Buddhist ceremonies, so they shifted their interest to Buddhism or Daoism.

**Franciscans.** The Franciscan mission started its work in China around the middle of the thirteen century and continued throughout the Yuan dynasty until it was completely eliminated around the middle of the fourteenth century, a relatively short period of evangelization. The grand Mongol empire, after occupying the whole of Central Asia in the thirteenth century, carried out liberal policies toward religion, wanted to soak up foreign ideas, and employed distinguished and learned intellectuals, no matter what

## NESTORIANISM IN CHINA

Nestorianism, a branch of the Christian faith that was practiced in Syria, arrived in China in the seventh century. In 781 a stone was erected in Chang'an in honor of the faith. A portion of the inscription on the stela appears below:

The true Lord is without origin, profound, invisible, and unchangeable; with power and capacity to perfect and transform, He raised up the earth and established the heavens.

Divided in nature, he entered the world, to save and to help without bounds; the sun arose, and darkness was dispelled, all bearing witness to his true original.

The glorious and resplendent, accomplished Emperor, whose principles embraced those of preceding monarchs, taking advantage of the occasion, suppressed turbulence; Heaven was spread out and the earth was enlarged.

When the pure, bright illustrious religion was introduced to our Tang Dynasty, the Scriptures were translated, and churches built, and the vessel set in motion for the living and the dead; every kind of blessing was then obtained, and all the kingdoms enjoyed a state of peace.

When Kau-tsung succeeded to his ancestral estate, he rebuilt the edifices of purity; palaces of concord, large and light, covered the length and breadth of the land.

The true doctrine was clearly announced, overseers of the church were appointed in due form; the people enjoyed happiness and peace, while all creatures were exempt from calamity and distress.

When Hiuen-tsung commenced his sacred career, he applied himself to the cultivation of truth and rectitude; his imperial tablets shot forth their effulgence, and the celestial writings mutually reflected their splendors.

The imperial domain was rich and luxuriant, while the whole land rendered exalted homage; every business was flourishing throughout, and the people all enjoyed prosperity.

Sources: Charles F. Horne, ed., *The Sacred Books and Early Literature of the East*, volume 12, *Medieval China* (New York: Parke, Austin & Lipscomb, 1917), pp. 381–392.

"Ch'ing-Tsing: Nestorian Tablet: Eulogizing the Propagation of the Illustrious Religion in China, with a preface, composed by a Priest of the Syriac Church, 781 A.D.," *East Asian History Sourcebook* <http://www.fordham.edu/halsall/eastasia/781nestorian.html>.

religion they practiced. In 1280 Kublai Khan established an office in charge of supervising Christian activities.

**Visiting Priest.** At that time the Roman Catholic Church in Europe was interested in Asia and determined to send a mission to the Mongol empire. John of Montecorvino (Giovanni da Montecorvino), the first Roman Catholic priest to visit China, was permitted to construct a church in Beijing in 1300. He began to evangelize the Chinese, and by 1305 he had converted about 6,000 persons to Catholicism. He took about 150 boys under his protection and educated them in the Christian faith, helping them to learn Greek and Latin and then hiring them to transcribe Christian texts.

**Growth.** Early in the fourteenth century the Pope sent another mission to Beijing in order to help John increase Roman Catholic influence in China, while promoting John to archbishop and patriarch of East Asia. In 1313 a rich woman donated money to construct a church in the port city of Chuanzhou (Zayton), which had a close trade relationship with the Persian Gulf. This church was later made a cathedral to which a friary was attached, and other churches were constructed in the city in the following year. Undoubtedly, the Christians, part of a large foreign commercial population in Chuanzhou, needed these churches. By the time of Archbishop John's death (1328) the Roman Catholic Church was well established in the capital and other cities, such as Hangzhou. Among its believers were some remnants of the Nestorian church, Armenians, and members of a Caucasian tribe who in the beginning were adherents of the Eastern Orthodox faith.

**Decline.** The Christian missionary force in China was relatively small and was repeatedly reduced by death. The Pope tried several times to send groups of missionaries from Europe to China, but few of them were able to finish their lengthy and dangerous trips to the East. Maintaining the mission was nearly impossible, despite the aggressive efforts of the Roman Catholic Church. Few native Chinese were converted to Christianity, and the Church comprised mainly foreign merchants, businessmen, alien Christian residents, and some Nestorians who were persuaded to join the Catholics. Subsequently, when a fierce persecution of foreign religions started again in the early Ming period, the missionaries were driven out of China. The scattered groups of Christians did not have any native leaders to hold them together and the influence of the Catholic Church declined.

Sources:

E. R. Hughes and K. Hughes, *Religion in China* (London & New York: Hutchinson's University Library, 1950).

François Jullien, *The Propensity of Things: Toward a History of Efficacy in China,* translated by Janet Lloyd (New York: Zone, 1995).

Frederick W. Mote, *Intellectual Foundations of China* (New York: Knopf, 1971).

D. Howard Smith, *Chinese Religions* (New York: Holt, Rinehart & Winston, 1968).

## RELIGIOUS POLICIES OF THE YUAN

**Shamanism.** Originally, Mongol religion was a form of shamanism, the religious practices of certain native peoples of northern Asia who believed that good and evil spirits pervaded the world and could be summoned or heard through inspired shamans (priests) acting as mediums. Kublai Khan had performed its rituals before his occupation of China.

**Tolerance.** The Mongol tolerance of foreigners extended to their religions. The early khans supported religious debates at their courts and granted tax exemptions to all religions. Nestorians, Muslims, Christians,

Painting of a Buddhist missionary reading a Sanskrit manuscript, Yuan dynasty, 1279–1368 (National Palace Museum Collection, Taipei, Taiwan)

and Jews were welcomed. The religious policy of the Yuan (1279–1368) government consecutively supported different sects, following the interests of the moment, and handed over to them the general direction of religious affairs of the dynasty. The Yuan empire, famous for its religious freedom, did not impose Mongol religious beliefs on the Chinese.

**Daoism.** After the Daoist master Qiu Chuji visited Genghis Khan in Central Asia, his faith was particularly favored by the ruler. The emperor belonged to a sect founded in Shandong by Wang Chongyang, who attempted to purify Daoism. Genghis respected Qiu Chuji and made him patriarch of all religious orders in the Mongol empire and later authorized Daoists to answer all religious questions in 1223.

**Buddhism.** Kublai Khan, who succeeded his grandfather Genghis and established the Yuan dynasty, promoted

Illumination of the demon queller Chung K'uei in different poses, circa 1300
(Metropolitan Museum of Art, New York)

open discussion between Buddhists and Daoists, who were involved in a bitter rivalry. Influenced by the monk Haiyun, the Mongol emperor transferred his preference to the Chan school of Buddhism after 1242. Buddhism enjoyed a dominant position in the Khitan, Tangut, and Jurchen empires and its influence increased within the Mongol empire.

**Great Debate.** While Lamaism, a form of Mahayana Buddhism that incorporated elements of Tantrism and shamanism, enjoyed the favor of the Mongols, Daoists and Buddhists fought a series of great religious debates at court. Daoists used wartime chaos as an opportunity to occupy Buddhist temples and began to distribute pamphlets claiming that Lao Zi, the founder of Daoism, had "civilized" and converted Buddha himself. When Buddhists complained, the Mangu Khan organized several court meetings (1255 to 1258) to consider the Daoist-Buddhist charges and countercharges. The last meeting, directed by Kublai Khan, was a great event that gathered about three hundred Buddhists, two hundred Taoists, and two hundred Confucian scholars. The Daoist assertions were pronounced untrue in all cases, possessions appropriated from Buddhist plaintiffs were returned, libelous Daoist books on the Buddha were destroyed, and several chief Daoists were forced to withdraw and take Buddhist pledges.

**Suppression.** After this famous debate it became obvious that many Daoists were not remorseful, and Kublai ordered in 1281 that since the Buddhists had won the competition, Daoist excesses should be restricted. During this persecution the millennium-old dispute over the sequential priority of Lao Zi and Buddha vanished steadily; Daoists lost their reputation and riches, and their power declined. Daoism did not disappear, although Buddhism became popular in the Mongol empire. The emperors continued to tolerate Daoism and Chinese Buddhism, although they favored the faith of Tibetan lamas.

**Lamaism.** After the Mongols invaded Tibet, their interest in Chinese Buddhism soon surrendered to an energetic interest in Tibetan Buddhism, which played a significant religious role in the Yuan empire. After receiving the obedience of Tibetans, the Mongols employed a Tibetan abbot to rule on their behalf over Tibet. Lamaism was more complicated and worldly than the native shamanism of the Mongols. Impressed by the Lamaist methods and charms infused with magic power to heal or harm, Mongol emperors thereafter engaged in the Tibetan religion as a form of Buddhism.

**'Phags-pa.** The Tibetan lama 'Phags-pa went to Beijing in 1253; in 1260 he invented an alphabetic script for the Mongolian language. As a result, Kublai appointed him as imperial mentor and state tutor. As Kublai's intimate adviser, 'Phags-pa began to introduce lamas into government service in China and became responsible for the affairs of all Buddhist monks. In return, he recognized Kublai as the universal emperor of the Buddhist tradition.

**Senge.** A multilingual Uighur lama called Senge became Kublai's religious supervisor and favorite monk. The power of the lamas in China enabled them to take advantage of religious communities. Engaging in financial speculation and forced exaction of funds, Senge was later found guilty of plundering and of committing several murders.

**Yanglian Zhenjia.** After occupying southern China, the Yuan established a new office of religious affairs at Hangzhou. Beginning in 1277 the Mongols trusted a Tibetan monk called Yanglian Zhenjia, who became famous for his bad behavior. His most terrible crime was to open the tombs of the Southern Song (1127–1279) emperors in an effort to possess their treasures. After this period the government, as did Kublai's heirs, favored Lamaism. In 1309 the Yuan court issued an edict that anyone caught beating a lama would have his hand cut off; anyone convicted of affronting a lama was sentenced to lose his tongue.

**Confucianism.** The Mongol emperors' stance toward Confucianism was more cautious. Since Kublai did not understand the written Chinese language, he had little knowledge of the Confucian texts. Recognizing the importance of the philosophy, however, he hired Confucian officials and encouraged the translation of the classics into the Mongolian languages. When Ayurbarwada came to the throne (1311), for the first time a Mongol emperor had a knowledge of written Chinese. He reintroduced Confucianism to the state and society to modify the Mongolian culture, but Confucian elements remained superficial. Early in Toghon Temur's reign (1333–1368), when Chancellor Bayan controlled the government, Confucian scholars were disappointed by his attempt to turn the tide of sinicizing (making things more Chinese) by repealing civil service examinations as a route of entry into government service. After the fall of Bayan in 1340 Confucianism recovered some of its ideological supremacy, and the Yuan government restored the examination system, offering the opportunity not only to Chinese applicants but also to Mongols as part of a common objective and commitment to establishing a unified state.

**Dilemma.** In Yuan times Confucians were put in a dilemma. Some scholars claimed that their Confucian obligations required them to serve the Mongols in order to civilize them, while other intellectuals declined to condone the Mongol presence in China and refused to compromise or accept any government positions. Liu Yin was a distinguished example; in 1291 he turned down an offer to become an academician at the Imperial Academy. His refusal to commit himself to public service was regarded as an instance of Confucian eremitism, a removal of intellectuals from worldly affairs as a protest against the Mongol regime. Another type of resistance by the Confucians emerged through drama; they wrote plays that contained protests against the Mongol presence, and the popular response to their productions in part resulted in the downfall of the Yuan empire.

**Islam.** Central Asia was converted to Islam during the Tang period (618–907), and many Muslims settled in the western part of China Proper during Yuan times. The Mongol emperors favored the introduction of Islam into China. In the Yuan era, Islamic communities were founded in northern China and the Yunnan province, to which a Muslim governor had been appointed since 1274. Some of these Muslim communities gradually combined with the local Chinese, while others tried to preserve their own personality, showing a marked trend toward autonomy. Thousands of Chinese in northern China were converted to Islam during this period.

**Influence.** Islamic Iran had a significant impact on the Chinese world during the Mongol era. Mongols built a Muslim temple in Beijing, and there were many examples of Islamic architecture in Mongolia and China. Mosques were established in Yunnan, Gansu, and Guangzhou. Mongols began to translate Arabic texts at the Islamic Academy, founded during the reign of Kublai Khan, and

they set up a Muslim observatory in Beijing. Yuan emperors tolerated all religions and coped kindly even with representatives of Islam, Nestorianism, and Christianity.

Sources:

Kung-Chuan Hsiao, *A History of Chinese Political Thought*, translated by F. W. Mote (Princeton: Princeton University Press, 1979).

Charles O. Hucker, *China's Imperial Past: An Introduction to Chinese History and Culture* (Stanford, Cal.: Stanford University Press, 1975).

Frederick W. Mote, *Intellectual Foundations of China* (New York: Knopf, 1971).

## ZOROASTRIANISM, MANICHAEANISM, AND ISLAM

**Persian Faith.** Zoroastrianism, a Persian monotheistic religion whose adherents believed in the dualism of good and evil and who practiced their faith in a ceremony that included fire as a major element, began to appear in China during the Tang dynasty (618–907), mostly to meet the needs of Persian refugees who fled to the east after the downfall of the Sassanian empire and the conquest of Persia by Muslims between 637 and 642. The last Sassanian ruler, Yesdegerd (Yazdegerd III), asked the Chinese for help against the Arabs, but the Tang court refused to send military forces to assist him. Later, Firuz, the son of Yesdegerd, together with other refugees, fled to Chang'an where he was appointed a general of the imperial guard. After Firuz's death the Tang government allowed Persian refugees to construct temples in order to practice their faith, but Zoroastrians were not aggressive in trying to convert the Chinese. During the great persecution of all foreign religions between 842 and 845, Zoroastrianism vanished from China.

**Manichaeanism.** The influence of Manichaeanism, another Persian religion that accepted a dualistic view of the world (good versus evil) and said that the spirit was released from its material form at death, was far more extensive than Zoroastrianism. Manichaeanism, which emerged in the third century, appeared as early as 694 in China, but it was not until the early eighth century that Uighurs were converted to the faith, from whom the Chinese later learned of it. Since Uighurs gave useful military assistance to the Tang emperor during the rebellion of An Lushan (755), after the revolt was suppressed, the Tang court allowed the Uighurs to settle within China and tolerated the spread of Manichaeanism and the construction of their temples. From 766 to 779 Manichaean shrines were built at Jingzhou in Hebei, Yangzhou, Nanking and even as far south as Shaoxing in Zhejiang, where many Chinese were converted to Manichaeanism.

**Port Cities.** Trade relations by sea with the Persian Gulf in the Song (960–1279), Yuan (1279–1368), and Ming (1368–1644) periods resulted in the construction of temples to serve the needs of different foreign communities located in big commercial ports. Manichaeanism was one of the allowed religions. The picture of Mani, placed in the central hall of the temple, was totally different in style from any Buddhist image. A great halo of light surrounded his

Porcelain bowl painted with a good-luck formula written in Persian, sixteenth century
(Smithsonian Institution, Washington, D.C.)

head and two long plaits of hair trailed down past his shoulders.

**Decline.** After the Khirgiz defeated the Uighurs in 840, Manichaeans in the Tang empire could no longer depend on Uighur protection. Thus, in 843 the Tang emperor confiscated their properties, burned Manichaean manuscripts, and destroyed their temples and images. More than seventy Manichaean nuns were killed in Chang'an, and everywhere in China Manichaean monks were forced to throw out their characteristic clothes and accept lay status. Manichaeanism in China never restored the influence it enjoyed before the persecution, although its teachings wielded extensive influence down to the Song and Yuan dynasties. The believers of Manichaeanism were slowly absorbed into Buddhist or Daoist sects in the later Ming period.

**First Contact.** Arabic kingdoms became more powerful in the seventh century, and by 713 they posed a threat to both India and Tibet, whose governments asked the Tang court for military aid. Recognizing the gravity of the situation, Tang leaders dispatched an army to Tibet, but it was defeated by the Arab army. The Mohammedan general then sent to China a group of ambassadors, whose approach was so arrogant and aggressive that the emperor met them with every token of favor and sent them back with letters of companionship. This policy, together with internal rebellions within the Muslim empire, saved the Tang empire from attacks by the Arabs.

**Muslims in Tang.** Led by a Tartar chief named An Lushan, an awful rebellion against the Tang dynasty started in 755 in northwestern China. An Lushan, who had been the general in charge of the northwestern frontier, declared his independence and attacked the capital. The emperor called for help from Arab and Uighur armies stationed on the borders of Turkestan. An army of several thousand soldiers came to help the Tang government, defeated the rebellion, and restored the dynasty. Thereafter, many of these soldiers settled near Chang'an and married Chinese women, which resulted in the expansion of the Muslim population. The first mosque was constructed as early as 742, and more were built in the following years. Toward the end of the eighth century, Arab troops again fought alongside Tang armies against Tibet in the southwest; as a result of this activity, many Muslims settled in Yunnan after the campaign.

**Arab Technology.** When Mongol troops invaded countries occupied by Muslims in Central Asia and eastern Europe, many Muslims were slaughtered, but Genghis Khan saved the intellectuals and craftsmen, sending them back to China. Thereafter, many distinguished Muslims served in the Yuan government and its armies. With them they brought Arabic sciences, technology, and other technical skills. Muslims presented Kublai Khan with seven astronomical instruments, and they also impressed him with the skill of manufacturing catapults for military use in siege warfare. In Ming times the first Chinese emperor to retake the throne even ordered Arabic books on science for the Imperial Library and hired scholars to translate them into Chinese. Introduced into China from outside, Islam, though influential in the West, was not an important part of Chinese religious life, affecting only a small fraction of the population.

Sources:

E. R. Hughes and K. Hughes, *Religion in China* (London & New York: Hutchinson's University Library, 1950).

Jonathan N. Lipman, *Familiar Strangers: A History of Muslims in Northwest China* (Seattle: University of Washington Press, 1997).

D. Howard Smith, *Chinese Religions* (New York: Holt, Rinehart & Winston, 1968).

# SIGNIFICANT PEOPLE

## LIU YIN

### 1249-1293
### SCHOLAR AND PHILOSOPHER

**Charmed Start.** Liu Yin's father, who at the age of forty had not yet had an heir by his wife, dreamed that a spirit delivered a baby boy on horseback and then departed with the words, "Raise him well." When his son was born, he named him Yin, "Two-colored Horse." An intelligent child, Liu Yin began his studies at the age of three. Liu Yin's mother died in 1256; his stepmother then took care of him, and he displayed intense filial piety toward her. Liu began a career as a private teacher in 1260 and soon became well known. During this time, Liu Yin made rapid progress in classical studies and literary composition and impressed his father with his abilities.

**Official Service.** In 1275 Liu showed his sympathy for the dilemma faced by the Song dynasty. He proclaimed his support for unity and accepted as inevitable the defeat of the Song. He expressed positive views on Kublai Khan's conquest of the Song and claimed that it was the only way to save China from fragmentation. His praise of Kublai Khan's efforts to reunify China was not unique among northern Chinese intellectuals at that time. In the meantime, Kublai Khan's reunification appeared to have awakened Liu Yin's interest in government service. In 1281 he was recommended to the court, and in 1282 he was called to the capital to serve as grand instructor in the newly established Household Department of the Heir Apparent. Liu Yin served only for a brief period, however, and then became more interested in philosophy than politics. In doing so, he remained faithful to the teachings of Confucius and Mencius, the guiding lights of an ethical philosophy that emphasized devotion to the pursuit of moral improvement. For that reason, Liu was appropriately called a leading representative of Confucian eremitism (living as a religious hermit).

**Developed Views.** Liu's opposition to aspects of Daoist ideas endured for all of his life. His views, as expressed in his 1270 essay, were developed in later writings. Liu's essential position was that Lao Zi's methods of self-preservation must be based on honesty and selflessness. During the decade until his death in 1293, Liu Yin lived in his native province and engaged in teaching and writing. He attracted many students, some of whom later gained distinction as scholars. Liu Yin became famous for his erudition, poetry, and character. One of the leading literati of northern China in early Yuan times, Liu left a considerable amount of prose, poems, and philosophical essays.

**Source:**
Igor de Rachewiltz and others, eds., *In the Service of the Khan: Eminent Personalities of the Early Mongol-Yuan Period (1200–1300)* (Wiesbaden, Germany: Harassowitz, 1993).

## LU JIUYUAN

### 1139-1193
### CONFUCIAN SCHOLAR

**Education.** Born in Jiangxi in 1139, Lu Jiuyuan was taught privately by his father and other tutors. In 1172 he successfully earned the *jinshi* degree and entered the National Academy, situated in Hangzhou, the capital of the Southern Song dynasty (1127–1279). Later he became a recognized instructor at Elephant Mountain in Jiangxi and hence took the name of Xiangshan.

**Official.** As a magistrate at Qingmen in Hubei province, he carried out reforms in the administration of his office. Lu was popular and often gave speeches on civic duty. Although he consecutively held several official positions, he was seemingly more interested in education than in government affairs.

**On Learning.** Lu maintained in the *Total Collections of Lu Xiangshan* that the goal of learning was to clear the mind of all things by which it is blinded, allowing the mind to go back to its initially uncontaminated state. All people, he advised, were responsible for their own beclouded state of mind and had to struggle to clean their vision in order to keep away material desires and self-assertive dogmatism. Reaffirming his dependence on the idea of "principle," he asked people to avoid selfish, sly manipulation to reach the objective of developing a state of fairness.

**On Buddhism.** Claiming that it was impossible to realize the goal of impartiality, Buddhists tried to escape from the world; Confucians regarded life in the world as well worth the attempt to accomplish impartiality. Confessing that evil in man was unavoidable, Lu opposed any theory of original sin and disapproved of the Buddhists. He maintained that when accepting bodily needs, man actually permitted evil to move in quietly, and therefore the Buddhists undercut their own arguments. The entire goal of Confucian teaching was to help men develop their innate ability for thoughtful knowledge.

**On Education.** In his educational philosophy, influenced by Buddhism, Lu jumped the dualistic gap left by Zhu Xi and linked the mind of man with principle, while Zhu Xi asserted that the earthly human mind could be transformed only with prudent encouragement in the spirit. Recognizing that Zhu Xi's structure was too complicated, Lu based his own philosophy on the foundation of universal law, refusing to regard as important any acquisition of truthful information by outside study.

**Conferences.** In 1175 Zhu Xi met with the younger scholar, Lu, but they could not reach any agreement during the conference. In 1181 they met again, and Lu was asked to teach Zhu's students at White Deer Grotto Academy. In 1187 they began their long communication on the "Illustration of the Supreme Ultimate." However, since Lu held on to a monistic, and Zhu to a dualistic, vision of the nature of reality, their discussions could never reach any conformity.

**Differences.** Among the four virtues—humanity, justice, propriety, and wisdom—Lu favored justice, while Zhu concentrated on humanity. Among later philosophers several accepted Lu's model. His followers carried on monistic idealism, regarding Lu's idea of principle as infusing all things at all times and all places. More particularly, Lu had a great impact on the philosopher Wang Yangming.

Sources:

Clarence Burton Day, *The Philosophers of China: Classical and Contemporary* (London: Owen; New York: Philosophical Library, 1962).

E. R. Hughes and K. Hughes, *Religion in China* (London & New York: Hutchinson's University Library, 1950).

D. Howard Smith, *Chinese Religions* (New York: Holt, Rinehart & Winston, 1968).

# MATTEO RICCI

## 1552-1610
### JESUIT MISSIONARY

**Confucian Scholar.** Born at Ancona, Italy, in 1552, Matteo Ricci quickly showed his scholastic aptitude and attractive character. At the age of sixteen he moved to Rome to study law. While there he joined the Society of Jesus in 1570, where he showed a talent for arithmetic and

geography. In 1577 he decided to practice his missionary career in Asia, and he arrived in Goa (on the western coast of India) in 1578. Goa was under Portuguese rule. After finishing his spiritual education he lectured in the college there until 1582, when he was called to Macao to prepare himself to visit China. He studied written and spoken Chinese, and in 1583 he became the first Jesuit to enter into China, near Guangzhou in the South although at first he was regarded as only a guest. He began to study Confucianism, and in 1589 he used a Chinese architectural design to build a church. He adopted the clothing, as well as the behavior and learning, of a Confucian scholar.

**Characteristics.** Ricci was a forceful, energetic person with blue eyes, a booming voice, and a curly beard, which he used to assure the Chinese of his sagacity. The Chinese called him Li Matou. He also impressed the Chinese with his extraordinary knowledge of current Western accomplishments as well as his command of classical Chinese learning. Furthermore, he had an extraordinary, almost photographic, memory and used a variety of mnemonic devices to improve it. This method was a wonderful assistance to an intellectual, particularly for studying the difficult Chinese language. At that time some scholars, who desired to do well in the national examinations or see their sons succeed in the tests, sought out Ricci's assistance, since he got along well with the Chinese. For this reason he was accepted by the Confucian scholars, as he had been at Macao after separating himself totally from the Portuguese dealers. In 1595 he and his missionary fellows were allowed to move north to the Yangzi valley and in 1601 founded their permanent base in Beijing.

**Court.** By the end of the sixteenth century the Emperor Wanli had become useless and was interested only in chasing pleasures; the government was corrupt and crammed with devious groups. The emperor's fancy was caught ultimately by Ricci's gifts—two clocks, a clavichord, and a precursor of the piano. Before performing on these instruments, Ricci composed some enlightening songs for the ruler to sing. Afterward, the emperor employed him at court as an excellent and helpful scholar. Since Ricci was the first Jesuit missionary to enter China and he knew how the hierarchical Chinese society functioned, he focused his attention on the court, avoiding any conversation of Christian theology. To keep from isolating the Chinese and to make it more comprehensible and attractive, he represented Christianity as a scheme of morals comparable to Confucianism. He excluded such potentially offensive elements as the act of crucifixion, the virgin birth, and equal opportunity for all men.

**Evaluation.** Staying away from sermonizing or obvious efforts at evangelization, Ricci and his fellows won few converts, but they claimed that their efforts had laid the groundwork for later conversions. They knew how to make the Chinese accept the less-controversial aspects of Christianity and to pretend to be Confucian scholars. With his sharp mind and vast education Ricci was the perfect man for such a position. His selective description of Christian theology, however, landed Ricci in trouble with Rome, but he argued that his goal was to interest Chinese in the faith. After he died in 1610, his body was buried in Beijing in a special area awarded by the emperor.

**Sources:**

Marcel Granet, *The Religion of the Chinese People,* translated by Maurice Freedman (Oxford: Blackwell, 1975).

Charles O. Hucker, *China's Imperial Past: An Introduction to Chinese History and Culture* (Stanford, Cal.: Stanford University Press, 1975).

D. Howard Smith, *Chinese Religions* (New York: Holt, Rinehart & Winston, 1968).

# WANG YANGMING

## 1472-1529
### PHILOSOPHER

**Early Life.** When Wang Yangming, son of an official in Zhejiang province, was a boy, he became versed in government fields that required great common sense, such as military protection. Like the philosopher Zhu Xi, he was determined to become a sage. At eighteen he met, in Jiangxi province, the famous scholar Lou Liang, who discussed with him the exploration of things. Wang won his *jinshi* degree in 1499. He declared that it was absolutely possible to become a sage through study. Later, after reading the books of Zhu Xi, he gradually believed that, in line with Confucianism, all things—outside or inside, excellent or poor—contained within them the supreme principle. In 1498 he started to learn in a systematic way, but for him, mind and principle remained unconnected. After hearing a Daoist monk's lecture on the principle of nurturing life, he once again gained control of his life.

**Official Career.** Wang soon became one of the best-known statesmen of his times, especially famous for his successful repression of rebels and development of socioeconomic stability. He was a commander in the military and provided logistical management of more than five provinces in southern China. He served with courage and distinction as a civil administrator and as a military officer. Wang had a dynamic career, though it was briefly interrupted when he fell into disfavor at court.

**Exile.** After Wang opposed and offended a disreputable authoritarian eunuch faction, who at that time controlled Emperor Wuzong, he was sent to prison in 1506 for two months. He was later given forty strokes and was finally exiled in shame. He spent three years among the native tribes of Guizhou, then an uncultivated and thinly populated province in the southwest.

**Enlightenment.** He studied the Chen-Zhu doctrines diligently but later realized that his efforts to practice them, by intensely observing a bamboo stem for seven days, not only gave him no insight into the principle of bamboo, but the effort actually made him sick. He studied Buddhism and Daoism too, but he concluded they were as wrong as Zhu Xi's ideas. After meeting with disciples of Chen Xianzhang, who guided him in difficult philosophical directions, including serious consideration of the teachings of Lu Jiuyuan, he finally gained a Chan-style enlightenment. The essential insight came suddenly after a period of intense thought, while Wang was serving his exile. In 1508 Wang realized that mind and universe were united and that all principles, far from being external, were complete within oneself. This realization guided him finally to expound the doctrine that moral virtues, such as humanity, were parts of the instinctive knowledge of the individual mind.

**Philosophy.** The central idea of his philosophy was that moral knowledge was innate. Wang's most famous saying emphasized the organic connection between knowledge and behavior: knowledge was the beginning of conduct, and conduct was the completion of knowledge. The fundamental nature of the mind, according to Wang, was its capacity for love. In its pristine goodness the human mind created a union between heaven and earth, and as a result, the ideal man regarded all things as one and expanded a universal love to all things. This worldwide love was the basis for all existence and all relationships. He was monistic (believing in one principle) in his views. He recognized the reality of external things but highlighted that it was only through consciousness, or reason, that one became aware of things. As a consequence, the mind was the main reality.

**Educator.** The realization of this basic principle directed Wang through the rest of his life. He further crystallized his concepts when in 1514 he began to teach students about the extension of intuitive knowledge. He continued to teach until he died in 1529.

**Contribution.** As a moderate, restrained individualist, Wang was not only a successful and well-liked officer but also an excellent writer. However, his creative philosophy, rather than his beautiful prose, established his name in Chinese history. He standardized the long-ignored ideas of Lu Jiuyuan and expanded them into a self-assured individualism that openly questioned the totalitarianism of the orthodox Chen-Zhu school. Wang exceeded the neo-Confucianism of Zhu Xi in pushing for both a thoughtful and instinctive self-cultivation, an argument much influenced by Buddhism, and an activist moral role in society. Opening up this new intellectual outlook within neo-Confucianism, Wang's ideas were a major part of the lively diversity that typified sixteenth-century life during the Ming period (1368–1644). Esteemed by Confucians in China, Korea, and Japan, Wang's enduring influence addressed some of the lasting concerns of East Asian philosophers and activists.

**Sources:**

Joanna F. Handlin, *Action in Late Ming Thought: The Reorientation of Lu Kun and Other Scholar-Officials* (Berkeley: University of California Press, 1983).

Huang Tsung-hsi, *The Records of Ming Scholars,* translated by Julia Ching and Chaoying Fang (Honolulu: University of Hawaii Press, 1987).

Wang Yang-ming, *The Philosophy of Wang Yang-ming,* translated by Frederick Goodrich Henke (London & Chicago: Open Court, 1916).

# XUAN ZANG

## 596-664
### PILGRIM AND TRANSLATOR

**His Goal.** In the early Tang period (618–907), Xuan Zang, one of the greatest persons in the history of Chinese Buddhism, was the most prominent pilgrim and translator. At the age of thirteen he went into the Buddhist temple, and in 629, provoked by a strong wish to visit the holy places in India, he began a journey that made him famous. When Xuan started out alone across the deserts of Central Asia, he was already one of the authorities on Buddhist beliefs. His goal was to obtain a manuscript of the great treatise on metaphysics titled *Land of the Masters of Yoga* and to expand his understanding so as to be able to solve the inconsistencies among the different philosophical schools of Buddhism.

**Expedition.** After a dangerous trip through the deserts and mountains of Central Asia, during which Xuan Zang several times barely escaped death, he arrived in India in 633. After spending two years in Kashmir he arrived at the holy ground of early Buddhism in Magadha and spent five years learning in the famous Buddhist monastery of Nalanda near Rajagrha (Rajgir). He then traveled around India listening to the most-renowned masters. By that time he had an excellent knowledge of Sanskrit. He spent the next ten years traveling and learning before starting his trip home, again across Central Asia. He had collected much information about the foreign countries he visited and carried home a total of 657 Buddhist texts.

**Return.** In 645 he returned to the Chinese capital, Chang'an, and was welcomed in triumph. Emperor Taizong received the respected monk and tried to convince him to return to lay life and become a foreign policy adviser. Xuan refused the offer. Taizong, however, sponsored the translation of the texts, a project to which the scholarly Xuan committed himself for the rest of his life.

**Translation.** Alongside his pupils Xuan directed the most productive translation teams in Chinese Buddhist history. In eighteen years his team of 185 workers translated about a quarter of the Indian texts—1,338 chapters out of 5,084. Xuan translated at least 75 works himself, which both in style and accuracy are regarded as the first Chinese translations of Sanskrit.

**Achievements.** Xuan was largely concerned with bringing to China the specific form of Buddhism that was developed by Vasubandhu in the fourth century and Dharmapala in the fifth century. Xuan's writings were more Indian than Chinese in spirit and provided an interesting contrast with the more purely Chinese responses to Buddhism. His account of the pilgrimage was one of the most valuable records of India of that time, as well as of the countries located between India and China. From 644 to 648 Xuan translated the great *Summa* of the *Land of the Masters of Yoga.* He introduced the learned and complicated philosophy of the Vijnanavada epistemological school, which argued that the world observed by the senses was a creation of the mind.

**Books.** A year after Xuan's return to China one of his students used Xuan's travel journals to produce a general work on the kingdoms where he had traveled, from Central Asia to the southern Deccan and from the Kabul area to Assam. This book was the *Datang Xiyouji* (The Record on the West in Great Tang). It provided information on the weather, goods, behavior, ways of life, political systems, and history—in addition to the state of Buddhism—in those regions of Asia. The biography of Xuan was finished soon after his death and was rewritten in 688. It focused mainly on a detailed account of his trip, which thereafter provided motivation for the sixteenth-century novel, *Journey to the West* (1592), a major work of the Ming dynasty.

**Significance.** Xuan's influence on his disciples, as well as on Japan, was not limited to the monastic circles. As an extraordinary scholar of India and an exacting philologist, he created a system of tremendously exact regulations for translating. He was the only Chinese scholar successfully to master the enormous field of Buddhist philosophy in all its width and complexity.

Sources:

Jacques Gernet, *Buddhism in Chinese Society: An Economic History from the Fifth to the Tenth Centuries,* translated by Franciscus Verellen (New York: Columbia University Press, 1995).

Peter N. Gregory, *Inquiry into the Origin of Humanity: An Annotated Translation of Tsung-mi's Yüan jen lun with a Modern Commentary* (Honolulu: University of Hawaii Press, 1995).

Gregory, *Tsung-mi and the Sinification of Buddhism* (Princeton: Princeton University Press, 1991).

# DOCUMENTARY SOURCES

Li Zhi, *A Book to Burn* (1590)—Collection of letters, poems, and other writings that advocate that individuals follow their own ideas.

*Poxiechi* (Compilation of Disproved Heresies, 1639)—Early Chinese anti-Christian treatise.

Wang Yangming, *Instructions for Practical Living* (1524)—Idealistic dialogue between teacher and students that promoted the idea that the mind was everything and one should empty it of selfish desires in order to reach a state of nature (principle of heaven). The author argued that knowledge came first, only then to be followed by action.

William of Rubrouck, *Recueil de Voyages et de Mémoires* (circa late thirteenth century)—Account of the Franciscan's 1253–1256 trip to the Mongol empire.

Yi Jing, *Account of Buddhism Dispatched from the South Seas* (692)—A work by this famous pilgrim and translator on Buddhism in India and Southeast Asia.

Yi, *Account of the Distinguished Monks Who Traveled to Look for the Laws in West in Times of Great Tang* (692)—This work focuses on the travels by Chinese pilgrims to several Buddhist countries during the seventh century.

Yuan Liaofan, *Record of Silent Recompense* (1602)—Daoist treatment on the principles of karma, which called for people to be loving and charitable, and which set out a system of merits and demerits for individual acts.

Yuan Shu, *Narratives from the Beginning to End from the Comprehensive Mirror* (circa twelfth century)—A strict chronological presentation, covering Chinese history from the fifth century B.C.E. to the tenth century C.E., based on the work of Sima Guang, which reveals the philosophy of this historian. It is arranged according to major incidents.

Zhang Zai, *Zheng-meng* (Correcting Youthful Ignorance, circa 1070)—Primer for youth that called for individuals to be sincere, show integrity, love everyone, and search for higher understanding of oneself.

Zhu Xi, *Jinsi lu* (Mirror Image of Things at Hand, circa 1176)—Handbook on the principles of the True Way School of Confucianism for beginning students.

Zhu, *The Outline and Details of the Comprehensive Mirror* (circa late twelfth century)—A history of the major events from 403 B.C.E. to 959 C.E., providing much supporting evidence. It stresses the moral judgments and differences between legitimate and false claimants to the mandate of Heaven.

# SCIENCE, TECHNOLOGY, AND HEALTH

by GUANGQIU XU

## CONTENTS

*Sidebars and tables are listed in italics.*

**624**
- The Grand Medical Office, which is one of the earliest known schools for teaching medicine under state supervision, is founded.

**643**
- The famous physician Chen Quan dies. Before his death he uses hormones from the thyroid glands of gelded male sheep as a treatment for goiter and explains the practice in his book, *Experienced Old and New Prescriptions* (seventh century).

**655**
- The physician Sun Simiao publishes his book, *A Thousand Golden Therapies.*

**688**
- A temple, the largest cast-iron building made by the Chinese, is constructed under the order of Empress Wu Zhao.

**695**
- Empress Wu orders the erection of an octagonal cast-iron column known as the Celestial Axis Memorializing the Goodness of the Great Chou Dynasty with its Numberless Areas. This column is 20 feet high and is located on a base 170 feet in perimeter.

**725**
- The Chinese Buddhist monk and mathematician Yixing creates the world's first mechanical water clock.

**800**
- In his book *Miscellany of the Yuyang Mountain Cave,* Duan Chengshi mentions the relationships between the types of plants that grow in some regions and the minerals to be discovered underground at the same locations.

**850**
- *Secret Basics of the Strange Dao of the True Source of Things* is published and preserved in the great collection of Daoist literature. The first textual record of a protogunpowder formula is found in this treatise.

**904**
- Lu Chen mentions the first use of a crude flamethrower in *Historical Record of the Nine Countries.*

**905**
- The "fire-lance," the first protogun, is invented.

**919**
- Gunpowder begins to be used on the battlefield.

* Denotes Circa Date

**954**

- The emperor of the Later Zhou dynasty (951–960) orders the building of the Great Lion of Zangzhou as a memorial to his military victory over the Liao Tartars. This remarkable object is twenty feet high, sixteen feet long, and weighs forty tons. It is the largest single cast-iron object ever made at the time.

**975**

- In *Discussion at Fisherman's Rock,* Shi Xupai notes the use of flamethrowers in a naval battle on the Yangzi (Yangtze) River.

**976**

- Zhang Sixun builds a clock and uses a chain drive for transmission of power. Unlike Yixing's earlier version, Zhang uses mercury because it does not freeze at any temperature.

**1040**

- A gunpowder formula is published for the first time in history.

**1062**

- Su Song publishes his book called *Illustrated Pharmacopoeia,* pointing out that a specific plant of purslane contains sufficient mercury for the metal to be extracted from it by careful squeezing, ventilation, and natural organic decay.

**1067**

- The Song government begins a monopoly of gunpowder production by prohibiting private processing of sulfur or saltpeter and the sale of either item to foreigners.

**1068**

- A crossbow capable of penetrating a large elm tree from a distance of 140 paces is developed.

**1083**

- The Song army has a stockpile of 250,000 gunpowder-armed arrows.

**1086**

- The great scientist Shen Kuo publishes *Dream of Pool Essay.* In this book, Shen discusses the erosion of mountains and lofty peaks and describes sedimentary deposits.

**1090**

- Su Song constructs an astronomical clock with an escapement (a device that controls the motion of the wheelwork), cogs, and a transmission chain called the "celestial ladder." Later, he draws an illustration of the chain drive and prints it in his manuscript *New Design for an Astronomical Clock.* It is the oldest illustration of a continual chain drive for power transmission in the world.

\* DENOTES CIRCA DATE

**1092**
- Su Song builds the largest astronomical clock tower in the world. It is more than thirty feet high and represents one of the greatest mechanical achievements in the world at the time.
- *Archaeological Plates* is published and provides scientific classification and dating of bronze artifacts of the second and first millennia B.C.E.

**1100**
- Mathematician Liu Ruxie publishes "the tabulation structure for unlocking binomial coefficients" (a triangular array of numbers used as an aid in answering mathematical problems) in *Piling-up Powers and Unlocking Coefficients.*

**1137**
- Kang Yuzhi writes *Dreaming of the Good Ancient Times*, which contains an illustration of the storage and use of flammable liquid.

**1150**
- Rockets are invented and begin to be used in warfare.

**1161**
- Thunderclap bombs (paper cartons filled with lime and sulfur) are used for the first time during a sea battle.

**1187**
- Yuan Haowen publishes a book that has a description of a hunter using a thunderclap bomb.

**1231**
- The term *thundercrash bomb* is used by historians when they describe the battles between the Jin armies and the Mongols in Shangsi province. This device is a more powerful version of the thunderclap bomb.

**1233**
- The Jurchens use fire-lances against the Mongols.

**1245**
- Numerical equations of higher degrees than the third, involving powers higher than cubes, appear in *Mathematical Treatise in Nine Sections.*

**1247**
- A symbol for zero appears in Chinese books.

\* Denotes Circa Date

**1270**

- Astronomer Guo Shoujing improves upon the Arab version of the armillary sphere (a device for representing the great circles of the heavens with the horizon, meridian, equator, tropics, polar circles, and an ecliptic hoop).

**1293**

- A Japanese illustration shows a Chinese-style thundercrash bomb in a cast-iron shell exploding in the air.

**1299**

- Over the next four years, Zhu Shijie completes two well-known mathematical books, the *Introduction to Mathematics* and the *Emerald Mirror of the Four Rules*. The rule of signs for plus and minus is discussed completely in these volumes.

**1300**

- A medical encyclopedia is printed and includes commentaries by four famous physicians of internal medicine.

**1305**

- The Imperial School of Medicine is founded.

**1320**

- Daoist and geographer Zhu Siben finishes a massive atlas after spending nine years on it. He draws the maps with a grid system superimposed. The atlas exists in manuscript form for two centuries and is printed in 1555 in the *Enlarged Terrestrial Atlas*.

**1360**

- The flint-and-steel trigger is invented, which is the forebear of the flintlock musket.

**1412**

- *The Fire-Drake Artillery Guidebook* is published and includes detailed information on military weapons.

**1421**

- A book called *Signs of Metals and Minerals* is published, claiming that mineral trace elements can be retrieved from certain plants.

**1506**

- Syphilis, one of the first Western diseases to reach China, begins to appear. Since the first cases occur in Guangdong province, it is called "boils of Guangdong" or "plum boils." Present-day medical experts theorize that Portuguese merchants brought it into the area.

**1564**

- An epidemic of cholera erupts and kills an estimated ten million Chinese over the course of the next few years.

* Denotes Circa Date

**1578**
- Li Shizhen finishes the *Compendium of Materia Medica*. Its fifty-two chapters detail the medical uses of more than two thousand plants and animals. The manuscript is printed for the first time in 1593; a Japanese edition with color plates appears three years later.

**1596**
- *The Great Pharmacopoeia* is published. It holds that the thyroid glands of different kinds of animals have the same function in treatment for goiter in human beings.
- Li Shizhen correctly distinguishes glowworms, whose glowing tails are able to be seen at night over long distances, from fireflies and other evidently luminous insects, such as mayflies or midges infected with luminous bacteria.

**1601**
- An encyclopedia of acupuncture, written in short lines of rhythmic verse, is published.

**1622**
- An anthology of Daoist works divides the human body into three anatomical areas and regards unawareness and greed as the primary causes of physical sickness and mental pain.

**1643**
- Yu Chang finishes writing *Various Thoughts in Medicine*, which discusses traditional Chinese smallpox inoculation.

**\* DENOTES CIRCA DATE**

沉鉛結銀圖

Drawing of laborers refining silver, from *The Exploitation of the Works of Nature*, 1637 (Colin Ronan, *The Cambridge Illustrated History of the World's Science*, 1983)

# OVERVIEW

**Tang and Song Dynasties.** There were more scientific and technological achievements in the Song dynasty (960–1279) than in the Tang dynasty (618–907) because the two dynasties had completely different environments. The Tang period was humanistic while the Song era was much more scientific and technological. During the Song dynasty the pure sciences began to appear. Improvements in hydraulic engineering occurred, including the caisson, used either as an underwater foundation or as a floodgate. Shipbuilding technology was improved greatly when the sternpost rudder became common, and seagoing junks of substantial size were built. Chemical science, practiced in the little-known laboratories of Daoist shrines in Tang times, was applied to devastating effect on the battlefield when armies began to use gunpowder. The biological sciences thrived too and were applied for the benefit of society. Also, well-known physicians appeared in Song times, and many books on pharmaceutical botany and zoology were published.

**Yuan and Ming Dynasties.** Science and technology did not decline in the Yuan dynasty (1279–1368) because the Mongols greatly respected Chinese craftsmen and technicians. Technical books, which appeared before the collapse of the Ming dynasty (1368–1644), indicated obvious improvements made in textiles (cotton looms and silk looms with three shuttle winders), publishing (wooden blocks in five colors and a new alloy of copper and lead for casting movable characters), and food preparation (the refining of white sugar). In agriculture, books on farming techniques illustrated new equipment for cultivating soil, sowing seed, irrigating lands, and selecting good strains of crops.

**Agricultural Science.** Chinese agriculture depended on fertile lands located along the two major rivers, the Yellow and Yangzi (Yangtze). Struggling to raise enough food for a growing population, Chinese peasants practiced a cereal agriculture, rather than a combination of pastoral and arable methods used by Europeans. The intensive cultivation employed by the Chinese was more like gardening than farming. By the sixth century Chinese peasants had clearly identified the value of crop rotation. They used fertilizers, such as mud unearthed from the canals of the Yangzi, in addition to applying animal and human manure. During the Song dynasty peasants began to develop land reclamation procedures. Terraced mountain regions became a well-established feature in China. In addition to these terraced fields, lakes were drained and transformed into fields that were protected by earthen walls to keep out water. Chinese peasants even created floating fields on bamboo rafts that were covered with water weeds and earth. Therefore, after the eleventh century, intensive cultivation expanded when land reclamation expanded areas available for farming. In addition, the Chinese had produced many agricultural implements by the Tang dynasty, including the mould-board plough, which could invert the soil. There were also a variety of harrows, rollers, and the seed-drill plough. Thirteenth-century Chinese peasants used the rotary winnowing fan extensively, while European farmers were not aware of it until the eighteenth century.

**Botany.** The Chinese, like the Greeks, were interested in learning about and illustrating plants. They continually developed their botanical studies from the first century B.C.E. until the Ming dynasty. Botany was promoted because there were many kinds of plants in China, far more varieties than were found in Europe. In addition, the imperial government facilitated botanical studies. In Ming times, for example, the Chinese were interested in discovering plants that could be eaten in times of food shortages. Scholars created encyclopedic masterpieces of applied botany, listing and describing wild (emergency) food plants. The greatest botanist was Li Shizhen, who in 1583 finished writing a huge pharmaceutical natural history. Developing a predecessor of the modern international nomenclature system, Li Shizhen presented facts critically and chose a preferred name for each plant; he also included common names for the plants. He established both natural and pharmaceutical classifications of plants. By the Ming period many monographs and tracts on particular species or genera had been published, especially on such useful plants as the orange and such ornamental plants as the chrysanthemum, peony, and rose. These plants were grown in Chinese gardens at that time and were introduced into Europe thereafter.

**Earth Sciences.** The original Chinese concepts about the creation of minerals within the earth seem to be close to ideas formulated by the Greeks; it is likely that both civilizations based their understanding of mineralogy on earlier sources written by the Babylonians and Egyptians. In the eleventh century the Song people paid great attention to geological symbols that indicated the presence of ore beds and to the kinds of plants that grew in close proximity to specific mineral deposits. Herein the Chinese were the first people to employ geological and geobotanical prospecting, which began to appear in Europe only in the eighteenth century. By the twelfth century the Chinese used many specific minerals—particularly alum, ammonium chloride, asbestos, borax—and a variety of valuable stones, such as jade. Since China experienced much seismic activity, the Chinese kept extensive reports of earthquakes. By 1644 Chinese observers had recorded 908 shocks, for which there were precise dates, and records indicated that there were twelve peaks of frequency between 479 and 1644. Chinese theories explaining the cause of earthquakes focused on the escape of *qi* (gas) from below ground, a concept similar to Greek philosophy that explained the escape of vapor.

**Mathematics.** Chinese mathematical thought was fundamentally algebraic. The Chinese thought in terms of general relationships between quantities, unlike the Greeks, whose viewpoint was essentially geometric. During the Song dynasty the trend by Chinese mathematicians to think in algebraic patterns contributed to the use of a matrix, or square of compartments, filled by equations. Several such matrix boards could be used at the same time to solve equations, and the method was an enormous success. Song algebraists discovered the Binomial Theorem, which specified the expansion of a binomial to any power without requiring the explicit multiplication of binomial terms. European algebraists had not identified this theorem until the seventeenth century. In the centuries following the Song period, however, Chinese algebraists added little knowledge to the theory of equations. The Chinese seemed to have received scant mathematical inspiration from Mesopotamia or Egypt, but their mathematical ideas—which appear to have been transmitted from China to the south and to the west—included such concepts as the extraction of square and cube roots, fractions expressed in a vertical column, the employment of negative numbers, an independent verification of Pythagoras's theorem, and the fundamentals of coordinate geometry. Chinese mathematics was hence equal to pre-Renaissance European achievements.

**Astronomy.** Since the mainly agricultural people in imperial China required good information for planting and harvesting—and the Chinese emperors needed a reliable calendar—astronomy and calendrical science came to be the realm of government control. Astronomers were appointed as government officials. Chinese scholars established the oldest continuous series of astronomical observations of any civilization in the world. Astronomy in imperial China was founded on a structure dissimilar to that employed in Europe. The Europeans calculated celestial positions by observing ecliptic orbits and chiefly the constellations of the Zodiac, while the Chinese paid attention to the celestial pole and the celestial equator. In the eighth century the Chinese invented the first escapements (a device that controls the movement of gears) so that they could use clocks to compare the motions of the heavens, which helped them to detect quickly any discrepancies. Westerners did not create automatically driven observation instruments until the eighteenth century. Chinese interest in equatorial coordinates also contributed to the creation of a sort of dissected armillary sphere, an instrument that made positional observation of all celestial bodies significantly easier. This distinguished accomplishment enabled an observer to follow the path of a celestial body across the sky in one unbroken movement, rather than the two that were previously necessary. The Europeans did not introduce the equatorial mounting of telescopes until five hundred years later. By the thirteenth century the Chinese had embraced the Arabic-Indian procedure of constructing big stone instruments to observe solar shadows and make other measurements. Other instruments were invented, such as the clepsydra (water clock), in which water flow was thoroughly controlled either by using a series of water tanks or by fitting an overflow (constant-level) tank, or by both. The most significant of all Chinese inventions in physics was the magnetic compass; the Chinese discovered, between the first and sixth centuries, that the directive properties of the lodestone could be induced in small pieces of iron that were floated on water. In the Tang dynasty pivoted needles were introduced to provide more-accurate readings. During that time the Chinese also discovered magnetic declination and understood that the needle did not accurately show an astronomical-geographical north-south. The Chinese were concerned with the cause of declination long before Westerners were aware of polarity. The Chinese used the magnetic compass to measure the layout of sites long before employing it in navigation; the first magnetic compasses were used aboard Chinese ships between 1111 and 1117, while the Europeans adopted their use one hundred years later.

**Gunpowder.** Alchemy was chiefly studied by the Daoists, who carried out experiments on applied chemical and physical procedures in their pursuit of material immortality. Their experiments, however, brought them significant discoveries of quite a different kind. In Tang times alchemists learned to distill alcohol, a procedure that required a still with a cooling system to condense the distillate in order that the alcohol would not be lost. In the eighth century Chinese alchemists were familiar with the salts of alkaline metals and were able to separate them out. They identified saltpeter—potassium nitrate—and thereafter invented gunpowder, a mixture of saltpeter, charcoal, and sulfur. The Chinese did not use gunpowder in military campaigns until the tenth century, when it became prevalent during the Song dynasty. The use of gunpowder then began to spread to Arabs in the thirteenth century and finally to Europeans in the fourteenth century. Every phase in the growth of firearms development, from the gunpowder formula to the propellant metal-barrel cannon first used by the Europeans in 1327, can be identified as being discovered and initially used in China.

**Shipbuilding.** The Chinese were interested in ship-building because of two large waterways, the Yellow and Yangzi Rivers, and almost four thousand miles of coastline. By the Song dynasty the Chinese had invented junks, which had a flat or slightly curved bottom without a keel, and sides of planking that curved upwards in a design similar to half of a hollow cylinder. A junk had a square-ended bow and stern, without stempost or sternpost, and solid partitions without skeletal ribs. This unique construction not only produced great strength but also gave the vessel watertight compartments. By the sixteenth century the Chinese had designed another amazing vessel—the articulated junk, which was a long, narrow barge of shallow drought—that was built from two separable parts. Without difficulty the two halves could negotiate shallow, winding channels that were silting up. A longer vessel had to await a rising water level; the articulated junk, however, worked well on the Grand Canal.

**Mechanical Clock.** The clock is the oldest and most significant of complex scientific machines. In the eighth century the Chinese invented a device showing astronomical phenomena six hundred years before the Europeans did so. In 1080 the great scientist Su Song invented the astronomical clock tower, the basic drive of which was a water-wheel with scoops or buckets on its rim that were filled with water coming from a constant-level tank; an arrangement of linked works operated each time a full bucket was brought into place. This device—the first escapement—was really the core of mechanical timekeeping. Westerners were able to increase the accuracy of mechanical clocks in the fourteenth century, chiefly by refining the escapement mechanism and increasing the precision of the short intervals that measured time.

# TOPICS IN SCIENCE, TECHNOLOGY, AND HEALTH

### DISEASES AND IMMUNOLOGY

**Crossroads.** China was always exposed to epidemic diseases. Trade along the old silk route, war with the northern barbarians, and travel to and from India and Indochina all helped the spread of smallpox, pulmonary diseases, febrile illnesses, dysentery, and plague. With the emergence of European traders to China's southeast coast and the increase of international commercial activities in Southeast Asia during the sixteenth century, new epidemic illnesses, such as scarlet fever, cholera, diphtheria, and syphilis, appeared in the region.

**Malaria.** The mention of malarial fevers initially appeared in medical texts in the seventh century. Temperatures during the Tang period (618–907) were most likely higher than those of today, which meant that the diseases associated with the southern climates, such as malaria, schistosomiasis, and dengue fever, could be found further north. Some specialized treatises in the twelfth century suggested that the miasma of certain regions caused malaria.

**Bubonic Plague.** The history of bubonic plague in China is a controversial subject. Some scholars believe that it arrived in China in the early 600s, while others suggest the first appearance was in the 1130s in Guangzhou. (It is known that plague epidemics swept through the Roman Empire and present-day Iraq and Iran from the mid sixth century to the late eighth century.) Both of these views are based at least in part on simple descriptions of symptoms, such as congestion of the throat, chills, fever, vomiting, diarrhea, and buboes. A devastating epidemic occurred in China in the early thirteenth century, and it might have been related to the European Black Death at that time.

**Smallpox.** The first treatises on smallpox appeared in the late eleventh century. Qian Yi, an eleventh-century pediatrician, was among the first to identify smallpox, as well as chicken pox, measles, and scarlet fever. Pediatricians suggested that by that time smallpox had developed into a childhood illness among the Chinese population. The technique of variolation (inoculation with the small-pox virus) using human pox was first practiced in the lower Yangzi (Yangtze) region by the second half of the sixteenth century. Despite the early practice of variolation, smallpox was widespread in China, especially in the North.

**Inoculation.** The origins of inoculation against small-pox in China are rather mysterious. Daoist alchemists

Painting of a scholar boiling herbs for medicinal use, Ming dynasty, 1368–1644 (National Palace Museum, Taipei, Taiwan)

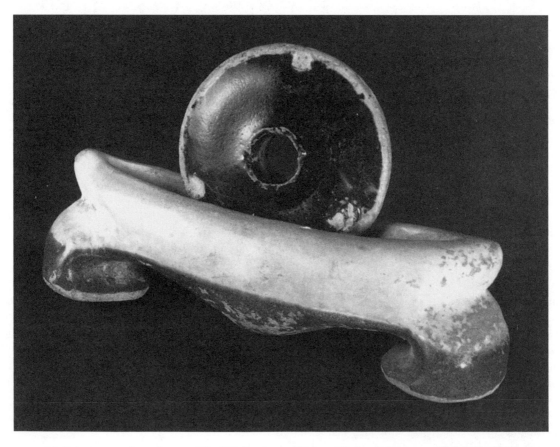

Medicine mortar, Song dynasty, 960–1279 (Institute of Cultural Relics, Shijiazhuang, Hebei Province)

who lived as hermits in caves possessed the secret of smallpox inoculation in the tenth century. They evidently first brought the technique to public attention after the eldest son of Prime Minister Wang Tan died of smallpox. Wang badly desired to prevent this disease from infecting any other members of his family, so he convened a meeting of physicians, wise men, and magicians from throughout the empire, and it was then that he stumbled upon the treatment.

**Delicate Process.** Chinese inoculators practiced various methods so that the chances of obtaining the full-blown disease were reduced while the chances of immunity were raised. The primary procedure used was to put the pox material on a plug of cotton, which was then inserted into the person's nose. The pox was therefore absorbed, by breathing, through the mucous membrane. Inoculators usually chose pox material from the scabs of someone who had been inoculated previously.

**Contribution.** Traditional Chinese smallpox inoculation was relatively safe, but it did not become widely known and practiced until the period 1567–1572, as indicated by the author Yu Chang in his book *Various Thoughts in Medicine*, published in 1643. During the seventeenth century the Chinese practice of inoculation spread to the Turkish regions and later to Europe.

Sources:

Edward H. Hume, *The Chinese Way in Medicine* (Baltimore: Johns Hopkins University Press, 1940).

Kenneth F. Kiple, ed., *The Cambridge World History of Human Disease* (Cambridge & New York: Cambridge University Press, 1993).

Walther Riese, *The Concept of Disease: Its History, Its Versions, and Its Nature* (New York: Philosophical Library, 1953).

Henry E. Sigerist, *Civilization and Disease* (Ithaca, N.Y.: Cornell University Press, 1943).

## DOMESTIC AND INDUSTRIAL TECHNOLOGY

**Cast Iron.** The Chinese used blast furnaces for making cast iron as early as the fourth century B.C.E. The largest cast-iron building was a temple constructed in 688. Ordered by Empress Wu Zhao, this 284-foot-high building was in the form of a 3-story pagoda (300 square feet), and a 10-foot cast-iron phoenix covered in gold plate was on the top of the building. In 695 Empress Wu ordered the erection of an octagonal cast-iron column known as the "Celestial Axis Memorializing the Goodness of the Great Chou Dynasty with its Numberless Areas." This 20-foot-high column was on a base of cast iron 170 feet in circumference. In 954 the emperor of the Later Zhou Dynasty (951–960) ordered the building of the Great Lion of Zangzhou as a memorial of his military victory over the Liao Tartars. This remarkable object was 20 feet high, 16 feet long, and weighed 40 tons. It was not solid; its walls varied from 2 inches to 8 inches in thickness. This enormous object was made four hundred years before any cast iron was made in Europe, and it was the largest single cast-iron object ever constructed at that time.

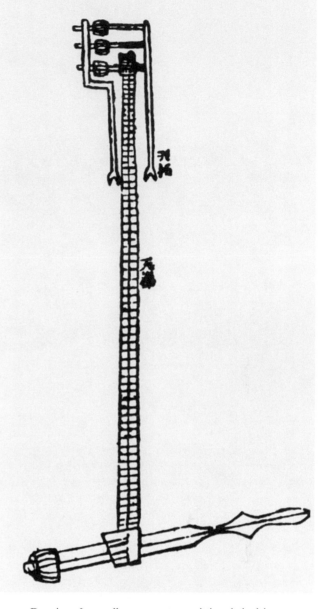

Drawing of an endless power-transmitting chain drive, from Su Song's *New Design for an Astronomical Clock,* 1094 (from Robert Temple, *The Genius of China,* 1986)

**Chain Drive.** Square-pallet chain pumps were extant in China since the first century C.E. Influenced by the sprockets of common chain pumps, the inventor Zhang Sixun saw the possibilities of replicating a similar design in order to solve the problem of transmitting power in a clock. In 976 he invented the chain drive to solve this problem, and by the tenth century hundreds of thousands of them were in use throughout the empire. In 1090 Zhang's better-known successor, the great inventor Su Song, attempted to build a gigantic astronomical clock tower, using a main vertical transmission shaft, but failed. As a result, he installed in it the chain drive, which he named "celestial ladder." Later, Su Song drew an illustration of this chain drive

Yuan observation tower that once had a gnomon twelve meters tall and was used to measure the shadow of the Sun

and printed it in his manuscript *New Design for an Astronomical Clock*. (It is the oldest illustration in the world of a continual chain drive for power transmission.) Eventually a shorter and tighter chain drive was installed in the clock as a means of removing any slack in the links. The Europeans did not make a real chain drive until Jacques de Vaucanson produced one in 1770 for silk reeling and throwing mills.

**Buoyancy Techniques.** By the eleventh century the Chinese had developed a technique for recovering weighty items from a river or seabed. Between 1064 and 1067 the renowned pontoon bridge near Puzhou over the great Yellow River was smashed by an unexpected flood. This bridge, which had been built three centuries earlier, was a major crossing of the river. It was composed of floating boats firmly connected together by a huge wrought-iron chain. The ends of the chain were fastened to eight gigantic cast-iron figures in the shape of recumbent oxen put in the sandy beaches on the two banks. When the flood carried away the bridge, the iron oxen were dragged into the river and sank deep underwater. Distressed local administrators made an announcement to solicit suggestions for recovering the iron oxen. A monk, Huaiping, answered this call. Directed by Huaiping, workers loaded two big boats with soil, and divers fastened cables from them to the oxen in the riverbed. Soil was slowly unloaded from the boats, which caused them to rise higher and higher in the water. As a result, buoyancy was created and raised the oxen from the riverbed. Workers then hauled the iron oxen by sailing boats into shallower water toward the shore. This event represents the first recorded attempt in world history to employ buoyancy techniques successfully in an underwater salvage operation.

**Astronomical Clock.** The Chinese Buddhist monk and mathematician Yixing created the world's first mechanical clock, which was in fact an astronomical instrument. Completed in 725, the clock was known for its accuracy and was placed in the palace where many officials observed it. In 730 candidates in the imperial examination were required to write an essay on the new astronomical clock. Yixing's machine was, like water clocks, subject to changes of climate. For example, cold temperatures could freeze the water inside such clocks, and attendants had to keep them warm by placing lit torches nearby. Since mercury does not freeze at any temperature, Zhang Sixun used it instead when he built another clock in 976. Representing a substantial amplification and enhancement of Yixing's device, Zhang's clock was much larger and more complicated.

**Su Song.** Su Song built the largest clock in the world in 1092. It is known in significant detail because his book, *New Device for a Mechanical Armillary Sphere and Celestial World*, has been preserved. Like the earlier clock by Zhang, Su Song's device was actually an astronomical clock tower more than thirty feet high. On top of the tower was an enormous bronze astronomical apparatus, with which people could watch the location of stars. A celestial globe within the tower turned in harmonization with this sphere above so the two could continually be contrasted. On the front of the tower was a pagoda

Model of Su Song's astronomical clock of 1092 (Science Museum, London)

**Blue-and-White Ware.** The attainment of certain colors and effects in porcelain was the consequence of complicated and clever control of the firing conditions of the kilns. Porcelain could be produced either in oxidizing or deoxidizing fires. A variety of metals, used as coloring agents, spread themselves chemically throughout the bodies of the porcelain objects in fairly different ways, relying on whether oxygen was being absorbed or emitted. When the blaze was reduced, it caused porcelain to emit oxygen, contributing to some of the most beautiful effects. In the Ming era (1368–1644) the Chinese learned how to manufacture the famous blue-and-white ware. As gifts for kings and queens porcelain objects were not popular in Europe until the fifteenth century, and Europeans did not produce porcelain themselves until three hundred years later.

**Economic Lamp.** By the fifth century B.C.E. the Chinese frequently used long-lasting asbestos wicks for lamps. The oil-and-wick lamp was actually a cup full of oil with a wick sticking out of it. However, the lamp had one major problem: the heat of the burning wick made much of the oil evaporate before it could be productively burnt. To save oil, the Chinese devised a method by the ninth century to cool the lamp in an effort to prevent evaporation. They invented the economic lamp, which had a reservoir of cold water below the oil and could save one-half the oil used. The economic lamp, normally made of glazed earthenware, was illustrated in Lu Yu's book *Comments from the Hall of Learned Old Era* (1190).

**Spinning Wheel.** The spinning wheel had its origins in China. The Chinese invented the quilling machine in the first century B.C.E. in order to process cotton fibers. Domestication of the silkworm and development of the

structure of five stories, each having a door through which figures of servants rang chimes and gongs and grasped tablets to show the hours and other special times of the day and night. All of these time indicators were maneuvered by the same huge clock mechanism that concurrently moved the sphere and the globe. Europeans did not develop a similar mechanical clock until the fourteenth century.

**Porcelain.** A hard, white, translucent ceramic, porcelain is made by firing pure clay and glazing with variously colored fusible materials. It is burned at a high temperature of 1,300 degrees. (Earthenware or common pottery is made from clay heated in a furnace at temperatures between 500 and 1,000 degrees.) The Chinese invented porcelain as early as the third century; by the tenth century it had reached high levels of artistry. Porcelain production was an extremely well-organized enterprise employing hundreds of thousands of people. While some workers specialized in cleaning the clay, others did the glazes. Large ovens could handle 25,000 pieces of porcelain at a single firing. The typical kiln was constructed on the slope of a hill, and the mild incline of about 15 degrees could help to decrease the speed of flames and thus control the firing. Some kilns were fired with either wood or charcoal. Chimneys were obviously used, along with sophisticated layers of insulation, buttresses, and clay linings.

---

### MECHANICAL CLOCK

The first mechanical clock in the world was built by the Buddhist monk and mathematician Yixing in 725. A contemporary text described it as follows:

[It] was made in the image of the round heavens and on it were shown the lunar mansions in their order, the equator and degrees of the heavenly circumference. Water, following into scoops, turned a wheel automatically, rotating it one complete revolution in one day and night [24 hours]. Besides this, there were two rings fitted around the celestial sphere outside, having the sun and moon threaded on them, and these were made to move in circling orbit. Each day as the celestial sphere turned one revolution westwards, the sun made its way one degree eastwards, and the moon 13 7/19 degrees eastwards. After 29 rotations and a fraction of a rotation of the celestial sphere, the sun and moon met. After it made 365 rotations the sun accomplished its complete circuit.

**Source:** Robert Temple, *The Genius of China: 3,000 Years of Science, Discovery, and Invention* (New York: Simon & Schuster, 1986).

---

silk industry in China had taken place by the fourteenth century. The inherent strength of silk made it stronger than any other plant fiber known at the time, and from the beginning there was an urgent need for silk-winding machines to deal with the enormously long fibers. (A single continuous strand of silk could run up to several hundred yards and had a tensile strength of 65,000 pounds per square inch.) Spinning wheels began to appear in China by the eleventh century, and these machines were first illustrated in the book *Pictures of Tilling and Weaving* (1237).

Sources:

Derk Bodde, *Chinese Thought, Society, and Science: The Intellectual and Social Background of Science and Technology in Pre-Modern China* (Honolulu: University of Hawaii Press, 1991).

E-tun Sun and Shiou-chuan Sun, trans., *Tien-kung k'ai-wu: Chinese Technology in the Seventeenth Century* (University Park: Pennsylvania State University Press, 1966).

Robert Temple, *The Genius of China: 3,000 Years of Science, Discovery, and Invention* (New York: Simon & Schuster, 1986).

## GUNPOWDER

**Overview.** Europe did not learn of gunpowder until the late twelfth century. By that time, the Chinese had perfected the "barrel gun" and the cannon. However, it was not invented by people looking for better weapons or even explosives, but by alchemists in search of the elixir of immortality.

**Saltpeter.** Gunpowder has three main ingredients: saltpeter or potassium nitrate, sulfur, and charcoal. Long before saltpeter could be used as a component of explosives, it was used for its capability to turn ores into liquid and to dissolve other indissoluble minerals, such as cinnabar, into water solutions. Saltpeter was used for this purpose at least by the second century B.C.E., as well as for a flux to help metallurgical processes. The potassium flame test is crucial for detecting saltpeter, which burns with a violet or purple flame. This test for true saltpeter was used in China by at least the third century C.E., and the test was carried out by putting a sample of the saltpeter on a piece of charcoal and watching it burn. Sheng Xuanzi, in his book *Illustrated Handbook on the Control of Mercury* (1150), described the details of this kind of procedure.

**Sulfur.** The Chinese had the ability to purify sulfur by the second century C.E. By the eleventh century the Chinese had identified the method of obtaining pure sulfur by roasting iron pyrites piled up with coal briquettes in an earthen furnace. In 1067 the Song emperor issued an edict prohibiting the sale to foreigners of either sulfur or saltpeter and the private production of both commodities altogether. Large private enterprises in those commodities were thus forced to close their business, and the government established a monopoly.

Cast-iron Chinese cannon, fourteenth century

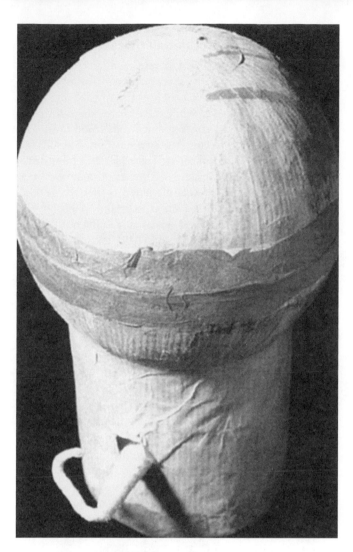
Chinese bomb with a fuse, early seventeenth century. This type of bomb was fired into the clouds in an attempt to start rain (Ontario Science Center, Toronto).

**Three Formulas.** It was not until the year 1040 that an actual gunpowder formula was published for the first time. Certainly, true gunpowder and its uses had been known by this time for at least 100 years. Three gunpowder formulas were identified for three different weapons: a quasi-explosive bomb to be thrown by a kind of catapult; a burning bomb with hooks which could catch on to wooden structures and set them on fire; and a poison-smoke ball for chemical warfare. The gunpowder in these weapons was not explosive but burned with a sudden and sparkling combustion, creating a noise like a rocket. The bomb did not yet hold enough saltpeter to explode.

**Small Explosion.** In the gunpowder mixture, whatever the proportions, it is the sulfur that reduces the ignition heat to 250°C and, on combustion, raises the heat to the fusion point of saltpeter (335°C). It also helps to increase the speed of combustion, but the explosive element in gunpowder is saltpeter, which burns at different rates even on its own. Gunpowder burns by taking oxygen from the saltpeter within it. The more saltpeter in the gunpowder, the more explosive it becomes. In the eleventh century Chinese gunpowder tended to hold about 50 percent saltpeter, and therefore was not really explosive. For a big explosion about 75 percent saltpeter is needed. The Chinese were slowly making progress toward this stronger proportion, which would eventually enable them to produce bombs, grenades, and mines in the following centuries.

Sources:

Brian Hook, ed., *The Cambridge Encyclopedia of China* (Cambridge: Cambridge University Press, 1982).

Denis Twitchett and John Fairbank, eds., *The Cambridge History of China* (Cambridge: Cambridge University Press, 1978–1995).

David C. Wright, *The History of China* (London and Westport, Conn.: Greenwood Press, 2001).

## MATHEMATICS

**Overview.** There were great achievements in Chinese mathematics in the Song dynasty (960–1279) and Yuan dynasty (1279–1368). The great mathematicians Shao Yong, Li Zhi, and Qin Jiushao made remarkable strides in the development of algebra. Qin was the first Chinese mathematician to use zero; at the same time the Italians began to use it as an Arabic numeral. Another famous mathematician, Zhu Shijie, completed two well-known books in 1299 and 1303, the *Introduction to Mathematics* and the *Emerald Mirror of the Four Rules,* respectively.

**Blank Space.** Zero is fundamental to effective mathematical operations, and its discovery was of the greatest significance. The traditional story of the invention of the sign *0* for zero is that the Indians created it in the ninth century. As early as the fourth century B.C.E., the Chinese invented the use of a blank space for zero. For example, the number "302" would be written as 3 blank 2, or three hundreds, no tens, two units. After almost 1,000 years the Chinese still did not have an actual sign for zero. On the accounting board, the blank space was entirely sufficient because the Chinese were used to solving problems without signs and calculations in mathematical treatises. When this process finally was seen to be inadequate, it is likely that the zero sign was developed as a circle drawn

**Mixture.** With saltpeter, sulfur, the readily available charcoal, and other substances, it was inevitable that alchemists would eventually put these things together and invent gunpowder. By the mid seventh century Chinese alchemists made some preparations, which included sulfur and saltpeter, but they were not flammable. By the beginning of the ninth century the Chinese had identified the method of subduing alum by fire through the mixture of two ounces of sulfur, two ounces of saltpeter, and one ounce of dried birthwort herb, which would contain sufficient carbon to make this mixture ignite suddenly and burst into flames, though it would not actually explode.

**Protogunpowder.** The first textual record of a protogunpowder formula is found in a book titled *Secret Basics of the Strange Dao of the True Source of Things,* published in 850 and preserved in the great collection of Daoist literature. The book included thirty-five dangerous elixir formulas, three of which involved saltpeter. Therefore, by 850 Chinese alchemists had created a formula that can be genuinely described as a gunpowder mixture.

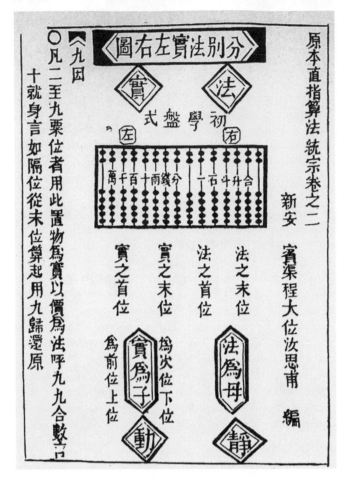

Ink drawing of an abacus, 1593 (Arnold Toynbee, *Half the World*, 1973)

The first actual solutions of cubic equations were not found in Europe until the thirteenth century.

**Negative Numbers.** The Chinese recognized and used negative numbers as early as the second century B.C.E. They occurred frequently on the counting board and were represented by black rods, while the red rods stood for positive numbers. Also, square-sectioned rods stood for negative numbers, while triangular-sectioned ones stood for positive numbers. The rule of signs for plus and minus was partly mentioned in a Chinese mathematical treatise of the first century C.E., but it was discussed completely in the book *Introduction to Mathematical Learning*, published in 1299. Negative numbers were not used in India until 630.

**Old System.** In the seventeenth century the French scientist and philosopher Blaise Pascal used his name to identify the following triangular array of numbers, beginning:

$$1\ 1$$
$$1\ 2\ 1$$
$$1\ 3\ 3\ 1$$
$$1\ 4\ 6\ 4\ 1$$
$$1\ 5\ 10\ 10\ 5\ 1$$
$$1\ 6\ 15\ 20\ 15\ 6\ 1$$
$$1\ 7\ 21\ 35\ 35\ 21\ 7\ 1$$

Every number in the triangle is equal to the total of the two numbers above it. From this triangle many mathematical relationships can be derived, including prime numbers; it

around the blank space. By 1247 the sign of zero had appeared in Chinese books, and an actual symbol for zero was written in the blank space.

**Roots and Equations.** In the first century the Chinese mathematical classic, *Nine Chapters on the Arithmetical Skills*, was published. One of the algebraic problems given in this book was to find the cube root of the number 1,860,867. (The answer is 123.) Mathematician Wang Xiaotong in the seventh century was the first to find the actual solution of the cubic equations. Numerical equations of higher degrees than the third, involving powers higher than cubes, began to appear when the book *Mathematical Treatise in Nine Sections* was published in 1245, including equations involving a higher power, such as:

$$-x^4 + 763,200x^2 - 40,642,560,000 = 0$$

The Chinese did not write such equation in signs but spelled them out. They were, however, proper equations. In two books published in 1248 and 1259 equations appeared as follows:

$$ax^6 + bx^5 + cx^4 + dx^3 + ex^2 + fx + g = 0$$

AND

$$-ax^6 - bx^5 - cx^4 - dx^3 - ex^2 - fx - g = 0$$

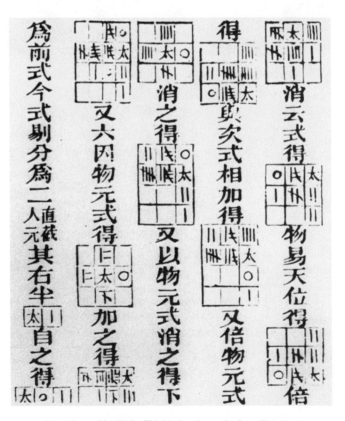

Page from Chu Shih-Chieh's book on algebra, *Precious Mirror of the Four Elements* (1303), showing both zero and negative terms (from George Beshore, *Science in Ancient China*, 1988)

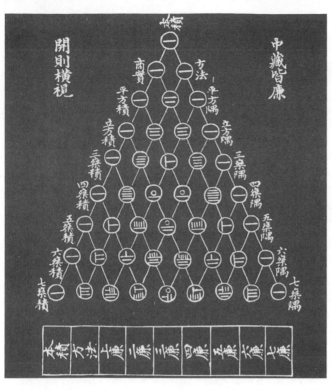

"Pascal's Triangle" as depicted by Chu Shih-Chieh in
*Precious Mirror of the Four Elements,* 1303 (from
Colin Ronan, *The Cambridge Illustrated
History of the World's Science,* 1983)

is a magnificent time-saver and one of the major contributions to mathematic operations. Although it is called "Pascal's Triangle," it was not invented by Pascal, who simply put it in a new style in 1654. The Chinese actually invented this triangle in 1100 and called it "the tabulation structure for unlocking binomial coefficients." It first appeared in a book titled *Piling-up Powers and Unlocking Coefficients,* published by mathematician Liu Ruxie. In 1303 this triangle was included in *Precious Mirror of the Four Elements,* and the caption called it the "Old System."

Sources:

Patricia B. Ebrey, ed., *Chinese Civilization and Society: A Sourcebook,* second revised edition (New York: Free Press, 1993).

F. W. Mote, *Imperial China, 900–1800* (Cambridge, Mass.: Harvard University Press, 1999).

Joseph Needham, *Science and Civilization in China,* 7 volumes (Cambridge: Cambridge University Press, 1954–present).

## MEDICINE AND HEALTH

**Characteristics.** Chinese medicine from the seventh century to the seventeenth century provided many diagnostic and prognostic options, therapeutic alternatives for most health problems, and a rational philosophical basis that could be applied to psychological illnesses. It also strongly stressed public health measures. More important, centralization and bureaucratization resulted in open access to the system for both rich and poor. The greatest weakness of Chinese medicine during this time was limited improvement in surgical procedures.

**Developments.** From 618 to 741 the relative stability of the Tang dynasty (618–907) contributed to major achievements being made in the field of medicine. Under the Song dynasty (960–1279), a new intellectual climate transformed the conceptual framework of medicine. Two significant changes occurred. First, specialized fields developed along with a trend toward prominent reductionism in concept of the cause, nature, and treatment of illness. Second, intensive research in practical drug therapy occurred.

**Official Control.** The Grand Medical Office (founded in 624) of the early Tang dynasty represented one of the earliest known models of state-supervised medical teaching. Significant works appeared during this era dealing with the study of leprosy, smallpox, measles, scabies, dysentery, cholera, dropsy, beriberi, rickets, and goiters. The Song government established a formal examining and grading system for physicians, medical schools, hospitals, and dispensaries. Physicians of the State Bureau of Medical Care visited the poor in their homes or in the hospitals. The Imperial School of Medicine was founded in 1305.

**Specialists and Practitioners.** During the Tang dynasty the first types of full-time specialists appeared—physicians, acupuncturists, masseurs, and exorcists. Each type was ranked, and the specialist seemingly could subspecialize in one of the recognized branches of medicine. The practitioners of state-supported medicine were only men, and most of them were among the privileged members of society. In Song times there were four classes of practitioners: Confucian medical theoreticians; amateur experts; full-time experts; and traveling doctors who provided mainly symptomatic and supportive therapy.

**Observation on Diabetes.** The Chinese were the first to realize that diabetics had too much sugar in their urine.

### ON DIABETES

In the seventh century the physician and bureaucrat Li Xuan wrote a monograph on diabetes and attempted to explain the reason for the sweetness of the urine in diabetic patients. He observed:

This disease is due to weakness of the renal and urinogenital system. In such cases the urine is always sweet. Many physicians do not recognize this symptom . . . the cereal foods of the farmers are the precursors of sweetness . . . the methods of making cakes and sweetmeats . . . mean that they all very soon turn to sweetness. . . . It is the nature of the saline quality to be excreted. But since the renal and urinogenital system at the reins is weak it cannot distill the nutrient essentials, so that all is excreted as urine. Therefore the sweetness in the urine comes forth, and the latter does not acquire its normal color.

Source: Robert Temple, *The Genius of China: 3,000 Years of Science, Discovery, and Invention* (New York: Simon & Schuster, 1986).

Painting of a patient being treated by moxibustion (cauterization of the skin),
Song dynasty, 960–1279 (National Palace Museum, Taipei, Taiwan)

(Europeans did not make this discovery until the late eighteenth century.) Diabetes in the Chinese language means "dissolutive thirst," obviously in reference to the sufferer's unusual thirst. In the seventh century, the physician and bureaucrat Li Xuan wrote a book on the subject, asserting that diabetes was caused by weakness in the renal and urinogenital system. Diabetics were discussed by the physician Chen Quan in *Experienced Old and New Prescriptions,* also published in the seventh century. Wang Tao's *Significant Medical Methods and Treatments Exposed by the Governor of a Remote Province* (752) quotes the details of Chen Quan's comments on diabetes. According to Chen there were three types of diabetic disease. In the first type the patient suffered severe thirst, drank a lot, and passed large amounts of urine, which was sweet when tasted. In the second type the patient ate vast quantities of food but had little thirst. In the third type the patient suffered thirst but could not drink much. During this time other Chinese physicians theorized that metallic poisoning caused diabetes among rich people who took the notorious elixirs of immortality, which tended to be full of lead, mercury, and even arsenic.

**Treatment.** The physician Sun Simiao in *A Thousand Golden Therapies* (655) wrote that a diabetic had to give up three things: wine, sex, and eating cereals and salted foodstuffs. (Dietary treatment for control of diabetes, such as keeping away from alcohol and starchy foods, is close to the modern treatment.) By 1189 the physician Chang Kao had identified in his book *Medical Discourses* the significance of skin care and the threat to diabetics of the slightest cut or abrasion.

**Goiter.** A chronic, noncancerous enlargement of the thyroid gland, a goiter is visible as a swelling at the front of the neck, occurring without hyperthyroidism, and associated with iodine deficiency. As early as 239 B.C.E. the Chinese began to identify the environmental causes in terms of the nature of the water and the soil. Later they began to use seaweed as treatment for this disorder.

**Thyroid Glands.** By the seventh century Chinese physicians had clearly identified the differences between solid neck swellings (tumors), which could not be healed, and movable ones (goiter), which could be healed. Treatment consisted of using the thyroid hormone. The physician Chen Quan, who died in 643, explained the practice in his book *Experienced Old and New Prescriptions,* presenting the uses of the hormone obtained from thyroid glands of gelded male sheep. He suggested that the physician first wash one hundred thyroid glands in lukewarm water, remove the fat, and then cut them into pieces. He should then combine them with jujube dates and ground the entire mixture into pills. Another method he suggested was removing the thyroid gland from the sheep and immediately giving it to the patient to eat. Wang Xi utilized the thyroid glands of a variety of animals, including pigs, for the treatment of goiter. His technique was to reduce these glands by air-drying to powder, which was to be taken every night in cold wine. He used fifty pigs' thyroid glands at one time for such a preparation. *The Great Pharmacopoeia* (1596) recommended the use of a water buffalo's thyroid gland.

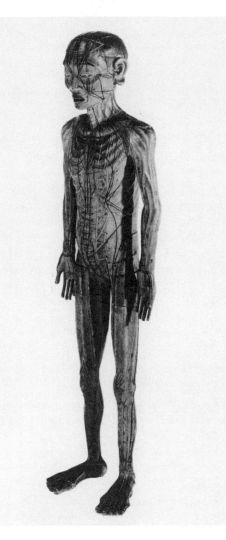

Acupuncture figure, showing the system of main
and subsidiary channels, seventeenth century
(from Alasdair Clayre, *The Heart
of the Dragon*, 1985)

record of unwritten traditions as well as the classics. In addition, this work included thorough technical, clinical, and remedial sections. The last chapter dealt with pediatric diagnosis and massage therapy for children.

**Internal Medicine.** A fourteenth-century medical encyclopedia included the writings of four famous physicians of internal medicine. Each section of the encyclopedia had a pathogenic structure, which was the basis for study in medical schools. One commentary was on the appearance of bluish white spots in the mouths of some individuals, but at the time the Chinese did not see the diagnostic value of such an observation (it is presently known as the premonitory symptom of measles).

**Alimentary Canal.** During the Ming period (1368–1644) the Chinese became interested in the course of the alimentary canal and the digestion of food. They viewed the bolus (a small mass of chewed food) as being divided into impure parts and pure parts, the former being evacuated through the pylorus (opening to the intestines) while the latter became blood.

**Syphilis.** The venereal disease syphilis began to appear in Europe around 1506 and was treated by mercurial preparations. One of the first new diseases that reached China, it was probably introduced to Guangdong province through Portuguese merchants in the early sixteenth century. A 1502 medical record indicated that syphilis was called the "boils of Guangdong" or "plum boils." Medical texts of the late Ming dynasty discussed the disease in great detail, some of which clearly stated that it was transmitted through sexual intercourse.

**Tumors.** With regard to tumors, Sun Simiao of the Tang dynasty identified bone tumors, adipose tumors, purulent tumors (ulcers), and vascular tumors. Chao Yuanfang classified them as belonging to either of two groups: enduring, palpable tumors or minor, changeable tumors.

**Yin and Yang.** The essential hypothesis underlying the medicine of systematic correspondence is that all phenomena can be grouped in either of two categories: yin (the feminine passive principle in nature that is exhibited in darkness, cold, and wetness) or yang (the masculine active principle in nature that is exhibited in light, heat, and dryness). All the phenomena within one category correspond to each other. The various categories themselves form a complicated, but logical, system of interdependencies and mutual interactions. So the human body is a complicated system of tangible anatomical elements and abstract functions. The Song doctor Lou Wansu and the Yuan doctor Zhu Tanji both theorized that the causes of all diseases can be traced to an excess of yang. Lou published *Compendium of Medicine*, a book on the circulation of the breath. Zhu devised the theory of internal fires in pathogenic conflict and asserted that the yang element always predominated in the yin-yang conflict.

**Daoist Influence.** The influence of Daoism in medicine is found in an anthology published in 1622. Daoists divided the human body into anatomical areas. The upper

**Deficiency Diseases.** Beriberi is caused by a deficiency of vitamin B1. The late-eighth-century literary figure Han Yu remarked in one of his essays that the disease was more common south of the Yangzi (Yangtze) River than north of it. He noticed that in the southern area people ate rice, while in the northern region the population ate wheat and millet, which today is known to have a high content of vitamin B1. (His observations were confirmed in a twentieth-century medical study.) Another author on the subject of dietary deficiencies and diseases was Hu Sihui, the imperial dietitian between 1314 and 1330. His book, *The Standard of Correct Diet*, was considered the classic work in the field because it compiled the best research of other scholars. In this book Hu explained two kinds of beriberi, the wet and the dry, and he suggested the remedies, many of which were diets rich in B1 and other vitamins.

**Acupuncture.** Wang Weiyi, a doctor and sculptor, composed a compendium of acupuncture in the Song dynasty. An encyclopedia on the subject, composed in short, rhythmic lines in an effort to help readers memorize the text, appeared in 1601. It provided an outstanding historical

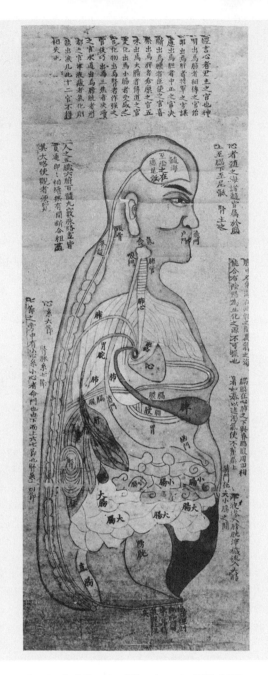

Anatomical diagram, Ming dynasty, 1368–1644
(Wellcome Historical Medical
Museum, London)

Sources:

Nathan Sivin, "Science and Medicine in Imperial China–The State of the Field," *Journal of Asian Studies*, 41 (1988): 41–90.

Robert Temple, *The Genius of China: 3,000 Years of Science, Discovery, and Invention* (New York: Simon & Schuster, 1986).

Paul U. Unschuld, *Medicine in China: A History of Ideas* (Berkeley: University of California Press, 1985).

## MEDICINE: THE IMPACT ON OTHER COUNTRIES

**Koreans.** The Korean peninsula played an important part in transmitting Chinese medicine to Japan. From the seventh to the eighth century Korean magician-healers, herbalist apothecaries, and doctors were frequently responsible for the care of Japanese emperors. Eventually the Japanese did away with these mediators and instead sent their own students to China directly or brought over Chinese masters. Korean medical texts were written in Chinese. In the fifteenth century the Korean court physicians and medical officials were required to produce an encyclopedia containing the Chinese classical prescriptions of all periods from the Han dynasty (206 B.C.E.–220 C.E.) to the Ming dynasty (1368–1644). *Collection of Classified Medical Prescriptions* (1445) provides an excellent introduction to the history of medicine in China.

**Japanese.** As early as 608 two Japanese studied medicine in China and returned home after fifteen years to spread their knowledge. The Zen sect was interested in Chinese medicine, poetry, and arts, playing a part in distributing respiratory techniques and judo (a martial art form) from China to Japan. Through the religious sects the Song era (960–1279) classics became available to the Japanese and thus continued to provide the foundation of Japanese medicine. The majority of books published in Japan were still written in Chinese, but a few were phonetically transcribed into Japanese characters, while others were completely translated. Many monk-doctors traveled to China during the Yuan period (1279–1368) and Ming period. As in China, there were many medical schools in Japan. In 1593 Li Shizhen published his great book, the *Compendium of Materia Medica*, which excited great interest in Japan. Its fifty-two chapters detailed the medical uses of more than two thousand plants and animals. It was translated into Japanese in 1596 and republished many times thereafter.

**Indians.** The golden age of Chinese Buddhism was from the fourth century to the tenth century, during which time pilgrim-monks established relationships between China and India. The late-seventh-century monk Yi Jing compiled the accounts of earlier trips made by Faxian (399–414) and Xuan Zang (629–645). The Buddhist monks brought to China Indian medical works advocating a theory of four elements, which most likely owed something to Greek influence. This theory established the number of recognized diseases at 404, each element being responsible for 101 diseases. Lack of harmony among the elements was the reason for illness. Although Chinese medical schools, apart from those of the Tang period (618–907), hardly ever resorted to Indian etiology, the Chinese found it necessary to combine their pathogenic systems with those of India.

or cephalic region was the source of spirits that dwelt in the body. Called the "pillow bone" or "pillow of jade," the occiput was found low in the back of the skull. The "palace paradise" or the "sea of bone-marrow," located in the brain, was the source of the decisive spirit. Daoist doctors regarded unawareness and greed as the primary causes of physical sickness and mental pain.

**Buddhist Hospitals.** At the institutional level Buddhists took part in a variety of charitable actions and organizations. Therefore, it was not unusual for convents and monasteries to use their dispensaries to provide treatment to lay patients. Empress Wu, a sponsor of Buddhism, assigned these hospitals to a special department at the beginning of the eighth century.

In terms of medical use, many plants were common to both India and China. The Chinese imported Indian hemp, chaulmoogra, sandalwood, camphor, long pepper, cane sugar, and cinnamon. Buddhist hospitals, leper wards, and dispensaries in the larger temples received revenue from private donors. This system was secularized toward the middle of the ninth century, and Chinese medicine acquired ethical principles of the highest order.

**Persians and Arabs.** The transfer of the imperial capital to Hangzhou under the Southern Song dynasty (1127–1279) contributed to the expansion of trade by sea with east Asia, India, and Africa. While chaulmoogra, alcohol, and opium were imported from the Indians and the Persians, the Arabs learned of Chinese medicine. Tabriz, a major city in northwestern Iran, was the main link for these Chinese, Iranian, and Mongol encounters during the Yuan dynasty. Rashid al-Din, a physician and prime minister to Mahmud Ghazan Khan (ruled from 1295 to 1304), acted as a facilitator. He constructed hospitals where Indian, Syrian, Iranian, and Chinese doctors worked together. Rashid al-Din also took advantage of his lofty position to compile an historical encyclopedia that embraced almost all the peoples of Eurasia, from China proper to the Holy Roman Empire.

**Tibetans and Mongols.** From the seventh century to the ninth century the Mongols were converted to Buddhism and to the medicine of Tibet. Tibeto-Mongolian medicine combined popular remedies with scientific findings. Chinese influence in Tibetan medicine was evident in the use of acupuncture and in the inspection of the tongue for diagnosis. The doctrine of the pulse appeared as early as the eighth century in Tibeto-Mongolian medical texts.

Sources:
Pierre Huard and Ming Wong, *Chinese Medicine* (New York: McGraw-Hill, 1968).

Manfred Porkert, *The Theoretical Foundations of Chinese Medicine: Systems of Correspondence* (Cambridge, Mass.: MIT Press, 1974).

Robert Temple, *The Genius of China: 3,000 Years of Science, Discovery, and Invention* (New York: Simon & Schuster, 1986).

## MILITARY TECHNOLOGY

**Impact of Gunpowder.** The first use of gunpowder in bombs in the military did not revolutionize war. About 919 gunpowder was used in the form of a flamethrower. When explosive gunpowder did appear, real explosive bombs, rather than merely incendiary bombs, were produced in large quantities. As the proportion of saltpeter in the gunpowder mixture was increased, up to 75 percent of the gunpowder was saltpeter, roughly the proportion used in modern gunpowder. Upon ignition, gunpowder of this type rapidly created three thousand times its bulk in gas, reaching a temperature of 3888°C. The speed of the occurrence was made possible because oxygen was in the saltpeter within the mixture, so that no oxygen needed to be sucked in from the nearby air. When the Chinese reached this stage, "barrel guns" and cannons became available.

**Protoflamethrowers.** A flamethrower is a device to produce an incessant stream of flame in warfare. As early as 675 the Byzantines used such a device to defend their

empire. It had a "siphon," which seemingly pumped flame by means of a single-acting force pump that looked like a large syringe. The protoflamethrower of the Byzantines was actually unable to eject a continuous stream of flame. It sent out a burst of flame with each pumping.

**Flamethrowers.** By the tenth century B.C.E. the Chinese were able to produce a continuous stream of flame because of the invention of a double-acting piston bellows, which was used in chemical warfare in the fourth century B.C.E. for spraying soldiers with clouds of poison gas. The Chinese device was the first genuine flamethrower. The superiority of Chinese metallurgy was obvious because the flamethrower was made of the best cartridge-quality brass, having 70 percent copper. The first use of the flamethrower in China probably was in the year 904; Lu Chen in *Historical Record of the Nine Countries* mentioned it. This dreadful mechanism sprayed enemies with burning liquid. As the liquid passed from the pump, it was ignited by the gunpowder-impregnated fuse, so that a sheet of flame fell on them. Shi Xupai's *Discussion at Fisherman's Rock* has a clear account of flamethrowers in the naval battle on the Yangzi (Yangtze) River in 975. In the same year another book, *Record of the Southern Tang Dynasty*, recorded their use. *Dreaming of the Good Ancient Times*, published in 1137 by Kang Yuzhi, illustrated the storage and use of flammable liquid for flamethrowers. A military encyclopedia, *Compilation of the Most Significant Military Techniques* (1044), illustrated design details.

**Color Fireworks.** Color fireworks appeared in China as early as 200 B.C.E. when pieces of bamboo were thrown into fires and exploded in bright colors. After gunpowder was invented, the Chinese quickly developed every conceivable type of fireworks and colored explosions, using a wide variety

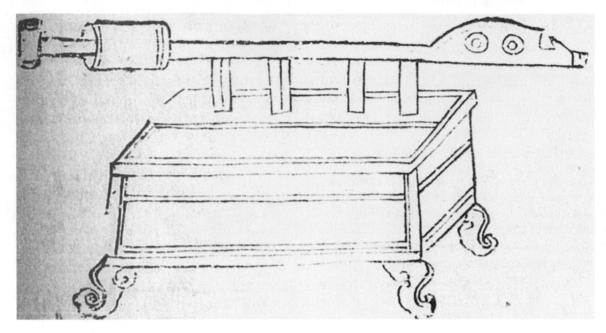

Woodcut of a Chinese flamethrower, 1601. Made of brass and powered by a double-acting piston bellows, it emitted a continuous stream of flame (from Robert Temple, *The Genius of China*, 1986).

of special materials. They could obtain luminous sparkling effects by mixing gunpowder with steel dust or tiny shavings of cast iron, which were reduced to powder. Blue-green flashes could be gained by utilizing indigo; white flashes by utilizing white lead carbonate; red flashes by utilizing red lead tetroxide; purple flashes by utilizing cinnabar; black flashes by utilizing lignite and soap beans; and yellow flashes by utilizing arsenical sulfides.

**Fire Arrows.** There was a long history of incendiary weapons of all kinds throughout the world, but when gunpowder became available in China it was incorporated into incendiary weapons to deadly effect. The first bombs used gunpowder with insufficient saltpeter to cause a proper explosion. By the tenth century new types of incendiaries had appeared. Fire arrows were tipped with little gunpowder bundles folded into papers sealed with wax and had gunpowder-impregnated fuses. These projectiles would set fire to anything inflammable, such as tents, wagons, clothing, besieging engines, trench walls made of wood, and stores of hay or food. In 1083 the Song army had a supply of 250,000 gunpowder-armed arrows.

**Thunderclap Bombs.** By the first half of the eleventh century a new kind of gunpowder bomb became available. Called the "thunderclap bomb," this device had a high percentage of saltpeter. Enclosed in a weak casing of bamboo or paper, the thunderclap bomb was hurled from trebuchets. Thunderclap bombs were efficient in starting fires and terrifying the enemy's horses with explosive sounds, and many barbarian soldiers were demoralized by the noise. These bombs either had fuses or were ignited by a red-hot poker just before being thrown. One eyewitness account details the successful employment of such weapons during a siege in the late eleventh century.

**Thunderclap Grenades.** Thunderclap bombs also appeared in the form of grenades that could be thrown by

hand. In 1187 the scholar Yuan Haowen recounted the use of thunderclap grenades by a hunter. This grenade would most likely have been housed in a narrow-mouthed pottery vessel, and the hunter almost certainly used a match to light the fuse.

**Soft-Shelled Bombs.** The Chinese invented the soft-shelled bomb in the thirteenth century. In 1276 they fired flares to send messages to distant troop detachments when the city of Yangzhou was being attacked. These soft-shelled bombs were timed to explode in midair, possibly colored like fireworks.

**Thundercrash Bomb.** By 1221 a new type of bomb had appeared in China. It was called the "thundercrash bomb." These bombs were much more deadly than earlier versions because, rather than having soft casings, they were hard bombs with casings of metal, similar to modern ones. The shrapnel would kill and wound many more of the enemy. Since their purpose was to burst the metal casings asunder, these new bombs were made with gunpowder containing a higher content of saltpeter. Gunpowder of this strength was equal to the modern version. The Jin armies probably first used thundercrash bombs around 1221 at their successful sieges of cities of the Song empire (960–1279). Since the new bombs were in cast-iron casings, they made a noise like thunder, shook the walls of houses, and killed and wounded countless people. The term *thundercrash bomb* was not used until 1231 when the Jin armies were overwhelmed by the Mongols in the Shanxsi province. The Jin general fled down the Yellow River with three thousand soldiers, pursued along the northern bank by fierce Mongol armies who fired a constant rain of arrows upon him. Historians used the term *thundercrash bomb* when writing of this battle. The only surviving picture of a bursting bombshell of the period was a Japanese depiction made in 1293, showing a Chinese-style thundercrash bomb in a cast-iron casing exploding in the air. Europeans probably did not use cast-iron bombshells until 1467.

**Other Bombs.** By the thirteenth century the Chinese developed a variety of bombs with special uses. Some were filled with antipersonnel material in order to increase the shrapnel result. There were also poison bombs, gaseous bombs, and bombs packed with feces. Some of the well-known bombs and grenades were the "bone-burning and staining fire-oil magic bomb"; the "magic fire dramatic bomb that flies against the wind"; the "dropping-from-sky bomb"; the "bee-swarm bomb"; the "equal to 10,000 enemies bomb discharging 10,000 fires"; the "flying-sand mysterious bomb"; and the "wind and dust bomb."

**Land Mines.** By 1277 the Chinese had developed land mines, and in the middle of the fourteenth century illustrations of how to make land mines were published in books. *The Fire-Drake Artillery Guidebook,* published in 1412, included some information on the land mines of the fourteenth century, such as a network of mines called the "ground-thunder explosive site." Another land mine illustrated in the same book was called the "highest pole mixture mine," which had a battery of eight small guns pointing in different directions, all detonated by an automatic trigger device. (The first appearance of land mines in Europe was not until the war between Pisa and Florence in 1403.)

**Trigger Devices.** Some of the trigger devices of Chinese land mines involved arrangements of flint and steel. These land mine triggers trace back to 1360 and seemed to be the forebear of the flintlock musket (first appearing in Europe in 1547). The first European land mines using triggers for ignition at a distance were not created until 1573.

**Sea Mines.** The Chinese also developed sea mines, which are recorded in *The Fire-Drake Artillery Guidebook.* Called the "submarine dragon-king," the sea mine made of wrought iron was carried on a submerged wooden board. The mine was enclosed in an ox bladder, and a thin joss stick in a container was arranged to drift above the mine. The burning of this incense stick determined when the fuse caught fire, but without air its flame would certainly go out, so the container was linked with the mine by a long piece of goat's intestine through which the fuse went. At the upper end the joss-stick container was kept drifting by an arrangement of goose and wild-duck feathers, so that it floated unevenly with the ripples of the water. At night the mine was sent downstream toward the enemy's ships, and when the joss stick burned down to the fuse, a great explosion occurred. The Chinese sea mine of the fourteenth century was two hundred years earlier than the European one, which did not appear until 1574.

**Rockets.** The rocket, a great technological contribution to the world, was perhaps the most significant invention of the Chinese. They invented rockets by 1150 and used them in warfare by 1206. By 1280 the Arabs called rockets "Chinese arrows." The Europeans did not develop rockets until the beginning of the fifteenth century.

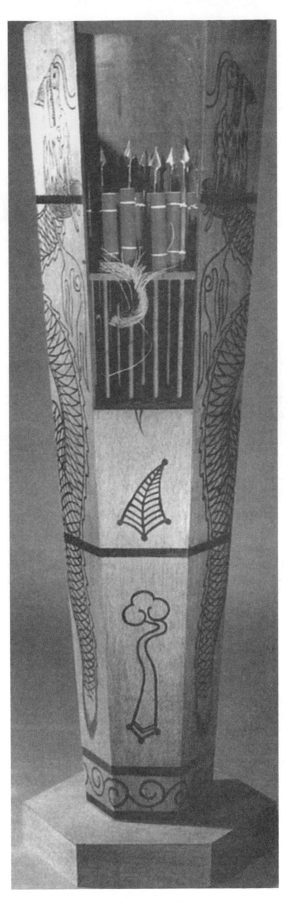

Reconstruction of a fourteenth-century bees' nest rocket launcher (Ontario Science Center, Toronto)

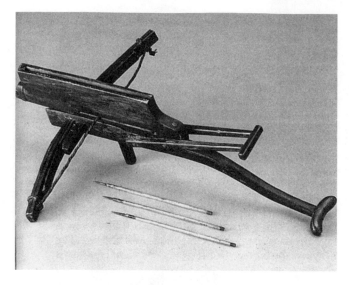

Reconstruction of a repeating crossbow, capable of firing eleven shots in fifteen seconds and invented circa eleventh century (Manchester Museum, Manchester, England)

**Early Types.** Inspiration for the rocket came from a type of firework known as the "ground rat" or "earth rat" that sped along the ground sending out flames behind it. Another type of firework, known as the "water rat," was tied to floats or little skis and went skidding across lakes or pools in firework festivals. The book *Traditions and Organizations of the Old Capital* (thirteenth century) illustrated celebrations of the 1100s and mentioned fireworks of those days. Some were similar to wheels while others resembled comets. The Chinese introduced stabilizing devices such as fins and wings for rockets soon after 1300.

**Weight Balancing.** By the twelfth century the Chinese had identified weight balancing. An iron weight was fastened at the rear end of the rocket arrow behind the feathering. These counterweights allowed the rockets to move significant distances by holding down their ends so as to prevent the rocket arrows from hitting the ground.

**Delicate Procedure.** When the gunpowder inside a rocket burns, there needs to be equal areas of combustion along the internal cavity. Illustrations from the twelfth century demonstrate that if the hole bored through the gunpowder charge was straight sided the arrow would fly straight, and if angled the arrow would fly off at a tangent. If the hole was too deep the rocket would lose too much flame at the rear; if it was too shallow, it would not have enough power, so the arrow would fall to the ground almost immediately.

**Modification.** By 1300 extreme modification of rockets had taken place, whereby the orifice of the rocket tube was narrowed to increase the flow velocity of the issuing gases, providing greater strength. This choke or nozzle results in the Venturi-tube effect, which is one of the most basic rules of aerodynamics, allowing for lift in connection with the use of wings. (The rule was not discovered in Europe until the eighteenth century.) Gunpowder used in these early Chinese rockets is thought to have had about 60 percent saltpeter, and they could fly for a distance of 50 to 1,150 yards.

**Basket Launchers.** The Chinese soon saw the military advantage of mass rocket firings. By fixing the rockets within frames of launchers, the Chinese could control them better. Conical basket launchers would not survive one mass firing, but were easily replaceable.

**Wheelbarrow Launchers.** Wheelbarrows were frequently used as portable batteries and were called "flames-frame-fighting-vehicles." The splayed rocket launchers had internal diaphragms with holes in them to keep the rockets separate, and the launcher was broadened at the top from a narrower base in order to insure a wide area of dispersion of the points of impact of the rockets. Each battery could dispatch 320 rockets at one time. These batteries consisted of four long-serpent rocket launchers in rows on wheelbarrows, together with two rectangular wooden hundred-tiger rocket launchers, one on either side. In Ming times (1368–1644) a super-battery was supposedly able to launch 32,000 rockets at a single moment, and during a battle approximately one million rockets might be used.

**Multistage Rockets.** By the early fourteenth century the Chinese had developed multistage rockets. According to *The Fire-Drake Artillery Guidebook,* the Fire-Dragon rocket had a range of one mile. When the gunpowder in the rocket tubes was nearly finished, the rocket continued to fly because of the automatic lighting by a fuse of its second stage. This rocket was a forerunner of the modern multistage version.

**Fire-Lance.** By 905 the Chinese had developed the first protogun, called a "fire-lance." A silk banner painted no later than 950 illustrated comprehensively the world's oldest gun. In the picture Buddha was contemplating while the demons of the evil goddess Mara the Temptress were attempting to sidetrack him. One demon held a fire-lance while the other demon wielded a bomb from which fire had already begun to come out. This unquestionable historical statement indicated the invention of the gun occurred much earlier than other monographs described. In the beginning the fire-lance was basically a Roman-candle firework fixed firmly to a spear. It was exceptionally useful for defending city walls against besiegers. Large numbers of fire-lances were wheeled around in trolleys. In 1233, when Mongols were besieging Jin armies in a city, Jin troops launched a brave night raid using the fire-lances. In following decades fire-lances were modified. Starting as lengths of bamboo tube that simply spurted fire, fire-lances advanced to metal barrels, so they could function as pikes in close battle. Later, fire-lances dropped their spear points, especially when they proceeded to stronger and longer metal barrels. The earliest description of fire-lances in Europe was a Latin manuscript of 1396 illustrating them clearly with a picture of a mounted horseman. Even after the true gun was invented, fire-lances remained popular and were used until the middle of the twentieth century in China as protection against pirates.

**Cannons.** Illustrated in *The Fire-Drake Artillery Guidebook*, a Chinese protocannon called the "eruptor" first appeared in the thirteenth century. Its projectile was a hollow shell of cast iron; inside, it held half a pound of powerful gunpowder. An early European cannon, depicted in a German manuscript circa 1450, was virtually identical to the earlier Chinese one. The first true cannon, the "long-distance grand cannon," weighed seventy-two kilograms. The barrels were more than half covered by large flattened bands.

**Firearms.** The true handgun was developed in the thirteenth century. A bronze handgun made in 1288 was excavated in Manchuria; it was more than one foot long and weighed about eight pounds. The gunpowder chamber had a small touchhole for ignition and a bulbous shape so as to prevent it from breaking up under the force of its own internal explosion. The Chinese also began to develop repeat-firing guns by doubling the rate of fire with small cannons. This type of gun was composed of two small cannons whose rear ends joined together in one long barrel. After the first one was fired the barrel was quickly rotated so that the second one fired. Another type was developed called the "cartwheel gun." It had thirty-six barrels radiating from its center like the spokes of a wheel. These guns were so small that a single mule could carry two, one on each side of its pack. In the following centuries hand-held guns proliferated in China.

**Tear Gas.** The prototype of modern tear gas was a blinding smoke, caused by thinly powdered lime that made the eyes tear profusely. During a sea battle in 1161 thunderclap bombs made with paper cartons and filled with lime and sulfur were launched from trebuchets. When they hit the water, the sulfur they contained burst into flames. The carton case rebounded and broke, spreading the lime to create a smoky fog that blinded the eyes of enemy sailors. A classic tear-gas combination was called "five-league-fog," containing about 29 percent each of saltpeter and sulfur and 45 percent of charcoal. Burning little by little, it included arsenic, sawdust, resin, human hair, and chicken, wolf, and human excrement. Smoke from burning wolf excrement, which looked red both in the daytime and at night, could also be used for sending warning signals.

**Poison Bombs.** Poison bombs such as the "bee swarm bomb," "poison-fog magic-smoke eruptor," and others came about in the fourteenth century. The Chinese combined animal, plant, and mineral poisons into one mixture. The resulting smoke from an exploding shell would attack defenders' noses, mouths, and eyes. The improvement of rockets for warfare added a new method of delivering poisonous bombs. Some bombs would also produce fire. The "flying-sand powerful bomb," for example, consisted of a tube of gunpowder put into an earthenware pot containing quicklime, resin, and alcoholic extracts of poisonous plants, and its explosion would discharge the deadly poisons. Another poison gas bomb called the "soul-hunting-fog" held a strong explosive with 83 percent saltpeter, 9 percent sulfur, and 8 percent charcoal, together with arsenic sulfides and lethal animal poisons.

Drawing from the early seventeenth century of soldiers firing arrows from special containers filled with gunpowder (from Alasdair Clayre, *The Heart of the Dragon*, 1985)

**Crossbows.** The Chinese used crossbows in combat as early as the fourth century B.C.E. A crossbow presented to the emperor in 1068 could penetrate a large elm tree from a distance of 140 paces. Consisting of two bows tied together, a crossbow catapult took several soldiers to draw its string and could shoot several arrows at the same time. The greatest range of a large winch-armed crossbow was about 1,160 yards.

**Repeating Crossbows.** The attempt to improve the firepower of the crossbow resulted in the invention of machine-gun crossbows in the eleventh century or twelfth century. This improvement solved the problems of arming the slow-loading crossbow. A magazine of bolts was fixed above the arrow groove in the stock of the crossbow, and after each bolt was shot, another would drop into its place. Therefore, twelve arrows could be shot in a minute. Using these repeating crossbows, one hundred soldiers could discharge two thousand arrows in fifteen seconds, but ranges of repeating crossbows were limited. It had an extreme range of two hundred yards with an efficient range of only eighty yards. Although the repeating crossbows were not as powerful as regular crossbows, such vast, rapid, and continuous showers of bolts raining down on soldiers would be tremendously frightening, particularly when the bolts were usually poison tipped. By the beginning of the seventh century repeating crossbows were used extensively throughout China.

**Frankish Bombards.** Cannons of the Chinese type widely used in Ming times played an important role in military campaigns, but the German monk Berthold Schwarz, after many experiments, developed more-effective firearms. Perfected in Europe, these new weapons were introduced by the Portuguese to east Asia in the sixteenth century. At the beginning, the Chinese did not value them and continued to use their traditional bombards. The Japanese, however, greatly appreciated the new European weapons. Japanese pirates who devastated the east coast of China in the middle of the sixteenth century used these new weapons to deal a great blow to the Ming armies in battles in Korea between 1593 and 1598. Thereafter the Ming government sought to adopt European cannons known as "Frankish bombards." In order to resist Manchu attacks, the Ming government asked the Jesuits to arrange for the purchase of European cannons from Macao.

**Sources:**

Hsiao Ch'I-ch'ing, *The Military Establishment of the Yuan Dynasty* (Cambridge, Mass.: Harvard University Press, 1978).

Wolfgang Franke, *An Introduction to the Sources of Ming History* (New York & Oxford: Oxford University Press, 1969).

Charles O. Hucker, *The Traditional Chinese State in Ming Times (1368–1644)* (Tucson: University of Arizona Press, 1961).

Robert Temple, *The Genius of China: 3,000 Years of Science, Discovery, and Invention* (New York: Simon & Schuster, 1986).

**Magnetism.** The Chinese were the first to study theories of magnetism: polarity (the condition of opposite properties); induction (the process by which an object becomes magnetized); retentivity (the capacity for retaining magnetism); and variation (the measurement of change in magnetism). These theories were identified much earlier in China than in Europe, although Europeans performed the first experiments relating to electric charges and magnetism in the seventeenth century. Chinese notions about magnetic phenomena were connected with cosmic theories that probably made their influence felt in Europe by the eighteenth century. The magnetic North Pole is about 1,200 miles from the geographical true north of the earth. The difference between the true geographical North Pole and the magnetic North Pole was identified as the angle of declination. (It is not constant and frequently shifts.) By the ninth century the Chinese had discovered this magnetic declination. The oldest, most accurate, and completely clear description of the declination appeared in an eleventh-century poem on the magnet written by Wang Chi, founder of the Fujian school of geomancers (scholars who performed divination by means of figures, lines, or geographic features). The magnetic compass and the polarity of the earth's field were not discussed in any Western literature until the end of the twelfth century. In addition, the Chinese had described explicitly the induction of remanent or residual magnetism in iron by the eleventh century, referring to a fish-shaped magnet.

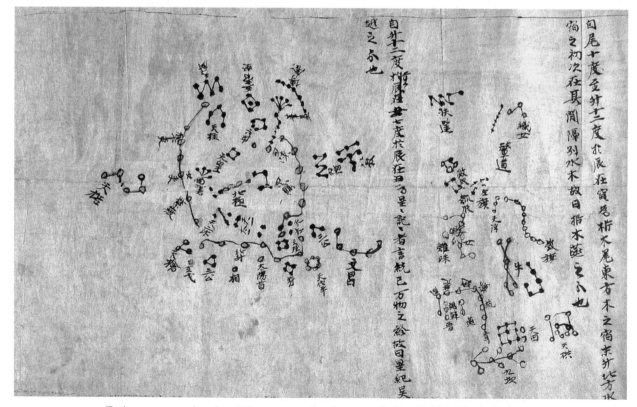

Tunhuang manuscript, circa 940, a star map showing constellations (British Library, London)

Artisans drawing steel wire and making needles to be magnetized and used for compasses; drawing from
*The Exploitation of the Works of Nature,* 1637 (from Robert Temple, *The Genius of China,* 1986)

**Archaeology.** The twelfth-century discovery of antique objects such as bronzes and jades in the area of Anyang, the last capital of the Shang dynasty (circa 1766–circa 1122 B.C.E.), spurred widespread interest in archaeology. In turn, increased enthusiasm for antiques contributed to a rise in epigraphy, the study of inscriptions. *Archaeological Plates,* a scientific classification and dating of the bronzes of the second and first millennia B.C.E., was published in 1092. By the end of the twelfth century *Ancient Coins,* the first book on numismatics in Chinese history, was available.

**Astronomy.** In 1090 an important development occurred in the field of astronomy. Su Song produced an astronomical clock actuated by an escapement system, cogs, and transmission chains. The machine had a wheel turned by the successive filling of pivoting cups fed by a tank with a constant level. This clock was the most precise thus far developed, and it was one of the oldest mechanisms in the history of the world, with a slow, regular, continuous rotation.

**Equatorial Instrument.** Astronomical observatories helped Chinese scientists to understand the positions of stars. The Arabs first invented an astronomical instrument that improved upon the ancient Greek armillary sphere (a device for representing the great circles of the heavens with the horizon, meridian, equator, tropics, polar circles, and an ecliptic hoop). With this Arab instrument all the various rings were not nested together in a single sphere but were mounted on a set of struts. In 1270 astronomer Guo Shoujing adapted this instrument to the equatorial system of the Chinese but with all the Arab ecliptic components left out. In this regard he anticipated the equatorial mounting so extensively used in contemporary telescopes.

**Star Map.** Chinese cartographers used the cylindrical projection centuries before the sixteenth-century German scholar Gerardus Mercator devised his projection map (a type of map that allows for the globe's surface to be projected onto a flat surface). By 940 they created the first star map with the cylindrical technique. The sky was divided into twenty-eight regions, which were similar to the sections of an orange. They were lunar mansions—stages of the moon's progress through the sky—with the pole as their base. In the star map the sections were represented as long rectangles centered on the equator and extremely dis-

Armillary sphere built in the late thirteenth century, Nanking observatory

torted in the direction of the poles. In 1094 Su Song illustrated this type of map in his book *New Design for a Mechanized Armillary Sphere and Celestial Globe.*

**Quantitative Cartography.** Two important maps were created in the eleventh century. (Both were carved in stone, and they currently reside in the Pei Lin Museum in Xi'an.) The "Map of the Paths of Yu the Great" has a rectangular grid laid over it. Superior to the other map with reference to the coastal details, this map includes the Shandong Peninsula. The other map, however, has more precise information on the southwestern rivers. In 1320 the Daoist and geographer Zhu Siben published a reliable map in an atlas. The map was not printed again until 1555, when it appeared in the *Enlarged Terrestrial Atlas.* This map was prepared with a network of squares that presented an accurate geographic picture. If the map was divided and then reassembled, the individual parts in the East and West fitted together perfectly. The grid was used successfully to reduce the size of the map in a manner similar to present-day photographic decrease. However, the map was seven feet long and thus difficult to unroll.

**Geobotanical Prospecting.** The use of botanical observation to find minerals is known as geobotanical prospecting. The Chinese were the first people to become aware of and use the link between the types of vegetation that grow in certain regions and the minerals to be discovered underground at the same area. In the first half of the sixth century there were no less than three guidebooks dealing with systematic accounts of geobotanical mineral prospecting and listing different kinds of plants and their related minerals. Duan Chengshi in his *Miscellany of the Yuyang Mountain Cave* (800) is the first to propose the relationship

between plant types and mineral deposits. In 1062 Su Song published his *Illustrated Pharmacopoeia*, which maintains that a specific plant of purslane contained sufficient mercury for the metal to be extracted from it by careful beating, ventilation, and natural organic decay. In 1421 a book called *Signs of Metals and Minerals* was published claiming that mineral trace elements could be found in and could be taken out of certain plants. Gold was found in the rape turnip; silver in a type of weeping willow; lead and tin in

## MAGNETIC COMPASS

Below is an account of the use of the magnetic compass for navigation from a book by Zhu Yu, son of a former port official and governor of Canton. The book is called *Pingchow Table Talk* and dates from 1117. Zhu writes:

According to the government regulations concerning sea-going ships, the larger ones can carry several hundred men and the small ones may have more than a hundred men on board. . . . The ship's pilots are acquainted with the configuration of the coasts: at night they steer by the stars, and in the day-time by the Sun. In dark weather they look at the south-pointing needle. They also use a line a hundred feet long with a hook at the end, which they let down to take samples of mud from the sea-bottom; by its appearance and smell they can determine their whereabouts.

Source: Robert Temple, *The Genius of China: 3,000 Years of Science, Discovery, and Invention* (New York: Simon & Schuster, 1986).

chestnut, barley, and wheat; and copper in Indian sorrel. Europeans did not understand geobotanical concepts until the seventeenth century.

**Geology.** In 1086 the great scientist Shen Kuo published his book *Dream of Pool Essay* in which the principle of modern geology was included. In his work Shen discussed erosion of mountains and lofty peaks and described sedimentary deposition. Although Shen Kuo was not the first person to have these ideas, he explained them thoroughly and included his personal observations in the field.

**Natural Luminescence.** The Chinese became interested in natural luminescence as early as the third century. They observed the relationship between the bioluminescence of fireflies and the glowing of certain kinds of rotting vegetation. This discovery resulted in the use of natural luminescence in the manufacturing of phosphorescent paints in the eleventh century, if not earlier. In 1596 Li Shizhen correctly distinguished glowworms, whose glowing tails were able to be seen at night over long distances, from fireflies and other evidently luminous insects, such as mayflies or midges infected with luminous bacteria. Luminescence and phosphorescence called "Yin fire" enthralled the Chinese for centuries, and they collected naturally luminescent pearls and glowing minerals. The West did not make any phosphorescent substance until 1768, when John Canton utilized oyster shells to prepare a mixed calcium sulfide by calcining the carbonate with sulfur.

Sources:

Joseph Needham, *Clerks and Craftsmen in China and the West* (Cambridge: Cambridge University Press, 1970).

Needham, *Science and Civilization in China,* 7 volumes (Cambridge: Cambridge University Press, 1954–present).

Edward H. Schafter, *Pacing the Void: Tang Approaches to the Stars* (Berkeley: University of California Press, 1977).

# SIGNIFICANT PEOPLE

## LI SHIZHEN

### 1518-1598
#### PHARMACOLOGIST

**Great Medical Book.** Born in 1518, Li Shizhen began editing a major work in 1552 and did not complete it until 1578; it was first printed in 1593 and color plates were added in 1596. Known as the *Compendium of Materia Medica,* this vast work described almost two thousand animal, vegetable, and mineral drugs and provided more than eight thousand prescriptions. As a great pathological and therapeutic work and a masterpiece of Ming era (1368–1644) medicine, this book provided discussions on botany, dietetics, acupuncture, gynecology, hygiene, smallpox inoculation, distillation, and the use of mercury, iodine, chaulmoogra oil, ephedrine, and other items. It also mentioned syphilis, which appeared in China in the sixteenth century and was treated throughout Eurasia. In addition, there were chapters on chemical and industrial technology, geography, history, cosmology, philosophy, and philology.

**Significance.** This book represented a culmination of the greatest scientific achievements of the Ming dynasty and was one of the few great scientific works written in the sixteenth century outside of the West. It was translated into all the major languages of east Asia and the West.

Sources:

Wolfgang Franke, *An Introduction to the Sources and Ming History* (New York: Oxford University Press, 1969).

L. Carrington Goodrich and Chaoying Fang, eds., *Dictionary of Ming Biography, 1368–1644,* 2 volumes (New York: Columbia University Press, 1976).

## LI ZHI

### 1192-1279
#### SCHOLAR AND MATHEMATICIAN

**Early Life.** Li Zhi was born in Shandong, where his father practiced medicine. His father later became so unsure of his diagnoses that he ended his participation in the profession. Li Zhi then studied law but soon gave it up for the Confusican classics and became an expert on belles lettres. In 1191 the father obtained the *Jinshi* degree in the category of prose literature and was employed as a magistrate. Li Zhi had been tremendously intelligent and an enthusiastic student since boyhood, but his early years were influenced by his father's career. Li Zhi dedicated himself seriously to study and began to show a genius in literature.

**Scholar-Official.** Li Zhi became close friends with future eminent men of letters and emerged as a literary celebrity and well-educated scholar whose reputation became well known in Henan. In 1230, at the late age of thirty-eight, he gained his *Jinshi* degree in prose literature and was employed as a county registrar in Shanxi. By that time Henan was threatened by the Mongol invasion. Li assumed personal charge of the accounting office, where he achieved excellent results, unquestionably owing to his mathematical skills. In 1232, however, Jin forces were defeated by the Mongols. In the following year many famous Jin scholar-officials became prisoners of war and refugees. Li Zhi, like many of his former colleagues and friends, wandered homelessly in Hebei, Shanxi, and Henan.

**Teaching.** During these years, Li Zhi had the time to improve not only his literary skills but also his mathematical knowledge by studying ancient treatises and devoting himself industriously to scholastic inquiry. In 1251 he returned home and established, with the assistance of the local populace, a private academy. Soon students from far and near came to his academy. Li Zhi began six years of concentrated teaching and research, until he was summoned by the Mongol government.

**Qubilai.** In 1257 the future Mongol khan Qubilai, acting on the recommendation of his Chinese advisers, summoned Li Zhi, as well as other Chinese scholars, to the capital. Qubilai was greatly impressed by Li Zhi's suggestion on how to rule China, but he was unable to implement the proposal, or those suggested by other intellectuals, since he did not hold any position as yet. Even so, from such contacts Qubilai understood more clearly the problems of governing China, and he implemented some of these recommendations after his accession to the throne.

**Mathematician.** Since Qubilai did not appoint Li Zhi to any official position, Li returned to his former residence and resumed his mathematical research. He continued working on circular measurements. Dissatisfied with traditional computation methods, he corrected and elaborated them in a treatise called *Yigu Yanduan* (New Steps in Computation) in three chapters. This work was completed in August 1259 but was published posthumously in 1282. Li Zhi's other existing works are two treatises on mathematics. His major contribution to mathematics consisted of verifying and elaborating solutions to complex problems of circular measurement that were proposed by earlier and contemporary scholars.

**Scholar.** In 1260, shortly after his enthronement, Qubilai called several Jin scholars and notables to serve his new government. Li Zhi was among those men invited, and he went to the Mongol's capital with several former colleagues and friends. In September he was appointed as Hanlin academician in charge of imperial documents. Li Zhi, however, declined the offer on the grounds of ill health, and his

request was granted. A year later Li Zhi was called to court for the second time and reappointed Hanlin academician. He quit because of sickness after a month in office. Li Zhi did not have any achievements in government affairs but was a versatile scholar and prolific writer on the subject of the classics, devoting most of his life to study and authorship. He deserves to be regarded as one of the greatest mathematicians in Chinese history.

**Sources:**

Yoshio Mikami, *The Development of Mathematics in China and Japan*, second edition (New York: Chelsea, 1974).

Li Yan and Du Shiran, *Chinese Mathematics: A Concise History*, translated by John N. Crossley and Anthony W. C. Lun (Oxford: Clarendon Press; New York: Oxford University Press, 1987).

# SHEN KUO

## 1031–1095
## SCIENTIST

**Reputation.** Shen Kuo's reputation has been mostly in the field of scientific writing: he was the first to illustrate and build orographic maps; the first to illustrate accurately the source of fossils and the marine origin of some rocks; and the first to hint at atmospheric refraction. Furthermore, his inquisitiveness aroused his interest in such subjects as music, painting, calligraphy, and philosophy, in addition to the technical applications of science, such as the workings of armillary spheres, dams, sluices, and calendars.

**Early Life.** In 1040, when Shen Kuo was only nine years old, he was fond of reading. His mother, a learned person, had a great impact on the boy. When he was eleven he started receiving a formal education, and in 1043 he followed his father to a new city, observing many towns on the way. Shen Kuo then began to study calligraphy. As a child his health was poor, and he suffered eyestrain when he was eighteen years old because of reading too often at night. In 1054 as a registrar Shen Kuo channeled and drained several rivers to gain 100,000 acres of land for farms. During this period his interest in geography increased while he corrected some mistakes in a book and studied the East Sea and surrounding areas. In 1061 he became subprefect of Ningkuo where at Wu Lake he built a barrage that withstood the great Yangzi floods of 1065. In the same year Shen Kuo finished writing a treatise on music, and the following year he became subprefect of Wanqiu. In the autumn of the same year he passed the law examination and was awarded the honor of an interview with the emperor in the capital. In 1064 he became inspector of police in Yangzhou.

**Scholar and Official.** Shen Kuo first held office in the central government in 1066 when he became collator in the Imperial Library; he studied astronomy and wrote a manual on the subject. At the same time he studied the details of a treaty of 1044 between the Song empire (960–1279) and the Liao empire (916–1115), thus obtaining detailed knowledge of diplomacy and military strategy that soon proved to be significant in his official work. In 1071 he filled a newly created post, Controller of Public Affairs of the legal department in the General Secretariat, which allowed him to enter the inner circle of government. Shocked by the lack of skill among officials in the Directorate of Astronomy, Shen Kuo carried out reforms in 1072. He created an armillary sphere (an astronomical instrument), clepsydras (water clocks), and gnomons (sundial pins). He hired a talented official to prepare a new calendar for 1075–1092 and recommended another official for the task of inspecting the canal. At the same time he composed more than two hundred astronomical charts. Two years later, in 1074, he was promoted to executive assistant of the Court of Imperial Sacrifices and Imperial Recorder, which provided some chances to see the emperor.

**Later Work.** His other intellectual work included the amplification of several maps. In 1075 he presented his "Regulations of the Method of Repairing Strongholds"; investigated the records of past intercourse between Song and Liao states; took notes on geography, animal and plant life, and climate; and produced a map of the Song frontiers. In addition, he was sent by the Song court as imperial ambassador to negotiate with the Liao government, who demanded more territory. From 1076 to 1078 he held a variety of offices in the central government, mostly concerned with financial and military matters. In 1087 he completed the *Atlas of China*. In 1091 Shen Kuo became ill and died four years later.

**Sources:**

Etienne Balazs and Yves Hervouet, eds., *A Sung Bibliography* (Hong Kong: Chinese University Press, 1978).

Herbert Franke, ed., *Sung Biographies*, four volumes (Wiesbaden: Steiner, 1976).

# SU SONG

## 1020-1101
### SCIENTIST

**Official.** The son of a high-ranking official, Su Song successfully passed his *Jinshi* degree examination and was offered a post in the Imperial Library in 1053. In 1057 the Song court appointed him to revise the medical classics. By 1062 he revised and enlarged a massive work on pharmacology and natural history in China.

**Minister of Justice.** After having served for nine years in the Imperial Library, Su Song accepted a position in local government in order to improve his family's economic situation. He was, however, unable to work his way up in the central administration because he and other conservative officials did not like Wang Anshi's reforms. He served as envoy to the Khitan state Liao and governor of the capital of Kaifeng in 1078. He was demoted for a short time because a member of his staff had failed in certain assignments. However, he eventually became Vice-minister of Personnel Affairs and Minister of Justice in 1086.

**Astronomy.** In the same year the Song government issued orders for the inspection of existing astronomical equipment and the creation of an astronomical clock. Two years later a wooden model was presented to the emperor and in 1090 the metal parts for an armillary sphere and a celestial globe were cast in bronze. The emperor appointed Su Song deputy prime minister in 1090 and prime minister in 1092. He then submitted to the emperor *Xin I Xiang Fayao*, a thesis describing the construction of a mechanical clock. He retired in the same year when the reform party controlled the Song court. One of his descendants compiled Su Song's collected works under the title *Su Weigong Wenji*.

**Sources:**

Etienne Balazs and Yves Hervouet, eds., *A Sung Bibliography* (Hong Kong: Chinese University Press, 1978).

Robert Wilson, *Astronomy through the Ages* (Princeton, N.J.: Princeton University Press, 1997).

# SUN SIMIAO

## 581-682
### DOCTOR

**Canonization.** Sun Simiao was one of the most important monk doctors of the Tang Dynasty (618–907). Born in Shanxi province, he was the son of a scholar. At the age of seven he was a devoted and diligent student. As a youth he studied the great Daoist writers as well as the Buddhist Canons. Early in his life he lived as a recluse in the mountains, but he was so famous that two emperors offered him high positions in their courts. He refused on the pretext of illness and returned to his hermitage in keeping with the tradition of the great Chinese sages. He died at an advanced age in 682 and was canonized after his death under the name *Sun Zhenren*.

**Medical System.** His medical system is a combination of Indian doctrine of the four elements (earth, water, fire, and wind) and the Chinese doctrine of the five viscera. When the fire's breath was disturbed, the body became burning hot. If the breath of the wind was disturbed, the stomach was blocked. If the water was disturbed, the body swelled and the breathing was deep, panting, and thick. If the breath of the earth was disturbed, the four limbs were slow. If the fire was suppressed, the body grew cold. If the wind stopped, the breathing was interrupted. If the water failed, there was no more blood. If the earth was scattered, the body burst. If the four breaths combined their qualities, the four spirits were in peaceful harmony, but should one of the breaths be disturbed, 101 ailments were produced, and if all four spirits were shaken simultaneously, then 404 illnesses occurred.

**Sources:**

Charles O. Hucher, *China to 1850: A Short History* (Stanford, Cal.: Stanford University Press, 1978).

William H. Nienhauser Jr., *Bibliography of Selected Western Works on Tang Dynasty Literature* (Taipei: Center for Chinese Studies, 1988).

# XU GUANGQI

## 1562-1633
### TRANSLATOR OF SCIENTIFIC WORKS

**Official.** Xu Guangqi was born to a landholding family near Shanghai. Successful in the doctoral examination in 1604, Xu was one of the first Chinese men to make contact with the Jesuit missionaries. Hired as tutor by a wealthy family, he met first Father Lazare Carraneo and then Matteo Ricci in Nanking in 1600. From 1604 to 1607 Xu lived in Beijing and there received instruction from Ricci. As a government minister, Xu used his Jesuit instructor's talents not only in the mathematical bureau of the Board of Rites but also as artillery adviser in the war against the Manchus and the rebels. Through his influence the Ming court (1368–1644) turned to the Portuguese for help and enlisted the first European forces to serve in China.

**Translator.** As a disciple of Ricci, Xu started to translate European scientific works such as guidebooks on mathematics, astronomy, geography, and hydraulics, thereby becoming the first Chinese translator of Western books. From 1606 to 1608 he engaged in the translation of a work on trigonometry of the *Elements of Euclid* and of a treatise on hydraulics, realizing that Chinese and Western trigonometrical methods were the same. His famous treatise on agriculture was published after his death in 1639 and titled *Encyclopedia of Agricultural Techniques*. Overall, with the help of Xu, Western science and geography were available to the Chinese, but European influence still remained limited.

**Impact.** Xu returned to the lower Yangzi in 1607 where he had new contacts with the Jesuits. He retired in 1621 and lived in Shanghai, where he translated *Treatise on the Soul*. In 1630 he recommended to the imperial court that Adam Schall be employed to create a new calendar and that Father Longobardo be appointed for negotiations with the Portuguese to buy cannons at Macao. Later, he bestowed his property on the mission, and after his death a small church was built near his home in the family township of Xu.

Sources:
William Theodore de Bary, *Self and Society in Ming Thought* (New York: Columbia University Press, 1970).

L. Carrington Goodrich and Chaoying Fang, eds., *Dictionary of Ming Biography, 1368–1644,* 2 volumes (New York: Columbia University Press, 1976).

Rear of bronze mirror, eighth century, showing the Earth and the four cardinal points (Seattle Art Museum, Washington)

# DOCUMENTARY SOURCES

Rashid al-Din, *The Il-Khan's Assets of the Sciences of Cathay* (1313)—An historical encyclopedia in the Persian language consisting of four volumes and compiled by the prime minister of a Mongol prince. The first book had illustrations by various Chinese scholars. Volume two dealt with the circulatory system and cauteries, caustic agents used to destroy aberrant tissue. The third volume included dialogues between rulers and their ministers, a classification of old books, the therapeutic effects of certain medicines, and the methods used in the treatment of illnesses by the Chinese Turkestan doctors before they gained knowledge of Greek medicine. The last book was devoted to medical doctrine and its classification of diseases.

Duan Chengshi, *Assortment of the Yuyang Mountain Cave* (800)—Identified the connection between certain types of plants that grew in some regions and the minerals to be discovered underground at the same locations, such as onions and silver, shallot and gold, and ginger and copper and tin.

*The Fire-Drake Artillery Guidebook* (1412)—Military manual.

Li Shizhen, *Compendium of Materia Medica* (1593)—Vast work on biology, chemistry, cosmology, geography, history, philology, and philosophy.

Li Zhi, *Ceyuan haijing* (Sea Mirror of Circle Measurements, 1248)—Written by a great mathematician of the early Yuan period, this book comprises twelve chapters that form a clever exposition of algebraic and geometric knowledge in medieval times.

Liu Ruxie, *Piling-up Powers and Unlocking Coefficients* (1100)—A discussion of what becomes known as Pascal's Triangle, an array of numbers used as an aid in answering mathematical problems.

Lu Chen, *Historical Record of the Nine Countries* (904)—This treatise has a description of the first use of a flamethrower.

*Secret Basics of the Strange Dao of the True Source of Things* (850)—Provides a crude formula for gunpowder.

Shen Kuo, *Dream of Pool Essay* (1086)—A treatise on geology.

Song Yingxing, *Industrial Technology Handbook* (1637)—A well-illustrated book describing the methods and instruments used in the production of rice, salt, silk, pottery, metals, coal, ink, paper, ships, weapons, and many other items.

Song Zi, *Siyuanlu* (On the Redress of Injustice, 1247)—Song Zi was an accomplished scholar with an interest in the neo-Confucianism of Zhu Xi. He was appointed administrative official at Kanzhou, then the superintendent of justice in Canton and Hunan, and finally inspector-general. A study in forensic medicine, *Siyuanlu* consisted of only two chapters.

Su Song, *Illustrated Pharmacopoeia* (1062)—Notes the chemical content of certain plants.

Su, *New Design for a Mechanized Armillary Sphere and Celestial Globe* (1094)—Contained illustrations of Mercator-style map projections. One of these had a straight line running across the middle of the map as the equator and an arc above it, the ecliptic. Rectangular boxes of lunar mansions were clearly identified, with stars near the equator being more tightly packed together and those near the poles spread further apart. This book included the oldest published star maps in the world.

Yu Chang, *Various Thoughts on Medicine* (1643)—Analyzes smallpox and the prevention of epidemics.

Zhu Shijie, *Introduction to Mathematics* and *Emerald Mirror of the Four Rules* (1299–1303)—These treatises explain the rule of signs for plus and minus.

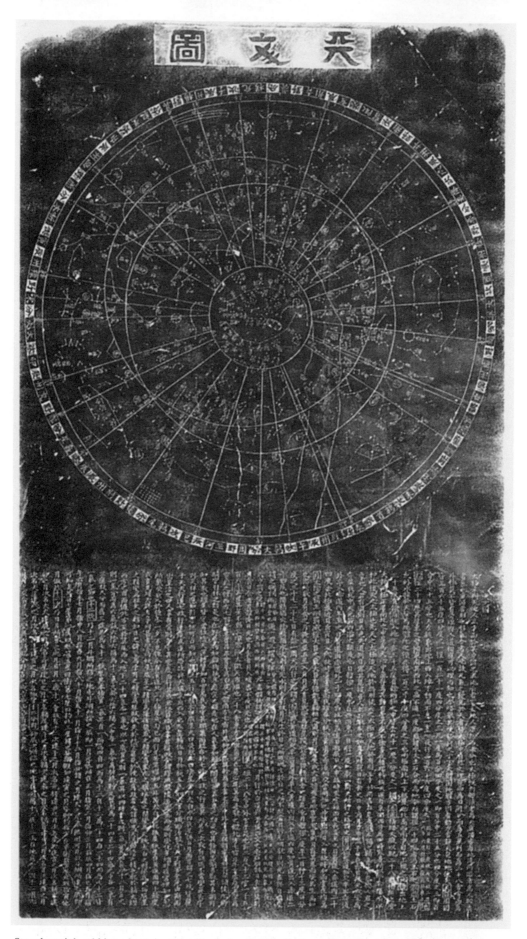

Star chart; ink rubbing of a stele at the Confucian Temple, Suzhou, 1247 (Stone Carving Museum, Suzhou)

# GLOSSARY

**Acupuncture:** The practice of piercing the skin with needles at certain points in order to alleviate pain and cure illnesses.

**Annam:** Kingdom on the eastern coast of Indochina (present-day Vietnam); first conquered by the Chinese in circa 200 B.C.E., it received its independence in the early fifteenth century.

**Arhat:** A **Buddhist** who has reached the stage of enlightenment.

*Bai Nian:* Literally, "New Year's greetings"; salutations practiced during the New Year celebration that served as a means to bond common folk together.

**Banner:** Group of fifteen thousand households in the **Manchu** system of military organization.

*Baojia:* A military registration system introduced in the late eleventh century by the **Song** (960–1279) reformer Wang Anshi; each household in an area provided and equipped a set number of militiamen; ten households made one *jia*, and ten *jia* made one *bao*.

**Beijing:** Literally, "northern capital"; capital city of the **Liao, Jin, Yuan,** and **Ming** dynasties located in northeastern China.

*Bo:* A board game played with dice and twelve colored pieces.

*Bonzes:* Buddhist monks.

**Buddhism:** The dominant religion in China and most of Asia, based on the teachings of the Indian Gautama Buddha; followers believe that all humans suffer, a condition that can be overcome by self-purification through meditation.

**Censorate:** Branch of government in the **Tang** dynasty responsible for hearing complaints from the general public and for preventing official corruption.

**Chang'an:** Capital city of the **Tang** dynasty located in east central China on the Wei River.

**China Proper:** Present-day People's Republic of China except for **Manchuria** and the island of Hainan.

**Chinese Arrows:** Rockets.

*Chiyuan Xinge:* Legal code of the **Yuan** dynasty that was only applicable to the Chinese population.

*Ci:* The ancestral hall where family ancestors were worshiped.

**Commercial Revolution:** A period of economic expansion that occurred during the **Song** dynasty, when technological advances, trade growth, handicraft industries, the use of paper money, and urbanization all reached unprecedented levels.

**Confucianism:** The state religion of China that was largely adopted by the scholarly class; based on the teachings of the ancient philosopher Kongzi (K'ung Ch'iu, or Confucius), Confucianism advanced the ideal of an educated, ethical, sympathetic, and wise elite.

*Corvée:* Forced labor; used by the Chinese as an early form of taxation.

*Daming Ling:* Great **Ming** Ordinance of 145 articles issued in 1368.

*Daming Lu:* **Ming** Legal Code of 606 articles issued in 1397.

**Daoism:** A mystical philosophy founded in the sixth century B.C.E. that was popular in China; it stressed working in harmony with nature.

*Di:* Younger brother.

*Dibao:* Village constable.

**Dragon Boat Festival:** Boat races celebrating the dragon who was believed to control rivers and rainfall.

**Eight-legged Essay:** A civil government examination of the late **Ming** dynasty administered in eight parts.

**Equal Field System:** A landholding system practiced during several dynasties in which equal amounts of agricultural land were held by adult peasants. First implemented by the Northern Wei in 485, the system was continued by the Sui (589–618) dynasty and was applied to the entire country. Although implemented by the **Tang** dynasty, the system was officially abolished in 780 as redistribution practices broke down.

*Fengzheng:* Kites.

**Fire-lance:** A crude firearm developed by 905.

**Fish Tally:** An adornment made of copper and carved with Chinese characters that was hung from the waist to indicate the rank of the wearer.

**Five Dynasties:** Succession of northern rulers from 907–960; they included the Later Liang dynasty (907–959), Later Tang dynasty (923–936), Later Jin dynasty (936–946), Later Han dynasty (947–950), and Later Zhou dynasty (951–960).

**Flying Cash:** Paper money used to pay for goods bought from distant regions and reimbursed at the capital.

**Footbinding:** A practice believed to have been started by palace dancers during the **Tang** period and introduced among upper-class women during the **Song** period, in which a young girl's feet were tightly wrapped by a long piece of cloth until all the toes, except the big toe, were broken and bent under the arch. This triangle-shaped "lily-foot," about half the size of a normal foot, crippled women for life, effectively confining them within the boundaries of the home.

**Forbidden City:** A general term given to the imperial palaces located in the capital cities of ruling dynasties between 617 and 1644. However, the name *Forbidden City* is used chiefly to refer to the palace complex in Beijing commissioned by the **Ming** emperor Yung-lo in 1406. It is located in the heart of the city on Tiananmen (Gate of Heavenly Peace) Square. First occupied in 1420, it encompasses 250 acres; it has walls 35 feet tall and a moat 171 feet wide. Twenty-four **Ming** and **Manchu** rulers lived here in several palaces, which have a total of 9,000 rooms. The Forbidden City received its name because commoners could not enter the complex; in fact, most government functionaries and imperial family members had only limited access. The emperor alone could move about at will.

**Frankish Bombards:** Cannons made in Europe and imported into China by **Ming** rulers.

*Fu:* Special prefectures or districts of the **Tang** empire; also means father.

*Fubing:* Militia.

*Gao Zhu Fu:* Great-great-grandfather.

*Gaoling:* A special clay used for making porcelain in the city of Jindezheng.

**Genghis Khan:** Literally, "Universal Ruler"; name given to the great **Mongol** leader Temüjin.

**Gentry:** The privileged class of official degree holders and landlords that emerged during the later **Tang** and **Song** periods and was considered the backbone of the government in traditional China.

**Gobi:** Desert in **Mongolia** about 500,000 square miles in size.

*Gong:* The artisan class.

**Grand Canal:** A series of waterways in **North China** connecting **Beijing** and Hangzhou. The longest man-made waterway in the world, it is 1,085 miles in length. Construction began during the Sui era (589–618) and the canal was extended by subsequent dynasties in order to facilitate the transportation of grain from the rich farmlands of the **Yangzi River** valley to heavily populated areas in the North.

**Great Wall:** Series of earth and stone fortifications built by individual kingdoms in **North China** and intended as a barrier to barbarian invasions. The state of Chou erected an early defensive system in the seventh century B.C.E., and other portions were completed in the third century B.C.E. The Great Wall was repaired, strengthened, and extended by various dynasties, especially the Han (206 B.C.E.–220 C.E.), Sui (589–618), and **Ming**. It is approximately 4,500 miles in length and averages anywhere from 15 to 30 feet in height and 15 to 25 feet in width.

**Greeting Tea:** The custom of offering tea to guests when they arrived at one's home.

*Gu or Gu Ma:* Aunt on father's side.

**Gunpowder:** An explosive mixture of potassium nitrate (saltpeter), sulfur, and charcoal, first used in China around the ninth century.

*Guo Zi Jian:* Literally, "State Academy Directorate"; the body overseeing Chinese education and examinations.

**Hakka:** A group of northern Chinese who migrated to southern China in the 1270s during the last years of the **Song** dynasty.

**Han:** The Chinese people, as opposed to the non-Chinese elements (Mongolians, Tibetans, etc.) in the population.

*Han ren:* Northern Chinese.

*Hang:* Trade guilds.

*Hao:* A nickname often adopted by a literary or elite individual.

**The Himalayas:** Vast mountain system covering most of Nepal, Sikkim, Bhutan, and southern **Tibet**; average elevation is 20,000 feet; the world's highest peak, Mount Everest (29,028 feet), is located here.

*Huchuang:* "Barbarian couch"; a type of chair used by Central Asian peoples.

*Jia:* The family.

*Jia Pu:* A record of a family's genealogy.

*Jia Zhang:* The family head or father.

*Jian:* The space between two beams in a building's wall.

*Ji Fu:* Stepfather.

*Ji Mu:* Stepmother.

**Jin:** Literally, "gold"; **Jurchen** dynasty during the period 1115–1234 characterized by military conquests.

*Jinshi:* Literally, "presented scholars"; **Ming**-era students who passed the metropolitan exam and were appointed to high government office. See *Juren* and *Xiucai.*

*Jiu:* Maternal uncle.

*Jiulianhuan:* Ring game.

**Jurchens:** Seminomadic and war-like people from **Manchuria**; called the Ruzhens by the Chinese. See **Jin**.

*Juren:* Literally, "elevated men"; **Ming**-era students who passed the provincial exam and were appointed to low-level positions in the government. See *Jinshi* and *Xiucai.*

**Karakorum:** Mongolian capital of **Genghis Khan** in the thirteenth century.

*Kesig:* Imperial palace troops of the **Yuan** dynasty.

**Khitans:** Turco-Mongolian tribesmen from southern **Manchuria**; called the Qidans by the Chinese and the Cathay by medieval Europeans. *See* **Liao.**

**Korea:** A peninsula on the eastern coast of Asia that fell under Chinese suzerainty during the imperial era (617–1644).

**Lamaism:** A form of Mahayana **Buddhism,** initially from **Tibet,** that incorporated elements of **Tantrism** and **Shamanism.**

**Leeboard:** A board attached to the hull of a sailing ship in order to prevent leeway or off-course lateral movement.

*Li:* The abstract form, or principle, believed to be the key in formulating things out of *qi* (matter) in the universe; also, a person's ultimate identity; it can refer to politeness in complying with all hierarchical orders and rites.

*Liang shui fa:* Literally, "Double Tax System"; a reform established by the **Tang** government in 780—to deal with fiscal problems resulting from the An Lushan rebellion (755)—that abandoned the **equal field system** and levied taxes twice a year on the amount of land held by peasant households.

**Liao:** **Khitan** dynasty during the period 916–1115 characterized by military conquests.

*Lijia* **system: Ming** administrative system in which families were grouped into tens and hundreds for local self-governance.

*Li Xue:* Literally, "Study of Principles"; the Chen-Zhu school of **neo-Confucianism.**

**Lion Dance:** A dance originally meant to frighten enemy soldiers and wild animals; it was later performed at New Year celebrations.

*Ma or Mu:* Mother.

*Majiang:* Mahjong; a game originally played with dice and 136 tiles.

**Manchuria:** Mountainous region in northeastern China; homeland of the **Jurchens, Khitans,** and **Manchus.**

**Manchus:** Nomadic and war-like tribesmen from the northeast who overthrew the **Ming** dynasty and established the Qing dynasty (1644–1912).

**Manichaeanism:** A Persian religion that accepted a dualistic view of the world (good versus evil) and a belief that the spirit was released from its material form at death.

*Mei:* Younger sister.

**Ming:** Literally, "radiance"; Chinese dynasty during the period 1368–1644 known for its political, economic, and cultural revival.

**Mongolia:** Region in eastern Central Asia inhabited by nomadic peoples united by the **Mongol** chieftain **Genghis Khan** in the thirteenth century.

**Mongols:** War-like tribesmen from present-day **Mongolia.** *See* **Yuan.**

*Nai Min:* Literally, "milk name"; a name given to a child by the mother.

*Nanquan:* A type of martial art stressing hand techniques.

*Nan ren:* Southern Chinese.

**Neo-Confucianism:** A new formulation of **Confucian** principles in reaction to the dominance of the **Buddhists** and the social upheaval caused by the An Lushan rebellion (755); adherents looked back to ancient traditions to design a philosophy that promoted the strength of family and state and emphasized personal improvement.

**New Laws:** Radical fiscal, military, and administrative reforms of **Wang Anshi** in the late eleventh century.

*Nong:* The peasantry.

**North China:** The **Yellow River** valley and surrounding areas.

**Ordos:** Desert region in **North China.**

**Pagoda:** A multistory tower, often part of a **Buddhist** temple complex, that functions as a tomb or monument.

**Pascal's Triangle:** A triangular array of numbers used in solving mathematical equations. First invented in China around 1100, it is usually attributed to the seventeenth-century French mathematician and philosopher Blaise Pascal. Every number in the triangle is equal to the total of the two numbers above and on either side of it (not including the ones). The Chinese called it "the tabulation structure for unlocking binomial coefficients."

**Picul:** A weight measurement; the equivalent of about 60 kilograms or 133 pounds.

**Pound-Lock:** An enclosure in a canal with gates at each end used for "pounding up," or raising, water levels so boats can pass through.

*Qi:* The single primal substance believed to make up the universe.

**Qing Ming Festival:** A spring celebration when people cleared and repaired the grave sites of their ancestors.

**Qinling Mountains:** Mountain range running east to west and dividing **North China** from **South China**; highest peak is 13,474 feet.

*Qiqiaoban:* A type of puzzle; known as Tangram in Europe.

**Red Turbans:** Secret political organization during the **Song** and **Yuan** periods.

*Ren:* Literally, "patience"; humanity or benevolence exhibited in performing all activities.

**Rhyton:** A drinking vessel shaped like an animal or an animal head.

*Ru Mu or Ru Ma:* Wet nurse.

*Sanjiao:* Literally, "Three Religions"; a philosophical system that integrated aspects of **Buddhist, Daoist,** and **Confucian** beliefs.

*Semu ren:* Western and Central Asians.

**Shamanism:** A religious practice based on the belief in good and evil spirits that can be summoned or heard through mediums.

*Shang:* The merchant class.

*Shangdi:* Supreme God.

*She:* A **Yuan** social structure that organized fifty households under the direction of the village leaders.

*Shi:* The family-clan organization; also the name for the scholar-official class.

*Shuangliu:* A board game similar to backgammon.

*Shu Mu:* Literally, "second mother"; concubine.

*Shupu:* A board game played with twenty colored pieces and five bamboo sticks.

*Shuyuan:* Private academies.

**Silk Road:** Also called the Silk Route, the Silk Road was approximately four thousand miles in length and linked the East and West. This ancient trade route (actually a caravan track) started in Sian in West China and led westward. The road followed the **Great Wall** before splitting: the South Road went through the mountain passes of the Pamirs and Hindu Kush to the Oxus River and India; the North Road skirted the northern edge of the Takla Makan Desert to the Jaxartes River and **Turkestan** and eventually the Levant. Shipments of silk came westward while wools, gold, and silver flowed eastward. Ambassadors, pilgrims, and missionaries also used the Silk Road. **Mongol** patrols thwarted the activities of bandits and made it safer to travel in the thirteenth and fourteenth centuries. Marco Polo used the route for part of his extensive journeys.

**Sixteen Prefectures:** Group of strategic northeastern border provinces.

*So:* Battalions or companies in the **Ming** military system.

**Song:** Chinese dynasty during the period 960–1279 known for civil administration and cultural achievements.

**South China:** The **West River** valley and surrounding areas.

**String of Money:** A string normally holding one thousand copper coins.

**Supreme Ultimate:** The principle of universal goodness in the **neo-Confucian** cosmology.

*Ta Cha:* Literally, "tea contest"; a game in which participants attempt to guess the origins of mystery teas.

*Taihe Lu:* Legal code of the **Jin** dynasty.

*Taijiquan:* "Supreme Pole Boxing"; a martial art emphasizing boxing and natural breathing.

**Tang:** Chinese dynasty during the period 618–907 characterized by centralized authority, government bureaucracy, territorial expansion, and agricultural and communication improvements; known as the Golden Age.

**Tang Code:** Set of laws first issued in 619 and periodically revised thereafter; a model for later codes, it dealt with criminal and administrative issues.

**Tantrism:** A mystical branch of Indian **Buddhism** that became popular late in the **Tang** dynasty.

*Tao:* Provinces of the **Tang** dynasty.

**Tartar Hat:** A woman's headdress, originally used in western China, that was made of brocade and black sheep's wool and covered with flowers.

**Tea Master:** A professional preparer and server of tea, often employed by wealthy families as a sign of status.

**Ten Kingdoms:** Group of predominantly southern polities from 902–979; they included the Wu kingdom (902–937), Southern Tang kingdom (937–975), Former Shu kingdom (907–925), Later Shu kingdom (935–965), Southern Han kingdom (917–971), Chu kingdom (927–951), Wu-Yue kingdom (907–978), Min kingdom (909–945), Nanping or Jingnan kingdom (924–963), and Northern Han kingdom (951–979).

**Thunderclap Bomb:** An explosive device that first appeared in the early eleventh century; the casing containing the **gunpowder** was made of bamboo or paper.

**Thundercrash Bomb:** An explosive device developed by the early thirteenth century. With a casing made of metal, it was more powerful than the earlier **thunderclap bomb.**

*Tianjiu:* Dominoes.

*Tiao:* Remote ancestors.

**Tibet:** A high plateau located in Central Asia and the home of powerful **Buddhist** kingdoms that emerged in the seventh and eighth centuries; region conquered by the **Mongols.**

*Tou Fu* (tofu): Bean curd.

**Treasure Ships:** The fleet of ships used by Zheng He (Cheng Ho) on his seven expeditions between 1405 and 1433. The largest of these vessels was 440 feet in length and had a displacement of 3,100 tons.

**Tribute System:** A mechanism developed by the Chinese to deal with the outside world, in which a tribute state accepted its vassal status; the system required the exchange of envoys and gifts, monitored foreign trade, and handled diplomatic relations.

*Tuntian:* **Ming** military colony.

**Turkestan:** Historical region of Central Asia comprised of present-day Turkmenistan, Uzbekistan, Kyrgyzstan, Tajikistan, southern Kazakhstan, northeastern Afghanistan, and western China.

**Uighurs:** Turkic people from **Mongolia** and eastern Turkestan.

**Wang Anshi Reforms:** A series of economic, military, and educational reforms introduced by Wang Anshi in the eleventh century. The reforms included a government monopoly on trade; low interest government loans; graduated land taxes; a revival of a collective military responsibility, called *baojia*, which organized peasant households into groups of tens (*bao*) and hundreds (*jia*) to maintain local peace and to provide a trained and armed militia at local expense; and reforms to the civil service examination system.

*Wang Zu:* Powerful family clans that dominated regions and were closely tied to the imperial government.

*Wei:* Garrison troops of a **Ming** military colony.

*Weiqi:* A board game played with white and black stones; also known as *yi* or *go*.

*Weisuo* **System:** **Ming** military organization in which troops rotate between the various garrisons of the empire.

**West River:** Chinese "Xi"; a river approximately 1,200 miles in length in southern China; it flows into the South China Sea close to Guangzhou.

**White Lotus Society:** Secret religious sect founded in the twelfth century and dedicated to the worship of the Buddha Amitabha.

*Wokou:* Japanese pirates.

*Wu Fu:* Literally, "Mourning Grades"; categories of mourning garments and time periods to be observed according to the differing relationships with the dead.

*Wu Jing:* The core moral and literary texts used formally to educate young men.

*Wu Lun:* The fundamental hierarchal human relations as spelled out by **Confucius.**

**Xi Xia:** Also known as Xia; the northwestern border state of the Tanguts, an ethnic group related to the Tibetans. A war-like people, the Tanguts formed an independent kingdom in the eleventh century.

*Xian:* Districts during the **Tang** dynasty.

*Xiangqi:* A board game similar to chess.

*Xiangyue:* Literally, "community compact"; regular local resident assemblies used to facilitate communication among families.

*Xiao:* Filial piety.

*Xia Qi:* Literally, "second wife"; a term given to the primary concubine of a married man. Other terms for concubines were *Xiao Qi* (minor wife) or *Ce Shi* (companion).

*Xin:* Sincerity and honesty in performing all rites.

*Xingshang zoufan:* Petty traveling peddlers.

*Xinjiang:* Mountainous region in western China traversed by the **Silk Road** and conquered during the **Tang** and **Yuan** dynasties.

*Xin Nian:* New Year.

*Xin Xue:* Literally, "Study of the Mind"; the Lu Wang school of **neo-Confucianism.**

*Xiong:* Elder brother.

*Xiucai:* Literally, "cultivated talents"; **Ming**-era students who passed the basic certification exam and frequently tutored the children of the elite. *See Jinshi* and *Juren.*

*Xiu Qi:* Literally, "dismissing a wife"; obtaining a divorce.

*Yang:* The masculine, aggressive principle in nature, which was balanced by *yin.*

**Yangzi River:** Chinese "Chang"; also known as the Yangtze; a major waterway in Central China that is an estimated 3,434 miles long; it empties into the East China Sea near Shanghai.

*Yang Mu:* An adopting mother.

**Yellow River:** Chinese "Huang"; major river in northern Central and East China, flowing 2,903 miles into the Yellow Sea.

*Yezi:* Playing cards.

*Yi:* Justice or righteousness that one should have in performing all hierarchical rites.

*Yi* or *Yi Ma:* Aunt on mother's side.

*Yin:* The feminine, passive principle in nature, which was balanced by *yang.*

*Yi tiao bian* (**Single Whip Reform**): Literally, "combining many items into one"; an economic reform, undertaken from 1522 to 1619 to solve **Ming** fiscal problems, which combined and simplified taxes into monetary payments.

**Yuan:** Literally, "first"; **Mongol** dynasty during the period 1279–1368 characterized by military conquests.

*Yuan Zhu:* Distant ancestors.

*Zhen Zhu Fu:* Great-grandfather.

*Zhi:* Wisdom and knowledge of all appropriate behavior.

*Zhongguo:* "Middle Kingdom," or China.

*Zhou:* Prefectures or districts of the **Tang** empire.

*Zhu Fu:* Grandfather.

*Zhu Mu:* Grandmother.

*Zi* or *Jie:* Elder sister.

*Zong:* The genealogy of a family; recent ancestors.

*Zongzi:* Sweet rice balls wrapped in bamboo or lotus leaves.

*Zongzu:* Groups of people who had the same surname, shared the same descent line, and were organized in the same age hierarchy.

**Zoroastrianism:** A Persian monotheistic religion based on the idea of the dualism of good and evil.

*Zu:* The kin or clan unit.

*Zuogu:* Large wholesale merchants or brokers.

*Zu Zhang:* The male elders in a clan.

# GENERAL REFERENCES

## GENERAL

Etienne Balazs and Yves Hervouet, eds., *A Sung Bibliography* (Hong Kong: Chinese University Press, 1978).

William Theodore de Bary, *The Liberal Tradition in China* (New York: Columbia University Press, 1983).

Bary and others, eds., *Sources of Chinese Tradition* (New York: Columbia University Press, 1960).

Woodbridge Bingham, *The Founding of the T'ang Dynasty: The Fall of Sui and Rise of T'ang, a Preliminary Survey* (Baltimore: Waverly Press, 1941).

Julia Ching and Willard G. Oxtoby, eds., *Discovering China: European Interpretations in the Enlightenment* (Rochester, N.Y.: University of Rochester Press, 1992).

Wolfram Eberhard, *A History of China*, translated by E. W. Dickes (Berkeley: University of California Press, 1950; London: Routledge & Kegan Paul, 1950).

Patricia Buckley Ebrey, *The Cambridge Illustrated History of China* (Cambridge & New York: Cambridge University Press, 1996).

Ebrey, ed., *Chinese Civilization and Society: A Sourcebook*, second revised edition (New York: Free Press, 1993).

John K. Fairbank and Merle Goldman, *China: A New History* (Cambridge, Mass. & London: Belknap Press of Harvard University Press, 1992).

Fairbank and others, *East Asia: Tradition and Transformation* (Boston: Houghton Mifflin, 1973).

C. P. Fitzgerald, *China: A Short Cultural History*, edited by C. G. Seligman (London: Cresset Press, 1935).

Herbert Franke, ed., *Sung Biographies*, 4 volumes (Wiesbaden: Steiner, 1976).

Wolfgang Franke, *An Introduction to the Sources of Ming History* (New York & Oxford: Oxford University Press, 1969).

L. Carrington Goodrich, ed., *Dictionary of Ming Biography, 1368–1644: The Ming Biographical History Project of the Association for Asian Studies* (New York: Columbia University Press, 1976).

Brian Hook, ed., *The Cambridge Encyclopedia of China* (Cambridge: Cambridge University Press, 1982).

Charles O. Hucker, *China to 1850: A Short History* (Stanford, Cal.: Stanford University Press, 1978).

Hucker, *China's Imperial Past: Introduction to Chinese History and Culture* (Stanford, Cal.: Stanford University Press, 1975).

Donald F. Lach and Carol Flaumenhaft, eds., *Asia on the Eve of Europe's Expansion* (Englewood Cliffs, N.J.: Prentice-Hall, 1965).

Dun J. Li, *The Essences of Chinese Civilization* (Princeton, N.J.: D. Van Nostrand, 1967).

Michael Loewe, *Imperial China: The Historical Background to the Modern Age* (New York: Praeger, 1966).

F. W. Mote, *Imperial China, 900–1800* (Cambridge, Mass.: Harvard University Press, 1999).

Igor de Rachewiltz and others, eds., *In the Service of the Khan: Eminent Personalities of the Early Mongol-Yuan Period (1200–1300)* (Wiesbaden: Harassowitz, 1993).

Witold Rodzinski, *A History of China*, 2 volumes (Oxford & New York: Pergamon Press, 1979–1983).

Paul S. Ropp, ed., *Heritage of China: Contemporary Perspectives on Chinese Civilization* (Berkeley: University of California Press, 1990).

Denis Twitchett and Fairbank, eds., *The Cambridge History of China*, 10 volumes (Cambridge & New York: Cambridge University Press, 1978–1998).

David Curtis Wright, *The History of China* (Westport, Conn.: Greenwood Press, 2001).

## GEOGRAPHY

Caroline Blunden and Mark Elvin, *Cultural Atlas of China* (New York: Facts on File, 1983).

Kang Chao, *Man and Land in Chinese History: An Economic Analysis* (Stanford, Cal.: Stanford University Press, 1986).

George B. Cressey, *Asia's Lands and People: A Geography of One-third of the Earth and Two-thirds of Its People* (New York: McGraw-Hill, 1963).

Elvin, *The Pattern of the Chinese Past* (Stanford, Cal.: Stanford University Press, 1973).

John K. Fairbank and Edwin O. Reischauer, *East Asia: Tradition and Transformation* (Boston: Houghton Mifflin, 1989).

Albert Hermann, *Historical and Commercial Atlas of China* (Chicago: Aldine, 1966).

John Larner, *Marco Polo and the Discovery of the World* (New Haven: Yale University Press, 1999).

Dun J. Li, ed., *The Essence of Chinese Civilization* (Princeton, N.J.: D. Van Nostrand, 1967).

Michael Loewe, *The Pride that Was China* (New York: St. Martin's Press, 1990).

Milton W. Meyer, *China: An Introductory History* (Totowa, N.J.: Littlefield, Adams, 1978).

Leo J. Moser, *The Chinese Mosaic: The Peoples and Provinces of China* (Boulder, Colo.: Westview Press, 1985).

Pierre Pfeffer, *Asia: A Natural History* (New York: Random House, 1968).

Christopher J. Smith, *China: People and Places in the Land of One Billion* (Boulder, Colo.: Westview Press, 1991).

Thomas R. Tregear, *A Geography of China* (London: University of London Press, 1965).

## THE ARTS

Cyril Birch, ed., *Anthology of Chinese Literature: From Early Times to the Fourteenth Century* (New York: Grove, 1965).

Andrew Boyd, *Chinese Architecture and Town Planning, 1500 B.C.–A.D. 1911* (Chicago: University of Chicago Press, 1962).

Jonathan Chaves, ed. and trans., *The Columbia Book of Later Chinese Poetry: Yüan, Ming, and Ch'ing Dynasties (1279–1911)* (New York: Columbia University Press, 1986).

Eva Shan Chou, *Reconsidering Tu Fu: Literary Greatness and Cultural Context* (New York: Cambridge University Press, 1995).

Craig Clunas, *Art in China* (Oxford & New York: Oxford University Press, 1997).

Arthur Cooper, trans., *Li Po and Tu Fu* (Baltimore: Penguin, 1973).

Lucy Chao Ho, *"More Gracile than Yellow Flowers": The Life and Works of Li Qingzhao* (Hong Kong: Mayfair Press, 1968).

Dorothy Hoobler, Thomas Hoobler, and Victoria Bruck, *Chinese Portraits* (Austin, Tex.: Raintree / Steck-Vaughn, 1992).

Wilt Idema and Stephen West, *Chinese Theater 1100–1450: A Source Book* (Wiesbaden: Steiner, 1982).

Liang Ssu-ch'eng, *A Pictorial History of Chinese Architecture: A Study of the Development of Its Structural System and the Evolution of Its Types,* edited by Wilma Fairbank (Cambridge, Mass. & London: MIT Press, 1984).

Lin Yutang, *The Gay Genius: The Life and Times of Su Tungpo* (New York: John Day, 1947).

William Lindesay, *The Great Wall* (Hong Kong: Odyssey, 1998).

Wu-chi Liu and Irving Yucheng Lo, eds., *Sunflower Splendor: Three Thousand Years of Chinese Poetry* (Bloomington: Indiana University Press, 1975).

Colin Mackerras, *Chinese Drama: A Historical Survey* (Beijing: New World Press, 1990).

Mackerras, ed., *Chinese Theater: From Its Origins to the Present Day* (Honolulu: University of Hawaii Press, 1983).

Victor H. Mair, ed., *The Columbia Anthology of Traditional Chinese Literature* (New York: Columbia University Press, 1994).

Mair, ed., *The Columbia History of Chinese Literature* (New York: Columbia University Press, 2001).

William H. Nienhauser Jr., *Bibliography of Selected Western Works on Tang Dynasty Literature* (Taipei: Center for Chinese Studies, 1988).

Stephen Owen, ed. and trans., *An Anthology of Chinese Literature, Beginning to 1911* (New York: Norton, 1996).

Michèle Pirazzoli-T'Serstevens, *Living Architecture: Chinese,* translated by Robert Allen (London: Macdonald, 1972).

Ru Jinghua and Peng Hualiang, *Palace Architecture: Ancient Chinese Architecture,* translated by Zang Erzhong and others (Vienna & New York: Springer, 1998).

Conrad Schirokauer, *A Brief History of Chinese and Japanese Civilizations* (Orlando: Harcourt Brace Jovanovich, 1989).

Rosemary E. Scott, ed., *The Porcelains of Jingdezhen* (London: Percival David Foundation of Chinese Art, 1993).

Shi Yongnan and Wang Tianxing, *Gugong: The Former Imperial Palace in Beijng* (Beijing: China Esperanto Press, 1995).

Laurence Sickman and Alexander Soper, *The Art and Architecture of China* (New York: Penguin, 1984).

Joan Stanley-Baker, *Japanese Art* (London: Thames & Hudson, 1984).

Michael Sullivan, *The Arts of China,* fourth edition, expanded and revised (Berkeley: University of California Press, 1999).

Nicole Vandier-Nicolas, *Chinese Painting: An Expression of a Civilization,* translated by Janet Seligman (New York: Rizzoli, 1983).

Marsha L. Wagner, *Wang Wei* (Boston: Twayne, 1981).

Dorothy B. Walmsley, *Wang Wei, the Painter-Poet* (Rutland, Vt.: Tuttle, 1968).

Burton Watson, ed. and trans., *The Columbia Book of Chinese Poetry: From Early Times to the Thirteenth Century* (New York: Columbia University Press, 1984).

Roderick Whitfield, Susan Whitfield, and Neville Agnew, *Cave Temples of Dunhuang: Art and History on the Silk Road* (London: British Library, 2000).

Zhang Tingchen and Wei Bosi, trans., *100 Tang Poems* (Beijing: Chinese Translation Company / Hong Kong: Business Press, 1994).

## COMMUNICATION, TRANSPORTATION, AND EXPLORATION

Thomas T. Allsen, *Mongol Imperialism: The Policies of the Grand Qan Mongke in China, Russia, and the Islamic Lands* (Berkeley: University of California Press, 1987).

Christopher I. Beckwith, *The Tibetan Empire of Central Asia: A History of the Struggle for Great Power among Tibetans, Turks, Arabs, and Chinese during the Early Middle Ages* (Princeton: Princeton University Press, 1987).

Thomas F. Carter, *The Invention of Printing in China and Its Spread Westward,* revised edition by L. Carrington Goodrich (New York: Ronald, 1955).

Jack Dabbs, *History of the Discovery and Exploration of Chinese Turkestan* (The Hague, Netherlands: Mouton, 1963).

George H. Dunne, *Generation of Giants: The Story of the Jesuits in China in the Last Decades of the Ming Dynasty* (Notre Dame, Ind.: University of Notre Dame Press, 1962).

J. J. L. Duyvendak, "The True Dates of the Chinese Maritime Expeditions in the Early Fifteenth Century," *T'oung Pao,* 24 (1938): 349–355.

C. P. Fitzgerald, *The Southern Expansion of the Chinese People* (London: Barrie & Jenkins, 1972).

Robert A. D. Forrest, *The Chinese Language* (London: Faber & Faber, 1973).

Richard von Glahn, *The Country of Streams and Grottoes: Expansion, Settlement, and the Civilizing of the Sichuan Frontier in Song Times* (Cambridge, Mass.: Harvard University Press, 1987).

James M. Hargett, *On the Road in Twelfth Century China: The Travel Diaries of Fan Chengda (1126–1193)* (Stuttgart: Steiner Verlag Wiesbaden, 1989).

Ryoichi Hayashi, *The Silk Road and the Shoso-in* (New York: Weatherhill, 1975).

Louise Levathes, *When China Ruled the Seas: The Treasure Fleet of the Dragon Throne, 1400–1433* (New York: Simon & Schuster, 1994).

Chih-Ch'ang Li, *The Travels of an Alchemist,* translated by Arthur Waley (London: Routledge, 1931).

Brian E. McKnight, *Village and Bureaucracy in Southern Sung China* (Chicago: University of Chicago Press, 1971).

Jerry Norman, *Chinese* (Cambridge & New York: Cambridge University Press, 1988).

Robert Payne, *The Canal Builders: The Story of Canal Engineers through the Ages* (New York: Macmillan, 1959).

Edwin G. Pulleyblank, *Middle Chinese: A Study in Historical Phonology* (Vancouver: University of British Columbia Press, 1984).

Edwin O. Reischauer, *Ennin's Travels in T'ang China* (New York: Ronald, 1955).

E-tun Sun and Shiou-chuan Sun, trans., *T'ien-kung k'ai-wu: Chinese Technology in the Seventeenth Century* (University Park: Pennsylvania State University Press, 1966).

*Transport in Transition: The Evolution of Traditional Shipping in China,* translated by Andrew Watson (Ann Arbor: Center for Chinese Studies, University of Michigan, 1972).

Denis Twitchett, *Printing and Publishing in Medieval China* (New York: Frederic C. Beil, 1983).

Herold J. Wiens, *Han Chinese Expansion in South China* (Hamden, Conn.: Shoe String, 1967).

Ch'en Yüan, *Western and Central Asians in China under the Mongols,* translated by Ch'ien Hsing-hai and Goodrich (Berkeley: University of California Press, 1966).

## SOCIAL CLASS SYSTEM AND THE ECONOMY

Kwan Man Bun, *The Salt Merchants of Tianjin: State-making and Civil Society in Late Imperial China* (Honolulu: University of Hawaii Press, 2001).

Robert Collins, *East to Cathay: The Silk Road* (New York: McGraw-Hill, 1968).

John Winthrop Haeger, ed., *Crisis and Prosperity in Sung China* (Tucson: University of Arizona Press, 1975).

Ping-ti Ho, *The Ladder of Success in Imperial China: Aspects of Social Mobility, 1368–1911* (New York: Columbia University Press, 1962).

Ayao Hoshi, *The Ming Tribute Grain System,* translated by Mark Elvin (Ann Arbor: Center for Chinese Studies, University of Michigan, 1969).

Charles O. Hucker, *The Ming Dynasty: Its Origins and Evolving Institutions* (Ann Arbor: Center for Chinese Studies, University of Michigan, 1978).

John D. Langlois Jr., ed., *China under Mongol Rule* (Princeton: Princeton University Press, 1981).

James T. C. Liu, *Reform in Sung China: Wang An-shih (1021–1086) and His New Policies* (Cambridge, Mass.: Harvard University Press, 1959).

Robert B. Marks, *Tigers, Rice, Silk, and Silt: Environment and Economy in Late Imperial South China* (Cambridge & New York: Cambridge University Press, 1997).

Edward H. Schafer, *The Golden Peaches of Samarkand: A Study of T'ang Exotics* (Berkeley: University of California Press, 1963).

Paul J. Smith, *Taxing Heaven's Storehouse: Horses, Bureaucrats, and the Destruction of the Sichuan Tea Industry, 1074–1224* (Cambridge, Mass.: Council on East Asian Studies, Harvard University, 1991).

Chiang Tao-chang, *The Significance of the Salt Industry in Ch'ing China* (Singapore: Institute of Humanities and Social Sciences, College of Graduate Studies, Nanyang University, 1976).

Denis Crispin Twitchett, *Financial Administration under T'ang Dynasty* (Cambridge: Cambridge University Press, 1963).

Pan Yihong, *Son of Heaven and Heavenly Qaghan: Sui-Tang China and Its Neighbors* (Bellingham: Center for East Asian Studies, Western Washington University, 1997).

Shiba Yoshinobu, *Commerce and Society in Sung China*, translated by Mark Elvin (Ann Arbor: University of Michigan Press, 1970).

## POLITICS, LAW, AND THE MILITARY

Etienne Balazs, *Chinese Civilization and Bureaucracy* (New Haven: Yale University Press, 1964).

Derk Bodde, *Law in Imperial China* (Cambridge, Mass.: Harvard University Press, 1967).

Albert Chan, *The Glory and Fall of the Ming Dynasty* (Norman: University of Oklahoma Press, 1982).

Hok-lam Chan, *Legitimation in Imperial China: Discussion under the Jurchen-chin Dynasty (1115–1234)* (Seattle: University of Washington Press, 1984).

Paul Heng-chao Chen, *Chinese Legal Tradition under the Mongols: The Code of 1291 as Reconstructed* (Princeton: Princeton University Press, 1979).

Hsiao Ch'i-ching, *The Military Establishment of the Yuan Dynasty* (Cambridge, Mass.: Harvard University Press, 1978).

Tung-tsu Chu, *Law and Society in Traditional China* (Paris: Mouton, 1961).

John W. Dardess, *Confucianism and Autocracy: Professional Elites in the Founding of the Ming Dynasty* (Berkeley: University of California Press, 1983).

Richard L. Davis, *Wind Against the Mountain: The Crisis of Politics and Culture in Thirteenth-century China* (Cambridge, Mass.: Harvard University Press, 1996).

Edward Dreyer, *Early Ming China: A Political History, 1355–1435* (Stanford, Cal.: Stanford University Press, 1982).

Elizabeth Endicott-West, *Mongolian Rule in China: Local Administration in the Yuan Dynasty* (Cambridge, Mass.: Harvard University Press, 1989).

Edward Farmer, *Early Ming Government: The Evolution of Dual Capitals* (Cambridge, Mass.: Harvard University Press, 1976).

C. P. Fitzgerald, *Son of Heaven: A Biography of Li Shih-min, Founder of the Tang Dynasty* (Cambridge: Cambridge University Press, 1933).

Herbert Franke, *China Under Mongol Rule* (Aldershot, U.K.: Variorum, 1994).

R. W. L. Guisso, *Wu Tse-t'en and the Politics of Legitimation in T'ang China* (Bellingham: Western Washington University, 1978).

Charles Hartman, *Han Yu and the Tang Search for Unity* (Princeton: Princeton University Press, 1986).

Ray Huang, *1587, A Year of No Significance: The Ming Dynasty in Decline* (New Haven: Yale University Press, 1981).

Charles O. Hucker, *The Traditional Chinese State in Ming Times (1368–1644)* (Tucson: University of Arizona Press, 1961).

Hucker, ed., *Chinese Government in Ming Times: Seven Studies* (New York: Columbia University Press, 1969).

Wallace Johnson, trans., *The Tang Code*, volume 1: *General Principles* (Princeton: Princeton University Press, 1979).

Adam T. Kessler, *Empire Beyond the Great Wall: The Heritage of Genghis Khan* (Los Angeles: Natural History Museum of Los Angeles County, 1993).

Edward A. Kracke, *Civil Service in Sung China: 960–1067* (Cambridge, Mass.: Harvard University Press, 1953).

Thomas H. C. Lee, *Government Education and Examination in Sung China* (Hong Kong: Chinese University of Hong Kong, 1985).

R. P. Lister, *Genghis Khan* (New York: Stein & Day, 1969).

James T. C. Liu, *China Turning Inward: Intellectual—Political Change in Early Twelfth Century* (Cambridge, Mass.: Harvard University Press, 1988).

Brian E. McKnight, *Law and Order in Sung China* (Cambridge: Cambridge University Press, 1992).

Ann Paluden, *The Imperial Ming Tombs* (New Haven: Yale University Press, 1981).

James B. Parsons, *The Peasant Rebellions of the Late Ming Dynasty* (Tucson: University of Arizona Press, 1970).

Paul Ratchnevsky, *Genghis Khan: His Life and Legacy*, translated by Thomas N. Haining (Oxford: Blackwell, 1992).

Edwin Reischauer, *The Background of the Rebellion of An Lu-shan* (London: Oxford University Press, 1955).

Morris Rossabi, *The Jurchens in the Yuan and Ming* (Ithaca, N.Y.: Cornell University Press, 1982).

Rossabi, *Khubilai Khan: His Life and Times* (Berkeley: University of California Press, 1988).

Edward Schafer, *The Divine Women: Dragon Ladies and Rain Maidens in T'ang Literature* (Berkeley: University of California Press, 1973).

Romeyn Taylor, trans., *The Basic Annals of Ming T'ai-tsu* (San Francisco: Chinese Materials Center, 1975).

Shih-shan Henry Tsai, *Perpetual Happiness: The Ming Emperor Yongle* (Seattle: University of Washington Press, 2001).

Denis Twitchett and Arthur F. Wright, eds., *Perspectives on the Tang* (New Haven: Yale University Press, 1973).

## LEISURE, RECREATION, AND DAILY LIFE

E. N. Anderson, *The Food of China* (New Haven: Yale University Press, 1988).

Hilary J. Beattie, *Land and Lineage in China: A Study of T'ung-ch'eng County, Anhwei, in the Ming and Ch'ing Dynasties* (Cambridge & New York: Cambridge University Press, 1979).

Charles D. Benn, *Daily Life in Traditional China: The Tang Dynasty* (Westport, Conn.: Greenwood Press, 2002).

Andrew Boyd, *Chinese Architecture and Town Planning, 1500 B.C.–A.D. 1911* (Chicago: University of Chicago Press, 1962).

Victoria Cass, *Dangerous Women: Warriors, Grannies, and Geishas of the Ming* (Lanham, Md.: Rowman & Littlefield, 1999).

K. C. Chang, ed., *Food in Chinese Culture: Anthropological and Historical Perspectives* (New Haven: Yale University Press, 1977).

Kit Chow and Ione Kramer, *All the Tea in China* (San Francisco: China Books, 1990).

Hugh R. Clark, *Community, Trade, and Networks: Southern Fujian Province from the Third to the Thirteenth Century* (Cambridge & New York: Cambridge University Press, 1991).

Richard L. Davis, *Court and Family in Sung China, 960–1279: Bureaucratic Success and Kinship Fortunes for the Shih of Ming-chou* (Durham, N.C.: Duke University Press, 1986).

John C. Evans, *Tea in China: The History of China's National Drink* (New York: Greenwood Press, 1992).

Valery M. Garrett, *Chinese Clothing: An Illustrated Guide* (Hong Kong & New York: Oxford University Press, 1994).

Henry Inn, *Chinese Houses and Gardens*, edited by Shao Chang Lee (Honolulu: Fong's Inn Limited, 1940).

Ronald G. Knapp, *China's Traditional Rural Architecture: A Cultural Geography of the Common House* (Honolulu: University of Hawaii Press, 1986).

Lu Yu, *The Classic of Tea*, translated by Francis Ross Carpenter (Boston: Little, Brown, 1974).

John Curtis Perry and Bardwell L. Smith, eds., *Essays on T'ang Society: The Interplays of Social, Political and Economic Forces* (Leiden: E. J. Brill, 1976).

Edward H. Schafer, *The Vermilion Bird: T'ang Images of the South* (Berkeley: University of California Press, 1967).

Frederick J. Simoons, *Food in China: A Cultural and Historical Inquiry* (Boca Raton, Fla.: CRC Press, 1991).

Reay Tannahill, *Food in History* (New York: Stein & Day, 1973).

William H. Ukers, *All About Tea*, volume 1 (New York: The Tea and Coffee Trade Journal Company, 1935).

James C. Y. Watt and Anne E. Wardwell, *When Silk Was Gold: Central Asian and Chinese Textiles* (New York: Metropolitan Museum of Art, 1997).

Zhao Feng, "Art of Silk and Art on Silk in China," in *China: 5000 Years,* edited by Howard Rogers (New York: Guggenheim Museum Publications, 1998), pp. 98–102.

Zhao, *Treasures in Silk: An Illustrated History of Chinese Textiles* (Hong Kong: Edith Cheung, 1999).

Zhou Xun and Gao Chunming, *5000 Years of Chinese Costumes* (San Francisco: China Books & Periodicals, 1987; Hong Kong: Commercial Press, 1987).

## THE FAMILY AND SOCIAL TRENDS

Hugh D. R. Baker, *Chinese Family and Kinship* (New York: Columbia University Press, 1979).

Patricia Buckley Ebrey, *The Aristocratic Families of Early Imperial China: A Case Study of the Po-ling Tsui Family* (Cambridge & New York: Cambridge University Press, 1978).

Ebrey, *The Inner Quarters: Marriage and the Lives of Chinese Women in the Song Period* (Berkeley: University of California Press, 1993).

Ebrey and James L. Watson, eds., *Kinship Organization in Late Imperial China, 1000–1940* (Berkeley: University of California Press, 1986).

Ebrey, trans., *Chu Hsi's Family Rituals: A Twelfth-Century Chinese Manual for the Performance of Cappings, Weddings, Funerals, and Ancestral Rites* (Princeton: Princeton University Press, 1991).

Werner Eichhorn, *Kulturgeschichte Chinas,* translated as *Chinese Civilization: An Introduction,* by Janet Seligman (New York: Praeger, 1969).

Han-Yi Feng, *The Chinese Kinship System* (Cambridge, Mass.: Harvard University Press, 1967).

Maurice Freedman, *Chinese Lineage and Society: Fukien and Kwangtung* (London: Athlone Press, 1966; New York: Humanities Press, 1966).

Freedman, *Rites and Duties, Or Chinese Marriage: An Inaugural Lecture Delivered 26 January 1967* (London: London School of Economics, Bell, 1967).

Freedman, ed., *Family and Kinship in Chinese Society* (Stanford, Cal.: Stanford University Press, 1970).

Shen Fuwei, *Cultural Flow between China and the Outside World Thru out History* (Beijing: Foreign Language Press, 1996).

R. H. van Gaelic, *Erotic Colour Prints of the Ming Period: With an Essay on Chinese Sex Life from the Han to the Ch'ing dynasty, B.C. 206–A.D. 1644*, translated as *Mi Xi Tu Kao: Fu Lun Han Dai Zhi Qing Dai Di Zhongguo Xing Sheng Huo, Gong Yuan Qian 206 Nian–Kung Yüan 1644 Nien* by Yang Quan (Guangdong, China: Guangdong People's Press, 1992).

Paul Rakita Goldin, *The Culture of Sex in Ancient China* (Honolulu: University of Hawaii Press, 2002).

Richard Gunde, *Culture and Customs of China* (Westport, Conn.: Greenwood Press, 2002).

Isaac Taylor Headland, *Home Life in China* (New York: Macmillan, 1914).

Dorothy Ko, *Every Step a Lotus: Shoes for Bound Feet* (Berkeley: University of California Press, 2001).

Li-Ch'eng Kuo, *Chung-Kuo Min Su Shih Hua* (Tales of Chinese Folk Customs) (Taiwan: Hankuang Press, 1983).

Norman Kutcher, *Mourning in Late Imperial China: Filial Piety and the State* (New York: Cambridge University Press, 1999).

Olga Lang, *Chinese Family and Society* (New Haven: Yale University Press, 1946; London: Cumberlege, 1946).

Thomas H. C. Lee, *Education in Traditional China: A History* (Leiden & Boston: E. J. Brill, 2000).

Howard S. Levy, *Chinese Footbinding: The History of a Curious Erotic Custom* (New York: Rawls, 1966).

James T. C. Liu and Wei-Ming Tu, eds., *Traditional China* (Englewood Cliffs, N.J.: Prentice-Hall, 1970).

Ta-lin Liu, *Chung-kuo Ku Tai Hsing Wen Hua*, translated as *The Sex Culture of China* (Ningxia, China: Ningxia People's Press, 1994).

Wang Ping, *Aching for Beauty: Footbinding in China* (Minneapolis: University of Minnesota Press, 2000).

Yongzhou Qin, *Zhongguo She Hui Feng Shu Shi* (History of Chinese Social Customs) (Shangdong, China: Shangdong People's Press, 2000).

Shuang Ren, *Tang Dai Li Zhi Jiu* (The Rites of the Tang Dynasty) (Changchun, China: Northeast University Press, 1999).

Weiming Shi, *Yuan Dai Shen Huo* (Social History of the Yuan Dynasty) (Bejing: Chinese Social Sciences Academy Press, 1996).

Leon E. Stover, *The Cultural Ecology of Chinese Civilization: Peasants and Elites in the Last of the Agrarian States* (New York: Pica Press, 1974).

Sing Ging Su, *The Chinese Family System* (New York: International Press, 1922).

Hoyt Cleveland Tillman, *Confucian Discourse and Chu Hsi's Ascendancy* (Honolulu: University of Hawaii Press, 1992).

Hui-Chen Wang, *The Traditional Chinese Clan Rules* (Locust Valley, N.Y.: Association for Asian Studies, Augustin, 1959).

Rubie S. Watson and Ebrey, eds., *Marriage and Inequality in Chinese Society* (Berkeley: University of California Press, 1991).

H. P. Wilkinson, *The Family in Classical China* (Shanghai: Kelly & Walsh, 1926).

Zhenman Zheng, *Ming Qing Fujian jia zu zu zhi yu she hui bian qian*, translated as *Family Lineage Organization and Social Change in Ming and Qing Fujian*, by Michael Szonyi and others (Honolulu: University of Hawaii Press, 2001).

Ruikai Zhu, *Zhongguo Hun Yin Jia Ting Shi*, translated as *History of the Family and Marriage in China* (Shanghai: Xueling Press, 1999).

## RELIGION AND PHILOSOPHY

William Theodore de Bary, *Neo-Confucian Orthodoxy and the Learning of the Mind-and-Heart* (New York: Columbia University Press, 1981).

Alison Harley Black, *Man and Nature in the Philosophical Thought of Wang Fu-chih* (Seattle: University of Washington Press, 1989).

Judith M. Boltz, *A Survey of Taoist Literature: Tenth to Seventh Centuries* (Berkeley: Institute for East Asian Studies and Center for Chinese Studies, University of California, 1987).

Timothy Brook, *Praying for Power: Buddhism and the Formation of Gentry Society in Late-Ming China* (Cambridge, Mass.: Harvard University Press, 1993).

Wang-tsit Chan, *Chu Hsi: New Studies* (Honolulu: University of Hawaii Press, 1989).

Chan, ed., *Chu Hsi and Neo-Confucianism* (Honolulu: University of Hawaii Press, 1986).

Chan, ed., *A Source Book in Chinese Philosophy* (Princeton: Princeton University Press, 1975).

Carson Chang, *Development of Neo-Confucian Thought*, 2 volumes (New York: Bookman, 1957–1962).

Kenneth K. S. Chen, *Buddhism in China: A Historical Survey* (Princeton: Princeton University Press, 1964).

Chen, *The Chinese Transformation of Buddhism* (Princeton: Princeton University Press, 1973).

Julia Ching, *To Acquire Wisdom: The Way of Wang Yang-ming* (New York: Columbia University Press, 1976).

Clarence Burton Day, *The Philosophers of China: Classical and Contemporary* (London: Owen; New York: Philosophical Library, 1962).

Jacques Gernet, *Buddhism in Chinese Society: An Economic History from the Fifth to the Tenth Centuries,* translated by Franeisus Verellen (New York: Columbia University Press, 1995).

Gernet, *China and the Christian Impact: A Conflict of Cultures,* translated by Janet Lloyd (Cambridge & New York: Cambridge University Press, 1985).

Marcel Granet, *The Religion of the Chinese People,* translated by Maurice Freedman (Oxford: Blackwell, 1975).

Peter N. Gregory, *Inquiry into the Origin of Humanity: An Annotated Translation of Tsung-mi's Yüan jen lun with a Modern Commentary* (Honolulu: University of Hawaii Press, 1995).

Gregory, *Tsung-mi and the Sinification of Buddhism* (Princeton: Princeton University Press, 1991).

Joanna F. Handlin, *Action in Late Ming Thought: The Reorientation of Lu Kun and Other Scholar-Officials* (Berkeley: University of California Press, 1983).

John B. Henderson, *The Development and Decline of Chinese Cosmology* (New York: Columbia University Press, 1984).

Kung-Chuan Hsiao, *A History of Chinese Political Thought,* translated by F. W. Mote (Princeton: Princeton University Press, 1979).

Charles O. Hucker, *China's Imperial Past: An Introduction to Chinese History and Culture* (Stanford, Cal.: Stanford University Press, 1975).

E. R. Hughes and K. Hughes, *Religion in China* (London & New York: Hutchinson's University Library, 1950).

Christian Jochim, *Chinese Religions: A Cultural Perspective* (Englewood Cliffs, N.J.: Prentice-Hall, 1986).

Francois Jullien, *The Propensity of Things: Toward a History of Efficacy in China,* translated by Janet Lloyd (New York: Zone Books, 1995).

Max Kaltenmark, *Lao Tzu and Taoism,* translated by Roger Greaves (Stanford, Cal.: Stanford University Press, 1969).

John M. Koller, *Oriental Philosophies* (New York: Scribners, 1970).

John Lagerwey, *Taoist Ritual in Chinese Society and History* (New York: Macmillan; London: Collier-Macmillan, 1987).

Kenneth Scott Latourette, *A History of Christian Missions in China* (London: Society for Promoting Christian Knowledge; New York: Macmillan, 1929).

Jonathan N. Lipman, *Familiar Strangers: A History of Muslims in Northwest China* (Seattle: University of Washington Press, 1997).

Henri Maspero, *Taoism and Chinese Religion,* translated by Frank A. Kierman Jr. (Amherst: University of Massachusetts Press, 1981).

Thomas A. Metzger, *Escape from Predicament: Neo-Confucianism and China's Evolving Political Culture* (New York: Columbia University Press, 1977).

Mote, *Intellectual Foundations of China* (New York: Knopf, 1971).

A. C. Moule, *Christians in China before the Year 1550* (London: Society for Promoting Christian Knowledge; New York: Macmillan, 1930).

W. Pachow, *Chinese Buddhism: Aspects of Interaction and Reinterpretation* (Washington, D.C.: University Press of America, 1980).

Kristofer Schipper, *The Taoist Body* (Berkeley: University of California Press, 1993).

D. Howard Smith, *Chinese Religions* (New York: Holt, Rinehart & Winston, 1968).

Laurence G. Thompson, *Chinese Religion: An Introduction* (Belmont, Cal.: Dickenson, 1969).

Huang Tsung-hsi, *The Records of Ming Scholars,* translated by Julia Ching and Chaoying Fang (Honolulu: University of Hawaii Press, 1987).

Arthur F. Wright, *Buddhism in Chinese History* (Stanford, Cal.: Stanford University Press, 1959).

Wang Yang-ming, *The Philosophy of Wang Yang-ming,* translated by Frederick Goodrich Henke (London & Chicago: Open Court, 1916).

Feng Yu-lan, *A History of Chinese Philosophy,* second edition, translated by Derk Bodde (Princeton: Princeton University Press, 1952–1953).

Erik Zurcher, *The Buddhist Conquest of China: The Spread and Adaptation of Buddhism in Early Medieval China* (Leiden: E. J. Brill, 1959).

## SCIENCE, TECHNOLOGY, AND HEALTH

William Theodore de Bary, *Self and Society in Ming Thought* (New York: Columbia University Press, 1970).

Derk Bodde, *Chinese Thought, Society, and Science: The Intellectual and Social Background of Science and Technology in Pre-Modern China* (Honolulu: University of Hawaii Press, 1991).

Pierre Huard and Ming Wong, *Chinese Medicine* (New York: McGraw-Hill, 1968).

Edward H. Hume, *The Chinese Way in Medicine* (Baltimore: Johns Hopkins University Press, 1940).

Kenneth F. Kiple, ed., *The Cambridge World History of Human Disease* (Cambridge & New York: Cambridge University Press, 1993).

Yoshio Mikami, *The Development of Mathematics in China and Japan*, second edition (New York: Chelsea, 1974).

Joseph Needham, *Clerks and Craftsmen in China and the West* (Cambridge: Cambridge University Press, 1970).

Needham, *Science and Civilization in China*, 7 volumes (Cambridge: Cambridge University Press, 1954–present).

Manfred Porkert, *The Theoretical Foundations of Chinese Medicine: Systems of Correspondence* (Cambridge, Mass.: MIT Press, 1974).

Walther Riese, *The Concept of Disease: Its History, Its Versions, and Its Nature* (New York: Philosophical Library, 1953).

Edward H. Schafter, *Pacing the Void: Tang Approaches to the Stars* (Berkeley: University of California Press, 1977).

Henry E. Sigerist, *Civilization and Disease* (Ithaca, N.Y.: Cornell University Press, 1943).

Nathan Sivin, "Science and Medicine in Imperial China—The State of the Field," *Journal of Asian Studies*, 41 (1988): 41–90.

E-tun Sun and Shiou-chuan Sun, trans., *Tien-kung k'ai-wu: Chinese Technology in the Seventeenth Century* (University Park: Pennsylvania State University Press, 1966).

Robert Temple, *The Genius of China: 3,000 Years of Science, Discovery, and Invention* (New York: Simon & Schuster, 1986).

Paul U. Unschuld, *Medicine in China: A History of Ideas* (Berkeley: University of California Press, 1985).

Li Yan and Du Shiran, *Chinese Mathematics: A Concise History*, translated by John N. Crossley and Anthony W. C. Lun (Oxford: Clarendon Press; New York: Oxford University Press, 1987).

# CONTRIBUTORS

**Jieli Li** received his education in China, England, and the United States. He is Associate Professor of Sociology at Ohio University, and his research interests center on comparative and historical sociology. He has published articles in *Sociological Theory, Sociological Perspectives, International Journal of the Sociology of Law, Michigan Sociological Review,* and other professional journals.

**Huping Ling** has her doctorate from Miami University (1991). She is presently Associate Professor of History at Truman State University, where she teaches Asian American and East Asian history. Her publications include *Surviving on the Gold Mountain: A History of Chinese American Women and Their Lives* (1998), *Jinshan Yao: A History of Chinese American Women* (1999), and *Ping Piao Mei Guo: New Immigrants in America* (forthcoming). She has contributed articles to such professional journals as *Journal of American Ethnic History, Journal of Urban History, Missouri Historical Review, History Teacher,* and *American Studies*. Her articles have also appeared in such anthologies as *Origins and Destinations* (1994), *Asian American Encyclopedia* (1995), *Ethnic Chinese at the Turn of Centuries* (1998), *New Studies on Chinese Overseas and China* (2000), and *Intercultural Relations, Cultural Transformation, and Identity* (2000).

She is also a recipient of the Ford Foundation Book Award (1999).

**C. X. George Wei** has a Ph.D. in History from Washington University (1996), and he is currently Associate Professor of History at Susquehanna University. He is the author of *Sino-American Economic Relations, 1945-1949* (1997) and co-editor of *Chinese Nationalism in Perspective: Historical and Recent Cases* (2001) and *Exploring Nationalisms of China: Themes and Conflicts* (forthcoming). He has also written many scholarly articles in both English and Chinese.

**Guangqiu Xu** received his bachelor's degree in Chinese history (1983) and his master's degree in modern Chinese history (1986) from Zhongshan University, Guangzhou, China; he received his doctoral degree in History from the University of Maryland, College Park (1993). He is currently Associate Professor of History at Friends University, Kansas, where he teaches courses in Chinese and Japanese history as well as Western civilization. He is the author of *War Wings: The United States and the Chinese Military Aviation, 1929-1949* (2001). His articles and book reviews have appeared in several professional journals both in China and the United States, including *Modern Asian Studies, Asian Survey,* and *Journal of Contemporary History.*

# INDEX OF PHOTOGRAPHS

Chu Shih-Chieh's book on algebra, *Precious Mirror of the Four Elements* (1303), showing both zero and negative terms (from George Beshore, *Science in Ancient China*, 1988) 420

Copper coin production; woodcut, 1637 (from Arnold Toynbee, *Half the World*, 1973) 203

Copper plate for printing money (left) and an imprint on paper, from the Southern Song capital of Hangzhou, circa 1127–1279 (Ontario Science Center, Toronto) 210

Court lady playing with two children, early twelfth century (from Wen C. Fong, *Beyond Representation*, 1992) 327

Court scene in which an adulteress (lower right) is being whipped, Song dynasty, 960–1279 (from Norman Kotker, ed., *The Horizon History of China*, 1969) 339

Daoist hanging scroll of the pantheon of gods, Ming dynasty, 1368–1644 (Nelson-Atkins Museum of Art, Kansas City) 387

Daoist tablet used during ritual audiences with deities, Ming dynasty, 1368–1644 (Staatliches Museum für Volkerkunde, Munich) 386

The Daxiongbao Hall of the Fengguo-si, built in 1020 300

Demon queller Chung K'uei in different poses, circa 1300 (Metropolitan Museum of Art, New York) 397

*Diamond Sutra*, originally published in 868 (British Library, London) 182

Disciples of Buddha giving alms to beggars, twelfth century (Museum of Fine Arts, Boston) 381

Dragon Boat Festival, Yuan dynasty, 1279–1368 (Palace Museum, Beijing) 353

Dragon King, ruler of the water world, surrounded by a bodyguard of water deities, Song dynasty, 960–1279 (Museum of Fine Arts, Boston) 389

Earthenware figure of a tomb guardian trampling a demon, Tang dynasty, 618–907 (Asian Art Museum, San Francisco) 126

Emperor and his chief adviser kneeling before an altar, circa 1041–1106 (Metropolitan Museum of Art, New York) 378

Emperor berating a court lady, circa seventh century (British Museum, London) 330

*Emperor Ming Huang's Journey to Shu* (hanging scroll); Song-era copy of the eighth-century original (National Palace Museum, Taipei, Taiwan) 247

*Emperors of the Successive Dynasties*, painting by Yan Liben, circa 650 (Museum of Fine Arts, Boston) 136

Endless power-transmitting chain drive, from Su Song's *New Design for an Astronomical Clock*, 1094 (from Robert Temple, *The Genius of China*, 1986) 415

Family gathering, Ming dynasty, 1368–1644 (Metropolitan Museum of Art, New York) 341

Family painting, Ming dynasty, 1368–1644 (Metropolitan Museum of Art, New York) 358

Family relationships, chart (from Caroline Blunden and Mark Elvin, *Cultural Atlas of China*, 1983) 340

Farmland at Roungshui in southeastern China 91

Feihongta (Pagoda of the Flying Rainbow) in Hongdong County, Shanxi Province, 1515–1527 121

Figurine of a Persian trader carrying a wineskin, Tang dynasty, 618–907 (Seattle Art Museum) 218

Figurines of female musicians from Chinese Turkestan, seventh century (from Bradley Smith and Wan-go Weng, *China: A History in Art*, 1973) 133

Figurines of horses, Tang dynasty, 618–907 (from Bradley Smith and Wan-go Weng, *China: A History in Art*, 1973) 190

Flat-bottomed ocean junk, Song dynasty, 960–1279. The ship has floating rudders for stabilization in high seas (from Louise Levathes, *When China Ruled the Seas*, 1994). 173

Flat-bottomed river barge carrying grain to the capital city of Beijing, Ming dynasty, 1368–1644 (from Louise Levathes, *When China Ruled the Seas*, 1994) 202

Footbinding materials: rolls of binding cloth; jar of medicinal foot powder; bamboo cage for fuming binding cloth; scissors; and box of fragrant foot powder (Bata Shoe Museum, Toronto, Canada) 344

Four-string pipa, a type of lute of Iranian origin, circa 700 (from Patricia Buckley Ebrey, *Cambridge Illustrated History of China*, 1996) 155

Genghis Khan and Mongol horsemen pursuing enemy forces, thirteenth century (Bibliothèque Nationale, Paris) 223

Giraffe; description of a gift sent to the Emperor Yung Lo, early fifteenth century (from Norman Kotker, ed., *The Horizon History of China*, 1969) 204

Glazed teacup and stand, Song dynasty, 960–1279 (Hong Kong Museum of Art) 306

*Going on the River at the Qing Ming Festival* (scroll), depicting the Northern Song capital of Kaifeng, 1111–1126 (Palace Museum, Beijing) 354

The Great Stone Bridge spanning the River Chiao Shui, the world's first segmental arch bridge built by Li Chun in the early seventh century 170

Great Wall, initially built in the third century B.C.E. to thwart raids by northern tribes 87

Green porcelain bottle; Yaozhou ware, circa 1100 (Museum of Oriental Ceramics, Osaka) 142

Guanyin Hall at the Duleshi (Temple of Lonely Happiness), Jixian County, Hebei Province, 984 116

Horsemen; tenth-century scroll (Museum of Fine Arts, Boston) 177

*Hsu-t'ing Mi-shih-so-ching* (Jesus Messiah Sutra), which summarizes Christian precepts for daily living, circa 635–638 (from P. Y. Saeki,

Noblemen riding carriages, circa 1070–1150 (Metropolitan Museum of Art, New York) 178

Offerings from the tomb of Zhang Wenzao, Liao dynasty, 916–1115 (Institute of Cultural Relics, Shijiazhuang, Hebei Province) 346

Officials receiving foreign guests; Tang-era tomb painting, circa 711 (Shensi Provincial Museum, Sian) 176

Oldest standing dwelling in Beijing; plans showing characteristics of a Ming-style residence (from Ronald Knapp, *China's Old Dwellings*, 2000) 298

*Old Trees by a Cold Waterfall* by Wen Zhengming; hanging scroll, 1549 (National Palace Museum, Taipei, Taiwan) 139

Paddle-wheel warship, 1637 (from Norman Kotker, ed., *The Horizon History of China*, 1969) 184

Pagoda of Sakyamuni at the Fogongshi (Temple of the Buddhist Palace), Ying County, Shanxi Province, 1056 118

Painted wooden figurine showing women's dress, excavated from the tomb of a Chinese official, Xinjiang province, Tang dynasty, 618–907 (Chinese Historical Museum, Beijing) 292

Palace women bathing children; detail from a fan mounted as an album leaf, circa thirteenth century (Smithsonian Institution, Washington, D.C.) 317

Paper money made from the bark of a mulberry tree, Song dynasty, 960–1279 (from Robert E. Murowchick, *Cradles of Civilization: China*, 1994) 212

"Pascal's Triangle" as depicted by Chu Shih-Chieh in *Precious Mirror of the Four Elements*, 1303 (from Colin Ronan, *The Cambridge Illustrated History of the World's Science*, 1983) 421

Patient being treated by moxibustion (cauterization of the skin), Song dynasty, 960–1279 (National Palace Museum, Taipei, Taiwan) 422

Peddler; handscroll illumination, circa 1190–1230 (Palace Museum, Beijing) 213

Porcelain bowl painted with a good-luck formula written in Persian, sixteenth century (Smithsonian Institution, Washington, D.C.) 399

Porcelain phoenix-head ewer; white ware with green-tinged glaze, circa twelfth century (British Museum, London) 143

Pottery figures of a flutist and dancer, Yuan dynasty, 1279–1368 (from Colin Mackerras, *Chinese Theatre*, 1983) 148

Pottery figurines of women doing kitchen chores, Tang dynasty, 618–907 (National Palace Museum, Taipei, Taiwan) 331

Qianxunta pagoda, circa 850 162

Red Cliff Ode, copied by Su Shih, early twelfth century (National Palace Museum, Taipei, Taiwan) 127

Repeating crossbow, capable of firing eleven shots in fifteen seconds; invented circa eleventh century (Manchester Museum, Manchester, England) 428

Rice paddies in Guizhou Province, southwestern China 90

Rice production, Yuan dynasty, 1279–1368 (Smithsonian Institution, Washington, D.C.) 296

River barges transporting goods; from the hanging scroll *Traveling on the River in Clearing Snow*, circa 975 (National Palace Museum, Taipei, Taiwan) 199

St. Paul's Church at Macao, built by the Jesuits at the beginning of the seventeenth century 383

Scholar boiling herbs for medicinal use, Ming dynasty, 1368–1644 (National Palace Museum, Taipei, Taiwan) 414

Scholar relaxing and listening to music, Southern Song dynasty, thirteenth century (National Palace Museum, Taipei, Taiwan) 156

Scholars at a banquet, Tang dynasty, 618–907 (from Patricia Buckley

Ebrey, *Cambridge Illustrated History of China*, 1996) 294

Scholars studying the yin-yang symbol, early seventeenth century (British Museum, London) 392

Seated Buddha (with restored head) from T'ien-lung-shan, Shanxi Province, Tang dynasty, 618–907 (Shansi Fogg Art Museum, Cambridge, Massachusetts) 144

Shoes with embroidered uppers and stitched soles made for bound feet, Ming dynasty, 1368–1644 (from Valery Garrett, *Chinese Clothing*, 1994) 293

Silk painting of a Song official and an attendant, Song dynasty, 960–1279 (Musee Guimet, Paris) 243

Silver bottle, Tang dynasty, 618–907 (Shaanxi Provincial Museum, China) 215

Silver tea grinder dated 869 (from Patricia Buckley Ebrey, *Cambridge Illustrated History of China*, 1996) 304

*Six Gentlemen* by Ni Zan; hanging scroll, 1345 (Shanghai Museum) 138

Sleeveless court vest belonging to Empress Dowager Li, made for her fiftieth birthday in 1595 (Asian Art Museum of San Francisco) 290

Soldiers firing arrows from special containers filled with gunpowder (from Alasdair Clayre, *The Heart of the Dragon*, 1985) 429

*A Solitary Temple amid Clearing Peaks* by Li Cheng; hanging scroll, circa 960 (Nelson-Atkins Museum of Art, Kansas City, Missouri) 137

Song emperor Huizong with advisers, circa 1102 (Palace Museum, Beijing) 241

Song official on horseback, 1296 (Palace Museum, Beijing) 265

Song seal (left) with its imprint, 1055 (Field Museum of Natural History, Chicago) 124

Star chart; ink rubbing of a stele at the Confucian Temple, Suzhou, 1247 (Stone Carving Museum, Suzhou) 438

# INDEX

*This index is sorted word by word. Page numbers in bold type indicate the primary article on a topic. Page numbers in italics indicate illustrations.*

and Nestorianism, 395
observances, 307–308
overview, 371–372
sculptures, 143–145, *144, 145, 146*
statues, 293
Tang (early), **372–375,** *373*
Tang (late), **375–377**
Wu (empress of China), 359–360
Yuan, 396–397
*See also* Religion and philosophy
Buddhist genre shows, 152
Buddhist hospitals, 424
Buddhist printing, 181–182, *182,* 183
Bukong (Amoghavajra), 375
Buoyancy techniques, 416
Bureau of Military Affairs, 241, 242, 243

# C

Cai Jing, 267
Cai Xiang, 123, 124
Cai Yuanding, 134
Calendar, 187
Calicut (India), 188, 189
Calligraphy and seal making, **123–125,** *124, 127, 180*
    *See also* Arts
*Camellias* (Zhu Kerou), 311
Canal pound-locks, 183–184, 189, 441
Canals, 187
Canglangting (Garden of the Blue-Waves Pavilion), 119
*Canjunxi* (adjutant play), 134, 149
Cannons, *418,* 429, 430
*Canon of Rites,* 327–328, 345, 347–348
Cantilever bridges, 170
Cao You, 134
Capitals
    Ming, 260
    Song, 117, 209, 265
    Tang, 115, 175, 178–179, 244, 282, 283, 359
    Yuan, 119
    *See also* Beijing, Chang'an (China)
Caravan road system, 174
Cards, playing, 301–302
Carriages. *See* Horses and carriages
Cartography, quantitative, 432
Carving, 126, *126*
Cast iron, 415
Cave decorations, 144
*Ce Shi* (companion), 346, 443
"Celestial Axis Memorializing the Goodness of the Great Chou Dynasty with its Numberless Area," 415
Censorate, 241, 242, 439
Central China, 89
Central economic manipulation policy, 214
Ceramics. *See* Porcelain
*Cha jing (Tea Memoir,* or *Tea Scripture)* (Lu Yu), 310
Chain drive, *415,* 415–416
Chan (Meditation) School (Buddhism), 380
    and neo-Confucianism, 393
    Song, 387
    Tang, 374–375, 377
    Wang Yangming, 402

writing, 388, 390
Yuan, 397
Chang Chun, 186
Chang De, 186
Chang River. *See* Yangzi River
Chang'an (China), 439
    city life in Tang, **282–283**
    conquered, 227
    contact with the West, 328–329
    cultural exchange, 154, 155
    development, 215
    diagram, *284*
    dress and costumes, 281
    foreign influences, 175
    layout, 115
    occupation, 246
    prostitutes, 356
    Tang, 244
*Changhenge (Song of Lasting Pain),* 157
Changling (Long Tomb), 146
*Changlun (Vocal Theory)* (Zhi An), 134
*Changzhuan* (singing show), 153
Chanism. *See* Chan (Meditation School)
Chastity, cult of, *329,* **329–330,** *330*
Chen Hao. *See* Cheng Hao
Chen Hongshou, 140, *333*
Chen Liang, 393
Chen Quan, 422
Chen Shi-Mei, 350
Chen Xianzhang, 393
Chen Yang, 134
Chen Yi, 320, 347, 360, 388, 392
Chen Ziang, 127–128
Cheng Dayue, **95**
Cheng Hao, **268–269,** 360, 385, 388, 392–393
Cheng Ho, **188–189,** 204–205, *205*
Chengzu. *See* Yongle (emperor of China)
Child brides, 348
Childbirth, 326
Child-rearing ceremonies, *317,* **324–328,** *325, 326, 327, 328*
*Children Playing in the Palace Garden,* 326
China Proper, **87–89,** *88, 262,* 439
Chinese arrows, 427, 439
Chinese Wall. *See* Great Wall
*Chiyuan Xinge,* 251, 439
Chongshanshi (Temple of Holy Goodness), 145
Chongshenshi (Lofty and Saint Temple), 115–116
*Chouhai Tubian* (Zheng Ruozeng), 95–96
Chronologies
    arts, **98–112**
    communication, transportation, and exploration, **164–168**
    family and social trends, **314–317**
    geography, **82–84**
    leisure, recreation, and daily life, **276–279**
    politics, law, and the military, **232–238**
    religion and philosophy, **364–369**
    science, technology, and health, **406–410**
    social class system and the economy, **192–199**
    world events, **1–80**
Chu K'o-Jou, **311**
Chu Shih-chieh, *420,* 421, *421*
*Chuanqi* (marvel tales), 129, 151
Chuanzhou (China), 210–211, 396
Chung K'uei, 397
*Ci* (ancestral hall), 318, 439

*Ci* (lyrics), 129–130
Circuit, 242–243
Cities
    Song, 117, 211
    Tang, 215, **282–284,** *284*
Civil service examination system. *See* Examination system, civil service
Clarity Tomb, 145
*Classic of Changes,* 390, 392
Clay models, 298–299
Climate, 85, **89–90**
"Climbing the Stork Pavilion" (Wang Zhihuan), 128
Clocks
    astronomical, *416,* 416–417, *417,* 431, 435
    mechanical, 413, 417, 435
    water, 187
    *See also* Science, technology, and health
Cloisonné, 125
Clothing
    for dead, 344
    men's, **286–289,** *287, 288*
    and social status, **284–286,** *285*
    women's, 285–286, **289–293,** *290, 291, 292, 293*
Coastal routes, **178–180,** *179, 180,* 187
Coffins, 344–345, *345*
Coins, *203,* 205, 211, 283, 442
*Collected Writings of the North Hall* (Yu Shinan), 133
*Collection of the Most Important Military Techniques* (Zeng Kongliang), 425
*Comments from the Hall of Learned Old Era* (Lu Yu), 417
Commercial policies, Yuan, 221–222
Commercial revolution, *199,* **209–211,** *210,* 212, 439
Communication, transportation, and exploration, **163–190**
    Arabs in Canton, 174
    bridge technology, *170,* **170–172,** *171*
    Chinese maritime expansion and Western navigators, **172–173,** *173*
    Chinese migration to South China, **173–175**
    chronology, **164–168**
    documentary sources, **190**
    horses and carriages, *177,* **177–178,** *178, 190*
    inland waterways and coastal routes, **178–180,** *179, 180,* 187
    language, 156, 169–170, *180,* **180–181,** 185, 304
    overview, **169–170**
    printing, *181,* **181–183,** *182*
    savage waves, 172
    significant people, **187–189**
    Tang foreign influences, *175,* **175–176,** *176*
    testing scholars, 183
    transportation technology, **183–184,** *184*
    Yuan travel, **184–186**
Compass, magnetic, 430, *431,* 432
*Compendium of Materia Medica* (Li Shizhen), 424, 433
*Compendium of Medicine* (Lou Wansu), 423
*The Complete Collection of the Revered Wang Wengcheng* (Wang Shouren), 134
Concubines, 346, 347
Confucianism

divorce, 347, 349–350, 443

documentary sources, **362**

family and child education, **332–333**, *333*, 335

family as a medium of social control, **338–339**, *339*

family authority, *331*, **331–332**, *332*

family composition, **335–336**, *336*, 358

family ethics: filial piety, 330, 331, 335, **336–338**, *337*, *338*, 443

family nomenclature, **339–341**, *340*, *341*

family patrilineage, **341–343**, *342*

footbinding, *343*, **343–344**, *344*

funeral ceremonies, **344–346**, *345*, *346*

Ghost Festival, 352

love and marriage: social regulations, **346–350**, *349*

mate selection and marriage, *350*, **350–352**, *351*

overview, **318–320**

popular festivals, **352–355**, *353*, *354*

*Qing Ming* festival, **322**, 323, 324

schedule of learning, **334**

sex life, **355–356**, *356*, *357*

significant people, **359–361**

wedding customs, **357–358**

*See also* Social class system and the economy

"Family Instructions of the Grandfather," 332–333

Fan Kuan, 138

Fan Zhongyan, 265

Fans, 292–293

*Faqu* (Buddhist melody), 132

*A Father's Instructions* (Guo Xi), 138

Faxian, 424

Feasts, 324, 326–327

Feihongta (Pagoda of the Flying Rainbow), 122

Fengxian (Ancestral Reverence) Temple, 143–144

*Fengzheng*, 301, 439

*Fenshu (Books to be Burned)* (Li Zhi), 132

Festival of "Cow Boy" and "Weaving Girl" Union, 354

Figure painting, 139–140

Filial piety, 330, 331, 335, **336–338**, *337*, *338*, 443

Finger guards, 304

Fire arrows, 426

Firearms, 429

*Fire-Drake Artillery Guidebook*, 427, 428, 429

Fire-lance, 428, 439

Fireworks, 425–426

Firuz (king of Persia), 175, 398

Fish tally, 288, 294, 439

Five Dynasties, 136, 138, 246, 440

Five Punishments, 251

Five virtues, 337–338

Flamethrowers, 425, *426*

Flower and bird painting, 139

Flying Cash, 211, 440

Fogongshi (Temple of the Buddhist Palace), *118*, 119

Foguang Shizheng (Temple of Buddhist Light), 115

Folk dancing, 148–149

*See also* Dance

Folk festivals, 319–320

Food, 280, **293–297**, *294*, *295*, *296*, *297*, 308

Footbinding, 213, 304, *343*, **343–344**, *344*, 440

Forbidden City, 115, 440

Foreign quarter

in Canton, 216

in Chang'an, 282

Tang, 216

*Four Books*, 336, 361, 390

"The Four Dreams of Linchuan" (Tang Xianzu), 151, 160

Four virtues, 348–349, 401

Franciscan missions, 185, 186, *394*, **394–396**

*See also* Religion and philosophy

Frankish bombards, 430, 440

Frontier armies, Tang, 253

*Fu* (father; head or family head), *339*

*Fu* (special prefectures), 242, 253, 440

Fu Yi, 375

*Fubing* (militia) system, 253, 255, 440

Funeral ceremonies, **344–346**, *345*, *346*

Furniture, 300–301

Furs and hats, 285

# G

Game (meat), 295

Games, 281

Gansu Province, *84*

Gao Zecheng, 151

*Gao Zhu Fu* (great-great-grandfather), 339, 440

*Gaoling*, 203, 440

Gaozong (emperor of China), 145, 270, 359, 374, 395

Garden of Five Mountains, 123

Garden of Perfect Clarity, 123

Garden of the Blue-Waves Pavilion, 119

Gardens, 116, 119, 123

Gate of Origin, 122

Gembo, 176

Genghis Khan, *269*, **269**

Daoism, 381, 396

Mongol empire, 184, 223, 261

travel, 185, 186

Genre music, 134–135

Genre painting, 140

Genre show, *152*, **152–154**

*See also* Arts

Gentlemanly behavior, 207

Gentry, 201, 207–208, 212–213, 258, 318–319, 440

Geobotanical prospecting, 432–433

Geography, **81–96**

agricultural conditions, 85

barbarians, 92

border regions, **86–87**

China Proper, **87–89**

chronology, **82–84**

climate, 85, **89–90**

cultural groups, **90–91**

documentary sources, **96**

environment, **91–92**

loess, 85

mountains and rivers, *84*, **92–93**

neighboring countries, **94**

overview, **85**

relations with Japan, 94

significant people, **95–96**

terrain, 85

*See also* Maps

Geology, 433

Ghost Festival, 352, 354–355

Giovanni da Montecorvino, 185, 186, 395–396

Giraffes, *204*, 205

Glossary, 439–443

Gobi Desert, 87, 440

Goddess Hall, 117, 144

*Going on the River*, 354

Goiter, 422

*Gold Vase Plum*, 132

*Gong* (artisans), 218–219, 440

Government personnel, 239–240, *248*, **248–250**, *249*

*See also* Politics, law, and the military

Grand Canal, 440

economic significance, 186, 218

first, 178–179

Ming, *180*

and sea transport, 189

second, 179

technology, 184

Grand Capital, 119

*Grand Dictionary of Kang Xi*, *339*

Grand Hall of the Temple of Chinese Rigorousness, 119

Grand Khan. *See* Kublai Khan

Grand Secretariat, 241, 242, 249, 256

"Grandfather's Instructions," 332–333

Grave-Sweeping Festival. *See Qing Ming* Festival

*Great Learning* (Confucius), 361

Great Lion of Zangzhou, 415

Great Stone Bridge, *170*, 171

Great Wall, *87*, 89, 117, 255, 271, 440

Great Wild Goose Pagoda, 115

Greeks, and science, 411–412

Greeting Tea, 280, 304, 440

*Groanings* (Lu Kun), **207**

Gu Hongzhong, 136

*Gu* or *Gu Ma* (paternal aunt), 339, 440

Guan Hanqing, 149, *158*, **158**

Guan Tong, 138

Guangdong. *See* Lingnan

Guangshengshi (Temple of Wide Victory), 119, 140

Guangxi. *See* Lingnan

Guangzhou (China), 215, 216

Guanyin Hall, *116*, 117, 119, 125, *146*

Gugong (Forbidden City), 120, 121–122

*Guide to Calligraphy* (Sun Guoting), 124

Guizhou Province, *90*

Gunpowder, 412–413, *418*, **418–419**, *419*, 425, 428, 440

*See also* Science, technology, and health

*Guo Jia*, 331–332

Guo Mian, 133

Guo Shoujing, **187**, 431

Guo Xi, 138

*Guo Zi Jian* (State Academy Directorate), 333, 335, 440

Guo Zixing, 272

*Guzici* (poetic drum) music, 135

# H

Hai Rui, **225–226**, 260

Hakka, 440

Hall of Central Peace, 121

# W

Wan Guifei, **310–311**
Wang Anshi, 159, 214–215, **227**, 241, 265
Wang Anshi Reforms, 227, 254, 266–267, 268, 390, 442–443
Wang Bo, 127
Wang Changling, 128
Wang (empress of China), 359
Wang Fuzhi (Wang Fu-chih), 92, 134
Wang Jian, 128–129
Wang Shen, 138
Wang Shihfu, 149
Wang Shouren, 134
Wang Tan, 415
Wang Wei, 128, 136, **160**
Wang Weiyi, 423
*Wang Wencheng Gong quanshu (The Complete Collection of the Revered Wang Wengcheng)* (Wang Shouren), 134
Wang Xianzhi, 123, 246
Wang Xiaotong, 420
Wang Xi, 422
Wang Xizhi, 123
Wang Yan, 401
Wang Yangming, 385, 386, 388, 393, 394, **402**
Wang Zhihuan, 128
*Wang Zhu (families of nobility)*, 342, 350
Wang Zhuo, 134
*Wang Zu (eminent family-clan)*, 335, 443
Wanli (emperor of China), 227, 229, 258, 266, *288*, 401, 402
*Washi (spontaneous market)*, 149
*Water Margins*, 131, 131–132, 150, 302
Waterways, inland, **178–180**, *179, 180*, 187
Wedding customs, **357–358**
*Wei*, 255, 443
Wei Liangfu, 135
Wei Zhongxian, 257, 258
Wei Zhuang, 130
*Weiqi*, 154, 281, 301, 443
*Weisuo* system, 255, 443
Wen Peng, 125
Wen Tingyun, 130
Wen Tong, 139
Wen Zhengming, *139*, 140
West, contact with, **328–329**
West River, 85, 89, 443
Western and Eastern cultural exchange, 114, **154–156**, *155, 156*
*The Western Chamber—Multiple Palace Tunes* (Dong Jieyuan), 149
Western Market (Chang'an), 282
Wheat, 294
Wheel ships, 183, *184*
Wheelbarrow launchers, 428
*Whispering Pines on a Mountain Path* (Tang Yin), *141*
White Deer Grotto Academy, 361, 388, 393, 401
White Lotus Society, 264, 271, 443
*The White Rabbit*, 151
Widowhood, 329–330
William of Rubruck, 185, 395
*Wokou (Japanese pirates)*, 95–96, 257–258, 271, 443
Women
    clothing, 285–286, **289–293**, *290, 291, 292, 293*
    social conditions, 213, 355, 356

Woodblock printing, 181–182, *182*, 183, 209
Work, Tang, 283
World events chronology, **1–80**
Wrapped turbans, 286
*The Wronging of Dou E* (Guan Hanqing), 158
Wu Chengen, 131
Wu Daozi, 136, 155
*Wu Fu (Five Mourning Grades)*, 345, 443
*Wu Jing (Five Classics)*, 335, 443
*Wu Lun*, 336, 443
Wu Qiuyan, 125
Wu (Wu Zhao) (empress of China), **359–360**
    Buddhism, 374, 375, 424
    technology, 415
    tomb sculpture, 145
    and Wan Guifei, 310
Wufengyuan (Garden of Five Mountains), 123
*Wujian (sword dance)*, 148
*Wutongyu (Rain on the Plantain Tree)* (Bai Pu), 150
Wu-tsung (emperor of China), *256*
Wuzong (emperor of China), 376, 380, 402

# X

Xavier, Francis, 382
Xi (West) River, 85, 89, 443
Xi Xia, 220, 223, 269, 443
Xia Baiyan, 146
*Xia Qi (second wife)*, 346, 443
*Xian (districts)*, 218, 443
*Xiang Huo Xiong Di (Brothers of Burning Joss-Stick)*, 356
*Xiangqi*, 281, 443
Xiangshan. *See* Lu Jiuyuan
*Xiangyue (Community Compact)*, 336, 443
Xiannongtai (Temple of Architecture), 120
Xianzong (emperor of China), 246, 375–376
*Xiao (filial piety)*, 331, 443
*Xiao Qi (minor wife)*, 346, 443
Xiao Wu Di, 328
Xiaoling (Filial Piety Tomb), 146
*Xiaoqu (mini melody)*, 134
*Xin*, 338, 443
*Xin Nian (New Year)*, 308, 352, 443
Xin Qiji, 130
*Xin Xue (Study of the Mind)*, 390, 393
*Xingshang zoufan (petty traveling peddlers)*, 210, 443
*Xinjiang (China)*, 86, *86*, 443
*Xiong (elder brother)*, 339, 443
*Xishan qinkuang (Zither Conditions from Creek Hill)* (Xu Shangyin), 134
*Xiu Qi (divorce)*, 347, 349–350, 443
*Xiucai (flowering talent)*, 207, 219, 249, 443
    *See also Jinshi; Juren*
*Xixiangji zhugongdiao (The Western Chamber—Multiple Palace Tunes)* (Dong Jieyuan), 149
Xiyuan (Western Garden), 119
Xu Guangqi, 384, **436**
Xu Shangyin, 134
Xu Xi, 139
Xuan Zang, 375, **403**, 424
Xuande (emperor of China), 125
Xuangzong. *See* Xuanzong (emperor of China)
*Xuanhe yinpu (Xuanhe Guide to the Seal)*, 125
Xuanwu Gate Incident, 244

Xuanzang, 270, 328
Xuanzhangta, 115
Xuanzong (emperor of China)
    Buddhism, 374
    concubine, 147, 150, 157
    dance, 147
    Daoism, 380
    expeditions, 189
    finances, 217
    music, 132, *133*, 154
    poetry, 158
    revolt, 245
    and Zhong Kui, 352–353

# Y

Yan Liben, 136, *136*
Yan Lide, 145
Yan Shi, **227–228**
Yan Yu, 130
Yan Zhenqing, 123
Yang (emperor of China), 226–227
Yang Guifei, 245
Yang Guozhong, 245
Yang Huan, **228–229**
Yang Jiong, 127
Yang Jung, *248*
Yang Kuei-fei, 245
*Yang (masculine, aggressive principle)*, 390, *392*, 423, 443
*Yang Mu (adopting mother)*, 341, 443
Yang Pu, *248*
Yang Shih-chi, *248*
Yang Tingyun, 384
Yang Weizhen, 124
Yang Yen, 217, 244
Yang Yuhuan, 147
Yanglian Zhenjia, 397
Yangtze River. *See* Yangzi River
Yangzhou (China), 119
Yangzi River, 85, 89, 93, *93*, 443
Yangzi Valley, 218
*Yanhai Tuben* (Zheng Ruozeng), 95
Yao Niang, *343*
Yazdegerd III (king of Persia), 175, 398
Yellow River, 93, 443
    bridge near Puzhou, 416
    change in course, 264, 272
    navigation, 187
    overview, 85
Yelu Chucai, 261
*Yezi*, 443
*Yi*, 338, 443
*Yi Jing (Classic of Changes)*, 390, 392
Yi Jing, 375, 424
*Yi or Yi Ma (maternal aunt)*, 339, 443
*Yi tiao bian (Single-Whip Reform)*, **205–207**, *206*, 261, 443
Yide (empress of China), 130
*Yigu Yanduan (New Steps in Computation)* (Li Zhi), 434
Yiheyuan (Summer Palace), 123
*Yin (feminine, passive principle)*, 390, *392*, 423, 443
*Yinpin (Seal Articles)* (Zhu Jian), 125
Yixing, 416, 417
Yongdingmen (Gate of Lasting Peace), 120

✓